# POPE INNOCENT III

# Europe in the Middle Ages
## Selected Studies

# Volume 12

*General Editor*
## RICHARD VAUGHAN
*University of Hull*

NORTH-HOLLAND PUBLISHING COMPANY – AMSTERDAM · NEW YORK · OXFORD

# POPE INNOCENT III

*By*
## HELENE TILLMANN

*Translated by*
## Walter Sax

1980

NORTH-HOLLAND PUBLISHING COMPANY – AMSTERDAM · NEW YORK · OXFORD

North-Holland ISBN: 0 444 85137 2


Published by:
North-Holland Publishing Company – Amsterdam/New York/Oxford


Distributors for the U.S.A. and Canada:
Elsevier North-Holland, Inc.
52 Vanderbilt Avenue, New York, N.Y. 10017


**Library of Congress Cataloging in Publication Data**
Tillmann, H.
  Pope Innocent III
  (Europe in the Middle Ages; 12)


This volume was originally published in German in 1954 by Vandenhoeck & Ruprecht, Göttingen.
© Vandenhoeck & Ruprecht, Göttingen


Printed in The Netherlands

# General Editor's note

English-speaking students and lovers of history have for long lacked a scholarly biography of the greatest of medieval popes. The gap has now been filled by this translation of Helene Tillmann's classic study of 1954. The author herself has collaborated in the translation, which is the work of Professor Dr Sax of the University of Würzburg although, in the case of the notes, my colleague Dr Alan Best of the German Department, University of Hull, helped by providing a draft translation. I for my part have here and there lightly revised both text and notes, and made the index.

October 1979

Richard Vaughan

# Author's foreword

What follows is a translation of my biography of Pope Innocent III which first appeared in German in 1954. I am grateful to the editor and publishers of the series Europe in the Middle Ages: Selected Studies for commissioning this translation and thereby allowing English-speaking students easier access to my work than has hitherto been the case.

Owing mainly to the intricacies of the German text, it has proved advisable to have it translated by someone whose native language is German and who at the same time has a passable knowledge of English. I was happy to find this someone in the person of my colleague Dr Walter Sax, professor of law at the University of Würzburg, who had already helped me with the completion of the German version of 1954. It is due to his painstaking and conscientious efforts that a translation has been brought about which is faithful to the German original both as to wording and meaning. I sincerely thank him for his efficient work. Last but not least my thanks must go to the general editor, Professor Vaughan, who was kind enough to undertake the toilsome task of revision.

Since 1954 a number of significant studies of the pope's character and influence have appeared. Michele Maccarrone, perhaps the most knowledgeable scholar of Innocent III's work in general, has provided an exhaustive bibliography of the individual studies and biographies of the pope and his work as well as an account of the revised editions of aspects of Innocent literature. This is to be found in the *Dictionnaire de spiritualité ascétique et mystique*, 1971. In addition the article enriches Innocent scholarship by a detailed study of the religious and spiritual education of Lothair of Segni and by an analysis of his writings.

The following titles should be added to the bibliography:

Kempf, Friedrich, *Papsttum und Kaisertum bei Innocenz III.*, Miscellanea Historiae pontificiae 19, Roma, 1954.

Maccarrone, Michelle, *Studi su Innocenzo III*, Italia sacra 17, Padova, 1972.

Tillmann, Helene, *Datierungsfragen zur Geschichte des Kampfes zwischen Papst Innocenz III. und Kaiser Otto IV.*, Hist. Jahrbuch der Görresgesellschaft 1964.

May 1979                                                        Helene Tillmann

# Contents

General editor's note      v
Author's foreword      vii
Abbreviations      x
Bibliography      xi
Addenda      xix

Chapter 1.    Lothair of Segni      1
Chapter 2.    Called to the fullness of power      21
Chapter 3.    On the chair of justice      51
Chapter 4.    The champion of ecclesiastical liberty      79
Chapter 5.    Under the pressure of politics      103
Chapter 6.    The pastor and reformer      189
Chapter 7.    The defender of the faith      229
Chapter 8.    Towards the unity of the Church      261
Chapter 9.    "For the inheritance of Christ crucified"      273
Chapter 10.    The man      289
Chapter 11.    The verdict of history      317
Appendix 1.    Innocent III's alleged claim for the fullness of temporal power      321
Appendix 2.    The marriage case of Philip Augustus of France and other marriage cases under Innocent III      333
Appendix 3.    Conrad of Würzburg's alleged 'treachery'      349
Appendix 4.    The timing of Emperor Otto IV's revocation of the papal recuperations      357

Index      361

# Abbreviations

| | |
|---|---|
| Arch. Soc. Rom. | Archivio della Società Romana di Storia Patria |
| DA | Deutsches Archiv für Erforschung des Mittelalters |
| EHR | The English historical review |
| HJb | Historisches Jahrbuch der Görresgesellschaft |
| Jen. Hist. Arb. | Jenaer Historische Arbeiten |
| MG. Const. | Monumenta Germaniae historica. Constitutiones et acta publica imperatorum et regum |
| MG. SS. | Monumenta Germaniae historica. Scriptores |
| MIÖG | Mitteilungen des Instituts für österreichische Geschichtskunde |
| NA | Neues Archiv der Gesellschaft für ältere deutsche Geschichtskunde |
| QFIAB | Quellen und Forschungen aus italienischen Archiven und Bibliotheken |
| ZRG | Zeitschrift für Rechtsgeschichte, Kanonistische Abteilung |

# Bibliography

The works included in this list are those to which repeated and widespread reference has been made throughout this book. They are listed here according to the identifying abbreviation used both in the body of the text and in the notes. Those titles to which reference is made only once, or more than once but in a restricted portion of the text, are given their full references on each occasion.

AASS: *Acta Sanctorum quotquot toto orbe coluntur vel a catholicis scriptoribus celebrantur*, quae ex latinis et graecis aliarumque gentium antiquis monumentis collegit, degessit, notis illustravit J. Bollandus; operam et studium contulit G. Henschenius. Ed. novissima, curante J. Carnadet, t. 1–61, 1863–1867.

Acta Inn.: *Acta Innocentii PP. III* (1198–1216) e registris Vaticanis aliisque eruit, introductione auxit, notisque illustravit P. Th. Haluscynsky (Pont. Comm. ad redig. Cod. iur. can. orient., Fontes ser. III, vol. 2) 1944, quoted according to Introd(uctio) or P(ars) I or II, no. and p.

Ambrose of S. Teresa: Fr. Ambrosius a S. Teresia, OCD, *Untersuchungen über Verfasser, Abfassungszeit, Quellen und Bestätigung der Karmeliter-Regel*, Ephemerides Carmeliticae II, 1948, p. 17ff.

Andrieu, Le Pontifical: M. Andrieu, *Le Pontifical Romain au moyen-âge* 2, Studi e testi 87, 1940.

Ann. Casin.: Annales Casinenses (MG. SS. 19).

Ann. Cecc.: Annales Ceccanenses (MG. SS. 19).

Ann. Marbac.: Annales Marbacenses qui dicuntur, SS. rer. Germ., ed. H. Bloch, 1907.

Ann. Placent. Guelfl: Annales Placenti Guelfi (MG. SS. 18).

Ann. Romani: Annales Romani, in Lib. Pont. (see below) Vol. 2.

Anonymous Halberst.: Anonymi Halberstadensis *De peregrinatione in Graeciam et adventu reliquiarum de Graecia libellus*, in Riant (see below) Vol. 1.

Arnold of Lübeck: *Arnoldi Chronica Slavorum, SS. rer. Germ.*, ed. *G. H. Pertz*, 1868.

Baethgen, Philipp: Fr. Baethgen, *Die Exkommunikation Philipps von Schwaben, MIÖG* 34, 1913.

Baethgen, Regentschaft: *Die Regentschaft Papst Innocenz' III. im Königreich Sizilien*, 1914.

Baluze, Misc.: S. Baluze, *Miscellaneorum libri VII seu Collectio veterum monumentorum, quae hactenus latuerunt in variis codicibus ac bibliothecis*, 7 vols, 1678–1715.

Barraclough: G. Barraclough, *Papal provisions; aspects of church history, constitutional, legal and administrative, in the later middle ages*, 1935.

Belperron: P. Belperron, *La croisade contre les Albigeois et l'union de Languedoc à la France 1209–1249*, 1942.

Berlière: D.U.B. Berlière, Innocent III et les monastères bénédictins, *Rev. Bénéd.* 32, 1920.

BF: J.F. Böhmer, *Regesta Imperii V. Die Regesten des Kaiserreichs unter Philipp, Otto IV., Friedrich II., Heinrich (VIII.), Conrad IV., Heinrich Raspe, Wilhelm und Richard. 1198–1272*. New and revised ed. by J. Ficker and E. Winkelmann, 3 vols, 1881–1901, quoted by the Regest number.

Böhmer, Acta: J.F. Böhmer, *Acta Imperii selecta. Urkunden deutscher Könige und Kaiser, mit einem Anhange von Reichssachen*, 1870.

Böhmer, Analekten: J.F. Böhmer, *Analekten zur Geschichte des Franziskus von Assisi*, Sammlung ausgewählter kirchen- und dogmengeschichtl. Abh. 4, [2]1930.

Bonazzi: L. Bonazzi, *Storia di Perugia dalle origini al 1860*, Vol. 1, 1875.

von Borch: L. von Borch, *Geschichte des kaiserlichen Kanzlers Konrad, Legat in Italien und Sizilien, Bischof von Hildesheim und von Würzburg*, 1882.

Browe: P. Browe, *Die Pflichtkommunion im Mittelalter*, 1940.

Burchard of Ursberg: *Die Chronik des Propstes Burchard von Ursberg*, SS. rer. Germ., ed. O. Holder-Egger and B. v. Simson, [2]1916.

Burdach, Walthers Kampf: K. Burdach, Der Kampf Walthers von der Vogelweide gegen Innocenz III. und gegen das vierte Lateranische Konzil, *ZKG* 55, 1936.

Cabrol-Leclercq: F. Cabrol-H. Leclercq, *Dictionnaire d'archéologie chrétienne et de liturgie*, Vol. 1ff., 1924ff.

Caesarius (Hilka): *Die Wundergeschichten des Caesarius von Heisterbach*, ed. A. Hilka, Publ. d. Ges. f. Rhein. Geschichtskunde 43, 3 vols, 1933ff.

Caesarius (Schönbach 1): Schönbach, Studien zur Erzählungsliteratur des Mittelalters, Part 4: *Ueber Caesarius von Heisterbach I.*, SB Wien 144, 1901, 9. Abt.

Caesarius (Schönbach 2): Schönbach, Studien zur Erzählungsliteratur des Mittelalters, Part 7: *Ueber Caesarius von Heisterbach II.*, SB Wien 159, 1908, 4. Abt.

Caesarius (Strange): *Caesarii Heisterbacensis Monachi ordinis Cisterciensis Dialogus Miraculorum*, ed. J. Strange, 1, 2, 1851.

Carlyle: R. W. Carlyle, The claims of Innocent III to authority in temporal matters, *Tijdschrift voor Rechtsgesch.*, 1926.

Chanson (Chabot): *Guillem de Tudele. La Chanson de la croisade albigeoise*, ed. Chabot, 1931.

Chanson (Meyer): P. Meyer, *La Chanson de la croisade contre les Albigeois, commencée par Guillaume de Tudèle et continuée par un poète anonyme*, 2 vols, 1875, 1879.

Cheney, Master Philip: C.R. Cheney, Master Philip the Notary and the fortieth of 1199, *EHR* 63, 1948.

Chron. Andr.: *Willelmi Chronica Andrensis*, ed. D. Heller, MG. SS. 24.

Chron. Angl.: *Radulphi de Coggeshall Chronicon Anglicanum*, ed. J. Stevenson, Rer. Brit. med. aev. SS. No. 66, 1875.

Chron. Evesham: *Chronicon Abbatiae de Evesham ad annum 1418*, ed. W.D. Macray, Rer. Brit. med. aev. SS. No. 29, 1863.

Chron. Mont. Ser.: *Chronicon Montis Sereni*, ed. E. Ehrenfeuchter, MG. SS. 23.

Chron. regia Colon.: *Chronica Regia Coloniensis (Annales maximi Colonienses) cum continuationibus*, SS. rer. Germ., ed. G. Waitz, 1880.

Chron. Reinhardsbr.: *Chronica Reinhardsbrunnensis*, ed. O. Holder-Egger, MG. SS. 30$^1$.

Chron. Sublacense: *Chronicon Sublacense*, a cura di R. Morghen, SS. rer. Italicarum, rev. ed. 24$^6$, 1927.

Clary: Robert de Clary. *La prise de Constantinople 1203*, in Hopf (see below).

Cod. dipl. d'Orvieto: *Codice diplomatico della città d'Orvieto, documenti e regesti del secolo XI al XV e la carta del popolo*, ed. Fumi, 1884.

Cramer: V. Cramer, *Die Kreuzzugspredigt zur Befreiung des Hl. Landes 1095–1270*, Studien zur Geschichte und Charakteristik der Kreuzzugspropaganda, 1939.

Davidsohn, Gesch. v. Florenz: R. Davidsohn, *Geschichte von Florenz*, 8 vols, 1896–1927. English translation also available.

Davidsohn, Forsch.: R. Davidsohn, *Forschungen zur älteren Geschichte von Florenz*, 4 vols, 1896–1908.

Davidsohn, Philipp II.: R. Davidsohn, *Philipp II. August von Frankreich und Ingebourg*, Heidelberg thesis, 1888.

Davy: M. Davy, Les sermons universitaires Parisiens de 1230–1231. Contribution à l'histoire de la prédication médiévale, *Etud. de philos. médiév.* 15, 1931.

Delisle, Cat.: L. Delisle, *Catalogue des actes de Philippe-Auguste*, 1856.

Delisle, Lettres: L. Delisle, Lettres inédites d'Innocent III, *BECH* 34, 1873.

Domerham: Adamus de Domerham. *Historia de rebus gestis Glastoniensibus* descripsit primusque in lucem protulit T. Hearnius. Qui et Guilielmi Malmesburiensis librum de antiquitate ecclesiae Glastoniensis, et E. Archery excerpta e registris Wellensibus praemisit, 2 vols, paged consecutively, 1727.

Devastatio: *Devastatio Constantinopolitana a. 1204 ab auctore Germano descripta*, in Hopf (see below).

Eichmann, Acht und Bann: Ed. Eichmann, *Acht und Bann im Reichsrecht des Mittelalters*, 1909.

Elze: R. Elze, Die päpstliche Kapelle im 12. und 13. Jahrhundert, *ZRG* 37, 1950.

Epp. Cant.: *Epistolae Cantuarienses*; The letters of the prior and convent of Christ Church, Canterbury. From A.D. 1187 to A.D. 1199, ed. W. Stubbs, Rer. Brit. med. aev. SS. No. 38, 1865.

Falco: G. Falco, *L'amministrazione papale nella Campagna e nella Marittima dalla caduta della dominazione Bisantine al sorgere dei Comuni*, Arch. R. Soc. Rom. stor. patr. 38, 1916.

Fejér: G. Fejér, *Codex diplomaticus Hungariae ecclesiasticus ac civilis*, 11 vols, 1829–1844.

Ficker, Forsch.: L. Ficker, *Forschungen zur Reichs- und Rechtsgeschichte Italiens*, 4 vols, 1868–1874.

Fliche: A. Fliche, Innocent III et la réforme de l'église, *RHE* 44, 1949.

Fliche, Chrétienté: A. Fliche, *La Chrétienté romaine (1198–1274)*, Histoire de l'église depuis les origines jusqu'à nos jours 10, 1950.

Forest-van Steenberghen-de Gandillac: A. Forest, F. van Steenberghen, M. de Gandillac, *Le mouvement doctrinal du XI$^e$ au XIV$^e$ siècle*, Histoire de l'église depuis les origines jusqu'à nos jours, 13, 1951.

Friedberg: E. Friedberg, *Quinque compilationes antiquae*, 1882.

Gervase of Canterbury: *Gervasii Cantuariensis Opera historica*, ed. W. Stubbs, Rer. Brit. med. aev, SS. No. 71, 1879f.

Gesta: *Gesta Innocentii PP. III*, in Migne PL. (see below) Vol. 214.

Gesta Episc. Halberst.: *Gesta episcoporum Halberstadensium*, ed. L. Weiland, MG. SS. 23.

Gibbs and Lang: M. Gibbs and J. Lang, *Bishops and Reform, 1215–1272*; with special reference to the Lateran Council of 1215, 1934.

Girald. Cambr.: *Giraldi Cambrensis Opera*, 8 vols, ed. J.F. Dimock, G.F. Warner, J.S. Brewer, Rer. Brit. med. aev. SS. No. 21, 1861ff.

Gottlob, Servitientaxe: A. Gottlob, *Die Servitientaxe im 13. Jahrhundert. Eine Studie zur Geschichte des päpstlichen Gebührenwesens*, Kirchenrechtl. Abh., ed Stutz, No. 2, 1903.

Grabmann: M. Grabmann, *I divieti ecclesiastici di Aristotele sotto Innocenzo III e Gregorio IX*, Misc. Hist. Pont., 5, 1941.

Gregorovius: F. Gregorovius, *Geschichte der Stadt Rom im Mittelalter*, 8 vols, ⁴1886ff. English translation also available.

Grundmann: H. Grundmann, Religiöse Bewegungen im Mittelalter. Untersuchungen über die geschichtlichen Zusammenhänge zwischen der Ketzerei, den Bettelorden und der religiösen Frauenbewegung im 12. und 13. Jahrhundert und über die geschichtlichen Grundlagen der deutschen Mystik, *Hist. Stud.* 267, 1935.

Guébin-Lyon: see Peter des Vaux.

Gunther of Pairis: *Historia Constantinopolitanea seu De expugnatione urbis Constantinopolis*, in Riant, Vol. 1 (see below).

Hagemann: W. Hagemann, Fabriano im Kampf zwischen Kaisertum und Papsttum, *QFIAB* 30, 1940.

Hahn, Coll.: S.F. Hahn, *Collectio Monumentorum veterum et recentium* 1, 1724.

Haller, Heinr. VI.: J. Haller, Heinrich VI. und die römische Kurie, *MIÖG* 35, 1914.

Haller, Inn. III.: *Innocenz III. und Otto IV.*, in Papsttum und Kaisertum, Festschr. f. P. Kehr, 1926.

Haller, Papsttum: *Das Papsttum. Idee und Wirklichkeit*, Vol. 3, *Die Vollendung*, 1952.

Hampe, Registerbände: K. Hampe, Aus den verlorenen Registerbänden der Päpste Innocenz III. und Innocenz IV., *MIÖG* 23, 1902.

Hampe, Sommeraufenthalt: K. Hampe, Eine Schilderung des Sommeraufenthaltes der römischen Kurie unter Innocenz III. in Subiaco 1202, *HV* 8, 1905.

von Heckel, Dekretalensammlung: R. von Heckel, Die Dekretalensammlung des Gilbertus und Alanus nach den Weingartener Handschriften, *ZRG* 29, 1940.

von Heckel, Ordination: Die Verordnung Innocenz' III. über die absolute Ordination und die Forma "Cum secundum apostolum", *HJb* 55, 1935.

Heiler: Fr. Heiler, *Altkirchliche Autonomie und päpstlicher Zentralismus*, 1941.

Heller: E. Heller, Der kuriale Geschäftsgang in den Briefen des Thomas von Capua, *AUF* 13, 1935.

Heyer: Fr. Heyer, Ueber Petrus Collivaccinus von Benevent, *ZRG* 6, 1916.

Hilpisch: S. Hilpisch, *Geschichte des benediktinischen Mönchtums. In ihren Grundzügen dargestellt*, 1929.

Hist. Damiat.: *Historia Damiatina des Oliverus*, ed. Hoogeweg: Die Schriften des Kölner Domscholasters, späteren Bischofs von Paderborn und Kardinalbischofs von S. Sabina Oliverus, Bibl. d. Lit. Vereins in Stuttgart Vol. 202, 1894.

Hon. Reg.: *Honorii III papae registrum*, in Horoy (see below).

Hopf: Ch. Hopf, *Chroniques Gréco-Romanes inédites ou peu connues*, 1873.

Horoy: *Medii aevi bibliotheca patristica sive eiusdem temporis Patrologia ab anno MCCXVII usque ad Concilii Tridentini tempora*, ser. prima, 5 vols, 1879ff.

Hoveden: *Chronica Magistri Rogeri de Houeden*, ed. W. Stubbs, Rer. Brit. med. aev. SS. No. 51, 4 vols, 1868ff.

Huck: J. Ch. Huck, *Joachim von Floris und die joachitische Literatur*, 1938.

Huillard-Bréholles: J.L.A. Huillard-Bréholles, *Historia diplomatica Friderici secundi* . . . , 1852–1861.

Hurter: Fr. Hurter, *Geschichte Papst Innocenz des Dritten und seiner Zeitgenossen*, Vol. 1, [3]1841, 2–4, [2]1842–1844.

d'Irsay: S. d'Irsay, *Histoire des universités françaises et étrangères*, vol. 1, 1933.

James of Vitry (Moschus): *Jacobi de Vitriaco Libri duo, quorum prior orientalis sive hierosolymitanae: alter occidentalis Historiae nomine inscribitur*, ed. D.F. Moschus, 1597.

JL: *Regesta Pontificum Romanorum ab condita ecclesia ad annum post Christum natum MCXCVIII*, ed. Ph. Jaffé, 2 ed. rev. S. Loewenfeld, F. Kaltenbrunner, P. Ewald, 2 vols, 1885, 1888.

Jordan: K. Jordan, Zur päpstlichen Finanzgeschichte im 11. und 12. Jahrhundert, *QFIAB* 25, 1933/1934.

Kantorowicz: E. Kantorowicz, *Kaiser Friedrich der Zweite*, 1927. Ergänzungsband, Quellennachweise und Exkurse, 1931. English translation also available.

Kauffmann: H. Kauffmann, *Die italienische Politik Kaiser Friedrichs I, nach dem Frieden von Constanz 1183–1189*, Greifsw. Abh. z. Gesch. d. MA 3, 1933.

Kehr, Briefbuch: P. Kehr, Das Briefbuch des Thomas von Gaeta, Justitiars Friedrichs II., *QFIAB* 8, 1905.

Kehr, Gött. Nachr. 1898: *Papsturkunden in Benevent und der Capitanata*, Gött. Nachr., 1898, Vol. 1.

Kehr, Gött. Nachr. 1903: *Papsturkunden im westlichen Toskana*, Gött. Nachr., 1903, Vol. 5.

Kehr, It. Pont.: *Italia Pontificia sive repertorium privilegiorum et litterarum a Romanis Pontificibus ante annum MCLXXXXVIII Italiae ecclesiis, monasteriis, civitatibus singulisque personis concessorum*, Regesta Pontificum Romanorum, 8 vols, 1906ff.

Kempf, Die Register: Fr. Kempf, *Die Register Innocenz' III. Eine paläographisch-diplomatische Untersuchung*, Misc. Hist. Pont. 9, 1945.

Kempf, Regestum, or Kempf: *Regestum Innocentii III papae super negotio romani imperii*, Misc. Hist. Pont. 12, 1947.

Kempf, Die zwei Versprechen: Fr. Kempf, *Die zwei Versprechen Ottos IV. an die römische Kirche 1200–1201*, Festschr. f. Stengel, 1952, pp. 359ff.

Kuttner, Joh. Teutonicus: S. Kuttner, *Teutonicus, das vierte Laterankonzil und die Compilatio quarta*, Misc. G. Mercati, Studi e Testi 125, 1946, pp. 608ff.

Leclercq: *Histoire des Conciles d'après les documents originaux* par Ch. J. Hefele. Nouv. trad. franç. faite sur la 2e éd. allem. par . . . (H. Leclercq), Vol. 5, in two parts, consecutive pagination, 1912f.

Lib. cens.: P. Fabre and L. Duchesne, *Le Liber censuum de l'Eglise Romaine*, 2 vols, 1910.

Lib. Pont.: *Liber pontificalis*. Texte, introduction et commentaire publ. par L. Duchesne, 2 vols, 1886, 1892.

Luchaire, Innocent III: A. Luchaire, *Innocent III*, 6 vols, 1904–1908.

Luchaire, L'avènement: A. Luchaire, *L'avènement d'Innocent III*, Séances et travaux de l'Acad. des scienc. morales et polit., Compte rendu 158, 1902.

Luchaire, Les ligues: *Innocent III et les ligues de Toscanie et de Lombardie, ibid.*, Compte rendu 161, 1904.

Maccarrone, Chiesa: M. Maccarrone, *Chiesa e stato nella dottrina di papa Innocenzo III*, Lateranum, nov. ser. 6, 1940.

Maccarrone, Innoc.: *Innocenzo III primo del suo pontificato*, Arch. Rom. stor. patr. 66, 1943.

Mandonnet: P. Mandonnet, *Saint Dominique. L'idée, l'homme et l'oeuvre.* Augm. de notes et d'études critiques par M.H. Vicaire, 2 vols, 1937f.

Mansi: J.F. Mansi, *Sacrorum conciliorum nova et amplissima Collectio...* vol. 22, 1903.

Marchetti-Longhi: Marchetti-Longhi, *Ricerche sulla famiglia di Gregorio IX*, Arch. Rom. stor. patr. 10, 1944.

Martini: Martini, *Innocenzo III ed il finanziamento delle crociate*, Arch. Rom. stor. patr. 10, 1944.

Maschke: E. Maschke, Der Peterspfennig in Polen und im deutschen Osten, *Königsb. hist. Forsch.* 5, 1933.

Mercati: A. Mercati, *La prima relazione del cardinale Nicoló de Romanis sulla sua legazione in Ingilterra 1213*, Essays on hist., pres. to R.L. Poole, 1927.

Meyer: see Chanson (Meyer).

Migne, PL.: J.P. Migne, *Patrologiae latinae cursus completus*, 1844–1864.

Migne, PG.: J.P. Migne, *Patrologiae Graecae cursus completus*, 1857–1886.

Mochi Onory: S. Mochi Onory, *Fonti canonistiche dell'idea moderna dello stato*, Pubbl. dell'univ. catt. del Sacro Cuore, Vol. 38, 1951.

Müller: E. Müller, Der Bericht des Abtes Hariulf von Oudenburg über seine Prozessverhandlung an der römischen Kurie im Jahre 1141, NA 48, 1930.

Muratori: L.A. Muratori, *Antiquitates Italicae medii aevi*, 17 vols, ²1777–1780.

Norden: W. Norden, *Das Papsttum und Byzanz. Die Trennung der beiden Mächte und das Problem ihrer Wiedervereinigung bis zum Untergange des byzantinischen Reiches (1453)*, 1903.

Ott: L. Ott, *Untersuchungen zur theologischen Briefliteratur der Frühscholastik*, Beitr. z. Gesch. d. Philos. und Theol. des MA 34, 1937.

Otto of Sankt Blasien: *Ottonis de Sancto Blasio Chronica*, ed. A. Hofmeister, SS. rer. Germ. 1912

P. or Potthast: *Regesta Pontificum Romanorum unde ab a. post Christum natum MCXCVIII ad a. MCCCIV*, ed. A. Potthast, 2 vols, 1874–1875.

Peter des Vaux: P. Guébin and E. Lyon, *Petri Vallium Sarnaii Monachi Hystoria Albigensis*, 3 vols, 1926–1939.

Recueil: *Recueil des historiens des Gaules et de la France*, founded by M. Bouquet. Reprinted and continued by L. Delisle, 25 vols, 1869–1904.

Reg. (if no brackets follow): *Innocentii III Romani Pontificis Regestorum sive Epistolarum libri*, in Migne PL. (see above) Vols 214–216 and Supplementum Vol. 217, quoted by book number (Rom.) and letter number (Arabic).

Reimchronik: *Braunschweiger Reimchronik*, ed. L. Weiland, MG. Dt. Chron. 2.

Reiner of Liège: *Reineri Annales*, MG. SS. 16.

Reuter: A.E. Reuter, *Königtum und Episkopat in Portugal im 13. Jahrhundert*, 1913.

Riant: P. Riant, *Exuviae sacrae Constantinopolitanae...*, 2 vols, 1877.

Richard of S. Germano: *Ryccardi de Sancto Germano notarii Chronica*, ed. G.H. Pertz, SS. rer. Germ. 1864.

Rich. of S. Germ. (Gaudenzi): *Ignoti monachi cisterciensis S. Mariae de Ferraria Chronica, et Ryccardi de Sancto Germano chronica priora*, ed. A. Gaudenzi, Soc. napol. di stor. patr., Monumenti stor., ser. 1, chronache, 1888.

Rigord (Delaborde): see William Brito (Delaborde).

RNI (if no brackets follow): *Regestum Domini Innocentii III super negotio Romani imperii*, in Migne PL. (see above) Vol. 216 (see too Kempf, Regestum), quoted by number of letter.

Rob. Autissiod.: *Roberti Canonici S. Mariani Autissiodorensis Cronicon*, ed. O. Holder-Egger, MG. SS. 26.

Roul. de Cluny: J.L.A. Huillard-Bréholles, *Examen des Chartes de l'église Romaine contenus dans les rouleaux dits Rouleaux de Cluny*, Notes et extraits des mss. de la Bibl. Nat., 1865.

Rymer: *Foedera... Cura et Studio Thomae Rymer*, new ed. by A. Clarke, F. Holbrooke, J. Caley, 1816ff.

Santifaller: L. Santifaller, *Beiträge zur Geschichte des lateinischen Patriarchats von Konstantinopel (1204–1261) und der venezianischen Urkunde*, Hist. diplom. Forsch. 3, 1938.

Sappok: G. Sappok, *Die Anfänge des Bistums Posen und die Reihe seiner Bischöfe von 968–1498*, Deutschl. u. d. Osten 6, 1937.

Schnürer: G. Schnürer, *Kirche und Kultur im Mittelalter*, Vol. 2, 1926.

Schöppenchronik: *Die Magdeburger Schöppenchronik*, Die Chroniken der deutsch. Städte v. 14. bis ins 16. Jh., ed. Hist. Comm. b. d. Königl. bayr. Ak. d. Wiss. 7, 1869.

Seeger: J. Seeger, *Die Reorganisation des Kirchenstaates unter Innocenz III. Grundlagen und Durchführung*, Kiel thesis, 1937.

Singer: H. Singer, *Die Dekretalensammlung der Bernhardus Compostellanus antiquus*, SB Wien, Vol. 171, Part 2, 1914.

Stickler: A. Stickler, *Der Schwerterbegriff bei Huguccio*, Ephemerides Juris Canonici Ann. III num. 2, 1947, pp. 201ff.

Tangl: M. Tangl, *Die päpstlichen Kanzleiordnungen von 1200–1500*, 1894.

Tellenbach: G. Tellenbach, *Libertas. Kirche und Weltordnung im Zeitalter des Investiturstreites*, Forsch. z. Kirchen- u. Geistesgesch. 7, 1936.

Tenbrock: R.H. Tenbrock, *Eherecht und Ehepolitik bei Innocenz III.*, München thesis, 1933.

Thomas of Celano (Alençon): *Sancti Francisci vita et miracula additis opusculis liturgicis auctore fratris Thomae de Celano*, ed. Ed. Alençon, 1906.

Tillmann, Legaten: H. Tillmann, *Die päpstlichen Legaten in England bis zur Beendigung der Legation Gualas (1218)*, Bonn thesis, 1926.

Tillmann, Rekuperationen: Das Schicksal der päpstlichen Rekuperationen nach dem Friedensabkommen zwischen Philipp von Schwaben und der römischen Kirche, *HJb.* 51, 1931.

Tillmann, Ueber päpstliche Schreiben: Ueber päpstliche Schreiben mit bedingter Gültigkeit im 12. und 13. Jahrhundert, *MIÖG* 45, 1931.

Tillmann, Zum Regestum: Zum Regestum super negotio Romani Imperii Innocenz' III, *QFIAB* 23, 1932.

Tillmann, Zur Frage: Zur Frage des Verhältnisses von Kirche und Staat in Lehre und Praxis Papst Innocenz' III, *DA* 9, 1951.

Tiraboschi: G. Tiraboschi, *Vetera humiliatorum monumenta...*, 3 vols, 1766, 1777.

Vaissete: *Histoire générale de Languedoc... composé... par...* C. de Vie, J.J. Vaissete, 16 vols, 1872ff.

Villehardouin: Geoffroi de Ville-Hardouin, *De la Conquête de Constantinople par les Français et les Vénétiens*, Recueil, Vol. 18, 1879.

Vincke: J. Vincke, *Der Eheprozess Peters II. von Aragon (1206–1213)*, Ges. Aufs. z. Kulturgesch. Spaniens 5, 1935.

Wenck, Päpste: K. Wenck, *Die römischen Päpste zwischen Alexander III. und Innocenz III. und der Designationsversuch Weihnachten 1197*, in Papsttum und Kaisertum, Festschr. f. P. Kehr, 1926.

Wendover: *Rogeri de Wendover liber qui dicitur Flores historiarum...* ed. H.G. Hewlett, Rer. Brit. med. aev. SS. No. 84, 3 vols, 1886f.

William Brito (Delaborde): H.F. Delaborde, *Oeuvres de Rigord et de Guillaume le Briton*, 3 vols, 1882–1885.

William of Puylaur: Beyssier, *Guillaume de Puyslaurens et sa chronique*, Bibl. de la fac. des lettres de l'univ. de Paris 18, 1904.

Winkelmann, Philipp u. Otto IV.: E. Winkelmann, *Philipp von Schwaben und Otto IV. von Braunschweig*, 2 vols, separate pagination, 1873–1878.

Zoepffel: R. Zoepffel, *Die Papstwahlen und die mit ihnen in nächstem Zusammenhang stehenden Ceremonien in ihrer Entwicklung vom 11. bis zum 14. Jahrhundert*, 1871.

# Addenda

Chapter 2, and in particular n. 121, cf. Maccarone, *Il papa 'Vicarius Christi'. Testi e dottrina, dal sec. XII al principio del XIV*, Misc. Pio Paschini, 1948, 1, 427ff.

Chapter 3, litigation between Evesham and Worcester, see D. Knowles, *The monastic order in England*, 1950, 363ff.

Chapter 4, the dispute with the English church, see Knowles, 363ff.

Chapter 6, n. 64, the effect of the Fourth Lateran Council on the reform of the English monasteries, see Knowles, 370ff.

Neither of the above works was available until after the text of the German edition of this book was printed.

# CHAPTER 1

# Lothair of Segni

Pope Celestine III died on 8 January 1198 at a moment of highest historical tension and import. Three months previously the Emperor Henry VI had passed away. A sudden death had annihilated the ruler's world-embracing designs and projects. The lands over which he had firmly held sway, Germany, Central Italy and the Sicilian kingdom, threatened to lapse into anarchy. The collapse of the imperial power in Italy removed a heavy pressure from the papacy. Paralysingly the emperor's hand had weighed upon it. It had been powerless politically and restricted in its free scope ecclesiastically. The question of the emperor's succession was yet unresolved and the import of his death not to be foreseen. In the forthcoming election of the new pope the college of cardinals, therefore, was burdened with the heavy task of choosing the man who would best use the advantage of the historical juncture and, at the same time, know how to obviate the dangers it involved.

The cardinals who remained by the pope's death bed in the Lateran Palace, looked forward to the election not without concern. They seem to have feared an infringement on their freedom of decision by attempts of the Romans[1] at interfering with the election or disturbing it.[2] Rome was not in the hands of the Curia. A senator apparently not bound to allegiance to the Roman Church ruled in Rome at that time, and outside Rome, in the Sabina and Marittima, officials of the Roman commune held office instead of papal justiciars.[3] In weakness and indulgence Celestine III had allowed the Romans to usurp the sovereign rights in the city and its environs. For Rome's leading figures much depended upon the attitude the pope to be would take up regarding the usurpations by the commune.[4] The masses will have been affected more strongly by the question whether the newly-elect would pay the large election presents[5] which the Romans claimed as their due by right.

In view of the unsafe conditions in Rome some of the cardinals left the Lateran immediately after the pope's death and resorted to the Septizonium of Septimius Severus on the southern slope of the Palatine.[6] The strong walls of the debris of the ancient imperial palace, now transformed into a fortress, which were in the hands of the Frangipani,[7] gave the cardinals greater protection than the poorly protected Lateran.[8]

Amongst the cardinals who thought it appropriate to remain in the Lateran until the funeral ceremonies had been concluded[9] and only then joined their brethren-cardinals in the Septizonium, was Lothair of Segni, cardinal deacon of SS Sergius and Bacchus.

Already at the first ballot, in which four candidates had been nominated,[10] he received, though at only thirty-seven years of age the youngest of the college, a majority of votes. At the second ballot, after some discussion about his youthfulness, he was unanimously elected pope the very same day.[11]

The crowd which had waited outside for the outcome of the election may have regarded and cheered Lothair, now Innocent III,[12] as a Roman citizen. Born in 1160 or in the first days of 1161[13] in the castle of Gavignano[14] as son of Trasimund of Segni of a propertied[15] noble family of the Roman Campania,[16] Lothair belonged to the Roman-civic patrician family of the Scotti on the side of his mother Claricia.[17] It is possible that his family moved to Rome in his early youth.[18] In any case it was in Rome that Lothair received his elementary schooling. By Peter Ismael, whom Innocent III later promoted to be bishop of Sutri, he was initiated, possibly in the school of the monastery of St Andrew,[19] into scholastic studies. In his clerical career young Lothair has enjoyed the special favour of highly-placed clerics of Roman-civic descent, such as Paul Scolari, the future Clement III, and the influential Octavian of SS Sergius and Bacchus, the later cardinal bishop of Ostia, who may have been relatives or friends of his family.[20] During Lothair's years of study in Rome the Curia was not resident in the city, since even after the disaster suffered by the imperial army in the fever-heat of August 1167, the ruling faction in the city still supported the emperor and his anti-popes Paschal III and Calixtus III.[21] Thus the antagonism between pope and emperor was already imprinted on the mind and feelings of the boy or adolescent young man.

Like so many of his fellow-Italians Lothair, who was perhaps already then a canon of St Peter,[22] was drawn to France by the high reputation which the Paris schools enjoyed in the philosophical and theological disciplines. To this country and to the University of Paris which, later on effectively supported by him,[23] began to emerge from the *universitas* of students and teachers at the Paris schools,[24] Innocent throughout his life extended a feeling of connection and indebtedness.[25] The thoughts of the pope often turned to his student days in Paris.[26] Peter of Corbeil,[27] his teacher of theology, was later promoted by the grateful[28] student to be bishop of Cambrai and afterwards archbishop of Sens. The Parisian masters Stephen Langton[29] and Robert Courçon[30] he called to the college of cardinals. Odo of Sully, the distinguished bishop of Paris who, like Robert and Stephen, was a possible fellow student of Lothair during his student days in Paris,[31] became one of the men of his trust in the French episcopate. It may have been in Paris that Lothair also became acquainted with Conrad of Querfurt, the later bishop of Würzburg and chancellor of Philip of Swabia, as well as with Master David of Dinant, the later heretic. It is said that, even after he became pope, he enjoyed conversations with David to the offence of many.[32] Conrad of Querfurt was to meet the erstwhile friend[33] again under dramatic circumstances.[34]

During Lothair's years of study as well as during his pontificate a conservative line of thought prevailed at the Paris schools which was but little interested in the interpenetration of theology by philosophy and which offered resistance to the growth of Aristotelianism.[35] It centered on the study of the Holy Scriptures and on the practical questions of morals and sacramental doctrine. Its mode of thought was more pastoral than speculative.[36] Nevertheless, the trinitarian and christological controversies, particularly those having reference to the teachings of Peter Lombard, the celebrated and at the same time very controversial sometime Parisian teacher,[37] may then have been passionately discussed.[38] Peter of Corbeil, as regards the question of the character of the reunion of the two natures in Christ, was an exponent of the *assumptus*-theory,[39] according to which in the incarnation a finite substance of flesh and blood has been assumed by the Logos, and thus rejected the *habitus*-theory[40] probably shared by the Lombard, namely the view that the Logos had taken on body and soul only like a habit or garment.

Lothair, whose later writings clearly show the pastoral attitude of the conservative mode of thought,[41] still enjoyed taking up his own position in the theological questions, thereby making use of the panoply of dialectical philosophy. It is not certain that he followed his teacher in the rejection of the *habitus*-theory. In a letter from his papal years, incorporated into the first collection of his decretals, he still cites without further commentary the *habitus*-doctrine already condemned by Alexander III[42] as one of the attempts at solving the vexed christological question.[43] At the Lateran Council of 1215, however, the *habitus*-doctrine was finally abandoned by the Council's profession of Christ as the truly incarnate Logos who, as man being composed of rational soul and human flesh, is one person in two natures.[44] At this same Council Innocent in a most singular manner conferred honour on the Lombard: *Nos autem, sacro et universali concilio approbante, credimus et confitemur cum Petro. . . .* With these words begins the Council's solemn avowal of the disputed Trinity-doctrine of the Lombard, which was preceded by the condemnation of Joachim of Fiore's counter-theses.[45] In these words may well ring the echo of many a discussion on the Lombard's theology, in which Lothair had taken part during his Paris years and later.[46] When pope, Lothair was, however, more sceptical than in his student years as regards the applicability of the dialectical method to the mysteries of Christinanity, and many a problem discussed in the schools he later dismissed as futile and sophistic or inappropriate. He had become vividly aware of the limits of theological cognition,[48] an experience which the young Lothair had not yet felt when he, sharpwitted, glib of tongue, and fond of dealing with words,[49] discussed the theological school-problems[50] in the circle of his fellow students or in the community of teachers and students.

It was during his days in Paris, probably in the beginning of 1187, that Lothair made a pilgrim's visit to the grave of St Thomas of Canterbury, the martyr of ecclesiastical liberty.[51] It must have been a deeply impressing experience for the man who, as pope, showed how vividly he was affected by the idea of the *libertas ecclesiae*. If at that time in England he was in company with the cardinal legate Octavian of SS Sergius and Bacchus, his fatherly friend, he had the opportunity of seeing with his own eyes that, despite Becket's martyrdom, the king continued to hold sway over the English church. He did not foresee that it would be his destiny to carry on Thomas Becket's fight and to bring it to a victorious end.

In autumn 1187 at the latest Lothair returned from France to Italy where he intended to continue his studies in Bologna.

It is to the University of Bologna that Lothair owes his excellent knowledge of jurisprudence,[52] in which field, though not the center of his interests, his supreme talent came into its own. One of the university teachers was Uguccio of Pisa, whom Innocent later promoted to be bishop of Ferrara. The famous canonist offered opposition to the extreme hierocratical ideas of his time as regards the relationship between spiritual and temporal power.[53] He taught that both powers, though equally from God, were independent from each other as regards their institution (*quoad institutionem*).[54] Lothair's own earlier view must have been somewhat shaken when Uguccio cited the passage of the *decretum*, according to which the Lord transferred to Peter power over the terrestrial as well as the celestial realm;[55] a spiritual interpretation[56] and expressly opposed to those who, in view of this passage, attributed to the pope both swords, the spiritual as well as the temporal one.[57] Uguccio also held the view that the emperor had received the power of the sword and his office not, in the first place, by way of his coronation by the pope, but from the people and the princes by virtue of his election.[58] Uguccio exercised a strong and lasting influence on the later pope's views on church policy.[59]

In the first months of his studies in Bologna, or shortly before, Lothair had been ordained subdeacon by Pope Gregory VIII, possibly during the latter's stay in Bologna on about 18 or 20 November 1187.[60] Gregory did not belong to the circle of men with which Lothair was closely connected by descent or bonds of relationship. Gregory's elevation to the papacy and the defeat of Paul Scolari, Lothair's patron, in the papal election of 1187, may have been an indication that a movement of a more spiritual approach, supported by cardinals of non-Roman descent, had gained the ascendancy over a more worldly-directed movement, which was rooted in the Roman-civic clergy.[61] Whatever tensions may have existed between Gregory VIII and Paul Scolari, they did not impair the veneration the young cleric held for the saintly pope.[62]

The very Paul Scolari, who as Clement III followed Gregory on the throne of Peter as early as December of the same year summoned the not yet twenty-nine years old Lothair of Segni, possibly in December 1189,[63] to the college of cardinals and in token of special favour invested him with the deaconship of SS Sergius and Bacchus,[64] which he had himself held as cardinal-deacon. The promotion of the young man, who may have completed his studies not long before,[65] is likely to have caused the same discontent as Clement's cardinals' promotions in the summer of 1189, by which cardinal Octavian had been appointed bishop of Ostia. But the new cardinal of SS Sergius and Bacchus did not feel indebted to any faction. "Without quarrel he lived with the brethren and stood aloof from taking sides."[65]

Lothair enjoyed the favour of a pope during the few months only in which Clement III was destined to sit on the throne of Peter, though we do not know whether the new pope, Celestine III, made the cardinal pay for the family enmity existing between the Boboni, the pope's family, and the Scotti, Lothair's family by his mother's side.[67] During Celestine's reign Lothair was attached to the Curia and frequently employed as *auditor* in legal proceedings.[68] Celestine even made the cardinal a present for his titular church.[69] That the highly qualified cardinal was not in any particular degree charged with dealings of political import,[70] need not necessarily be explained in terms of the enmity between the two families. It was not to be expected that the pope in his old age would credit a man as young as Lothair with being mature enough to handle affairs in the difficult field of church and world politics.

It is, therefore, unlikely that up to the pope's last serious illness[71] the cardinal of Segni in any substantial degree influenced the decisions of high politics which the Curia had to take during Celestine's pontificate. Unless special circumstances prevented his attending, Lothair would on 15 April 1191 have been, among the other cardinals, the displeased witness of the coronation as emperor, reluctantly performed by Celestine III, of Henry VI, the 'persecutor' and member of the 'house of persecutors'.[72] When Henry by his subsequent conquest of the Norman kingdom of Sicily deprived the Roman Church of its feudal sovereignty over the Sicilian vassal state, and when he arbitrarily disposed over the church and the churches of the kingdom, Lothair felt as if the Roman Church was trodden underfoot by its persecutor.[73] Lothair's indignation at the cruel punishment of the Sicilian conspiracy of 1197, and perhaps also the disappointment he felt at its failure, re-echoes in the pope's impassioned accusations against Henry and his helpers for their inhuman ravaging in the unfortunate country.[74] The pope's aversion to the Germans, the *gens robusta* whose language was not understood in Italy,[75] may be rooted in the experience he had in the years of his boyhood of the fierce struggle between Alexander III and Frederick Barbarossa. Later on Innocent denounced Frederick in front of the envoys of the latter's son Philip as a cruel and persistent persecutor of the Church.[76]

The impotence of the papacy, the vacillations of papal policy in the face of events, may be reckoned among the adversities from which Lothair himself tells us[77] he suffered during his cardinalcy. In other respects, too, conditions were disagreeable at the Curia. Clement III, Lothair's patron, had become a laughingstock because of his almost beggarly scramble for presents,[78] and Celestine, by his fickleness, was no less detrimental to the reputation of the papacy. It will not always have been easy for the high-spirited[79] young cardinal to curb his indignation at the erratic course and unreliability of papal policy and at the very volatile and arbitrary decisions of Celestine III which he witnessed in his capacity as *auditor* in many a legal proceeding. Innocent revoked a number of decrees of his predecessor as being contrary to law.[80] He was not alone in his indignation. A great part of the cardinals refused to sanction a privilege of Celestine III for a Spanish monastery, because it obviously encroached on the rights of the competent bishop.[81]

The care for the restoration of his dilapidated titular church in the first two years of his cardinalcy[82] and his activities as an author may, apart from his work in the service of the Curia, have distracted Lothair from all that weighed heavily upon him. Three of his works originate from his years as cardinal: the book on the misery of human condition (*De misera condicione hominis*),[83] the book on the 'fourfold species' of marriage (*De quadripartita specie nuptiarum*),[84] and the book on the mysteries of the Mass (*De missarum mysteriis*).[85] The treatise on the misery of human condition seems at first sight to mirror the author's gloomy disposition. In the first part, written probably much earlier than the other two parts,[86] he assembles all that is evil, nay loathsome in life, into a repellant picture of human existence which, though sinewy of style, by modern standards is schoolboy-like and tastelessly exaggerated.[87] In the second part, which deals with the cardinal sins, and in the third part on the penalties of hell, there is no more trace of the rhetorical delight in word-sound and word-play. The second part contains beautiful passages, not at all in keeping with the exposition of human misery, like the address to the greedy one: "Do you want to know why you continue to remain empty...? Your measure is not filled because it can always hold more than it just contains. For the human mind is able to hold God Himself. Whatever it contains, it is, therefore, never filled if it does not possess God".[88] The work is, in its first part at least, characteristic neither for Lothair's personality nor for his then mood nor for his outlook on life. In his preface he states that it is with

intention that he treats his subject from a one-sided point of view. He
had described, he writes, the baseness of human nature in order to
curb pride, and was thinking of describing its dignity, too, in order to
promote humility.[89] The second treatise, consequently, he would have
couched in light colours in the same degree as the first delights in dark
colours. He applies here the same method which later when pope
guided him when he delivered his judicial decisions. He preceded
them by so effective an exposition of the arguments for and against
the parties that each party, as long as he was exposing the arguments
in its favour, expected to win the day.[90] The treatise on human misery
enumerates the encumbrances only of human life. The necessary
counter-part was never written.

The book on the fourfold species of marriage is another piece of
occasional writing with little personal touch.[91] It deals with
marriage in its four outward forms, the association between man and
his lawful wife, between Christ and the Church, between God and the
soul and between the Logos and human nature, resorting to the
allegoric mode of expression then so popular, but so hard for the
modern mind to appreciate, and indulging, just as in the treatise on
human misery, in a fatiguing excess of quotations from the Holy
Scriptures.

The book on the mysteries of the Mass has survived only in its
revised form dating from the time as pope,[92] but in view of Lothair's
predominant interest in liturgies the original version, too, is sure to
have been a work which, more than the other two works, was
expressive of the author's personal attachment. The solemn ceremonies of the papal services[93] and the liturgical texts in the papal
library as well as historical works such as the *Liber pontificalis*, were
for him rich sources of research material.

If in the last weeks or months of the decrepit and sick Celestine
III's life the college of cardinals was responsible for the shaping of
papal policy, Cardinal Lothair must have shaken off the reserve he
had guarded so far[94] and have assumed his own share of responsibility. It was at this moment that, by the emperor's death, the Curia
was faced with momentous decisions. Otherwise there would be no
explanation for the majority of votes he received right away at the first
ballot. The election of the cardinal of SS Sergius and Bacchus may have
meant the victory of a specific view as to the political needs of the hour,
but there is nothing to indicate that by his election a political tendency had
triumphed over a religious one.[95]

## Notes to Chapter 1

[1]Ten years earlier, the influence of Leo del Monumento, Roman consul and leader of the imperial faction in Rome, had contributed to the election of Clement III. (Ann. Romani 349. Cf. Wenck, Päpste, 431; on Leo del Monumento see Kauffman, 140ff.). Since the election of 1187 took place outside Rome, the Romans were unable to bring any meaningful pressure to bear. See Zoepffel, 15, for the general threat posed to the independence of papal elections by the Romans.

[2]See below, n. 6.

[3]Gesta c. 8, 133. Cf. also Reg. II 239 (Migne PL. 214, 800).

[4]Cf. Gesta c. 133.

[5]Cf. Wenck, Päpste, 419f., 437.

[6]See Maccarrone, Innoc., 127, for the location of the election. For the Septizonium see (in addition to the literature given in Maccarrone): Wenck, Das erste Konklave der Papstgeschichte Rom August bis Oktober 1241 (QFIAB 18, 144); Gregorovius, Vol. 3, 567f., Vol. 4, 230, Vol. 5, 646 and Luchaire, L'avènement, 684.

[7]See Bartoli, La diaconia di S. Lucia in Settizonio (Arch. R. Soc. stor. patr. 50, 1927), 63ff. They belonged to the monks of St Andrew's, who had rented them to the Frangipani. The cardinals' decision to hold the election under the protection of the Frangipani suggests a combination of interesting circumstances which cannot be fully unravelled. At the schismatic papal election of 1130, which was also held under the auspices and protection of the Frangipani, it was their candidate, Innocent II, who was elected. The majority of the cardinals, those who were later to support Anacletus II, Pierleone, had already left the bedside of the dying Honorius II before he passed away, (cf. Haller, 33f.). It provides a strange parallel to the election of 1198.

[8]*Ut liberius et securius ibi possent de successoris electione tractare* (Gesta c. 5) – *Secessimus ut tanto licentius et tutius de substitutione pontificis tractaremus* (Reg. I 1). For the significance of the location as a means of securing a properly held election see Zoepffel, 13ff. and 159.

[9]Gesta c. 5.

[10]For the nomination of candidates at the pope's election see Zoepffel, 31ff.

[11]Gesta c. 5; Reg. I 1. Hoveden's account of events during the election (4, 174) is unconvincing in its detail (but Wenck, Päpste, 462 disagrees). Maccarrone (Innoc., 128) also casts some doubts on Hoveden's account but on the grounds of minor inaccuracies in such matters as time, and Lothair's age, details which scarcely suffice to discount Hoveden's account as a whole. Hoveden is wrong to suggest that John of Salerno gained ten votes in the first ballot. There were some nineteen cardinals involved in the election, not the twenty-seven or twenty-eight Wenck assumes. According to the Gesta (c. 7) the new pope's consecration as bishop on 22 February was attended by fifteen cardinal priests and cardinal deacons. Of the cardinal bishops not mentioned by name in the Gesta it is probable that only those of Ostia and Porto took part in the ceremony. The cardinal bishop of Sabina, Conrad of Mainz, was in the Holy Land, Praeneste and Tusculum were probably vacant, as was Albano. (It was not until 1199 that a bishop of Albano signed the papal documents.) Between the pope's election and consecration John of St Paul, cardinal priest of S Prisca, Cinthius and Gregory of S Maria in Porticu left the Curia, while Peter of Capua, on the other hand, returned (Gesta c. 7). If, of the three candidates whom the Gesta records as having stood against Lothair, the one to

whom Hoveden refers gained ten votes, and the other two only one vote each, Lothair would have gained neither an absolute nor a relative majority in the election. John of Salerno would have gained more than half the votes cast if he had indeed received ten votes. Hoveden's claim that Octavian of Ostia, Peter of Porto, Jordan of Novafossa and Gratian, indeed that every cardinal had sought the papacy for himself is most improbable. Such ambitions must have been curbed with considerable alacrity to allow Lothair to be elected on the first day of the electoral process. Nor is it altogether clear whether Celestine III did in fact, as Hoveden suggests (4, 32), attempt to designate his own successor. (Cf. Wenck, Päpste, 458, and Maccarrone, Innoc., 125.) Clearly Hoveden's sources were in Rome itself, but seem to have relied more on rumour than fact.

[12]For the procedure of changing the pope-elect's name, see Zoepffel, 166ff.

[13]According to the Gesta Innocent was thirty-seven years old at his election on 8 January 1198 (c. 5).

[14]See Maccarrone, Innoc., 66f.

[15]See Maccarrone, *loc. cit.*

[16]The statement of the Gesta of the pope that Innocent was a member of the house of Segni (c. 1) shows, according to Maccarrone (63f.), that the nobles were among the governors of the city of Segni. (On the designation of the city governors in the cities of the Campania as *comites* see Falco, 695.) Maccarrone believes that the designation of office became a family name after the family moved into the city. However, Innocent's brother Richard is not referred to as count before 1208, the year in which he received the county of Sora as a Sicilian fief (cf. Marchetti-Longhi, 280). It is my belief that the designation of the family as 'Conti', simply meaning 'counts', is linked to the loss of the county of Sora in 1225. To style Lothair, as is often done, 'count of Segni', is altogether arbitrary, since it was not then the custom for the sons of counts to bear their father's title. On the origins of the pope's family and its relationships to other noble families, which has been the subject of much invention and unsupportable attestation, see Maccarrone, Innoc., 61ff., and Marchetti-Longhi, 275ff.

[17]On the Scotti see Maccarrone, Innoc., 65f., Marchetti-Longhi, 298f.

[18]Cf. Maccarrone, Innoc., 68f.

[19]This according to Maccarrone, Innoc., 69, on the basis of Gesta c. 147 and probably Reg. X 145, where Peter Ismael is described as sometime abbot of St Andrew's.

[20]There is insufficient evidence to support the argument that these two men and Cardinal John of Anagni were closely related to Lothair (see Maccarrone, Innoc., 64ff.). There were certainly close links between them, however. Lothair's links with Octavian which predate Innocent's election as pope are discussed below, Chapter 10, n. 58. It is significant for Lothair's relationship with Paul Scolari that Scolari, as Clement III, summoned the twenty-eight year old Lothair into the college of cardinals and, as the Gesta emphasize (c. 3), bestowed upon him his own former titular church. There does seem to be some justification for supposing a relationship between the three men, though probably a rather distant one. Innocent III and Octavian were both described as *consanguinei* of Philip of France (Innocent: RNI 13, Octavian: Hoveden 4, 148). According to Hurter (1, p. 6, n. 30) Clement III was also a *consanguineus* of the king. Hurter refers for this assertion to a letter from Stephen of Tournai, then abbot of St Geneviève's' to a papal *consanguineus* of the king of France (Migne PL. 211, 427ff.), but this letter was written during the king's crusade and not, as the editor believed, in 1190 on the feast of St John the Baptist, the day on which Philip took the cross. It

could therefore also have been addressed to Celestine (1191–1198). No matter how far-fetched the blood relationship between the king and the Roman clerics may have been, such a relationship between a Roman civic and a Campanian nobleman and the king of France seems so strange that we can scarcely expect to find the names of two simple noble families from Rome or its environs independently of each other in Philip's pedigree. There is one further factor which supports a family link between Lothair, Octavian and Clement III: it was a favourite papal custom to bestow their former titular churches or those of cardinals who had died or been promoted on their own relatives and on the latter's respectively (see Wenck, Päpste, 454). Now the list of cardinal deacons of SS Sergius and Bacchus for the end of the twelfth and the beginning of the thirteenth centuries presents the following picture: Paul Scolari (Clement III), Octavian, Lothair of Segni (Innocent III), Octavian (*consobrinus* of Innocent III, Gesta c. 23 [Migne PL. 214 XLII] and c. 147; cf. Elze, 184). In addition I should like to point out that Octavian's successor in Ostia was Ugolino, who was in turn followed by Rainald, both of whom were commonly regarded as belonging to the house of the counts of Segni, the Conti, until Marchetti-Longhi's investigations (275ff.). Haller, Papsttum, Vol. 3, 535 and Vol. 4, 381, still insists on Ugolino's membership of the pope's family. Since John of Anagni was close to Clement III (cf. Wenck, Päpste, 436) and received his own cardinal see, Palestrina, from him, he may well have been related to Clement in some degree, and hence also to Innocent III.

[21]Calixtus III may even have been elected by a Roman civic faction without the prior knowledge of the emperor (see Holtzmann, Quellen und Forschungen zur Geschichte Friedrich Barbarossas, NA 48, 1938, 404).

[22]See Maccarrone, Innoc., 70ff.

[23]See Maccarrone, Innoc., 70ff.; Gilson–Böhmer, Die Geschichte der christlichen Philosophie von den Anfängen bis Nikolaus von Cues (1937), 376ff.; Rashdall, The universities of Europe in the middle ages (new ed. by Powicke and Emden, 1936), 292ff.; Halphen, Les universités au XIIIe siècle (Rev. hist. 167, 1931) 4f.

[24]Cf. S. d'Irsay, 53ff.; Haskins, The Renaissance of the twelfth century (1928), 383f.

[25]Innocent to Philip of France: *Tibi et regno tuo specialiter nos fatemur teneri, in quo nos recolimus in studiis litterarum aetatem transegisse minorem, ac divino munere quantaecunque scientiae donum adeptos, beneficorum impensam multiplicem suscepisse* (Reg. I 171). Innocent to the French bishops: *Reducentes ad mentem et infra nos ipsos saepius recolentes beneficia nobis olim in ipso regno scholasticis insistentibus disciplinis impensa, nos tam regi quam regno specialiter teneri fatemur* (Reg. II 197). Cf. also Reg. XVI 3. *Regnum benedictum a Deo* is how he refers to France in Reg. VII 42.

[26]Innocent bestowed the mitre on Abbot John of St Geneviève's in Paris, who had been one of his student friends in the French capital (see the letter written by Stephen of Tournai in Migne PL. 211, 530), on 10 June 1199; he holds out to him a prospect of higher honours, referring to the special love which he, already before he became pope, had felt and still feels towards him and his monastery (Migne PL. 217, 52f.). On one occasion he recalls a theological view he had defended while still a student (Migne Pl. 217, 1175f.). When he has occasion to reproach the chancellor for his harsh treatment of the students, he points out that in his own student days students had never been treated in such a manner (Denifle, Chartularium Universitatis Paris. 1889, 73). In a conversation with a monk from the abbey of Andres near Boulogne he told him of a visit he had paid to the abbey while he was a student in Paris on a journey to England (Chron. Andr. 737f.).

[27]Grabmann, 5f., 61f. On Peter, see Maccarrone, Innoc., 73ff.

[28]Reg. I 478, 480; VI 236. See also Gesta c. 56.

[29]For Stephen Langton see F.M. Powicke, Stephen Langton (1928), 30, and Maccarrone, Innoc., 76f. Moreover, for the dates of Langton's residence and teaching activities in Paris, see G. Lacombe, Studies in the Commentaries of Cardinal Stephen Langton (Arch. d'hist. doctr. et litt. du moyen-âge 5, 1930) 8, 22f., 166.

[30]By means of this man who, at that time cardinal legate in France, was in close touch with the University, Innocent in 1215 gave the University a rule of studies (d'Irsay, 69f, see also Maccarone, Innoc., 78).

[31]According to a letter written by Peter of Blois (published by Denifle, Chartularium 1, 36) Odo was still a young man when he visited the Curia at the time of Gregory VIII's accession to the papal throne in 1187. In the few months of his pontificate, Gregory ordained Lothair of Segni subdeacon (Gesta c. 3). Lothair had but recently returned from France, whether immediatly after the completion of his studies or in his capacity as a companion of the Cardinal Legate Octavian on his journey back from England (see n. 50 below).

[32]See below Chapter 7, n. 93.

[33]Innocent III refers to him as *olim dilectum nobis, cum in minori essemus officio constituti* (Reg. I 574).

[34]See Chapter 10 below.

[35]In accordance with the Provincial Council of Paris in 1210 the cardinal legate's rule of studies of 1215 forbids lectures on the metaphysical and scientific writings of Aristotle (cf. d'Irsay, 69f., and Grabmann, 6ff.). Given Innocent's broadmindedness and freedom from over-cautious concern it seems doubtful to me whether the prohibition can be attributed to the pope's initiative. For the struggle against Aristotelianism at the University in the first half of the thirteenth century see Davy, 82ff., 115.

[36]Grabmann, 37ff, 61ff. Cf. also Powicke, 54, and Forest-van Steenberghen-de Gandillac, 190ff.

[37]He died in 1160. See de Ghellinck's article 'Pierre Lombard' in Dict. de théologie cath. 122 (1935), cols. 1941, 1949f. For Peter Lombard and the christological disputes of the twelfth century see amongst others: de Ghellinck, cols. 1941ff., and, by the same author, Le mouvement théologique du 12e siècle (1948), 250ff.; Ott, 168ff.; Landgraf, Einführung in die Geschichte der theologischen Literatur der Frühscholastik (1948), 93ff., 109ff.; Forest-van Steenberghen-de Gandillac, 157ff.

[38]An insight into such discussions within the Parisian students' circles in the latter half of the twelfth century is offered by a letter edited by B. Barth (Ein neues Dokument zur Geschichte der frühscholastischen Christologie, Theol. Quartalsschr. 100, 1919, 409ff.).

[39]See Barth, 255f.

[40]Ott, Untersuchungen, 103.

[41]Grabmann, 68.

[42]Cf. Barth, Ein neues Dokument... (Theol. Quartalsschr. 101, 1920), 247ff., and de Ghellinck's article on Pierre Lombard, quoted above, col. 2003ff.

[43]*Compostellano archiepiscopo* (Pr. Coll. Tit. 1, Migne PL. 216, 1176).

[44]Can. 1 (Leclercq 1325) c. 1 X 1.1t.1.

[45]Can. 2 (Leclercq 1327) c. 2 X 1.1t.1. For the doctrinal decisions reached by the Lateran Council on the Trinity, see A. Michel's 'Trinité' in Dict. de théologie catholique 15² (1950), col. 1727ff. For Joachim, see Huck, 5ff., 16ff., 39, 131, and also 175ff., 266ff.

[46]Even after having become pope, Innocent had to deal with the accusations made against the Lombard. Stephen Langton reports as an eye-witness that Innocent had Lombard's work read to him at meal times and then formulated his judgement in the words: *Relatorem invenio, non assertorem* (cf. Lacombe in The new Scholasticism 4, 1930, 59). De Ghellinck (Article 'Pierre Lombard' in Dict. de théologie catholique 12[2], 1935, col. 1983, 2009) concludes from this statement that the pope believed that it was Peter's practice not to take up a definite position. However, in view of Innocent's veneration of the Lombard it would perhaps be more accurate to relate the pope's words to the doctrinal views which were under challenge rather than to the *Sententiae* as a whole. If that were the case Innocent would have considered only the disputed doctrines as not being Lombard's own ideas.

[47]*Ego solebam concedere, quando scholasticis studiis incumbebam, quod tam persona quam natura divina proprium nomen poterat habuisse* (Migne PL. 216, 1175ff.). – *Haec ergo tibi scholastico more respondemus. Sed si oporteat nos more apostolico respondere, simplicius quidem sed cautius respondemus, quod humana mortalitas proprium nomen secundum proprietatem ipsius quod videlicet certum et determinatum tum experimeret intellectum, non posse imponere Deo sive personae sive naturae, cum Deus . . . non possit in hac mortali vita certa determinatione vel determinata certitudine comprehendi, cum quid non sit possit intellegi, sed quid sit non possit agnosci (ibid. 1178).*

[48]See Migne PL. 216, 1178; 217, 346, 861, 862, 867, 868, 869, 870, 871.

[49]An echo of the young Lothair's diction is perhaps still traceable in the first book of his work *De misera condicione hominis*, On the misery of the human condition.

[50]Migne PL. 216, 1175f.; see n. 47 above.

[51]Both the chronicler of Andres and Gervase of Canterbury mention a stay of Lothair at Canterbury. The pope himself told the chronicler of the warm hospitality he had received at the monastery of Andres when, in his own student days in Paris, he had made his pilgrimage to the shrine of St Thomas (Chron. Andr. 738). Gervase records that the pope had seen for himself the oppression suffered by the church of Canterbury, that is by the convent of the cathedral church (Op. 1, 551). It follows that the *terminus a quo* of Lothair's visit to England, discounting the possibility of a second journey across the English Channel, is the first suspension of the prior by Archbishop Baldwin in December 1186 (Gervase 1, 345. Cf. also the subprior's statement of 24 March 1189 that the monks had been harried for some two years, *ibid.* 442) and that the *terminus ad quem* must be the late autumn of 1187, since Lothair was ordained subdeacon by Gregory VIII between the end of October and the middle of December of that year (Gesta c. 3). If Lothair had travelled to England after that date it would not have been as a student at the Paris schools, since he cannot have returned to Paris on leaving the Curia at the end of 1187, for he also studied at Bologna between his time in Paris and his promotion to cardinal in 1189. The *terminus ad quem* can in fact be even more precisely fixed, for it is known that Lothair, together with two legates, Cardinal Octavian and the English bishop, Hugh Nonant, attended a chapter at Grammont in 1187 (cf. Tillmann, Legaten, 81 n. 21, where I mistakenly refer to Lothair as a cardinal). Now the legates had also attended a meeting at Gué Saint Remy near Nonancourt on 5 April to try to negotiate a peace between the kings of England and France (Legaten, 81) and Octavian returned to the Curia in July or August. His signature does not appear on papal bulls dated 2 June, 30 June and 2 July (Migne PL. 202, 1517, 1522, 1523) but reappears on the bull dated 25 August (Kehr, Gött. Nachr. 1903, Vol. 5, 627). It follows

that Lothair must have been in Grammont between the end of April and the end of July. Now considering that it can hardly be assumed that between May and December, the latest date at which Lothair could have arrived at the Curia, he could have gone from Paris via Limoges to Grammont and thence to England and from England to Italy, but that in all probability he visited Grammont on his journey back to Italy, it follows that his journey to England must have taken place in the period between December 1186 and July 1187. This period would become even shorter if we were allowed to stretch William of Andres's statement that Lothair visited England whilst a student in Paris, since in that case Lothair would have had to return from England to Paris to resume his studies. Between December 1186 and September 1187, the limits we have established for Lothair's journey to England, the two legates in whose company we find Lothair in Grammont were in England too, that is between 25 December and 17 February (Tillmann, Legaten, 80f.). Given the close relationship between Lothair and Cardinal Octavian (see above and the final paragraph of this note), it is likely that Lothair accompanied his fatherly friend to England or, alternatively, went to see him when he himself arrived from Paris. Since the chronicler of Andres described Lothair's journey as private, which he had undertaken as a pious pilgrim, this latter seems the more probable, the more so since it is difficult to envisage Lothair as one of the many members of the two legates' retinue. In addition, Lothair will have crossed the Channel from Calais to Dover, not as the legates did to Sandwich (Tillmann, Legaten, 80). It may well be that Cardinal Octavian's presence in England was the motive for Lothair to make his pilgrimage at that particular time.

Early in February one of the legates, Hugh Nonant, acting with the full authority of the king, attempted to persuade the monks of the cathedral convent to be more conciliatory towards the archbishop. Together with the king and Cardinal Octavian, Hugh visited Canterbury on 11 February (Tillmann, Legaten, 81). If Lothair had been amongst the legates' entourage he would have had an excellent opportunity to see the oppression suffered by the church of Canterbury for himself.

As a further comment to n. 20 above regarding the discussion of Innocent III's relationship to Cardinal Octavian and other cardinals from the nobility of Rome and surrounding regions, I would like to point to the links between Victor IV, the imperial anti-pope to Alexander III, and the royal house of France. Victor IV, or Octavian, from the Roman family Montecelli or Maledetti, was a blood relation of Adela of Blois, the third wife of Louis VII of France (Kahr, Zur Geschichte Viktors IV., NA 46, 1925, 56ff.) and the mother of Louis's son and successor Philip II Augustus. Victor IV resided in Segni during the early days of his pontificate, from the end of October to early December 1159. From this Haller suggests a relationship between Victor and the counts of the Campania (Papsttum, 3, 504), i.e. the family of Innocent III. This suggestion is supported by the fact that both Victor IV and Innocent III are described as blood relations of Philip Augustus. In this connection it is worth noting that both Victor IV, Octavian of Ostia, and Innocent III's cousin, Octavian of SS Sergius and Bacchus, share the same forename.

[52]During his papacy Lothair testified to his high regard for Bologna in that in 1209/1210 he promulgated a series of decretals from the first twelve years of his reign, the first official collection of decretals, by way of depositing them at the University (Friedberg, 105. See also Kuttner, Repertorium der Kanonistik, Studi e Testi 71, 1937, 355 and by the same author, Johannes Teutonicus, Das vierte Laterankonzil und die Compilatio quarta, Studi e Testi, 125, 1946, 621).

[53]For the views of the canonists and theologians on the relationship between Church and state up to the end of the twelfth century see Maccarrone, Chiesa, 59ff.; Mochi Onory, 86ff., 110ff., 124ff., 143ff., 162ff., 192ff. (this latter includes the canonical controversy during Innocent III's life); for the middle ages as a whole see Eichmann, Acht und Bann, 27–63. For the doctrines of Uguccio see Maccarrone, Chiesa, 68ff.: Stickler, 203ff.; Mochi Onory, 143ff.

[54]*A Christo distincta sunt iura et officia imperatoris et pontificis et alia sunt attributa imperatori, scilicet temporalia, et alia, scilicet spiritualia, concessa sunt pontifici, et hoc est factum causa humilitatis servande et superbie vitande. Hinc aperte colligitur, quod utraque potestas, scilicet apostolica et imperialis, instituta sit a Deo et quod neutra pendeat ex altera et quod imperator gladium non habeat ab apostolico* (Text in Stickler, 210, 211, and Mochi Onory, 148f., n. 3).*.. ergo neutrum pendet ex altero, verum est quoad institutionem...* (Mochi Onory, 153, n. 1). However, see below Chapter 2, n. 31.

[55]*Terreni simul et celesti imperii iura* (c. 1 D 22).

[56]*Apostolicus potestatem habet imperii super laicos quoad spiritualia et preceptum celestis id est ecclesiastici imperii id est universitatis clericorum* (Mochi Onory, 152). Cf. Stickler, 208f.

[57]Cf. Maccarrone, Chiesa, 70.

[58]Texts in Mochi Onory, 149, and Stickler 209, n. 2, 211, n.1. Eichmann, Kirche und Staat (Quellensammlung z. kirchl. Rechtsgesch. u. z. Kirchenrecht, Vol. 2, 1914), 120. See also Maccarrone, Chiesa, 76.

[59]Ugoccio's decisive impact on Innocent III's conception of the relationship between Church and state is well brought out by Maccarrone (Chiesa). See also Stickler, 233ff., and Mochi Onory, 46, 64, 147, 157, 183f., 272. Cf. also below, Chapter 2.

[60]Gesta c. 3.

[61]In his fascinating essay on the Roman popes from Alexander III to Innocent III Karl Wenck endeavours to prove the existence of two opposing movements, the one with a rather temporally-directed Roman-civic approach, the other with a more spiritually-directed approach supported by the cardinals and popes originating from outside Rome. Wenck cites Clement III and Cardinal Octavian amongst others as exponents of the Roman approach and Gregory VIII as representative of its counterpart. Haller rejects Wenck's conclusions with considerable acerbity (Papsttum, 533f.). I must confess that I cannot follow Wenck in every regard either. Wenck is wrong to accuse Pope Clement III of a regime of cliquery on the basis of Epp. Cant. 296 p. 280 (Päpste, 434). He seems to have misread *de quo prae aliis confidere dinoscitur*, which refers to John of Anagni, as *de quibus...*, which would have to refer to a group of the cardinals. However, it does seem to me that Wenck has established the existence of these two differing approaches, at least for the decade 1180 to 1190. I can offer some support to Wenck's thesis by referring to two letters written by Stephen of Tournai when he was abbot of St Geneviève's in Paris. The first (Migne PL. 211 Ep. 103 col. 393) is addressed to Chancellor Albert de Morra, the future Pope Gregory VIII (according to Wenck one of the representatives of the non-Roman movement), and it must have been written shortly before Gregory was elected pope, or before Stephen had learnt of Gregory's election. The second letter (Migne PL. 211, Epp. 102 col. 393) sent to Cardinal Octavian, on Wenck's argument a representative of the Roman movement, belongs to the early days of Clement III's pontificate, who like Octavian ought to be considered an exponent of the Roman movement. Both letters deal with a dispute amongst foreign students in Paris in which were involved on the one side a nephew of

Clement III and a nephew of Cardinal Hyacinth, member of the Roman-civic family of the Boboni and future Pope Celestine III, and on the other side two nephews of Albert de Morra, the future Gregory VIII and one John of Naples. The former are described as *Cives Romani* and their opponents as *Apuli* as if merely indicating their native background were sufficient to indicate the nature of their antagonism. It is also significant that, after the death of Gregory VIII and the election of Clement III, Gregory's nephews seem to feel urged to clear themselves in front of Octavian from the charges of hostility and scheming against their Roman fellow students, amongst them the nephews of the new pope. The Epp. Cant. also reveal that during the papal election of October 1178 the Roman Paul Scolari, the future Clement III, was the fellow or rival candidate of Albert de Morra, the man from Benevento or, to use the contemporary tag, the Apulian (Epp. Cant. 135, 108; cf. Wenck, Päpste, 428). According to the same source two cardinals, who are designated as the 'Tuscans', are said to have demonstratively left the Curia as a reaction to the cardinals' promotions made by Clement III in 1189, in which two of the three promotions went to Romans, one of whom was Octavian himself (Epp. Cant. 315, 301; cf. Wenck, Päpste, 440). Could it be that strained relations between the leading figures of the Curia have painfully come to a head amongst their young relatives at the University of Paris?

[62]Of all the popes of his time it is for Gregory that Innocent reserves the epithet of man of saintly memory (Reg. I 244, 282, 432, V 42, VII 24, IX 140, Gesta c. 84: letter of the pope). Reg. I 432 is particularly informative. Here successively are designated: Urban III as *felicis record.*, Gregory VIII as *sanctae memoriae*, Clement III and Celestine III as *bonae memoriae*, Clement III for a second time, now as *piae recordationis*, and Celestine III as *bonae memoriae*. The contemporary Gesta of the pope adopt the designation of Gregory VIII as a man of saintly memory as their own (c. 3). In perhaps two passages of the Register Gregory's name is accompanied not by *sanctae memoriae* but by a *felicis recordationis* (Reg. I 59 and VI 88). Of the pope's other contemporaries only Peter of Castelnau and Albert of Liège are for him men of saintly memory (Reg. XI 30, 32, 33; XII 31; XV 102; V 155; RNT 33, 56, 80) doubtless on account of the kind of deaths they suffered, which were considered martyrs' deaths. Of the earlier popes Innocent styles 'men of saintly memory' Nicholas I (Reg. VII 127; XI 181), Silvester II and in two letters strangely enough Innocent II (Reg I 427 and 555; *felicis recordationis* or *felicis memoriae* however Reg. I 56 II, 82 col. 627, II/38bis, XII 33). In collective lists more recent popes, too, are included in a *sanctae memoriae* (Reg. I 56). On Gregory VIII see Haller, Heinrich VI. 645.; Kehr, Papst Gregor VIII als Ordensgründer (Misc. Fr. Ehrle 2, Studi e Testi 38, 1924) 248ff.; Wenck, Päpste, 428ff. (also for the earlier literature on the pope).

[63]According to the Gesta (c. 3) Lothair was twenty-nine years old. Since he was thirty years of age on 8 January 1198 he must have become cardinal before 8 January 1190 if we are to believe the dates given. The diaconate of SS Sergius and Bacchus only fell vacant in the summer of 1189 on the promotion of Octavian (see n. 51 above). So if, as appears to be the case, only those three named in the Epp. Cant. were promoted and it was still the custom to announce the creation of cardinals on ember-days (Maccarrone, Innoc., 84) we could fix Lothair's promotion to cardinal precisely to September of 1189. Strangely enough Maccarrone takes as *terminus ad quem* 22 September 1190, even though he himself refers to the timing given in the Gesta: *vigesimum nonum aetatis suae annum egentem*.

[64]See n. 20 above.

[65]The view shared also by Maccarrone (Innoc., 70) that Lothair had served at the

Curia already during the papacy of Lucius III (1181–1185) is due to a misunderstanding. The pope who states in Reg. I 150 that before his elevation (*nobis adhuc in minori officio constitutis*) he had under Lucius III acted together with two cardinals as auditor in a matter concerning the monastery of Vézelay is not Innocent III but Urban III, whose sentence has been incorporated into Innocent's document.

Stubbs, editor of the Epistolae Cantuarienses, identifies the *dominus Lotharius* in Ep. 80 p. 68, a colleague of the monks' procurator at the Curia, as Lothair of Segni (2, 570). Maccarrone tends to support this view (Innoc., 81ff.). However Lothair was not so unknown a name at the Curia as to justify this identification. In 1185 a Magister Lothair appears at the imperial court as an emissary of Urban III (I. Friedlander, Die päpstlichen Legaten in Deutschland und Italien am Ende des XII. Jahrhunderts (1181–1198), Berlin thesis, 1928, 21). Innocent himself mentions a papal subdeacon of the same name in a letter of 9 July 1198, a *juris peritus*, who is active at the Curia (Reg. I 314). The letter from the convent referring to the *dominus Lotharius* was written between 23 June and 25 July 1187 at which time Lothair was either on his journey back to Rome from France or England or had recently arrived (see n. 51 above). He can scarcely have been known to the convent as a colleague of their procurator. It is true that Ralph of Coggeshall suggests that before his pontificate Innocent III had been attorney (*advocatus*) of the monks of Canterbury (Chron. Angl. 89). But the chronicler of the dispute, Gervase, a monk from Canterbury, can record no more than that the new pope had seen the oppression suffered by the church of Canterbury with his own eyes and had known that the matter had been settled and decided at the Roman Curia (1, 551). The first letter sent by the convent of Canterbury to the new pope (Epp. Cant. 2, 430, p. 387) shows, in spite of the high sounding words with which the monks greet Innocent's elevation, that the convent, so familiar with curial matters, knew very little or nothing at all of the new pope and of his attitude in the Canterbury conflict. Innocent's decisive readiness to stand for their rights was received, therefore, as a pleasant surprise (*ibid.* 451, 411f.). Nowhere in the correspondence between the convent and its representatives is there any mention of Cardinal Lothair.

[66] *Inter fratres sine querela conversans, non dividens se in partem* (Gesta c. 4). In considering Lothair's position, aloof from the antagonism subsisting at the Curia, between a more spiritual and a more temporally-directed faction, his high regard for the Cistercian Order carries weight, whilst Clement III, as the representatives of the convent of Canterbury at the Curia report, held that Order in lower estimation (Epp. Cant. 210, p. 195. See Wenck, Päpste 433).

[67] The Gesta read *veteres aemulationes* (c. 135).

[68] See Maccarrone, Innoc., 87ff. It should be noted that on one occasion Innocent repeats a remark which Celestine allegedly often used in his and other cardinals' presence.

[69] Reg. II 102.

[70] At the time of his election Lothair seems to have been unknown beyond the inner circles of the Curia. The monks of Canterbury, so familiar with curial affairs, knew scarcely anything of the new pope (see n. 65 above). We may also assume that Lothair's significance was unknown even at the English court in view of the patronizing warnings sent him by King Richard, to which Innocent more than once replied with ironic thanks and expressions of recognition (Ref. I 230, 485; II 57).

[71] Cf. Wenck, Päpste, 460f., 464.

[72] RNI 33 (Kempf, Regestum, 105, 107), RNI 62 (Kempf, 173, 174, 179, 180), RNI 92

(Kempf, 243f.), RNI 165 (Kempf, 370), RNI 29 (Kempf, 80, 83ff., 87, 89), RNI 18 (Kempf, 52) and more pointedly in the unrevised version of RNI 18 in the Siena Codex (Kempf, 411f.; cf. Tillmann, Zum Regestum, 23).

[73]Reg. I 159; see also I 413.

[74]Reg. I 356, II 221. Cf. also RNI 80.

[75]Reg. V 89. See Maccarrone, Chiesa, 150. I cannot accept the conclusions Maccarrone draws in the passage referred to (see below, Chapter 5, n. 8).

[76]See the unrevised version of RNI 18 in the Siena Codex (Kempf, 411f.)

[77]*De misera condicione hominis* (Migne PL. 217), 701, 921f.

[78]See Wenck, Päpste, 434ff.

[79]See below, Chapters 3 and 10.

[80]Reg. I 61, 253, 267; II 151, Compil. III c. 1 t. 18 1.2 (Friedberg, 115ff.). In the first year of Innocent III's pontificate a privilege granted by Clement III is also quashed as illegal and having been obtained by deception (Reg. I 245).

[81]Reg. I 253. This is probably one of the privileges JL. 17135, 17137–1739 of 14 July 1194. It was not possible to determine this precisely since I was unable to obtain Escalona, Historia de Sahagun, in which the documents are published.

[82]Gesta c. 4.

[83]Migne PL. 217, 701ff. As Maccarrone has shown (Innoc., 93ff.) the commonly used title *De contemptu mundi* is incorrect. The final two chapters of the second book in Migne PL. 217, 734ff., are not from Lothair's pen (Maccarrone, Innoc., 101).

[84]Migne PL. 217, 921ff.

[85]Gesta c. 2. Cf. below.

[86]In a lecture to the Third Congress of Medievalists in Cologne, October 1952, Professor Wili of Bern drew attention to the stylistic discrepancy between the first book and the last two books, and to an alteration in the plan, which suggests that the two sections were written at different times. In the first book he points to the delight taken in the sound of and the play with words and in descriptions which were often in contrast to the content. We might find easier to understand the rhetorical self-indulgence and lack of seriousness, which occasionally embarrass the reader in the first book and give it an exceptional place in Innocent III's writings, if we could date it as belonging to an earlier period, say, prior to Lothair's appointment as cardinal. The fact that the dedication is indubitably from Lothair's cardinalate need not affect such a view.

[87]Maccarrone's detailed assessment of the work (Innoc., 93ff.) is more positive.

[88]Migne PL. 217, 720.

[89]Migne PL. 217, 701.

[90]Gesta c. 41.

[91]*De misera condicione hominis* was written during an otherwise unoccupied leisure period (Migne PL. 217, 704), *De quadripartita* in response to the promptings of a third party (*ibid.* 922).

[92]The work named in the Gesta is generally identified as *De sacro altaris mysterio* (Migne PL. 216, 773ff.). Maccarrone concurs with this identification (Innoc., 110). In fact it cannot belong to the period of Lothair's cardinalate in its present form. The author of *De sacro alt. myst.* refers (in Book 6, Chapter 9) to the fact that the subdiaconate used to be considered one of the lower grades of ordination whereas it was now classed amongst the higher grades (Migne PL. 217, 911). It was Innocent himself who first determined this graduation (c. 9 X 1, 14; Reg. X 164). Contradictory

statements as to the admissibility of the use of unleavened bread in the mass are readily explained if the final version was written after the so-called restoration of the union of the Greek and Latin Churches (see below, Chapter 8). Only the pope can have written the Conclusio: *cum ex officio tot causarum sim impeditus incursibus, tot negotiorum nexibus irretitus, ut infra breve temporis spatium nec ad meditandum otium nec ad dictandum quiverim nancisci quietem* (Migne PL. 217, 914. Once again we can hear the pope's eternal complaint; cf. below Chapters 6 and 10). Lastly, while revising the final version, Innocent also had in front of him the letter he wrote to the resigned archbishop John of Lyons (Reg. V 121), in which he replies to questions posed by John concerning the ritual of consecration and the transformation of water into wine, questions which the pope deals with in Book Four (Migne PL. 217, 858, 975.). While composing c. 54 (Migne PL. 217, 794) Innocent most probably also had Reg. XII 148 of 7 January 1210 to hand as well. I cannot decide whether Innocent had already received a letter from Peter of Blois containing suggestions for the improvement of the canon (only part of this letter is reproduced literally by R.W. Southern, Some new letters of Peter of Blois, EHR 53, 1938, 422ff.). Innocent does, however, provide more detailed explanations for most of the passages of which Peter complained, for example for *Accepta habeas. . .sacrifica illibata* (Migne PL. 217, 842), *in somno pacis* (*ibid.* 892), *Misterium fidei* (*ibid.* 858), *Commemorantes* (*ibid.* 848), and for the disorderly and incomplete state of the catalogue of apostles and martyrs (*ibid.* 893). Had the text been in Innocent's hands there would be a new lead to the date of the composition of *De sacro alt. myst.* more surely since the letter was probably written between 1201 and 1212 (Southern, 415). The revised version appeared in 1208 at the earliest since the Gesta are familiar with the version from Lothair's cardinalate only.

[93]Innocent often refers to these ceremonies in his sermons and writings (see Migne PL. 217, 341, 393, 911, 395, 337).

[94]See above n. 68.

[95]Wenck construes Lothair's election as just such a victory (Päpste, 473). Wenck also indicates, however, that the deeply religious John of St Paul (see below Chapter 7) whom Celestine III is alleged to have wished to designate as his successor (see n. 11 above) in order to prevent Lothair's election, played a major part under Innocent III in carrying out the policy of recuperations (cf. Seeger, 28f.). He seems to have been in other respects too in Innocent III's particular confidence and trust.

# CHAPTER 2

# Called to the fullness of power

Lothair of Segni, now Innocent III, was in full possession of the papal supreme power since on 8 January 1198 he had accepted the election and the eldest of the cardinal deacons had put the purple mantle on his shoulders with the words: "I invest you with the Roman pontificate so that you preside over the city and the whole world".[1] His order remained that of a deacon for another six weeks.[2] Not until 21 February was he ordained priest, and on the following day, the feast of St Peter's chair, he was consecrated bishop and solemnly took possession of the chair of the princes of apostles.[3]

".... So that you preside over the city and the whole world" – this mission might be interpreted in a purely spiritual sense, but also be understood in the sense, advocated by the hierocratic idea, of the pope holding the spiritual as well as the temporal swords, the offices both of high priest and emperor. How did the newly-elect interpret the words? In a sermon preached either on the day of consecration or on a day of its commemoration,[4] Innocent seems to put in a claim for a quasi-divine power vested in the Vicar of Christ, which in itself would mean that it embraced both the spiritual and the temporal spheres. "Now you see, what kind of servant he is who commands the household, truly the Vicar of Jesus Christ, the successor of Peter, Anointed of the Lord, God of the Pharaos,[5] who is the mediator between God and man, placed below God but above men, who is less than God, but greater than man." These words seem to herald revolutionary and shocking news.

But in the context of the address they lose much of what appears strange to us and is offensive to our feeling. The sermon is based on the text: "Who, then, is the faithful and wise servant whom the Lord has set over his household so that he may serve him the meal in season?[6] To interpret the *super familiam*, "over the household," is the purport of the presumptuous ringing words just quoted. He, the pope, is the servant who is set over the household; he, consequently, stands above the other servants, but below the master of the house. The words, therefore, though strikingly formulated, say no more than that all those belonging to Christ's family are subordinate to the pope as the Lord's steward, that he as the Lord's Vicar has precedence over all others. Moreover, the words themselves express audacity of style rather than a manifestation of excessive papal self-assertion. In the same sermon Innocent tells his listeners that there is *one* sin for which he could be judged by the Church, the sin against faith.[7] It was the wish to emphasize the contrast between the inferiority of the person and the dignity of the office which induced him to use so exaggerated a style.

But a reliable assessment of the meaning and import of these words is only possible in the light of Innocent's general view on papal dignity and power. The pope who has been looked upon as having brought papal kingship to completion,[8] and who is said to have, as Vicar of God, claimed the plenitude of power,[9] the fullness of both spiritual and temporal authority,[10] the very same pope has in fact, at different times and on different occasions, clearly and distinctly given voice to the limitation of his power.[11] The *plenitudo potestatis*, the fullness of power, which the Lord has assigned to the Roman bishop alone, is in no way the totality of all spiritual and temporal power, but, according to Innocent's often repeated own statement, nothing else but the *plenitudo ecclesiasticae potestatis*, the fullness of ecclesiastical power,[12] in the same way as the *plenitudo potestatis*, which Innocent ascribes to the emperor,[13] denotes the fullness of temporal power. Innocent has not succumbed to the temptation of the medieval papacy to lay claim to both swords,[14] the spiritual and the temporal one.[15] The kings and princes, above all the emperor, in whom all temporal power attains its height, are vested with the temporal sword by the Lord Himself: "We are both of us," the pope writes to Emperor Otto, "*principaliter* entrusted with the rule of this world. If we are of one mind and harmonious in the pursuit of that which is good, then, as the prophet testifies, sun and moon will stand in their order, since with God's help nothing can hinder or resist us, *we both having the two swords* of which the apostle said to the Lord 'Behold, two swords', and with regard to which the Lord replied 'It is enough'.

The high-priestly authority and the royal power, *which both are supreme in us* and which are designated by the two swords, are in themselves completely sufficient to a happy performance of their offices, if only the one vigorously supports the other."[16] Bernard of Clairvaux, with whose ideas Innocent was well acquainted and whom he often followed in his writings, had interpreted the *hic* in *Ecce duo gladii hic* as meaning "in the pope's hands".[17] But Innocent, in a letter to King Philip of France, expounds the *hic*, with the intention of forestalling a possible misunderstanding, by *id est simul*, "that is together", in the sense that it is God's will that the sword which the king has received from God be joined in action with the sword held by the pope.[18] While occupying Peter's chair, Innocent kept loyally to the doctrine of his teacher Uguccio, who defended the old Gelasian view of the axiomatic separation and independence of the two powers against the emerging hierocratic doctrine.[19] Although, in Innocent's view, the spiritual power has a higher rank by far than the dignity of the temporal power,[20] he, yet, deems it God's will that the temporal authority be autonomous in its domain,[21] just as the Church is in its own sphere. Frankly, Innocent also repeatedly confesses to the limits which in the Gospels God Himself has set to his power by separating that which is God's and that which is Caesar's due. Thus he guards himself against the insinuation that he intended to extend his prerogatives at the expense of the temporal power: "Not that we intended to infringe upon the rights of others or to arrogate an undue power to ourselves, as we know well that Christ answered in the Scriptures: 'Give to Caesar what is Caesar's', and that, when he was asked to divide a heritage between two heirs, he replied: 'Who has made me judge over you?' "[22] At the Lateran Council, with reference to the above-mentioned passage of the Scriptures, he again forbids all clergy to extend their jurisdiction at the expense of the temporal authority under pretence of ecclesiastical liberty.[23] When Innocent speaks of the royal dignity which God had vested in the Roman bishop, so that he be in truth the Vicar of the divine priest-king, of the priest according to the order of Melchisedech, he has only in mind the domination over the Papal States.[24] In his reference to Melchisedech, exposing its mystical sense, he justifies for himself and for the papacy what he normally felt to be condemnable and unnatural: the union of spiritual and temporal sovereign power.[25]

Innocent did not claim world domination by virtue of his office, nor did he strive to establish it by way of feudal policy. It is wrong to talk at all of Innocent engaging in a feudal policy. He never attempted to change a hitherto independent country into a vassal state,[26] and the bonds of vassalage already existing when he entered upon his office, and bonds of a similar kind between several countries and the Apostolic See, he has visibly held to be of little importance,[27] unless political interests were involved as in the cases of Sicily and Sardinia.

Though Innocent confesses in principle to the separation and independence of spiritual and temporal power, he yet laid claim to a conditional temporal power within the whole Christian world,[28] a power which the pope exercises occasionally (*casualiter*) only and in respect of certain circumstances (*certis causis inspectis*), well knowing that such a measure was something extraordinary, since the temporal jurisdiction, in general, belongs to that which is the Caesar's, and the Vicar of Christ is usually not the judge of the legal affairs of laymen. Innocent has in view those law cases which are *brought before him*, because they cannot be settled in due course of law, be it that the legal position is ambiguous and no temporal instance available to clarify it, or be it that law cases or litigation are involved which have no, or no common, superior judge. But it is essential that at least one of the parties concerned appeals to the pope.[29] This condition of prior appeal from the first sets bounds to the scope of this extraordinary papal jurisdiction.

In his doctrine of the pope's supplementary temporal jurisdiction Innocent only draws the consequences which resulted for the papacy from the medieval doctrine of the law of emergency,[30] a doctrine which, in default of a worldly judge, entitled the Church, as already in late Roman times, to encroach even upon matters of state. Here, too, Uguccio had paved the way for him, for on the basis of Justinian's legislation in which the competence of the bishops' courts for lawsuits of the poor and in default of a superior judge is regularized, Uguccio had maintained a certain jurisdiction of the clergy, and of the pope in particular, in temporal matters.[31]

It is in exercise of jurisdiction of this kind that Innocent, on the appeal of Philip of France, legitimized the children Philip had from his alliance with Agnes of Meran. It must have seemed unjust that the king should be excluded from a benefit of law which he could grant to any of his subjects. Some, though, held the view, and Innocent himself did not reject it, that Philip could exercise his right of legitimization in favour also of his own children. But any doubting as to such legitimization being legally binding could have led to disastrous consequences if, for example, Philip's sole legitimate son should have died without issue. We may speak of a gap in the law which Innocent was requested to fill and which he thought himself entitled to fill. Innocent rejected a similar appeal for legitimization made by Count William of Montpellier, giving as one of his reasons that this was not a case which could not be settled in due course of law.[32] William was not sovereign and, therefore, could not submit himself to papal jurisdiction without infringing upon the rights of a third party.

Innocent exercised the power of extraordinary temporal jurisdiction sparingly and in cases of little historical moment.[33] He was able to exercise a greater influence on events in the lives of kings and states by way of his jurisdiction *ratione peccati.*[34] Just as the actions of private persons, as regards their moral aspect, are subject to the judgement of the Church, so are the actions of the rulers, not only concerning their private lives, for instance in matters concerning their marriages, but also as regards their public activities. In reply to Philip of France's view that the conflict of the kings, meaning his war with King John of England, was none of the pope's business, and that in feudal matters he was not bound to answer papal judgement or command, Innocent gives this principle its classic formulation: it is not *ratione feudi* that he is entitled to judge on the conflict, as in feudal matters the king is competent, but *ratione peccati*, since it is doubtless the pope's office to adjudicate on sin and since he can, and is obliged to, exercise this office on everybody.[35] Innocent substantiates his standpoint in the following way. The king of England complained that the king of France was sinning against him, and finally appealed to the Church, as the Gospels prescribe. What could he, the pope, do other than treat the king of France, in accordance with the selfsame prescription, as a heathen and public sinner, unless he listened to the Church and showed that, far from sinning against John, he as liege lord was only claiming seignorial rights over a vassal? Although the jurisdiction *ratione peccati* over rulers and kings opens no end of possibilities for the pope to interfere with state affairs, Innocent keeps within the bounds of his spiritual competence when he prosecutes public mortal sins of temporal rulers in the same way as those of other laymen and when he characterizes political actions which are mortal sins, as for instance breaches of oaths[36] and waging unjust wars,[37] as such and punishes them with the Church's own correctional measures, ban and interdict.[38]

This judicial function was liable to be misused and was misused by Innocent for political ends. In Germany he tried to estrange former partisans of Otto of Brunswick, the anti-king recognized by him, from his Staufen opponent by threatening them with the punishment for breach of oath, and his intervention in the conflict between France and England was for a time conditioned by his wish to set the English king's forces free for the support of Otto's cause. But Innocent never used the jurisdiction *ratione peccati* as a pretext to find a possibility of interfering in the secular sphere without a stringent reason.[39]

The result of our analysis may be summarized as follows. Innocent neither asserted papal world domination in the sense of a papal universal monarchy, i.e. of a union of both powers in the person of the Roman bishop, nor claimed it for himself in the sense of a fundamental subordination of the temporal to the spiritual power. What he claimed of temporal jurisdiction was *in substance* no more than a certain right of emergency to settle questions of law and litigations when the secular law failed and at least one of the parties concerned had appealed. He disregards this exceptional case when he clearly and firmly confesses to the principle that the sphere of secular affairs is as such no business of the pope's and that his power has been limited by God Himself in the Gospels by the distinction between that which is God's and that which is Caesar's.[40] When interfering in secular matters *ratione peccati* Innocent in general keeps within the bounds of his spiritual competence. Where he misuses this jurisdiction for worldly ends, he is motivated by political necessities of the moment, not by the intention to extend papal jurisdiction at the expense of temporal jurisdiction.

Though Innocent clearly marked off the limits of the authority he exercised over the temporal powers, in practice he transgressed these limits in crucial moments, most conspicuously when he released those who had sworn allegiance to Emperor Otto IV from their oaths,[41] when he prepared the same measure against King John of England,[42] and when he required that the papal recognition of Otto of Brunswick and the rejection of Philip of Swabia be binding on all imperial subjects[43] and that the bishops in particular be bound to obedience to him in the imperial cause.[44] These cases are not in contradiction to the results of our inquiry, because Innocent was at pains to prevent these measures from appearing as acts of temporal sovereignty. Thus he explains the release from the oaths of allegiance as being the declaration of their nullity on the grounds of disloyalty to God and the

Church and of the excommunication therefore inflicted, so understanding it as the ultimate consequence of the prohibition of intercourse and communion with excommunicates.[45] The authoritative
declaration of the legitimacy of Otto's kingship Innocent never truly
justified,[46] precisely because from his fundamental point of view he
was in no position to justify it.

The measured cautiousness of Innocent's attitude stands out in full
relief if contrasted to the attitude adopted by Gregory VII and
Innocent IV. These popes have not only released subjects from their
oaths of allegiance, but laid, theoretically as well as practically, claim
to the right of deposing emperors and kings.[47]

Innocent III cannot be regarded as the representative of a secularized papacy, which Innocent IV was to become some twenty-five
years later.[48] The conviction that Christ's realm was not of this world
and that his Vicar's task, in essence, was of a spiritual nature,[49] was
unfalteringly alive in the pope whose actual position of power
resembled that of a pope-emperor. He explained and excused his
being overburdened with worldly affairs[50] with the phrase *temporis
exigente malitia*, because of the malice of the time. If Innocent's reign
was a stage on the disastrous way of the papacy to a spiritual-
temporal monarchy, this is not because of the principles for which he
stood, nor because of the highest ends at which he aimed. Though his
more spiritual and more religious mode of thought explains many a
difference between his own aims and claims and those of Innocent IV
or even of Boniface VIII, it cannot explain the contrast between him
and Gregory VII as regards the Roman bishop's position of power. It
is precisely by passionately assuming his spiritual task that Gregory
arrived at comprising all worldly matters in the papal sphere of
influence.[51] How is it that Innocent came to see things differently, to
recognize the limits of papal power and to respect an autonomous
sphere of temporal power? Perhaps a distinction between concepts
comes into play here, which in another field, the Investiture Contest,
once allowed the antagonistic positions to be resolved. Innocent was
able to distinguish more strictly than Gregory between the temporal
power as such and certain of its manifestations which come under the
jurisdiction of the Church *as sins*, not as actions of a subordinate
instance. Moreover, Gregory had intended to make the kingdom of
Heaven come true, to realize Christ's sovereignty by submitting all
temporal matters to the Vicar of Christ. Innocent knew that the
papacy attempted the impossible if it tried to combine both powers in

itself. "Why should we", he replied to those who reproached him with having transgressed the limits of his jurisdiction, "why should we arrogate to ourselves 'foreign' jurisdiction, when we are unable fully to exercise our own?"[52] Innocent took a more sober view of things than Gregory and, taught by an experience which was not yet at Gregory's disposal, realized that combining both powers in the papacy must needs result not in Christianizing the temporal sphere, but in dragging down the spiritual to the level of the temporal sphere. Innocent himself feared becoming involved in worldly affairs. At the beginning of his papal reign he appeals to the general chapter of the Cistercians, an Order of which he thought highly, for their intercessory prayer that God might show him the way to salvation and cheer him up as once He had St Peter, so that he might not be embroiled in worldly affairs more than is good.[53] This concern may well be founded in the pope's awareness of the threatening danger of secularization with which the papacy was faced at that time.

The difference between Gregory and Innocent cannot be explained by the later pope's more moderate approach and more mature discernment, but is partly to be understood in the light of the changed circumstances. Gregory saw the spiritual sphere serving the temporal sphere, the Church being subservient to the state; he had just recently witnessed the subjection of the papacy to the Empire and found the question of the relationship between both powers unresolved. In the accomplishment of internal church reform he met with the resistance of most of the temporal powers, and it must have seemed to him as if the principles of reform were only attainable by defeating these potentates like enemies. Hence the fanaticism with which Gregory at times sought to humiliate secular authorities, and his indulgence in concepts of papal omnipotence over the kingdoms of the world. On the other hand, Innocent's juvenile years, the time of his service at the Curia as subdeacon and cardinal, fell, it is true, within a period of declining papal prestige. But the essence of the papal position had not been shaken by adverse circumstances and the personal shortcomings of some popes. The dignity and independence of the supreme spiritual power was in principle no longer threatened and Innocent had no trouble at all in restoring the authority of the papacy and raising it to the pink of perfection. The unparalleled position which the papacy enjoyed under his reign doubtless made it easier for Innocent to assess the relationship between *sacerdotium* and *imperium* more moderately and to do justice also to the function and position of the

state.[54] The episode of the impassionate struggle wit
was too brief to have exercised any decisive influen
basic outlook. At the back of the excessiveness of
under Gregory IX and Innocent IV there was surely
weapons in the deadly fight, lasting for decades, a
Frederick II, the need to justify the measures taken, and also an
impassionate hatred against the Emperor's person. Thus the claims of
these popes can hardly be deduced from the hierocratic idea alone,
even if from the outset they may have been more alive to it than
Innocent III.

That Innocent III had a more friendly approach to the secular
power than Gregory VII, was due also to the fact that it was now no
longer necessary, as in the period of church reform, to enforce
ecclesiastical demands mainly by fighting against the secular authorities, though Innocent had to dispute with many a ruler about the
remnants of state-churchism. The threats with which the Church was
now faced, emanated much more from below, from heresy, which the
Church was unable to bring under control with her own means of
power, and which flourished precisely in those regions, which, like
southern France and northern Italy, lacked a strong centralized
supreme power, and it was not the kings, but the Italian communes
which offered the most obstinate resistance to the ecclesiastical
claims, in this instance to the immunity of the clergy.[55]

As little as Innocent comprises temporal matters in the sphere of
his competence, so little did he attempt to transgress the limits which
are set to all human and also to papal activities in relation to God.
Even by law the Roman bishop cannot act as he pleases in the
Church. For Innocent too an unsurmountable barrier was set to papal
authority by the *ius divinum*, the divine law. The pope has power only
over that which in the Church exists by virtue of human institution,
not over that which is of divine ordinance. Should he take a decision
contrary to the *ius divinum*, he would run the risk of being charged
with heresy and thereby incur the danger of being dismissed from
office. To the insistent demand of Philip of France for dissolution of
his marriage, Innocent repeatedly replies that he has no right of
dispensation in view of our Lord's words: "Man may not separate
what God has joined".[56] Without consulting a general council he dare
not decide in the marriage matter as the king wished; he would
thereby jeopardize office and priestly order, since papal authority
could not grant dispensation in contravention of these words of

truth.[57] He was not allowed to extend his permission to separate married couples further than the examples of the saints and the decrees of the Fathers admit, lest it should seem as if human arrogance infringe on the divine ordinance.[58] With regard to another divorce case he declares that in matrimonial matters he was bound to incline more to upholding the marriage than to separating it, lest men should venture to separate what God has joined.[59] The range of the unimpeachable divine law for Innocent is wide, wider than for the Church of the present day. Monks' vows too,[60] and the marriage-impediment of a close degree of affinity,[61] which for Innocent is not confined only to the closest ties of consanguinity, are beyond his power of dispensation. There is, however, one case in which the pope may dispose of that which, in his belief, exists by virtue of divine law: the union of the bishop with his church.[62] This union being a spiritual marriage is, like a corporal marriage, not dissoluble by human decree, and yet God had authorized His vicar on earth by *special privilege* to terminate it in His stead. He alone, therefore, is entitled to depose, to translate the bishop and to allow him to resign. But how does the pope know that, in the case of the *causae maiores* of the bishops, something beyond his ordinary competence is due to him by virtue of this extraordinary authorization? He deduces it from the fact that the canonical decrees and custom, the best interpreter of law, bestow this power upon the Roman bishop.[63] In a negative form this reasoning recurs in Innocent's refusal to extend, without consulting a general council,[64] the grounds for divorce on his own account beyond the decisions of the Fathers and the examples set by the saints.[65] There are, of course, no decisions of the Fathers and no decrees of a council, which could hold against the ordinances of divine law, but they may serve to interpret these ordinances when they are ambiguous, as for instance in the question whether an unconsummated marriage is dissoluble, a question which was relevant in the royal marriage cases.

Here we meet with another barrier, most effective in practice, which Innocent sets to papal power. In cases of doubt he dare not draw the line of his own accord between that which exists by divine law and that which is by church law, between that which lies within his competence of decision and that which is beyond it. In such cases he is dependent on the teaching of the Fathers, on the decrees of the councils, on the custom prevailing in the Church and on its legal rules, on the lines of conduct of the saints, i.e. the view held by ecclesiastical tradition, and on the consultation of a general council where even tradition fails to give an unambiguous answer. Only if he is in accordance with these holders, wardens and interpreters of tradition does Innocent feel sure that his decisions cannot amount to heresy.

Just as Innocent does not arrogate to himself any arbitrary infringement of the domain of divine law, just as he does not even feel himself unconditionally authorized to interpret the divine law on his own account, so he also upholds the ultimate freedom of conscience of the individual against ecclesiastical and even papal decisions. When he insists on suffering excommunication rather than committing a mortal sin, because what is not from faith is sin and what is done against conscience leads on to hell,[66] Innocent shows that for him conscience is the ultimate instance to decide on good and evil and that he does not concede that anyone can be relieved from responsibility by the command of an ecclesiastical superior, not even by that of the Roman bishop himself. This command is of course binding in conscience, within the limits of competence of him who commands. But it never holds 'against God'. And it is precisely this decision, whether a command is against God, which the individual can only take in his or her own conscience. Innocent never curtailed this right. Yet, for the sake of ecclesiastical discipline, he had to insist that the individual accept the consequences of acting contrary to it, i.e. even submit to a possible exclusion from the community of the Church. In this spirit Innocent decides that a partner in marriage, positively knowing of an impediment to his marriage, but unable to furnish proof before the Church, is on no account allowed to continue his marriage in obedience to the decision of the ecclesiastical judge, even if he thereupon becomes liable to excommunication.[67] In order to anticipate a possible rejoinder of Ludolf of Magdeburg against the charge of obstinate disobedience in the imperial cause, perhaps even to meet an objection of his own, Innocent asks the archbishop: "Or do you perhaps believe that the mandate served to you is against God?" For answer he is himself, though, unable to put forward anything but the reference to his personal conscience: "If you do, you are indeed foolish. For we also are human and fear the Lord of heaven and never intend to give orders in disregard of Him nor to arrogate anything to ourselves which is not our due".[68] In principle Innocent also recognizes the reference to the conscience in this case, but he denies that it is relevant here. He has tacitly recognized the principle in the schedule of an oath of obedience drawn up for a bishop of the Empire in the imperial cause: the person concerned has to declare that by his oath he is bound to obey the pope in matters concerning the Roman Empire as well as in others, but under the proviso *secundum Deum*.[69] Innocent often and decidedly gave voice to the fact that the tribunal of God and *the tribunal of the Church are not always* in accord. The tribunal of God always bases its decisions on the truth, which neither deceives nor is deceived, whereas the tribunal of the Church sometimes follows opinion, which often deceives and is deceived. It occasionally happens, therefore, that he who is bound in God, is loosed in the face of the Church, and he who is free before God, is bound by the judgement of the Church. By forgiving the guilt the ropes were untied with which the sinner is fettered before God, whereas he became free before men only by the annulment of the sentence.[70]

Innocent in principle concedes to the individual not only the right and the duty to follow his conscience even in defiance of the command of an ecclesiastical superior, but he also recognizes the possibility that man, by divine inspiration, may offend against a general law of the Church or even against divine law, and of course also against the instruction of an ecclesiastical superior, because he who is moved by the Spirit of God is not under the law, and where there is the Spirit of God there is freedom – in juristic parlance, because the *lex privata* has precedence over the *lex publica*.[71] It is conceivable for Innocent that someone, by virtue of divine inspiration, assumes competences which are usually due only to the hierarchy or in its gift, as for instance the office of preaching. But as this inner vocation is concealed, it is not sufficient for someone to pretend that he acted on God's mission. Every heretic made that pretence. Rather he had to verify his vocation, as the Disciples had done, by miracles.[72] Innocent rejects the view that an unconsummated marriage could be dissolved by one of the partner's joining an Order, since some saints had been called away from their wedding feast to a monastery. The example of some, particularly of those who are held to have acted by divine inspiration, did not make a general law, for where there is the Spirit of God there is freedom, and those moved by the Spirit of God were not under the law.[73] Innocent thus admits at least the possibility that saints by virtue of divine inspiration may have acted contrary to the generally accepted law of the indissolubility of marriage. A bishop who had requested to be allowed to resign his bishopric, is disallowed by Innocent to plead the *lex privata*, as nobody could be moved by the Spirit of God who acted contrary to it, i.e. who for the sake of personal profit in spiritual matters or of other private reasons evades the obligation to the Church which, by spiritual marriage and in consequence irreversibly, had been entrusted to him.[74] Innocent thus denies that the *lex privata* is in question in the bishop's case. This solution is unsatisfactory in practice, but in actual life there are no satisfactory solutions if the general law of the Church and the law of freedom are at variance. He who is subject to the *lex privata* will, therefore, always find himself confronted with the insistence, as Innocent pointed out, that excommunication is to be preferred to mortal sin, i.e. in this case to opposition to the Holy Spirit.[75]

That for Innocent the divine law ranks before ecclesiastical demands if the two are at variance, needs no further emphasis. A cleric, who after separating from his wife had himself ordained subdeacon, is compelled by Innocent to continue his marriage,[76] thereby of course forfeiting the right of the order. Confronted with the wife's divine right to her husband, of the divine law of the indissolubility of marriage, the law of continence, which the Church imposes upon a cleric of higher orders, must give way.

As regards the limits of papal power in spiritual matters, attention may also be drawn to the pope's explanatory comments on the nature of saintliness and the significance of canonization, laid down in the canonization bull of St Homobonus. Persistence alone would in the end be sufficient for the saintliness of man in the Church triumphant, for he who held out to the end would be blessed. Two things, however, were necessary for anyone to be deemed saint in the Church militant, strength of morals and strength of tokens; works, that is, of piety in life and tokens and wonders after death, because only the concurrence of both warranted saintliness.[77] Only if God Himself testifies to the saintliness, is the Church, in this case the Roman bishop, able and allowed to declare a man to belong to the host of the blessed. Innocent postponed the canonization, repeatedly requested from him, of Archbishop William of Bourges, until the wonders giving evidence of his saintliness had become so numerous and so conspicuous that he could proceed safely in this difficult matter. For a decision was involved here which was due to God rather than to man,[78] and it was difficult for mortal man to judge upon those who, clad as we believed in the mantle of immortality, lived in Christ.[79]

The pope's views and decisions just mentioned show that not even

by a hair's breadth has he shifted the confines between God and man
in favour of the Vicar of Christ, and that he has by no means laid
claim to a semi-divine status. The realm of divine law, of divine acts
of grace, of the inner divine life of the soul, is beyond the reach of
any human discretion as well as of any act of arbitrariness on the side
of the pope. Neither does Innocent arrogate to himself the binding
declaration as to whether certain cases fall within the reach of divine
or of human law, but commits them for deliberation with the general
council.[80]

Within the whole range of human law in the Church, however, the
full and unlimited *potestas* of the pope is valid for Innocent, the
*plenitudo potestatis* in the strict sense of the word. The *canones*, the
ecclesiastical ordinances, are for him in force only because they have
either been promulgated by the Apostolic See or have become his by
way of some form of approval.[81] Since each pope is in possession of
the same power as his predecessor, he too is entitled to create new
law. In exercising this power Innocent has, by way of amending the
existing law, developed a grandiose legislative activity.[82] By heavenly
dispensation the Apostolic See has been endowed with the *plenitudo
potestatis super universas ecclesias*[83] *et tam res quam personas
ecclesiasticas*,[84] over churches, over church property as well as over
the members of the clergy. Not by canonical statute only, but by
virtue of divine ordinance, the Apostolic See alone is competent in all
*causae maiores* of the Church.[85] The *plenitudo potestatis* vested in
Peter and his successors rests undivided with them, even if they call
others *in partem sollicitudinis* to share their burdens and honours.[86]
Though they have appointed bishops in all corners of the world and
allotted each province its share of ecclesiastical offices, it is yet to
them that is due the magistral office and the jurisdiction over all the
churches, all the believers, and all expose themselves to doom and
perdition who, like Dathan and Abiron, rebel against them. At the
Lateran Council Innocent defined the position of the Roman Church
as a *principatus ordinariae potestatis*, as a primacy of ordinary power
over all the churches by virtue of divine law.[87] Innocent, therefore,
deems himself entitled to exercise concurrently in every respect the
rights of the bishops, archbishops, primates and patriarchs. If he
takes over a function himself, which is normally the business of
another ecclesiastical office holder, he wrongs nobody, since he who
is only exercising his right cannot do wrong to anyone.[88] If he refrains
from encroaching on the sphere of jurisdiction of an ordinary

ecclesiastical superior where such a course of action was, for some reason or other, readily to be expected, he likes to point out that such indulgence implied his goodwill.[89]

Innocent's claim to the fullness of ecclesiastical power was in itself no innovation;[90] only he enforced this claim more consistently than his predecessors. It was decisive for ecclesiastical practice that he strictly interpreted the principle that the pope alone was competent in *causae maiores*, i.e. the deposition, resignation and translation of bishops.[91] Prior to Innocent's reign the exclusive power of the pope was, indeed, recognized only in deposition. Innocent's predecessor, Celestine III, had *admitted* the already effected resignation of a bishop[92] and, stating the principle that the translation (*mutatio*) of bishops could lawfully take place by virtue of papal authority, had *confirmed* the election of a bishop to another see.[93] Innocent takes up a much clearer position. For him there is no resignation of bishops except by papal authority, and there is no election of a bishop to another see, but only a postulation, i.e. a resolution to request the pope to translate the elect to another see of his own accord. The reason for this claim of Innocent's is already known to us. It follows from the concept of the union of the bishop with his church being a spiritual marriage[94] which is insoluble in itself, but which, for the sake of the benefit of the Church, may be dissolved by the Vicar of Christ by virtue of a special privilege. It was of far-reaching practical importance that Innocent enforced the sole right of the pope to effect translations. The need for such translations in the Christian world was extremely great. Kings often wished that successful men in the episcopate of their countries should be raised to the archiepiscopal and primatial sees, and that the career of ambitious or active men was not cut off by their accepting a small bishopric. Innocent relentlessly punished any unauthorized transition from one bishopric to another by deposition from both sees, even though the humiliated culprit was often restored to one of the bishoprics by act of grace. Innocent further strengthened the power of the pope in the Church by claiming and enforcing the right of devolution, in the case of ecclesiastical elections in which the electors had made themselves guilty of a grave offence against the *canones*, be it that they neglected the canonical impediments to election, or be it that the election was simoniacal or otherwise criminal. As such impediments were many – for instance, *defectus nativitatis, ordinis, aetatis* and being bound to another church – the right of appointment, in the beginning of the pope's reign, devolved more frequently on him. In the exercise of this right of devolution Innocent appointed among others the archbishops of Palermo,[95] Rheims and Sens. In consequence of the general acceptance of papal claims, such uncanonical elections happened less frequently. They were replaced by postulations in which the nominee, though, acquired no proper legal title and which the pope was free to turn down or to grant.

On the basis of his *plenitudo potestatis* over church property and over the members of the clergy Innocent could perhaps have justified the weighty innovation which he introduced in the form of a tax on the clergy for the benefit of the crusade. Yet the only reason he alleges for the levy of the fortieth in 1199 is the emergency,[96] and at the same time he asserts that thereby no precedent was set against the clergy and that the fortieth should by no means be regarded in future as a due and customary payment.[97] Nor is disobedience to the demand threatened with ecclesiastical punishments as an offence against church discipline, but as a breach of moral duty it is left to the judgement of God. Before he imposed, in the course of the preparations for the Fifth Crusade, a crusading tax on the clergy on pain of excommunication, Innocent made sure of the consent of the general council.[98] He had no intention of introducing general papal taxation of the Church,[99] but the precedent was set. There was, however, still a long way to go from this tax in a cause which the whole of Christendom regarded as its own and which was approved by a general council representing the entire Church, to the imposts which under the name of crusading taxes Innocent's successors, in their fight with Frederick II and other political adversaries, exacted from the clergy for the cause of the Curia.

Where the pope's fullness of ecclesiastical power was challenged in fact or in essence Innocent, particularly in the beginning of his reign, resorted to extremely rigorous and harsh measures. Archbishop Hubert Walter of Canterbury met with unusually harsh treatment at the hands of the new pope in his conflict with the monks of the cathedral chapter in the matter of the chapel of Lambeth, which Archbishop Baldwin, his predecessor, had built in disregard of the convent's appeal. On 31 May 1198 the news struck England like a bolt from the blue that the new pope had not only refused to renew the archbishop's legation,[100] which the archbishops of Canterbury almost held to be their due by prescriptive right,[101] but also seemed determined to enforce with the most stringent measures the destruction of the chapel, and that he had threateningly demanded from the archbishop a public statement declaring void all ecclesiastical punishments laid upon the members of the convent and had threatened to excommunicate all those who had laid hands on the monks' belongings and revenues.[102] No pope had ever used such bold language against the holder of one of the noblest sees of the Occident, which in this case was backed by the king with his full prestige. A few months later the archbishop is even faced with the threat of deposition if he continues to be disobedient. The sore limb, which defies all medicine, was to be cut off with the iron instrument, Innocent writes to him.[103] Apparently Innocent intended to redress a lasting derision of papal authority by king and archbishop.[104] Even Archbishop Peter of Sens, Innocent's otherwise highly esteemed and honoured erstwhile teacher, had to accept harsh censure and grave threats when he failed to execute a papal mandate.[105] In the first years of his pontificate Innocent threateningly required the Greek Church to submit at once to the Apostolic See without taking the thought of a council of union into consideration.[106]

Innocent, however, never regarded the fullness of ecclesiastical power as a *carte blanche* for papal arbitrariness. This power, though it knows no legal barriers, does have moral limitations, which are binding in conscience and which Innocent does not think of transgressing. When faced with the question whether he should allow a bishop, who had resigned from his see, to accept a new see contrary to the decrees of the Council of Constantinople, he comes to the conclusion that in three cases the prohibition laid down by the Council had no standing. If none of these three cases was in question, the postulation was to be rejected. It seemed to him, he writes, impossible to decide in this matter against one of the Councils in question which were venerated by the Church like the four gospels.[107]

Innocent feels bound not only to the old councils, but also, not legally, but morally, to the *canones*,[108] even if as *moderator canonum* he is in individual cases allowed to dispense from their strictness,[109] i.e. to reconcile the demands of the law with the needs of practical life and, on paramount grounds, to substitute for them new ones of his own accord. A modification of canon law as weighty as the abrogation of the impediments to marriage beyond the fourth degree of consanguinity and affinity, thus repealing opposing time-honoured constitutions,[110] Innocent may only have dared to effect *approbante sacro concilio generali.* The proclamation of an innovation as im-

...ant as the precept of yearly confession and communion on pain of exclusion from the Church[111] he also reserved to the general Lateran Council.|

Innocent feels bound not only to councils and *canones*, but also to decrees issued, and to the examples set, by his predecessors, unless there are reasonable grounds for divergence.[112] A question of marital law he decides, though personally inclining to a differing decision, on the lines set by his predecessors, because he does not wish to depart in this matter rashly (*subito*) from the way they had shown,[113] and in a patronage case he follows, in awe of Pope Alexander III, a distinction between lay and clerical patronage, which he would not have drawn of his own accord.[114] He declines to repeal reasonable regulations enacted by his predecessors, he does not wish, by frequent modifications, to give rise to grumbling, nor to set an example for his successors unscrupulously to repeal his own statutes,[115] thus causing insecurity of law. As the Holy Scriptures forbid us – thus Innocent neatly expressed his conservative attitude – to transgress the limits set by the Fathers, so he, too, was obliged to follow their example in the government of the Church as best he could, and to maintain its meritorious customs and traditions reverentially and unhurt, lest he should prove faithless to the Fathers and to be their successor as to the place only, not as to intention and goodwill.[116] The pope has also to respect vested rights or rights inherent in the nature of an office. Innocent refuses to believe that his predecessor had knowingly curtailed an archbishop's right of absolution in favour of a third party,[117] and already as cardinal he had either refused, together with other cardinals, to approve of a privilege granted by Celestine III amounting to a violation of the rights of the competent bishop, or, if he himself was not directly involved, at least approved of the refusal by his brother cardinals.[118] He did not exercise his concurrent power without reason, as he was in all matters whatever a foe to arbitrariness.[119]

To sum up, Innocent regards himself as the holder of the fullness of spiritual power. This spiritual power is not unlimited, but yields to divine law in the Church and to the immediate relations between God and the soul of the individual. In difficult cases Innocent did not dare to decide whether a matter fell within the reach of divine or of human law, but reserved the decision for deliberation with a general council. He considers himself unbound in the sphere of church law and of church government, but bound both factually and morally to the decisions of the four old general councils as well as to the *canones* in general, to the tradition of the Holy Fathers, to the reasonable rulings of his predecessors, in short to the whole weight of ecclesiastical tradition. A dispensation on reasonable grounds does not loosen these bonds, since it only harmonizes the general law with the needs of the individual case, that is the individual person's life. In the sphere of church government he claims concurrent authority with all ecclesiastical organs, but in general did not exercise it without reasonable grounds founded in the merits of the individual case. The pope is forbidden any arbitrary use of his power by his duty to show justice and love, which he owes to all and which cause him to maintain everyone in their vested rights. He is the first to have claimed a right of devolution in the case of uncanonical elections and to have exercised in the Church the right of taxation. He is stricter than his predecessors in insisting on the exclusive right of deciding the *causae maiores* of the bishops, and it is precisely by this last measure that he immensely enhanced papal prestige within the Church.

Under Innocent III the pope's position in the Church underwent no fundamental change. But he gave the doctrine of primacy a strict formulation and a systematic justification,[120] and he deeply inculcated into the consciousness of the occidental Church the position of the Roman bishop as the ordinary holder of all ecclesiastical power, of the *plenitudo potestatis*, the papal universal episcopate. Innocent was the first pope to style himself *vicarius Christi*, Vicar of Christ,[121] and to describe his office as a representation of God.[122] The title Vicar of Christ and the designation of the office as the representation of God, raised, indeed, the pope out of the rank and file of the bishops in a more emphatic degree than the title of Vicar of Peter, they gave widely visible expression to his unique position within the Church and his unique rank within mankind. They placed the Roman bishop, as is stated in Innocent's sermon on the day of his consecration – without obscuring the difference between God and man –, "below God but above men."[123]

## Notes to Chapter 2

[1]Ordo X ed. by Andrieu, Le Pontifical, 526. On the *immantatio* see Zoepffel, 168ff.
[2]See below, Chapter 5.
[3]Gesta c. 7.

[4]Migne PL. 217, 658. According to Maccarrone (Innoc., 133), Innocent did not actually preach any of the extant sermons *in consecrat. pont.* on the consecration day itself. I am not fully convinced on this point. The programmatic nature of *Sermo II in consecrat.*, as well as the lively manner of the references to Innocent's own elevation, seem to indicate that, despite the objections which doubtless militate against this view, the sermon was in fact preached on the day of his consecration, especially since otherwise it could only have been preached on the second anniversary at the earliest (the first anniversary is fixed as the date of *Sermo III* in view of the close relationship between Reg. II 4 and the sermon, Migne PL. 217, 665. See Tillmann, Zur Frage, 148f.).

[5]On this phrase and its use referring to the pope by Bernard of Clairvaux and Peter of Blois see Rivière, Sur l'expression "Papa-Deus" au moyen-âge (Misc. Fr. Ehrle 2, Studi e Testi 38, 1924), 278. John of Damascus uses the expression, which derives from Exodus and the metaphorical sense of which seems to have been familiar to Innocent from ecclesiastical literature, with reference to the saints being Gods, not by nature, but by having overcome their passions (Bibl.d. Kirchenväter 4, 1923, 15). Gregory of Nazianzus, in a eulogy delivered in the presence of St Basil the Great, addresses him: "But I call you also the God of Pharaoh, that is God of the whole Egyptian enemy power" (Bibl. d. Kirchenväter 18, 1923, 352). Cf. also Tellenbach, 12, 61f.

[6]Matthew 24: 45.

[7]Innocent expresses the same idea of his being subject to the jurisdiction of the Church in two other sermons on the anniversary of his consecration (*Sermo III* and *Sermo IV in consecrat.*, Migne PL. 217, 665, 670), once in *Sermo IV* even using the striking formulation, "In truth the pope may not flatter himself with his power and praise his magnificence and honour to excess, for the less he is judged by men the more he will be judged by God. I say the less, because he can be judged by men or rather be proved to have been judged if he succumbs to heresy".

[8]So most recently Bihlmeyer-Tüchle, Kirchengeschichte 2 (1948), 258.

[9]E. Kantorowicz, 40.

[10]I do not intend to give an exhaustive list of the literature taking this line. For a revision of his interpretation see Maccarrone, Chiesa, and Tillmann, Zur Frage.

[11]A privilege of 1198 for two noblemen from the Patrimony declares it to be a custom of the Apostolic See to give particular protection and favour to those who serve it not merely as *everyone* is subjected to it *spiritually*, but also to those who *additionally* come under its *temporal* jurisdiction (Reg. I 378). He inaugurates a donation for the church of St Peter with the statement that God had placed St Peter and in him his successors above *everyone* in *spiritual* matters and had also enriched the Church in *temporal* matters (*dilatarit*, Reg. I 536). According to Innocent's sermon on the first anniversary of his consecration the Roman Church, his bride, has given him at their marriage an immeasurably precious dowry, the *plentido spiritualium* and the *latitudo temporalium* (*Sermo de diver. III*, Migne PL. 217, 665). In a letter to a city in the Patrimony of the same year Innocent states that, whereas the *spiritual* jurisdiction of the Holy See is subject to no restriction, but *has attained power over kingdoms and nations*, yet its *temporal* jurisdiction by the grace of God extends also over many matters. Towards the end of 1202 he writes to William of Montpellier that not only in the *Patrimony* of the Church which is subjected to his *full* power *in temporalibus*, but in other countries as well he exercises *certis causis inspectis* temporal jurisdiction *casualiter* (Reg. V 128). A letter to the clergy and laity of the diocese of Fermo states that the bishop of Rome had been vested by the Lord himself not only with the totality

of power (*summam potestatem*) in *spiritual* matters, but also with a *great* power in *temporal* matters (Rev. VIII 190). Innocent remarks to Philip of France in October 1203 that the God-man had extended the jurisdiction of the Apostolic See *in spiritualibus* so extensively that it could not be increased since fullness allows of no increase (Reg. VI 163, P. 2009).

[12]The pallium, Innocent informed the Bulgarians, is carried during the celebration of the mass always and everywhere by the pope alone because he is accepted *in plenitudinem ecclesiasticae potestatis*, which the pallium symbolizes. Others are allowed to use it, but not always and not everywhere since they are called *in partem sollicitudinis*, not *in plenitudinem potestatis* (Reg. VII 10). On another occasion Innocent points out that in order to maintain in force the full measure of the ecclesiastical jurisdiction the Lord had conferred *magisterium* and the primacy over the entire Church and all the faithful on the Apostolic See. It in turn, though retaining the full power, calls many in *partem sollicitudinis* by allotting to them parts of its burden and honour in such a way that its own rights remain unimpaired and its jurisdiction uncurtailed (Reg. II 60). Innocent also indicates the limited sense of the concept by stating that it was by divine ordinance that the Apostolic See gained the *plenitudo potestatis* over all the churches and the church property and the clergy (Reg. VIII 153, X 56, 200). The pope frequently uses the more precise concept of the plenitude of the ecclesiastical power. St Peter was granted the *plenitudo ecclesiasticae potestatis* (Reg. VI 67, IX 82). The Lord said to Peter: 'You follow me', that is, become like me in the office of the true shepherd *et potestatis ecclesiasticae plenitudine* (Reg. VII 1). The pope then in his turn received the *plenitudo ecclesiasticae potestatis* (Reg. I 536) from the Prince apostle through the merits of Peter. The vicar of Christ received in Peter the *plenitudo ecclesiasticae potestatis* (Reg. VII 209). Not a man, but God, or rather the God-man, has granted in St Peter the *plenitudo ecclasiasticae potestatis* to the Roman Church (Reg. VIII 19). God has founded the *plenitudo ecclesiasticae potestatis ecclesiasticae dignitatis* in the Apostolic See (Reg. VII 119, VIII 137). The Apostolic See is accepted *in plenitudinem ecclesiasticae dignitatis* (Reg. VI 188). The Roman Church allots to those whom it summons *in partem sollicitudinis*, burdens and honours in such a way that it retains the care for all the churches and is graced by the *plenitudo ecclesiasticae potestatis* (Reg. VIII 20; Hampe, Registerbände, 560). On Innocent's use of *plenitudo potestatis* and the history of the term see Maccarrone, Chiesa, 5ff.

[13]RNI 33. This concept is also used in other respects to describe imperial power. The crusaders do not fear their words would be misconstrued when they report to the pope that the imperial diadem had been restituted *cum plenitudo potestatis* to the prince they had led back to Constantinople (Reg. VI 211).

[14]See Maccarrone's detailed account, Chiesa, 82ff. Cf. also Carlyle, 146. Heiler (268) is mistaken when, referring to Reg. V 128, he attributes to Innocent a claim both to the "authority of the *summus pontifex* as well as to the power of the *supremus princeps*". The passage reads: *Id* [a right of legitimization] *autem in patrimonio b. Petri libere potest Apostolica sedes officere, in quo et Summi Pontificis auctoritatem exercet et supremi principis exsequitur potestatem.* In fact the passage speaks for the limitation of the pope's claim to temporal power, not against it.

[15]On the doctrine of the two swords see W. Levison, Die mittelalterliche Lehre von den beiden Schwertern, DA 9 (1951), 14ff.

[16]RNI 179. This statement would seem to confirm the interpretation of Uguccio who

had cited the *Ecce duo gladii* to support his view that both powers were derived from God, were independent of each other, and that the emperor did not receive his sword from the pope (the relevant passage of the *Summa* is printed for instance in Hugelmann, Die Wirkungen der Kaiserweihe nach dem Sachsenspiegel, ZRG 9, 1919, 22f., and glossed in Maccarrone, Chiesa, 69ff.). Innocent derives the temporal sword or temporal power from God in many other passages, too, in Reg. I 18, III 3, VI 94, VII 79, 113, IX 127, XIII 67, XIV 131, XVI 2, Pr. coll. 2 (Migne PL. 216, 1184), RNI 2, 32; Hampe, Registerbände, 562; cf. also c. 8 of the council of legates for the Empire of Vulk of Dioclea and Dalmatia of 1199, Reg. II 178. On occasion Innocent does describe the spiritual sword as the sword which Peter *per se ipsum exercet* (Reg. VII 212, XIV 63). This expression derives from similar phrases used by Bernard of Clairvaux (cf. Maccarrone, Chiesa, 86ff.): *Petri uterque [scil. gladius] est, alter suo nutu, alter sua manu... evaginandus.... Ergo suus erat et ille, sed non sua manu utique educendus* (Migne PL. 182, 464; cf. Maccarrone, Chiesa, 62). *Uterque ergo ecclesiae et spiritualis [scil. gladius] et materialis, sed is quidem pro ecclesia, ille vero ab ecclesia exserendus: ille sacerdotis, is militis manu, sed sane ad nutum sacerdotis et iussum imperatoris* (Migne PL. 182, 776). If Bernard really meant this passage to characterize the pope as the bearer of all spiritual and temporal power (cf. Stickler, 237, and n. 17 below), Innocent's phrasal borrowing does not imply that in the passages cited he has, in contradiction to his other statements on the relationship of the two powers, ascribed to the Church the plenitude of temporal power too (cf. Maccarrone, Chiesa, 86ff.). While the concept of the sword which Peter *per se ipsum exercet* does seem to require as complement the concept of a further sword which Peter has others wield, Innocent may well have been thinking in terms of a right of disposing which the Church held over the temporal sword in that it had by right a claim on the state's support in certain circumstances. In the letter in which this noteworthy phrase occurs Innocent appeals to Philip of France to use the material sword against the heretics who had shown no fear of the sword which Peter *per se ipsum exercet* (Reg. VII 212). In the same letter, in which he describes the spiritual sword as the sword which Peter *per se ipsum exercet*, Innocent confesses that God, from whom all power derives, had given the sword to the king. It would be a forced interpretation to suggest that in all passages in which Innocent derives the temporal sword from God he only intended to point to the supreme creator of all power. It is significant that Reg. X 28 interprets the *hic* by *id est simul*. Does Innocent intend to refute the interpretation as being *in manu Petri*? In future, as a consequence of Stickler's arguments in his study of Uguccio's conception of the sword, we must draw a clear distinction between a political and a coercive-legal concept of the sword and in each individual case take pains to scrutinize the sense in which the concept of the sword is being used (see Stickler, 232ff.). Where the Church's or pope's sword is used in the coercive-legal sense it merely refers to the Church's right to use temporal power too or to have temporal power used to intervene on its behalf so that the Church may achieve its religious and spiritual goals (*ibid.* 212ff.). Innocent's assertion in RNI 18 that the kingdom was established in the children of Israel *per extorsionem humanam* or that it was *extortum ad petitionem humanam* should not be construed as denying the divine origin of the state's supreme power. The reference here is to the origin of the kingdom in one particular instance and not to the origin of the state's supreme power as such (cf. Maccarrone, Chiesa, 81f.).

[17] *Alioquin, si nullo modo ad te* [i.e. Eugenius III] *pertineret et is* [the temporal sword] *dicentibus apostolis, 'ecce duo galdii hic' non respondisset Dominus satis est, sed nimis*

*est* (Migne PL. 182, 776). The *nullo modo* could point to a merely coercive-legal significance of the image of the sword (cf. Stickler, 212ff., 232ff. and n. 16 above).

[18]Reg. XI 28.

[19]See above, Chapter 1. For the Gelasian concept see also Tellenbach, 42ff., who rightly demands in his assessment of the ecclesiastical interpretations of the relationship between Church and state in the middle ages that a distinction be drawn between precedence and predominance (p. 46).

[20]RNI 16.

[21]In response to the Greek Emperor Alexius's claim that the *imperium* was superior to the *sacerdotium* both in dignity and power, Innocent replied in terms consistent again with Uguccio (the relevant passage from the *Summa* is printed for instance in Stickler, 212, note), that he did not deny that the emperor held precedence *in temporalibus* (*quin praescellat in temporalibus imperator*), but only in relation to those who received temporal gifts from him (i.e. in this connection not in relation to the clergy). The *pontifex*, however, held precedence *in spiritualibus* which were as superior to the *temporalia* as the soul was to be preferred to the body (Migne PL. 216, 1183). The supplementary sentence in no way restricts the pope's recognition of the supremacy of the emperor in the worldly sphere. In his letter to William of Montpellier of 1203 Innocent agrees that in *temporalibus* the king of France recognizes no one to be his superior (Rev. V 128). The feudal letter to King John of England states that the king has also agreed to submit himself and his kingdom *temporaliter* to him to whom he knows he is subject *spiritualiter*. God has ordained, Innocent writes, that those provinces which from old had the Holy Roman Church as their proper teacher *in spiritualibus* now had her as their peculiar sovereign *in temporalibus* (Reg. XVI 131). It follows that Innocent recognizes that England before becoming a fief of the Church was not subject to him *in temporalibus* (see Maccarrone, Chiesa, 54f.).

[22]Reg. V 128. Despite his legates' pressure Innocent therefore refused to force laymen to provide a contribution for the costs of the heresy crusade without the prior consent of their lords (Reg. XII 87). See n. 99 below.

[23]Can. 42 (Leclercq 1366). It is perhaps significant that Can. 42 is one of the two canons of the Council which were not incorporated into the decretals of Gregory IX.

[24]See Tillmann, Zur Frage, 150.

[25]On Bishop Waldemar of Schleswig's attempt to seize the Danish crown Innocent gave the opinion that Waldemar had wished to unite in his person both *regnum* and *sacerdotium* and had thus wished to become the monster with many heads (Reg. VI 181).

[26]See Tillmann, Zur Frage, 169ff.

[27]*Ibid.* 175ff.

[28]Reg. V 128. See Molitor, Die Dekretale *Per venerabilem*, Maccarrone, Chiesa, 118ff., and Tillmann, Zur Frage, 137ff. Molitor and Maccarrone do not draw any or sufficient distinction between this extraordinary jurisdiction and the jurisdiction *ratione peccati*. On the significance of the decretal for contemporary canonistics see Mochi Onory, 209ff., 271ff.

[29]See Tillmann, Zur Frage, 138f.

[30]See Maccarrone, Chiesa, 74ff., 89f., 114, 123ff. Cf. also Kempf, Regestum, 75, n. 3.

[31]See Maccarrone, Chiesa, 73ff. The text is in Mochi Onory, 149 note, 153 n. 1, 155f. nn. 1, 2; see also p. 156f. When dealing with the alleged deposition of the last Merovingian king by Pope Zacharias Uguccio states that the pope could depose a king

who has been committed for trial to his tribunal by the princes of the kingdom (Maccarrone, Chiesa, 74ff. Text in Mochi Onory, 155f. n. 2). The request of a third party proves to be essential also for Uguccio. Innocent himself, who normally followed Uguccio very closely, never laid claim to a papal right to depose rulers (see Tillmann, Zur Frage, 139ff.), and thus adopted a more moderate approach than Uguccio, whose account of the alleged procedure adopted to dethrone the last Merovingian king would have served Innocent as a convenient precedent to dethrone Otto IV since his committment to the papal court by the (rebellious) princes could well have been construed.

[32]Here too Innocent follows Uguccio's doctrine (see Maccarrone, Chiesa, 78).

[33]See Tillmann, Zur Frage, 138f.

[34]See Maccarrone, Chiesa, 108ff. (and see n. 28 above).

[35]Reg. VI 163, VII 42.

[36]See RNI 16, 26, 27, 111, 120, 121; Reg. VII 42.

[37]Reg. VI 163, VII 42, VIII 114. See also RNI 2, Reg. XI 174.

[38]His jurisdiction *occasione peccati* in temporal matters should not be confused with a jurisdiction over the temporal power as such, in the way Hugh of St Victor attributes it to the ecclesiastical order, as being of higher rank, over the temporal order being of lower rank: "But as much as the ecclesiastical life ranks above the temporal in dignity and the spirit above the body, so much the ecclesiastical power stands ahead of the mundane or temporal power in honour and dignity. The ecclesiastical power has to institute the temporal power in order that it can exist and to adjudicate it if it has proved inadequate." (*De sacram.* c. 4.1.2 pars 2, Migne PL. 176, 417f.). Innocent, who knew Hugh's conception (compare Hugo *op. cit.* with Innocent *De sacro alt. myst.*, Migne PL. 217, 844 and RNI 18) does agree with him as to the reasons given for the incomparable pre-eminence in dignity of the ecclesiastical power over the temporal (RNI 18), but does not draw Hugh's conclusion and does not impair the independence of the temporal power, but in his theological work draws a very sharp line between the two spheres by ascribing the *spiritualia* and *coelestia* to the Church and the *carnalia* and *terrena* to the laity. When the pope judges *occasione peccati*, he does not sit in judgement on the temporal power as such, nor on the king as its bearer but on the mortal sinner, who accidentally is the bearer of the temporal power, being the coordinated principle; he adjudicates on human actions which involve a mortal sin and which also happen to be acts of royal prerogative and state affairs, and in so judging, and this must be emphasized again, he applies only the Church's own disciplinary measures against laymen, and not such punishments as the deposition which Hugh of St Victor declares applicable.

[39]It is utterly devious when Meyer (Staatstheorien Papst Innocenz' III., Jen. Hist. Arb. 9, 1919, 28) asserts that Innocent had felt competent to intervene in all temporal matters since he needed only to interpret worldly actions as sins, a procedure which in view of the relative meaning of the word had been applicable to any case whatever. In the first place the concept of a manifest mortal sin is by no means so relative as to allow any worldly matter to be so classified, as Meyer suggests; it is by no means indiscriminately that Innocent hallmarks an action as being a mortal sin.

[40]This basic standpoint does not impinge on the paternal care for the temporal welfare as well which the pope, the common father of Christendom, is bound to show for the individual as well as for peoples and realms (see Reg. I 5, 271, 558; II 245; VII 1, 8). Innocent does not intend to manifest indifference to temporal matters but to delimit

his legal competence regarding them. Hauck (Der Gedanke der päpstlichen Weltherrschaft bis auf Bonifaz VIII., 1904, 40 n. 1) would have the pope's pastoral obligations extend to such details as the minting of full-weight coins in Spain. That is out of the question. The letter on which Hauck bases his proposition (Reg. II 28) is in fact in answer to a question of conscience raised by Peter II of Aragon relating to the oath he had sworn to maintain the circulation of debased coinage. The king had turned to the highest spiritual authority as a Christian, not as a worldly subordinate. From the mentioned obligation to pastoral care Innocent has hardly deduced a right to intervene in state matters beyond the limits fixed by his jurisdiction *occasione peccati*, by the supplementary temporal jurisdiction and by the obligation to support the temporal power. It is not possible to follow this argument further here.

[41]See below, Chapter 5, and Tillmann, Zur Frage, 140 n. 17.

[42]See below, Chapter 4, and Tillmann, Zur Frage, 141f.

[43]See below, Chapter 5.

[44]See below, Chapter 5 and nn. 101, 108, 109, 115.

[45]See Tillmann, Zur Frage, 142f.

[46]See below, Chapter 5.

[47]See Tillmann, Zur Frage, 144f. also regarding the attitude of Alexander III, who contents himself with releasing from the oaths of allegiance but effects this release in a much more pretentious form. For Gregory VII see Tellenbach, 179ff. As far as the attitude of Innocent's successors is concerned, Gregory IX stands closer to Innocent III than Innocent IV. Even though Gregory threatens Frederick II with depriving him *iure feudi* of the Sicilian kingdom, being a fief belonging to the Roman Church, he contents himself with announcing the release of Frederick's subjects from their oaths of allegiance, and later puts this into effect. He manifests a juxtaposition of both attitudes, that of the judge and the proclaimer: *absolvimus et denuntiavimus absolutos*, MG. Epp. saec. XIII 1, 731; see also 319, 638.

[48]See also Martini, 335.

[49]See also Migne PL. 217, 311, 381, 398 (*Sermo de temp.* 18; Reg. I 176, 366).

[50]Migne PL. 217, 311.

[51]See Tellenbach, 182, 194ff.

[52]Reg. VII 42.

[53]Reg. I 358. See also Reg. I 176; see also below, Chapters 5 and 10.

[54]See Maccarrone, Chiesa, 80ff. 91ff.; Kempf, Regestum, 49, n. 13.

[55]See below, Chapter 4.

[56]Reg. XI 182, XV 106. See also Reg. VII 227.

[57]Reg. XV 106.

[58]Reg. XI 182.

[59]Reg. VII 227. See also Conc. Lateran. can. 52.

[60]Cap. 6 X 3, 35. Here too Innocent follows Uguccio's doctrine (cf. Maccarrone, Chiesa, 68f.).

[61]Cap. 13 X 2, 13.

[62]Reg. I 117 (Rainer of Pomposa, Migne PL. 216, 1199), 326, 335, 602, 532 (Rainer of Pomposa *op. cit.* 1197); II 78; IX 172.

[63]Reg. I 326, 335, 490.

[64]Reg. XV 106.

[65]Reg. XI 182.

[66]Cap. 13 X 2, 13.

[67]Reg. XI 269; c. 13 X 2, 13. Innocent warns Philip of France of the possibility of just such a conflict if the king should secure a divorce by deceit (see below, Appendix 2).

[68]RNI 109.

[69]RNI 114.

[70]Rainer of Pomposa, Pr. coll. t. 31 (Migne PL. 216, 1248).

[71]Reg. II 141; IX 1 (Migne PL. 215, 807), 62; XI 182; VIII 195; XII 195. The expression refers to the Decr. Grat. c. 2 C XIX qu. 2. Relating to the *lex privata* Urban II allows a secular priest to yield to the inspiration of the Holy Ghost and to turn monk, in contradiction to the *lex publica*, i.e. without the otherwise obligatory permission of his bishop. In a learned opinion Stephen of Tournai declared admissible the transition of a monk from Grammont into the Cistercian Order, referring to the word of St Paul cited above and to the pertinent decretals (Migne PL. 211, 362, 366f.) Innocent greatly extended the scope of this principle.

[72]Reg. II 141.

[73]Reg. XI 182. See Reg. VIII 195 and c. 2 C XIX qu. 2 (see Tellenbach, 31 n. 43).

[74]Reg. IX 1.

[75]Reg. XI 269.

[76]Reg. XI 204.

[77]Reg. I 530.

[78]... *quod huiusmodi judicium divinum sit potius quam humanum* ... (quoted Hon. Reg. 6, 44).

[79]*Ibid.*

[80]See n. 110 below.

[81]Reg. II 278.

[82]A detailed assessment would require a detailed and exhaustive knowledge of the canonical literature of the pre-Innocentian and Innocentian times. On the pope's legislative activity see pp. 37–8 above and pp. 57ff., 62, 190ff., 192ff., 197 and 201ff. below.

[83]Reg. X 56, 200, 316; VIII 153.

[84]Reg. X 200.

[85]Reg. II 133.

[86]Reg. VIII 35.

[87]Can. 5. See Maccarrone, Chiesa, 5, 17. Uguccio already had designated the Church of Rome as the *commune et generale forum omnium clericorum et omnium ecclesiarum* and the pope as the *index ordinarius omnium, scil. maiorum et minorum prelatorum et subditorum* (Mochi Onory, 160 n. 1, 166 n. 1).

[88]Reg. X 35.

[89]Reg. VIII 13, 153; X 52, 56.

[90]Nicholas I already had, in principle, laid claim to this totality of power (see Maccarrone *loc. cit.* and Reinacher, Die Anschauungen des Papstes Nickolaus I. über das Verhältnis von Staat und Kirche, Abb. z. mittl. u. neuerer Gesch. 1909, 8ff.).

[91]Innocent III emphatically laid claim also to canonization as being a papal reservation, a claim which hitherto, at least in the emphatic form used by Innocent, had never been expressed. Cf. Kuttner, La réserve papale du droit de canonisation (Rev. de droit franç. sér. 4 t. 17, 1938, 172ff.).

[92]JL. 17209 (Migne PL. 206, 1077).

[93]JL. 16731 (Migne PL. 206, 886). Alexander III considered a bishop's resignation not to be legally binding before the papal approbation and denies the bishop's metropolitan the right to accept the resignation without the pope's mandate (Compil. I c. 11. 2 t. 5), but granting a dispensation tolerates in the end what had happened.

[94]On this conception see Tellenbach, 154ff.

[95]See below, Chapter 4, n. 88.

[96]See Martini, 315f., 320.

[97]Reg. II, 270. On Innocent III's crusade taxes in general see, in addition to Martini, Gottlob, Die päpstlichen Kreuzzugssteuern im 13. Jahrhundert (1892).

[98]See below, Chapter 9. See also Martini, 322.

[99]He also rejected his legates' proposal that he should tax the clergy, in those areas where the nobility had taken up the cross against the heretics, in favour of the Albigensian Crusade. He replies that it seemed to him and to his cardinals too harsh a measure to bring pressure to bear where requests and admonitions were more seemly. He would, he wrote, consider imposing such a tax only if it were the sole means of preventing the dissolution of the crusading army, and even then, only if it would not create considerable resentment (Reg. XII 87, XIII 87). In 1208 the archbishop of Sens and his suffragans had on their own initiative placed a tenth of their income at the pope's disposal for the Crusade. Referring to this example Innocent in the same year recommends to the French bishops and prelates to bring their influence to bear upon clergy and laity in the territories of those nobles who had taken the cross against the heretics, to contribute their tenths (Reg. XI 158). In addition to this the legates had applied for coercive measures which Innocent firmly refused to take against laymen without the consent of their lords.

[100]Gervase of Canterbury 1, 551.

[101]On the legations of the archbishops of Canterbury up to Innocent III's pontificate see Tillmann, Legaten, 30ff.

[102]Reg. I 111, Epp. Cant. 394ff.

[103]See Tillmann, Legaten, 23ff.

[104]Reg. I 432, 433–435.

[105]Reg. VI 151.

[106]Reg. I 353, 354; II 209, 211 (Acta Inn. 1 Nos. 4, 5, 9, 10).

[107]Reg. XI 249.

[108]Reg. V 99, X 5.

[109]Reg. XVI 154.

[110]Can. 50 (Leclercq 1372f.). These constitutions are at the same time characterized as being the expression of human law. The pope may not have come to the firm conviction of the competence of human, i.e. here the ecclesiastical law, in this question until the general council gave its approval (see Chapter 1 above).

[111]Can. 21 (Leclercq 1350).

[112]Reg. I 172, 118, 215, 267, 357; II 38 bis.

[113]Reg. VIII 195.

[114]Reg. VII 169 (Migne PL. 215, 481); similarly Reg. IX 25.

[115]Reg. I 357.

[116]Migne PL. 217, 66.

[117]Reg. I 61.

[118]See above Chapter 1. In a number of cases Innocent himself did indeed grant to bishops whom he had consecrated a privilege under which they could not be excommunicated without the consultation of their consecrator, (i.e. of the pope himself) (Reg. VIII 179f., IX 196). When circumstances so required, Innocent did not even shrink from altering the legal status of churches for political reasons. For example he deprived exempt churches of their exemption or at least threatened so to do (Reg. I 121–123). In such cases he may simply have claimed his *plenitudo potestatis*, which does not allow,

as he points out, of any surprise if he now raises the humble, now strikes down the obstinate (Reg. I 123).

[119]In this respect it is characteristic how Innocent responded to requests that he should administer the consecration of bishops. Archbishop Siegfried of Mainz had postponed the consecration of his Strasbourg suffragan for various reasons and pretexts, despite receiving a papal mandate. When the bishop elect came to Rome to request that he be consecrated there Innocent required Siegfried to state his opinion, adding that if he, the pope, were to proceed with the consecration, he would sufficiently guard the archbishop's rights and dignity (Reg. VIII 90). In the event Innocent, despite the elect's insistence, granted Siegfried's request that the elect should be sent back to him for consecration. However, should Siegfried place further obstacles in the bishop-elect's path, the archbishop of Sens, Innocent stipulates, is to proceed with the consecration by virtue of papal authority, but is to accept the elect's *professio* in Siegfried's name and order the newly-consecrated bishop to present himself to Siegfried as soon as possible in order to acknowledge the *professio* (Reg. VIII 138). The electors of William of Staufen, the bishop elect of Constance, informed the pope that for fear of Philip of Swabia they were not applying for the confirmation of this election by the archbishop of Mainz. They asked Innocent to confirm William's election by virtue of his apostolic authority and to accord the elected candidate the administration of the spirituals and temporals since harm could come to the Church should any delay occur. Innocent grants William the *administratio*, materially the most urgent point to be decided, but refers him to the archbishop for confirmation and consecration (Reg. IX 163). Where Innocent personally administered the confirmation of ordination of suffragan bishops we know or may guess the special reason. Thus he consecrates a suffragan of Constantinople because the patriarch who had confirmed him had as yet no fellow bishops and was obliged to send the bishops elect of Athens and Thebes to Syria to receive their consecration (Reg. X 35). Innocent confirms the election to the see at Winchester of Peter des Roches because it had taken place at the Curia (Reg. VIII 108); it seems likely that Peter's consecration did not take place until later (Reg. VIII 179) when the death of the archbishop of Canterbury was already known in Rome. Innocent confirms the bishop elect of Sées and has the archbishop of Sens consecrate him, since the archbishop of Rouen for fear of King John had not dared to carry out either function and probably would not dare to do so in the future. Although the archbishop had approved the election, he declined to confirm it and the king had explicitly forbidden him to perform the consecration. Innocent makes it plain to the archbishop that he has not acted to his prejudice, but for the sake of ecclesiastical liberty and that on the occasion of the consecration the rights of the church of Rouen had been safeguarded (Reg. VI 73). In the few cases where Innocent granted exemptions for special reasons he did his best to preserve the rights and prestige of the diocesan bishop (Reg. XI 65, XIII 21, 89). If requested for grants which impinge on the rights of the diocesan bishop or another church superior, he only makes them reserving these rights or else he forwards such requests to the competent prelates with his own recommendation (Reg. I 9, 134, 400, 508; XV 240).

[120]In particular see Reg. II 209 to Patriarch John Kamateros of Constantinople. See Maccarrone, Chiesa, 3ff., 16ff. On the development of the concept of primacy and the conflict between episcopalism and papalism see Tellenbach, 164ff. (for further literature *ibid.* 167 n. 15).

[121]Maccarrone, Chiesa, 34ff.; Tellenbach, 230. It is not clear whether Innocent used

this designation for the bishop of Rome already before his pontificate (Maccarrone, Chiesa, 35) since the only extant final version of *De secro alt. myst.* dates from the time of Innocent's pontificate (cf. pp. 8 above and 300–301 below). The designation itself is not new (cf. Maccarrone, Chiesa, 34ff. In 1141 Abbot Hariulf of Oudenburg addressed Innocent II as *Christi vicarius*, see Müller, 111). Following the pope's example it is then used not·only by Otto IV in the Promise of Speyer (RNI 189) when the Curia's influence will have been at work, but also by Philip of Swabia in his letter of justification to the pope (RNI 136: *Christus cuius vicem in terris geritis*, Kempf, Regestum, 322).

[122]The term *vicarius* Dei is not used in an isolated form but either in paraphrase or, in special circumstances, indeed in the original wording, but always linked with a quotation from a literary text (see Maccarrone, Chiesa, 36f.; for further examples: Tillmann, Zur Frage, 145f.).

[123]The description of the bishop of Rome as the vicar of Christ by Innocent III gave an unfortunate impetus to the elaboration of the hierocratic idea, since theologians and decretists, contrary to Innocent III's conception, deduced from the idea of the Kingdom of Christ the world domination of the vicar of Christ (Maccarrone, Chiesa, 38ff.).

# CHAPTER 3

# On the chair of justice

"When I had stayed some time at the Curia I found much that was contrary to my way of thinking. People were so intensely occupied with temporal and worldly affairs, with kings and kingdoms, with lawsuits and quarrels that it seemed hardly permissible to talk, even only a little, about spiritual matters." In these words James of Vitry,[1] bishop of Acre, later cardinal of the Roman Church, describes the impressions he had at the Curia when in 1216, immediately after Innocent III's death, he came to the papal court at Perugia. It was mainly the host of litigations with their accompaniments which gave life at the Curia an unspiritual appearance and which in fact contributed to its becoming secular. There was a throng at the Curia of those who for themselves or for their mandators sought right or what they regarded, or gave out, as right; members of all nations, of all social ranks, of all stages of education, rich and poor, men and women, laymen and clerics, and above all monks and priests of all ranks. One monastery sued another for subordination or independence, cathedral chapters, bishops, canons sued for rights, revenues, offices and honours. Attorneys and legal advisers offered the litigants their services and enlarged the body of followers of the Curia. The litigants and the legal advisers were joined by money-lenders and money-changers who, up to Innocent III's accession to the throne, ran a changing office in the kitchen yard of the Lateran for their own and for their customers' convenience and to the offence of the pilgrims in Rome.[2] The huge staff of officials, which the growing centralization of all ecclesiastical affairs at the Curia made necessary, had no little share in intensifying the impression of worldly dealings.

The administration of justice was, in principle, gratuitous, as was the decision on all applications and the granting of acts of indulgence. Innocent III, though, by establishing a scale of fees, initiated the remuneration of scriveners and sealers, but in other respects upheld the principle of gratuity. This was due perhaps to fundamental considerations, perhaps to the scruple that the general introduction of fixed charges would have heavily burdened the less well-off and hindered the Curia from causing the well-to-do to share, beyond the costs of their transaction, in the financial burdens it had to bear. Such burden-sharing was indispensable, since the Curia was not in a position to meet the costs of government and administration of justice for the entire Church. The curial officials, who had no fixed salary and were insufficiently provided with benefices,[3] were, therefore, dependent on being paid by way of presents from those who availed themselves of their services. The position was similar for the pope and the cardinals themselves. The visitors did not see this interrelation and regarded the demand for presents as the outcome of greed or blackmail. In times of desperate pecuniary straits overcharges may easily have occurred, as well as that hunt for presents which, under Clement III, often made the Curia the laughing-stock of its visitors.[4] How far the reproach, so often alleged, of venality is true we cannot ascertain. There certainly were cases of bribery, and it is just as certain that bribery often was unjustly assumed or alleged. For the losing parties, their opponents' money in most cases seemed the only reason for their defeat. Moreover, dishonest procurators may more than once have embezzled sums of money which, allegedly to bribe pope and cardinals and other influential persons, they demanded from their mandators.[5]

Innocent allowed the curials to accept presents and himself accepted presents and promises of presents.[6] The only presents tabooed were gifts by the parties to persons of great influence or to those engaged in conducting the case, before the case was settled. When Thomas of Marleberge, monk and procurator of the abbey of Evesham, on the occasion of his farewell visits, handed the pope and the cardinals one hundred marks each, the cardinals did not accept the money before making sure that for the time being the monks had no litigation pending at the Curia.[7] Yet the principle was not always observed in its full strength. Thomas was not turned away when, filled with joy after a favourable interlocutory decision, he handed the pope a silver vessel to the value of six marks.[8]

Innocent emphasized that such gifts were voluntary.[9] But it is certain that well-to-do visitors of the Curia, after having successfully transacted their business, were – rightly – expected to make presents, and by this expectation alone moral constraint was brought forth. There is no doubt that Innocent would have taken in bad part any neglect, for instance by great abbeys, to express thanks and devotion in the usual manner.[10]

Although during Innocent's time, too, presents may have been exacted at the Curia from high and low places, it is certain that right and indulgence were not then for sale. It is strange to see how much even prelates close to the Curia were none the less mistaken in the assessment of the role which money and presents played for Innocent. With resentment the pope as late as 1211 reacts to an instruction by the bishop of Alessandria to his procurators to take up a loan varying in amount from one hundred to three hundred pounds according to the result they can achieve in his cause. Innocent holds that this instruction clearly showed how low the bishop rated him, the pope, since he believed that he could influence him by money to grant church property. It also showed what the bishop was prepared to pay for church property, for he had precisely fixed how much his agents were to give for this and that. Innocent suspended the bishop from his episcopal and priestly office, so that others, alarmed by his example, might guard themselves from acting in a similar way. On this occasion he called God to witness that he had handled and carried out blamelessly and honestly the matters brought before the Apostolic See and that he abhorred the vice of venality which resulted from greed. Those who frequently came to the Roman Church to transact their manifold business could bear witness to the truth. He was careful, he continues, to keep this blemish away from the Roman Church and to give without payment whatever he had received without payment. He would not tolerate anything being transacted in ecclesiastical lawsuits on the basis of a pact, an agreement or a promise, so that presents sometimes[11] given after the settling of the case were seen not to be exacted by necessity, but to be made from devotion.[12] In his presence, Innocent wrote to the bishop of Fiesole, he would be able to prove before the pope whether his money could, as he had boasted, buy him out of his guilt.[13]

The visitors to the Curia to whom Innocent appeals, have in fact borne witness to his incorruptibility. Thomas Marleberge calls him a just judge precisely in connection with the pope's intercession for his (Thomas's) opponent.[14] The monks of Canterbury, who without mercy and with mockery had laid bare the venality of Clement III, though he, too, was surely well-disposed towards them, report to their convent towards the end of 1198 that their opponents had offered an immense sum of money[15] in order to estrange the pope's mind from the convent or at least to place obstacles in the way of the convent's cause, but in vain because that man was founded in Peter and there was with him no respecting of persons or gifts.[16] Before this letter arrived, the prior himself had set out for Rome since the convent doubted the steadfastness of the Curia. He was able to send the soothing message from Pisa that he had come to know the new pope's steadiness and justice: he would not deny to them or to others anything that demonstrably had to be done by the dictates of justice.[17] In a letter sent from the Curia he expresses his conviction that their cause, being just, could not end in failure since neither greed moved the pope to wrong anyone nor did indolence restrain him from reprimanding, and that the pope was so possessed by the love of virtue that he omitted nothing that befits a good shepherd.[18] Towards the end of the following year he praises to his convent again, saying that Innocent would not deliberately leave the path of law.[19] The pope himself declared to King Richard, the protector of the opposing party that, if he respected persons and wished to be made presents, he would certainly have favoured the archbishop's side before the monks' side.[20] Only Gerald of Wales pretends that pope and cardinals, being bribed, had decided against him. Innocent had intended to appoint him, after quashing, as it seems, his election, bishop of St Davids. But the archbishop of Canterbury had thwarted the appointment by offering subsidies from the part of the English clergy.[21] By bribing the Curia with a huge sum of money, Gerald alleges, the archbishop had brought about the final cassation of the election at the next hearing. He, Gerald, had not noticed anything of the machinations until after the pronouncement of judgement.[22] The good archdeacon, who in his unshakeable self-consciousness remains convinced of the transparent justice of his cause even when all the world think differently, seems to have inferred from the judgement back to the motivation underlying it. Moreover, it is clearly shown by two detailed accounts of the hearings, each drawn up by one of the litigants involved, that money and presents played no part in the decision. The one case is the already mentioned[23] suit of Evesham versus Worcester, the other the suit of Andres versus Carrefou. The monastery of Andres was shorter of ready money than its opponent, the abbey of Carrefou, whose procurator managed to win over nine attorneys for his cause, whilst the procurator of Andres could only produce two.[24] The compromise which Innocent negotiated with gentle pressure was none the less favourable to Andres. According to the statement by the monk of Andres, which is of course to be accepted with all reserve, his opponents paid 200 marks to have a decision already taken in favour of Andres cancelled and the old privileges renewed. The Curia, he alleges, used to such practice, though retaining the money, had fobbed off the opponent with some useless commissions and sent him back home.[25] If one of the parties did in fact offer bribes and if any curial quarters did accept them, then their endeavours were of no avail since Innocent neither consciously nor unconsciously allowed these machinations to influence his decisions.[26] We have every reason to assume that Innocent was in earnest about the sharp condemnation with which as cardinal, in his treatise on the misery of human condition, he turned against those judges who loved presents, who dispensed justice with respect to persons, who showed themselves severe to the poor party and indulgent to the rich one, who neglected the cause of the former, but eagerly pursued that of the latter, who delayed the proceedings so that the parties lost more than the whole, that is more than the value of the object of litigation, because the expenses were greater than the profit gained.[27]

Innocent deemed his judgeship highly. "We have," he declares, "the unalterable will and the unbending intention not to deviate from the path of law, neither for pleas nor for reward, neither for love nor for hate, but, walking in the royal ways, not to turn to the right nor to the left and to sit in judgement without respect of persons because God is no respecter of persons."[28] That Innocent did not fear the countenance of the mighty he showed in the divorce suit of the king of France.[29] At a moment in which it was a matter of great consequence for him to win the king for Otto of Brunswick's, his protégé's, cause, and in which his legate, therefore, was inclined to meet Philip Augustus half-way in the marriage case, Innocent strictly declared that he would not tolerate foul play in the matter.[30]

Innocent conceived the objective of administering justice wider than in the sense only of rightfully deciding the suit just pending or even the current phase of a far-reaching dispute.

In the long, annoying dispute between Archbishop Geoffrey of York and his cathedral chapter Innocent recognizes the root of the evil to be a privilege granted by Celestine III to the canons which, though not directly in contradiction to the rights of the archbishop since it was hedged with clauses in almost every stipulation, still was interpreted by the chapter in its own favour. Instead of taking a decision in the legal question at issue on the basis of the privilege, Innocent orders an inquiry to be made into the law possibly wronged by the privilege as well as into the use and misuse of the privilege, lest injustice should emanate from where justice starts and lest on the occasion of the privilege the Apostolic See, while preaching peace to others, should be regarded as the creator and increaser of discord.[31]

Innocent did not settle the cases brought before him by the letter only of the law. He was not concerned only to give his formal opinion apparently unassailable from the juridical point of view and founded solely on the pleadings of the litigant parties, but he tried to get down to the core of the case. Where he saw that the litigants resorted to falsehoods which, given the conditions of traffic and communication of that time, were not easily to be proved, he enforced the confession of the truth, apparently by the force of his personality. When Innocent directs a sharp glance at the glib and not very scrupulous lawyèr, the pert Thomas Marleberge of Evesham, and orders: "Procurator, tell the truth! Are there baptisteries in those churches?", he dares not suppress the truth so disadvantageous for him.[32] Counsellors for the defence who had shifted from one party to the other he compels to admit on the spot that they had changed parties.[33] The bishop of Pecs had been landed in an evil plight by his adversaries and overzealous friends, if friends they really were, and would have had difficulty in extricating himself from it if Innocent had not entered the lists on his behalf. King Imre of Hungary had accused the hated bishop of a grave offence and asked the pope to abate the alleged nuisance. Innocent, who knew that the accusation sprang from hatred, made cautious inquiries which compassed the expected favourable result. Unfortunately, however, an adversary got sight of the confidential letter in which Innocent exhorted the bishop to proceed with more caution, so that the bishop could falsely appear to be suspect to the pope. On the ill-advised pressure of the episcopal procurator Innocent was eventually obliged to assent to the bishop's offer of compurgation. But he told the procurator, whom he did not fully trust, beforehand that the suffragans of Gran would hardly purge the bishop, meanwhile postulated archbishop, because they were opposed to his translation to Gran, and that the suffragans of Kalocsa would not purge him either because of the dispute between the churches of Gran and Kalocsa. When things turned out as Innocent had feared, he instructed his delegates to see that the pitiable bishop did not fall victim to machinations, and menacingly warned those bishops who had previously declared the harrassed prelate to be without guilt, that they made themselves suspicious of lying or of hatred if they refused to purge their fellow bishop.[34] The abbess of Montmartre had lodged an appeal against a decision taken by papal delegates on the grounds of an alleged misrepresentation of the facts of the case by the plaintiff. When the latter, a poor widow unacquainted with law, appeared before Innocent he sees at once that she is wholly unable to plead her cause and that it was by clumsiness only that she had not represented the facts correctly in all respects. He, therefore, orders the delegate to grant the woman her right irrespective of possible errors in the simple description of the facts.[35] The abbot of Prüm himself observed how Innocent saw to the rights of a poor illiterate priest who was unable to plead his own cause against a rich opponent well versed in law who had deprived the poor man of his church.[36] In the event of awkwardness on the part of procurators Innocent takes care of the rights of their mandators. Against an intercession of the pope in favour of the bishop in the suit of Evesham versus Worcester the procurator of Evesham once demurred: "Holiest father, you are called to the fullness of power and, therefore, anything is allowed to you. But by civil law judges are only allowed to redeem errors of the advocates as far as the law is concerned, not in regard to the facts of the case." Innocent, who could put up with contradiction, retorts without any sign of indignation that such a view was wrong.[37]

Numerous constitutions promulgated by the pope provide for the administration of justice, beginning with the chancery rules dating from the first years of the pontificate,[38] which were to impede irregularities, collusion and fraud in the conduct of curial business, particularly when petitions were entered,[39] and with the contemporaneous ordinance against the nuisance of conterfeiting,[40] which at that time had become rampant at the Curia, and ending with the *canones* of the Fourth Lateran Council which deal with legal procedure. The conduct of a law case at that time was, mainly on account of the adverse traffic conditions, extremely dragging.[41] A suit filed at the Apostolic See could not be dealt with immediately on the spot, but first a date, perhaps long ahead, had to be fixed for the hearing of the parties. If one of the parties was unable to observe it, an extension was necessary. Even in the case of the unexcused non-appearance of a party the proceedings could not be carried through straight away. The party present, therefore, suffered waste of money and time. If a party raised objections they had, with the possible effect of a considerable loss of time, to be examined by delegates on the spot. This often meant that a new date of hearing had to be fixed for the judge's ruling. The work of the delegates was often hampered by malevolent appeals and other tricks. The danger of a wilful protraction of the proceedings in these circumstances was given full scope.

Innocent is at pains to prevent these tricks and chicaneries of the one party against the other. With the explicit determination to put an end to litigations in such a way that the parties were not unduly clogged with useless efforts and expenses, he decides that anyone that raises an *exceptio*, an objection, which entails an adjournment is to refund the costs incurred to the opponent if in the end he is unable to prove his objection to be justified,[42] and later on he decrees that objections of this kind are to be entered simultaneously within a period of time fixed by the judge.[43] If Innocent delegates inquiry and decision to judges outside the Curia he often energetically forbids them to comply with obviously frivolous objections, tricks and appeals, and he reprimands the delegates who had allowed themselves to become influenced by them.[44] Innocent sought to safeguard against a misuse of appeals even in the case of appeals by which law cases were first brought before the Apostolic See; that is, he sought to reduce the number of law cases brought before the Curia in the interests of those seeking relief, who were thus spared great costs and efforts, in the interests of the judges ordinary and, in a wider sense, of the Apostolic See itself. It had often happened that, by appeals to the pope which then were not pursued, cases remained unsettled which otherwise could easily have been ended. It is not sufficient for Innocent that, according to the decrees of the Third Lateran Council, the appellant in such cases had to pay the costs incurred to the opposing party, since thereby the protraction of the proceedings was not prevented, but he prescribes that after the term of hearing has expired the defaulting party is to be proceeded against as if it had been summoned peremptorily, under the threat of forfeiting its claims.[45]

|The *canones* of the Fourth Lateran Council of 1215 contain

effective regulations against chicanery at the hands of the parties and against the misuse of appeals./Often litigants obtained mandates in an underhand way by which a law case was transferred to a delegate residing far away in order to force the defendant, by causing him efforts and costs, to give in./The Council counters such practices by decreeing that nobody must be summoned by papal writs to a court more than two days' journey distant from his diocese, unless both parties have agreed otherwise or the decree has explicitly been suspended in the case at issue.[46] The same canon threatens with punishment as forgers all those who without being commissioned have themselves drawn up writs, by which suits already settled are renewed or new ones brought in, with a view to selling them to one of the two parties. At the Council Innocent also forbids the lodging, without legitimate reason, of an appeal with a higher judge before the judgement is delivered.| If such a reason is alleged the higher judge has first to rule on the admissibility of the appeal. If necessary, he has to recommit the appellant to the lower judge and to condemn him to the costs caused to the opposing party.[47] If someone challenges as suspect the judge who has pronounced to him the admonition preceding every excommunication, he has to prove before an arbitration court that his reproach is justified. An appeal of the admonished person is inadmissible if his offence is notorious. If his guilt is doubtful the higher judge, before accepting the case for decision, has to judge on the admissibility of the appeal and, when occasion arises, to recommit the appellant to the lower judge.[48] An analogous procedure prevents a party from appealing without legitimate reason to a higher judge before a judgement is delivered.[49] Innocent cannot be reproached with having had litigations transferred, if possible, to the Curia, nor of having protracted proceedings in order to keep the source of income flowing.[50]

In the interests of the parties and on ideal grounds Innocent sought by preference to arrive at an amicable agreement;[51] particularly in those litigations which he tried to settle by compromise and which owing to the difficult legal situation had been dragging on for decades or longer. He cleared away by compromise the suit between the Spanish bishoprics of Osma and Lerida[52] and partly also the suit between the church provinces of Braga (Portugal) and Compostela:[53] the former had engaged the Curia since the days of Eugenius III (1145–1153), the latter even longer. A settlement by judicial decision would indeed have made it necessary to ascertain the confines of the bishoprics and church provinces at a time before the Moorish conquest.

Litigations often dragged on for decades or even centuries because popes allowed proceedings to be renewed which had been settled by judicial decision, as in the case of the suit of Tours against Dol for the metropolitan authority over the churches in Brittany which dated back to the days of Nicholas I, that is to the ninth century. Innocent regrets that his predecessors had frequently renewed the suit and decides definitely that the church of Dol is for ever to be subordinate to the church of Tours.[54] Documents in favour of Dol which might be found later are declared null and void in advance. Innocent often takes such precautions in his judgements, he even declares void all the evidence already offered by or to be expected from the parties, as in the case of a suit of the Roman Church against the abbey of Bobbio which a papal chaplain had conducted and lost.[55] Innocent insists on the strict observance of the principle that a judgement lawfully pronounced and having become absolute is inappellable, in the case of decisions by the lower judge as well as in the case of a ruling by the Apostolic See. In a suit in which after fifty years an appeal was lodged against a judgement on the basis of newly found documents Innocent decides against the admissibility of the appeal because the legal position of the parties now was founded on the absolute judgement.[56] No more than an absolute decision does Innocent allow a formal compromise, a *compositio*, to be called in question.[57] The release from a sworn obligation to a compromise which his predecessor once had granted, he regards as surreptitious and therefore void.[58]

In conformity with an ancient custom, but no more observed prior to his pontificate, Innocent three times a week held a consistory in open court[59] in which he heard suits and petitions, examined himself the cases of major importance with the assistance of the cardinals, had the less important ones examined by the cardinals, and pronounced the judgements. These public consistories were attended by many lawyers and law scholars[60] who sought to improve their schooling from the pope's way of conducting the cases and substantiating the judgements. The sharp-witted criticism Innocent often passed on the documents produced as evidence aroused quite a stir[61], but the main attraction came from the pronouncement of judgements. Innocent used to precede the decision by an exposition of the arguments in favour of each party, and he emphasized what was to be said in favour of the one as well as of the other party so shrewdly and effectively that each party hoped to carry the day as long as he was dealing with its arguments.[62] We can still experience to-day the impression which such judgements and the exposition of their grounds had on parties and listeners, if we read the pope's famous *Deliberatio*,[63] the formulation of the legal position he took up on the rights of the three aspirants in the German throne contest. Here, too, the arguments for the recognition of Philip of Swabia and of Frederick of Sicily respectively, and for the rejection of Otto of Brunswick, appear to be of such force that, while Innocent is expounding them, the respective decision seems to be established. In this case, though, the visibly weak arguments in favour of Otto turn the scale, since here, in the form of a juridical deliberation, a political decision is taken.[64] Where Innocent decided the case in his capacity as judge we cannot prove him to have twisted the law for political reasons.

We must not visualize Innocent as presiding in the consistory sessions in unapproachable sublimity. It did not appeal to his lively ways to display dignity, to put on a mask. Even as pope he preserved his natural human manner. A litigant once notes how Innocent with a facetious word in Italian turns smilingly to the cardinals,[65] and these freely intervene in the interrogation of the parties.[66] Innocent found it hard to bear the verboseness of attorneys and procurators. Brusquely he cut short the procurator of the bishop of Worcester in his elaborate prefatory remarks adorned with sententious quotations and expounding profound mysteries: "We do not want such a preface. Come to the point!".[67] To the allegation that the rights of the bishop did not fall under the statute of limitations, as he had learnt at the university and as was taught there still, the same procurator is reported to have received the unpolished answer: "You and your teachers must have drunk much English beer when you learnt that".[68] Innocent tolerated liberty of speech to such a degree that the procurator of Evesham already known to us, the monk Thomas Marleberge, once went to the length of brazen-facedly questioning the pope's sense of justice. To his importunate insistence that a mandate in favour of the opposite party be revoked Innocent in the end indignantly replied: "We have issued this letter to the bishop in the full knowledge of the facts and, therefore, have no intention of withdrawing it. Do you have your answer now?". "Indeed, my lord", Marleberge ventures, "the answer is given, but by authority (*de potestate*)." "And not by right?", comes the sharp retort from the pope. On the pert answer "I don't know", Innocent angrily orders him to hold his tongue and to be gone.[69] One of the reasons why Rainer of Pomposa, as he himself relates, compiled decretals of the first three (more exactly four) years of the pope's reign was to meet the requirements of lawyers who had come from afar to listen to the wisdom of the "new Solomon"[71] and who wished to have a report handy on the course of proceedings and on the sentences passed (*iustitia et iudicia*).[70] In 1208 Bernard of Compostela made a second collection covering the first ten years of the pope's reign.[72] As Innocent took exception to the selection,[72] he had his notary Peter Collivaccini of Benevento,[74] the later cardinal, compile a new collection of his decretals, the so called Compilatio III, the first official collection of decretals. A collection of decretals mainly from the later years of his reign, the Compilatio IV,[75] was again turned down by Innocent. The most prominent canonists of that time, Silvester, Johannes Galensis, Laurentius Hispanus, Vincentius Hispanus, Johannes Teutonicus, Tancred, glossed the decretals. They upheld, though, their liberty of comment even in front of the new Solomon.[76] In his gloss to the Compilatio III the aggressive Laurentius Hispanus even repeatedly attacks the pope sharply, nay disrespectfully. In his commentary he often qualifies a remark of the pope's as superficial.[77] On the other hand Vincentius Hispanus, Laurentius' countryman, in his apparatus to the Compilatio III, styles Innocent the holiest pope, the father of eminent knowledge and of an extremely perspicacious mind, *pater eminentis scientiae et perspicacissimi ingenii.*[78] Even if they were not in every respect in accord with Innocent, the canonists were doubtless aware of the importance which the decretals had particularly for the development of canon law as well as for the furtherance of an administration of true justice. Innocent often personally conversed with the canonists on questions of law.[79]

Innocent did not look upon the cases brought before him only with the eyes of the lawyer, but in lively sympathy he also saw their human aspect. Already in a treatise dating from the time of his cardinalcy the compassion takes shape which he had for the unfortunate litigant who, though in the end he was granted his right, ended poorer than he was before; his compassion also for the poor wretch whose cause was neglected all too readily whilst everybody hastened to be at the service of the rich one.[80] He himself witnessed at close quarters the tragic lot of a poor *magister* in whose case he had acted as *auditor*. The *magister* had come to the Curia at great expense and

effort and, after a long wait which had brought his weakened body to
the verge of the grave, had obtained a favourable decision in his fight
about a canonry. After his departure his opponent contrived to have
the decision quashed. The unfortunate *magister* appeared a second
time at the Curia and appealed for the new pope's compassion.
Innocent, who remembered the man and his deplorable lot, mercifully
procured him a provision in the church of Laon.[81] Even in cases in
which not just bare survival was at stake, Innocent felt the disappointment of the loser. William of Andres, whose election as prior the
pope by judicial decision had quashed as void, is summoned one
evening before him. Innocent wants to tell him that he should not be
grieved at the issue, God was his witness that he had acted not from
anger but from love. He, William, was not even harmed so much
since he could be elected again. If he so wished he would draw him
up letters to that effect.[82] Gerald of Wales also stresses the efforts the
pope made to console him for, or, as Gerald puts it, to reconcile him
with, the annulment of his election to the see of St Davids. The pope
had praised, Gerald reports, the zeal and effort with which he, Gerald,
had defended his and his church's cause against king and archbishop.
God would reward him for it, at least if he had done it as he, the pope,
believed, in pure mind.[83] The subtle appeal to self-examination Gerald
did not understand. He was dismissed with intimations of favour and
many indulgences. Thomas Marleberge reports to his convent that
Innocent had granted their defeated opponent, the bishop of Worcester, many indulgences so that he might not depart in grief. Thomas
came to know during his long stay at the Curia that it was Innocent's
nature to console the oppressed generously.[84]

Innocent feels obliged to stand for law and justice even outside the
sphere of jurisdiction. In the first years of his pontificate he
announces that it was his intention to prevent the rights of his fellow
bishops from being diminished during his pontificate.[85] The course
and issue of proceedings at the Curia in which bishops were involved
as litigants give no wholly adequate picture of the realization of this
intention. The cases were mostly concerned with decisions based on
privileges which Innocent had not granted, but which he also could
not unlawfully set aside. The pastoral authority of the bishops, their
most original right that is, had been curtailed in the course of time in
many respects by privileges. Where Innocent created law himself, as
in the *canones* of the Lateran Council, he strengthened the
bishops' position. He considerably cuts down the possibility of ap-

peals by which subordinates, secular and regular priests, and even the bishop's own cathedral chapter, only too often paralysed the bishops' official authority.[86] He decrees that the establishment of chapters of the monastic Orders was not to prejudice the bishops' duty of correction towards the monasteries subordinate to them.[87] He prohibits the monastic Orders from infringing, which often happened, on the bishops' rights.[88] He limits privileges granted to monastic Orders which are detrimental to the bishops' prestige.[89] He extends preferences granted to monastic Orders to the bishops[90] and checks the inroads of cathedral chapters on their bishops' standing.[91] The bishops' authority will also have profited from can. 35 of the Lateran Council which admits the appeal of a person sued before a judge ordinary only if he produces reasonable arguments on the validity of which the higher judge has to decide before he accepts the appeal.[92] Innocent rigorously safeguards the bishops' standing and right also in their administrative practice, especially as regards the power of correction over subordinates, the appointment to the office of parish priest, and the revenues.[93] He severely punishes machinations of clerics against their bishop. On one occasion he transferred canons who had malevolently worked against the bishop-elect to different monasteries for penance.[94] One canon who had brought serious charges against his bishop, which later he was unable to prove, he suspended from office and benefices in order to warn others against being too quick in defaming their superiors.[95] In a wider sense he also safeguards the bishops' rights in that he does not, by virtue of his concurrent authority, encroach discretionarily upon their competences, he does not easily accept charges laid against them, he invites them during their visits to the Curia to attend the deliberations of the consistory, and he lays stress on their consent. An event which has by chance come down to us shows how Innocent tries to pay respect and honour to his brothers and fellow bishops: he orders Bishop Hugh of Auxerre, who had died while at the Curia, to be buried in the Lateran basilica, and with the cardinals himself attends the funeral.[96]

Convinced of the appropriateness of a state of order in the relationship between state and Church in which "in just distribution Caesar is given what is Caesar's and God what is God's", Innocent, within the limits as he sees them, also gives the state its due. At the Lateran Council he formally pronounced that as little as he wanted an arrogation by laymen of rights which belonged to the clergy, so little could he tolerate clerics usurping rights for themselves which belonged to the laity. Referring to the Lord's word just quoted he prohibits the entire clergy from continuing, under the pretence of the liberty of the Church, to extend its jurisdiction in prejudice of the temporal jurisdiction (*iustitiae*).[97] But Innocent also concedes to the state that justice which is not based on the letter of the law, but on the recognition of the moral relevance of state authority. When Innocent demanded free canonical elections he did not mean to keep the chapters from electing men who also suited the king. The concordat he transacted with Constance of Sicily made it a legal duty for the electors to have regard for the king's wishes. In England, in view of a special emergency threatening the king, he puts the elections to the then vacant bishoprics under the supervision of his legate who is to ensure that persons are elected who are loyal to the king.[98] Also in other cases of appointments to bishoprics he was ready to be accommodating to the kings in the question of persons.[99]

A complaisance shown to Andrew of Hungary which was hardly justifiable, reluctantly given and soon regretted, is Innocent's assent to the postulation of Provost Berthold of Bamberg, the queen's brother, to the archiepiscopal see of Kalocsa.[100] Less than nine months previously he had quashed Berthold's election since the elect was little more than twenty-five years old and had had an utterly insufficient theological schooling.[101] Before the scrutiny Innocent had promised the king, yielding to his wishes or rather to necessity, that he would grant the provost dispensation provided his knowledge was but moderately sufficient and that he was near the canonical age.[102] The necessity which thereupon induced Innocent to assent after all, contrary to his principles, to the young man's elevation, to all appearances was no necessity of *papal* policy.[103] It is possible that Andrew had convinced him that in view of the unreliability of the Hungarian magnates he needed an absolutely devoted partisan in the archiepiscopal see.

In other respects too Innocent takes into account the necessities and exigences of states in many ways. He allows Peter II of Aragon to reclaim even from churches and pious foundations the revenues which had been unlawfully given away during the king's minority.[104] In Sicily, during his regency, he tries in the most adverse circumstances to preserve and to regain for the crown domains and sovereign rights.[105] After the death of King Imre of Hungary he prohibits, under the threat of God's wrath, the *regalia* being alienated during the minority of the king's son Ladislas.[106] He acknowledges without reserve that the late King Cnut of Denmark is not to be blamed for having taken prisoner Bishop Waldemar of Schleswig, an illegitimate offspring of the royal house, on the latter's incursion into the king's realm, and for having thus taken away from him the means to do damage. He, though, requires Cnut's successor King Waldemar to hand over the bishop, who was being kept in harsh imprisonment, but at the same time promises to keep the dangerous man in Italy and never allow him to return to Denmark without the king's permission.[107] In the quarrels between Alfonso II of Portugal and his sisters on the subject of their father's will which Innocent had probated, he seeks and finds a solution which gives the princesses their right and still safeguards essential public interests.[108] In Hungary, during the period of disorders, he grants the trusty followers of the king a reprieve for their start on the vowed crusade,[109] and later on allows the king himself to delay his departure for the Holy Land, and tolerates, in defence of a peace settlement confirmed by the pope,[110] his taking hold of the person of his untrustworthy brother. In a period in which John of England was entirely dependent on his mercy, Innocent does not demand from him the dissolution of his alliance with Emperor Otto whom the pope had rejected and anathematized, since, in view of the mortal enmity of Philip Augustus of France, this dissolution would have been for John tantamount to suicide.

The benevolence which Innocent himself generally shows to the rulers he expects also the episcopate to show. He is angry with the Latin patriarch of Constantinople about the difficulties which he puts in the hard-pressed emperor's way. In view of the heavy burden of the Empire, Henry deserved to be alleviated and not encumbered by the men of the Church. Moreover, St Peter himself taught how obligingness was to be shown to the kings.[111] Innocent finds it hard when the English bishops after the victory of the Church disregard his wish to avoid difficulties in the conflict with the king, and when, because of the damages, they obstruct the raising of the interdict in a manner, as it seems to him, not becoming to the clergy.[112] The excommunication privilege for the king, issued in the following year,[113] shows that Innocent regards it as a matter of necessity to support the king against the inwardly unreconciled English church.

Innocent often expressed his view that just as the temporal sword has to protect the spiritual sword against those who show contempt for it, so the spiritual sword must intervene where the temporal sword fails.[114] It is the business of the Church and its head to support the legitimate public powers. With great energy he intercedes for King Imre of Hungary against his rebellious brother[115] and strives to enforce and to safeguard the regimentation of state affairs, set up by Imre in the event of his absence on crusade, even against the opposing episcopate[116] whose open defection was, indeed, only prevented by the pope's line of conduct.[117] In Sweden Innocent supports the legitimate, or supposedly legitimate, king against a real or presumed usurper.[118] He provides ecclesiastical punitive measures against rebellious subjects of John of England many years prior to the great revolt of 1213.[119] During the revolt he anathematizes John's enemies and sends one of the most energetic cardinals, Guala of SS Silvester and Martin, as legate to help him. With unyielding energy, shrewdness and unusual devotion the legate defended, under often truly desperate circumstances, John's and, after the king's death, the young Henry III's kingship against the rebellious barons and against the pretender, the French Dauphin Louis, whose assistance they had called in. With his mandator he shares the first rank among the men who saved England from a new foreign rule or a continuance for years of the horrors of civil war and from the disaster of a baronial regime.[120]

But mutual support of the two swords implies no unconditional solidarity between Church and worldly powers, no alliance between throne and altar as it sometimes fatally manifests itself in modern European history. Innocent regards the relationship between the public powers and their subjects not simply as the power to command on the one side and the duty to obey on the other, but as a legal relation in which ruler and subjects have their position assigned to them by law and custom. English history provides the most impressive example of Innocent's will to support the legitimate ruler and still to maintain the rights of the subjects. If we wish to do justice to the pope's line of conduct in the conflict between King John and his barons we must, though, neglect the opinions of historical tradition laid down in not strictly contemporary chronicles which look upon the events one-sidedly from the standpoint of the barons and the clergy and which project back to the time of King John experiences of the period of conflict between barons and king in the reign of Henry III.

Papal policy in the conflict between king and barons is, as the documents prove, clearly and plainly orientated towards peace in the kingdom, a peace which safeguards to the king what is due to him and which gives the subjects the liberty to which they have a right; that is to say Innocent rejects both royal arbitrariness and baronial anarchy and demands an amicable settlement which excludes both extremes. Immediately after the termination of the church contest he requires all those conspiracies and groupings to be dissolved which had been formed on the occasion of the discord between *regnum* and *sacerdotium* and, referring also to the special obligation he had to his new vassal, ḥe calls on all subjects to be loyal to the king.[120] But at the same time he prevails on the king through his legate to adopt a policy of reform and appeasement.[122] The legation of the barons which in February and March 1215 stays at the Curia with a view to presenting their complaints to the sovereign lord,[123] returns with the ruling that Innocent is not willing to tolerate a forcible infringement on the royal prerogatives,[124] but that he also demanded from the king to be accommodating to the just claims of the barons.[125] Innocent did not think of leaving it to the king's discretion to decide on the extent of this accommodation. If no amicable settlement came about the dispute was to be decided in a judicial way by judgement of the Court of Peers, in compliance with the customs of the realm.[126] Innocent's rejection of the great charter of liberty, Magna Carta, extorted from the king by force of arms, as being ignominious, wrongful and evil, mainly on account of the way it had been brought about,[127] shows the pope consistently in keeping with his line of policy. Innocent, though, disapproved with regard to substance of the article which submitted the crown to a humiliating tutelage of twenty-five barons. But together with the rejection he promises the barons that if they give up the charter in its present form, he would persuade the king to give them their right. Just as he did not wish the king to be deprived of his right, so on the other hand he wanted the king to refrain from encumbering the barons lest the kingdom, under papal sovereignty, should be oppressed by evil customs and unlawful imposts. Whilst the English bishops, their friends, were assembled at the Council, they might send procurators and safely put their trust in him because he would ensure that all encumbrances and all abuses in England were removed, that the king contented himself with the rights and honours due to him, and that clergy and people should enjoy the peace and the liberty to which they had a right.[128] Innocent without reserve acknowledged that there were abuses, wished to see them redressed and was doubtless in a position to obtrude his will on John. The way Innocent proposed was the only one leading to peace. It is hardly to be denied that the charter in its then form and in view of the manner in which it had been brought about, did not serve peace. How would the crown have lastingly put up with the tutelage of the twenty-five? The outcome of Innocent's proposal would probably have been a second Magna Carta similar to that of 1217, which was negotiated with the decisive co-operation of the legate, appointed still by himself, and which would not have been purchased with three years of devastating war and the danger of a French domination. The barons did not put their trust in the pope, possibly because they did not want a fair compromise with the king; instead they thought of making capital out of their superiority with a view to paralysing and humiliating the king, and perhaps they were already resolved to overthrow him.[129] Too much hatred was bottled up for any real readiness to reconciliation. Some of the barons may also have thought that the time was ripe to set up a baronial oligarchy.[130]

A policy of fairly balancing the rights of the sovereign and those of the subjects is also pursued by Innocent in the territories under his own rule. His programme of government he once described by saying that he wished the land to be governed in justice by the Church, which in truth could say of itself: My yoke is sweet and my burden light.[131] But by a government in justice Innocent means a government which maintains to the individual as well as to the bodies corporate and to the communes the position which is due to them by law, privilege or good custom. Innocent readily tolerated the diversity of rights and liberties, if only he retained the possibility and the means to fulfil his task as sovereign, that is to defend the Patrimony against attacks from outside and to safeguard peace and law inside.[132]

Appealing above all is the humane way in which Innocent stood for the right of those who were themselves unable to defend it. The case has already been mentioned of the poor widow unacquainted with law, in which he turned from judge to legal adviser.[133] After a visitation of the monastery of Monte Cassino he prohibits abbot and convent from continuing to exact from their dependants unjust and excessive charges and at the same time makes it easier for the monastery to do without these charges by renouncing in its favour certain revenues due to him.[134] When establishing a Land Peace in Provence he orders his legate to renew the prohibition decreed by the Lateran Council of unjust duties and to ensure the execution of both this prohibition and the Land Peace by having the magnates pledge fortified places to the Apostolic See.[135] When defending the interests of young King Frederick of Sicily, Innocent surely advocated his own interests, but it would be wrong to say that he pedantically measured to what degree royal and papal advantages were identical, for he, indeed, truly held up the right, vested in the king by the concordat, to consent to the ecclesiastical elections. On the news of the king of Hungary's death and of the regency having been assumed by the late king's unreliable uncle, the later Andrew II, Innocent, deeply worried, takes care of little King Ladislas and his mother.[136] Winning are the words with which he recommends the child to his uncle's love and care, referring to the purity of intentions the regent had expressed to him.[137] The child's death a few months later spared the pope from fighting for his right. Innocent became the fatherly protector of his little vassal James I of Aragon, son of Peter II who in 1213 was killed in the Albigenesian war against Simon de Montfort. He requires Simon to hand the child over to Cardinal Legate Peter of Benevento,[138] has him escorted by the cardinal to Aragon,[139] has the Cortes swear him the oath of allegiance and, by the hands of the legate who stayed in Aragon for months despite urgent business in southern France, has conditions in the kingdom put in order and peace and concord safeguarded.[140] Innocent himself prudently settled the delicate question of guardianship. Count Sancho, the child's great uncle, could not be excluded without driving him to open rebellion. But Innocent in large measure banished the danger threatening from the guardianship of a man who himself aspired to the crown, by placing at his side as the king's advisers such men of far-reaching influence as the archbishop of Tarragona, head of the church of Aragon, and the master of the Order of Templars.[141] King James always felt indebted to the protector of his childhood; he styled him in his chronicle the best of popes.[142]

We would put the picture of the pope as a servant of law and justice in a one-sided light if we did not call to mind here too that where *questions of high politics* were involved law and justice were not always the leading stars of his actions. Vital interests of the Church sometimes compelled him to call right what was wrong.[143] We cannot doubt that in such cases Innocent felt the tragedy of the antagonism.

## Notes to Chapter 3

[1]See his letter in Böhmer, Analekten, 67f. See also Schnürer, 336, who mistakenly attributes the passage to James of Vitry's Historia occidentalis c. 32.

[2]Gesta c. 41.

[3]The pope could not provide sufficient benefices within the diocese of Rome or the Roman church province. To provide benefices outside these regions was often difficult and for the beneficiary was often the source of considerable inconvenience, for it was not always easy for him to come to enjoy the revenues, even if no ill-will put obstacles in his way. For the non-resident incumbent the returns of only one prebend were mostly insufficient, since the full sum was generally not paid out or a representative had to be funded.

[4]Wenck, Päpste, 433ff.

[5]It is very probable that the chief procurator for Glastonbury, Magister Martin de Summa from Milan (see Royal and other historical letters illustrative of the reign of Henry III, ed. W.W. Shirley, RS., No. 27, Vol. 2, 1862, 216), whom the monks believed to be conducting their case at his own expense (Domerham, 371), reimbursed himself with at least part of the money since he and his companions, the monks, who were not necessarily aware of possible foul play, write about a loan of 900 marks, while at the same time Innocent himself is aware only of a loan of 750 marks. See also Gottlob, Servitientaxe, 16ff. Gottlob refers to an ordinance of Innocent IV (Tangl, 59, cf. *ibid*. p. xxviiif.) by which anyone who paid the pope or any curial official a *servitium* of more than twenty solidi must take care to be given a receipt, the procurator in the same way as the party negotiating in person. The receipt was to serve, in the interest of the reputation of the Curia, as a certificate proving that only the amount indicated had been paid and no more. In addition the mandator is explicitly committed to examine such receipt. Honorius III, too, had turned against those unreliable travellers to Rome who wasted their mandators' money and then, to justify the deficit, held Roman greed for money responsible (Gottlob, 18).

[6]Thomas of Capua, Summa dictaminis 18 (Heller 268).

[7]Chron. Evesham 146. The pope's Gesta mention with praise that as cardinal he never permitted anyone to promise or give him anything as a present before the case was settled (Gesta c. 4). Once, protesting against the belief that presents of money could influence his decisions, he admits presents or promises of presents to be permissible once the case has been decided (Reg. XIV 114).

[8]Chron. Evesham 142.

[9]Reg. XIV 114.

[10]The procurator of Glastonbury informs the convent that the pope expected some reward for the favours he had shown their church (Domerham, 404). He also complains to the convent that the pope had not taken care to obtain a present from the bishop, their opponent (Domerham, *loc. cit.*). The bishop had not lost on every point and the abbey's representatives probably felt that the pope, therefore, should have awarded part of the presents due to him, in modern parlance: part of the costs of the proceedings, to the bishop. When a promised money-present is long in arriving Innocent, as a papal notary records, takes up an unfriendly attitude in other affairs of the petitioner (Thomas of Capua, Summa dictaminis 18, Heller, 268, cf. also *ibid*. 211). Matthew Paris, a wholly unreliable source, however, in these matters, says of Innocent – who according to Matthew in his insatiable greed for money could be brought by money to any crime (Chronica majora, ed. H.R. Luard, RS., No. 57, Vol. 2, 1874, 565) – that after the Lateran Council he extorted a huge sum of money from every single participant (*ibid*. 635). The abbot of St Albans is reported, when taking leave, to have offered the pope fifty marks, but to have been given to understand that it must be one hundred marks (MG. SS. 28, 438). It must be said, however, that the expenses

incurred by the Curia in preparing and running the Council sessions were enormous. From a notice accidentally extant we know that Innocent promised the senator Pandulf that the Curia would defray all the costs he incurred in securing the safety of those attending the Council, and that he would add to that sum a special reimbursement *cum munere*. Pandulf had, among other tasks, to secure the roads on the outskirts of Rome, and to take the city towers into his hands and to guard them (Lib. cens. 1, 259). It is true that no visitor to the Curia, at least no-one who had to carry out a legal transaction, was allowed to depart without papal permission. Thomas Marleberge, who did not obtain such permission, assumes that the pope will refuse it until he has made his farewell gifts to the pope and the cardinals in a manner befitting someone who has won his case. Since he is unable to raise the money, he stealthily leaves the Curia (Chron. Evesham 200). Whether Marleberge was right in his assumption or not, to prevent an unauthorized departure from the Curia was, on the whole, a reasonable measure. It was designed to prevent the parties from using chicanery against each other, for example by the untimely departure of a legal representative with the intention of delaying the proceedings (see Reg. I 360, II 80), and to obviate other evil machinations (for example obtaining papal mandates surreptitiously: Reg. XIV 132, Migne PL. 216, 489, XVI 53) or irregularities (cf. Reg. I 68, XIII 203), since such dishonest practices were more than likely to be discovered if the individual concerned had personally to apply for permission to leave. The prohibition was perhaps also designed to ensure that obligations were performed which visitors to the Curia had incurred (Reg. I 68; cf. Chron. Evesham 198). In one instance Innocent stresses that a visitor to the Curia had left without his permission even though he, the pope, had not burdened him in any way, nor ever intended so to do (Reg. I 68).

Innocent himself disliked any tenacious pursuit of financial rights and obligations. Once he replies to an inquiry, concerning a payment due to the church of Compostela, by stating that since it had originally been voluntary the church's officers should not be too strict in claiming its performance. Otherwise it might seem as though, like *exactores*, they were excessively greedy of worldly profits (Reg. IX 32; see also Reg. XVI 6 and VI 128). Innocent himself waived payments due to him for a time or for good if they were too heavy a burden for the debtor (cf. below, Chapter 10). Occasionally he also assigned parts of his income to churches and monasteries which were in financial difficulties (Reg. XI App. Migne PL. 215, 1593; Reg. I 296, V 78, VIII 186). He transferred the total revenues due to the Apostolic See from the churches of Lombardy to the bishop of Piacenza and his priests who, presumably at the pope's command, had left the city during the fight for immunity of the clergy (Reg. VII 174).

[11]The "now and again" may be justified in that the majority of cases will not have been conducted by wealthy parties, and it is these latters' experiences at the Curia which we usually alone come to know of.

[12]Reg. XIV 114.

[13]Reg. VII 20.

[14]Chron. Evesham, 190f.

[15]Accounts furnished by procurators and plaintiffs of their opponent's machinations are, of course, always to be treated with discretion.

[16]Epp. Cant. 457.

[17]*Ibid.* 458.

[18]*Ibid.* 478.

[19]*Ibid.* 482.

[20]*Ibid.* 484.

[21]Girald. Cambr. 3, 178f. Cf. also *ibid.* 84, 95f. If Innocent had in fact wished to proceed with Gerald's appointment despite his election, he would have had to hold Gerald's election to be invalid. Quashing the election at a later stage would then have been the proper action. However, if the election were invalid it seems most improbable that Innocent would have considered appointing Gerald. There is nothing that could have given him the idea of insisting on the appointment of this quarrelsome man in defiance of both the king's and the archbishop's reluctance, especially as Gerald lacked sufficient claim to the see and had no backing in the chapter of St David's either.

[22]Girald. Cambr. 3, 263f. The Episcopal Acts relating to Welsh Dioceses 1066–1272 (Vol. 1, ed. J.C. Davies, Hist. Soc. of the Church in Wales 1, 1946), which contain rich material on the vacancy at St David's from 1198 to 1203, were not accessible to me.

[23]See Chapter 3 above. When at the end of his second stay in Rome, Marleberge left the Curia without permission because he could not afford the usual presents, he regretfully writes to the convent that he would have been able to achieve the renewal of the privileges, the incorporation of new chapters, the reimbursement of the bishop's expenses and many other things, if he had made the farewell visits (Chron. Evesham 200). To some extent these are no more than acts of indulgence, as for example the renewal of privileges, kindnesses which could be returned with, or which had been prepared by, kindnesses. As far as anything more is concerned, Thomas may be thinking of concessions which he might have been able to pursue if he had stayed longer. There can be no question of Thomas accusing the pope, whom he himself describes as a just judge (Chron. Evesham 190), of corruption.

[24]Chron. Andr. 744.

[25]Chron. Andr. 740.

[26]This holds true for political decisions as well. The payments which in February 1207 King John of England orders to be assigned to Richard, the pope's brother, and to Richard's son Paul, his thanks to the papal notaries and chaplains for their help and his request for further support, such as the annual payments to Ugolino of Ostia, the pope's confidant, and to other influential cardinals (see Brem, Papst Gregor IX. bis zum Beginn seines Pontifikats, Heidelb. Abh. z. mittl. u. neuer. Gesch. 32, 1911, 9f.), did not prevent Innocent from consecrating Stephen Langton in June of the same year (see Chapter 5 below). On one occasion we hear that a cleric, despite many petitions by cardinals and blood relations of the pope, had not been granted a provision (Reg. I 349). Under a less independent pope the acceptance of pensions and favours by colleagues and other persons of the pope's entourage naturally could have had much worse consequences than was the case under Innocent III. Numerous examples of assignments of this kind are extant from England (Rotuli litterarum patentium 1201–1216, ed. T.D. Hardy, 1835, 118, 138; Rotuli litterarum clausarum 1204–1227, ed. T.D. Hardy, 1833, Vol. 1, 156, 157, 180, 488, 168, 58lb, 654f; Rymer 1[1] 95; see also Cheney, Master Philip, 343). Of course there can be no certainty, and in the case of a man such as Cardinal Ugolino, the later Gregory IX, it is totally inconceivable, that the recipient should have felt obliged to advocate the interests of the donor at every turn.

[27]Migne PL. 217, 718f.

[28]Reg. I 171.

[29]See Appendix 2 below.

[30]*Ibid.* and Chapter 5 below.

[31]Reg. VII 35.

<sup>32</sup>Chron. Evesham 185.

<sup>33</sup>Chron. Andr. 744.

<sup>34</sup>Reg. IX 113.

<sup>35</sup>Reg. X 34.

<sup>36</sup>Caesarius (Strange 1), 381.

<sup>37</sup>Chron. Evesham 191.

<sup>38</sup>Tangl, 54f. (Constitutiones II, sections 1–10); cf. von Heckel, Studien über die Kanzleiordnung Innocenz' III (HJb. 57, 1937) 259ff.

<sup>39</sup>Heller, 205f., shows that parties none the less found ways and means of circumventing what the constitutions decreed.

<sup>40</sup>Reg. I 235, 349, Rainer of Pomposa 1, 14 (Migne PL. 216, 1221, cf. von Heckel, Studien, 265 and Heller, 229 n. 1).

<sup>41</sup>Vincke's essay on the marriage case of Peter II of Aragon (108ff.) is a good indication of the difficulties of such cases.

<sup>42</sup>Rainer of Pomposa, Pr. Coll. t. XXVIII (Migne PL. 216, 1241).

<sup>43</sup>Reg. VII 169 (Migne PL. 215, 483). Exceptions raised later are not to be accepted unless they have arisen at a later date or have only later come to the party's notice.

<sup>44</sup>Reg. I 39, VIII 154, IX 109, XV 49, XVI 4.

<sup>45</sup>Reg. VII 169.

<sup>46</sup>Can. 37 (Leclercq 1363) c. 28 X 1, 3.

<sup>47</sup>Can. 48 (Leclercq 1370f.) c. 61 X 2, 28.

<sup>48</sup>*Ibid.*

<sup>49</sup>Can. 35 (Leclercq 1362) c. 59 X 2, 28.

<sup>50</sup>See Fliche, 97ff. for the pope's measures against the growing centralization of the affairs at the Curia.

<sup>51</sup>Reg. I 108, 427; II 106; V 3.

<sup>52</sup>Reg. VI 75.

<sup>53</sup>Gesta c. 42; Reg. II 133.

<sup>54</sup>Gesta c. 42; Reg. I 168, II 82, 83.

<sup>55</sup>Reg. X 212, 213.

<sup>56</sup>Reg. I 283.

<sup>57</sup>Reg. I 30, 161, 188; II 38; VI 75.

<sup>58</sup>Reg. I 164. If Inocent, in exceptional instances, had cases retried which had been judicially decided by his predecessors, he did so only because the sentence had already been questioned by other popes, and even then only on mature deliberation with the cardinals and under the explicit recognition of the principle that it was no easy matter to allow an appeal against the *res iudicata.*

<sup>59</sup>Gesta c. 41, Rainer of Pomposa, Pr. coll. praef. (Migne PL. 216, 1173). Abbot Hariulf of Oudenburg (see Müller, 102ff.) gives a graphic illustration of the session of a consistory court in earlier times under Innocent II. A comparison between the legal procedure in Hariulf's case and the practice by Innocent III's time testifies to the progress in the judiciary which the Curia had made. It would have been unthinkable, under Innocent III, that as happened in Hariulf's case, simply on the strength of the statement made by the one party, a far-reaching decision should have been passed against the opposite party (see Müller, 107). Still for Celestine III, Innocent III's immediate predecessor, such arbitrary decisions are provable, and in one case even for Clement III (see Chapter 1 above).

<sup>60</sup>Amongst them the famous canonist Tancred of Bologna (*Hoc saepe vidi fieri . . . in*

*curia Romana a domino Innocentio papa tertio felicis recordationis, cum prolixas ferebat sententias* (Mochi Onory, 58 n. 2f.).

[61]See Chapter 10 below.

[62]Gesta c. 41.

[63]RNI 29.

[64]See Chapter 5 below.

[65]Chron. Evesham 160f.

[66]Chron. Andr. 747, Girald. Cambr. 3, 270.

[67]Chron. Evesham 151f. The same spirit is seen in Innocent's admonitions against longwindedness in prayer in *De sacro alt. myst....* Many clerics so multiplied the orations at mass that they aroused the disgust of the audience (Migna PL. 217, 814).

[68]*Ibid.* 189.

[69]Chron. Evesham 143.

[70]Rainer of Pomposa, *op. cit.*, Cf. Heyer, ZRG 4, 1914, 495ff.

[71]Thus Innocent was styled at the Curia, see Rainer of Pomposa, Pr. coll. praef. (Migne PL. 216, 1173) and Chapter 10 below.

[72]Singer, Die Dekretalensammlung des Bernardus Compostellanus antiquus, SB. Wien 171², 1914; cf. Heyer *op. cit.* 602ff.

[73]See Singer, 3, 4, 29ff. Cf. Kuttner, Johannes Teutonicus, 630, 633 n. 13.

[74]See Chapter 7 below.

[75]See Kuttner, Johannes Teutonicus, 617ff. For the other, smaller collections of Innocent III's decretals, see Kuttner, Johannes Teutonicus, 622.

[76]See Mochi Onory, 75.

[77]Gillmann, Laurentius, 94f.

[78]Text in Mochi Onory, 27, note.

[79]As is shown by occasional comments made by canonists such as Bernard of Compostela (Singer, 114), Johannes Teutonicus (von Schulte, Johannes Teutonicus, Zeitschr. f. Kirchenrecht 16 N.F.1, 1881, 123 n. 51), Magister Albertus (Mochi Onory, 58 n. 2) on their discussions with the pope.

[80]*De misera condicione hominis* (Migne PL. 217) 718f.

[81]Reg. I 103.

[82]Chron. Andr. 748.

[83]Girald. Cambr. 3, 271f.; cf. also *ibid.* 179.

[84]Chron. Evesham 199.

[85]Reg. I 222. See Berlière, 27ff., 31f. for Innocent's concern to protect the rights of the bishops against the monasteries.

[86]Can. 7 (Leclercq 1335f.), c. 13 X 1, 31; can. 36 (Leclercq 1361f.), c. 59 X 2, 28.

[87]Can. 12 (Leclercq 1342f.) c. 7 X 3, 35.

[88]Can. 60 (Leclercq 1380), c. 12 X 5, 31.

[89]Can. 57 (Leclercq 1378), c. 24 X 5, 33. See also Reg. VII 169 (Migne PL. 215 481f.), X 121.

[90]Can. 58 (Leclercq 1379), c. 25 X 5, 33.

[91]Can. 7 (Leclercq 1336), c. 13 X 1, 31.

[92]Leclercq 1362.

[93]Reg. I 222, 224, 394, II 49, 150, V 77, VII 27, 169 (Migne PL. 215, 481f.), IX 43, X 45, XVI 85 (Migne PL. 215, 1599).

[94]Reg. IX 138.

[95]Reg. X 58, see also *ibid.* XI 102.

[96]Hist. episcop. Autiss. (Recueil 18) 730.

[97]Conc. Lateran. can. 42 (Leclercq 1366). The law conforms to the practice Innocent always observed (see for instance Reg. VIII 180, IX 72, XIV 128; Hampe, Regestum, 556f.). See also Maccarrone, Chiesa, 90f.

[98]See Chapter 4 below.

[99]When the appointment to the archbishopric of Palermo devolved to the pope in 1213, Innocent appointed Archbishop Berard of Bari, Frederick's companion on his journey to Germany, stressing the fact that the archbishop had been loyal and devoted both to him and to the king (Reg. XVI 110). Examples for the Angevin Empire may be found in Chapter 4 below; for Poland, Chapter 4 below; for Hungary, Chapter 3 above and Chapter 4 n. 57; and for Denmark, Chapter 3, n. 107 below.

[100]Reg. X 177.

[101]Reg. X 39.

[102]Reg. IX 74.

[103]When he approved the postulation in 1207/1208 Innocent was politically rather untrammelled. Moreover, in such a case he would scarcely have openly confessed to being bound by political necessity. In the postulation the chapter of Kalocsa points to the pressing necessity and to the obvious advantage of Berthold's postulation (Reg. X 177), the king, for his part, to the necessity and to the advantage that would accrue to him and his kingdom (Reg. IX 74).

[104]Reg. XIV 28.

[105]See Baethgen, Regentschaft, 117f.

[106]Reg. VIII 39.

[107]Reg. VI 181, VIII 193. Although Innocent is later tempted to dispose of considerable political obstacles by agreeing to Waldemar's postulation to Bremen (see Tillmann, Rekuperationen, 352), he refuses the translation in deference to the king of Denmark (Reg. XI 10). When at the same time he declares Waldemar's restitution to the bishopric and to his paternal inheritance, there is no doubt that in practice only the revenues were involved, not the administration of the see, for which the archbishop of Lund had appointed the procurator, and even less a repeal of the restrictions of residence. Immediately after the pope's decision Waldemar fled from Rome. Innocent sent ban and anathema after the perjurer (Reg. X 209, XI 10).

[108]Monarchia lusitana (ed. by Brandão, 1632) P. IV Esc. VIII 264; Quadro elementar das relacões politicas e diplomaticas de Portugal com as diversas potencias do mundo, pelo Visc. de Santorem, continuado por Rebelle de Silva, 1842ff., 9 p. 62. The pope's final sentence delivered on 7 April 1216 after much confusion and difficulty (see Reg. XVI 52, Mon. lus. IV App. Cont. 8), grants the king sovereignty over the places in dispute, which are given into the Templars' care, and adjudges the revenues to his sisters. Cf. Reuter, 13f; see also Tillmann, Zur Frage, 175f.

[109]Reg. I 270, P. 290.

[110]Reg. VI 156, VII 127.

[111]Reg. X 120.

[112]Notwithstanding the undeniable total untrustworthiness of the king, the bishops' rejection of all the king's proposals, which remitted the question of restitution to the pope's decision, can in fact only be explained by their fear that the pope would reduce the creditors' money-claims, and was a symptom of unspiritual self-interest or any equally unspiritual insistence on their rights or else of an insulting lack of confidence in the pope.

[113]Rymer 1[1], 119 dated 15 April 1214.

[114]See Maccarrone, Chiesa, 92ff.

[115]Cf. Reg. I 7, 10, 270, 271, 510, 511; P. 978; Reg. VII 127.

[116]Cf. Reg. VI 4; P. 1431–1434.

[117]For the attitude of the episcopate towards the king, see Roul. de Cluny 344, 341; Reg. I 511 and IX 76.

[118]Reg. XI 174.

[119]Reg. V 31.

[120]Cf. Tillmann, Legaten, 107ff.

[121]Reg. XVI 134, 135.

[122]Cf. Tillmann, Legaten, 104. The mission of the legate Nicholas of Tusculum served positively to restore internal peace in England and apparently had been requested by the bishops themselves (Reg. XVI 81, 82, 89). The king is required to follow the advice and the admonitions of the legate who was fully informed as to the pope's intentions (Reg. XVI 79).

[123]Rymer 1[1], 120.

[124]*Ibid.* 127, 128.

[125]*Ibid.* 127.

[126]*Ibid.* 135f.

[127]*Ibid.* 136.

[128]*Ibid.* 136.

[129]In letters, written at the same time and, as it seems, for conditional delivery only, in which Innocent excommunicates all disturbers of the peace and lays the interdict on their territories, the bishops are charged with the solemn publication of the censures, and are designated as being worse than the Saracens, since they were attempting to deprive the one man (John had taken the cross) of his crown who could be counted on to come to the succour of the Holy Land (Wendover 2, 152; Rymer 1[1], 138). Shortly after the conclusion of Magna Carta Stephen Langton and a number of bishops together with the papal nuncio Pandulf had testified to the king that the barons had refused the allegiance to which they had pledged themselves at the conclusion of peace (K. Major, Acta Stephani Langton, Canterbury and York Series, Vol. 50, 1950, 24f..

[130]There is no reason to assume that this refusal was a matter of principle. The barons themselves had requested Innocent at the beginning of the year to act as feudal lord and oblige his vassal, if necessary, to leave them their ancient liberties unimpaired (Rymer 1[1], 120). It is true that John maintains the barons were holding his act of vassalship to Innocent against him, but the barons had already some time before attempted to win Innocent's favour by putting forward the counter-argument that the king had granted the annual tribute and other honours to the Roman Church not voluntarily nor from a sense of piety, but from fear and because the barons had forced him.

[131]Reg. I 356.

[132]He lays claim to the oath of allegiance by his subjects, to military service to a limited extent, to the delegation of representatives to diets, to appellate jurisdiction, in most cases also to tributes, procurations and other revenues due to the territorial lord and, in addition, to certain rights in respect of the installation of the municipal governments. He also demands the restitution of alienated domanial estates including the castles, without which the territorial lord was totally dependent on the good will of the local powers. On the nature of papal rule in the Papal States see Ermini, I rettori

provinciali dello stato della chiesa da Innocenzo III all'Albornoz (Rivista di storia del diritto italiano 1931, 45f.).

[133]See Chapter 3 above.

[134]Reg. VI 281.

[135]Reg. XII 106; *Forma iuramenti* (Migne PL. 216, 127ff.). Innocent agreed with Bishop Peter of Ivrea that, despite the poverty of the church, he must forgo the traditional but unjust revenues.

[136]Reg. VIII 36, 40, 41.

[137]Reg. VIII 36.

[138]Reg. XVI 171. Cf. Peter des Vaux 2, 201.

[139]Rod. Tolos. (Recueil 19) 230.

[140]Heyer, 398. For the course of events see also Schäfer, Geschichte von Spanien 3 (1861), 71ff.

[141]P. 5314 identifies Sancho as procurator appointed by the legate. In a document dated 28 September 1218 James names Archbishop S. of Tarragona, Count Sancho, his great uncle, and G(uillelmus) de Monterotondo, the *magister militie templi* and the other spiritual advisers given him by the pope, *a domino papa nobis datis et assignatis* (Vaissete 8, 714f.). It seems that the three first-mentioned were the most prominent of the *praelati et nobiles*, who according to the rubrics in Theiner (P. 5181) were appointed by the pope to serve the young king as *consiliarii*. In Theiner (P. 5183) the people from Montpellier are instructed *ut de universis proventibus et iuribus ad dictum pupillum spectantibus magistro militiae templi in Ispania pro conservatione dicti pupilli responderi procurent*. In a document dated 19 June 1220 James states that Innocent had consigned him to the care and protection *magistri militie templi* and had appointed the latter as well a number of magnates of the country as his advisers (Huicci, Coleccion diplomatica de Jaime I el Conquistador 1, 1918, 33). Cf. also the *Gesta Comitum Barcionensium*, according to which Sancho receives the regency, while the child is given into the Templars' care (ed. by L. Barrau-Dihigo and J. Masso Torrents in Croniques Catalanes 2, 1925, 19, 56f.). Innocent also reserved Montpellier, the disputed maternal inheritance, for the child (P. 5183, 5220).

[142]Forster, The Chronicle of James I, king of Aragon (1883), 18.

[143]See Chapter 5 below. Though this cannot be denied, it must be denied that decisions made by the pope in issues which have or could have been of political moment, are from the outset arbitrarily conceived as political decisions. The pitfalls of such an assumption are well revealed in Innocent's attitude in the matter of the conferment of the pallium on the bishop of Antivari. Innocent had an interest in granting the request made by King Vulk of Dioclea (see Chapter 8 below) and the envoys delegated to Dioclea were given the pallium to take with them (Reg. I 526–528). But after the legates' departure the pope is informed and confirms for himself from the *Liber censuum* that the church of Antivari is numbered among the suffraganships of Ragusa. Reproaching the chaplain and legate John, who had scrutinized the book and given the pope inaccurate information, Innocent forbids the legates to hand over the pallium to the elect of Antivari unless they had satisfied themselves that his predecessors had been archbishops. He has all the letters redrafted, with the relevant passage omitted in which the conferment of the pallium is mentioned, so that the legates could use the first or the second copies as the situation required (Reg. I 535). As it turned out the entry in the *Liber censuum* was erroneous (cf. Tangl, p. xviii). Cf. also the pope's decision in the electoral conflict of Constantinople (Chapter 4 below).

# CHAPTER 4

# The champion of ecclesiastical liberty

Raised to the chair of justice to protect the rights of all, Innocent regarded it as one of his noblest tasks to establish order in the relationship between state and Church, in which "in just distribution be given to Caesar what is Caesar's, and to God what is God's", thereby maintaining the liberty of both.[1] State-churchism violated this God-willed order by withholding from the Church the independence without which it could not fulfil its spiritual tasks. Innocent III redemanded or defended the liberty of the Church against the long-standing claims of state-churchism as well as against more recent attempts to sway the Church to other forms of State requirements.

The essential claims which Innocent advocated in the name of *libertas ecclesiae* are contained in two *canones* of the Fourth Lateran Council. Canon 25 decrees that any election taking place under lay pressure is void, that the elect assenting to being thus elected is ineligible in future, and that the electors are suspended from office.[2] Canon 46 prohibits the taxation of the clergy by laymen and allows voluntary contributions by clergymen only in special cases and on prior consultation with the Roman bishop.[3]

Innocent fought the hardest and most momentous struggle for the liberty of appointment to ecclesiastical offices in England. The pope's powerful and successful advance in the Canterbury dispute in the beginning of his reign[4] was meant no less for the king than for the archbishop, and was doubtless intended to give new heart to the friends of ecclesiastical liberty in England.

Prior to Innocent III the struggle against state-churchism had been fought more by personages within the English church than by Rome itself. The popes had never let matters arrive at a rupture with the

kings since they were dependent on their support in the struggles with
the Empire. The English kings, though, no longer stood on the
ecclesiastical prerogatives of the crown, the 'ancient customs of the
realm', since Henry II in 1172 atoned for the murder of Archbishop
Thomas Becket, the defender of ecclesiastical liberty and of the
immunity of the clergy against these customs. But nothing had
changed in the practice of elections being held 'according to the
ancient customs of the realm'. The king's candidate was now as
before 'elected' at the court by representatives of the chapter.
Through this filling of bishoprics and abbacies after the king's will the
crown had retained the key to its domination of the English church.

Innocent did not intend either to break off the traditional friendly
relations with the English kings by unleashing a struggle of principle
against the 'ancient custom'. He hoped to abolish it gradually by
supporting the wish for liberty of the cathedral chapters and convents.

During King John's reign Innocent had for the first time to deal
with double elections in the Angevin realm. They were the surest
indication of a movement towards emancipation within the electoral
chapters since part of the electors must have had the courage to
nominate their own candidate against that of the king. On the
occasion of a double election in the Norman bishopric of Sées
Innocent in 1202 quashes the election of the royal candidate for
formal reasons, that is without mentioning the king's intervention, and
confirms the candidate freely elected by the majority.[5] When John
refuses to acknowledge the elect, Innocent threatens to lay Normandy under interdict[6] and now justifies the confirmation also with
his duty to stand for ecclesiastical liberty. He expects that John, in
view of the threat to his possessions in northern France from Philip
of France, will not carry the conflict to extremes.[7]

The first double election in England itself which was brought
before the pope, happened, as was to be expected, in one of the
numerous monastic cathedral chapters, in Winchester. Both the freely
elected and the royal candidate were rejected by the pope, the one
because of the irregularity of the election, the other because force
had been used against the electors. The new election held at the Curia
in 1205 was again split, but in the end the electors, perhaps not
without the pope's conciliation, agreed upon the royal candidate.[8]

Innocent alleged as reason for the rejection of the royal candidate
after the first election the force used against the electors; formerly he

had annulled elections held under force on the grounds of other defects[9] which also in the Winchester case were not missing. He had thus made a conspicuous advance against the royal right of appointment. But he contents himself with maintaining the principle of free elections theoretically and he is sure to have been glad that he could humour the king's wishes in the question of persons. But Innocent was unable to prevent the king from wreaking his vengeance upon the elect of the opposite party and his friends.

At the beginning of 1206 unprecedented happenings were disclosed in Rome. It was learned that in Canterbury two candidates had been 'freely and unanimously' elected to the archiepiscopal see. The monks had sent their subprior, whom they had elected secretly and on a specific condition, together with a delegation to the Curia, but had then disavowed the election before the king[10] and postulated the king's candidate, Bishop John of Norwich. With no little astonishment and indignation Innocent greets the request for the translation of the second 'freely and unanimously' elected candidate. They had, he reproaches the electors, offered their mother like a whore to different lovers.[11] The course of events in Winchester seems to be repeating itself. Both elections are quashed, at the new election at the Curia the votes are at first again split. Innocent may not have been disinclined to approve of John of Norwich on the basis of a new election,[12] but did not think of bringing pressure to bear in that direction. The election of Cardinal Stephen Langton he may have proposed as a compromise.[13] Stephen was English, his parents lived in England, John had only recently congratulated him on his promotion to cardinal and had amiably held out to him a prospect, now shattered, of calling him to his court.[14] The pope may have hoped that the man who had had no share in the happenings and quarrels would still be the most acceptable alternative for the king if he had to renounce the elevation of a candidate nominated by himself. With urgent requests, and doing his best to be convincing, he appeals for the king's consent, but also cautions him against getting enmeshed in difficulties of which it would not be easy for him to get out.[15] Innocent still hopes that the king will give in, but is determined otherwise to fight the matter out and to take up, beyond the individual case, the struggle for the liberty of the English church. Though John refuses to approve of Stephen, Innocent on 17 June 1207 takes the decisive step,[16] having first declared to the king that for his conscience sake he could not act otherwise and that the victory would go to Him whose place he

took.[17] Innocent did not work up the struggle which now became
inevitable, but neither did he shirk it; no occasion was more propitious for the initiation of a struggle for the liberty of the English
church than the appointment to the archiepiscopal see of Canterbury,
the election of a successor to St Thomas at a moment in which the
unmasking of outrageous machinations disclosed to all the world the
servitude of the church for which the martyr had shed his blood. In
March 1208 three English bishops, in their capacity as papal commissaries, published the interdict over England, and towards the end
of 1209 solemnly laid John under ban. The issue of the negotiations of
the preceding years had been less the recognition of the archbishop in
itself than the conditions of that recognition, on the occasion of which
John wished to maintain his and his heirs' rights, honour and liberties,
namely the ancient royal prerogatives, against the English church.
Innocent was prepared, though, to be accommodating to the king and
to respect his honour,[18] but only as far as this was reconcilable with
the objective of the struggle, the liberty of the English church.[19]
John's fight was hopeless from the moment it became evident that the
English church supported the pope loyally against the king, though
from his brutality and cruelty the worst was to be feared. The fact
that even his most loyal followers in the episcopate, the bishops of
Norwich and Winchester, observed the interdict in their diocese[20]
and that his chancellor, elected to be bishop of Lincoln, had himself
consecrated by Stephen Langton and henceforth joined him and the
other bishops in exile, could have brought home to him how hopeless
his resistance against Innocent was. These men knew which of their
two lords they had to accept as the stronger.

After the publication of the ban Innocent still waited more than
two years before he confronted the king with the option between
capitulation and ruin. In view of the public feeling in England, the
king's inevitable overthrow was imminent if the pope released the
subjects from their oaths of allegiance and declared John an enemy
and persecutor of the church. The ultimatum closes with the threat[21]
that, if John did not give in now, he would, following the example of
Him who with a strong hand saved his people from the serfdom of the
Pharaoh, seek to rescue the English church with a strong hand from
its servitude. He predicted, in truthfulness and unshakable determination, that, if he did not want peace now that he could have it, he
would not be able to get it when he would want it. Repentance after
the ruin would be in vain, as he could see by the example of those

who in these days had ventured on a similar course,[22] that is by the example of Emperor Otto. In Otto's fate John could see the course of events approaching also for himself: after the anathema the release of his subjects from their oaths of allegiance, the call on the trusty supporters of the church to defend it against its enemies, the defection of the vassals, the elevation of an anti-king who in the person of the French dauphin stood ready against John just as Innocent had opposed to Otto the person of Frederick of Sicily. In the first days of June 1213 Innocent will have received the news that John had accepted the ultimatum and, in view of the constant threat by France and his own subjects, had surrendered his realms of England and Ireland to the Church to receive them back as fiefs.

One is easily tempted to think that Innocent took advantage of the victory to bring about a radical change-over in the relationship between state and Church in England and to humiliatingly subdue the crown to the triumphant hierarchy. In actual fact this was so far from happening that the misconception could arise that Innocent, in blind partiality to his new vassal, had sacrificed to him the interests of the Church. This view fails to recognize how little, relatively, Innocent valued the establishment of such feudal bonds for the Roman Church. Even in victory Innocent adhered to the principle that it was befitting and necessary for him to maintain ecclesiastical justice and liberty in such a way as not to infringe upon the royal jurisdiction and honour.[23]

The programme of his future English church policy is laid down in a letter to the English bishops issued a few days after the receipt of the news of the victory. It is a document of wisdom, moderation and justice. The pope calls upon and admonishes the bishops with regard to the peace between *regnum* and *sacerdotium* to be in all respects disposed to furthering it and to cause no difficulties nor delays. He would always be intent on heeding justice and ecclesiastical liberty and take care that those who had fought for the just struggle would also carry off the desired palm.[24] The liberty of the Church is, thus, to be restored and those who have suffered for this cause are to be justly indemnified, but the king, too, is to have true peace and to receive that which, though not by law, is required on the grounds of fairness. Correspondingly he replies to the king on his first complaints about the bishops that he could honour the church in his own realm and allow it to enjoy the liberties due to it, so that he might prove himself a true son of the Church. He recommends him not to quarrel with the archbishops and bishops, especially about spiritual matters and the rights of the church, since he could turn to him, the pope, and achieve with honour much through him which on his own he could not honourably do. He could rest assured that he, the pope, would be careful to grant his requests effectively as far as decency allowed.[25] Innocent was aware from the first that he would often have to reconcile John with the episcopate. Stephen Langton had always struck a somewhat sharper tone than the pope. During the struggle Innocent had, on the occasion of the election affair of Lincoln, already once recommended him not to overdraw the bow.[26] At least some of the bishops had returned from exile unreconciled inwardly and disposed to exploit to the last extremities the victory over the tyrant who rightly was not to be trusted. Clerical circles demanded that all those who had suffered for the liberty of the Church be first fully indemnified, and that the numerous vacancies among bishoprics and abbacies be filled by free canonical elections without royal influence.[27] These demands were in themselves justified. But Innocent could not shut his eyes to the fact that in view of the threatening conditions in the country it was impossible for John to come up then and there with the total amount of damages, the payment of which was to be the condition for the raising of the interdict. John need not have been the pope's vassal to meet with his understanding also of the fact that it was a question of existence for him whether the bishops and abbots to be elected would strengthen the opposition against him or support him. In the matter of damages Innocent himself brought about a just and fair settlement,[28] and in the question of episcopal elections he took precautions that men who were loyal to the king were elected to the bishoprics vacant at the time.[29] It is not Innocent who should be blamed for the way that the legate, who, not without the bishops' fault, found himself in antagonism with the episcopate,[30] favoured the king more than was fitting when executing the papal mandate on the elections.[31] After the legate had been recalled, John, who, encouraged by the legate's complaisance, had been bold enough to order elections to be held again 'according to the ancient custom of the realm',[32] had to acknowledge formally and generally the liberty of elections. The royal decree of 21 November 1214 reserves to the crown only the honorary rights of permitting, and consenting to, elections, both of which must not be withheld.[33] Therewith the objective of the great struggle was obtained. State-churchism in England was annihilated.[34]

Owing to favourable circumstances it was easier in Sicily than in England for Innocent to succeed in causing the crown to give up state sovereignty over the church. In the Sicilian kingdom, though, the spirit of state-churchism was, at the end of the pope's reign, not so mortally stricken as in England, since the Sicilian church at the time of Innocent's accession to the throne was not yet susceptible to the idea of ecclesiastical liberty in the same degree as the English church already had been some decades earlier.

The popes themselves had surrendered the Sicilian church to the Norman kings because they needed their political and military support against the emperors. By the ecclesiastical privileges granted to William I by Hadrian IV in the treaty of Benevento of 1156, a unique position had been conceded to the kingdom in ecclesiastical matters. The appointment to bishoprics and abbacies lay in the king's hands owing to his unrestricted right to reject any candidate elected by the chapters and convents, and owing to the stipulation that the voting return had to be kept secret until the king had been informed. Appeals to the pope were not permitted in Sicily, and in other parts of the kingdom they were liable to restrictions. No legate was allowed to be sent to the island without request by the king. It was for the king to decide whether priests from Sicily summoned to the Apostolic See could obey the summons.[35] When the privilege was renewed by Celestine III, Tancred, the 'usurper', had had to acquiesce in considerably reduced rights, but had yet retained important prerogatives as to legation and ecclesiastical elections.[36] Henry VI and Constance did not recognize Tancred's concordat. In gruff, insulting terms Constance on one occasion entered a protest against an infringement of her and her husband's ecclesiastical prerogatives by Celestine III.[37]

Constance fought for almost a year against Innocent III for the ecclesiastical privileges of the Sicilian rulers. She was, indeed, not directly dependent on the pope's protection. In the first months after Innocent's accession to the throne her and her son's rule was hardly threatened, and Constance had no reason to reckon with exceptional difficulties.[38] Her position was surely more favourable than Tancred's when he negotiated the concordat. Although the return of Sicily into the system of feudal relationships of the Roman Church depended on the issue of the negotiations, Innocent had informed the empress from the beginning that he would never concede her the objectionable chapters of the concordats of William I and William II.[39] It is to this firmness and to his ability to wait until the right moment had come, that Innocent owes his ultimate success. In the last days of her life, under pressure perhaps of the disturbances prevailing in the kingdom at that time or perhaps in presentiment of her imminent death, Constance waived the extraordinary prerogatives of the Norman kings. Only in the question of elections did Innocent make a concession; this, however, was in keeping with the general course of his church policy, which was inclined to compromise. Under the terms of the concordat of late 1198 the chapter is to notify the bishop's death to the crown, then to effect the election canonically, but to elect a candidate to whom the king could not reasonably refuse to give his consent. The election return is to be published at once, that is before the royal consent is applied for. But the enthronement of the elect may only take place after the king's consent has been given.[40]

Even before the new concordat, from the first days of his reign onward, Innocent set out actively to break down the lay domination in the Sicilian church. Already before his consecration he rejects a candidate forced by lay pressure upon the Greek chapter of Santa Severina[41] in Calabria as bishop who, as Innocent finds, should be styled a Barbarian rather than a Latin, allows[42] the chapter to hold a free new election, and requires the empress to refrain from obstructing this canonical appointment to the church.[43] All official acts transacted by the procurators of the archbishopric, whom Henry VI had installed after the arrest of the archbishop of Salerno, Nicholas de Ajello, are declared void.[44] A bishop is authorized to proceed with the ban against clerics who dare to bring him up before the temporal court even in ecclesiastical matters.[45] An inquiry is instituted against another bishop charged by his canons with having, among other things, taken legal proceedings against clerics before the imperial court.[46] With the pope's support the churches seek to repossess themselves of that which they had alienated under lay pressure or had lent out as benefices.[47]

The period of the papal regency following Constance's reign was naturally of great assistance to the Sicilian church in emancipating itself from the crown and establishing closer ties with the Roman Church. As soon as he had been declared of age King Frederick himself tried to re-establish the state sovereignty over the church set up by his ancestors. As early as 1208 he exiles three canons of the church of Palermo, because they had appealed to the Apostolic See when their brother canons were about to proceed to the election of the candidate apparently nominated by the king. The scarcely fourteen-year-old king is bold enough to write to his former guardian explaining that only reverence for the Apostolic See has caused him to let it go at this punishment. For answer Innocent sends him an excerpt from the electoral stipulations of the concordat concluded with Frederick's mother, declares that he would have them published all over the kingdom, and requires that the exiled be recalled.[48] In Policastro and probably also in Sarno about the year 1210 Frederick again forced his will upon the electors by brutal pressure.[49] When the archbishop of Palermo informs the elect of Policastro, the physician-in-ordinary to the king, that by papal order he was not allowed to consecrate him for the time being, the physician angrily exclaims that he would return to the king's court and seek the help of those who had had him elected. A papal legate does the king the favour of having the elect consecrated. But Innocent declares the election void, prohibits the king's minion from exercising the unlawfully obtained episcopal office, and orders the chapter to present the candidate, whom before the king's intervention they had unanimously elected, to the archbishop of Salerno for scrutiny.[50] Even towards the end of Innocent's pontificate, a bishop is said to have declared that he would never give up his see on the pope's orders since he held his church not from the pope but from the king.[51] We must not, though, attribute too much significance to the attitude of the clergy in the kingdom. The vicious prelate had nothing to lose. Since he stood condemned by the pope, he intended to try and hold his own in the pope's despite under the protection of Lupold of Worms, who was active in the kingdom as Frederick's legate. He was obviously aware of Frederick's view of the king's position in the Sicilian church. Naturally, the young king had in the end to defer to the pope's will in every individual case, but Innocent is sure to have observed with no light concern his protégé's bearing. If he had stayed alive longer, Innocent would have been spared an incomparably harder fight for the liberty of the Sicilian church only if he had ensured that Sicily was transferred to the young son of the emperor to be.

In Germany Innocent eliminated to the last shreds the state's sovereign rights over the church, which emperors and kings had retained since the end of the Investiture Contest. The kings of the period of the throne disputes, who were dependent on Innocent or strove for papal recognition, were in no position to refuse to accede to his demands. Possibly following the precedent set by Philip of Swabia in the peace negotiations with the Curia,[52] Otto IV, in the

Privilege of Speyer of 1209,[53] renounces any obstruction of appeals and his participation in ecclesiastical elections. In order to remedy, Otto declares, the abuse which, as the saying is, some of his ancestors had practised on the occasion of the election of prelates, he decrees that elections should be held freely and canonically and that the candidate elected unanimously or by the greater and saner part of the chapter should be given the church, barring canonical impediments. The king's right to have the elections held in his presence and his competence to decide, with the advice of the metropolitan, between the candidates in the case of double elections, was thereby implicitly disavowed. That the elect before his consecration had to accept the *regalia* from the king might continue to hold good as a custom, but was scarcely any longer to be regarded as binding law for the Church, all the more since the Privilege, in connection with the abandonment of the rights of *spolia* and *regalia*, leaves the disposition of all *spiritualia* to the pope and the prelates. The decrees of the Privilege, which "in just distribution tries to give Caesar what is Caesar's, and God what is God's", Frederick II on 12 July 1213 re-affirmed in the Golden Bull of Eger. That the imperial princes were witnesses of, and consented to, the promise, measures which Innocent, after his experiences with Otto, will have regarded as necessary, safeguarded its binding force in imperial law.

The new or, as Innocent would have said, the proper order in the relationship between state and Church in Germany was perhaps less secured by these privileges than by the fact that Innocent had accustomed the German bishops to regard the pope, in all ecclesiastical matters at least, as their true lord against whose displeasure no royal or imperial grace could protect them. In the Mainz election dispute King Philip had to abandon his supporter Lupold of Worms, who had been elected by the great majority of the Mainz cathedral chapter and whom he had invested with the *regalia*, in favour of the candidate approved by the pope, Siegfried of Eppenstein, whose election was supported only by three or four canons and whom Philip's opponent Otto had invested with the *temporalia*. At the beginning of the peace negotiations Philip had at once declared himself prepared to abandon Lupold, who as bishop of Worms ought not to have changed over to Mainz without papal permission, but for the sake of the honour of the Empire had demanded from the pope the resignation also of Siegfried, thus thinking of an issue similar to that in the Trier election dispute in his father's lifetime. But a settlement by compromise was just what Innocent did not want in this test case and what caused him to reject the demand as *iniquum, frivolum et absurdum*. Siegfried was one of the first to desert the emperor after Otto's breach with the pope. His rise and the fall of others, most conspicuously the fall of Archbishop Adolf of Cologne, had shown him that it was Innocent's, not the emperor's, will which could hold the princes of the Church in, and sweep them from, their seats. At the peace negotiations Philip was also compelled to abandon Adolf who had been deposed by Innocent for breach of oath, i.e. for defection from the Welf to the Staufen. The proceedings against Adolf were, though, to be reopened, but the decision fell within the exclusive competence of the papal court.[54] Adolf's second successor was deposed for his communion with the excommunicate emperor and had not dared defy the sentence. In the long dispute whether the German bishops were to be imperial princes in the first place or servants of the Church, Innocent decided that the principality was to be regarded as an annex only to the spiritual office. As regards the elevation and deposition of bishops, Innocent proceeded according to the law without having regard to their position as imperial princes. When rejecting, or approving of, elections he did not take into account whether or not the elect had received the *regalia*, and he considered it self-evident that an elect whose election was quashed and a bishop who was deposed had to return the *regalia*.[55]

Did the renunciation by the German kings of their participation in ecclesiastical elections signify a new weakening of the kingship intended by Innocent? Everywhere, even where the bishops had not become reigning princes, the ruler had a vital interest in the appointments to the episcopal sees. It does not seem that the French episcopate since the early freeing of canonical elections from royal intervention had been less loyal to the kingdom. English church history, on the other hand, reports many and serious conflicts between king and bishops, though up to 1214 the appointment to the bishoprics lay in the king's hands. The English and French examples also show that the enforcement of papal authority in the national churches did not need to imply a disadvantage for the ruler. By way of applying to Rome, the king could often enforce his will more effectively and more easily than by using force against the electors. In general, the papacy regarded it as in its and the Church's interest to co-operate with, not to work against, state authority. Nothing was more detrimental for the Church than the dissolution of public order, than the anarchy of territorial and local potentates. In southern France, and to some extent also in Lombardy, the Church had before it an example of the consequences which the lack of a strong central power had for the life of the Church. In Germany since the Concordat of Worms the influence of the territorial powers on the appointment to bishoprics had ousted the royal influence. In the case of a new election the king could often maintain his interests only by playing the territorial powers off against each other. In alliance with the pope the king would have been in a position to counter the influence of the territorial powers much more effectively. If the fundamental antagonism between Empire and Church had been overcome,[56] the Curia would hardly have refused to act as the Empire's ally, since from the standpoint of the Church too the domination of the bishoprics by the territories must appear unwelcome throughout.

In the remaining countries of occidental Christendom Innocent's fight against state-churchism did not lead to such a dramatic culmination nor to such revolutionary results as in England, Sicily and the Empire. But there is, surely, no country, in which the position of Church and state had stayed unaffected by Innocent's government.[57] In Aragon Peter II, the pope's devoted adherent, grants the liberty of canonical elections as a permanency and, waiving the right of assent, makes only the proviso that the freely and canonically elected candidate, in token of loyalty, personally call on the king.[58] In 1210 three Polish dukes guaranteed the liberty of the Church to Archbishop Henry of Kietlicz and to the bishops of Poland.[59] That the dukes were open to the efforts of Archbishop Henry Kietlicz of Gnesen and to the pope's views,[60] may in part be due to their antagonism to the fourth duke, Ladislav Lakonogi, Henry's sovereign lord, against whom they sought to win the pope's and the Church's favour.[61] But even this man so apt to violence, who at that time was under ban for having banished the archbishop and for his acts of violence against clerics and churches, began to show himself in some degree accommodating to the demands of the Church. When filling the see of Posen at about the same time, he for the first time renounced the idea of conferring the bishopric by investing the candidate with ring and staff at pleasure. Master Paul, the duke's trusted chaplain, whom the chapter naturally had elected at the duke's request, was himself allowed to take up the ring and staff from the altar.[62] Innocent realized that in the Polish church internal conditions were not yet ripe for the liberty he was then engaged in winning for the English church.

He therefore holds the view, in this case differing from Archbishop Henry, that it was expedient to deal more benevolently with the church of Posen, which at the election had begun to enjoy a new liberty, and to approve of the elect despite some scruples on account of his earlier attitude.[63] But before confirming the elect in July 1211 he strictly binds him to stand truly and devotedly by the archbishop for the maintenance of ecclesiastical liberty. The most effect for the independence of the Polish church, in particular for the establishment of its inner preconditions, Innocent achieved by the support and furtherance he gave to Archbishop Henry Kietlicz of Gnesen whom he sincerely venerated,[64] in his reforming efforts as well as in his attitude to the episcopate and in his quarrels with his duke.[65] In a similar way he to a large extent gave a free hand to the primate of Sweden, Archbishop Andrew of Lund, one of the king's friends and at the same time a champion of ecclesiastical liberty.[66] It was difficult, almost impossible, for the pope to form a correct picture of conditions in those far-off countries and of the expediency of measures to be taken. Whether he was right in his harsh rejection of King Sverre of Norway and whether his fight against him rebounded in fact to the advantage of ecclesiastical liberty, is impossible for us to decide.

It was not a fight against state-churchism which was in question in the quarrel between state and Church in the Latin Empire of Constantinople erected in 1204. By reorganizing the Greek church, by erecting the Latin patriarchate and by disposing of churches and church possessions,[67] the conquerors had, though, made themselves guilty of a trespass which no western monarch would have dared. But the originators of this new order did not appeal to state sovereign rights over the Church. Their only intention was to convey to safety the spoils of the Greek church before the pope could contest their right to them. The lawless happenings, therefore, did not result in a fundamental conflict between Innocent and the wielders of power. The fight for the liberty of the Church within the area of the Latin Empire meant for Innocent the resistance not to state-churchly, but rather to national, claims of the Venetians to the appointment of their fellow-countrymen to the patriarchate and to the most prominent bishoprics;[68] it further meant the defence of the property and revenues of the Church against the potentates as a whole.

Innocent first contents himself with declaring void the election, effected by the newly installed Venetian canons of Hagia Sophia, of the

Venetian Thomas Morosini as patriarch and to appointing him patriarch on his own authority.[69] He gave way in the substance of the matter, because he could not undo what had happened without seriously endangering the new Empire and the crusade in whose realization he still believed. But he was determined not to surrender the church of Constantinople to the Venetians for ever.

A silent, tenacious fight begins against a tenacious opponent, who as such hardly comes to view, but whose cause is, more or less voluntarily, pursued by the patriarch and the cathedral chapter. For the outcome of the confrontation everything turned on one factor: whether the canons of Hagia Sophia, namely the electors of the patriarch to be, were drawn exclusively from within the ranks of the Venetians or whether access to the cathedral chapter was open also to clerics of non-Venetian provenance. Innocent broke the Venetian monopoly of the canonries by granting provisions in Hagia Sophia to non-Venetians, personally or through his legates,[70] and by enforcing their installation by the patriarch.[71] Thomas, who after his elevation in Venice had bound himself to grant the canonries of his episcopal church to Venetians only,[72] was obliged towards the end of 1208 by papal order to revoke this obligation before the body of the clergy of the city and to promise on oath an impartial appointment to canonries.[73] The vast majority of the canonries naturally remained then as before in the hands of Venetians.[74]

To forestall the Venetian claims to the exclusive possession of the patriarchate Innocent had further conceded participation in the election of the patriarch to the prelates of all the conventual churches in Constantinople.[75] When, in consequence of the heterogeneous composition of the constituent body, on two occasions double elections came about after Morosini's death, Innocent in both cases quashed the election or postulation on account of the irregularity of the transactions[76] and, at the Lateran Council, finally elevated Archbishop Gervase of Heraclea to the patriarchate on his own authority.[77] He thereby appointed the candidate of the non-Venetian faction,[78] but did not overdraw the bow, since Gervase was a Venetian by birth.[79] The fight between the papacy and the republic of Venice was not definitely settled, but Innocent had achieved a success in that he had at least wrested from his powerful, tenacious and unscrupulous antagonist[80] unlimited disposal of the church of Constantinople.

In the pact of partition by which the Conquerors arranged for the reorganization of the church of Constantinople, they had also agreed to secularize the entire church property except for that which was indispensable for its sustenance.[81] This was not the only act of outrage; new acts of robbery often supervened on old ones.[82] Testamentary dispositions or other donations of landed property in favour of the church were forbidden,[83] the tithes due to the churches by the lords of the manor were often not paid, and those owed by the subjects even withheld by the lords. Those in power aimed at obtaining immediate hold of the church property, at preventing its growth, and at curtailing church revenues in favour of their own or to utilize them for state purposes. Whilst the states of the West were still endeavouring to benefit from the moral and economic influence of the Church by way of their influence on appointments to ecclesiastical offices or simply through feudal procedures we are confronted in the Latin Empire of Constantinople with the forerunners of a state policy which aimed at secularizing church property itself. None the less, in unending negotiations about the restitution of, or compensation for, church property, and by an admonishing, threatening, occasionally punishing intervention in individual cases, Innocent achieved more than he might at first have expected.[84] It was not yet possible at that time to realize the policy of secularization, because the Latin Empire was too much dependent on the support of the Roman Church and because the potentates, with the possible exception of the Venetians, were not yet ready for the idea of secularization, that is were themselves not yet sufficiently secularized.

Aspirations similar to the attempts at secularization in the Latin Empire, namely the tenacious and purposeful endeavours of state authorities to incorporate the clergy into the general community of subjects and to have the church property share in the financial burdens of states and communes, led in Portugal and in the large Italian communes, particularly in northern Italy, to conflicts of a new kind between Church and temporal power.

When Innocent III like Gregory VII demanded that in the lands of Christendom "God be given what is God's" he did not forget as readily as Gregory to give Caesar what is Caesar's. But that which is Caesar's Innocent saw in the light of the needs of a feudal state. Less understandingly he valued demands upon the Church which were made as soon as a state began to throw off the loose garment of feudalism. Just as the feudal state had utilized the influence and possessions of the Church in the forms of feudalism, so the emergent new state sought to bend the wealth of the Church to its needs by submitting the clergy to the general civic duties, and particularly to taxation. Innocent, who recognized the duties of the Church arising from feudal tenure,[85] countered these tendencies in a way exceeding the bounds of ecclesiastical necessity by sticking to the principle of the immunity of the clergy, of its special legal domicile, and of its freedom from civic charges,[86] a principle which was not called for by the nature of the spiritual office. Innocent's intention though, was not to forbid the clergy any service to the state.[87] But he insisted on the principle of voluntariness and sought to check pressure even when disguised under the masks of which he had acquired ample knowledge in the disputes of one and a half decades, by decreeing at the Lateran Council that any grant of taxes was subject to prior consultation with the Apostolic See.[88]

Most of the states might then have still been in a position to rest satisfied with an appeal to the clergy for a voluntary contribution on special occasions. But for a small country like Portugal, which had to gather up all its strength to be equal to the demands of the permanent Saracen wars and of the conflicts with Christian neighbours, it was apparently no longer sufficient to have the Church participate in the financial burdens of the state by way of occasional voluntary contributions.[89] These were of even less use to the Lombard cities, in view of their pressing need for money resulting from campaigns against each other and from the necessity to be constantly prepared for battle. Both Portugal[90] and the Lombard cities, therefore, heavily attacked the immunity of the clergy. They met with Innocent's unbending resistance, yet the quarrel with the Portuguese kings did not lead to so radical a final reckoning as that with the communes.[91] King Sancho I of Portugal had written to the pope himself claiming that there was no better way to break up the idol of arrogance and sumptuosity of those who feigned to be religious, namely the clerics and prelates, than to deprive them of the abundance of worldly possession which they had received from him and his father, to his own and his successors' greatest detriment, and to give it to his sons and to the defenders of the realm who were short of much.[92] But he died[93] before Innocent could proceed from fatherly admonitions and warnings to punitive measures. His successor, Alfonso II, recognized the immunity of the clergy to its full extent,[94] until under Honorius III new needs or the dissipation of his fear of a powerful adversary caused him to take up the fight again.

The struggle between Innocent and the Lombard communes was

fought on both sides in full awareness of its fundamental import and, therefore, with full engagement of forces. Those responsible for the struggle on the side of the cities were less vulnerable to spiritual weapons than the rulers of the states. Responsibility was divided among many, the magistracy changed every year, and the magistrates did not conceal the fact that they did not fear the ban because they could easily get rid of it after the term of their office had expired, and even believed they were released from it with the discharge from office. Moreover, the institution of the office of podestà enabled the cities, in times of fighting with the Apostolic See, to call from outside a head of the city who cared little for the ban, for instance a supporter of heresy.[95] Innocent employed, or at least threatened to employ, the usual and some unusual measures: the ban the raising of which is reserved to the pope;[96] the prohibition for every Lombard of communion with the excommunicates under pain of solemn excommunication; the decree that the descendants of the excommunicates are incapable up to the third and fourth generation of obtaining ecclesiastical offices and benefices;[97] the nullification of ordinances and sentences issued by magistrates under ban; the interdict over cities; the order to detain all citizens of interdicted cities on all the markets of Lombardy and to seize their wares;[98] the withdrawal of the bishopric or its subordination to another church.[99] The threat of the withdrawal of the bishopric and its transference to the neighbouring dioceses was sufficient for Piacenza, the most obstinate opponent of clerical immunity, to surrender unconditionally.[100] The withdrawal of a bishopric would not only have impaired the honour of a city, but also have jeopardized its material interests. In Lombardy the concepts of bishopric and county tallied to such a degree that the loss of the one could jeopardize the possession of the other, the more so as the possessions and castles of many a city were nominally still under the sovereignty of the bishop.[101] A dreadful weapon was then as before the interdict. Hardly any city sustained it longer than a few years. But the sword cut both ways, since the cessation of service and sermon encouraged the loosening and spoiling of religious and moral life and made the way free for the spread of heresy, even if the town afflicted did not refuse, as Treviso had done in 1198, to execute the heresy decrees on the grounds that it did not intend to fight against these enemies of the Apostolic See since they were themselves its adversary.[102]

Though Innocent had in every individual case succeeded in making the communes renounce the extension of civic duties to the clergy, and though the number of conflicts diminished considerably in the later years of his reign, his fight still proved fruitless in the end as regards ultimate aim and ultimate success, because the pope was opposed to the inescapable development of the idea of state, and it proved detrimental to the inner life of the Church on account of the means he used and the embitterment he created. Innocent may, indeed, have come to realize this in the end, for the Lateran Council provides for no punishments other than the ban against the guilty, and the nullification of their constitutions and judgements. Does this imply mitigation of the fight in principle or the abandonment of interdict and of temporal punishments because of their moral questionableness,[103] or is the reason rather that Innocent, following his own scruples or that of the Council, merely did not want to legalize the use of these means?

Innocent fought the struggle with the communes, even in its outward form, with a rigour otherwise foreign to him, without the inclination to reconciliation and the constant readiness to make peace which he shows to the kings even in serious conflicts. It seems that he had taken an aversion to these emerging city states. In their aspiration for centralization and levelling he may have seen dangers which were greater than the threat to the Church from the state-churchism, inwardly already discarded, of the feudal states. These aspirations may have been all the more odious to him since perhaps for him the cities were not even exercising legitimate authority, and as he regarded the state of affairs in Lombardy as a civic anarchy, to which, as in the case of the anarchy of the nobility in southern France and indeed any anarchy in general, he was at heart opposed. Our own time, which has come to know the idea of the total state in its terrible consistency and has been the victim of its consequences, is perhaps able to understand Innocent better than could earlier times, since our eyes are opened to recognize the seeds of totalitarian aspiration germinating in the cities of northern Italy.[104]

### Notes to Chapter 4

[1]On the concept of freedom in the middle ages see Tellenbach, 230ff., on the concept of *libertas ecclesiae* in particular, 151ff., 236ff.
[2]Leclercq 1354, c. 43 X 1, 6.

[3]Leclercq 1368, c. 7 X 3, 49.

[4]Reg. I 432, 433–435. See Chapter 2 above.

[5]Reg. V 70.

[6]Reg. VI 73.

[7]The king may have made his peace with the elect forthwith; if he did not, the dispute would in any case lose its basis with the conquest of Normandy by the French king.

[8]Reg. VIII 104.

[9]In addition to the election at Sées, the elections in Angers and Avranches under King Richard (Reg. I 447, 532). In Avranches he accommodated the king by personally conferring the see of Angers on the elect, who had been declared to have forfeited both sees on the grounds of unauthorized changeover from Avranches to Angers (Reg. I 532). In Avranches he would probably even have allowed the re-election of the elect if he had not been unacceptable on personal grounds.

[10]Gervase of Canterbury 2, 99. Cf., on the events, the detailed account by M.D. Knowles, The Canterbury election of 1205–6 (EHR. 53, 1938, 211ff.). C.R. Cheney has published a letter by the pope dated 1 December 1205 in which Innocent, apparently not yet aware of what had happened, commends the subprior to the king as elect (Bulletin of the Institute of Hist. Research 21, 1948, 237).

[11]Reg. IX 34.

[12]Apart from the re-election of the bishop by part of the chapter, this is perhaps suggested also by the pope's demand to King John to send a procurator to uphold his interests, since he, the pope, as far as with God's help he could, wished to be regardful of his right and honour (Reg. IX 36).

[13]In view of the condition the pope's initiative is to be assumed and furthermore is confirmed by William of Andres who was at the Curia at that time. He reports that it was commonly held that the election had taken place on the pope's advice (Chron. Andr. 737).

[14]Migne PL. 215, 1328.

[15]Reg. IX 206.

[16]Gervase of Canterbury 2, App. to Pref. LXI.

[17]Ibid. LXXIV ff.

[18]Cf. Tillmann, Legaten, 94 n. 122. In 1208 Innocent recommended the archbishop, who was inclined to gruffness, to confirm the election of the royal chancellor as bishop of Lincoln, if the chapter, in response to the king's requests and without pressure, had voted for him (Reg. XII 56) and, in other respects, too, he advised him not to be too rigid (Reg. XII 91).

[19]Gervase 2, App. to Pref. LXI, Reg. XI 141, 211, 221.

[20]Their sees, too, had been temporarily sequestered by the king (Rymer 1¹, 100).

[21]In the ultimatum (Reg. XV 234) which he then accepted John is only threatened with deposition, it cannot therefore have been pronounced, cf. Tillmann, Legaten, 96, n. 130. On the pope's letters see ibid. 193f. and Zur Frage, 141f.; in addition see C.R. Cheney, The alleged deposition of King John (Studies in med. hist. pres. to F.M. Powicke, 1948), p. 100ff. Poole (456 n. 3) ascribes to Cheney the overthrow of the legend of John's deposition, but I myself had disproved it as early as 1925 (thesis) and, in slightly enlarged version, in 1931 (MIÖG 45). Cheney, who quotes the thesis, seems to have overlooked this.

[22]Reg. XV 234.

[23]Reg. V 145.

[24]Reg. XVI 81.

[25]Reg. XVI 130.

[26]See Chapter 4 above.

[27]Cf. Gibbs and Lang, 59.

[28]See Tillmann, Legaten, 98, n. 149. Towards the end of the year the bishops agreed with the king upon the supersession of their claims by privileges of sundry kinds (*ibid.* 103. n. 183). John instructed the executors of his will to provide compensation for the damages and grievances he had inflicted on God and the Church (Rymer 1[1], 144). According to the statement of the contemporary Gerald of Wales (4, 192) who by no means took the king's part, the Church was fully recompensed.

[29]Migne PL. 216, 928. See Tillmann, Legaten, 99f., Gibbs and Lang, 59ff. 70f.

[30]See Mercati, 285ff.

[31]See Tillmann, Legaten, 100ff. Innocent did not approve of the legate's attitude (*ibid.* 102ff.).

[32]See Tillmann, Legaten, 102; Gibbs and Lang, 60ff.

[33]Stubbs, Select Charters, ed. H.C. Davis (1913), 283f. Cf. Tillmann, Legaten, 103f., Gibbs and Lang, 58. The restoration of the freedom of canonical elections naturally did not cut off every influence of the king on the elections. On the later electoral practice in England and on influences on the elections from outside, particularly from the king's and the pope's sides, see Gibbs and Lang, 53ff., 69ff.

[34]Gerald of Wales, in retrospect, speaks of the times when the English church had yet to gain its liberty (3, 157, 163, 339), and explicitly testifies that the old electoral practice was abolished in Innocent's last years (4, 337).

[35]M.G. Const. 1, 588f.

[36]*Ibid.* 1, 593f.

[37]Cf. Kehr, Briefbuch, 50.

[38]For conditions in Sicily see below Chapter 5, n. 18.

[39]Reg. XI 208.

[40]Huillard-Bréholles 1[1], 16.

[41]See Acta Inn., 170 n.

[42]Reg. I 16, Acta Inn. I n. 1.

[43]Reg. I 18, Acta Inn. I n. 2.

[44]Reg. I 65 P. 524.

[45]Reg. I 72 P. 519.

[46]Reg. I 21.

[47]Reg. I 105, 250, 180, 414, 294, 72, 64, 566, P. 259, 161, 307, 519, 518.

[48]Reg. XI 208.

[49]Reg. XIV 81.

[50]*Ibid.*

[51]Thomas of Capua, Dict. epist. (Hahn, Coll. 1) 343f.

[52]The offer of peace made by Philip in 1203 included the assent to canonical elections of bishops and prelates and the devolution of all *spiritualia* to the pope (M.G. Const. 2, 2, 8f). Being in peace with the pope Philip was in no position to refuse Innocent the concessions in ecclesiastical matters which he had declared himself prepared to grant in 1203. It is probable that the stipulations of the Privilege of Speyer relating to ecclesiastical matters are identical with those accepted by Philip. In part they resemble Philip's secret offers of 1203, which they formulate in more detail and precision.

[53]RNI 189.

[54]Reg. IX 88. Until the outcome of the proceedings, in which Adolf's chances were

extremely small, his opponent, Bruno of Sayn, was to exercise all archiepiscopal rights, while Adolf was to hold only those castles which he had held before Bruno's capture.

[55]Thus he proceeded in Mainz and Cologne, thus in Hildesheim and Würzburg on the occasion of the deposition of Chancellor Conrad of Querfurt, and in Naumburg. After Bishop Engelhard of Naumburg had resigned at the Curia at the pope's request he travelled to Philip's court to return him the *regalia* (Chron. S. Petri Erford., MG. SS. 30[1], 380). See also Innocent III's letter of 6 April 1206 in UB des Hochstifts Naumburg (ed. by the Hist. Komm. f.d. Prov. Sachsen u.f. Anhalt, 1925) p. 384.

[56]See Chapter 5 below.

[57]Occasional reports on the pope's efforts to secure the liberty of the Church are recorded for Bohemia (Reg. I 78), for Ireland (P. 5241), for Cyprus (Reg. XV 206), Tripoli (Reg. XV 219). For Hungary it is to be supposed that Innocent, in view of his amicable relationship with the Hungarian kings, exercised a greater direct or indirect influence in favour of the liberty of the Church than the sources reveal. Still during Innocent's reign, in one of Hungary's neighbouring countries, the king's brother Andrew as duke of Croatia and Dalmatia, as he himself relates, transferred the bishopric of Phara to a canon of Spalato (Fejér 2, 318ff.). The king himself refused the monks of the Latin monastery of Wgyed at Samogyvar his assent to their abbot, though elected according to traditional custom, with the argument that he would only accept a Hungarian, and he then transferred the abbacy to another Latin priest, the archbishop of Spalato (Reg. VII 128). Innocent intercedes to maintain the rights of the monastery. In 1204 the canons of Gran do not dare, as they say, proceed to an election which is not agreeable to King Imre, and then postulate the royal candidate, Archbishop John of Kalocsa (Reg. VII 159). After Imre's death a section of the chapter postulates the bishop of Pecs (Reg. VI 139), the candidate of the regent, later king, Andrew. Innocent quashes both postulations as being uncanonical and himself transfers John to Gran for whom also Andrew had in the end decided. It was certainly on Andrew's initiative that his young brother-in-law Berthold of Bamberg was elected to Kalocsa. Despite the suspicious circumstances, an investiture of these bishops by the king, as was customary for instance in England before the great conflict, is hardly to be presumed. It is not merely the pope's silence which militates against such presumption. Direct pressure was out of the question at least in the case of the more important churches. That the pope's protection against oppression would not even have been necessary is shown by the example of the suffragans of Gran, who were opponents of the royal candidate and who were partly in opposition to the king; an opposition which bordered on treason and which did not lead to open rebellion only because Innocent stood behind Imre. The statement by the chapter of Gran, that it did not dare elect a candidate who was not acceptable to the king, namely the bishop of Pecs whom the king hated so bitterly, does not by a long way imply that the chapter felt obliged to accept the king's nominee. The chapter may well have been so ready to accommodate the king's wishes in the hope of securing an ally against the suffragans of Gran who challenged the chapter's exclusive right to effect the election. Not even the suffragans claimed that the chapter had accepted the candidate named by the king; their only complaint is that the chapter had informed the king before the election of the candidate whom it was intending to elect. No matter how the elections in Gran, Kalocsa and other episcopal churches may have been effected, Innocent certainly complained about single acts of violence by the king against high-placed clerics and infringements of the Church's right of sanctuary (Reg. I 388), but not about encroachments on the canonical elections.

[58]Reg. X 144.

[59]Reg. XIV 43. It is indeed possible that by this liberty only the immunity is meant.

[60]Reg. IX 223, 227.

[61]Duke Lesko of Silesia had requested the pope's help in maintaining his position in Cracow, which was his due by virtue of the right of seniority approved by the pope and protected by threat of interd. Innocent instructs the episcopacy on 9 June 1210 to secure compliance with the constitutions enacted in the interest of the peace of the land by ecclesiastical punitive measures (Reg. XIII 82). Early in 1207 Innocent takes the duke of Cracow (Reg. IX 229), and in 1213 Vladislav of Kalish and Greater Poland into the shelter of the Church against a voluntarily offered payment of four marks every three years (cf. Lib. cens. p. 151 and P. Fabre, La Pologne et le Saint Siège du douzième au treizième siècle, Etudes d'hist. du moyen-âge, déd. à Monod, 1896). Innocent stresses the duke's honest love for the liberty of the Church, which he had bestowed on the churches and clerics of his country.

[62]Reg. XIV 89.

[63]Ibid.; cf. Sappok, 99.

[64]Innocent styles him *vir eximiae sanctitatis* (Reg. IX 217).

[65]Cf. Reg. IX 217, 218, 220–223, 227, 228, 230–232, 234–236. Cf. Sappok, 93f., 97, 99, and also Maschke, 49, 50, 53f.

[66]See Chapter 6, n. 113 below.

[67]Reg. VII 205.

[68]Reg. IX 130, XII 105 (Migne PL. 216, 122) cf. also Reg. XII 94.

[69]Reg. VII 203 (Acta Inn. P. I no. 68, 285f.).

[70]Reg. VIII 62, 136; IX 100, 129, 134, 148; XI 76; XII 105 (Migne PL. 216, 122); XII 113. Cf. Santifaller, 147f., 149ff.

[71]Reg. XII 105.

[72]Reg. 130; XII 105 (Migne PL. 216, 122).

[73]Reg. XII 105. Innocent expresses the opinion that as the Venetians demanded that only Venetians be appointed to the bishoprics in their sphere of influence, so the Romans could combine to prevent a non-Roman from becoming pope or cardinal and to force him, the pope, to promise to appoint only Roman patriarchs, archbishops and bishops all over the world (Reg. XI 76).

[74]Along with the repudiation of the obligation assumed in Venice, the patriarch had voluntarily appointed a cleric from Piacenza as canon of the church of Hagia Sofia, to show the world that he was willing to stand by the oath he had just sworn (Reg. XII 105). But it was not long before Innocent, on the complaint of Emperor Henry, had to reprimand the patriarch again, because he summoned only Venetians or their subjects to the cathedral chapter (Reg. XIII 18).

[75]P. 2508, Reg. XIV 97, XV 156.

[76]The decisive factor in deciding electoral matters was their legal aspects, not political reasons. This is shown by the pope's detailed instruction to his agents for the examination and decision of the second election and the postulation (Reg. XV 156, Acta Inn. P.I. no. 200). At first the majority of the cathedral chapter had elected the dean of the chapter, a Venetian, and the prelates had postulated three candidates at a time from outside, of whom the pope was to appoint one to be the head of the church in Constantinople. Innocent quashed both the election and the postulation as being irregular. In the next election the votes were divided between the parish priest (*plebanus*) of St Paul in Venice and the archbishop.

[77]Cf. Santifaller, 30.

[78]Reg. XVI 91.

[79]Reg. XV 156 (Migne PL. 216, 680, Acta Inn. P.I. no. 200, P. 436).

[80]See Chapter 9 below.

[81]Reg. VII 208.

[82]Reg. XI 12–15, 24; XIII 99, 100, 105–109, 112, 152–154; XV 22, 65, 66, 76, 77; XVI 98. Cf. Acta Inn. P. I Introd. 128f. Honorius III, Innocent's successor, still states that the magnates of the Empire from the beginning had, arbitrarily, now conveyed property to and now seized it from the Church.

[83]Probably in the first half of 1210 Emperor Henry together with the barons issued such a prohibition by formal decree (Reg. XIII 98, 110). Despite the pope's protest it was still in force two years later (P. 4480 Migne PL. 216, 968).

[84]In 1206 a legate by the pope's order (Reg. VIII 135, Acta Inn. P. I no. 88), mediated an agreement of compensation between the imperial administrator, the later Emperor Henry, and the patriarch, under the terms of which a fifteenth of all estates, duties and franchises is allotted to the Church (Reg. IX 142, Acta Inn. P. I no. 92) as compensation for the confiscated church property. In the treaty of Ravennika of 1210 the lords of northern and central Greece, who seem not to have been affected by the agreement of Constantinople, even returned all church property against the promise of the churches to pay the ground rent as far as they had been liable to it before the conquest (Acta Inn. P. I no. 217, 462ff.; Migne PL. 216, 970ff.). Cardinal legate Pelagius of Albano later quashed this agreement and replaced it by another, which in Innocent's opinion was less useful. The pope reinstated the old treaty early in 1216 and extended its former scope of application (Acta Inn. P. I no. 217, 462f., wrongly dated by the editor to 1215, although the document refers to a resolution of the Lateran Council). There is no mention of any refund of church property or of any compensation for acts of plunder on the part of the Venetians.

[85]Reg. IX 87, XIV 52, XV 40.

[86]Innocent also maintained this principle as regards the crusade taxes by taking into his own hands the taxation of the clergy for the purposes of the crusade (cf. Martini, 315ff.).

[87]Reg. VI 45; Conc. Lateran. can. 46 (Leclercq 1368).

[88]Can. 46, c. 7 X 3, 49.

[89]It speaks in favour of this assumption that for several generations the struggle concerning the immunity of the clergy and the status of the ecclesiastical possessions in general was always taken up again. Sancho I, Alfonso II, Sancho II and his rival brother and successor Alfonso III fought for it. It was not brought to an end until 1289 under King Diniz by a concordat. Both Alfonso II and Alfonso III died under interdict (for these struggles see Reuter, 7ff.).

[90]Reg. XIV 8.

[91]For the struggles between Innocent III and the Lombard cities in general see Luchaire, Les Ligues, 504ff.

[92]Ibid.

[93]In the face of death he did not maintain his anti-clericalism (Reg. XIV 58, 59, 60).

[94]Reuter, 11ff. Laws which contradict canon law are declared void from the beginning. Even so the acquisition of real property for churches and monasteries is limited by purchase restrictions. In view of the extraordinary readiness to make concessions to the Church in other respects this restriction seems to have had its cause in so

conspicuous a state necessity that Innocent, especially with regard to the Saracen war, could not shut his eyes to it.

[95]William of Pusterla, podestà of Alessandria in 1213, was suspected of heresy (Reg. XVI 58).

[96]Reg. VI 45.

[97]Reg. VI 184, VII 41.

[98]Reg. VI 45, 184; VII 173; IX 131.

[99]Thus for instance in the cases of Piacenza (Reg. I 123, X 166–168, X 222), Bergamo (Reg. VI 184), Modena (Reg. VII 41), Milan and Alessandria (Reg. XV 189), yet in the two latter cases not merely, nor in the first place, on account of the infringements of the immunity of the clergy. If we wanted to determine which punitive measures were actually applied or which threats of punishment were actually published in the single cases, we would have to decide whether or not the letters concerned were for conditional delivery only (cf. Tillmann, Über päpstliche Schreiben, 193, 199). Alessandria did in fact lose its see. In 1213 the bishop of Acqui as he calls himself (formerly he had been bishop of Acqui and Alessandria) requests permission to resign from office (Reg. XVI 58, 140).

[100]Reg. IX 169, X 64, 222. The city had already been laid under ban and interdict in 1203 (Reg. IX 167 Migne PL. 215, 999: *cum iam expectaverimus per triennium*), and at the end of 1204 in the archbishopric of Milan personal and business contacts with the citizens of Piacenza had been forbidden, their goods had been ordered to be confiscated (Reg. VII 173).

[101]For northern and central Italy cf. Kauffmann, 40ff., 58f., 73, 76ff., 81, 120f.

[102]Reg. II 27.

[103]Innocent shrunk from using the interdict from a growing concern about the spread of heresy and surely also for general pastoral reasons. At Bergamo in 1210, in order to achieve a speedier raising of the interdict, he contents himself on the request of bishop and clergy with a satisfaction to the clergy, which he would normally not have regarded as sufficient (Reg. XIII 43). In 1212 he threatened Milan with all kinds of punishment including the use of a crusading army against the city as being a protector of heresy, but the interdict is not referred to (Reg. XV 189). In England, too, Innocent in 1213 tried to prepare the ground for as swift a raising of the interdict as possible. In Spain the spread of heresy had caused him to mitigate the interdict as early as 1199 (Reg. II 75).

[104]According to Gibbs and Lang (134) the decree of immunity passed by the Lateran Council has a special place in the development of a tradition which was later to protect England from subjection to arbitrary taxation.

# CHAPTER 5

# Under the pressure of politics

Emperor Henry's sudden death on 27 September 1198 had opened the way for the Roman Church to regain its lost independence and liberty of action and to secure them lastingly. Innocent III was determined to resolve the question of the security of the papacy for good. This unshakeably fixed objective, though not sanctified, yet inescapably prescribed to him the means which seemed necessary to attain it.

To resolve the question of security it was indispensable for the papacy to define definitively its relationship to the Empire. Innocent explicitly declared that the Roman Church was not willing to forgo the imperial advocate.[1] Indeed, it needed the emperorship to escape the danger of becoming dependent on Italian territorial powers, on local potentates and on faction leaders within its own territory. The emperorship was a counterweight against any power on Italian soil which might be tempted to bring Rome and its bishop under its control.[2] But on the other hand, and this was the hopeless dilemma in the relationship between the two powers, the imperial protector must not be so strong in Italy as to become, by right or in actual fact, the pope's master. Every pope, no matter if the spiritual task was uppermost to him or if he was more worldly-minded, was obliged to maintain the balance between the imperial power and the particularist powers of the peninsula. A pope who, in a conflict with the emperor, stood to lose revenues, possessions, residence, personal liberty and even the papal dignity, was in a state of dependence also as regards the execution of his ecclesiastical office.[3] The pope needed the protection of the German sword, but he neither could nor would live under this sword. For the papacy the security question was the pivotal point of its imperial policy. The Investiture Contest would not have taken such destructive forms if it had not at the same time been a fight for the independence of the papacy. The course the Curia took up in the dispute over the Matildine estates,[4] over the central Italian territories as well as over the relationship of the two powers to the Sicilian kingdom and to the Lombard cities has its common denominator in the defence of the papal position against encirclement by the imperial power.

Innocent sought to resolve the security question by continuing the already adopted course of the policy of recuperations. When pursuing the attack on the imperial territories in central Italy which had already begun after Henry VI's death, thus under Celestine III,[5] Innocent's aim was not to enforce legal claims. He energetically urged the acquisition of the duchy of Spoleto and of Tuscany, though it is unlikely that the shrewd lawyer disguised from himself the dubious character of the papal claims to these imperial territories,[6] but on the other hand he was less eager in enforcing the far better founded claims to the exarchate of Ravenna and to the Matildine estates.[7] Nor did Innocent aim at scraping together the greatest possible share in the booty which had been left behind among the ruins of imperial rule in Italy. His objective rather was to build a powerful consolidated Papal State which, like a broad belt, would lie between imperial Italy and the Sicilian kingdom. Along with the support which a re-established Sicilian vassal state would give, the new patrimony was to guarantee the Roman Church the security it needed. On the other hand, in his sense for moderation and for what is possible and attainable, the idea had never entered Innocent's head of excluding the emperor from Italy[8] and of unifying the country under papal leadership.[9] The Lombard cities would no more, or even less, have conformed themselves to papal rule than to imperial rule, and, if the emperor were excluded from Italy, the papacy would have been dragged into the whirlpool of chronic struggles for power which then would have been inevitable in the peninsula.

Innocent won over for the Roman Church the duchy of Spoleto and, in his fight with the imperial margrave Markward of Anweiler, the major part of the March of Ancona.[10] In Tuscany, which he claimed in its totality,[11] he had to content himself with recovering the southern Tuscan territories of which the popes had been deprived by the last emperors, and with an eternal league with the cities for the defence of the Roman Church.[12] Innocent found it hard to give up his claims,[13] since the new Papal State was not yet consolidated and

Rome lacked a secure defence towards the north. Nevertheless the pope's success was great enough to fill Innocent with the exaltation which rings in the festal sermon on the commemoration-day of his consecration: "She ... [the Roman Church] has awarded me a rich dowry; but whether I, too, have made her a present on the occasion of the wedding, it is for you to see. I will not assert it boastfully ...".[14]

The development which had taken place meanwhile in the Empire and in Sicily will have made it easier for Innocent to give up his Tuscan plans.

The dissolution of the personal union between the kingdom of Sicily and the Empire had become a fact. The Staufen faction in Germany, too, had decided to ignore the rights of Henry's little son Frederick, the Roman king-elect, now king of Sicily as his mother's co-regent, and in early March 1198 had elected the child's uncle, Philip of Swabia, Henry VI's brother, to be king. In May Constance on her son's behalf renounced the right of bearing the title of Roman king.[15]

Innocent hardly had a decisive share in the dissolution of the union although this union of the two realms was so fateful for the Roman Church that his involvement has been taken for granted. Indeed, if the personal union had continued to exist, even the extended Papal State would have offered the pope no sufficient protection; it would on the contrary have been bound to give rise to a new and incurable antagonism between pope and emperor. A German ruler who at the same time was king of Sicily could not permanently accept the separation of the two territories under his rule by the Papal State. Anyhow, as matters then stood, we cannot contend that Innocent took any step to prevent Frederick of Sicily from succeeding to the German throne. When Innocent acceded to the papal throne the Curia was doubtless correctly informed that at least a unanimous recognition of Frederick was out of the question and that an anti-Staufen faction was looking for a pretender to the throne of its own. It may even have been known that Philip of Swabia was holding himself in readiness for his own candidature in case the child's election should prove impossible. But if Philip became king his intervention in Italian affairs was imminent. An anti-Staufen kingship must in itself be more agreeable to the pope, but given the ascendency of the Staufen house it had little prospect of winning through. In this state of affairs it was the right thing for Innocent to wait and see how Frederick's cause would prosper in Germany and not to expose himself unnecessarily to the reproach of having deprived the child of his well-founded rights.[16] Should part of Germany pronounce for Frederick, there was still time left to raise objection, quite apart from the possibility that Innocent even at that time might see a way of recognizing Frederick and yet at the same time obviating the danger of a renewed union of the kingdom with the Empire. The rule of a minor in Germany would have held out the prospect of an undisturbed realization of the recuperations and of a smooth completion and consolidation of the acquisitions. In any case, Innocent could no longer be greatly interested in Frederick's renunciation of the dignity of Roman king, since the child had but few chances of his rights being recognized. But after Philip of Swabia's election Innocent could even have taken advantage of the child's claims in the forthcoming negotiations with Philip.[17] It may have been Philip himself who brought his sister-in-law to the tacit renunciation by convincing her that the child's recognition was not attainable.[18]

Whatever possibilities Innocent may have had in mind as to Frederick's succession in the Empire, he will have been relieved when the bonds between Sicily and the Empire were broken by Philip's elevation and that, owing to the elevation of an anti-king in the person of Otto of Brunswick, Philip after all confronted the pope not as an uncontested ruler, but as one forced into negotiations with the Curia for his recognition. As long as two kings fought against each other in Germany, Innocent was in a position to pursue, unhampered from that side, his policy of recuperation and his Sicilian plans.

In the kingdom of Sicily he sought to re-establish the former feudal sovereignty of the Apostolic See. The empress was prepared to do what her husband had refused: to take the oath of allegiance for Apulia and Sicily. But Innocent was not willing to pay the price which she demanded and which his predecessors had paid by surrendering the Sicilian church to the Norman rulers. It is unlikely that for the sake of any political advantage he would have explicitly surrendered to any sovereign the church of his land. But in this instance even his own political advantage called for firmness. If he was the master of the Sicilian church, the Sicilian king's feudal vassalage would assume a relevance for the pope quite different from what it would have had if the church regarded the king as its lord and master. Constance, who during her husband's lifetime had harshly and passionately defended the ecclesiastical position her ancestors had held,[19] in the difficulties of the last days of her life saw herself forced to give in. She could not reckon on any support from the pope as long as the vassalage was not re-established.[20] On her deathbed Constance in November 1198 also transferred to the pope the guardianship over the young king and the regency of the kingdom.[21] The pope had achieved more than he had sought, the ground was prepared for a closer connection between Sicily and the Roman Church than he could have expected. Luck had been with him to a high degree, yet not luck, but his firmness alone, had prevented an intolerably high price being again paid for the close connection between the Apostolic See and the Sicilian kingdom.

The foundation was laid of a rather important body politic for the protection of the material existence and political independence of the papacy, and the support of the Sicilian vassal state was re-established. But the new creation still lacked stability both outwardly and inwardly. Peace and order had to be established in the Patrimony as far as in those days this was at all possible in an Italian community, and papal sovereignty had to be formed into more than a mere nominal rule. An indispensable precondition of success was the protection of the new political community against threats from outside, and this protection, as well as the safeguarding of the position of Sicily as a papal vassal state independent of the Empire and its rulers, could only be held to be achieved if a German king or emperor recognized the territorial changes in Italy as legally binding.

The position which the papacy had to take up in the question of the succession to Henry VI in the Empire was thus predetermined in one respect. The provisions stipulated by Celestine III's legates with the Tuscan League, which obliged it to recognize a holder or representative of the imperial sovereignty only with the consent of and on instructions from the Roman Church,[22] give rise to the conjecture that even at that time the Curia was determined to make the recognition of its recuperations a condition of its recognizing Henry's successor. To maintain and to secure the new territorial order in central Italy, *that* was Innocent's objective of his imperial policy.

The Curia had only been in a position to risk engaging itself in its policy of recuperation because it foresaw that the Empire would not be able to intervene in Italy for some length of time, either because it was ruled by a minor or because it lacked a generally accepted head. This span of time was to be utilized to make a lasting success of the policy of recuperations, in which we also include the acquisition of old and new rights in Sicily. There were two ways open for papal policy through which to obtain this objective. It could either endeavour to add fuel to the discord reigning in the Empire and to prevent the restoration of peace, or else try to cause the holder of the imperial sovereignty to recognize the recuperations. Innocent was not the kind of man to pursue a policy of war and destruction without dire necessity, although Walther von der Vogelweide laid it at the pope's charge[23] and many since have echoed Walther. So Macchiavellian a policy would not only have been unspiritual and un-Christian, but also dangerous and unwise, since the pope's authority was in reality founded on his moral prestige, and since the strength of the German kingship was still so great that a conflict with the restored imperial authority was bound to arise before long, but above all because the years of uncertain conditions in Germany meant years of uncertainty also in central Italy and Sicily. Germans still held strongpoints within the recuperated territories as well as in Sicily; both here and there numerous partisans of the Empire were holding out and many of them, undecided and indifferent, were prepared to support whoever for the moment held the power and guaranteed their advantage.

Innocent adopted the course of negotiating with the man who, though not uncontested, represented the imperial sovereignty, namely Philip of Swabia, Henry VI's brother, Barbarossa's son, the Staufen. A Staufen kingship in itself was not welcome to the pope. But as matters stood, only Philip's emperorship, in view of the power of the Staufen house, warranted the prospect of peace being restored in a measurable time for Germany and thereby for Italy, too. What mattered to Innocent was not the written confirmation of his claims by a Welf or any other anti-king, but only the recognition of the new territorial order in central Italy and Sicily by Philip, whom the Germans in opposition to the pope regarded as their lord.

Innocent's readiness to negotiate was met by an equal readiness on Philip's part. Philip who as duke of Tuscany had solemnly, though not by name, been banned by Celestine III for having despoiled the Patrimony,[24] had sought to come to terms with the Curia as soon as he received news in Montefiascone of the emperor's death.[25] His request for absolution and his promise to release Archbishop Nicholas of Salerno from captivity were apparently not the only commissions which Bishop Radulf of Sutri, a German by birth,[26] delivered to Celestine III. As guardian and representative of his nephew, the Roman king-elect, Philip seems even at that time to have entered into the questions which were vital to the Church and to the Empire and which pressed for decision. It was for Innocent to respond. Towards the end of February 1198 he sent Philip's own negotiator together with the abbot of S Anastasio's in Rome to Germany with the official mission to bring about, if needs be by resort to ban and interdict, the release of the Sicilian captives, among them King Tancred's wife and children, and to absolve Philip after he had redeemed his promise.[27] The authorization to absolve Philip was a marked sign of friendliness towards Philip, since Innocent is sure to have come to know meanwhile that a faction had formed amongst the imperial princes which was opposed to the kingship of Henry VI's son as, indeed, to any other Staufen throne candidature. Even after Philip's election as king on 8 March and the proclamation of a Welf anti-king on 9 June, the envoys were not recalled, though Innocent could not disguise from himself that their presence at Philip's court implied moral support for the Staufen. Philip might well boast of the favour of the pope,[28] whose envoys dealt with him as the legitimate king. Innocent, though, had avoided official communication with him ever since he knew of Philip's elevation,[29] but he did not care to keep secret the fact nor, to a certain degree, the subject-matter, of his negotiations with Philip.[30] Meanwhile his envoy, Philip's devoted follower Bishop Radulf of Sutri, had absolved the Staufen without strictly complying with the papal instructions. Knowing the pope's readiness to come to terms with Philip he probably believed that he was allowed to show to the *king* greater complaisance than to the duke. On 8 September he even attended Philip's coronation in his pontificals, thus not only in his private capacity. When, soon after, he returned to the Curia,[31] he had no proposals to deliver which could satisfy the pope. It is true that Philip, like his predecessors Frederick I and Henry VI, aimed at settling all the contentious issues between the papacy and the emperorship.[32] In view of the changes which had occurred in the balance of power, he may even have been inclined to greater complaisance than Henry VI in the negotiations of 1196/1197. He will have been ready to render the Apostolic See what Henry VI in his last will had offered the pope for his son's succession in the Empire and in Sicily, namely the March of Ancona and the exarchate. But he appears to have been unwilling to put up with southern Italy being cut off from the Empire or to renounce the German influence in Sicily. Weighty circumstances seem to indicate that relations between Philip and his sister-in-law, Empress Constance, were ruptured or at least strained by serious dissensions over the question of Sicily's feudal vassalage to the Empire.[33] After the empress's death in November 1198 Philip's and the pope's claims to Sicily became an issue of highest political moment. As next of kin and surely as head of the Empire Philip contested the pope's right to the regency and to the guardianship over the kingdom,[34] and charged Markward of Anweiler, the pope's enemy, with enforcing his claims. Already in the beginning of January Markward opened hostilities by assaulting Monte Cassino, the key to the kingdom. The pope's work was directly threatened by Philip and his followers.

Since the prospects of coming to terms with Philip had changed for the worse, Innocent thought it necessary to depose Bishop Radulf of Sutri for having acted on his own authority,[35] by this measure countering the impression that Radulf, who in Germany had passed for a legate,[36] had acted by the pope's order or in accordance with his intentions. The negotiations with Philip of Swabia, which Philip of France, the Staufen's ally, now joined,[37] were carried on without intermission throughout the first months of 1199[38], but met with failure.

Innocent found himself faced with the question whether he should now turn to Philip's opponent, the Welf Otto, for whom his uncle King Richard of England had from the first assiduously interceded at the Curia, and whose official legation, which was to notify his election and coronation, was at that time staying at the Curia.[39] Innocent could on no account let matters slide until Philip faced him as an uncontested ruler. But there were serious objections to taking sides for Otto. In view of the Staufen's ascendency and his incomparably greater following, the issue was uncertain, even if Innocent brought the whole weight of his prestige to bear. Legal arguments, to which Innocent, indeed, was not unsusceptible, spoke in favour of Philip, even though for the politician, for whom along with the maintenance of the independence of the papacy its very survival was at stake, the ultimate decision was dependent on other factors. It was even less irrelevant to Innocent that by siding with the weaker party he would be protracting the horrors of civil war.[40] Moreover, the war in Germany, which threatened to spread out also over the neighbouring countries, jeopardized the plans for a crusade which for Innocent was an innermost matter of heart.[41] From the summer of 1198 onwards he had been energetically pursuing the preparations for a new crusade.[42] It was in view of the cause of the cross that he sought to reconcile

France with England, Pisa with Genoa, that he strove for inner peace in Hungary, and that he required the Greek emperor, as a precondition of a political agreement, to take part in the concerted enterprise of Christendom. Could he, in the position he took up in the German throne contest, disregard the interests of the Holy Land? He had only just then pronounced harsh judgement on the kings who preferred taking revenge on each other for their own wrongs to revenging the wrongs done to Christ crucified by taking up arms against his enemies.[43]

And so it was that Innocent accepted the Welf legates' documentary consent to his Italian and Sicilian claims[44] and entered into friendly relations with the Welf faction,[45] but at the same time sought for a way in which he could bring Philip to be more compliant or in which he could with less scruples help the weaker Otto to win his cause. He tries to obtain his objective by acting as accepted arbitrator between the parties.[46] On 3 May 1199 he informs the German princes that in view of his office and of the close connection between *regnum* and *sacerdotium*, particularly between the Roman Church and the Roman Empire, he could no longer allow the internal war in Germany and the destruction of the Empire to go on. He had, he continues, waited in vain for the princes, if they themselves were unable to bring about an agreement,[47] to turn to him as the competent arbitrator in this matter. He now strongly admonished them to put an end to the hitherto existing state of affairs. Failing this, he would be obliged, since further delay would entail grave dangers, to grant the Apostolic favour to him who was recommended by the size of his following and by his greater merits. At the same time he directs Conrad of Wittelsbach, the archbishop of Mainz and cardinal bishop of the Sabina, to commit by letters patent, as far as his person was concerned, to the pope the arbitration of the throne contest, and to bind all vassals and dependents of the church of Mainz to accept as king the man whose nomination the Apostolic See would sanction.[48] At the time of his banishment through Frederick I, Conrad had been awarded by Alexander III, whose devoted follower he was, the suburbicarian bishopric. Innocent expects the archbishop, who is away in the Holy Land and, therefore, had not yet taken up a definite position in the throne contest, to bring to bear his prestige as archbishop of Mainz in the spirit not of the most prominent imperial prince, but of a cardinal bishop. If the leading imperial prince committed the decision to the pope, Innocent was a good part of the way nearer to his goal. He might well expect that the princes of the Welf faction, amongst them Adolf of Altena, would agree to his proposals. The third of the Rhenish archbishops to play a particularly important part in the election of a king, John of Trier, was well enough known to Innocent, from his rôle in the election of the two kings, to hold out hopes for the success of a papal intercession. Many who were undecided and longed for peace might follow the example of the leading imperial princes, and in the end even decided partisans of the Staufen might be faced with the necessity of accepting the papal arbitration. A success, at least with the princes of the Staufen faction who were not involved in the course of the negotiations, seemed all the less hopeless, since Innocent so far had not manifested any inclination towards the Welf faction, but appeared to favour the Staufen, at whose court the pope's envoys had been staying for months and in whose coronation one of them had taken part.

The pope's chances of maintaining and securing his achievements in Italy by way of his arbitration between the parties melted away when the impressive declaration was conveyed to him in which twenty-six German princes, not to mention an equal number of absentees who had allegedly given their consent by way of letters or messengers, entered a protest against the violation of Philip's and the Empire's rights in Italy and Sicily and demanded that Innocent recognize the Staufen as the unquestionably legitimate king and emperor to be. They request the pope not to reach out his hands unjustly for the rights of the Empire, and to bestow his favour to King Philip more fruitfully. The same favour they expect for their dear friend, Philip's truly devoted Markward, the "margrave of Ancona, duke of Ravenna, procurator of the kingdom", whose enemies the pope should cease to support. They further announce to the pope that they will support their lord so effectively that no one within the Empire, or *within the lands which had obeyed Emperor Henry*, would dare any longer to decline his rulership, and that they will soon be coming to Rome in order to procure the imperial crown for Philip.[49] Without knowing of Innocent's intention, the signatories of the Protest of Speyer showed how hopeless his attempt was to persuade the princes to agree on a court of arbitration which jeopardized what for them, with the exception of a few "who go against justice", was an incontrovertible fact: Philip's legitimate kingship. The arrival at the Curia of the archbishop of Mainz towards the end of July on his return journey from the Holy Land made it clear to Innocent that in the question of the court of arbitration he had also counted in vain on Conrad of Wittelsbach.

Innocent repudiates the princes' reproaches against his Italian policy in a generalizing form only. All the more thoroughly does he comment on the demand to recognize Philip without further discussion and on the intimation of their coming to Rome. He cleverly utilizes the tactical blunder the Staufen princes had made when, with the demand to recognize their elect, they invited the pope to take sides and thereby to interfere in the throne contest. They could not now hinder him if he did not keep one-sidedly to the presentation of facts given by the Staufen faction, but made his decision dependent on his own examination of the legal situation. Innocent emphasizes that he was informed of the persons elected, of the electors and also of the circumstances of election and coronation in each case, part of which indeed, to read between the lines, undeniably did not speak in favour of Philip. Innocent explains, therefore, that he was not wholly ignorant as to which of the kings-elect merited the apostolic favour. Since the conferment of the imperial crown fell within his competence, he was prepared, he writes, to *call* the candidate to receive it, who previously had been lawfully elected and likewise crowned king.[50] Against this argument not even a zealous defender of the honour of the Empire could raise any substantial objection. It was not the pope's fault if neither pretender fully met the obvious preconditions of the coronation as emperor. Philip had been elected first and by the majority, but yet in the absence of some electors who had an important rôle to play in the election, and he had only been the second to be crowned, and that at the wrong place and by the wrong consecrator. Philip was warned that, depending on the weight to be attached to the individual defects of election and coronation, even the recognition of his opponent's legitimacy was possible, and that in any case the coronation as emperor could only be the outcome of negotiations and could not be obtained by force. Innocent the sharp-witted dialectician and lawyer had spotted the weak point in the adverse demands and utilized it to parry the weighty blow dealt by the Protest. In the actual struggle for power, however, the pope was threatened with getting the worst of it.

In the Patrimony and in Sicily conditions had taken a turn which was contrary to all the pope's hopes and expectations. In 1198 he had been able to state with great satisfaction that the recuperated central Italian territories had returned to the sovereignty of the Roman

Church without bloodshed and with the free assent of their inhabitants. In those days he declared it to be his will that the land, freed from domination by the mighty nation which, perhaps owing to sins, God had led up from afar,[51] be ruled in justice by the hand of the Church which in truth could say of itself: my yoke is sweet and my burden light. And he already thought that he could apply the other scriptural passage, too: *Sedebit populus meus in plenitudine pacis et in tabernaculis fiduciae et in requie opulenta.*[52] As late as the spring of 1199 he made mention of the recuperations in proud blissfulness.[53] But already in October he confesses to bitter disappointment. In the Tuscan and Spoletan regions of the Patrimony there were many who, shamelessly abusing the patience of the Apostolic See, violated the peace, depraved the law, infested the roads and the country, and thus injured their own and the pope's honour.[54] Conditions in the March were probably far worse. The gloomy picture which Innocent, in that merciless clarity of sight peculiar to him, sketches, at the beginning of 1201, of dissension and feud, of destruction of churches and burning down of houses, of captivity and massacres, of outrage and robbery, this picture doubtless fits in with the situation prevailing at the turn of 1199/1200. He states that conditions in the March, since it was liberated, were worse than at the times of servitude, so that now he was more grieved than he had then been rejoiced at its return to the sovereignty of the Church.[55] Whereas the communities in Roman Tuscany, with the exception of Città di Castello in its farthermost corner[56] and the duchy of Spoleto, professed themselves, at least outwardly, loyal to the sovereignty of the Church, not even that was the case in all parts of the March. Innocent had not been able completely to conquer the March.[57] The year 1199 had even brought a set-back. Some of the cities which had first been on Markward's, the imperial margrave's, side, had fallen back upon a state of neutrality between Empire and Church, between Markward and the pope.[58] Innocent could not disguise from himself that Markward's return and the re-establishment of the imperial sovereignty was generally expected. The greatest and most immediate danger threatened from the situation in Sicily. Since the beginning of the year Innocent had been fighting with Markward for the regency, nay for the very possession of the kingdom.[59] Markward had failed, though, to establish an effective rule on the mainland, but a situation of utter anarchy had spread mainly within the important border district, the Terra di Lavoro, whence the Germans also harrassed the Roman Campania.[60]

In October at the latest Markward crossed over to the island with a view to taking hold of the young king and of the seat of government. Backed up by an alliance with the Sicilian Saracens, Markward, along with the Germans still remaining in Sicily and with the Genoese who had entered his service, constituted a terrible menace to the pope's Sicilian and entire Italian position at a moment when, in Germany, Philip's final victory was beginning to take shape, after Otto in April, with Richard of England's death, had lost his best supporter. Moreover, the Welf had so far not even seen his way to approve of the political concessions made by his legates.[61] Innocent must have felt how much his work was threatened, when even the man who was so much dependent on his benevolence was reluctant to agree to the new territorial order in Italy.

In these days of extreme tension in which the evil tidings from Germany and from the kingdom multiplied[62] and in which a letter from Markward to King Philip fell into Innocent's hands from which seemed to result their agreement upon "the spoliation" of young King Frederick, possibly meaning his transference to Germany,[63] in any case upon a solution of the Sicilian question dangerous to the Roman Church[64] – in these days Innocent received a Staufen legation in public consistory.[65] Relations must have been strained to the point of rupture, since Innocent in his address openly gives voice to his deep aversion for the Staufen and proceeds to unveiled threats. Not the superior statesman, not the calm and assured lawyer seems to stand before us, but the impassioned fighter who sees his work jeopardized and yet is determined to save it at all costs. Innocent brands Frederick I and Henry VI, Philip's father and brother, as persistent persecutors of the Church,[66] stresses the precedence of the priestly over the royal honour, and points out that God had always avenged opposition and schism against priesthood, but that sometimes he had even inspired schisms against the kingship, as in the case of the schism against Saul's kingship caused by David who, though having borne Saul's superiority for a long time, finally gained the upper hand because God's hand was with him. The allusion was easy to understand even without the additional reference: *Magna rei magnum est sacramentum et forsitan instantis temporis est parabola*, a great sign for a great thing and perhaps a parable of the events of a time at hand. A still broader hint is the reference to the schism between Innocent II and Anacletus and the coincident schism in the Empire between Lothair of Supplinburg, Otto's grandfather, and Conrad the

Staufen. Innocent II was victorious and Lothair won the throne because Innocent II crowned him. In calmer tones the pope finishes by justifying his right, apparently contested by Philip, to intervene in the throne contest and the moral duty of the parties to turn to the Apostolic See in this matter, by referring to the translation of the emperorship from the Greeks to the Occident and to the conferment of the imperial crown by the pope.[67]

If Innocent was unwilling to admit that the Roman Church attempted too much when it believed it could substitute its own rulership in central Italy and Sicily for the imperial rule, he had no option but to decide to prop up Otto's otherwise hopeless cause and to embark upon the dangerous and, from the point of view of law and morals, questionable fight with the Staufen and the German nation, which in its overwhelming majority stood behind him. And yet, once again Innocent puts off the decision despite the dangers inherent in any further letting things slide.[68] He resolves to wait for the development of the peace negotiations undertaken by Archbishop Conrad of Mainz, who after a stay of several months at the Curia, was just then about to depart for Germany. Conrad had promised him in public before the cardinals that in the throne question he would not make any final decisions without consulting him.[69] In all other respects the archbishop was given a free hand. His clever mediation might well still result in an unanimously recognized German king offering the Church what it felt it could not forgo, if its independence was to be safeguarded. That this king would be a Welf, Innocent could hardly expect.[70]

It was an unexpected blow for the pope[71] when he received news that the archbishop had proposed to have the conflict settled by a court of arbitration constituted on the basis of equality, which would soon come to a decision. There was no doubt how it would go. Innocent, therefore, had to try to prevent the award coming to pass by confidentially informing those princely members of the arbitration court whom he hoped were susceptible to papal intervention that Philip was unacceptable to him as emperor.[72] As causes of impediment he alleges the public excommunication which had still lain upon Philip at the time of his election, the perjured usurpation of the Empire in defiance of the oath of allegiance he had sworn to his nephew, the threat to the princes' liberty, and the persecution of the Church and the princes by Philip and his family. The only decisive reason, Philip's refusal to surrender to the pope the imperial

rights and claims in central Italy and Sicily, is not mentioned. The
curial cleric who delivers the message, Master Aegidius, is naturally
charged to work underhand for Otto.[73] A little later Innocent intercedes for Otto with the kings of France and England. He is particularly at pains to reopen for the Welf the flow of English money[74]
which had dried up at Richard's death, and to have the English
influence work again for him, particularly in view of the indifference,
nay alarming attitude, of some of Otto's Lower Rhenish partisans, the
archbishop of Cologne at their head.

The arbitration plan had failed with or without the pope's interference. Otto had only just escaped the catastrophe. But he was lost
all the same, if Innocent did not now intercede publicly for him;
meanwhile he had accepted all the pope's demands[75] and after that
had formally, presumably in a privilege sealed with his golden bull,[76]
recognized the recuperations and renounced the pursuit of an independent Italian policy.[77]

At the turn of 1200/1201 the momentous decision arrives. In the
consistory before the cardinals Innocent once more ventilates the
arguments for and against the pretenders, among them Frederick of
Sicily, arguments which he had been labouring to reason out in the
preceding years. Innocent spares himself nothing, not even the statement that it befitted the Apostolic See to recognize Philip, since
thereby peace could easily be restored in Germany and since it was,
indeed, the pope's task to work for peace. The pope's arguments are
strong and impressive as long as they center on Philip's and young
Frederick's rights, but they are weak and unsatisfactory when in
conclusion he declares that Otto alone is suitable. A legate is to work
upon the electors so that they themselves agree upon a suitable
person or confide themselves to the pope's arbitration. If the princes
do not make up their mind to follow either course, Innocent will
recognize Otto on his own authority and call on him to come to Rome
to receive the imperial crown.[78]

This last attempt on the pope's part to bring the princes to agree of
their own free will to Otto or to another throne aspirant agreeable to
him and thus to escape the hated necessity of deciding independently
in Otto's favour, did not come to pass. On his arrival in Germany the
legate Guido, cardinal bishop of Palestrina, comes to the conclusion
that Otto's recognition can no longer be delayed.[79] After Otto in the
Privilege of Neuss of 8 June 1201[80] had renewed his promise of the
preceding year and, in addition, had committed himself to conclude

peace and to come to an understanding with France in conformity
with the pope's wishes, the cardinal, at an assembly of the princes
convened by him in Cologne on 3 July which but few attended, at
once proceeds to publish the papal letter in which Innocent "by virtue
of the authority of Almighty God transferred to him by St Peter"
accepts Otto as king and orders that as such he be henceforth shown
reverence and obedience.[81]

Innocent thus requires by virtue of the authority of Almighty God
transferred to him by St Peter that his vote be decisive in the dispute
as regards the person to be considered legitimate king. There is only
*one* basis on which such a claim would be solidly founded, the
doctrine of the axiomatic subordination of the temporal to the spiritual power,[82] a view, though, which was in contradiction to Innocent's
own conviction of the interrelation of both powers. He had so far
only asserted and substantiated a right to concern himself with the
throne contest and under certain conditions to take sides.[83] When in
1200 on the occasion of Aegidius's mission he insists that the imperial
princes agree upon a candidate whom he could and must crown and
break with the candidate on whom because of obvious impediments
he could not bestow the apostolic favour, this duty is at that time,
indeed, posed as a moral one only. The consequence of acting to the
contrary is for Innocent not the invalidity of what is enacted, but the
offence taken by Rome and Italy, the conflict with the Church, and
the disaster for the Holy Land which would result from such a
course.[84] But now, quite unexpectedly and without any substantiation,[85] the pope's decision is vested with divine authority and with
binding force on all citizens of the Empire. By what right?

The Bamberg-Hall Protest of the Staufen princes compelled Innocent to answer this question. In their proclamation the princes
repudiate the pope's intervention in the election of the Roman king as
being unprecedented so far. How could the pope be allowed to claim
a right which he had never had, the less so as the emperors from piety
had renounced their legitimate rights to participating in the elections
of the popes? There was, they continue, no competence superior to
the princes as regards the election of the king. Also, a schism could
only be composed by their very own free will.[86]

In his reply to the princes' protest[87] Innocent bluntly ascribes to
the Apostolic See a right to reprobate an elected king and emperor
who in the light of the Church is unsuitable, with the consequence
that he also forfeits the right to the Roman kingship. The pope bases

this right on the general principle that he who has to effect the imposition of hands also has to examine the person to be consecrated. If this right was contested, he continues, the monstrous consequence would be that he could be compelled to anoint and to crown a sacrilegist, heathen, heretic, excommunicate, tyrant, or lunatic. In his reply Innocent further substantiates a conditional papal right to decide in the case of a double election. Who was to hinder the pope, after he had exhorted the parties to come to an agreement and had waited for concord to be established, from favouring one of the parties, above all since both parties demanded from him to be anointed and crowned? Should, indeed, the Apostolic See, which could not dispense with its defender, be punished for the princes' fault? The argumentation is telling and seems to have impressed the Staufen legation. With satisfaction Innocent states that it had recognized the papal right of examination. But the argumentation is sophistical all the same. It is true that the pope could not be hindered from informing himself as to the personal qualification of the man he was to crown and, when occasion arose, from refusing to anoint him. But it did not follow from this that the rejected candidate could not be German king and that the pope could release people from the oaths sworn to him as king. And so it is that Innocent himself does not advance his inference in the context of the substantiation of his right of reprobation, but that it appears quite unexpectedly at the conclusion of his argumentation. The mental bridge between the right to simply refuse the coronation of the emperor, which results from the consecrator's right of examination, and the right of reprobation, which Innocent claims on top of it, seems to be the consideration that the Apostolic See could not dispense with its defender. Since the right to the imperial crown was vested in the German king, this king, Innocent may have inferred, must be so qualified as to put no impediment in the way of his being crowned by the pope as emperor, that is his being accepted as the Church's advocate. But this inference, too, would not be conclusive. Indeed, a German king whose coronation as emperor was barred by impediments could, in the first place, only be challenged by the pope to eliminate these impediments if possible; he could for instance demand from Philip to have his excommunication lifted and to atone for the alleged breach of oath and for the offences committed against the Church. Only if this was refused or if the impediment could not be eliminated, did the pope have a right definitely to refuse the coronation. Neither did the arguments that the Roman Church could not dispense with its advocate and that the German king, the only legitimate expectant of the imperial crown, was permanently incapable, authorize the pope to deprive the king of his rights. They would only have entitled him to feel himself no longer bound to the exclusive expectancy of the German king to the emperorship and to look for another protector. After all, even in Innocent's own views of the translation of the *imperium*, the German kingship was not an annex of the German emperorship, but rather the emperorship an annex of the German kingship. It could not by right be forbidden to the pope any more than to the kings of England and France, to take sides in the throne contest, though for him such a course was far more dubious unless it was in favour of the obviously better legitimated claimant. But in Innocent's reasoning the simple taking sides is unobtrusively superseded by the authoritarian decision. Innocent's keen mind was surely aware of the weakness of his argumentation, but he saw himself obliged to advocate rights to which he had recourse from necessity only and which he wished to formulate as unobtrusively as possible. He could not help resorting to sophisms, because he could not bring himself to assert sovereign rights over the German kingdom nor over the temporal power, and because he could not admit that he had taken a political decision instead of deciding according to law.[88]

Under the pressure of politics Innocent had widely deviated from the path of truth and justice along which he was called to be the leader. A still deeper enmeshment in trouble and guilt was in store for him if he set out, or had to set out, to enforce his authoritative decision and to bring his prestige and the authority of his office, particularly his means of ecclesiastical punishment, to bear for Otto's cause.

With entreaties, admonitions and promises, with threats and punishments, and with the use of all political practices conceivable, Innocent in the ensuing years toils for Otto's cause in and outside of Germany. He strengthens the slackened relationship between the Welf and Duke Henry of Brabant by granting dispensation for Otto's marriage to Henry's daughter.[89] He threatens John of Trier with ban and deposition unless, pursuant to his oath, he recognizes Otto,[90] he gets the reluctant Adolf of Cologne to stick to Otto for another three years,[91] he brings effective pressure to bear on Ottokar of Bohemia by refusing to recognize the royal dignity conferred on him by Philip and at the same time allures him by holding out the prospect of the hereditary crown.[92] The zupans of Bohemia he animates by amiable thanks and friendly acknowledgements to further exertions for Otto's cause.[93] He tries to have the Lombards promise to support his protégé, probably in the event of his journey to Rome[94] which was to wipe out the blemish of anti-kingship lying on Otto's rule. He manages to have the Hungarians, his very close friends, send auxiliary troops.[95] He declares void the oath which forbade King John of England to support the Welf nephew,[96] he mediates an alliance between John and Otto, negotiates, too, by the hands of his legate, an alliance between Waldemar of Denmark and the Welf,[97] offers Philip Augustus of France to stand security for Otto,[98] and is unrelenting in his efforts towards establishing peace between France and the Anglo-Welf allies.

In his fight for Otto and for the maintenance of his own achievements in Italy Innocent did many a thing which his conscience must have condemned, but not all means were good to him: he was not prepared to pay any price for political advantage. When his legate in France, realizing that there were no political concessions for the Capetian to counterbalance the danger of a Welf kingship, sought to find a way for concessions in the king's personal sphere, in the matter of his marriage that is, the pope leaves both the king and the legate in no doubt that in the divorce suit he would not tolerate fraud and foul play.[99]

Innocent personally exercised reserve in the use of ecclesiastical punitive measures. He never ratified the general excommunication sentence which his legate had passed against Otto's adversaries. He was, as was his legate, far from regarding every partisan of the Staufen as excommunicate. Philip was not excommunicated by name, the territories under his sovereignty or his immediate rule were not laid under interdict. Innocent contents himself with challenging the legal validity of Philip's absolution effected years ago by the bishop of Sutri, and including him in the ban to which all the helpers of Markward were to be liable.[100] In the case of lay princes Innocent does not go beyond threats of excommunication which, besides, only take concrete shape when he has a special reason for intervention, as in the case of breach of oath and of contract.[101] As regards the spiritual princes, only one of them, Adolf of Cologne, met with ban and deposition after his defection from Otto. The legate excommunicated several bishops,[102] among them one, John of Trier, on the pope's special order.[103] It is striking how Innocent gives those

excommunicated bishops, who do not yield to pressure, ever and
again a chance to evade the consequences of their persevering in the
state of excommunication.[104]

Did Innocent shrink from a radical rupture with Philip? He surely
considered the possibility of being forced to make peace with his
opponent. Such a thought may have encouraged him to observe
reserve. But Innocent was not the kind of man to make only part-use
of his weapons, thinking of a possible defeat. He followed the
dictates of prudence, when he did not proceed against all the Staufen
bishops at a time and in the same way, when he molested but little the
bishops within the Staufen sphere of influence, when in Trier he
prevented the resignation of an undecided partisan of Philip,[105] and
when he was even prepared to tolerate in Worms a decided Staufen
partisan, provided that he renounced the important see of Mainz.[106]
But shrewd calculation is not the only reason for his treating Philip
with consideration. What in the end will have hindered Innocent from
fighting against Philip and his partisans in the same way as he later
fought against Otto and the Welf partisans, was his being aware that
in his fight against Philip's kingship, though it was for the sake of a
vital interest of the papacy, he did not stand on the side of law and
that he misused his means of spiritual power to enforce the defection
from the cause of law which was also the cause of peace. It is
significant that only in the case of Adolf of Cologne did full and
ultimate seriousness stand behind a measure taken by the pope
against a Staufen partisan. Adolf was the creator of Otto's kingship
and had pursued his recognition with Innocent. No sooner had it been
granted and Innocent moved heaven and earth to lead Otto to victory,
than Adolf began to beat a retreat and in the end, by his defection,
brought to pass Otto's catastrophe. There were in this case no
scruples of a moral kind to weaken the arm of the avenger when he
punished the oath-breaker. John of Trier, too, the other of the
ecclesiastical princes excommunicated by Innocent's order, had forfeited, by evil machinations at the beginning of the throne contest,[107] a
good part of his right to complain about restraint of conscience. In
other respects, too, Innocent is visibly reluctant to take ecclesiastical
measures or decisions in connection with the throne contest from a
politically influenced point of view. The reproach, therefore, is incomprehensible that it had become a custom at the Curia to refuse
bishops their confirmation as long as they sided with Philip, or that
any suit pending at the Curia was inevitably lost for a bishop who had

resisted an obligation in the imperial cause being extracted from him, and that this obligation always had been the precondition for the removal of canonical impediments which with ill-will could have been found in every election.[108] In 1203 Innocent sanctions as many as three postulations of partisans of Philip without expecting them to go over to Otto,[109] and Wolfger of Passau is allowed the transition to the patriarchical see of Aquileia without having to purchase this indulgence with defection from Philip.[110] The Liège election dispute was not decided for Innocent simply because one of the candidates, Hugh of Pierrepont, had accepted the *regalia* from Otto and the other, Henry of Jacea, enjoyed Philip's favour. As late as October 1201 Innocent reproves his legate for not executing a papal mandate against the Welf elect.[111] Guido, who seems to have been more an opportunist than Innocent wished,[112] wanted to secure this bishopric whose *temporalia* were held by the powerful Hugh, powerful also for the backing he received from his relatives, to the Welf cause at all costs. That in the end Innocent still left it to the legate to take the final decision,[113] shows that with him too political considerations turned the scale. The same may apply to the papal sanction of the legate's decision in the Mainz election dispute. The rejection, though, of Lupold, the Staufen candidate, who had changed over from Worms to Mainz on his own authority, naturally was unassailable. Innocent would have decided exactly in the same way, notwithstanding any political consideration whatever. But Siegfried of Eppenstein too, the Welf partisan, is hardly likely to have been rightfully elected.[114] At any rate, the Liège and Mainz cases show that Innocent did not decide easily and without further considerations on violating the law, not even for high-political reasons.[115] However little the pressure he brought to bear upon the German episcopate for the sake of his political objectives is justifiable,[116] and however little his imperial policy can at all hold its ground before the tribunal of law and thus of morality, a scrupulous policy[117] in the proper sense of the word he did not pursue and surely also was unable to pursue, since the principles of law and morality were alive in him and since his keen mind did not allow him to regard as always being justified morally what is indispensable politically.

Without excessive hopes Innocent watched the progress which Otto's cause made at first, thanks to the pope's intervention and to a series of happy circumstances.[118] Neither was he to be deceived by the surprisingly favourable development of affairs in the latter half of

1209 about the frailty of Otto's position who, unlike Philip, could not rely on his own forces and was thrown back upon the doubtful loyality of his adherents.[119] Innocent knew what it meant when he had to admonish the archbishop of Cologne and the duke of Brabant not to forsake Otto in the moment of triumph.[120] He seems to have then been thinking of inviting Otto, in case he should arrive at a decisive success, to come at once to Rome to be crowned emperor.[121] To all appearances, the imperial crown was to safeguard the legitimacy of Otto's rulership against any objection and to guarantee him the incontestable precedence over Philip. Innocent may have been prepared to accept the risks of Otto's absence from Germany, where he had to leave behind a scarcely completely overcome opponent, because he regarded a bold deed as being the only chance for Otto to maintain his ground lastingly.

The change for the worse, the possibility of which Innocent never lost sight of, the collapse of the Welf faction on the threshold of success, came to pass. The 'Job's news' of 1204, namely the outbreak of the Dutch war of succession which deprived Otto of his support from the Netherlands, Otto's brother's, the count palatine's, going over to Philip, the landgrave of Thuringia's subjection to the Staufen, the defection of the king of Bohemia, of the archbishop of Cologne, of the duke of Brabant and of most of the Lotharingian nobles, all these were forebodings of the imminent failure of the Welf cause.

The question whether Innocent's calculations were erroneous must be answered in the negative. Otto's recognition and the fight for his kingship were for the pope the only possible ways out of an extremely difficult situation. Innocent took the decision while fully aware of its dangers. The prospect of success depended on the degree to which his influence on the German princes, particularly on the ecclesiastical princes, would be effective. The influence proved to be great, but not decisive. The Staufen episcopate had been alarmed, partly paralysed in its strength, but had remained loyal to Philip with the exception of some few bishops who had been compelled by force of arms to submit themselves to the Welf. The bearing of the Welf princes too showed Innocent both the weight and the limits of his authority. The fear of the spiritual sovereign, though, made Adolf of Cologne stick to Otto's cause for three years, but in the fourth year it could as little prevent his going over to the Staufen as the defection of the Westphalian bishops in 1205. Innocent from the outset will have taken into account that in a purely temporal matter means of spiritual coercion would in the long run fail.

The question now was whether the pope's cause stood and fell with the Welf's cause, whether Otto's catastrophe was decisive for the break-down of the papal security policy. Innocent saw himself again faced with a situation which in 1201 he had warded off at the last moment by recognizing Otto: before long an uncontested representative of the Empire would be standing before him, with whom he had failed to arrive at an agreement on their mutual rights in the peninsula. Philip, indeed, showed himself determined to reclaim at once by force of arms the imperial rights in Italy and Sicily.[122] After his decisive success he sent the banned and deposed Staufen elect of Mainz, Lupold of Worms, who in the pope's despite held his ground in both bishoprics, across the Alps with an army in order to reconquer the territories lost to the Church and to put an end to the pope's Sicilian regency. In October 1204 at the latest the imperial legate arrived in the March of Ancona or his assault was imminent. Was the papal position in the Sicilian kingdom strong enough to bear up against the assault?

Conditions on the island and in the mainland parts of the kingdom had remained critical since 1199.[123] As long as the island itself was not threatened, the government in Palermo, the council of *familiares*, left it entirely to the pope to organize the fight against Markward. Owing perhaps to pecuniary difficulties it did not even place at the pope's disposal the means for the defence of the kingdom[124] which he could claim under the terms of the empress's last will.[125] In vain Innocent remonstrated with the *familiaries* that it would be better to spend once only a sufficient sum of money than to lose successively spent insufficient sums.[126] He himself did what lay in his power, he opened his treasury, raised loans, enlisted troops and had his money work also amongst the enemies.[127]

The results at first were poor, although Innocent in the person of his cousin, Marshal James, disposed of an efficient commander to confront the German forces in the kingdom. A second, even more efficient military leader he obtained in the person of Count Walter of Brienne, the husband of King Tancred's daughter.[128] After mature deliberation Innocent accepted the count's offer – he also held out the prospect of supplying a considerable contingent of his own troops – and at the same time recognized the count's claim to Taranto and Lecce which Henry VI had promised to Tancred's unfortunate son William and to William's heirs.[129] Innocent felt obliged to venture on the policy, dangerous in itself, of restoring the sovereign rights of Tancred's family since the defence of the kingdom overstrained his

own powers. He also thought that he might take this risk since he felt
he could so force the count's hand that he was no longer a menace to
the young king.[130]

Although the pope's association with Walter of Brienne resulted in
an alliance between Markward and the leading figures in the Sicilian
central government and in creating new adversaries to the papal
policy also on the mainland, the situation in Apulia in the ensuing
years fundamentally improved in the pope's favour. On the island
Innocent in 1202 was rid of his most dangerous enemy by Markward's
death, who on 1 November 1201 had taken hold of Palermo and of the
person of the young king. After then the college of *familiares* sought
to regain the pope's favour with unprecedented eagerness. Moreover,
in the days preceding the imperial legate's arrival William Capparone,
the German who held the young king in custody, committed himself
to obedience to the pope as the regent of the kingdom.[131] When the
imperial legate set out on campaign and perhaps had already crossed
the Sicilian frontier,[132] the pope was thus recognized as Frederick's
guardian and as regent of the kingdom by the king's custodian as well
as by the *familiares* and the greater part of the mainland. Wrestling
with no end of difficulties,[133] Innocent had brought about relatively
favourable conditions in the Sicilian kingdom for the confrontation
with the imperial power, though the utter unreliability of the Sicilian
people and of the nobility in particular left open the possibility of
matters taking an unexpected turn.[134]

How much these achievements were Innocent's personal work is
shown by an event which happened in autumn 1203 during a serious
illness of the pope. While Marshal James and Walter of Brienne, the
lord of Taranto and Lecce, as well as the justiciaries appointed by the
pope for Apulia and the Terra di Lavoro, are staying at the pope's
sick-bed in Anagni, the bogus news of his death spreads throughout
the territories under their rule. A number of cities at once revolt
against the unpopular foreigners. When the news turns out to be
wrong, they do not, though, submit themselves again to the counts'
rule nor do they by any means resort to the pope's German enemies
for support, but at once take the oath to the pope's guardianship.[135]
The papal regency had struck roots in the country which it would not
be easy to remove.

In the part of the Patrimony to be first threatened by a German
attack, in the March, the Empire still had many partisans.[136] Since the
Apostolic See disposed of no means of power of its own here the defen-

sive strength of the country was entirely dependent on the possibilities and on the goodwill of the papally-minded communes. In these circumstances it could be called an extraordinary piece of good luck that Innocent's lasting and thorny efforts to establish peace between the pro-papal cities which fiercely fought against each other,[137] had resulted in January 1202 in an apparently lasting peace.[138] In Roman Tuscany and in the duchy of Spoleto the papal position had gained in strength. Since the spring of 1199 Innocent had energetically and successfully been trying to re-establish security, law and peace, to arrange for defence,[139] and to bring his prestige to bear also on the more powerful communes, such as Orvieto, Narni and Viterbo.[140] The way to Rome he had, as far as possible, covered towards the north by fortifying the anyhow strong citadels of Montefiascone and Radico-fani.

For Innocent the situation in Rome was of greater moment than the conditions in any other part of the Patrimony. At the time of his accession to the papal throne the city was practically independent of the papal administrator. Just as the Lombard cities and other Italian communes had become the masters in the districts they governed outside the city walls (*comitatus*), so the city of Rome had seized upon the Sabina and Marittima.[141] By cleverly putting to use the contentedness the townspeople felt with the rich money presents they received after his consecration, Innocent succeeded in re-establishing the pope's authority as territorial sovereign in the city and its out-skirts. He first brought the senator to swear him the oath of allegiance and then managed to have a new senator appointed by the hands of a middle man appointed by himself, a so-called *medianus*.[142] He took over again the administration in Sabina and Marittima. At the same time he liquidated the imperial sovereignty in Rome by re-investing the city-prefect, who, contrary to the terms of the peace settlement of Venice of 1177, had held his office as an imperial fief, with the prefecture and by binding him to the papal sovereign by way of a detailed oath. Innocent had put off the distribution of the angrily claimed election presents until after his consecration[143] and had delayed this act for more than a month and a half, probably until the preparations for the overthrow of the independent city regime were completed.

Rome was left with a grumbling civic opposition which did its best to agitate against Innocent.[144] Its day of reckoning came when in September 1202, during a summer sojourn of the Curia at Velletri, the

enmity between the Scotti, Innocent's maternal relations, and the
Boboni changed into open feud. Innocent hurried back to Rome and
tried to quench the flames, but the death of a Boboni by the hand of
a Scotti frustrated his promising efforts. The houses of the Scotti
were stormed.[145] The Poli, a run-down noble family whose encumbered estates had come into the hands of Innocent's brother Richard
of Segni by way of a marriage agreement, added fuel to the excite-
ment. They pretended that the pope's brother had defrauded them of
their heritage, they marched demonstratively through the city in
pitiful attire, and they transferred their claims to the Roman commune. The commune demanded from Richard the surrender of the
Poli estates, though Innocent as feudal lord alone was competent in
this question of law, though he offered to do the Poli justice before
his own court, and though he even declared himself prepared to bear
the legal costs.[146] A similar trick played by the opposition once
already had gone wrong: its leaders had had themselves mortgaged
contested estates by noblemen who, like the Poli, disdained to take
their law from Innocent. The pope, then, had not shirked from the
test of strength. After their crops had been ravaged, their fruit-trees
felled, their mills broken and their movables carried away, the
noblemen found themselves forced to surrender the estates and to
revoke the mortgage-contracts.[147] Innocent had won the townspeople
over to his side by clearing himself, in a public address to them, of the
reproach that he intended to deprive the people of Rome of their
rights and liberties. In the case, though, of the Poli, and the parallel
case of the Abaiamonti, it was easier to cast suspicion on the pope's
intentions. The Abaiamonti were under the ban because in the lawsuit
of one of the pope's relatives they had refused to accept the pope as
judge despite the many securities they were offered.[148] No great skill
was necessary to dress up these happenings for the purposes of the
opposition.[149] With the pope's tacit consent, let alone his secret
collaboration, thus their spokemen's inflammatory talk will have run,
his relatives commit acts of violence and murder, shamelessly enrich
themselves with other people's goods and insolently disregard the
rights of the people of Rome.

On Easter Monday 7 April 1203 the solemn pontifical high mass
was disturbed by blasphemous interjections and Innocent, as he
returned to the Lateran in the traditional ceremonial procession, was
grossly insulted and threatened by the mob. With unruffled countenance and showing no sign of fear or commotion he continued his
way, because, as the contempory biographer tells us, his conscience

was clear and peaceful.[150] After the senator devoted to him had been banished from the city, the pope in the first days of May left Rome to her own doings.[151] Not until March 1204 did he return, greeted by the populace with cheers of welcome, after the city, tired of the continual disorders and the financial loss due to the absence of the Curia, had repeatedly implored him formally and urgently to return home. Now, Innocent is clever enough to have Gregory Pierleone Raynerii, a popular figure with the townspeople and, as it seems, a near relative of one of the leaders of the opposition, appointed senator by the hand of a *medianus* who was not even suspect to the opposition.[152] When the radicals after all constitute an anti-senate headed by John Capocci, a new struggle arises which dangerously links up with the imperial cause or is connected with it from the start.[153] Innocent faced the storm. Without regard for his health which was always threatened by the summer heat and against his wont he spends the summer in Rome and during the critical days of fighting far into September resides in the poorly protected Lateran. In June he issues an order in favour of his relative Johannes Oddonis for the transfer of possession in regard of the estates of the Abaiamonti claimed by him[154] and on 9 October he transfers in due form the fiefs held by the Poli to his brother until he is compensated for the damage he had suffered and the costs he had incurred.[155] The passage at arms he left to his brother Richard, to the ex-senator Pandulf and to his brother-in-law Peter Annibaldi. His adversaries lamented that the pope's money was working against them.[156] Innocent certainly did not spare his own money as long as the victorious Staufen's money was working in Rome.[157] Only after his success was beyond doubt, did he cleverly and conciliatingly show himself accommodating to his adversaries in the questions of the appointments to the senate and of the estates of the Poli. Innocent's prestige was more firmly established than ever, and, as his biographer writes, there was no more need for him constantly to buy himself free from his adversaries.[158] Henceforth he could vigorously bring to bear his sovereign rights in Rome.[159] Conditions no longer were such as Gerald of Wales remembers them when, apparently during the English church contest, he mockingly remarked that it was indeed queer that the pope by the very same words, with which he moved sceptres outside Rome, did not impress the most lowly inside, and that someone, who in Rome could not even recover a wrongfully alienated garden, intended to subject kingdoms to his will.[160]

Innocent could now confidently face the imperial legate's arrival.

His position in Rome and in the Patrimony as well as in the Sicilian kingdom could not easily be overrun. Lupold's despatch he must regard as a precipitate measure dangerous to the Staufen cause. Philip was totally unable to send an army across the Alps which would offer sufficient guarantee for obtaining its objective. Yet, if the expedition failed, this would strengthen his, the pope's, position in central Italy and Sicily, and weaken Philip's own position in the forthcoming peace negotiations.

It became in fact evident that Philip, unlike the pope, had no grasp of the high art of waiting for the right moment. After some minor initial successes the imperial legate was decisively defeated in the March of Ancona by an army of papal vassals under the command of Cardinal Cinthius. The vast majority of the communes and vassals in the Patrimony had stuck by the papal sovereign.[161] With his own forces Innocent had warded off the assault of the Empire.

In Germany Innocent continues to champion the Welf cause,[162] not because he wishes to hold onto Otto at all costs, but because the issue of the negotiations with Philip, which had begun in spring 1205 at the latest, is still uncertain. In spring 1206 the pope is engaged in the last effort for Otto's kingship. He apparently fosters the bold idea of having Otto come to Rome for his coronation as emperor in spite of, or rather because of, his desperate situation. England was to support the enterprise financially.[163] Since by crowning Otto as emperor Innocent would have linked his cause indissolubly with the Welf cause, the plan may have been conceived only as a last resort in case negotiations with Philip should again come to nothing.

It seems to have been Philip who opened the peace negotiations. Ever since Otto's recognition by the pope the Staufen had repeatedly tried to make his peace with Innocent,[164] and the pope, realistically sizing up Otto's position, had felt it useful at least to lend Philip an ear. In summer 1207 negotiations had progressed so far that Innocent could absolve the Staufen and order his legate to set out to bring about Otto's resignation.[165]

The official tradition leaves aside the questions of the basis on which the peace was settled and whether the restitution of the former imperial territories gave this peace the stamp of a papal defeat. But the facts available intimate that Innocent upheld what he had achieved in central Italy and in Sicily, that Philip either explicitly or tacitly renounced the reclamation of the duchy of Spoleto, the March of Ancona and, naturally, Roman Tuscany, and that he further waived

the guardianship over Frederick of Sicily and the imperial claims to
the kingdom.[166] What could bring Philip to give up as victor what, as
the general opinion goes, he had firmly held during the struggle? The
term 'victor' is equivocal in this connection. Philip was victor only
over Otto, not over Innocent. In his struggle, which was fought for
the Papal State and Sicily, not for Otto's kingship, Innocent had,
though, suffered a grave defeat on German soil, but he had by no
means lost the war as such. The pope's position in Italy was not
shaken, as is proved by the outcome of Lupold's expedition. Innocent
still had in reserve his strongest weapons. It rested with him to
unleash a fight of quite different dimensions, if Philip, after an
ultimate failure of the peace negotiations, personally took up arms
against the Apostolic See by an inroad on the Patrimony and on
Sicily. In such a case Innocent in all probability would not have been
short of allies in imperial Italy.[167] Moreover, Innocent could refuse the
imperial crown even to a king who was victorious in Italy. No power
on earth could force the coronation out of the pope. But in Germany,
too, peace would hardly have been achieved, let alone secured,
without the pope's reconciliation with Philip. A Welf kingship, which
the pope had recognized and which was supported by English money
and Danish arms, could not be eliminated by force, unless the lucky
chance was assumed of capturing Otto who, however, could always
escape to Danish soil. The Danish king, who owed to the throne
contest the possession of the Northalbingian territories, was doubtless willing to prevent the ultimate abolition of the Welf kingship.
Already at the beginning of 1207 he had garrisoned troops in Brunswick and had ordered Otto to be escorted to England by way of
Denmark. Bishop Waldemar of Schleswig's postulation in Bremen
shortly before Christmas 1207 threatened to lead to an embittered
fight for the archbishopric between King Waldemar, the postulated
archbishop's cousin and arch-enemy, and Philip of Swabia, his protector. But King John of England, after the conclusion of a two years'
truce with France in October 1206, took up the cudgels for his
German nephew with greater energy than before. Since at that time or
a little later there was also disagreement within the princely circles,
the dispute on the archbishopric could easily have become the signal
for the formation of a new English-Danish-Welf coalition.[168] Otto's
recognition by papal authority also provided the legitimate pretext at
any time for a defection from Philip. On the other hand, Innocent
offered the Staufen, as compensation for the peace, his help in the

attempt to bring Otto to renounce his claims, an issue in which Innocent took a lively interest, since only Otto's resignation of his own free will would have allowed him to recognize the Staufen without seriously damaging his honour.

A last trump card for Innocent to play in the negotiations, besides the general longing for peace in Germany, was the particular interest which the spiritual princes took in Philip's reconciliation with the pope. Innocent's authority, though, had not proved powerful enough to force the German episcopate to side with Otto. But still it had become evident that the bishops felt themselves to be very strongly tied to the pope. Even those bishops who had sided with Philip in general obeyed Innocent's summons, submitted themselves to his censures, if he left them no other way out, and obeyed his orders – barring the one order which obliged them actually to go over to Otto, but which Innocent was clever enough not to direct too often to a particular bishop personally.[169] From some of the bishops, in general those who, on the occasion of the receipt of the pallium or of their consecration at the Curia, had come to take the normal oaths of allegiance and obedience, Innocent held written declarations in which the signatories acknowledged that, in view of the oaths previously taken, they were obliged to follow the pope's directions in the imperial cause.[170] Two archbishops, Everard of Salzburg and John of Trier, had explicitly committed themselves to recognize Otto. Innocent could not bring, and in general did not even try to force, any of these men actually to go over to Otto. But these ties and declarations gave him the means to put pressure on a number of the most influential princes which was still effective when he could no more even think of enforcing accessions to Otto.[171] At any time it lay in his hands to land these men in a position which exposed them to the charge of, and to the penalty for, breach of oath. Even if their consciences absolved them, in that they regarded an order to disloyalty to Philip as being against conscience and therefore not binding, they would still have had to bear the external consequences of suspension and excommunication. It was important for the pope that, at the time of the peace negotiations, a number of prominent members of the episcopate were particularly interested in their successful progress. Wolfger of Aquileia, Everard of Salzburg and Albert of Magdeburg, three of those bound by their written or explicit declarations, went all out for peace between the Church and the Empire. They, as well as the other spiritual princes, could only escape from the dilemma which tormented them if their spiritual and temporal overlords became reconciled. It is, indeed, now, at the end of the throne contest, that the influence really bore fruit which the pope had exerted on the German episcopate whilst it was going on.

Philip had never been wholly uncompromising as regards the territorial questions of central Italy.[172] The Sicilian question had had a decisive share in the failure of the previous negotiations, but meanwhile it had lost much of its relevance. The course of time had worked for Innocent in this respect. It was no longer worthwhile to quarrel about the guardianship over the king. But with regard to the feudal sovereignty in Sicily and to even further-reaching claims Philip soon would have had to come to grips not only with the pope, but also with his own nephew. Conditions were again as they had been prior to Henry VI's conquest of the kingdom. If Philip was really determined to give up, for his own person and as the representative of the Empire, the luckless policy of conquest in southern Italy, the recuperated territories would lose their former relevance for the Empire. They were only indispensable as the connecting bridge between the Empire and a Sicily which was either linked up with the Empire by personal union or dependent on it as a vassal state. Otherwise the loss of two not exceedingly valuable provinces like the March of Ancona and the duchy of Spoleto could be accepted. But to the Tuscan recuperation the Church had an uncontestable right recognized right up to the times of Frederick Barbarossa. The losses suffered by the Empire would have been counterbalanced if, in the extended complex of northern Italian territories which remained to the Empire, it had been able to bring energetically to bear its right of sovereignty and possession without being hampered by the obstacles and set-backs constantly resulting from the conflicts with the papacy. The Lombard cities, which opposed a strong imperial authority and which were continually at variance with their clergy, which often manifested tolerance to heretics and sometimes even supported heresy, these cities would certainly not have had the possibility of relying in future on the sympathy of the Curia whenever they came into conflict with the emperors. In Germany a more or less lasting peace between the Church and the Empire would have removed one of the causes which ever and again led to weakening the king's power. Considerations of this kind cannot have been alien to Philip, who already in the first years of his kingship, like his predecessor, had striven for a peace with the Church which, by resolving all points at issue, guaranteed that it would last.[173]

It is likely that in the peace settlement the pope, too, made essential concessions which went beyond abandoning the Welf anti-kingship. He probably renounced the Matildine estates in favour of the Empire,[174] territories on which, prior to the collapse of imperial rule in Italy up to Henry VI's death, since the Peace of Constance,[175] the imperial power in northern Italy was mainly based. In the peace settlement a marriage was stipulated between Innocent's nephew, Richard of Segni's son,[176] and one of King Philip's daughters. If the king's son-in-law had been vested by him with imperial Tuscany and the Matildine estates, he would have held Philip's former fiefs in Italy.[177] Innocent may further have renounced claims and isolated possessions in the Romagna, as for instance Ferrara, probably also the exarchate, or have been prepared to return part of the recuperated territories.

Innocent and the Staufen must have come to an agreement on the compensation to be given to the anti-king. Otto probably was to be given Philip's eldest daughter in marriage and thereby to receive the Burgundian heritage of the Staufen house as well as the dignity of king of Burgundy.[178] But it was no easy task for the pope to bring the stubborn Welf to renounce his kingship, all the less since the Bremen quarrels seemed to offer him a new chance.[179] Yet, in spring 1208 Otto's envoys at the Curia, too, agreed to the terms of peace. Nothing was wanting but the ratification by both kings.

Innocent had accomplished a tremendous work. Ever and again obstacles had blocked his path and his plans had come to nothing. But his diplomatic talent had always found new ways, his energy always provided for new means. Amidst endless difficulties he had established and consolidated his position in Italy and Sicily, at the same time basis and objective of his claims, and even in the most adverse circumstances he had stuck to his aim with unshakeable perseverance. Innocent could tell himself that the peace not only gave the Church what it needed for its security, but that the Empire too was given what was the Empire's, not in the sense of historically founded rights, but in view of its vital interests to which a lasting peace with the Church belonged in the first place.

Since the course of the negotiations gave a secure prospect of peace being settled, Innocent began to put in order conditions in the Papal State or, rather, actually to form a state out of the various possessions.

While a legation of cardinal-legates is on its way to the Staufen court, Innocent starts on a journey through the Tuscan part of the Patrimony,[180] on which among other places he visits Montefiascone, the former imperial fortress, which King Philip had held as duke of Tuscany and from which at the end of 1197 he had fled to Germany. At Montefiascone he brought the pro-imperial Count Palatine Aldobrandino, who had probably fought on the imperial legate's side,[181] to commit himself to render vassalian service for the county of Rosellae, for Montalto and for any other place which he held as fief from the Roman Church as evidenced by its privileges.[182] From Corneto, where he himself built a new palace and where he re-seizes rights alienated from the Roman Church, he congratulates Philip on his absolution.[183]

The most important event of the pope's journey was the great Court held at Viterbo, to which Innocent on 23 September 1207 convenes the counts, nobles, consuls and podestà from both the old and the newly acquired papal territories of the Patrimony.[184] Here Innocent fixed the sovereign rights which he claimed for the Apostolic See and bound the participants by oath to the organization he was about to establish. He further accepted complaints and petitions, promulgated a heresy statute, passed a constitution guaranteeing the clergy its immunity in all the communes, and ultimately promulgated a land peace which forbade any armed self-aid, including also the individual waging of war. The land peace statute commits everybody to assist the rector at his request in the prosecution of robbers and outlaws. Complaints of individuals or of the communes are also to be submitted to the rector. Anyone failing to comply with the rector's award is to be attacked as a public enemy. It is significant that Innocent passes the two former statutes simply by virtue of the papal authority, whereas he imposes the stipulations of the land peace upon those assembled by virtue of the oaths they had previously taken and by which they had committed themselves to carefully guard peace, justice and security according to the papal orders. In this case an innovation was involved, the abolition of the right of feud previously practised by communes and nobles, to which those affected had to give and had given in advance their assent in the form of a general commitment. With the promulgation of the land peace in the Patrimony Innocent had achieved what even the Staufen failed to bring about in Germany. The new Papal State and the papal rule had proved their vitality.[185]

Within a wider compass, but under adverse conditions similar to those which due to the utter unreliability of nobility and populace hampered the constructive work in the Patrimony, the pope's Sicilian regency made its way. In the kingdom too Innocent reaps the reward of endless labours about the time of, and partly owing to, the conclusion of peace with the Staufen. The negotiations with King Philip had proceeded so far as to leave the Germans in the kingdom no hope of support from beyond the Alps. In spring 1208 Innocent by force of arms and by negotiation succeeded in enforcing the surrender of the fortresses still held by Germans in the Sicilian districts bordering the Papal State.[186]

It is Innocent's plan in the last year of his regency to settle the last remnants of discord and to re-establish security and order. On 22 June he arrives at the border-fortress of San Germano, whither he had summoned the counts, barons and town representatives of the kingdom. A few days previously, in the monastery of Fossanova, Richard of Segni, the pope's brother, had been proclaimed count of Sora by a royal protonotary, in which capacity he controlled the cities and castles which, partly with his assistance, had been liberated in the previous battles.[187] By enfeoffing Richard the Sicilian government not only, more or less voluntarily, rendered thanks to the pope for the labours of a decade of regency in the most adverse circumstances, but also contributed to the conclusion of peace, in that by Richard's elevation in rank it provided more appropriate preconditions for the stipulated marriage between Richard's son and the daughter of the emperor to be.

Just as the Court assembly of Viterbo is the monument to the ending of the struggles for the Papal State, so the assembly of San Germano marks the conclusion of the wrestling for Sicily. Just as at Viterbo for the Papal State, so Innocent at San Germano promulgated, and had confirmed by oath, a land peace at first probably for the northern provinces of the kingdom, the Terra di Lavoro, and fixed detailed regulations for its execution. The assembly further assents to support the king, who on the island still had to fight against a last remnant of German troops under the command of William Capparone and against the rebellious Saracens. Two hundred knights are to be placed at his disposal for one year without costs.[188] One of Innocent's last actions as guardian is the confirmation of the young king's engagement to Constance of Aragon,[189] which he negotiated with difficulty, even against the reluctant bridegroom himself, and which held out the prospect to the king of armed support from the bride's knightly retinue.[190] Innocent had to give up continuing his journey to Apulia and to leave it to a cardinal legate to organize the land peace there, because the heat was too much for him[191] and because he received the shocking news from Germany of the murder of Philip of Swabia who at Bamberg on 21 June had fallen victim to an act of private revenge. It is symbolic that the death-news forced Innocent to renounce the idea of personally realizing his work of pacification in the kingdom. Owing to Philip's death everything that had been achieved so far was once again jeopardized. The fruits of the papal labours for the inner consolidation of the Patrimony as well as of the Sicilian vassal state were not to ripen so soon because of the events which followed Philip's death.

What may Innocent have felt when he received the news? For all his abhorrence of the deed, he yet regarded the ghastly event as a conspicuous confirmation of the decision he had taken in the throne contest.[192] At the very moment in which he himself reversed it, God had interfered. He was spared the humiliation of recognizing the man whom he had rejected, perhaps even the ignominy of rejecting the man whom he had recognized, since it seems by no means certain that Otto, who still at the beginning of 1208 had asked for and received support from the Danes, would have consented to the peace which his envoys in Rome had accepted. A satisfying agreement had been settled with Philip, but Otto had long ago acquiesced in far greater concessions. By deed and by oath[193] he was committed to return all the territories to which the Roman Church since Henry VI's death had laid claim, barring imperial Tuscany.

But was it certain that Otto would take Philip's place? Would not the Staufen faction hold a new election and was not a candidate at hand in the person of Frederick of Sicily who was just coming of age, the only surviving Staufen who appeared able to play the rôle of a pretender?[194] Innocent did not take chances. That not even five months after Philip's death the vast majority of the German princes declared themselves for Otto, the Welf owed to the pope's actions during this time and to the results of his actions in the years before.

Everybody knew that the person of the pope was an unsurmountable obstacle to the only rival candidature which could have been opposed to Otto with the prospect of a sweeping success, namely the candidature of Frederick of Sicily.[195] After the issue of the mandate to the German bishops to do their best to prevent a new election, and of the threat of anathema and deposition to anybody that would dare to anoint and crown anyone else than Otto,[196] neither Frederick nor a third throne pretender could have reckoned on being crowned.

It was extremely propitious for Otto that, thanks to Innocent, the archiepiscopal sees of Mainz and Cologne were filled with reliable Welf partisans. Innocent had sent Siegfried of Eppenstein and Bruno of Sayn, who were staying at the Curia when the death-news arrived, immediately to Germany in order that they might throw their pregnant word into the scale. To Bruno's deposed predecessor, the still powerful Adolf of Altena, he holds out the prospect of another bishopric, if by his attitude to Otto he proved himself worthy of the pope's favour.[197] Notwithstanding the altered conditions, he eagerly intercedes with Philip's widow and his marshal, Henry of Kalden, for the maintenance of the marriage stipulated between Otto and Philip's eldest daughter Beatrice,[198] since this marriage was essential for the Swabian nobles and the imperial *ministeriales* to reconcile themselves with a Welf kingship. The pope's will, which everybody was sure to know even before the respective mandates arrived in Germany, most strongly influenced the bishops's attitude from the first. Two Staufenminded bishops, Albert of Magdeburg and Conrad of Halberstadt, who had recognized a particular commitment to the pope in the imperial cause,[199] at once went over to Otto. Adolf of Altena for his part, even before the ultimate papal demand reached him, swore obedience to his own successor, Archbishop Bruno, and brought his powerful adherents to swear allegiance to Bruno.[200] The haste in which Adolf reacted[201] shows that he wanted to gain the pope's favour.

Already in November 1208 Otto is the uncontested ruler; already in August of the ensuing year Innocent can send envoys to meet him in Lombardy; in September the two come to stand face to face at Viterbo.

Innocent no longer looked forward to the meeting with glad feelings. The relationship between him and the Welf was already in difficulties. The first frictions had arisen on the question of the Matildine estates.[202] Otto intended to seize them for the Empire in spite of the Promise of Neuss,[203] which assigned them to the Church. Innocent may have appreciated that Otto was not prepared to sacrifice more imperial rights and claims than had the Staufen. But it was impossible for Otto simply to enter into the territorial stipulations contained in the peace treaty with Philip, since they were linked with the marriage agreement. Innocent had left it to the Welf to decide on the marriage of the Staufen princess to his nephew[204] and had then abandoned the plan at Otto's request. That his house was denied a spectacular rise of prestige, seems not to have carried all too much weight with Innocent. But since the expected position of power of the papal nephew did not materialize, the Roman Church had to do without a bulwark which, though only temporarily, still for the reigning pope's lifetime and thus for the important years of inner consolidation of the new territorial order in Italy, would have been of relevance.

In these days the Sicilian question, too, had threateningly arisen again. On 10 March Innocent had to warn the Welf that he, the pope, could not refuse to succour Frederick, his vassal, whom Otto pleased to call 'the boy' and 'Emperor Henry's son',[205] in the matters relating to the *kingdom*.[206]

Moreover, the position Otto took up towards France and England encumbered the relationship between Innocent and the Welf from the first. Innocent neither could nor would tolerate that the powers of the emperor and of the English king were merged with a view to over-throwing France. Otto had had to commit himself in the Promise of Neuss to make peace with the king of France according to the pope's counsel and direction. He was averse to this commitment because of his deep personal hatred for Philip Augustus of France and his close relations to the English royal house. Besides, in the relationship to his English uncle John lay the germ of a personal opposition to the pope. There is no doubt that Otto bore him a grudge for the harsh line of action the pope had taken against the king of England, whose land at that time lay under interdict and whose excommunication was imminent.

The pope's answer to Otto's request for coronation as emperor immediately after the princes' assembly at Frankfurt, already reveals that the atmosphere is strained. Although his letter is most warmly worded, Innocent shows he is displeased that Otto had not sent a legation of princes,[207] as was customary on such an occasion. Besides, he felt obliged to warn the king against those who aimed at sowing the seeds of discord between *regnum* and *sacerdotium* with a view to fishing in troubled waters themselves.[208] Innocent also thought it necessary to make sure, before fixing the date of the coronation, whether Otto stood by the obligations he had accepted as anti-king. Thereupon at Speyer on 22 March Otto in almost suspicious haste issued his second privilege for the Roman Church, which repeated all his territorial concessions and added new ones in ecclesiastical matters, but in which the obligations were omitted, which tied Otto's policy towards the Lombard and Tuscan Leagues as well as towards France and the Roman commune.[209] It is probable that this privilege was not regarded, even by the pope himself, as having settled the whole complex of territorial questions once and for all. The territorial provisions simply may have been taken over from the previous privilege because, the journey to Rome being imminent, there was not enough time left for negotiations on its revision.[210] Otto may have agreed to, or even have suggested, the provisional solution with the arrière pensée that it would be easier for him to evade his obligations if the forthcoming negotiations proved abortive. Was it a political miscalculation that Innocent allowed Otto to come to Rome before the questions pending between them were settled?

News had soon been received from imperial Italy which gave rise to concern. The imperial legate Wolfger of Aquileia, who was to prepare Otto's journey to Rome,[211] began to demand the Matildine estates for the Empire.[212] He also arrested, as it seems on Otto's orders, French crusaders, former subjects of King John,[213] and revoked concessions which, as Philip's legate, he had made to Siena the previous year, giving as reason that times had changed, since now there were no longer two rulers, but only one, Otto, who wore the crown.[214] On the other hand, Otto will have greeted with indignation Innocent's intercession for those cities of imperial Italy which had been harshly treated by the imperial legate, and his reminder to the king on this occasion that in Lombardy and in Tuscany the legation would scarcely have taken such a successful course without the support of the pope's recommendations.[215]

Whilst Otto was on his way to Rome negotiations had never ceased. Innocent seems to have demanded from Otto the renewal by oath, and this time by way of a solemn declaration in public, of the recognition of his obligations in connection with the coronation as emperor[216] as was stipulated in the Promise of Neuss; and already he reminds the king that, though Otto's devotion was indispensable for the pope, the pope's affection was also very useful to Otto.[217]

If Innocent had still hoped to gain influence over the king by way of personal contact, he was in for a disappointment. This unwise prince, who like his uncle Richard of England was not troubled by any sense of responsibility, but instead was all the more eager for battle and conquests, knew of no limits to his will to power since his successes in Germany and Italy. He was not even able to realize the implications which were involved for him in a fight with a pope like Innocent. He saw only the brutal superiority of external power, which was on his side. The only lesson which the throne conflict had brought home to him seems to have been that his adversary Philip had been victorious though Innocent was opposed to him, rather than the fact that Innocent had attained his objectives in spite of Philip's victory. At the meeting of Viterbo[218] Otto in rude words refused to become reconciled with Philip of France and gave to understand that at least the first Privilege of 1201 was but a scrap of paper for him.[219] He refused to renew his oath of renunciation of the former imperial possessions sworn on the occasion of his coronation as emperor, arguing that it was against his honour, if he appeared to be acting under duress.[220] What was Innocent to do? It was impossible for him to refuse altogether to crown the man whom all the world regarded as his protégé, nay as his creation, and who now was standing at the gates of Rome in a menacing concentration of power; he could not even postpone the coronation until all the pending questions were settled, since Otto, if he was evil-minded, could always revoke such a settlement on the pretext that, by the refusal to crown him, pressure had been exerted on him.

On 4 October Otto was crowned without having given any other securities than those usual at a coronation as emperor.[221] What may Innocent have felt when he performed the solemn ceremony? Would not the sword with which he girded Otto this day be turned against him on the morrow? Would he not shortly be aiming at pulling off again from the Welf's head the crown which he now placed on it? The picture may well have appeared to him of Philip kneeling before him in Otto's stead, if he had not fallen victim to a senseless murder. The true relevance of the change of destiny on that 21 June 1208 had now become obvious. After a long fight Philip had been willing to conclude an honourable peace based on an understanding with the papal adversary whose strength he had come to experience during the struggle and of which to a certain degree he had always been aware. This responsible prince was now succeeded by an irresponsible warrior on whom in times of his distress certain obligations had been obtruded by the priest who now, seemingly helpless, could not but allow the course of events to drift. The emperor is reported to have said right to the pope's face, on the very day of his coronation, that he could not leave him the former imperial possessions.[221] We do not know whether the coronation day really ended in so outwardly dramatic a way. In any case Innocent knew what he had to expect from Otto.

Still on the day of his coronation, during which murderous fighting occurred between the Roman citizens and the imperial partisans, Otto left the town and pitched his camp in the neighbourhood near Isola Farnese. From here he invites the pope to a talk outside Rome since their short meeting had so far not allowed them to discuss thoroughly all the questions concerning the honour of God, the welfare of the Roman Church and the peace necessary for the entire Church. Failing this, he would not shrink from returning to Rome even at the risk of his own life. Yet the pope might consider the danger which could result for the Church from such a course.[223] Otto's letter shows how utterly he misjudges the situation. Not because he threatened to use force! His fatal error was his belief that only the Church, the papacy, was concerned in the negotiations which he demanded, whereas in fact, to a higher degree, the destiny of the Empire and of the emperorship was at stake.

Innocent's reply of 11 October does not reveal that he understood the threat. With polite firmness he declines the dangerous meeting.[224] The experiences he had had so far gave Innocent every reason to fear that Otto was no less capable of acts of violence than once Henry V was against Paschal II, and that Otto had not enough power of discrimination to realize that he would not be meeting another Paschal. At the same time Innocent expresses his readiness to come to an understanding. As to the territorial matter, the *negotium terrae*, the emperor might devise a solution which did credit to both of them, he would be doing the same in an attempt to find a way which would lead to their mutual advantage.[225]

Whether the *negotium terrae* is still to be understood as a simple revision of Otto's territorial obligations along the lines laid down in the agreement between Philip and the Roman Church, this question is hard to answer, although the expression seems to point to a single territorial question rather than to the whole complex of the recuperations. Otto, at that time, was certainly no longer willing to content himself with the concessions granted to Philip.[226] The pope's refusal to meet him personally may well have served him as a pretext to cry off from his obligations.

In the ensuing weeks and months Innocent has to watch Otto demolish his achievements in central Italy. News dating still from the month of the coronation comes to hand that the emperor regards the

March as an imperial possession.[227] In December reports are received of Otto's invasion of the duchy of Spoleto, in January that Dipold of Schweinspeunt, the old champion against the pope in the Sicilian kingdom, has been invested with the duchy and Marquis Azzo of Este with the March of Ancona.[228] In March at the latest Innocent is informed that Otto is also disregarding the rights of the Roman Church to Ferrara,[229] a long-standing possession of the Apostolic See. The occupation of Vetralla, Radicofani, Montefiascone and of other towns and fortresses in Roman Tuscany[230] in August and September 1210 leaves Innocent in no doubt that Otto is not contenting himself with reducing the possessions and the power of the papacy to the level of 1197, but that he aims at cutting them down beyond that.

Innocent also was already aware that Otto would not keep his promise regarding Sicily. The emperor disposed of offices and honours[231] and apparently had already sent troops across the frontier.[232]

All this happened without Innocent laying Otto under the ban. Had he lost his faith in being able to save his achievements or did he, at least for the moment, see no alternative to letting force take its course? It was not from pusillanimity nor from the feeling of impotence in the face of Otto's dreadful position of power that he spared him. But he wanted peace and had to want peace even at the cost of sacrifices until every possibility of coming to an understanding was exhausted. Without the most obvious reasons he could not now excommunicate the man for whose kingship he had fought for years and whom he had just now crowned. Otto's promises had been kept secret. Only a few knew of the surrender of extensive imperial territories to the pope. His rupture with Otto for the sake only of these matters and of the mere intimation of the intention to attack Sicily would have been likely to meet with little understanding and surely with little sympathy in Germany. But that was not even the decisive reason. Innocent had once already been forced to make peace with a king whom he had rejected. It could not happen a second time without papal prestige suffering an irreparable loss. Innocent could only strike a blow when he was sure that it would crush Otto. The final rupture with Otto, therefore, presupposed that he pitted against the emperor an opponent whose name in the Empire was not outshone by the emperor's name: Henry VI's son, Frederick Barbarossa's grandson, the last Staufen, Frederick of Sicily. On the other hand, Frederick's elevation would bring to pass just what

Innocent wished to prevent, the union of Sicily with the Empire. Besides, the experience the pope had had with the boy during the short span of Frederick's autonomous rule was not likely to lessen, not even for Frederick's lifetime only, his misgivings about such an union. From the first Frederick had given ear to the counsel of men who were not in the pope's confidence and whom Innocent as early as 1209 had threatened with his anger if they continued to offer their pernicious advice.[233] Innocent also disapproved of Frederick's way of treating those who, rightly or wrongly, were suspect to or discredited with him, because this was apt to drive those who were undecided or in disfavour over to the enemy's side.[234] In June he had to warn Frederick that, if he kept up his present course, the Church would be forced to conclude peace with the emperor at his cost, since it was not willing to be jeopardized by such imprudent actions. What he believes he may expect from Frederick or his entourage is shown by the fact that he thinks it necessary to protect the dismissed chancellor, Bishop Walter Pagliari of Catania, for whom he intercedes in his letter, by declaring that he would regard any action taken against the chancellor from whatever side as being directed against himself.[235] There were also clear intimations of Frederick's intention to follow in Henry VI's and his Norman ancestors' footsteps as regards his Church policy.[236] If Innocent should ever have counted on gratitude in political life, he surely never included Frederick's gratitude and devotion to the Apostolic See into his calculations.

It is in these circumstances that Innocent prepares for the decisive fight against Otto, but continues his attempts to come to an agreement with him. Towards the end of 1209 he issues a warning to the Sicilian court demanding that preparations be made against the imminent assault.[237] In January 1210 his attempts begin to undermine Otto's position in Germany and northern Italy, and to win over the likewise threatened kings of France[238] and Denmark[239] as allies. During this month he solicits help and counsel, in his oppression by the emperor, from the German princes and the German clergy, perhaps also from laypeople whom he could suppose to be sensitive to his complaint.[240] He already hints at taking extreme measures. An eventual excommunication of the emperor would entail, he writes, the release from all the oaths sworn to him and, besides, the legal validity of his coronation might well be open to question because of the suspicion that he had obtained it surreptitiously. Only with some reluctance does the pope appeal to Otto's arch-enemy, Philip of France, admitting that he had thoroughly deceived himself about Otto and describing the amount of derision and implacability with which Otto had rejected any peace with France and had talked big about intending to bring all the kings of the world into subjection.[241] Innocent knew that he need not convince the king of the danger involved for France in a Welf-English concentration of power, and yet it was his rôle to be the suppliant. He wished for armed help and financial support as well as for the king's intercession with the imperial princes, whose rebellion was to compel the emperor to evacuate papal territory,[242] and yet he was well aware that it was not at all in the interest of France if Otto, expelled from the Patrimony and Sicily with the help of French arms and French money, sought and found reconciliation with the Church. Indeed Philip, acting also on behalf of the imperial princes which were inclined to defect from the emperor, made the counter-claim that the princes be released from their oaths of allegiance, that assent be given to the elevation of an anti-king, and that the pope and the cardinals commit themselves in writing that the Curia would never again become reconciled with Otto.[243] As matters stood, the anti-king could only be Frederick of Sicily.

On 18 November 1210, immediately after Otto had crossed the frontier of the kingdom, Innocent pronounced the ban over him[244] and declared void the oaths of allegiance sworn to him, but for the time being put off the execution of the ban, probably meaning the order for its publication in Germany and in the kingdom of Sicily.[245] Innocent at that time knew that amongst the German princes a pro-papal faction had been formed with the aim of going to the length of dethroning the emperor. It consisted of the archbishops of Mainz and Magdeburg, King Ottokar of Bohemia, Landgrave Hermann of Thuringia, Bishop Egbert of Bamberg and the duke of Meran.[246] Innocent was sure, too, of Philip Augustus's help if he agreed to Frederick of Sicily's candidature, but he was not yet resolved to pay this price.

In the last months of 1210 and up to mid-February 1211 lively negotiations were kept going between him and the emperor. Innocent is reported to have offered to renounce the recuperations as compensation for Otto's renunciation of Sicily and of an assault on France.[247] But there is nothing at all to warrant this report.[248] Innocent's own statement, that he had offered to do Otto justice in the questions at issue before a court of arbitration,[249] tells us nothing as to the subject-matter of the negotiations. Whatever the pope may have offered, Otto, infatuated by his easy successes in Italy and on the

Sicilian mainland, did not want peace with the pope who kept him from subjecting the entire peninsula to his rule and from satisfying his hatred against the French king, with the pope who had just solemnly excommunicated his English uncle.[250] Otto was not willing to tolerate any obstruction in the pursuit of his imperial policy.

Thus the only way out for Innocent was to consent to Frederick's elevation. When giving his consent, he is sure to have had a clear idea as to the way in which a temporary union between the Empire and Sicily was again to be dissolved, yet it remained highly dangerous all the same. But whatever evil under Frederick and his heirs might *in future* be threatening from the union – if Innocent did not overthrow Otto now, the disaster, the incorporation of Sicily into the Empire, was *a present-day reality*. Frederick might turn hostile towards the papacy some time in the future; Otto was manifesting his brutal hostility this very moment. Besides, there was the threat of a Welf-English world-power being established which would have encircled and crushed the French kingdom, which Innocent, like his predecessors since the days of Louis VII, the *rex christianissimus*, regarded as a reliable support for the Roman Church.[251] A victory of the English-Welf coalition might also have entailed a sharp reaction within the clerical sphere. Reverence, if not for the Church, still for its servants, was alien to Otto. He never understood how to assess the relevance of forces which were not of a purely material nature. His own fight with the pope, his uncle's fight with the pope and with the church of his own country may in fact have aroused in him the anti-clerical feelings which his adversaries exaggeratedly laid to his charge.[252] It is indeed possible that he would have liked to shape his relationship to the German church on the lines of the English example, and it is probable that he would at least have adopted towards it the position which his Staufen predecessors had held, for already then Innocent had reason to complain that Otto, too, violated his ecclesiastical promises. General misgivings which the pope had for the future had to stand back in view of the threat of the worst fears being realized in the present day. Moreover, if the pope succeeded now in overthrowing Otto, his prestige was bound to increase so much that a recurrence of similar events was not easily to be expected. If on the other hand he impotently lets things slide, he exposed his political and partly also his moral prestige.

On Maundy Thursday, 31 March 1211, Innocent solemnly pronounced the excommunication sentence.[253] He declares anew all the oaths of allegiance sworn to Otto to be void and excommunicates and anathematizes all those who support the emperor against the Sicilian kingdom and the Patrimony.[254] Already some time before the papal letters had been dispatched which ordered the publication of the anathema and thereby set its execution going.[255] Innocent requires the imperial magnates[256] that as catholic princes they help their mother, the Church, and act in their own interest as long as they are still able to do so and their standing is not yet reduced to that of the English barons under Otto's uncle and grandfather. What kind of action he had in mind is shown by the reference to the giant Goliath's fall at the hands of little David as *instantis temporis figura*, as the example of happenings to come. Apparently in view of King Philip of France's demand,[257] Innocent commits himself, whatever the issue of the affair, effectively to support those who heeded his admonitions and commands. This guarantee could suffice for the princes. For Innocent had stuck to the bishops, who in the throne contest between Philip of Swabia and the Welf had stood by him to the last moment, against the victor who for his part had had to sacrifice his own partisans to them, and he had honourably and successfully been at pains to offer the defeated anti-king favourable terms. A formal commitment never to become reconciled with Otto would have been appropriate neither to the pope's interests nor to his spiritual position. Innocent had blazed the trail for the princely opposition, he had sanctioned their revolt as a fight for the defence of the Church against its persecutors and made it their duty to bring it about. It was for them to take the next step.

Meanwhile the emperor without effort had conquered nearly the entire mainland part of the kingdom. Only the border areas controlled by the pope had held firm.[258] When in 1211 he was about to cross over to Sicily, news reached him that in Germany a rebellion had broken out and that Frederick of Sicily had been nominated a candidate for the throne. On his hasty way back he was met by papal envoys in the district of Montefiascone. Innocent, before binding himself irrevocably by his answer to the envoy of the German rebels who had formally notified Frederick's nomination to him and to the king himself, for the last time invited the former protégé to accept reconciliation.[259] But the obstinate Welf was far from any complaisance, and so the pope's life-and-death-struggle against Otto began.

He proclaims Frederick, who himself had adopted the title of Roman emperor-elect, the champion of the Church, the head of the catholic party.[260] In April 1212 he receives the Staufen in Rome, equips him for his journey to Germany and provides for his escort by the Genoese and by the anti-Welf cities in Lombardy[261] on his dangerous way through northern Italy, where the powerful Milanese town-group stood firmly by Otto. It is probable that it was only just about this time that Innocent issued the order to all the citizens of the Empire to extrude Otto as an enemy of God and the Church from his rulership.[262] But he did not formally oust Otto from emperorship and royal dignity. Unlike Gregory VII he renounced the raising of so far-reaching and dangerous a claim.[263]

Fully convinced that his cause was a just one, Innocent uses his weapons against Emperor Otto, whom henceforth he styles the reprobate and 'maledict', *reprobus et maledictus*, quite otherwise than in his previous struggle with Philip of Swabia, who always had remained for him the high-born man, the duke of Swabia, *nobilis vir, dux Suevie*. Every single ecclesiastical prince was now faced with the decision between the pope and the emperor, and now no longer only suspension and excommunication are at stake, but office and title. Sweeping assertions of obedience no longer could help, but a clear and open rupture with the banned ruler was required. Archbishops Siegfried of Mainz and Albert of Magdeburg who, as papal legates, since the spring of 1212 had been organizing and directing the struggle against Otto in Germany, apparently were even authorized to exercise the right reserved to the pope of deposing bishops, and they reck-lessly put it to use.[264] Not even Otto's worldly supporters remained unscathed. Duke Henry of Brabant was excommunicated by name by the archbishop of Mainz, his land was laid under interdict.[265] As opposed to what happened during the recent throne contest, the consequences of the general excommunication sentence are now actually applied against those supporting the ruler whom the Church had rejected. When the monks of Ottobeuren allow their deceased provost, one of Otto's partisans, to be buried within their walls, the monastery has to suffer the interdict and the abbot the suspension.[266] No strong measures are necessary against the majority of the bishops. They are little inclined to bear the pope's dreaded indignation on behalf of the arrogant and brutal man[267] whom papal insistence and general war-weariness had made their sovereign.[268] When Frederick, having happily escaped all dangers, in September 1212 sets foot on German soil, the German church within a short time is almost completely on his side. In Trent and Chur he and his small escort had been met and then escorted on their way onwards by the local bishops. A decisive moment comes when Bishop Conrad of Constance, whose initial hesitation was quickly overcome when he remembered the emperor's excommunication, opens the gates of his episcopal city to the Staufen rather than to the emperor who was already near Constance at Ueberlingen. In Basel Bishop Lutold, who had been the first to publish the excommunication sentence against the emperor, joins Frederick, as does Bishop Henry of Strasbourg and, in Hagenau, Siegfried of Mainz, the Welf's arch-enemy, as well as Lupold of Worms. Even those bishops who, like Egbert of Bamberg and Otto of Würzburg, until recently had dared to hold open communion with the banned emperor, with few exceptions now seek to save their skins by going over to Frederick and by throwing themselves on the pope's mercy.[269] Dietrich of Cologne, who had been deposed by the legate, appeared at the Curia in spring 1213 at the latest with a view to having his suit revised.[270] It is significant of the measure of ecclesiastical obedience which in the matter of the emperor Innocent experiences with the German clergy, that Otto does not find a single priest to perform his marriage to Mary of Brabant.[271]

Just as the German episcopate so the Lombard clergy, including the bishops of the pro-imperial cities, loyally follow the pope in the fight against the banned and reprobate ruler.[272]

In Frankfurt on 5 December 1212 Frederick was elected king and thereafter recognized by the pope as Roman emperor-elect. In the Golden Bull of Eger dated 12 July 1213 and drawn up in the presence of the princes, the Staufen, doubtless pursuant to a previous promise, confirms to the Church its possessions and the realization of its claims as laid down in Otto IV's privileges.[273] But already once before, the obligations, stipulated in the days of the anti-kingship, had been regarded as void by a monarch. Probably after Otto's ultimate defeat at Bouvines in 1214, Innocent, therefore, provided against the recurrence of a similar event and at the same time gave the recuperations an unassailable legal basis. In a renewal of the Privilege of Eger Frederick not only restituted to the Roman Church the territories to which it laid claim, among which now are also named Sardinia and Corsica,[274] but also granted, conveyed and donated them to the Apostolic See with a view to "remove any doubt". The princes for their part agreed to the restitution and cession of the imperial territories by way of letters of consent.[275] It was not the ruler alone who declared the renunciation, but the Empire approved of it by the hand of its representatives. The renunciation was effected not only in view of the legal position as asserted by the Church, but it was also a donation from the emperor and the Empire to the Church in the interest of a lasting peace. The new Papal State now possessed all the securities which documents and the taking of oaths could give. It was a great satisfaction for Innocent that the lasting existence of this state was still not dependent on external security provisions only.

Otto's assault had not resulted, any more than Lupold of Worms' attack under Philip of Swabia, in an immediate and complete collapse of papal rule in the recuperated territories. The cities in Roman Tuscany had fought for the cause of the Church and the most important ones, like Viterbo and Perugia, had maintained their ground.[276] The cities in the duchy of Spoleto, too, had not without exception, and certainly not always voluntarily, submitted themselves again to the imperial rule.[277] Rome and Roman Tuscany as well as the neighbouring cities and counties had admirably stood their test as a bulwark for the pope's personal safety. Against this it was of minor relevance that the March proved less capable to resist the imperial troops. In the territories conquered by Otto in Roman Tuscany the emperor's position, which in other parts of imperial Italy was still strong, appears to have collapsed as early as the end of 1212[278] and in the duchy of Spoleto to have begun to waver not much later.[279] Only for the March of Ancona may the Church still in 1215 have been dependent on the support which the future emperor had promised it in his privilege.[280]

The question whether the pope's demand for new securities had only been a general precautionary measure or whether some particular occasion caused Innocent to make it, is hard to answer since our knowledge of the events in these last years of Innocent's life unfortunately is all too scanty. We have, however, good reasons for assuming that Lupold of Worms' appointment as Frederick's legate for Sicily about the beginning of 1215[281] and even more his activities in the kingdom caused ill-feeling[282] and perhaps even suspicion at the Curia, since Lupold had remained for years in the archiepiscopal see of Mainz in the pope's despite and, in his capacity as Philip's legate for Italy and Sicily, had confronted the pope in arms. But in any case Frederick, shortly before the convening of the Lateran Council of 1215, gave a token of his goodwill by donating to the Roman Church the county of Sora which he had enfeoffed to Richard, the pope's brother, with all the rights resting in it.[283] The county with its castles, from whence in the years 1198 to 1208 the Germans had molested the Roman Campania, provided the Patrimony with a rampart against the kingdom. Innocent now held all the strategically important border districts,[284] since Philip in Rome as early as April 1212 had conceded him the full disposition of the domain of Fondi bequeathed to the Apostolic See by its count[285] as well as all the territories this side the Garigliano, and had mortgaged Monte Cassino and the county of Aquino to the Roman Church as compensation for the expense it had incurred during the papal regency in Sicily.[286]

At the Council Innocent solemnly confirmed Otto's rejection and Frederick's recognition. It had been in vain that Milan defended the imperial cause in open Council session,[287] that King John of England, who since his reconciliation with the Church in May 1212 had zealously been advocating Otto's cause, interceded for him, and that Otto's friends actively promoted his cause in the college of cardinals.[288] Even if Innocent had had reason to distrust Frederick, there was no retracting without destroying the moral prestige on which his predominance in the Christian world was based. It was not for a pope of his time to change sides in the manner of a Renaissance pope. Moreover, Innocent more than ever strove for peace in the Occident, which nothing could have more hopelessly hampered than the revival of the throne contest in Germany. Since the spring of 1213 all the pope's hopes were directed towards a new crusade, for which in these years he made the most extensive preparations.[289]

There is no doubt that Innocent intended soon to call the king to Rome for his coronation and immediately thereafter to put an end to the personal union between the Empire and Sicily, as must have been stipulated between him and the Staufen before the latter's departure to Germany. The dispatch of a cardinal legate seems to have been a preparatory step. Before him, in Strasbourg, Frederick commits himself on 1 July 1216 by oath that immediately after his coronation as emperor he will release his son Henry, already crowned king of Sicily, from his fatherly authority and transfer the kingdom to him as the vassal of the Roman Church for good and all, but that he himself will resign both title and authority of king of Sicily and during Henry's minority have the kingdom administered at the pope's pleasure by a suitable personage. This personage is to be responsible to the Roman Church, being, as he states, the sole holder of the supreme authority in the kingdom, for the rights and the revenues due to it.[290] In unveiled words, doubtless inspired by Innocent, the true reason is given for the promise: the union of the Empire with the kingdom is to be prevented, because it could prove detrimental both to the Apostolic See and to the emperor's heirs. To the emperor's heirs! Innocent was aware of their being jeopardized, too, not only of the threat to the Church. The almost prophetic warning is impressive in view of the fate of Frederick's sons and grandsons who perished because the emperor broke his promise, the fate above all of the last true off-spring of his house, the high-minded young Conradin, for whom the ancestor's breach of promise prepared the scaffold at Naples.

Innocent never held the document of renunciation in his hands. Two weeks after the execution of the important act he unexpectedly departed his life at Perugia. In a fight, unparalleled in view of the scanty means of which he disposed, he had wrought from the holders of the imperial power the bulk of the territories to which after Henry VI's death the Curia had laid claim, he had defended the Sicilian kingdom against the German potentates in Sicily, he had then maintained Sicily and the recuperations against Philip's legate and ultimately secured them in the peace concluded with the Staufen who was victorious in Germany. He had struck down Emperor Otto who again had contested both acquisitions with him, and had brought Frederick II to give him an unassailable legal basis and every conceivable security for the newly constituted Papal State. Lastly he had also made preparations for a settlement which was to put an end to the deadly peril which ever since Frederick's elevation threatened from a union of the Empire with the kingdom.

Innocent's untimely death must be regarded as one of the events in medieval history fraught with the gravest consequences. In view of his successor's weakness Frederick dared to have his son come to Germany and in 1219, whilst negotiating with the pope on the renewal of the separation pact, to have him elected Roman king.[291] Honorius III allowed himself to be inveigled into crowning Frederick emperor, although young Henry continued to stay in Germany, and into tolerating Frederick's continued rule in Sicily. In these circumstances the fight had become inevitable. The emperor who at the same time was king of Sicily could not but attempt to overcome the separation of his realms caused by the barrier of the Papal State; the Church for its part was forced to set out to weaken and ultimately to destroy the power which encircled it. When Frederick II also began to subject northern Italy to his centralistic aspirations and the papacy saw its last bulwark in Italy thereby threatened, in a fierce fight it broke the ring which threatened to strangle it and crushed the imperial power. It drew support then from France, but found a new and no less dangerous threat to its liberty there. The French popes, during the times of Avignon, were tied much more inwardly than externally, they deserted their universal mission and had to put up with the new situation.[292] The Avignonese 'captivity' and the schisms it caused in the papacy and in Christendom, these are the results of the fight which the papacy began for the sake of securing its independence. An issue of this kind would not have been possible if the papacy had not long before suffered damage to the innermost heart of its existence. The popes were deeply enmeshed in worldly affairs. Politics must needs be an essential business for the papacy which saw itself faced with the necessity of preventing both the emperorship and any other power from becoming too powerful in Italy. This political objective could not fail to bring the popes into conflict with their religious duties and their moral convictions, all the more so the more the danger increased and the adversary gained in power. Under Innocent IV the fight of extermination against Emperor Frederick II absorbed almost every other function incumbent on the papacy. Not only were ecclesiastical punitive measures misused to exert political pressure, but also all the pope's ecclesiastical full powers, rights and duties were put to use in his fight. Bishoprics and benefices were conferred to this end, dispensations and indulgences were made to serve it, the funds of the churches were mobilized to finance the fight and the idea of the crusade was misused on its behalf. Under pressure of this distress centralism underwent an unsound increase. After the fight which had brought the Curia to financial ruin, in the times of Avignon, when the Curia was cut off from its natural base, and still more during the time of the Great Schism, a blatant fiscalism spread through the whole range of ecclesiastical administration, and finally an ugly traffic with offices and benefices, a systematic financial exploitation of the churches, took place. At the time of the fight between papacy and emperorship the basis was laid for the deplorable situation of the Church at the close of the Middle Ages. Avignon, Schism, Renaissance papacy, Reformation – one of the roots of these catastrophes in the history of the Catholic Church dates back to the fight between Church and Empire, to which Innocent III had sought to put an end by resolving the security question.

For Germany, Innocent's policy, balked as it was of its consistent realization, was disastrous. It had to pay for this with long years of inner war, which preyed terribly upon the strength of the kingship. If the pope's work had been realized, it would have made good to Germany what it had had to pay for it. The emperorship no longer would have wasted its means on the south, Frederick's genius would have been of service to Germany. After the situation had con-solidated, the Roman Church, far better protected than ever finan-cially, politically and militarily owing to the possession of extended territories in central Italy and with the backing it had in Sicily, would have been in a position to put up without distrust or ill-will with the strengthening of the imperial power throughout the imperial ter-ritories, in northern Italy too, and would even have been able to support it, since there was, indeed, so much which then linked up its interests with the existence of a strong emperorship: the crusade plans, the fight against heresy and anti-clerical tendencies in the Italian communes,[293] the dangers of anarchy. Innocent aimed at diverting the 'vehicle Empire' from the path which led to a fatal collision with the Church. At the moment in which he compelled the team to reverse, death tore the reins from his hands and the vehicle continued its course towards destruction without the weak hands of Innocent's successors being able to prevent disaster.

## Notes to Chapter 5

[1]RNI 62.

[2]This should not blind us to the fact that the popes may well have stirred up resistance to the Empire in the peninsula or used it for their own ends more often than they have allied with the Emperor against his opponents. Thus the Norman-papal friendship would not have been possible without the existence of the Empire, for otherwise there would necessarily have existed between the pope and the Norman state the same irreconcilable enmity as in earlier days existed between him and the Lombards. The Curia was considering in particular the re-establishment of a counter-weight to the Franco-Angevin power in southern Italy when it embarked on the policy of restoring an emperorship which had become less menacing.

[3]The lesson that for the papacy worldly dependence meant at the least a restriction of its spiritual independence and a curtailment of its range of activity had been brought home to the Curia under the domination by the East-Roman emperors and under the sceptre of Charlemagne, and this experience came home to the Roman Church anew when it set out to reform the church in Germany and Italy under a monarch hostile to the ideas of reform. When the fight for the independence of the papacy had in principle been decided, an ecclesiastical decision, Urban III's sentence in the election dispute of

Trier, resulted in the occupation and seizure of part of the Patrimony by Frederick I. The possibility of such actions being taken not only curtailed the pope's freedom of decision in ecclesiastical matters arising within the imperial sphere of influence, but, if taken, they would also impair the pope's power of action in general, since he depended on the Patrimony as the material base for the existence of the papacy.

[4]Cf. Overmann, Gräfin Mathilde von Tuszien (1895), 81ff., and also Kauffmann, 15ff., 33ff., 98f., 143ff., 174ff. Kauffmann's suggestion that the Curia had waived its claim to the Matildine estate in 1189 (146) seems to me not sufficiently founded.

[5]Immediately after Henry's death Celestine III laid claim to the Tiber counties, to the duchy of Spoleto and to the March of Ancona (Kehr, It. Pont., 4, 118, 138, 154; *ibid.* 4, 154 No. 2 in connection with Gött. Nachr. 1898, 43; *ibid.* 4, 24. Seeger, 23ff.) and had begun to enforce it. Celestine's legates took part in the formation of the Tuscan League of 11 November 1197 which only stipulates an alliance with the Roman Church for the purpose of defence and the commitment undertaken by the League to accept a bearer or representative of the imperial authority only with the consent of and on special instruction from the Roman Church (Ficker, Forsch. 4, 242f.). Unless the legates acted on their own initiative the Curia was then not yet laying claim to Lombard Tuscany for the Patrimony. However, on 23 December 1197, that is during the last days of Celestine's reign, the claims to all of Tuscany are documented (Kehr, Gött. Nachr. 1898, 43).

[6]The great imperial privileges of Louis the Pious, Otto the Great and Henry II, which the Roman Church believed it possessed in their original versions (Ficker, Forsch. 2, 335) formed, since the last days of Celestine's pontificate at least, the legal basis for the recuperations (*cum iuxta privilegiorum ecclesiae Romanae tenorem tota Marchia et Tuscia in patrimonio b. Petri existant*: Celestine III on 23 December 1197 – Kehr, Gött. Nachr. 1898, 43–; *ad has* [the possessions of the Roman Church] *pertinet ... cum aliis adiacentibus terris expressis in multis privilegiis imperatorum a tempore Lodoyci*: Juramentum Ottonis RNI 77 of 1201). On the contradictory statements of these documents all claims entered by the Curia, and more than these, could, in one form or another, have been founded. In the text of the documents were interpolated the statements of the *Liber pontificalis* on the donation of Charlemagne to the pope, which enclosed the duchy of Spoleto in the possessions of St Peter and according to which Tuscany, too, lay within the confines of the territories under papal sovereignty, in contradiction to a genuine passage of the text according to which the pope was only granted the revenues from both duchies, whereas the sovereignty itself was explicitly reserved to the emperor (MG Const. 1, 25. Cf. Ficker, Forsch. 2, 332ff. for all issues connected with the privileges). The Curia could hardly have been blamed if in guileless acceptance of the data in the documents it kept to those in its favour (cf. Kempf, Die zwei Versprechen, 371), the more so since they appeared to be supported by the *Liber pontificalis*. However, for a mind as acute as Innocent's (see below Chapter 10) such guileless acceptance cannot be presupposed.

[7]The legate who was to take control of the exarchate for the Roman Church does not seem to have been appointed until relatively late, towards the end of February in fact, and the commission is not given to a cardinal, but to a mere subdeacon (Reg. I 27, Gesta c. 12). But in view of the claims of the archbishop of Ravenna Innocent hastens to renounce the enforcement of his claims for the time being. He adopts a similar procedure when calling in the Matildine estate from these cities which had appropriated it. The communes were prepared to accept it as a fief from the Roman Church under

certain circumstances, but Innocent declines because the conditions seem unsuitable to him, and postpones the decision to a more favourable time (Gesta c. 13). The rejection of the communes' offer, the acceptance of which would have allowed the Curia the financial use of the Matildine goods, so desirable just at that time, suggests that Innocent valued the Matildine estate as an object of composition for future negotiations with the Empire. The Gesta (c. 13) see a connection, even though a temporal one only, between the postponement of this decision and the emergence of the imperial question (*Quia tamen pactiones illae convenientes non erant, noluit ex ipsa terra quidquam concedere, praeter id quod concessit episcopo Mantuano, differens in aliud tempus idoneum, quia tunc ei sollicitudo gravior supervenit ex divisione imperii et turbatione regni Siciliae quibus eum intendere principaliter oportebat*). If he had enfeoffed the cities Innocent would have reduced, if not destroyed, the value of the object of composition. The conditions laid down by the cities which Innocent considered unsuitable may have included the obligation not to sell the Matildine estate, that is, not to sell it to the Empire. We often meet with such conditions when cities and other places which had previously owed allegiance to the Empire come under the sovereignty of the Church. For example, Innocent commits himself towards Perugia never to dispose of the city and to retain it in his hands for ever (Reg. I 375). He assures Fano and Pesaro that they would remain for ever under the sovereignty of the Apostolic See (Böhmer, Acta, 907; Reg. III 29), Innocent's promise to the people of Montefiascone that he would conclude no definitive agreement with Philip (i.e. Philip of Swabia, duke of Tuscany) unless Philip renounced the *castrum* in favour of the Church (Reg. I 361) seems to carry the same meaning. Against suspicions voiced by the Tuscan League that he fraudulently reclaimed the castle of Assisi with a view to returning it to Conrad of Irslingen, the former duke, Innocent protests by declaring that he intended to recuperate the Patrimony of the Church once and for all *non ad opus alterius, sed ad eius dominium et profectum Italiae* (P. 82). In 1197 Celestine III had promised Rieti that he would retain the territory of the city in his hands as well as that of the cities of the Campania (Kehr, It. Pont. 4, 24; Ficker, Forsch 4, No. 325, p. 355).

[8]Maccarrone (Chiesa, 148ff.) regards Innocent III as the exponent of the anti-German and nationalist reaction in Italy and ascribes to him the idea of an Italy no longer subject to the Empire united in its autonomous communities. It is true that Innocent was no friend of Germany and loved his Italian homeland doubtless more than any other country with the possible exception of France (see Chapter 1 above and Seeger, 10). The German domination in Italy, that is the direct administration of the country by German magnates as it had existed in central Italy from the days of Frederick I to the death of Henry VI (cf. Kauffmann, Chaps. 5, 8, 9, 11) and for a time in northern Italy, he is sure to have repudiated. Yet, he had no intention of excluding Italy from the Empire. In the sources adduced by Maccarrone there is nowhere mention of a separation of Italy from the Empire. The *libertas totius Italiae* of which Innocent speaks in RNI 92, is not *libertas* from the Empire but within the Empire. The *libertas* to which he aspires for Lombardy and for all Italy Innocent contrasts with the *servitus* which the Staufen emperors sought to impose on Lombardy; the bearing of the Staufen rulers he contrasts with the benevolent demeanour of Henry the Lion, the father of Otto of Brunswick, the German king recognized by him. Another passage of the letter states that some emperors had cruelly persecuted the Roman Church, Lombardy and all Italy, while others had honoured and enriched the Apostolic See. The pope emphasizes in the same letter that he is not out to harm but to benefit the Empire, that

the Church cannot dispense with its imperial protector, and declares that he, the pope, had accepted Otto as king without the Lombards but on their behalf. For Reg. I 401, in which Innocent deals with the primacy of the ecclesiastical and temporal powers which by God's providence both had their seats in Italy, see the following note.

⁹There is no evidence to sustain allegations of papal intrigues in northern Italy at the beginning of Innocent's pontificate. It is true that Innocent carried on with the mission of a cardinal legate for Lombardy, which his predecessor seems to have ordered, and it may well be that his legate was to come to an understanding with the Lombards on the major political issues. This does not, however, imply that Innocent had any intention of encroaching on the status of the possessions or legal rights of the Empire in Lombardy. We only know of the legate's activity against heresy. That he had taken part in the renewal of the Lombard League on 27 April 1198, whose members pledged themselves not to enter into any alliance with the emperor or the king or with any other party except on a decision by the League (Gli atti del Comune di Milano fino all'anno 1216, ed. C. Manaresi, 1919, 287; BF. 12153), is only assumed (Winkelmann, Philipp, 342; Ficker, Forsch. 2, 285; Luchaire, Innocent III vol. 1, 126) in view of the fact that the legate issued his statutes against heresy in Verona (Reg. I 298, II 27). The treaty-act does not mention the legate's participation and it is hardly possible that by the *quidam sapientes* who partook in the deliberation of the *constitutio* against heresy were to be understood the consuls and podestà of the allied cities. The Trevisans who took part in the establishment of the league were themselves under ban and interdict at that time and refused to acknowledge the heresy statutes on the grounds that they, like the heretics, were enemies of the pope (Reg. II 27). The same applies to Piacenza, which had not yet joined the League, but whose representatives had attended its formation. The cardinal legate held papal documents giving him authority to impose stern measures, should the city fail to provide the satisfaction demanded by the pope (Reg. I 121, 122, 123). Innocent was equally severe in his measures against Parma (*ibid.* and BF. 5623) and he supported the bishop of Tortona who had answered the city's refusal to pay the tenths and first-fruits with a general interdict, in his dispute with the city (Reg. I 132, X 158). To take such a line against powerful communes would hardly be consistent with an attempt to win the Lombard cities over to an alliance. An approach by Innocent to the Lombards in matters concerning the Empire is first mentioned in July 1203 (RNI 87, 88). The only factor which directly indicates the pope's political interest in Lombardy is the obligation Innocent laid upon Otto before the latter's recognition, to conform his attitude towards the Lombard League, the Tuscan League and to France with the pope's counsel (RNI 77). Such an interest would have to be assumed anyhow. Naturally enough Innocent did not want the Peace of Constance, for the maintenance of which the Lombard League had been formed, to be jeopardized. But it may be that the obligation laid upon Otto had at that time only the same purport as the obligation regarding France: to win over opponents of Otto by way of possible papal guarantees or to disperse distrust of him.

¹⁰Cf. Seeger, 34ff.

¹¹*Immo, cum ducatus Tusciae ad ius et dominium ecclesiae Romanae pertineat, sicut in privilegiis ecclesiae Romanae oculata fide perspeximus contineri* (Reg. I 15).

¹²According to the Gesta (c. 11) the League pledged itself: (1) to sustain the League for the honour of the Apostolic See, (2) to defend in good faith all the possessions and rights of the Roman Church, and (3) to accept no king or emperor who had not been approved by the bishop of Rome. Luchaire (Les Ligues, 493, n. 1) accuses the Gesta of

falsifying the record, but as long as the modified treaty-act (see Reg. I 555) is not at our disposal, such a charge cannot be justified by a comparison between the act of 1197 which had been negotiated under the legates of Celestine III and the report of the Gesta on the act of 1198. Nor do I understand how Luchaire fails to find any trace of the obligations cited above under (1) and (2) in the treaty of 1197. Also the treaty of 1197 was completed amongst other reasons for the glory of God and the Roman Church. The rectors of the League had to swear to accept no king, emperor, duke or margrave nor any of their representatives without the prior approval and explicit direction of the Roman Church. They also pledge themselves to help the Roman Church, after joint decision, to recuperate and defend its possessions (except against members of the League) and on other clearly defined occasions, if for example a prince who had been recognized both by pope and rectors, on a joint decision, should later undertake a hostile action against the Roman Church (Ficker, Forsch. 4, 245; cf. Davidsohn, Gesch. von Florenz 1, 616f.).

[13]Relations between Innocent and the League were from time to time severely strained. The pope repudiated the agreement reached between Celestine's legates and the League and disputed the cities' right to form a league without the reservation of the law and authority of the Apostolic See (Reg. I 15). He forbids the cities of the Patrimony from joining the league for the time being (Reg. I 34). He also temporarily lifts the interdict which Celestine III had laid on the city of Pisa because Pisa as a city loyal to the Empire had refused to join the League, and thus supports Pisa in its resistance to the League (Reg. I 35, 56, 88, 555). For its part the League clearly supports those cities of Roman Tuscany which were reluctant to submit to the sovereignty of the Church's authority. On the occasion of the negotiations with Conrad of Irslingen the League accuses the pope of treachery against the national cause (Reg. I 88; cf. Gesta c. 9) and seeks to provide against a possible attempt by the pope to dissolve the League. In the spring of 1198 Certaldo pledged itself, on joining the League, to remain loyal to the League even if the pope were to release it from its oath (Luchaire, Les Ligues, 459; cf. Davidsohn, Gesch. von Florenz 1, 625).

[14]Migne Pl. 217, 665.

[15]On 30 April Frederick was still using the title of king of the Romans in a Sicilian document (Ries, Regesten der Kaiserin Constanze, Königin von Sizilien, Gemahlin Heinrichs VI., QFIAB. 18, 1926, 62f., Nos. 77, 78), but the title is missing in royal documents dated later than 17 May.

[16]Similar considerations will have induced Celestine III, or, in the case of his disability to carry out his office, the college of cardinals, to exercise restraint.

[17]If Innocent had arranged for Frederick's renunciation Philip would scarcely have failed to refer to this when in 1206 he apologized to the pope for taking the crown in defiance of the oath sworn to Frederick (RNI 136). It is also unlikely that Innocent in that case would have, up to 1201, ranked Frederick's rights as being theoretically equivalent to or level with the rights of the two anti-kings. The date at which the empress waived her sons's claim suggests a wholly different contingency of events (see the following note).

[18]Philip was elected on 6 March 1198. A delegation may have left for Sicily at about this time and by May have persuaded Constance to accept the facts given. A Staufen emperor, bound by considerations of kinship, may well have been more acceptable to the empress than one who, not hampered by such considerations, could have resumed the former imperial policy against the weakened Empire. That Philip and Constance

could have come to terms was possibly not taken into consideration because of the general assumption that immediately after her husband's death Constance had indulged in a policy of hateful reaction against all things German. Constance could scarcely have taken up a hostile attitude against the Germans immediately after Henry's death, since her son was in German care in the duchy of Spoleto at Foligno, a town which Conrad of Irslingen had held even after Frederick's transfer to the kingdom. It is, moreover, unlikely that she would have given vent to her alleged hatred against the Germans as long as she regarded her son as the German king and future emperor. It must be said, however, that Richard of San Germano (18) reports that the empress, for the sake of peace and order in the realm, had banished Markward and all Germans from the kingdom and indeed had made Markward swear that he would never return without her permission, and Innocent also refers to Markward's banishment from the kingdom. However, it is striking that the author of the Gesta, who as to time stood in much closer connection to these events than Richard and who was certainly not bent on passing over any hostile activities of Constance against the Germans, merely records that after Henry's death some of his confidants had *left* the kingdom (c. 20). See too the Ann. Casin.: *... tunc exiens de regno... Marcualdus* (p. 318). The well-informed Breve chron. de rebus Siculis (Huillard-Bréholles, $1^2$ 891) contains a most revealing piece of information. According to it Constance sent the German knights in her husband's retinue, after rewarding them with presents, to Germany to *Philip of Swabia*. That Philip is mentioned is significant, for whereas in Sicily the German knights were a burden if Constance wished to rule as a national queen, they could in Germany under Philip be of use to her son's cause. The dismissal will not have affected those Germans who by that time had become high Sicilian dignitaries such as Markward count of Molise and Dipold of Schweinspeunt, count of Acerra. We also know that Markward swore an oath of allegiance and service to the young Frederick for Molise (RNI 15). Markward, the most hated and most prominent of the emperor's followers, according to Innocent bore the prime responsibility for all the ghastly events which the Sicilians had suffered. Some time later he will have been required to leave the kingdom for the sake of peace and his own personal safety, but he was not dispossessed of the county of Molise (cf. Richard of S. Germ. 19). Dipold remained in the kingdom, apparently not in open rebellion against the empress since Innocent describes him in 1199 as formerly a secret, now an open, persecutor of the king and the kingdom (Reg. I 575). William Capparone remained on the isle proper and one Frederick of Malveti remained in Calabria (Gesta c. 20). Against this Frederick the empress later employed force, which the Gesta (c. 20) attributes not to his continued presence in the kingdom, but to his hostile activities against the empress.

[19] Cf. Kehr, Briefbuch, 50.

[20] Cf. the pope's promise of help in the future in Kehr, Briefbuch, 45f.

[21] Reg. I 557. For the papal regency in Sicily and conditions in the Sicilian kingdom see Baethgen, Regentschaft.

[22] See n. 12 above.

[23] Ahi, wie kristenlîche nu der babest lachet
swenne er sînen Walhen seit, ich hânz alsô gemachet.
(Daz er da seit, des solt er niemer hân gedâht)
er giht: ich han zwên Alman under eine krône brâht,
daz siz rîche sulen stoeren unde wasten,
ie dar under füllen wir die kasten:

Ich hâns an mînen stoc gement, ir guot ist alles mîn;
ir tiusches silber vert in mînen welschen schrîn.
Ir Pfaffen, eszent huener und trinkent win,
und lât die tiutschen . . . vasten.

The verses themselves refer to a later time, to the war between Otto IV and Frederick II. See Walther von der Vogelweide, Gedichte, Insel-Bücherei No. 105, 31.

[24]Cf. Kempf, Regestum, 80, which also contains the literature on the matter.

[25]His agent, the bishop of Sutri already mentioned, appears to have brought Philip's request for absolution still to Celestine personally (. . . *sicut b.m. Celestino papae . . . per te, frater episcope, obtulit . . .*, Reg. I 25). Accordingly the bishop's arrival at the Curia would have to be fixed to December 1197 at the latest. The choice of the agent is well explained if Philip had sought to be reconciled with the pope before returning to Germany from Montefiascone, the neighbouring town of Sutri (Burchard of Ursberg, 76). Certainly, once Philip learnt of his brother's death he will not have put off opening negotiations any further.

[26]Gesta c. 22. Bishop Radulf of Sutri acts as witness in a document of Henry VI on 17 August 1194 (Baethgen, Philipp, 210, n. 1). On 31 March 1195 he attached the cross to the emperor's breast in Bari (Annales Marbac. 65. Cf. Haller, Heinrich VI, 593). In 1198 Radulf consecrated the rebuilt collegiate church of Neustift near Brixen in the vicinity of the Brenner (Memoriale benefactorum of the convent, quoted in Schott, Gli avvenimenti storici della Prepositura dei Canonici Regolari di Nova Cella, Arch. per l'Alto Adige 33, 1938, 94f. n. 141. The memoriale reports him to be legate). According to Schott, Le relazioni della prepositura dei canonici regolari di Nova Cella con la curia Romana nel medio evo (Arch. Dep. Rom. di stor. patr. 67, 1944, 343f), he was the guest of Bishop Everard of Brixen in Neustift on his return to Italy.

[27]Reg. I 24, 25, 26 of 25 February, date in P. 27. A party to Philip's negotiations with the pope seems also to have been the provost Frederick of St Thomas's near Strasbourg, the confidant of both Barbarossa and Henry VI (Burdach, Der mittelalterliche Streit um das Imperium in den Gedichten Walthers von der Vogelweide, DViSchr f. LitWiss. u. Geistesgesch. 13, 1935, 528; cf. also Kauffmann, 142) and at the turn of 1199/1200 also Philip's envoy to the pope (RNI 17; cf. Kempf, Regestum, 44, n. 2). The benefice case, whose settlement by the provost's waive during his stay at the Curia Innocent makes public on 2 March (Reg. I 30), need not have been the sole nor yet the main reason for his journey to Rome.

[28]RNI 1.

[29]See Reg. I 230: . . . *quia circa personam nobilis viri ducis Sueviae quaedam audivimus immutata, eidem ad praesens scribere cautela prohibente nequivimus.*

[30]Innocent, at that time, pledged himself to the people of Montefiascone that he would conclude no definite agreement with Philip before the king had renounced the *castrum* in favour of the Church (Reg. I 361).

[31]He may have been accompanied by the abbot of Salem. People from the Swabian abbey were at the Curia during December 1198 (see Codex diplomaticus Salembitanus, UB. der Zisterzienserabtei Salem, ed. von Weech, 1 1883. N. 58, 59). The abbot acted as an intermediary between Philip and the pope (Reg. VI 160 of 27.10.1203. Cf. RNI 107 of January 1204 in which the pope requests Otto IV to give special favour to the monastery of Salem on his imminent raid into Swabia. There can be no doubt that members of the monastery were at the Curia when this letter was drafted. Reg. IX 177 of 4 November 1206 points to the same state of affairs. It may be that the patriarch of

Aquileia, Philip's agent, or the patriarch's delegate, was also at the Curia, cf. Reg. IX 178).

[32]Cf. Tillmann, Zum Regestum, 70ff. In addition to the literature there indicated see Kauffmann, 17ff.

[33]Markward had been mixed up with the confused happenings in the kingdom during the empress's last days. He was declared by the empress herself an enemy of the king and the kingdom (Gesta c. 23). Markward on the other hand was the pioneer of the Staufen cause in central Italy and we know that as such and as imperial representative for the March of Ancona and the Romagna as well as for the kingdom itself he was recognized by Philip at least in May 1199 (RNI 14). According to the Chronica regia Coloniensis the kingdom of Apulia is conveyed to Markward with the approval and on the instructions of King Philip (Reg. I 167). The *Deliberatio* styles Philip *non solum factor, sed auctor iniquitatis eius* (Markward's), RNI 29. On the relations between Philip of Swabia and Markward see Baethgen, Regentschaft, 131ff.

[34]For a consideration of Philip's ultimate aims in the kingdom see Baethgen, Regentschaft, 131ff. In my opinion there can be no unambiguous answer. We cannot forthwith give credit to Innocent's and his biographer's assertion that Philip intended to deprive his nephew of his maternal as well as his paternal inheritance, but it is equally inadmissable to accuse the pope straightaway of telling an open lie. When Innocent writes in RNI 47 to the king of France with reference to Philip: *cum ... imperium obtineret, saltem occasione nepotis ad regnum Sicilie ardentius aspiraret, cum ad illud iam manifestis indiciis ardenter aspiret ...*, these words cannot be read as admitting that Innocent himself did not believe the charge that Philip intended to deprive his nephew of his kingdom. Why should Innocent not have dared to repeat a lie in his letter to Philip of France which he had already dared pronounce in a letter to the German princes (RNI I 33), that is in Philip's face? It may be that the king of France, who at that time was acting as intermediary between Philip of Swabia and the Curia, had assured the pope that the Swabian had no hostile intentions against his nephew, and that Innocent now invited the king of France to consider the possibility that Philip, at least as guardian, would be willing to seize the kingdom. In RNI 64 Innocent warns Philip of France again that, if Philip of Swabia should gain the imperial dignity, he would lay his hands on the kingdom, at least with regard to the nephew whose care he would claim by virtue of his blood relationship, an aim which, with the help of his satellites, he was already at present, though in vain, actively trying to achieve. Once again Innocent declared his accusation to men who must have at least partly been aware of the truth, namely in his letter to the young king Frederick, that is to the government of Palermo, which had defended the chancellor Walter Pagliari, the ally of Markward, before the pope (see Baethgen, Regentschaft, 128f.). If Innocent's accusations had been a bold lie, he would hardly have upheld it in the secret consistory at the end of 1200 in the so-called *Deliberatio*. In the Protest of Speyer the German princes declared to the pope that the time would come when nobody in the Empire or in those countries which Emperor Henry had ruled, would dare to challenge Philip's rulership. That aims also at Sicily, and at Sicily in the first place, for what else could be meant by the countries mentioned besides the Empire? Considerable goodwill is necessary to interpret this statement as being no more than the claim to the power of a guardian or to suzerainty. Baethgen elsewhere (Regentschaft, 5 n. 1) points to Philip's possible intention to place Frederick next to him as Henry VI had stood beside his father. Philip may well have considered securing Sicily for the Empire and summoning

Frederick to Germany in order to bring him up as his successor to the Empire and in Sicily. Assuming this, we would perhaps do justice both to the pope's statements and to our view of Philip of Swabia's character.

[35]Gesta c. 22, RNI 29 (Kempf, Regestum, 81). Haller counters my interpretation of the negotiations between Philip and the pope up to May 1199 (in QFIAB 23, 69ff.), referring to the severe punishment received by the bishop of Sutri and the conditions of the peace of Andely mediated by a legate; a peace which had forced Philip of France to abandon his alliance with the Staufen ally and had left the way open for Richard of England to support Otto. He also objects that if my interpretation were conclusive then the pope would have acted in a precipitate and unwise manner needlessly to break all bridges of understanding at the first unfavourable impression of the negotiations with Philip. The fact is that in May 1199 Innocent did not in the least break these bridges, but was canvassing and preparing to take Otto of Brunswick's side in case his negotiations with Philip should definitely fail. Haller's further objections can be refuted by the reference to the pre-emptive measures Innocent took. Even if Innocent had seriously wished to come to terms with Philip he could not have wished Philip's victory to precede a final accommodation between them. Moreover, Richard was in a position to lay down the conditions for the five-year truce which he only accepted with considerable reluctance (see Tillmann, Legaten, 89). Moreover, the harsh punishment meted out to the bishop of Sutri after his return to the Curia need not in itself imply hostility to Philip, for the bishop in absolving Philip had failed to observe the pope's instructions and had attended Philip's coronation at the wrong place and by the wrong consecrator, being the only bishop, as the Gesta record, in his pontificals. (The Gesta's account is wholly reliable. The Staufen-minded bishops held back not because of the person of the man to be crowned but because of the circumstances of the coronation. The fact that the archbishop of Tarentaise undertook the coronation also indicates that no German archbishop was prepared to officiate in the stead of the lawful consecrator, the archbishop of Cologne. Participation in coronations of such an unusual nature could have most unfortunate consequences, as for instance had been experienced by those participating in the coronation of young Henry of England, Henry II's son, which had been effected by the archbishop of York in infringement of the rights of Canterbury.) Since the contents of Philip's offer had meanwhile shown that an agreement was still a good way off at least, Innocent must have felt the need to disavow, by a conspicuous punishment of his envoy, the latter's attitude in Philip's case which was indeed unjustifiable.

[36]See n. 26 above.

[37]RNI 13.

[38]In February 1199 two letters are issued to Bishop Wolfger of Passau giving him the full authority he requested (Reg. I 571, 572). At the same time a mildly worded letter is issued by the pope addressed to Philip's chancellor Conrad of Querfurt, whom Innocent had deposed for his arbitrary move from Hildesheim to Würzburg. By this letter Innocent seems to counter the view that his harsh action is connected with Conrad's support for Philip (... *nec credere de facile debuisses quod in exaltationem alicuius* [Otto?] *et depressionem alterius* [Philip?] *duximus procedendum*..., Reg. I 574, P. 611). Dated as late as 26 March is a favour granted to Archbishop Ludolf of Magdeburg (Reg. II 551), who was one of Philip's most prominent supporters, and to the dean of his cathedral church (*ibid.*). All these letters point to the presence of Staufen partisans in Rome.

[39]For the arrival and departure of the legation cf. Tillmann, Zum Regestum, 57ff. If the special register of the throne dispute was first begun at the end of August or in September 1199, as is made probable by Kempf, Die Register, 50ff. (cf. his Regestum 2), and not, as had been hitherto believed, in May, the date of the first entry, then all previous attempts to clarify the origins of the special register (Haller, Innocenz III. 484ff.; Peitz, Die Entstehung des Registrum super negotio Romani Imperii und der Anlass zum Eingreifen Innocenz' III in den deutschen Thronstreit, HJ. 46, 1926, 354ff.; Tillmann, Zum Regestum, 72) become irrelevant. The late date suggested for the inauguration of the special register tallies neatly with my assumption that in spring Innocent's relations with Philip had taken a turn for the worse but that the pope was not at that time by any means determined yet to recognize Otto. If Kempf's dating is correct the Protest of Speyer is likely to have caused the change of events which led to the inauguration of the special register (Kempf, Die Register, 52 and Die zwei Versprechen, 372f.).

[40]RNI 29. The objections raised in the *Deliberatio* against the rejection of Philip and the recognition of Otto had without doubt been the objectives of Innocent's earnest deliberation in the years which preceded the decision.

[41]See Chapter 9 below.

[42]See Reg. I 336 of 15 August 1198.

[43]Reg. I 336.

[44]RNI 20; cf. Kempf, Die zwei Versprechen, 371f.

[45]See Haller, Innocenz III., 492 and Tillmann, Zum Regestum, 73. Otto received no official response. The letter of 20 May (RNI 11) in which Innocent expresses his thanks for sending the legation is addressed to Adolf of Cologne. It is friendly but reserved and commits the pope to nothing. Besides his thanks Innocent merely states his readiness to support Otto as far as with God's help he can, adding that he hopes that Otto will continue to show the loyalty shown by his ancestors to the Apostolic See and even increase it after his elevation. Davidsohn (Gesch. von Florenz 1, 627) deduces the pope's secret plotting on Otto's behalf in the Florentine region during 1199 from the fact that the monks of Passignano, at the time when an emissary of the pope stayed in Florence, were forced to swear an oath that they would not enter into any conspiracy with the pope or the emperor or any emissary of either party. Since naturally the emperor referred to can neither be Otto nor Philip, the use of the imperial name rather suggests that the oath for the time being had no actual purport.

[46]Against Haller (Papsttum, 538) I must stick to the view that Innocent's decision to intervene was caused by the collapse of the negotiations of 1198 and early 1199, not by the news of the death of King Richard of England on 6 April (see Tillmann, Zum Regestum, 54). The letters sent to King Richard in favour of Archbishop Geoffrey of York on 28 April 1199 are not, as Haller will have it, letters to the English government sent under the king's address, but quite specially drafted hortatory letters to the king in person. It would have been incomprehensible that the archbishop, Richard's half-brother, had not had new letters to King John made out, if he came to know of Richard's death while still at the Curia. Hoveden's statement (4, 92) that the archbishop was surprised by the news of Richard's death eight days after he had started on his journey home, and had returned to Rome, is totally ignored by Haller. On 3 May, when Innocent announces his intervention in the throne dispute, Geoffrey of York was not yet in possession of the news of Richard's death. The pope may well have learnt the news before Geoffrey, but in no case before 29 April, the earliest possible date for the

archbishop's departure from Rome. It is certain that Innocent was well able to reach a decision within twenty-four hours, but in this case there were no reasons for a precipitate measure. It seems wholly improbable to me that a totally unexpected piece of news, which therefore could not have arrived at the Curia before 29 April, and probably did so later, was the cause of a crucial decision, whose written expression are two lengthy papers in which every word is weighed, which were executed in the papal chancery under the date of 3 May. It does not even strike me as surprising, let alone incredible as Haller suggests, that the news of Richard's death took more than three weeks to reach Rome from Poitou. For it is provable that the king's brother received it on his journey from Rome to the north at best one month after the event.

[47]RNI 2 (Kempf, Regestum, 8), cf. Tillmann, Zum Regestum, 74f.

[48]RNI 1.

[49]RNI 14. For the literature on the Protest of Speyer see Kempf, Regestum, 33. Cf. Tillmann, Zum Regestum, 64ff.

[50]RNI 15.

[51]This is rather a criticism of the direct administration of the country by Germans than a condemnation of the German Empire.

[52]Reg. I 356.

[53]Reg. II 4.

[54]Reg. II 203, P. 849.

[55]Reg. III 49.

[56]In the years 1200 and 1201 the dating here is according to Philip's reign (Magherini-Graziani, Storia di Città di Castello 2, 1910, 303, 312, 313).

[57]See Ficker, Forsch. 2, 381. In addition it should be noted that the dating in Fabriano in July 1198 is according to Philip's reign (Hagemann, 105). From 1199 onwards Fabriano, according to the dating of its documents, appears to have adopted a neutral position between Church and Empire (*ibid.* 107).

[58]In June 1199 the cities of Sanseverino and Fabriano pledge themselves to mutual support except against the pope, the margrave Markward or any other lord who might rule in the territory for the Empire (BF. 12190).

[59]Further details in Baethgen, Regentschaft, 10ff.

[60]Ann. Cecc., 294f.

[61]See RNI 20. Cf. Haller, Innocenz III., 489ff.; Tillmann, Zum Regestum, 73 n. 2; Grundmann in his review of Kempf, Die Register, ZRG. 37 (1951), 426; Kempf, Die zwei Versprechen, 373.

[62]The defection to Philip in August 1199 of Landgrave Hermann of Thuringia, the decision by the archbishop of Trier to support the Staufen cause, the submission of Conrad of Strasbourg to Philip, the ambiguous attitude of the archbishop of Cologne and of the duke of Brabant, Markward's crossing to and his early successes on the island of Sicily, perhaps also Dipold's raid into the Campania towards the end of November. The legation was received in mid-October at the earliest. For details on the legation and its reception see Tillmann, Zum Regestum, 76ff.

[63]See n. 34 above.

[64]Reg. II 221, RNI 33 (Kempf, Regestum, 105f.).

[65]RNI 18 (for the dating end of 1199/early 1200 see Kempf, Regestum, 45, n. 18, 409 n. 1). When drafting or registering the text Innocent suppressed the worst invectives, cf. Tillmann, Zum Regestum, 76ff.

[66]RNI 18 (a variant version recently edited by Kempf, Regestum, 409ff.).

[67]RNI 18. Significantly Innocent did not justify his intervention by the precedence of the priesthood over the kingship, which is explicitly referred to in the address, but rather by historical facts.

[68]His decision will not have been materially affected by the fact that he had yet to receive Otto's confirmation of the renunciation agreed upon by the Welf envoys at the Curia in spring. Otto's position did not allow him to resist the pope's demands for any appreciable period.

[69]RNI 22.

[70]According to a reliable source Conrad, who had played a part in 1184 and 1186 in the negotiations between Frederick I and the Curia in all the controversies between the two parties yet unresolved (cf. Kauffmann, 44, 96f.), intended to persuade one of the kings to renounce his claim (*ut alteruter eorum cessaret*) or else to establish a five-year truce, during which efforts could be made to resolve the throne conflict (Chron. Reg. Colon. Cont. I 168). This report is supplemented by the report of a second, albeit much less reliable informant, according to whom Conrad had gone for the kingdom of Frederick of Sicily (Chron. Reinhardsbr. 562). The latter information gains some support from the fact that Innocent in the following year, in the *Deliberatio*, also argues Frederick's candidature for the throne (cf. also K. van Cleve, Markward of Anweiler and the Sicilian regency; a study of Hohenstaufen policy in Sicily during the minority of Frederick II, 1937, 110, 113f.). In Germany the archbishop may have realized from the outset that peace could only be achieved by a consensus in favour of Philip. Since Otto was not prepared to renounce the throne the archbishop achieved an understanding with the Welf faction over Otto's head (cf. RNI 20, 22). As regards the decision of the throne question itself, the arbiter's sentence was surely only of formal relevance. Since the award of the court of arbitration was to be binding on all the princes, the Staufen faction must have concurred in toto or with a substantial majority, and it is out of the question that they would have left her cause which had come off so splendidly, to be decided by an uncertain arbitrament. The fact that Innocent, for all that, recommended the Welf faction to fall in with the archbishop's peace moves (Otto RNI 20: *ad hoc Moguntinum archiepiscopum elaborasse nostrosque principes consensisse iuxta admonitionem vestram ut colloquium esse debeat...*) shows how much he was interested in the action and how little he had become set on the Welf aspirant's succession to the throne. In 1210 the German public seems to have known little of the pope's favouring the Welf rather than the Staufen aspirant. According to the history of the diocese of Liège Henry of Jacea, the opponent of the bishop-elect of Liège who had been invested by Otto, went to Rome *favore ducis Suevorum animatus* in order to achieve the quashing of the election of his rival, Hugh of Pierrepont (Recueil 18, 652). This shows that at that time Philip's word carried weight at the Curia.

[71]Otto considers it necessary to offer Innocent the oath made on his behalf by his agents to prove that he holds true what he reports of the forthcoming colloquy.

[72]RNI 21.

[73]A series of papal letters in support of Otto, probably for conditional delivery only (RNI 23, 24, 26, 27), seem to have been sent on to the nuncio after his departure. These include the papal dispensation for Otto's marriage to the daughter of the duke of Brabant (RNI 23), a papal safeguarding of the possessions, dignity and honour of those princes who were prepared to side with a king favoured by the pope (*ibid.* 24), a letter in which the pope in his capacity as judge over breach of oath threatens Hermann of Thuringia with ban and interdict unless he resumes his loyalty to Otto or at the least

returns Nordhausen to Otto with which he had been invested as a reward for his homage to the Welf, and a mandate to John of Trier to accept, as he had sworn, the candidate supported by the archbishop of Cologne or else to return the church treasures which had been lodged with him as a pledge and to present himself in Rome by Lent on pain of suspension to account for his breach of oath (*ibid.* 26, 27). Kempf dates RNI 23 in July and the others in August-September, which in my view is questionable. If we rely as Kempf does on the chronological order of the rubrics in Theiner, then RNI 25 = Theiner 155 (P. 1130) and accordingly the associated group RNI 24, 26, 27 would belong to the first half of August. Theiner 143 belongs to 2 August, Theiner 170 to 4 September (Domerham, 399ff), Theiner 172 = Reg. III 3 to 11 October. Accordingly Theiner 155 (RNI 25) which is synchronous with Theiner 149 (both seem to have been sent to Octavian of Ostia, the pope's legate in France) is near to the date of Theiner 143 which is 2 August.

[74]RNI 28.

[75]RNI 20.

[76]MG. Const. 2, 20 No. 16 (with incorrect date). Cf. Kempf, Die zwei Versprechen, 362ff. Against Kempf, I agree with Grundmann (review of Kempf, Die Register, in ZRG. 37, 1951, 426ff) who places RNI 20 with the execution of the privilege.

[77]He promises to conform his attitude towards the Tuscan and Lombard Leagues as well as the Roman commune with the pope's wishes.

[78]RNI 29.

[79]According to the legate's report there was a danger the full extent of which he had not realized until later, that a number of princes might otherwise have elected a third king *in odium Romanae ecclesie* (RNI 51). Those princes still loyal to Otto will have left the legate in no doubt that they would no longer stand by Otto if the pope by recognizing Otto's kingship did not restore the already lost prospect of success. In a similar way the princes' opposition to Otto IV later, in 1211, demanded from the pope that he definitely abandon the emperor. Strangely enough Luchaire ascribes the discontent of the Welf faction to the pope's intervention in the throne dispute (Innocent III Vol. 3, 79). However, the Welf princes themselves had demanded the intervention (RNI 10). Moreover, such discord could not have been placated by a recognition of Otto by papal authority.

[80]RNI 77. On the privilege and its antecedents see Kempf, Die zwei Versprechen, 359ff.

[81]RNI 32, 33 doubtless given to the legate at his departure or sent after him for conditional delivery only. Both the legate and his companion Philip when reporting to the pope what had happened, know how disagreeable a piece of news they convey to him. Guido excuses the hastiness of his proceeding, alleging unavoidable necessity (RNI 51). His companion, the notary Philip, thinks it necessary to soften the information for Innocent by an exaggerated if not mendacious report on Philip's desperate situation and the brilliant prospects facing Otto, both resulting from the proclamation (RNI 52. The dubious role which Philip here plays vis à vis his mandator would tally well with that played by a certain notary and *magister* Philip in England in 1200, see Chapter 6 n. 136 below. The identity of the two is not certain, but probable, see Cheney, Master Philip, 344f.). The envoys were somewhat uneasy as to the possibility that Innocent might refuse to approve what had happened and might accept the proposals put forward by the opposite party. In his reply Innocent instructs his agents always to tell him the whole and unadulterated truth (RNI 56).

[82]The assertion of a subordination of the imperial to the papal power would be equivalent to this assumption since according to Innocent's view the imperial power signifies the highest mundane power, indeed ideally embraces it in its totality.

[83]In his first pronouncement on the throne dispute in May 1199 Innocent reserves to himself the possibility of giving his favour on certain conditions to one of the kings (RNI 1). In the Protest of Speyer the princes use the same expression, requesting Innocent to give his favour more fruitfully to their lord (RNI 14). Innocent picks up the phrase again in his answer (RNI 15... *ut non penitus ignoremus, si cui favor sit apostolicus impendendus*... Kempf, Regestum, 40). In the *Deliberatio* Innocent repudiates the person of Philip, decides to oppose his kingship and, on one particular condition, to give his favour to Otto and accept him as king.

[84]RNI 21.

[85]In the accompanying letter to the German princes (RNI 33) merely the decision for Otto and against Philip is substantiated, not the right to an authoritarian decision as such.

[86]RNI 61.

[87]RNI 62.

[88]*Ratione peccati* Innocent's decision in support of Otto could not be justified. Only a brazen-faced slight for facts could have led to the pretence that Philip was waging an unjust war against Otto or had deprived Otto of his rights. Not even the repudiation of Philip could be justified under this title since Innocent *ratione peccati* could bring to bear only ecclesiastical measures. The pope's extraordinary jurisdiction in temporal matters, which Innocent in the very same year proclaimed in the case of William of Montpellier, could not be claimed here either. The throne dispute could indeed be passed off as a case whose decision was difficult and unattainable through the normal channels, but then Innocent would have had to adjudge only the litigation between Otto and Philip, not the person of Philip and his attitude both in itself and towards the Roman Church, which alone could be the basis for Philip's repudiation. Innocent never claimed that Otto on his elevation had better rights than Philip.

[89]RNI 52.

[90]RNI 68, 75, 83, 84.

[91]His first letter to Adolf after recognizing Otto (RNI 55) already contained a warning against defection.

[92]RNI 44.

[93]RNI 102.

[94]RNI 92–95.

[95]Reg. VII 127.

[96]RNI 60.

[97]RNI 84.

[98]RNI 47, 50.

[99]Reg. III 16, 18. Cf. Appendix 2 below.

[100]RNI 33.

[101]RNI 120, 121, 111.

[102]John of Trier, Ludolf of Magdeburg, Conrad of Halberstadt, Diethelm of Constance, Dietrich of Merseburg (Reg. VII 114). The statement made by the Gesta Episc. Halberst. (116) that the legate had attempted to enforce a second election after Conrad's excommunication is at variance with the facts. Conrad was not and could not be deposed by the legate. The bishop avoided the consequences of excommunication

by lodging an appeal and by departing for the crusade. He was provisionally absolved by the crusading legate at Acre, and finally when he visited the Curia in 1205. In June Innocent dismisses him in grace though Conrad steadfastly refused to change over to Otto (Gesta Episc. Halberst., 118ff.). Either then or later Conrad declared that he was obliged to obey the pope also in the imperial cause, a declaration which at that moment had all but a formal significance (RNI 157). The alleged excommunication of Hartwig of Bremen by the legate (Chron. Reg. Colon. Cont. III 202) is unlikely to have taken place (cf. P. 2171, Migne PL. 217, 106). How should Hartwig ever have been able to defect from Otto while the Welfs and their allies the Danes dominated virtually all northern Germany to the north and west of the Elbe?

[103]Cf. RNI 68 and 83.

[104]As an example the pope's way of proceeding in the case of Ludolf of Magdeburg may be described in more detail. Innocent does not confirm Ludolf's excommunication by the legate, but recognizes that it possibly might not be legally binding on account of a well-timed appeal or on other grounds. The archbishop is required, though, to obtain absolution from the legate, but no term is fixed nor is any obligation to be imposed on him in view of the usual oath of obedience in matters of excommunication, if he can prove the sentence of excommunication to be contrary to law. This at least gave Ludolf a breathing space, since for the time being the much-feared papal confirmation and formal publication of his excommunication was held in abeyance. Even if he could no longer delay accepting the absolution he had the possibility left to him to put the publication of the mandate still further off by attempting to furnish the proof required. Ludolf used his chance and came round to apply for his absolution only after the pope's threatening request of October 1202 (RNI 73). In summer 1203, two years after he had first taken action against Ludolf, the legate handed over to the archbishop the pope's mandate to recognize Otto and again laid the ban on him for breach of oath (RNI 109, Reg. VIII 77, Chron. Mont. Ser. 170). Towards the end of January 1204 Innocent grants the archbishop, who did not consider himself to be under ban, a further month's grace in which to atone for the affront to the legate and in which to effect his change over to Otto (RNI 109). On 25 May 1205 Innocent allows Ludolf's absolution on condition that he take the usual oath of obedience in matters of excommunication (Reg. VIII 77).

Diethelm of Constance, who was probably excommunicated by the legate in 1203, is absolved by papal permission of 15 June 1204 on the usual conditions of taking the oath of obedience in matters of excommunication (Reg. VII 89). The personal integrity of the man who was to effect the absolution, the abbot of Salem, a loyal partisan of Philip (see n. 31 above), guarantees that in fact no other price was demanded for his absolution. Diethelm then continued to serve Philip as before and won great merits by mediating between Philip and Adolf of Cologne. Though by December 1205 he seems to be in disgrace with the pope (Reg. VIII 158), he was not placed under censure and in 1206 he died in peace with the Apostolic See (in Reg. IX 163 the pope styles him *bone memorie*).

[105]Innocent gives his permission for the archbishop to resign on condition that his resignation will not give rise to a material detriment to Otto's cause (RNI 76).

[106]In view of the arbitrary move of Lupold of Worms to Mainz Innocent could by rights have withdrawn his bishopric forthwith. He renounced doing so because he could hope that Lupold would give up Mainz sooner if Worms remained his (Reg. V 14).

[107]He had had the church treasures of Cologne delivered to him by the archbishop of Cologne against his promise on oath that he would vote for the archbishop's candidate, but then had neither supported Otto nor returned the treasures.

[108]Winkelmann, Otto IV, 1, 233, 301f.

[109]Egbert of Bamberg was required only a year after the papal dispensation to make a formal declaration of obedience in the imperial affair in view of the usual oath of obedience which as exempt bishop he had sworn at his consecration at the Curia (Delisle, Lettres, 415; cf. RNI 114). The very fact that he refused to give such a declaration makes it unlikely that he obtained his dispensation by making a political concession.

When Innocent quashed the election of Dietrich of Merseburg he left it to the chapter to postulate its candidate. He then approves the postulation on the basis of an investigation carried out by Ludolf of Magdeburg (Reg. VI 87) who was an enthusiastic partisan of the Staufen cause. Later Innocent allows Dietrich's absolution from the ban which the legate had laid on him, provided that Dietrich promise on oath to obey papal commands without demur (Reg. VII 114). Dietrich was not required to change over to Otto. The Welf Bishop Hartbert of Hildesheim consecrated the elect by the pope's order even though he refused to accept the regalia from Otto (Chron. Mont. Ser. 171). Innocent had quashed the election of Hartwig of Augsburg in November 1202 because of the elect's illegitimate birth, but at the same time allowed Hartwig to administer the diocese and held out the prospect of a future postulation (Reg. V 99). Siegfried of Mainz, who had examined the postulation as the pope's delegate, then interceded on Hartwig's behalf, describing him as an obedient son who was ready to obey the Church's orders (Reg. VI 158). This general wording is hardly to be understood as the promise of a defection from Philip. Philip's loyal negotiator Abbot Everard of Salem, strangely enough Siegfried's co-delegate, joined the legate and the archbishop in supporting admission of the postulation.

[110]Wolfger was not invited to declare his obedience to Otto until the pallium was sent to him, not as the price for his translation to Aquileia. After having sworn the oath due at the receipt of the pallium, he is to forward a declaration that by this oath he is bound to obey the pope's mandates in the imperial cause (RNI 114). It is certain that Wolfger was not thereupon obliged to recognize Otto. At the same court session of early June 1206 in which he carried out a papal mandate to Philip, Wolfger accepted the regalia from him, presumably with papal consent. Later Archbishop Everard of Salzburg complains to the pope that he was being denied what had been allowed to the patriarch (RNI 139). On 22 May 1204 Innocent attested to Wolfger, then bishop of Passau, that he had neither entered into obligations nor made promises which were at variance with the rights of the Empire (RNI 110). Wolfger had had personal contact with Philip up to his journey to Rome and had gone to see him immediately after his return to Germany in early July.

It should also be mentioned that the elect of Constance, William of Staufen, by indulgence of 30 September 1206, is allowed to assume the administration of the see before the confirmation by the metropolitan, because he had not dared accept it from the Welf archbishop of Mainz Siegfried of Eppenstein whom Philip had refused to recognize (Reg. IX 163) and, furthermore, that in October 1205 Innocent allows Henry of Veringen, the elect of Strasbourg, to have his consecration given to him by the archbishop of Sens if Archbishop Siegfried was not prepared to effect it at a place to which the elect could travel with safety, i.e. at a place outside the Welf sphere of influence, or if Siegfried should put off the consecration for some other reason (Reg. VIII 138). In May at the latest the elect had already received a friendly hearing at the Curia (Reg. VIII 90 of 7 June) and earlier, probably still in 1204, had obtained a mandate which directed the archbishop of Mainz to consecrate the elect or to have him consecrated (*ibid.*).

[111]P. 1506. Cf. P. 1215, 1180, BF. 5750; Reiner of Liège, 655; Hist. Leod. Episc. (Recueil 18), 651f.

[112]Guido's partisanship for the count palatine, Otto's brother, against Archbishop Hartwig of Bremen is severely disapproved of by Innocent in a letter of 5 April 1204, that is before he had learnt of Henry's defection. He even decrees the solemn excommunication of the count palatine if he should fail to compensate Hartwig for the loss of the county of Stade (Migne PL. 217, 206; P. 2171). Innocent did not even forsake the archbishop when the latter drew his attention to the pact of subjection to Otto approved by the legate, under the terms of which Stade was secured for the church of Bremen. In other matters, too, Innocent showed that he was not in any case prepared to sacrifice the protection of the churches and their servants, the maintenance of their rights and their possessions to political interests. In the same days when he was engaged in his defence of Bremen against the count palatine he had ordered the publication of the excommunication which Bishop John of Cambrai had laid on his enemies, in particular Philip of Namur, the regent of Flanders, but also on the dukes of Brabant and Limbourg and on the count of Loos (Reg. VII 45, P. 2176). It may well be, however, that these mandates were for conditional use only, and that John was only allowed to publish the mandate if Otto's cause thereby would suffer no material damage.

[113]Reiner of Liège, 655.

[114]Though Innocent rejects the legal objections to the election, yet he sought reassurance in the thought that if Siegfried's voters, too, had made themselves guilty of an offence similar to that of his rival candidate, the conferment would have devolved on him and that he could have appointed Siegfried forthwith (Reg. V 14). It is strange, though, that Innocent did not prefer the unimpeachable loophole of confirmation if he regarded the legal decision as untenable.

[115]In matters of law Innocent, in other cases too, proves himself to be more scrupulous and less orientated towards the interests of the moment than his legates (for example in the divorce case of Philip of France, see Appendix 2 below; in the case of Raymond of Toulouse, see Chapter 7 below; in his proceedings against guilty prelates, see Chapter 6 below).

[116]In addition to the above mentioned measures summonses issued against the bishops Aimo of Tarentaise (RNI 74), Amadeus of Besançon, Conrad of Speyer and Wolfger of Passau are to be named. Though certainly amounting to hostile measures taken against Staufen partisans, they must not be regarded as in themselves unjustified. The offences charged against the bishops, though connected with the throne dispute, are to a great extent subject also to jurisdiction according to canon law. None of the bishops had to pay or paid the price of defection from Philip for regaining the pope's grace. At Laetare 1203 the bishops were summoned. On 21 May 1203 Innocent replies to a canonical inquiry from the archbishop of Besançon (Reg. VI 72), on 22 May he confirms to the monastery of Maulbronn, under acknowledging mention of the bishop, the revenues with which Conrad of Speyer had endowed it (Württembergisches UB., ed. Königl. Staatsarchiv. Stuttg. 2, 1858, 345, P. 1916). Wolfger of Passau's summons

was (probably more than once) prolonged (cf. the note to Reg. VI 56, Migne PL. 215, 56, n. 118). Later on Innocent even allowed his move to the patriarchal see of Aquileia. The only prelate who was explicitly required to recognize Otto seems to have been Archibshop Everard of Salzburg (RNI 103, 139). It seems likely that Everard was the first of the bishops from whom Innocent by way of an oath of obedience required the declaration that the oath also obliged them to obedience in matters concerning the Empire. Apparently by reason of this declaration Everard was required to recognize Otto. He complied by words without drawing the consequence by deeds. In the majority of cases this special mandate was not issued. The enumeration in RNI 157, of the bishops who in 1208 in some way or another were bound by oath to the pope in the imperial cause, contains six names. Four of these bishops, in view of their ecclesiastical position, had had to swear oaths of loyalty and obedience usual on the conferment of the pallium: the archbishops Everard of Salzburg, Albert of Magdeburg, Siegfried of Mainz and Bruno of Cologne. We know that two of the bishops not named in this list, Wolfger of Aquileia and Egbert of Bamberg, were required by Innocent, on the basis either of the oath sworn on receipt of the pallium or of the oath of obedience which the exempt bishop had taken at his consecration at the Curia, to declare that by virtue of their oath they owed obedience to the pope even in the cause of the Roman Empire (RNI 114; Delisle, Lettres, 415; Reg. IX 15). The absence of these two names does not indicate that the list is incomplete for Germany in other respects. Egbert's name for instance seems to have been omitted because he was then (1208) under the suspicion of co-responsibility for Philip's death. The patriarch's name will be missing because he was an Italian bishop, for none of the identical letters which Innocent sent to bishops bound to him in the imperial cause is addressed to a member of the Italian episcopate, though several Italian bishops had entered the same obligation (RNI 114). The two other German bishops who were obliged to accept this obligation, according to the list, are Archbishop John of Trier and Bishop Conrad of Halberstadt. Conrad too had sworn an oath of obedience on which Innocent could have based the obligation in the imperial cause in matters of his excommunication, namely the normal oath of obedience which he had had to swear at the Curia in 1205 on the occasion of his absolution. In the case of John of Trier Innocent may have reverted to the former pallium oath, but it is also possible that John was absolved at the Curia and had had to swear the oath on that occasion. In John's case at least there may exist a direct obligation with regard to the imperial cause which Innocent perhaps extorted by reason of the archbishop's obligation sworn to the archbishop of Cologne to accept the latter's candidate as king.

[117]For a discussion of the alleged unscrupulous way by which Innocent is said to have driven Philip's chancellor, Conrad of Würzburg, to shameful treachery against his unsuspecting lord, see Appendix 3 below.

[118]To the exaggerating reports by his agents on the favourable state of Otto's situation as a result of the pope's recognition of his kingship (see above, n. 81), Innocent answers admonishing them to write him nothing but the plain truth (RNI 56).

[119]Cf. the sceptical end of the reply to Otto's message concerning his imminent ultimate victory (RNI 107).

[120]RNI 100, 99.

[121]RNI 65, 99.

[122]In the treaty between Philip and Henry of Brabant a marriage between Frederick of Sicily and Mary of Brabant was taken into consideration, with no regard to the duke's daughter's engagement to Otto nor to the marriage agreement negotiated by the

pope between Frederick and Sancha of Aragon (not her sister Constance, the widow of Imre of Hungary, who later became Frederick's wife) RNI 111; cf. Chapter 10 n. 117 below (Kempf, Regestum, 277). This clause of the treaty naturally had sense only if Philip intended to usurp at least the guardianship of his nephew, who was at that time in the care of a German, William Capparone.

[123]Cf. Baethgen, Regentschaft, 21ff.

[124]Reg. III 23; Gesta c. 33; Huillard-Bréholles 1, 82.

[125]Reg. I 557.

[126]*Ibid.*

[127]See Gesta c. 23, 24, 28, 30, 33; Reg. I 557, 558, 560; Reg. III 23; Ann. Cecc. 294f.; Rich. of S. Germano, 19, 22.

[128]For details of the pope's agreements with Walter and their consequences see Baethgen, Regentschaft, 25ff. On Walter of Brienne cf. also L. Böhm, Johann von Brienne, König von Jerusalem, Kaiser von Konstantinopel (Heidelberg thesis 1938), 16ff.

[129]Gesta c. 25.

[130]The count, his wife, and Tancred's widow were obliged to swear on oath that they would do nothing to impair the person or the honour of King Frederick or the kingdom of Sicily, and to recognize in advance that any infringement of the oath would lead to immediate excommunication and interdict as well as to the loss of all the rights they had in respect of the territories mentioned and of the kingdom. In the same oath the count pledges himself that as soon as he received his fief, he would render allegiance and service to King Frederick, swear the oath to the pope on the guardianship and fight against the Germans in the kingdom (Gesta c. 25, BF. 5709). The king's real safeguard was that the pope's opposition would prove an unsurmountable obstacle should Walter of Brienne be tempted to lay hands on the crown of Sicily. For the Germans the restoration of Tancred's dynasty was intolerable; but the national king was Frederick, Constance's son, and Walter could never have hoped to gain the crown against the pope's will, unless he could gain the support of one of the two combatants. Walter's resistance to the pope's urging to cross over to the island and take up the fight against Markward (Reg. V 38, 39, 84–87) suggests that the count was well aware of this state of affairs. The objectives for a pretender to the throne had to be to gain Palermo and a position of power on the island.

[131]Reg. VII 129–31, 135; Gesta c. 36; Cf. Baethgen, Regentschaft, 85f.

[132]Cf. Hampe, Deutsche Angriffe auf das Königreich Sizilien im 13. Jahrhundert (HV. 7) 474, and Tillmann, Rekuperationen, 354f.

[133]Innocent had to try and preserve the rights due to him as regent without restricting too much the free scope of the council of the *familiares*; he had to advocate the king's rights without antagonizing the powerful nobility, and generally to neutralize the conflicting tendencies. One example must suffice for many. Sergius Scrofa, the bailli of the duchy of Amalfi, shortly after he had his justiciarship confirmed by Innocent (P. 1607), early in 1202, when Innocent calls on him to pay the revenues drawn from the royal tributes, refuses any rendering of accounts and publicly challenges the pope's right to the rule of the kingdom (Reg. V 76).

[134]A cardinal legate in Apulia has sketched out to the pope a vivid picture of his thankless task. It is a sad picture of unreliability, treachery and indifference of the inhabitants of the country (Hampe, Ein sizil. Legatenbericht an Innocenz III. aus dem Jahre 1204, QFIAB. 20, 1928/9, 52).

[135]Reg. VI 191; see also Gesta c. 37, 38.

[136]In Tolentino in 1201 Margrave Walter Guarnerii is mentioned as podestà; he was a partisan of Markward (Ficker, Forsch. 2, BF. 12228) and castellan of the castle. In other cities, too, the pro-imperial nobility will have succeeded in sustaining or newly establishing its influence by joining the communes (Zonghi, Carte diplomatiche Fabrianesi (1011–1299), Coll. doc. stor. Marchig. 2, 1872, 23ff., 32, 33, 35, 163, 49). On 2 June 1201 the Camaldulenses of Fonte Avellana in the north-west of the March have their immunity from certain tributes granted by Philip (BF. 54).

[137]Reg. III 28; Ciavarini, Collezione di documenti storichi antichi delle città e terre marchigiane, 1870ff, 4, p. 177ff.

[138]In the peace treaty the pope is not named as intermediary, but his co-operation in one way or another is probable in view only of his preceding efforts. With reference to one particular issue the treaty provides for a court of arbitration consisting of legates or cardinals (Ciavarini 4, 122).

[139]The newly appointed rector of the duchy and of the Tuscan patrimony, a cardinal legate, is instructed to take care, in co-operation with the city prefect, of the security of the highways, of the promotion of justice, of the maintenance of peace and of the defence of the territory (Reg. II 203, P. 849). By force of arms Innocent puts an end in 1201 to the criminal activities of two noblemen highway robbers who ever since the days of Innocent's predecessors had been infesting the road from southern Tuscany to Rome from their robbers' nest of Raspampano, and had even managed to detain a papal castellan with impunity (Gesta c. 15; P. 1514). It had been to Raspampano that in 1199 had fled the betrayers of Peter Parenzi whom the Patarenes had then murdered, and the murderers themselves had pondered whether they should lug their victim there (AASS. 21 maii 5, 88f.).

[140]The pope's disputes with the major cities of the Patrimony are mostly connected with the latters' aspirations to extend their power, which Innocent, as far as was feasible, resisted both in the interests of the smaller communes and of his own rule.

[141]See Chapter 1, p. 1 above.

[142]Gesta c. 8. This procedure probably is not a fundamental innovation after all. The restitution of the senate in the charter of 1188 seems to refer not only to the recognition of the papal right to invest the senate. The fact that *prior* to 1188 the senators were freely elected and that even under Celestine III the pope seems to have taken no part in their election (Cf. Halphen, Etudes sur l'administration de Rome au moyen-âge (751–1252), 1907, 69ff.) does not prove that the popes were not legally entitled to participate in elections after 1188. Innocent's control over the city in the early days of his reign surely was not such that he could have introduced such an innovation on his own or that he could have brought it about with the goodwill of the commune.

[143]Gesta c. 8.

[144]Gesta c. 134–142.

[145]Gesta c. 135–137.

[146]Gesta c. 137; Reg. VII 133.

[147]Gesta 135–137.

[148]Reg. VII 102.

[149]The Gesta's report about the pope's actions can be accepted as accurate. We would offend, if not against his sense of justice, in any case against Innocent's shrewdness, if we were to presume that in these critical times he had played into the hands of the opposition merely to serve the interests of his brother or even of a more distant

relative. The marriage contract between Richard and the Poli had been arranged by Cardinal Octavian, the uncle of Odo of Poli. The court of arbitration later instituted seems to have adjudged the estates to Richard.

[150]Gesta 135–137.

[151]Gesta c. 137. Cf. Girald Cambr. 1, 16.

[152]Gesta c. 139.

[153]Cf. the text following.

[154]Reg. VII 102, P. 2253.

[155]Reg. VII 133; P. 2297. At the same time Richard pledged himself to deliver the estates to the pope against compensation if the peace between pope and commune, Richard and the Poli, should make it necessary.

[156]Gesta c. 140.

[157]RNI 153.

[158]Gesta c. 141.

[159]Once peace has been restored Innocent enforces the handing over of a fortified tower built against his will next to the Lateran Palace and has it torn down (Gesta c. 141). From one of the members of the opposition he requires the return of the property of the Roman Church in Tusculum, excommunicates him and after his death compels his relatives by the denial of a Christian burial to give guarantee for the reparation promised, but not provided by the deceased (*ibid.* 142).

[160]Girald. Cambr. 1, 377, 374.

[161]Tillmann, Rekuperationen, 355ff., 379.

[162]RNI 111, 113, 116–135.

[163]RNI 131, 132.

[164]The Staufen legation which delivered the Protest of Bamberg-Hall also had to convey a peace offer. With regard to the latter, Innocent writes to Otto to explain that it had not been able to dissuade him from his project *licet multa nobis et magna promissa fuissent* and warns him for his part to guard against a circumvention which his opponents were sure to attempt (RNI 65). The Staufen legation was supported by an envoy from the French king, Marquis Boniface of Montferrat, who also advocated the interests of the crusade. He delivers Philip of France's protest against the acceptance of his Welf enemy by the pope as well as a guarantee that, should Philip of Swabia gain the imperial crown, he would not turn against the Roman Church (RNI 63). In 1203 the Staufen put forward a detailed offer of peace in which he proposes territorial concessions not qualifiable as to detail, and a marriage between his daughter and one of the pope's nephews, and in which he offers to undertake a crusade to restore the union of the two Churches should the Greek Empire get into his hands or into the hands of his brother-in-law, the Prince Alexius, and to make concessions in the ecclesiastical sphere (cf. MG. Const. 2, 9 and RNI 90 of 9 September 1203). The statements given by the pope and Philip of Swabia as to the mission of the prior of Camaldoli, the mediator, do not agree. It should be borne in mind that if Innocent had an interest in denying that he had commissioned the prior, Philip for his part had no less an interest in emphasizing the part that the pope had played in the negotiations. Moreover, Philip states no more than that Innocent had *allowed* the prior to make the journey and to enter into negotiations on the basis of the offers Philip had made (MG. Const. 2, 10). The commission entrusted to the abbots of Salem and Neuburg in October 1203, to remonstrate with Philip personally on account of the favour shown to the deposed Lupold of Worms (Reg. VI 160), shows that the pope, too, did not wish to allow contacts with Philip to break down completely.

[165]For the negotiations see Tillmann, Rekuperationen, 343ff. By an examination of the handwriting Kempf (Die Register, 53ff.) shows that the entries in the special register were discontinued from about July 1206 to August 1208 and that letters 140 to 159 beginning with the authentication of Philip's peace mission (No. 140) and the announcement of the cardinal legates by Innocent (No. 141), were entered at the same time, probably by August 1208, that is after Philip's murder. The discontinuance of the register or its interruption certainly indicates a turning-point in events, namely Innocent's changing sides to Philip. Kempf also indicates that a letter to Philip's wife, written in February 1208 (Reg. X 209), is addressed *illustri reginae Mariae* (Die Register, 58). Cf. also Kempf, Regestum, 338, n. 4 on RNI 143, on Philip being addressed as *serenitas*, and the suggestion that the original address of the letter which was not registered until after Philip's death does not necessarily have to have been *Duci*.

[166]I have justified this view in detail in Rekuperationen, 341ff. Cf. also Chapter 5 above.

[167]The alliance between Milan and a number of other Lombard cities of 16 June 1208 (BF. 12324), pledged to uphold the Peace of Constance, represents an act of mistrust if not of hostility towards Philip, whose march to Rome owing to his reconciliation with the pope, seemed to be palpably on hand.

[168]Cf. Tillmann, Rekuperationen, 353.

[169]Cf. *ibid.* 361.

[170]Cf. n. 115 above.

[171]A great many of the obligations derive from the period after Otto's catastrophic defeats and cannot, therefore, have been intended to help Otto's cause. When Innocent demanded the declaration from Wolfger, the latter had already begun to be active as intermediary between Philip and the pope. Early in 1206 the mediation is performed by Egbert of Bamberg (Delisle, Lettres, 415; Reg. IX 15) who in 1204 had refused to undertake it (cf. RNI 114, 139). Albert of Magdeburg took it up towards the end of 1206 on the occasion of his consecration and receipt of the pallium in Rome, Conrad of Halberstadt in 1205 (cf. n. 102 above) and Archbishop Bruno of Cologne in the same year at the earliest.

[172]Cf. Tillmann, Zum Regestum, 69ff.

[173]Cf. Tillmann, Zum Regestum, 70ff.

[174]Cf. Chapter 5 above and n. 7 above.

[175]Cf. Kauffmann, 15f.

[176]In Rekuperationen, 359 I point out that the designation of Richard of Segni as count of Sora by the chronicler Burchard of Ursberg was inaccurate for the time Burchard had in mind. Richard was surely not yet in possession of the county when negotiations were concluded, though his elevation was then probably intended. The considerable difference in rank between the betrothed would have been somewhat diminished if the princess were to become engaged to the son of the count of Sora rather than to an insignificant Campanian nobleman.

[177]Cf. Tillmann, Rekuperationen, 360.

[178]Geoffrey of Viterbo Cont. (MG. SS. 22) 369. See also Annales Marbac. 77. According to Otto of Sankt Blasien (80) Otto was to have received the duchy of Swabia. A conferment of the Arelate is very likely to have been considered, since in this way Otto would have retained the royal dignity without which he would, by all we know of him, certainly never have been prepared to resign (see also A.L. Poole, England and Burgundy in the last decade of the twelfth century, in Essays in History pres. to R.L. Poole, 1927, 262).

[179]Cf. Tillmann, Rekuperationen, 352.

[180]See Gesta c. 127 for details of the journey.

[181]The Aldobrandini had adhered to Henry V and later sided with Otto IV against the Church.

[182]Migne PL. 217, 298f.; Gesta c. 127.

[183]RNI 143.

[184]Haller (Papsttum, 544) rejects the argument I put forward in Rekuperationen, 346f, and argues that the legislation of Viterbo by no means referred to the whole of the Papal State but only to the Campania and Roman Tuscany from the latter of which, as being the Patrimony proper, the March and the duchy had always been sharply distinguished. He argues that the Gesta (c. 124) seem to have arbitrarily added the names of the two latter provinces. In fact it is Haller who is being arbitrary. How and why should the almost contemporaneous notes of a man who was closely connected with the Curia ever have come to report that the estates were convened for Spoleto and the March, too, if they were only summoned for the old territory of the Patrimony? We also know that, at about the time of the court session in Viterbo, citizens and nobility from the new regions (the county of Todi and the March) were staying at the Curia (Tillmann, Rekuperationen, 348f.) In any case, during Innocent III's reign the Patrimony was not understood to embrace only the old territories including Roman Tuscany. The *cura et provisio* which Innocent bestowed on the apostolic Patrimony by appointing a legate in October 1199 doubtless refers also to the duchy of Spoleto (Reg. II 202, 203). When the duchy was regained by the Church Innocent expresses his pleasure that the *patrimonium b. Petri* had been restituted without force (Reg. I 356). At the beginning of his reign Innocent states that despite Markward's offences against ecclesiastical liberty and the Church's Patrimony he had postponed his excommunication (Reg. I 38). In the connection in which the term 'offences' occurs it can indeed only be meant to refer to the defence of the March and the duchy of Ravenna.

[185]Naturally it is possible that parts perhaps of the March continued to stand off. But in the south of the March the faction of the nobility hostile to papal rule had lacked any influence since the end of 1207 and had partly sought reconciliation with the Church (Regesta Firmana in Doc. di storia Ital. a cura della R. Dep. di storia patria per le provv. di Toscana, dell'Umbria e delle Marche, 4, 1870, 338).

[186]Gesta c. 39; Ann. Cecc. 296; Rich. of S. Germ. 27; Ann. Casin. 319.

[187]Ann. Cecc. 297; Gesta c. 39.

[188]Gesta c. 40; Reg. XI 131–133.

[189]Reg. XI 134.

[190]RNI 111; Reg. XI 4; Huillard-Bréholles 1¹, 131.

[191]Reg. XI 131; Huillard-Bréholles 1¹, 134.

[192]RNI 155, 180.

[193]RNI 77.

[194]Already in his first letter to Otto after Philip's death Innocent warns Otto of this opposition (RNI 153). In early March 1209 at the latest the Curia is in possession of a letter from Otto informing the pope that he was reliably informed that the Emperor Henry's son was wishing him ill and plotting against him with requests and promises (RNI 187). Winkelmann (Otto IV, 101 n. 5, 142) suggests that the allegation was invented by the pope in order to bring home to the Welf how much he was dependent on him and that Otto was merely repeating to the pope as *veridica quorundum relatio* what he had learned from the pope himself. Winkelmann argues that Innocent could not

have become aware of Frederick's attitude in so short a span of time. However, Otto was so completely dependent on the pope that it seems unnecessary for him to emphasize this dependence. The pope learned of Philip's death while staying in the kingdom, albeit in Terra di Lavoro. Frederick may well have taken immediate steps at the Curia or otherwise which were directed against Otto. If Otto had learned of Frederick's brisk agitation against him already by January or February there is no reason why Innocent should not have learned of Frederick's hostile intentions some time in August. As to the objection that Frederick had been too young and too dependent on the pope to act on his own initiative in the imperial cause see Reg. XI 208 (and above 144f.).

[195]Even Philip of France in view of the pope's attitude regarded a candidature of Frederick as impossible. Otherwise, given the great danger which the Welf kingship represented for him, he would not have promoted the installation of an anti-king so utterly without prospects of success as Henry of Brabant.

[196]RNI 154, 155.

[197]RNI 166.

[198]RNI 153.

[199]Cf. RNI 157.

[200]Chron. regia Colon. Cont. III, 226f.

[201]Still before November of the year, since Bruno died on 2 November.

[202]Chron. regia Colon. Cont. II 185, III 229f.; Weltchronik 238; Schöppenchronik 135; Caesarius (Hilka 3), 239. Before starting his imperial legation in January 1209 the imperial legate for Italy, Patriarch Wolfger of Aquileia, enquires of Innocent about the Matildine estate (RNI 186), probably to ascertain whether a waiver in favour of the Empire stipulated in the peace treaty with Philip, for whom Wolfger had acted as negotiator, would be recognized by the pope even in the new circumstances. However Innocent, referring to the Pledge of Speyer, a copy of which he sends him, requires the legate to re-claim it for the Roman Church. Reiner of Liège somehow came to know that the marriage plan in connection with territorial losses of the Empire played a rôle in Otto's dispute with the pope (Rein. Ann. MG. SS. 16, 662ff.).

[203]Cf. p. 117 above.

[204]See RNI 153.

[205]RNI 187.

[206]RNI 188.

[207]RNI 177.

[208]RNI 179.

[209]RNI 189.

[210]The legates, who are certain to have delivered the demand, Ugolino of Ostia and Leo of S Croce (RNI 179), the same men who had been spokesmen in the final stages of the peace negotiations with Philip, left Rome in the latter half of January at the earliest (letter of credence of 18 January, RNI 178). Within the short time between their arrival and the issue of the privilege no negotiations adequate for the difficulties of the matter at issue can have taken place. Cf. also Hampe, Deutsche Kaisergeschichte in der Zeit der Salier und Staufer ([10] 1949), 246f.

[211]The extension of Wolfger's authority to include also the March of Ancona and the duchy of Spoleto was perhaps not yet suspicious in itself. The provinces were important in view of the march to Rome, on which the Roman king had a claim to the fodrum even in the Patrimony, which in Innocent's view, however, was allowed to be

collected only by papal decree (RNI 77). Innocent had the letters of recommendation asked for by the imperial legate made out to him only for Lombardy and those regions of Tuscany which belonged to the Empire (RNI 185). The legate's activities in the Romagna need not necessarily have been an usurpation nor an infraction of the obligations of Neuss and Speyer. It is open to doubt whether the concept of the Exarchy used in the privileges is identical with that of the Romagna. In 1213, when Frederick II is still wholly dependent on Innocent, his legate exercises the same rights of sovereignty in the Romagna as formerly had Otto's legate, and the imperial rule goes unchallenged there until the reign of Gregory X. It is true that Innocent makes out to the imperial legate no letters of recommendation specifically for the cities of the Romagna, but it is possible that those cities were included in the letters for Lombardy. In a letter written by the legate Ugolino in 1221 Ferrara, a city in the Romagna, seems to be regarded as belonging to Lombardy (Registro del Cardinale Ugolino d'Ostia, ed. Levi, in Fonti per la storia d'Italia 8, 1890, 104f.). When Ugolino was entrusted with the legation in Lombardy, the March of Verona, Romagna and Tuscany (*ibid.* 138), Frederick II sends him his congratulations on his appointment as legate in Lombardy and Tuscany (*ibid.* 151).

[212]BF. 12340, Savioli, Annali Bolognesi (1784ff.) $2^2$, 297ff.

[213]Reg. XII 75–77.

[214]Böhmer, Acta, 824.

[215]Reg. XII 78. Cf. RNI 185.

[216]Reimchronik, vv. 6644ff. The information is confirmed by the fact that Innocent, besides the city prefect, sends Magister Philip, the nuncio of 1203 and witness of the Promise of Neuss, to meet the king in Lombardy (RNI 191).

[217]RNI 191.

[218]Cf. p. 138 above.

[219]Böhmer, Acta, 629; BF. 6082.

[220]Reimchronik, vv. 6656ff.

[221]Reimchronik, *ibid.* If it had been otherwise the imperial register would certainly have recorded the oath sworn. Those sources which seem to report differently either refer to the former oaths sworn by Otto or regard the normal coronation oaths as being special obligations accepted by Otto. Cf. also Winkelmann, Otto IV, 489ff. though I cannot wholly agree with his way of argumentation.

[222]William Brito (Delaborde 1), 237.

[223]RNI 193.

[224]RNI 194.

[225]RNI 194.

[226]See Appendix 4 below.

[227]Imperial privilege for Matelica of 12 October (BF. 306): investiture of the bishop of Ascoli with the *regalia* of his church and the county (*ibid.* 309). In Fabriano up to and including part of 1209 the dating is *imperio Romano vacante*, but after 20 January 1210 according to Otto's reign (Hagemann, 109). There is a privilege dated 9 December 1211 granted to Fabriano by Otto (Hagemann, 112).

[228]BF. 14633, 348.

[229]On Lupold's arrival the city had defected from the Church and may have been given up in the peace made with Philip. From this Otto could not deduce any rights, the less so as he no longer recognized the recuperations of the Roman Church.

[230]Cf. Winkelmann, Otto IV, 239f. For Radicofani see also BF. 12429.

[231]Cf. Winkelmann, Otto IV, 245 n. 1; BF. 12362; Ficker, Forsch. 4, 277.

[232]BF. 352b. Cf. Winkelmann, Otto IV, 245, n. 3.

[233]Reg. XI 208.

[234]In 1209 Frederick orders Amphusus de Rota, count of Tropea, to be treacherously imprisoned. As a consequence the counts of Calano and Fondi do not dare obey a royal summons and the abbot of Monte Cassino cancels a delegation he had proposed to send to the court (Richard of S. Germ., Gaudenzi, 74; BF. 14648). Then and later proscriptions and confiscations of property took place (BF. 14647a). Towards the end of 1209 Innocent vainly urges Frederick in view of the danger threatening by Otto to strengthen the loyal followers in his service by kindness and try and win for his cause those standing aside (Hampe, Beiträge zur Geschichte Kaiser Friedrichs II, HV 4, 1901, 193). In April or May 1210 Frederick dismisses his chancellor Walter Pagliari from his court in disgrace. On 20 June Innocent raises decided objections and demands that Pagliari be recalled (Reg. XIII 83).

[235]Reg. XI 208.

[236]Reg. XI 208, XIV 81.

[237]Hampe, HV 4, 193f.

[238]Böhmer, Acta, 629f.; BF. 10722. For the dating see Ficker, Erörterungen zur Reichsgeschichte des 13. Jahrhunderts, MIÖG 4 (1883) 338ff.

[239]On 30 January Innocent takes the Danish kingdom under his protection against invasion and safeguards the king against any infringement of his rights in a letter sent to the kings, princes and all Christian believers neighbouring the Danish kingdom, in so far as they maintain the Catholic unity (Reg. XII 157, P. 3898). Otto was doubtless planning to follow Philip's example and move against the Dane who had hitherto been his friend and ally. Immediately after Philip's death, before he had been generally accepted as king, Otto had opposed the candidate supported by Denmark for the see of Bremen (RNI 160). It seems likely that Otto, already at that time, would have been well content if Waldemar of Schleswig, the arch-enemy of the king of Denmark, had held the field.

[240]Only the letter issued to the bishop of Regensburg is extant (BF. 6081). It goes without saying that he was not the only prelate to whom Innocent turned, and this is also confirmed by the Schöppenchronik (135). Cf. Ficker, op. cit. n. 238. Similar letters were sent to the archbishop of Ravenna and his suffragans (Reg. XIII App. 210 of 7 March 1211) and certainly also to other bishops of imperial Italy. The activity of papal legates here is testified by BF. 12363, 12373, 12395, 12397, 12402. We can assume that their activities were directed against Otto.

[241]Böhmer, Acta, 629f.

[242]BF. 6092.

[243]BF. 10722 (draft of the letter edited by Tuetey, Archives des missions scientifiques, 3e sér. 6, 1880, 34, No. 2). To the deliverer of the papal request, his chaplain Peregrine, Innocent on 13 September writes in a Parisian prebend case (Reg. XIII 130, 131).

[244]Ann. Casin. 320; Rich. of S. Germano, 30; Ann. Cecc. 300.

[245]The Bolognese canonist Paulus Hungarus makes the interesting statement in his Notabili: potest ferri sentencia excommunicacionis et eius executio ad tempus suspendi, sicut etiam fecit Innocentius in Othonem temporibus nostris (quoted in Mochi Onory, 186). The excommunication was in fact published in Germany and, it seems, also in Italy including the Sicilian kingdom, not earlier than 1211, and probably not before February. For Germany see pp. 146ff. above. The Annales Casinenses report that Otto is

excommunicated on 18 November 1210, that the sentence is confirmed on 31 March 1211 and that the canons of Capua at the same time are excommunicated because they had celebrated mass while the emperor was present (Ann. Cas. 320. Cf. BF. 443d). The sentence must therefore have been published in the kingdom some time before the end of March, but on the other hand cannot be dated many months earlier since the canons who had continued to celebrate mass in the emperor's presence during his long stay in Capua (Otto remained there during the negotiations conducted by the abbot of Morimund between September 1210 and February 1211, see n. 247 below) would then have been excommunicated at an earlier date. The disputed validity of the interdict which Archbishop Anselm of Naples by papal mandate laid on his episcopal city for its support of Otto, was not confirmed by Innocent until 16 June 1211 (Reg. XIV 74). On 6 July 1211 (for the date see Ficker, MIÖG 4, 344ff). Innocent orders the publication of the ban in the diocese of Cremona (Böhmer, Acta No. 922, 631) and in the archdiocese of Ravenna (see Ficker *op. cit.*). Along with a letter dated 7 June (Reg. XIV 78) to Gerard, elect of Albano, the papal legate for Lombardy, mandates were issued to the patriarchs of Aquileia and Grado, to the archbishop of Genoa, as well as to the suffragans of Milan in which Innocent in a tone which indicates that he expects resistance, requires *ut excommunicationem in ipsum* [Otto] *et fautores eius prolatam postposita omni occasione solemniter innovent.* These letters were meant for the legate's use, who probably was to avail himself of them as and when he saw fit. They may not have been delivered and may have been replaced the following month by others, of which the letters sent to Sicard of Cremona and the archbishop of Ravenna are extant in their original wording. When in June the bishops are required to 'renew' the excommunication, this was, therefore, not a demand to renew a ban already published by them, but to renew the pope's sentence by publishing it. It is also unlikely that Wolfger of Aquileia, Otto's former legate in Italy, who in 1212 was still in friendly contact with him (see Winkelmann, Otto IV, 298), should have published the ban some time before June of that year. The assumption that the ban was at first suspended is to some extent challenged by Innocent III's letter of 22 December 1210 (Reg. XIII 193), in which he stresses that the Pisans *per censuram et denuntiationem apostolicam* had been released from their obligations of allegiance to Otto who is styled *dictus imperator, excommunicatus et maledictus.* Since Paulus Hungarus's statement of the suspension of the execution of the ban is beyond challenge, and since this suspension can hardly have been limited to a mere month starting from 18 November but must have lasted at least until negotiations had finally broken down, the only way out of the difficulty seems to be to assume that the *denuntiatio apostolica* was no more than a simple announcement to the Pisans of the excommunication executed against Otto and its legal consequences; in the case of Pisa it could not be postponed since the city was most actively supporting the emperor in his raid on the Sicilian kingdom. There is no mention of the competent Pisan church superior, the archbishop, having published the excommunication sentence, nor of the pope having instructed the archbishop to act accordingly.

[246]See the document in Bretholz, Ein päpstliches Schreiben gegen Kaiser Otto IV. von 1210, 30 October, Lateran, NA 22 (1897), 293ff.

[247]According to Burchard of Ursberg (100) negotiations lasted from 29 September to Lent. Ash Wednesday in 1211 was on 16 February.

[248]Cf. Tillmann, Rekuperationen, 365.

[249]Böhmer, Acta, 631.

[250]A letter from Otto urging John to be complaisant to the pope is extant under the title of emperor, but it remains questionable whether it belongs in fact to the time of his emperorship (cf. BF. 303). As the full title is not given, the phrasing *Romanorum imperator* should not be given undue significance. If the letter were actually written after Otto's coronation we would have to regard it only as a cheap expression of amiability by Otto towards his consecrator immediately after his coronation.

[251]The assertion that peace with France was the *conditio sine qua non* for the compromise with Otto (Böhmer, Acta, 630), is entirely credible.

[252]Cf. Winkelmann, Otto IV, 292ff. There was in fact among members of the imperial faction some playing with the idea of confiscating church property. Cf. Walther von der Vogelweide's verse quoted in Winkelmann *op. cit.* 296.

[253]Rich. of S. Germ., 31; Ann. Casin. 320.

[254]Böhmer, Acta, 630.

[255]According to a papal letter dated 6 April 1213 the provost of Marbach had *iam annis elapsis duobus* been driven from his church because he had, on the order of Bishop Lutold of Basel, published the papal letter of excommunication (Reg. XVI 24). It follows, then, that the sentence must have been published in the diocese of Basel in the first days of April *at the latest*.

[256]The letter in Böhmer, Acta, 630 is undated. According to the Schöppenchronik the papal letters announcing Otto's excommunication were dispatched in 1211 (135). Burchard of Ursberg states that Innocent did not begin to work for Otto's 'deposition' until the final collapse of negotiations, that is February 1211 at the earliest (100).

[257]BF. 10722 (Tuetey *loc. cit.*).

[258]Rich. of S. Germ. 30. In June 1210 Frederick had reimbursed the pope for his expenses, fixed at 12,800 gold ounces, for the defence of the kingdom during his administration as a guardian, by mortgaging to him the entire landed property of Monte Cassino, of the lords of Aquino and of Count Richard of Sora, Innocent's brother, with the reservation of the military service hitherto due to him (BF. 631, MG. Const. 2, 540). The mortgage was renewed and extended in December. All the revenues are to devolve to the pope and the Church, those named above are bound to loyalty to the pope as well as to the king, but on the pope's order have to render military service to the king (BF. 639, MG Const. 2, 541). It was not only the satisfaction of papal wishes which was involved here. The abbot of Monte Cassino was politically unreliable. To defy the pope directly would in any case have been riskier for the abbot than to do it indirectly by abandoning Frederick.

[259]Ann. Placent. Guelfi 425. The wording in Franciscus Pipini (Muratori, Antiqu. 9, 640) makes it doubtful whether we should read *sperans*, which would imply that Otto had hoped to achieve peace, or *sperantes*, which would refer to the papal legates. Luchaire (Innocent III, 3, 275) assumes that Innocent had now taken up an intractable posture. However, since Innocent sent the envoys, the attempt at peace must, indeed, have been his doing, or at least have suited him. William Brito (Delaborde 1 239) informs us that Innocent had not immediately approved the request for Frederick's designation made by the princely opposition. This may be explained not only by the *gravitas* with which, in the French court chaplain's view, the Roman Church was wont to deal with such matters nor by the aversion against Frederick's lineage, but rather by the wish to make one ultimate attempt with Otto.

[260]In his letters of 25 May and 6 June 1213 (P. 4736, 4746; Reg. XVI 56, 50), Innocent does not speak of a faction supporting Frederick or of a change over to Frederick, but of the *pars*

*catholica*, of the change over to the *pars catholica*. He did not recognize Frederick as Roman emperor-elect until after his election at Frankfurt on 5 December 1212 and the official report of that election to the Curia (see Tillmann, Rekuperationen, 362ff.).

[261]Reg. XV 189.

[262]Chron. Reinhardsbr. 578. The rendering given here of a papal letter against Otto, rubricated under the date 1211, cannot amount to a letter in all parts genuine. At that time Innocent cannot yet have in a formal manner demanded loyalty to Frederick, though a formal demand to take up arms against Otto or at the least a prohibition against fighting on Otto's side must have been issued at some stage. At first only those had been anathematized who were supporting Otto against the kingdom and the Patrimony. Later, all those who on the emperor's side fight in Germany against the Catholic faction are regarded as excommunicated. In July 1211 Innocent had apparently envisaged an alternative way to dethrone Otto. Early that month he issues letters in which he accuses Otto of contempt for the power of the keys of the Church because he continues to have masses celebrated in his presence, and Innocent threatens to declare him a heretic if he persists in doing so (BF. 6111, 6112).

[263]Cf. Tillmann, Zur Frage, 139ff. To the argument presented there the following comment may be added. The canonistic literature of the time was fascinated by the question of the pope's right to depose worldly rulers. How could it ever have failed to notice the deposition by Innocent III of the emperor if such deposition had indeed happened?

[264]Siegfried dismisses Archbishop Dietrich of Cologne as early as April 1212 for having refused to publish the ban on the emperor, for having celebrated mass in the emperor's presence, and for having removed opponents of Otto from their offices and benefices (Chron. regia Colon. 233; Reiner of Liège 664; cf. also Caesarius, Hilka 3, 239), and at the same time reinstates Adolf of Altena, who had been ousted in 1205. In the same year, in a procedure not free from spite and, therefore, later quashed by Innocent, Siegfried replaces the bishop of Würzburg by Henry of Ravensburg (cf. Reg. XV 226 of 3 February), and also opens legal proceedings against Egbert of Bamberg (cf. Reg. XV 225), who had been one of the leading conspirators against Otto but soon after had submitted to him. Albert of Magdeburg suspends and excommunicates the bishops of Halberstadt (Chron. Mont. Ser. 184) and Hildesheim. In early June 1213 Innocent himself orders their dismissal after having re-examined their cases, and orders new elections to be carried through (Reg. XVI 70, 71).

[265]Reg. XVI 56.

[266]Chron. Ottenburanum, ed. L. Weiland (MG. SS. 23) 623.

[267]Archbishop Everard of Salzburg, who, together with Duke Ludwig of Bavaria and Duke Bernard of Carinthia, had arrived at the emperor's court in Italy in June 1210, presumably to warn him or to mediate between him and the pope, had been required by Otto to swear an oath of unconditional loyalty, and on his refusal had been kept a prisoner. Everard finally swore an oath on 3 July that he would never abandon the emperor for the sake of the pope and that he would, in defiance of papal orders, support him even against the pope or anyone else (see Winkelmann, Otto IV, 237f.). There is no clearer indication of Otto's brutal use of his power and of the foolish delusions he harboured as to its extent.

[268]Otto's first court assembly after his return on 16 March 1212, which was generally well attended, had "only very few ecclesiastical princes" participating (Reiner of Liège 664). Two months later at Nürnberg a few more dared attend, or rather, did not dare

stay away. Egbert of Bamberg, one of the first conspirators against Otto, sought to regain the emperor's favour on this occasion (Chron. regia Colon. Cont. III 233). Further participants are traceable: Dietrich of Cologne, by that time already deposed, Hartwig of Eichstädt, Manegold of Passau, Engelhard of Zeitz. Certainly partisans of the emperor were the bishops of Würzburg, Hildesheim and Halberstadt. Wolfger of Aquileia had supported him in the summer of 1212 at least surreptitiously by words and deeds (Böhmer, Acta, 231).

[269]Even before the year was out Egbert of Bamberg and Otto of Würzburg had thrown themselves on the pope's mercy (cf. Reg. XV 226 of 3 February, XVI 50, XV 225). In early February of 1213 Innocent orders that proceedings to depose Egbert be halted, at the beginning of June he rejects Otto's anti-bishop and forbids Bishop Otto who had broken with the imperial faction for good and all and who effectively adhered to the Catholic faction, to be molested in future in the matter of the bishopric (Reg. XVI 50). Both Hartwig of Eichstädt and Manegold of Passau are known to have been with Frederick on 15 February 1213 (Huillard-Bréholles 1¹, 245). Frederick of Halberstadt, on the other hand, seems to have changed over to Frederick not earlier than January 1215 (cf. Winkelmann, Otto IV, 390), and Hartbert of Hildesheim to have never wavered in his loyalty to Otto. Even so Hartbert died in possession of his diocese in 1216. Did Innocent incline to lenience in view of the lie of the bishopric, after Otto had ceased to be a menace?

[270]BF. 15046 and Chron. reg. Colon. Cont. III 237.

[271]Reiner of Liège, 671.

[272]None of the Lombard bishops attended the imperial court session at Lodi on Otto's journey to Germany. The bishop of pro-imperial Como does not obey a summons of the excommunicated emperor in a legal proceeding (Reg. XV 31). Bishop Albert of Vercelli, a city sympathetic to Otto, together with Sicard of Cremona, is active as legate against Otto in northern Italy from the spring of 1212 onwards.

[273]MG. Const. 2, 57ff.

[274]The cause presumably was the pope's conflict with the Pisans in the preceding years. As early as 1210 Innocent had threatened the Pisans with excommunication as being the main supporters of Otto's Sicilian enterprise and for infringing papal sovereign rights in Sardinia (Reg. XIII 193). In early September he asks the Sardinian *judices* to offer armed resistance to the Pisans (Reg. XIV 101), whom some time before he had already declared to have forfeited all fiefs, privileges and dignities, i.e. in all probability their rights in Sardinia (Chron. Januense, Muratori, Antiqu. 9, 44f.). For some time Innocent had been endeavouring to bring the Sardinian magnates into a closer relationship to himself. A promising attempt in 1206 had been thwarted by the love or opinionatedness of a girl. Helen, the heiress of the Sardinian *judicatus* of Gallura, had been intended by Innocent, who was her liege lord and her guardian by appointment of her father, to marry his cousin Trasimund. It would in itself have been important for the realization of the papal objectives in Sardinia, if a pope's relative had obtained one of the *judicatus's*. But it was not the *judicatus* of Gallura alone which was concerned. Innocent aimed at the formation of a united front of the *judices* of Cagliari and Torres. At the end of 1200 he attempts to establish peace between the two *judices* in his capacity as liege lord (Reg. III 35). Since 1203 at the latest the peace, which had probably been established meanwhile, was being gravely threatened by the question of Helen of Gallura's marriage (Reg. II 29). Both *judices* held a relative standing by as a bridegroom, and William of Cagliari had seized several fortified places in Gallura as a

security (Reg. VI 145, 146; VII 104, 106). It is possible that Pisa then had a third candidate at hand, the Pisan Lambert. Peace could only be upheld in the country if the two *judices* abandoned their marriage plans and Helen were married off to a neutral party. Hence the project of a marriage to Trasimund seems to have come up. The project was probably at first approved by the *judex* of Cagliari who recalled his relative from Gallura (Reg. VI 145, VII 106). The *judex* of Torres, who had just sought Innocent's support against the Pisans (Reg. VI 18, 28), also seems to have resolved to abandon his plans for a marriage between his brother and Helen. The following year Helen declared her readiness to follow the pope's advice in choosing a husband (Reg. VII 103) and swore to the marriage pact with Trasimund in 1206. But she delays its fulfilment (Reg. IX 68, 147) and finally evades the pope's pressure by marrying the Pisan Lambert. The duped pope can punish the breach of oath, but not undo the marriage (Reg. X 143, 117, XI 80).

[275]One of these letters of consent, that of the count palatine of the Rhine Ludwig, dated 6 October 1214, is extant (Böhmer, Wittelsbachische Regesten, 1854, 135; BF. 749). On the different versions of the Privilege of Eger (MG. Const. 2, 57ff.) see Ficker, Forsch. 2, 421ff.

[276]Otto in vain laid siege to Viterbo (cf. Winkelmann, Otto IV, 239 n. 4). Orvieto, which as late as July 1209 had been in serious conflict with the pope regarding Aquapendente, also appears to have remained loyal to the Church. A privilege of Otto of 13 December 1209 (Cod. dipl. d'Orvieto, 56f.) seems to have been directed against Orvieto. On 4 September 1210 the city was certainly still determined on resistance to the emperor 1210 (*ibid.* 58). In 1212 it stands on the Church's side (*ibid.* 62, 65). Perugia in a treaty of 28 February 1210 pledges itself to defend the pope in the region between Perugia and Rome (Ficker, Forsch. 4, 276). Perugia did not fall into Otto's hands. An imperial confirmation of the privileges for Gubbio (BF. 449 of 14 December 1211) is clearly directed against Perugia. Early in September 1210 a papal legate at Perugia negotiates the peace between the Tiber counties of Todi and Amelia on the one side and Orvieto on the other (Cod. dipl. d'Orvieto, 58). In Radicofani, which he finally captured, the emperor meets with the resistance not only of the papal garrison but also of the townspeople, and he was only able to seize Montefiascone after a lengthy siege (cf. Winkelmann, Otto IV, 239).

[277]In contrast to the majority of the neighbouring towns Rieti, at Otto's arrival, did not give in to force and successfully withstood a siege (Ficker, Forsch. 4, 355). Foligno, too, is not likely to have decided forthwith in favour of the Empire. Dipold, the imperial duke, was obliged to make considerable concessions to the city in March 1210 (BF. 12362; Ficker, Forsch. 4, 277); it continued to incline to the Church's cause. A document of the podestà of Foligno, of 23 October 1211, is dated *tempore Innocentii papae III.* The concession confirmed therein for the monastery of Sassovivo is made, among other reasons, from reverence to the Roman Church (Jacobilli, Cronica della Chiesa di Santa Croce di Sassovivo, 1653, 314ff.).

[278]This is best seen in the hopeless position of the pro-imperial Tuscan nobles who submit themselves to the powerfully rampant pro-papal Orvieto or to its bishop: the counts of Ildebrandini on 17 September, the Visconti de Valentano on 17 November 1212 (Cod. dipl. d'Orvieto 65, 66), Count Bulgarello, an excommunicated partisan of the emperor who pledges himself in the same year to Bishop John of Orvieto for his fief of Parano against everybody except the pope and a Catholic emperor (*ibid.* 62). Some places such as Proveno may have continued to be held in imperial hands. Radicofani was regained by the Church in 1215 at the latest (P. 5283).

[279]A document issued by Dipold for the city of Spoleto on 16 July 1213 in Foligno's disfavour indicates that Foligno had returned to the papal faction and, by the nature of the concessions, that Dipold was in a difficult position (BF. 12444; Sansi, Storia di Spoleto 2, 1879, 222). On 20 March of that year only in Spoleto the dating was according to the pope's reign (Sansi 220). In Tuscany only Città di Castello, the most northerly and most exposed county of the Patrimony and one which had always been sympathetic to the Empire, seems to have still been loyal to Emperor Otto. In the spring of 1216 the citizens, it seems, submitted themselves to the Church (BF. 12493). The humiliating surrender of Narni in 1215, against which Innocent had called up Todi, Amelia and Terni the previous year, presupposes a very strong position of the pope at least in the southern regions of the duchy. Among other matters stipulated, the Castrum Stroncone, which Narni had destroyed and which it is now required to rebuild, is to belong for ever to the *domanium* of the Roman Church, unless the Church decides to grant it to the town by way of grace. The people of Narni must forswear all the alliances they had entered into during the period of their excommunication and are forbidden to form new alliances without the prior permission of the pope and the rector of the Tuscan Patrimony. They are further forbidden to retaliate against Todi, Amelia and Terni for the hostile activities committed by them on the pope's orders, and to elect a non-resident as podestà without the pope's approval (Lanzi, Un Lodo d'Innocenzo III ai Narnesi, Boll. della R. Dep. d. stor. patr. per l'Umbria 1, 1895, 131ff.). In the following year the podestà of Narni was a relative of the pope, Petrus Annibaldi (Liber cens. 459). On April 8 1215 Foligno and Terni form an alliance against Spoleto and all others except Todi, without prejudice to their loyalty to their lord the pope, the people of Rome and a Catholic emperor (document published in Boll. della R. Dep. d. stor. patr. per l'Umbria 10, 1904, 382f.). The document, though not genuine as a whole, seems to be genuine as to the details given above. On 5 May 1214 Innocent requires all the inhabitants of the duchy to support the papal Marquis Aldobrandino of Este who is on his way to the March of Ancona (BF. 6168; Migne PL. 217, 228). Since about May 1215 at the latest, Count James, a relative of the pope and his marshal, had been the rector of the apostolic Patrimony of Tuscany including the duchy (Lanzi 131; P. 5283, P. 5310). But Dipold of Schweinspeunt must still have held a number of strongholds up to the beginning of 1216. It is only then that he left the country stealthily (Richard of San Germ. 40). In the years 1214 up to 1216 Cardinal Guala and Stephen, the pope's chamberlain, are successfully active in the reorganization and pacification of the region. On 28 August 1215 Gimualdo of Fumone and Leo of Anticoli recognize before Guala the rights of the Apostolic See over Castel Fumone (Liber. cens. 469); in 1216 Narni before the chamberlain waives all rights to Stroncone (*ibid.* 459). In 1214 or 1215 Guala negotiates a peace treaty between Todi and Orvieto (Cod. dipl. d'Orvieto 69) and in 1214 the chamberlain together with the podestà a peace between the nobility and people of Perugia, a peace which was confirmed by Innocent on 19 September (Theiner, Codex diplomaticus dominii temporalis S. Sedis I (756–1334), 1861, 44; BF. 6174). Interesting is the stipulation that taxes may be imposed in four cases only: for the service of the Roman Church, of the people of Rome, of the emperor or his envoy and in the event of a war which Perugia might embark on in its own interests. The stipulation referring to the emperor contained in a treaty confirmed by the pope and inserted in a papal document shows that the Church, too, did not regard the territories of the Papal States as being wholly independent from the Empire.

Even at the time of Innocent's death only parts of the March of Ancona had reverted to the sovereignty of the Church, to which it probably never had totally submitted. The conferment of the March in May 1212 on Marquis Azzo of Este (P. 4446a. cf. Tillmann, Rekuperationen, 359 n. 90) indicates that Innocent at that time despaired of the possibility of establishing direct rule by the Church in those regions. In August 1213 he seems to have deemed conditions more favourable. He requires Aldobrandino, Azzo's son and heir, to put off no longer the march into the March, which he, the pope, could now easily regain for the Church; otherwise he would take such steps as he considered appropriate (Reg. XVI 102). Very few details of the conditions in the March in these years are known to us. We do know that Fabriano professed its loyalty to the Empire in October 1213 (BF. 12446). In October 1213 Dipold of Schweinspeunt himself was staying in Fabriano and granted the commune a privilege (Hagemann, 113f.). From 1214 onwards the pope's name is increasingly used in dating next to the emperor's (*ibid.* 114). An alliance of February 1214 between Fabriano and Camerino stresses that it is directed neither against the pope nor against the emperor (*ibid.* 114f.). On 22 May Fabriano has itself granted a privilege by the papally-appointed Marquis Aldobrandino of Este (*ibid.* 116f.). But it seems that Fabriano did not definitely change over to the pope's side, as is shown by the dating according to the emperor's reign in November 1214 (*ibid.* 114f. n. 4). Between 8 October 1218 and 1220, however, the dating in Fabriano is almost exclusively according to the pope's reign (*ibid.* 117f.).

[280]MG. Const. 2, 57f.

[281]According to a papal letter in the collection made by Thomas of Capua, a bishop threatened with deposition is said to have placed himself under Lupold's protection (Dict. Epist. Hahn, Coll. 1, 343f.). The pope threatens both the bishop and Lupold, whom he styles a former bishop, with his retaliation (BF. 6214). In BF. 6214 and apparently in Huillard-Bréholles 1[2], 377 n. 1, the letter is referred to Honorius III and as possible date of drafting the time shortly after Lupold's death (January 1217) is suggested. Yet it seems that the letter presupposes Lupold as still living and the occurrence, at which the queen was also present, as having happened not long before. Constance left for Germany as early as July 1216. Moreover, since the letter clearly presupposes as originator a pope who has been reigning for some length of time it is only Innocent III who can be meant. Just supposing the letter were a fabrication, it would be telling testimony as to the relationship between the pope and Frederick's legates.

[282]Cf. Huillard-Bréholles 1[2], 375.

[283]Gesta c. 39 col. LXXIIf. Cf. Seeger, 42.

[284]On the pope's methodical efforts to secure the southern borders of the Papal States see Seger, 42f.

[285]Migne PL. 217, 301. Cf. Seeger *loc. cit.*

[286]BF. 661.

[287]Rich. of S. Germano, 39.

[288]See Rymer 1[1], 120 (with incorrect date, cf. Winkelmann, Otto IV, 421, n. 6) and the catalogues of cardinals according to their political partisanship published by Davidsohn from the *regesta* of Philip Augustus (Forsch. 4, 318).

[289]For the reasons given I cannot agree with Haller's suggestion (Papsttum, 419) that Innocent prior to the battle of Bouvines had contemplated pardoning Otto. Innocent's failure to prevent John from fighting on Otto's side can, in my opinion, be explained on other grounds; cf. Chapter 3 above.

[290]MG. Const. 2, 72.

[291]To Winkelmann's question (Otto IV, 438f.) why Innocent did not provide against the eventuality of Henry's being elected Roman king, the answer must be that, since the pope intended to summon Frederick immediately to be crowned emperor, there could be no question of such election before the separation had been put into effect.

[292]A truly horrific example of this state of mind is seen in the ban which in the Angevin interest Martin IV published in 1281 against the Greek Emperor in whose reign, at the Council of Lyons in 1274, the Greek Church had been reunited with the Latin Church. The fact that this union would not have lasted anyway cannot excuse the fact that an act of friendship for the Angevins was the immediate cause of the schism. Again and again, too, French interests prevented the reconciliation of Ludwig the Bavarian with the pope.

[293]Cf. pp. 29, 90ff. and 133 above.

# CHAPTER 6

# The pastor and reformer

In a sermon Innocent on one occasion renounces going into detail on a thought, remarking that great, important and manifold pursuits took up his time, and adding: "In truth, manifold and, I hope, not also vain pursuits, for rightly is it said: vanity of vanities and all is vanity".[1] Is this only the conventional way of speaking about the futility of all earthly things, or is the papal preacher giving expression to his own experiences, to the knowledge and to the feeling that for him the essential duties of his office often have to give way to pursuits which, from the point of view of eternity, are vain?[2]

Innocent took the spiritual duties of his office very seriously. The Fourth Lateran Council,[3] which he celebrated in November 1215 in the presence of 412 bishops from all the countries in Catholic Christendom, became a monument to his sense of pastoral responsibility and to his reformating ardour. The Fourth Lateran Council makes us feel what is so rarely to be sensed in the councils of the twelfth century, whether Roman or non-Roman: the immediate concern for pastoral care. We feel as if we are breaking new ground in the conciliar field.

The Council does not focus its attention narrowly on the reform of the clergy, but extends it also to the religious needs of laity.[4] Innocent seeks to renew Christian spirit and Christian life in the people by reviving the much neglected people's sermon,[5] the receiving of the Eucharist, the pastoral care for the sick,[6] and the entire religious care for the believers. Canon 21, which is already styled the famous one by the rubricator of Gregory IX's decretals,[7] imposes the duty on every Christian, arrived at years of discretion, of confessing once annually and of receiving the Eucharist at least at Easter under penality of exclusion from attendance at church and church-burial.[8] By way of this rule, which in substance is identical with the fourth and fifth church commandment still in force, Innocent ensured throughout the centuries up to the present day that the sacraments of penance and of the Eucharist also exerted an influence on the lives of those relatively indifferent religiously and morally, since henceforth everybody once every year was bound to answer before himself for his conduct, to eschew sin and to raise his mind to God. Everybody, in some respect or other coming into conflict with divine or church law, within a relatively short time was obliged to make up his mind whether he should abandon his conduct or see himself excluded from the Church. After the Lateran Council King Richard the Lionheart, for instance, would no longer have been able to put off receiving the Eucharist for years because he was not prepared to show forgivingness to his enemy, Philip II of France.[9]

The demands[10] made by the Council upon the pastor implied a level of education of which the parish priests in general fell short. Not even the bishops, who in the practice of the early Church as well as in theory still were the pastors proper, were able sufficiently to fulfil the office of preaching and other pastoral duties, since their dioceses were widely extended, since they were overburdened with other tasks, and for other reasons, "not to say for lack of knowledge", as Innocent III remarked at the Council.[11] The pope, though, declared that such shortcomings would no longer be tolerated in future, but he hardly deceived himself that even in future want of knowledge would continue to hamper the spiritual engagement of a bishop. Though he took very seriously the episcopal duty of preaching to the people and though he himself frequently took up preaching,[12] he was grieved that, owing to the overstrain weighing upon him, he could not fulfil his episcopal duty of pastoral care in every single respect.[13] At the Council, therefore, he did not decree anything that was bound to remain dead-letter, but made it strictly incumbent upon those bishops who personally were unable to fulfil sufficiently the pastoral office, to appoint clerics at the cathedral church and at the conventual churches "for the administration of the holy office of preaching". These clerics, as the bishops' assistants and representatives, are to visit the parishes, to preach, to hear confession, and to take charge of all the tasks pertaining to the salvation of souls.[14] The bishops are also made responsible for the careful instruction of the candidates for the priestly office in liturgical duties and in the practice of administering the sacraments,[15] they are further charged with the painstaking

examination of the level of education, the conduct of life and the age
of the clerics presented to them for a pastoral office.[16] In addition to
the grammarian, who under the decrees of the Third Lateran Council
in every episcopal church is to teach its clerics and poor students,[17]
every metropolitan church has to appoint a theologian who is to
instruct the priest in theology (in sacra pagina) and in all the tasks
pertaining to the salvation of the souls.[18] For the sake of pastoral care
the incumbent of a parish church has to provide for it in person
or – but only in one specific exceptional case – through a *permanent*
vicar endowed with an adequate stipend,[19] and no custom must impair
the right of the parish priest to an adequate share in the revenues of
his church.[20] It is declared to be *de iure* impossible to hold two
benefices entailing pastoral care at a time.[21]

It was of no little relevance in pastoral terms that the impediments
of marriage beyond the fourth degree of consanguinity and affinity
were abrogated.[22] As reasons for his deviating from time-honoured
laws, a course which surely was not easy for his conservative mind,
the pope adduces the great difficulties which had often resulted from
the wide extension of these impediments, and the danger for souls
which they had sometimes entailed.[23] By restricting the scope of the
impediments of marriage Innocent put an end to situations which
were untenable from the point of view of private and public morals,[24]
though as a politician he would have been interested in the maintenance of the former marriage prohibitions, since they gave the
papacy a far-reaching means of interfering in the lives of the mighty.
In addition, the introduction of the churchly marriage banns for
engaged couples,[25] the aggravation of proof in the case of an action
for nullification of a marriage on the grounds of too close relationship,[26] and the renewed inculcation of the prohibition of clandestine
marriages,[27] serve to protect marriage and family morals. The Council
seeks to guard popular devotion against deception and misuse.[28] It
makes the public veneration of newly discovered relics dependent on
papal permission, it prohibits the preaching of alms without a papal or
episcopal letter of authorization, and forbids the preachers to expound
in their sermons anything not in keeping with the purport of these
letters. The prelates are to prevent church-goers from being deceived
by fabrications and falsifications, as used to happen in many places
for the sake of profit. In order to prevent damage to the ecclesiastical
penitential discipline and to the seriousness of the ecclesiastical
penitential practice the bishops, when granting indulgences, are to
keep within the limits which the pope applies to himself.[29]

Any legislation dealing with the reform of the clergy and the appointment to ecclesiastical offices is subservient to pastoral care. But the intention of the legislator may be directed more to the prestige or to the purity of the clergy and its pleasingness to God than to the needs of pastoral care. In his reforming legislation, which was directly concerned with the clergy and with individual churches, Innocent was just as much orientated by the needs of pastoral care as by the will to elevate the clergy and to further the interests of the Church. As reasons for the constitution, according to which no episcopal or regular church must remain vacant for longer than three months, he adduces the danger to souls which are without their pastor and the danger to church property.[30] He thereby indicates the points of view appropriate for the assessment of the other constitutions concerning the appointment to bishoprics and prelacies, among them the important canon which reduces the embarrassing variety of forms of election to three and exactly regularizes the electoral procedure.[31] In the inaugural address of the Council Innocent expressly subordinates the reform of the clergy to the pastoral point of view: he expresses his hope that by the Council, in the eighteenth year of his pontificate, the Church might be restored and the virtuous life of former times revived in the Christian people. Since depravity had started from the clergy, purification must begin in the sanctuary.[32]

At the Lateran Council Innocent assigns to the provincial synods[33] and to the the general chapters[34] an important task in the execution of the work of reform. Provincial synods were already prescribed by the canons of the early Church, and general chapters belonged to the permanent institutions of the Cistercian Order. Innocent revives the idea of provincial synods and assigns them a new or at least more firmly fixed task, and extends the institution of general chapters to all monastic orders. At the Lateran Council he seeks to make the provincial synods the central instance for the reform of the clergy, for the control of the execution of the canonical decrees, particularly of those enacted by the last general council, and for the punishment of their contravention. The provincial synod is, for example, charged with supervising the collation of benefices and with suspending possible culprits, after repeated admonition, from their right to be collated.[35] It is laid down that the synod convene annually. For its preparation the archbishop and the bishops are to appoint suitable persons for the single dioceses who, not vested with the power of jurisdiction, simply ascertain all the year round what is in need of

Affirmative
action.

reform and correction, and report on their findings at the next provincial council. The resolutions of the council are to be promulgated at diocesan synods. Anyone neglecting the decrees of the Lateran Council regarding the setting up of provincial synods is to be suspended from his benefices and from the execution of his office.[35] The Lateran Council assigns a corresponding task to the general chapters for the monastic orders and for the regular canons of the single provinces and countries who had not hitherto held such chapters. They are to take place every three years after the manner of the Cistercian chapters, with the initial support of Cistercian abbots. Among other things, the chapter is to appoint visitators to correct the single abbeys of the country or the province, monasteries and nunneries, according to the prescribed rules and, if occasion arrises, cause the superiors to be deposed by the diocesan bishop.

Why did Innocent establish such central instances? In his reforming legislation he did not take as basis the ideal case of every ecclesiastical superior being willing and able to carry the reforms through. The cathedral chapters, which elected the bishop, were in general the domains of the younger sons of the higher or lower grades of the territorial nobility. In most cases it was not inclination and qualification which made them take holy orders, but family interest. It was therefore possible, in some dioceses even probable, that unsuitable, unspiritual and even unworthy persons were called to be pastors of the Church. In these circumstances the degree to which the episcopate became worldly depended on the moral and religious qualities of the nobility in the respective region. The unparalleled degeneracy of the episcopate in southern France had its foundation in an equal demoralization of the nobility. The dissolute nobility, owing to the influence it had in the cathedral chapters, not only filled the bishoprics, but also appointed a good part of the parish priests. There are reports that the nobles and knights presented the sons of their dependents without any regard for qualification and worthiness and that, if the bishops refused to accept them, they pressed them upon the churches by force, that they withdrew unruly clerics and vagrant monks from their superiors' penal authority, that they misappropriated the church revenues for themselves and for their chaplains, and let the parish priests live in unworthy poverty.[37]

When introducing a central instance for the execution of church reform, Innocent took into account that, as matters stood, it was impossible to exclude the danger of bishoprics being unsuitably filled

and of unsuitable clerics being presented, however strongly the
Council might urge the competent *confirmator* and *consecrator* to
examine the candidate. The provincial synod was to see to it that
compliance with the canonical statutes and the execution of the
reforms of the Council where not solely dependent on the more or
less obliging will of the particular bishop and on the degree of his
personal qualification or external power. In the same way, the general
chapter was, to a certain degree, to compensate for the shortcomings
of individual superiors.

The course adopted by Innocent of involving provincial synods
and general chapters in reform made use of the advantages of
centralization and evaded its dangers. Provincial synods and general
chapters do not relieve the individual superiors of their burden and
initiative, but, on the contrary, they are apt to stir up and to stimulate
their activity. They do not deprive the bishop in his diocese, the abbot
in his monastery even of part of their jurisdiction and do not release
them from any responsibility. It is rather that he is answerable before
them for the conditions prevailing in his own church or his own
house. The central instance is no foreign body corporate either, no
superior authority to which opposition would be unfailing; it is a court
of peers which exercises its own jurisdiction over its members, a
community which passes its own rules and which gives support and
backing to the individual superior, for instance to the bishop, as far as
he is willing to fulfil his duty, vis-à-vis the incumbents.

Even if the provincial councils fulfilled the expectations placed
upon them, the strength and profundity of any reform was in large
measure dependent on the individual bishops' sense of duty. Their
readiness to remedy abuses vigorously Innocent III strengthened at
the Lateran Council by way of the rule that no custom and no appeal
was allowed to hinder the bishop from redressing and punishing
excesses perpetrated by his clerics,[38] and by seeking to strengthen
their position as superiors of secular priests and of the regular clergy,
and to restore their prestige where it had been impaired by privileges
granted, for instance, to monastic orders and cathedral chapters.[39]

This reforming legislation is the result of a true co-operation
between the pope and the participants in the Council. Innocent had
issued the summons to the Council, which was to convene in
November 1215, as early as April 1213.[40] He wished that those
summoned, bishops, superiors of monastic orders and representatives
of the chapters as well as the papal confidental agents appointed for

each church province, should have time for thoroughly preparing and elaborating the written reform proposals they were requested to hand in to the Council. The experiences of the pope and the participants in the Council were utilized in the church assembly, the views of both got a hearing, and it was not always Innocent who carried his point. None the less, its reforming achievements as a whole as well as the entire work of the Council[41] bear the stamp of his personality. The canons are often worded with reference to his person.[42] Detailed instructions,[43] and prudent precautions[44] reveal the practical mind of the pope who tries to prevent the decrees from remaining dead-letters. For some constitutions we can establish their connection with Innocent III's earlier measures and attempts at reform.[45] Other constitutions reveal by their subject-matter that they are the pope's work or came about with his decisive co-operation.[46] This may hold good for all reforms pertaining to the procedural sphere and to procedural questions, such as the introduction of written minutes for the course of the proceedings in all its stages and details,[47] and for measures which are designed to protect against the challenge, unjustified in substance, of the ecclesiastical judge of first instance,[48] or to prevent chicaneries on the part of the litigants.[49] The decrees relating to pastoral care, which the Council enacted, correspond to Innocent's frequently testified high esteem for the Eucharist,[50] the confession,[51] the sermon,[52] and to his pastoral attitude in general.[53]

How much the constitution relating to annual confession and Easter communion emanated from the pope's pastoral convictions is shown by a Good Friday sermon in which Innocent lets a dialogue between penitent and father-confessor unfold itself to an almost dramatic climax.[54] He puts the case that someone confesses to the priest that he has insulted father and mother, lied, committed perjury, and stolen other people's goods. The priest asks whether he feels penitence and in future would eschew sin. The other asseverates it from his heart. But the priest continues to ask: "Think, whether you have done still more. Tell me whether you have touched a whore!" Whereupon the other: "Is there anybody, my lord, who has not done that? Whoever would desist from that sin?" The priest: "Do not say that, do not say that, friend. If you do not confess this sin like the others and if you do not promise to amend as you did in respect of the other sins, you should know for certain that you neither deservedly receive the Eucharist, nor after this life will you gain the

heavenly life. Therefore, confess this sin, too, promise to amend and
receive the Eucharist." The penitent retorts: "Oh, my lord, I am very
ill, I cannot be continent, and so I dare not promise what I know I
shall be unable to keep. It is better not to promise anything than to
promise and not fulfil." The priest: "I do not demand that you make a
vow, but that you do what you promised. Did you not in baptism turn
away from the devil and his works? If, following my suggestion, you
promise to commit no carnal sin, you do what you must do. Even if
you do not promise it, you are still bound to it. A vow is taken by one
who by his own free will promises to do what he is not bound to do.
But he who promises to sin no longer against the sixth commandment,
does not take a vow, but resolves to do what he must do. I, therefore,
do not demand a vow from you, if I warn you to eschew *fornicatio*
and to be continent, but I simply demand that you act according to
your duty. But when you tell me that you are weak, that you cannot
be continent, then think over what you say. For I believe that you
could if you wanted to, that you could if only you loved God as much
as you love your eye." He then puts to the penitent the question
what would he do if being about to commit such a sin, he came to
know that it would cost him the loss of an eye. "Now," he continues,
"consider what you are wont to say: I should like to be continent, if I
could. But you could be if you feared to lose an eye. If you cannot do
for God's sake what you can do for the sake of your eye, this is only
because you love your eye better than God. Is your eye worth more
than God? Therefore do not say, I would be continent if I could, but
say, I could if I wanted to. Strengthen your will and go in for chastity
and you will gain the power to be continent. But if you pretend to be
ill, why do you not consult a doctor? If you are ill, why do you not
love health? If you know yourself to be powerless, why do you not
take the Almighty? He will be everything to you when He comes to
you. He will come to you, He will heal you, He will restore your
health, He will give you strength. For He Himself is the doctor, He
Himself is salvation, strength and health. Follow my suggestion,
eschew carnal sin, promise to be continent, and receive the Eucharist.
If you choose the one, you cannot have the other; therefore choose
what you want to have." The penitent: "If I cannot receive the
Eucharist without promising to be continent, I would sooner put off
communion than give a promise which is beyond my power." The
dialogue is over. "What a silly answer," the pope comments, "what a
Judaic choice! What did the Jews answer to Pilate? Not this one, but

Barrabas! If we weight the meaning of the former's words, what does he answer other than: Not Christ, but the whore! For what else does it mean when he says: I would sooner put off communion than promise to be continent? Would it not be better for you to withstand the temptation than to put off communion? For if you withstood the temptation, you would be blessed; putting off communion does not free from guilt, but increases it. Woe to him who for the love of sin puts off communion! What else does it mean to flee from carnal sin but to avoid the opportunity?" And turning to the listeners, Innocent finishes: "Therefore flee from temptation, choose Christ so that you deservedly may receive his communion in earthly life and arrive at possessing Him in future life!"

The legislation of the Lateran Council against the Jews[55] seems to clash with the pope's broad mind. And yet it too is probably due to his initiative, or at least came about with his decisive and unhesitating co-operation. The reasons alleged for the curfew imposed on the Jews during the Passion Week correspond to imputations which Innocent, as early as the beginning of 1205, raised against them in a letter to the king of France.[56] In this letter he had also demanded from the king the punishment of Jewish blasphemies against Christendom, just as at the Council he made it incumbent upon the Christian princes in general,[57] and had turned against Jewish usury,[58] which was also a topic of deliberation by the Council.[59] The harsh words Innocent uses against the Jews[60] and the serious imputations he raises against them or undiscriminatingly echos – he does not even hesitate to charge them with having foully murdered Christ[61] – also seem to indicate the pope's authorship of the decrees of the Council against the Jews. It needs no stressing that in these measures no hostility from racial grounds is involved.[62] We must not see a derogatory insult expressly and solely directed against the Jews in the curfew and in the order to wear distinguishing clothing, since both regulations also applied to Mohammedans living in Christian countries. According to the wording of the constitution the clothing decree is to prevent Christians, from ignorance of the differences in religion, becoming intimate with non-Christians – it thus has a pastoral meaning.

The reform work of the Fourth Lateran Council bore fruit. The fact alone that the canons were almost completely incorporated into Gregory IX's code of canon law, and thereby into the *Corpus iuris canonici,* secured them an efficacy lasting over the centuries. There are clear indications of preaching receiving an impetus and of pastoral activities being revived.[63] (Provincial councils, bishops' synods, diocesan constitutions and general chapters strive to execute the reform decrees. Responsible bishops school the parish priests in preaching and administering the sacraments, instruct them in the tenets of the sacraments, provide for the teaching of the people in the religious faith on the basis of the Creed established by the Fourth Lateran Council.[64] And yet, the fundamental renewal of the Church failed to materialize.[65] Death did not allow Innocent III to carry out himself the church reform on the basis laid down by the decrees of the Lateran Council. But even if he had still been granted years to sit on Peter's Chair, the renewal of the Church could not have been accomplished within the space of one pontificate. Innocent's successors, even if inspired with the same reforming energy as he was, would have had ever and again to give new impetus to the forces of reform in the single countries, would above all have had to take care that the canon concerning the annual holding of provincial councils was observed in letter and *spirit*, and that, thereby, the most important instrument which Innocent III had provided for church reform was actually put to use.[66] What has been said about the fate of the reforms of the Lateran Council in England may hold true for their fate in general: only a few bishops really understood Innocent's ideal of church reform, the work seen as a whole. The majority misunderstood the relative value of the single decrees, often neglected precisely the most important ones or observed them only in letter, not in spirit.[67] It is true that the decree concerning penance and communion is one of those decrees which was most quoted and had the most telling effect,[68] but no less strong was the after-effect of the fatal constitution which obliged Jews to wear distinguishing clothing and imposed a curfew on them during Passion Week.[69]

A problem of great moment to church reform, the provision for the lower grades of the clergy, was not resolved at the Lateran Council. From the beginning of his reign Innocent had strictly insisted on the bishops' obligation of maintaining those who, contrary to the canons, had been ordained without title.[70] This obligation which, particularly in the beginning, imposed a heavy burden on the bishops, was frequently greeted by them with indignation. Stephen of Tournai complains to the pope that, on the strength of papal hortatory or threatening letters, many in number, but few deservedly, demanded a provision from the bishops without their origins, their living conditions, their offences and crimes being examined, because they had been ordained by the bishops or their predecessors. Notwithstanding the reverence due to His Holiness, such a demand seemed new and unusual to him, since under the ancient canons and the regulations enacted by the Third Lateran Council it was only meant to apply to priests and deacons. The bishops were unable, he continues, to remember the names and number of all those they had ordained below the grade of deacon. They would sooner desist from further ordinations than take over such an unbearable burden.[71] A Portuguese bishop, too, complains that clerics promoted without title to the higher orders pestered him for benefices. All the revenues of his church were not sufficient to provide them. In addition, he continues, provisions were demanded for clerics who did not deserve benefices even in parish churches, let alone in the cathedral church, and for whom the pope would never intercede if he knew them.[72] It is possible that bishops, before ordaining the candidates, caused them to swear that they would not, by way of appealing to the pope, demand a benefice from them as their consecrators.[73] The complainants seem to have been wholly unaware how much their own arguments fell back upon them. They themselves had admitted to holy orders those whom they qualified as undeserving of an ecclesiastical benefice, and some of them even to higher orders. It was naive to demand that the pope from afar institute an examination of qualifications, which they, being near to the events, had forborne. Innocent, therefore, rightly replies to the archbishop that, by right, he could disregard the objection of non-suitability, since the archbishop and his predecessors, when bestowing holy orders, had had to take care to prevent unsuitable candidates from being ordained.[74] He would also have been right in asking the bishops whether they were aware of their responsibility, if they ordained so many clerics whose provision was not guaranteed, the great majority of whom, therefore, were forced to take to winning their bread in a manner which was discreditable to their profession and who, as *clerici vagantes*, often led a scandalous life, particularly if they, as Stephen of Tournai claims (thereby involuntarily incriminating himself and his fellow bishops), had only striven for tonsure and lower orders with a view of escaping temporal justice. The Fourth Lateran Council passed no regulations for the maintenance and provision of those ordained without title.[75] That the Council so conspicuously passed over in silence a matter which Innocent had very much at heart would easily be explained if we assume that Innocent, in view of the bishops' opposition, was not prepared to

enforce the extension of the obligation of maintenance to clerics in
lower orders by solemn resolution of the Council, but that, on the
other hand, he was not willing to agree to its restriction which the
explicit regularization of this obligation for clerics from the subdeaconship upward would have entailed. In any case, in 1212 he was
still abiding by the obligation of maintenance in its widest scope.[76]
The Church would have been spared many a contumely if Innocent's
demand had won through. A clerical proletariate would either not
have arisen or it would have been done away with. The Church would
in fact have had fewer, but better clerics. But already the extension of
the obligation of maintenance to the subdeacons which, owing to the
incorporation of Innocent III's corresponding decree into Gregory
IX's decretals,[77] remained operative law, was of great relevance, since
the subdeaconship, in view of the obligation to celibacy, meant an
undissoluble bond to the cloth.

Innocent did not let the bishops indiscriminately bear all of a
sudden the entire burden of maintaining clerics whom they or their
predecessors, wrongfully or following a custom, had ordained without
title, but shifted part of the burden on the wealthy churches. By far
the greatest part of papal provisions[78] served for the maintenance of
poor clerics in their own or in a foreign church. The *Gesta* rightly
point to provisions of this kind as being a title of fame for the pope.
He had been, they continue, so generous to honourable and educated,
particularly to poor, clerics that he had doubtless caused more clerics
to be provided with benefices all over the world than had been
provided by his predecessors within forty years.[79] Some of these and
other provisions, by the way, were wholesome punitive measures
against those ecclesiastical superiors who failed to re-fill vacant
benefices and prebends within six months after becoming vacant, as
prescribed by the Third Lateran Council.[80] Since the re-filling was
generally delayed or left undone in order that the bishop or the
chapter might continue to avail themselves of the revenues, it was
appropriate that the right to re-filling devolved to the superior and
ultimately to the pope. It is reported that at the approach of papal
legates in the churches belonging to their sphere of legatine jurisdiction vacant benefices and offices were re-filled in all haste.[81]

At the Lateran Council Innocent tried in vain to make secure
provisions for the maintenance of the Curia[82] and thereby to remove
one of the main causes for the evil conditions prevailing at the papal
court. It seems that in all cathedral and prebendal churches particular

prebends were to be reserved for the Apostolic See, and the monastery and collegiate churches as well as the bishops were to place takings equal to the value of one prebend at its disposal.\ These emoluments would be accumulated and used for the maintenance of the pope, the cardinals, the chaplains, the chancery officials, the door-keepers, and the other curial officials, and henceforth all transactions of visitors to the Curia would really be handled free of charge. Henceforth no curial would make any further demands, neither personally nor through a third party, neither explicitly nor tacitly, nor accept free-will offers.[83] As Honorius III attests, highly reputed prelates had judiciously identified themselves with the proposal, but, as was to be expected, they remained a minority. It was the greater, not also the better, part of the Council that wrecked this important attempt at reform. Innocent himself dropped the matter when he encountered strong opposition. As Honorius states, he wished to avoid the impression that he had convened the church assembly only for this purpose. Innocent would perhaps have rendered the Church a service which could not be rated too highly, if he had not minded the bad impression and had pushed his project through.[84]

A sharp weapon in the struggle for the reform of the clergy was solemnly sanctioned at the Lateran Council, the inquisitorial process. Already some years before Innocent had applied the inquisitorial procedure, until then applicable only in proceedings against heretics, also to other canonical criminal proceedings. He thereby extended the possibility of initiating legal proceedings *ex officio* without private accusation by a third party. According to the procedural law until then operative, a canonical criminal process, barring the proceedings against heretics, was only instituted on the grounds of a formal, though not official, accusation for which the responsibility and the burden of proof lay on the private accuser.[85] This burden was so onerous and, in the case of proceedings against highly placed persons or against powerful clerics who enjoyed the support of relatives and friends, also so dangerous that even in cases of serious crimes an accuser was not easily found. In territories such as southern France and Burgundy, which lacked a vigorous central power, it would have hardly been possible to call to account, by way of a private accusation, brutal or unsuitable and unworthy clerics who were supported by friends. Already in his first pontifical year Innocent found that the accusers of the seriously incriminated and doubtless guilty archbishop Amadeus of Besançon beat a retreat when it became a question of presenting a formal accusation in writing.[86] In the ensuing year an accuser forwent an accusation against a canon in view of threats expressed by his native township.[87]

It was only after some hesitation that Innocent, even in proceedings involving the suspicion of heresy, disregarded the time-honoured principle that, where there is no accuser, there is no judge. As late as 9 May 1199, not without hesitation and only in view of the extraordinary seriousness of the offence, he sanctions the action of a bishop who had heard witnesses against a cleric reputed to be a heretic, but not yet accused, and thus had instituted proceedings against him instead of imposing on him the canonical compurgation.[87] He himself then orders the defamed cleric to be admitted to the compurgation, though under aggravating conditions. But already at the end of the year Innocent resolutely follows the new course in that, on information from the monks and on the grounds of repeated complaints, he orders proceedings to be instituted *ex officio* against an abbot and witnesses to be heard,[89] and in that at about the same time, on information received from the cathedral chapter of Benevento, he orders an inquisition to be instituted against the brutal archbishop.[90] At the Lateran Council the inquisitorial process was institutionalized as a general form of procedure.[96]

Besides the inquisitorial process the accusatorial process continued to be legally relevant,[92] since the former, unlike the latter, could not lead to the degradation of the person found guilty, but only to his deposition. But in practice the new procedure, as might be expected, won through over the accusatorial process from the beginning, even though according to Innocent it was not to be initiated light-handedly and, above all, it was dependent on the public defamation of the accused.[93] The cleric against whom no accuser was found, also in future escaped trial, if his character was not decried in public, even though his offence might have become known to the ecclesiastical superior.[94] Innocent, who by nature was averse to revolutionary changes, was only prepared to depart from the time-honoured principle that, where there is no accuser, there is no judge, when it was imperative in view of the exigencies of time. Moreover, he feared that the ecclesiastical superiors, who "often incurred enmity, since sometimes they were obliged to censure and to punish",[95] might be enmeshed in endless suits to the serious detriment of their authority, since in any such suits their subordinates would have had to have been interrogated against them. The very fact of the perpetual quar-

rels between bishop and chapter would ever and again have given rise
to more or less malevolent imputations, for which little room was left
if the burden of proof was borne by the accuser. In spite of the
restrictions established on the institution of proceedings, under Innocent III a great number of unworthy bishops were removed, by
way of an inquisitorial process, from their offices who, by way of an
accusatorial process, would never have got their deserts. Under
Innocent III abuses were not, as they often were in the later Inquisition against heretics, connected with the inquisitorial process. Any
means of defence was open to the accused. The inquisition was to be
held in his presence, unless he malevolently stayed away. The points
at issue, to which the inquisition referred, had to be made known to
him beforehand, he had to be informed of the statements of the
witnesses and of their names, legitimate exceptions against the
person of the witness and against their depositions (the *exceptiones
legitimae* and the *replicationes*) had to be admitted.[96]

The extended applicability of the inquisitorial procedure and the
possibility of initiating the inquisitorial process were of the greatest
moment for the success of the visitations of entire countries, of
provinces, bishoprics[97] and single monasteries, which Innocent often
ordered to be carried through by legates[98] or special commissioners.[99]
In churches and monasteries which were ill reputed, these visitators
initiated inquisitions, in which the parties concerned, in episcopal
churches the bishop himself, the canons and the town-clergy were
obliged to depose on matters which they knew or believed to be in
need of reform in their church, barring offences which were not
notorious.[100] The result of such an inquisition could be the institution
of an inquisitorial process and, thereby, the deposition of the person
found guilty.[101]

In the heretical districts of southern France papal visitators had
been active for decades. Their resolute work resulted in the renewal
of the southern French and Provençal episcopate.[102] To what degree
trenchant measures were indispensable here is shown by the shocking
picture which Innocent, on the basis of reports received, sketches of
the conditions prevailing in the church province of Narbonne, even if
we have to make allowance for exaggerations on the part of the
informants. Owing to the prelates' remissness the church is enslaved.
The clergy is oppressed, the church reduced to poverty. With the
knowledge, even the consent of some prelates the churches are used
by laymen as fortresses whence Christians make war upon Christians

and carry out armed robbery. More heretics are to be found there than true believers, and the prelates indolently watch their doings. They only strive after presents, they are flatterers towards the mighty and judge the poor harshly, they call good what is evil and evil what is good. When conferring ecclesiastical offices and benefices they give preference to new-comers, to inexperienced and base persons. Uncouth youths who have not yet taken the higher orders are often vested with several offices at a time. Primarily to blame is the archbishop, Berengar II, whose God, as they say, is money, who simoniacally bestows holy orders and who within the ten years of his pontificate did not even once visit his diocese, let alone his church province. In his palaces he houses the excommunicated leaders of the bands of mercenaries banned by name by the Third Lateran Council as heretics, he neither shows hospitality nor bestows alms, often for a week or two fails to go to church and from avarice does not fill vacant churches. The number of canons at his cathedral had decreased from eighteen to nine, three of whom do not even reside. Things have come to such a pass that many monks and regular canons keep concubines, even live with married women, practise usury, indulge in dice-playing and hunting, take over the conduct of worldly business against payment, and practise non-clerical professions. Lay people follow their pernicious example in that many of them, in their wives' lifetime, keep concubines who are sometimes allowed by clerics to attend processions, to the offence of the people and under the mockery of the heretics. There are prelates who do not shrink from entrusting churches to supporters of heresy.[103] On the metropolitan of the neighbouring province of Auch, Archbishop Bernard, the pope passes the judgement that he not only failed to educate the people entrusted to him, but also corrupted them by the example of his odious life. He was, the pope adds, so much surrounded by and covered with sordidness that even if he was intent on amending the conduct of his subordinates, his teaching must prove void, since the teaching of one whose life is despicable, is despised itself. People styled him, Innocent continues, a protector and supporter of heretics, a gamester and notorious prodigal, a simoniac, perjurer and libertine, who did not even shrink from incestuous intercourse.[104] After the removal of such unworthy and unsuitable men a series of excellent monks and secular priests was raised to the episcopal sees in co-operation with the visitators and other authorized persons.[105]

In the years 1205 up to 1213 Innocent ordered intensive visitations to be carried through in the churches of Lombardy. Outrageous conditions prevailed here. Even though the state of affairs could not be compared with the conditions reigning in southern France, in northern Italy, too, heresy derived its strength and its right to exist from the evil state of the clergy, which was in any case unpopular in the Lombard cities for its claim to be by profession exempt from civic taxes. Innocent charged with these visitations excellent men from the resident secular and regular clergy who were well acquainted with local conditions.[106] They, too, carried through inquisitions and proceedings against some unworthy bishops and prelates.

Innocent's efforts towards reform in all countries of Christendom are characterized by the endeavour always to engage the best men for the reforming work. When in his attempts to arrange for the reform of the exempt monasteries, he decides in 1203 to institute, at first by way of trial, three visitation provinces in central Italy and France,[107] he appoints as visitators among others the saintly[108] Archbishop William of Bourges, the excellent Bishop Odo of Paris[109] and Peter of Arras as well as the prior of Camaldoli. Two years previously William of Bourges and Odo of Paris had already been commissioned with the correction of the Order of Grammont.[110] In 1208 the bishop of Florence, the abbot of Sassovivo and the afore-mentioned prior of Camaldoli, the Tuscan prelates in whom Innocent placed most confidence, are appointed visitators for all the monasteries in Tuscany, in the duchy of Spoleto and in the March of Ancona.[111] In Lombardy the saintly Cistercian abbot Peter of la Ferté, later bishop of Ivrea, was active as the pope's commissioner for church reform.[112]

Where Innocent found men in the episcopate who were filled with reforming ardour and enjoyed ample reputation to take up the work of church reform energetically in their sphere of jurisdiction, he vigorously supported them, for instance the great reformer of the Polish church Archbishop Kietlicz of Gnesen,[113] whom Innocent also esteemed as a man of excellent saintliness, Archbishop Andrew of Lund, primate of Denmark and Sweden, and Patriarch Albert of Jerusalem, the latter two also by investing them, along with the legation, with the authority to represent him.[114]

It is not easy to assess the success of Innocent's efforts towards reform in the single countries. He obviously succeeded in renewing the episcopate in the heretical districts of southern France. But this was only possible because Innocent focussed his energy on this end to a degree which was impossible everywhere, and because fear of the strength of the crusading army supported his measures at least in the later years. He was only able to remove the most powerful bishops, Berengar of Narbonne and Bernard of Auch, after the victory of the crusading army. In the territories adjacent to the heretical districts and in parts of the Sicilian kingdom the degeneracy of the churches was scarcely less alarming, but the pope's interference was far more cautious and the result much smaller.

Against the dissolute Elias Malmort of Besançon Innocent ordered an inquisition to be instituted and, on the basis of its result, he ordered the archbishop's deposition, unless he resigned within two months. It seems that the pope was only spared a fierce fight because the archbishop died in the ensuing year. The deposed bishop's adherents got the successor of a suffragan of Bordeaux, the bishop of Périgeux whom Elias had deposed, into much trouble.[115] Another prelate, the bishop of Poitiers, laid violent hands on a papal delegate and is said to have remarked on the occasion that in his bishopric he intended to be bishop and pope and that nothing should be effected in his diocese by the pope's judgelets.[116] Innocent had already before that threateningly reproached him with his sins, but for this time had left him to search his own conscience and called upon him to amend, so that he, the pope, would not be compelled to make him feel his hand.[117] It was not always easy to remove guilty bishops; one could say that the degree of difficulty increased in proportion to the degree of guilt, since the most unworthy prelates naturally owed their elevation exclusively to the power of their family or of their supporters, and since they scrupulously strove to maintain their position. The proceedings instituted by Innocent against Archbishop Rainald de Forez of Lyons,[118] if they really were carried through, did not result in the quarrelsome man's deposition. As an imperial bishop true to type he was at odds with his episcopal town, he is said to have devastated it and on his campaigns to have not even spared churches and monasteries. These were conditions against which Innocent too could scarcely prevail. The undutiful, simoniacal and incontinent archbishop Amadeus of Besançon only met with the well-deserved lot of deposition after the variegated course of a proceeding which spread over fourteen years. Considerations for the papal German policy may have occasionally hampered Innocent's course, but on the whole it was the archbishop's position of power which forced the pope to proceed with caution. In Sicily Innocent initiated and carried through a series of proceedings against bishops the result of which is not always known to us. It is significant that in most cases the accusation embraced the charge of acts of violence, sometimes of murder or manslaughter.[119] The archbishop of Benevento is reported , among other offences, to have burnt down a castle belonging to his adversary together with women and children, to have killed his cook with his own hands and to have so maltreated a peasant that he died from it.[120] It was not easy to remove such bishops and, at times of civil war, as during Frederick II's minority, and of threats from outside, as during Emperor Otto IV's campaign, such a course was most dangerous for the king's cause, which at the same time was the pope's cause. In the proceedings against Archbishop Alferius of Sorrento on the grounds of simoniacal elevation and of high treason Innocent threatens the accused with suspension if his powerful relatives obstructed the production of witnesses for the prosecution, since it was unlikely that he was not mixed up with their doings.[121] A bishop charged with serious offences three times refused to accept papal writs and threatened and maltreated the emissaries. When in the end he could not but accept the mandate delivered to him in the empress's presence, he is said to have exclaimed that the writ came from that bishop who had been king and emperor in one person. He would not succeed in bringing him, Alferius, to give up his bishopric on papal order, since he held his church not from the pope, but from the king.[122] In these circumstances Innocent was obliged to show much forbearance with a worldly-minded episcopate. He orders that the bishop of Melfi, who was suspected of being implicated in his predecessor's death, of uncanonical elevation, of perjury and of concubinage, be first served only with a copy of the charge sheet, so that he might be his own judge of his conduct and do penance. But instead of communing with himself, the bishop admitted his own son to the cathedral chapter, collated prebends and benefices to his little nephews who were hardly beyond the stage of infant's prattle, continued to sell right for money and to get up to his old tricks, even after he had promised the chapter and the representatives of his own episcopal town to remedy the abuses. Not until he went over to the banned emperor was he dismissed from his office.[123] The proceedings against the villainous Bishop Matthew of Toul engaged the Curia for eight years. During this period the legate in Germany, who had been charged with the inquiry, on one occasion brings the opposite party to desist from the accusation in view of the danger which threatened the accuser and the other opponents of the bishop from the brutal man and his

relatives, the Lorraine dukes; at another time Innocent himself gives
a conditional order for the proceedings to be quashed.[124] The assault
on the accuser at the hands of the bishop's brother, the duke of
Lorraine, and the murder of his successor in office at the hands of the
deposed bishop himself, justified the pope's misgivings to the full and
placed in its true light his forbearance with many an unworthy
member of the episcopate. Innocent held that, balancing the conditions of place and time, the rigour of justice must be somewhat
alleviated, particularly if the rigour of ecclesiastical discipline could
not be practised without harm to the Church.[125] In such cases he may
have staked more on the present moment than would have been
feasible for an ardent reformer in his fight for principle and ideal. But,
for all that, the reform of the Church and of the clergy may have been
as sacred a duty for Innocent as for the latter. But it was peculiar to
Innocent and his strength, also his limitation if that is the way to look
at it, that, whilst considering the general and principal aspect of
events, he never forgot their individuality and actuality, that he never
lost sight of the concrete reality. On the other hand, he never
regarded singularities as isolated items either, but always saw them as
part of a whole. In his actions he sought to do justice to both modes
of viewing events. The forbearance and patience Innocent seems to
show to unworthy prelates in many instances find their explanation in
that even in the case of persons charged with the most serious
offences he maintained the legal order and wished it to be maintained
by his representatives, who were inclined to exceed the bounds which
the existing law set to their reforming ardour.[126] Innocent knew that
arbitrariness, even where it is thought to serve justice, is a greater evil
than forbearance shown to a criminal who is out of the reach of law.
Moreover, he willingly practised mildness where he hoped to attain
his end without severity. At visitations of monasteries which he
carried through personally, he knew how to combine earnestness, nay
severity, in matter with benevolence and friendliness in manner
towards those visited, so that he left the monks, as far as they were
good-willed, in good cheer,[127] a way of proceeding which he once
recommended to visitators on the occasion of their authorization.[128]

Innocent's endeavours at reform did not halt at the Curia. By
introducing a more modest standard of living he counteracted for
himself and his surroundings the tendency of the Curia to worldliness,
as well as the bad example and the offence which the prelates often
gave to clergy and laity by a life of self-indulgence. At table he had

himself served by monks, no longer by laymen, except for ceremonial
occasions at which noblemen performed their habitual functions.[129]
No longer was a host of noble varlets met with in the papal chambers.[130] In order to be able to dismiss them, Innocent at great expense
provided them with other means of sustenance.[131]    When removing
lay officials from the Curia Innocent also tried to eliminate lay
influence. But he was unable to ward off completely from himself and
from the visitors to the Curia the unwelcome services of laymen. On
special occasions Roman citizens, associated in colleges, performed
honorary service, for instance when the consecration of bishops and
abbots was celebrated at the Curia.[132] They took advantage of the
occasion to rob and plunder by force the prelates who had to put up
with their services. In 1208, when after years of difficulties and
struggles he had firm hold of the city,[133] he caused these people to
swear that henceforth from no archbishop, bishop or abbot would
they, after their consecration, impetuously claim or forcibly seize the
horse which was their due, the cope or anything whatever; nor would
they do wrong to anybody in this matter, but would humbly accept
what the prelates offered them on their own accord or what the
chamberlain, on their request, could obtain in the form of presents.[134]
Innocent could not, then, venture on the attempt of ridding the Curia
of these guilds of brigands without getting himself again into serious
difficulties in Rome.[135] It is easy to imagine how much the reputation
of the Curia was impaired by the doings of these fellows.

   Innocent is sure to have made a quick end to the worst extortions
committed against the curials proper.[136] A measure dating from the
first days of his reign seems to belong here, when he ordered the
doorkeepers to be removed from the chambers of the notaries in
order to give free access to everybody.[137] At the same time he also
took up the fight against venality.[138] It was impossible to root it out
completely as long as it could be disguised under the form of
accepting presents. Though Innocent was intent on keeping up the
principle that justice and the services connected with it were to be
administered free of charge, he introduced fees only for *scriptores*
and *bullatores*. He allowed the other officials and, as matters stood,
could not but allow them to accept free-will presents,[139] as he himself
together with the cardinals accepted presents and was obliged to
accept them.[140] Circumstance were stronger here than the pope's will
to reform.

   The same holds good in part also for the reform of the entire

Church. In his reform work Innocent did not confine himself to treating the symptoms of decay, but he tried to get down to its roots. But it was beyond his power to tear them out. The basic evils from which the medieval Church suffered were the claims of the nobility to the higher ecclesiastical offices and benefices, and the system of patronage and benefices together with the restrictions of the bishops' governmental power they entailed.[141] Basically the same phenomena were at work here which in the sphere of state policy had a disintegrating effect and ever and again threatened to expose the medieval state to anarchy. They were founded in the economic conditions and the social order following from them, and in their origin, therefore, were out of reach for any state or ecclesiastical reforming activity. Any fundamental change was dependent on a change of the economic and social conditions, which at that time slowly began to take shape.

Innocent was aware of the prime causes of the evils, since they were clearly apparent to him for instance in southern France and in Burgundy. In the filling of bishoprics Innocent, surely also in the interest of the Church, was accommodating to the kings, since the royal influence, unless it impinged on the principle of ecclesiastical liberty, was welcome to counterbalance the preponderance of the territorial nobility in the cathedral chapters. Not only from military reasons, Innocent tried to bring Philip Augustus personally to take action against the supporters of heresy among the southern French potentates. He wanted the influence of royal power extended to the south and even requested the king to bring the land under his fortunate rule.[142]

To shake the dominant position which the nobility enjoyed within the Church, a revolution of immense dimensions would have been necessary which would also have had to embrace social and political life. In the last run the appointment of worthy and, from the point of view of the Church, suitable men to the ecclesiastical offices could only be secured to a certain degree if these offices ceased to be a stimulus to the striving after worldly possessions and worldly power. That such a revolution could ever happen was alien to Innocent's thoughts. He did not even try to diminish the influence the nobility exercised in the Church by attacking lay patronage. It is true that thereby he would have mobilized forces against himself which even his energy and skill would have been unable to check. But his successors might have brought the fight to a happy end, as Gregory

VII's successors did in the case of the quarrel about lay investiture, begun by Gregory without any prospect of success. On the other hand, it was not altogether surprising that in lay circles there was some apprehension as regards their patronal rights, so that, for instance, Stephen Langton had, also on the pope's behalf, to protest solemnly against the dissemination of the rumour that lay people should be deprived of their patronage over churches.[143] This may have been a matter of malevolent invention in King John's fight against the pope, but it might find credit because Innocent was, on the whole, so successful in his attempt to exclude lay people from disposing of church offices and church property, and because he fought the abuses of patronage. But he scrupulously guarded the patronal right itself both as regards clerics and laymen.[144] In his conservative mind he was far from modifying customs and vested legal positions which were neither immoral nor at variance with ecclesiastical principles. Thus, Innocent's reforms do not aim at subverting existing conditions, but they try to obviate the dangers resulting from them and to diminish their bad consequences.

Far beyond his personal engagement Innocent III promoted church reform by the understanding he showed of new forms of pastoral care and monastic life.

Since he had to take into account the deficiencies of the secular clergy, Innocent had early tried to engage the services of the Order of Citeaux, which he esteemed before others, for the renewal of the Church.[145] Under him Cistercians were frequently active as legates, visitators and commissaries in the field of church reform[146] and of the reform of monasticism in particular.[147] He drew upon Cistercians for preaching the cross[148] and for missions to the heathens.[149] In the heretical areas of southern France and in other regions,[150] where bishops and parish priests neglected their duties, Cistercians were to take over the office of preaching. The pope was convinced that the brethren were particularly qualified for these tasks, since, as he states, not even envy could find much fault with them and also those living in the world gave them a good character, testifying that with them the lives of the saints harmonized with sound teaching and that their manners manifested what their sermons expounded.[151]

The Cistercians could not fully meet with the pope's expectations, since preaching and performing pastoral care was alien to the objectives of their order and to those of the ancient orders in general.[152] To fulfil the tasks which the Order of Citeaux only shouldered hesitatingly and only for single members, new religious communities offered themselves to the pope. It redounds to Innocent's credit that, unlike his predecessors,[153] he did not reject them.[154]

In 1201 Innocent approbated the Order of the Humiliati[155] in its three branches, a community of canons,[156] a monastically living lay community,[157] and a community of lay people living in the world.[158] The approbation of the latter branch was an unprecedented novelty. The members, citizens of Lombard towns, lived in their families but were bound to a life of piety, simplicity and apostolic engagement. What Innocent now granted them, the right to hold meetings and to preach penitence, they, like Waldes of Lyons, had solicited from Alexander III at the Lateran Council of 1179. The pope, then, had approved of their way of living, but had set narrow bounds to their apostolic activity. Lucius III, in 1184, had banned them as heretics because they had not kept to these bounds. Innocent III widely reopened the gates of the Church to them,[159] and the major part of the Humiliati returned into the pale of the Church. James of Vitry, in a letter of October 1216, writes how, during his visit to Milan in the last days of Innocent's life, he had found there, admidst a saddening decay of churchly life in view of the rapidly spreading heresy, saintly men and pious women who alone withstood the heretics. Malevolent and worldly-minded people called them Patarenes, but the pope, who had empowered them to preach and to oppose the heretics and who had also approbated their order, named them Humiliati. For Christ's sake they had forsaken everything, they lived by the sweat of their brows, liked to hear the Word of God and often preached it. In the bishopric of Milan alone the order numbered 150 conventual congregations, not including those members who lived in their homes.[160] In another passage James reports that the brethren, clerics as well as educated lay people, had been authorized by the pope to preach not only in their own meetings, but also in the streets of the towns and in the churches of the secular clergy after having obtained the respective prelates' consent.[161] Not only ill-will was at the root of hostility against them. Narrow-mindedness opposes all that is new, particularly in times when novelty is easily confounded with heresy. Innocent was far from such anxiety. Even the apostasy or aberration of some few was no occasion for him to distrust a sound companionship which displayed a blessed activity within the lower social strata of the Lombard cities[162] and towards which he personally seems to have felt kindly disposed.[163]

Innocent in generous-hearted trust also allowed a community of converted Waldenses, the Catholic Poor of Durandus of Huesca,[164] whose members, unlike the Humiliati, were mostly clerics, to preach and to have schools of their own.[165] He took the community under his protection when the episcopate of the heritical provinces brought in an accusation against them, because they held communion with the Waldenses who were not yet reconciled with the Church, even invited them to go to mass with them, kept on wearing their former clothing to the offence of the believers, neglected the attendance of church in order to preach in their schools, and the like. In his reply Innocent did not, though, reject the possibility that the brethren's intentions were not honest, but he was inclined rather to believe that they adopted a somewhat doubtful course to win over their former fellow believers. He wishes on no account to quench the spirit before he was convinced that it did not come from God. He did not approve, he replies to the bishops, the brethren imitating the heretics, but he was willing to follow the example of Him who had become a sick one to the sick, nay everything to everybody, in order to win everybody over to His side, and who wanted all to be blessed and to arrive at the knowledge of truth. A doctor was not to blame if he sometimes allowed something injurious to the health of the all too desirous patient. He asks the bishops to tolerate the brethren in the spirit of gentleness and to win them over rather by way of kind-hearted admonition than by severity. Nor did the doctor use fire and iron if a badly healed wound broke out afresh, since then the sound parts could easily be affected.[166] The brethren for their part he asks to remedy what was offensive, also in regard to their clothing. For himself, he writes, such externals were irrelevant. Differences of customs, above all in formalities, were not, to his view, detrimental to the beauty of the Church. But just because the Kingdom of Heaven did not lie in clothing, so they ought to abate the offence which was taken at their former clothing and be careful not to destroy the Kingdom of Heaven for the sake of shoes, being remindful of the Word of the Apostle: "If your brother is annoyed at your food, you do not walk according to love. Do not, for the sake of your food, displease him for whom Christ died."[167] The bishops kept on making difficulties for the brethren; but despite these hostilities Innocent enabled the community to pursue their tasks actively. In apostolic spirit he once admonishes the bishops of the dioceses in which the Catholic Poor were active to show such a benignity to the brethren that, thereby, others too would

be encouraged to give up their error.[168] The opposition of the episcopate to communities of preachers which challenged the exclusive
right of the clergy to preaching did not restrain Innocent from also
approbating, in 1210, the companionship of Bernard Primus of
Milan,[169] though Bernard in southern France had preached against the
Waldenses without being authorized and by certain pronouncements
had exposed himself to the reproach of heresy. The companionship,
of lay people as well as clerics, was authorized to preach penance and
against the heretics.

The companionship of St Francis and his followers was no more
than a community of laymen when Innocent III allowed them to
preach penance. In the summer of 1210 Francis appeared before the
pope to request the approbation of his rule.[170] Innocent granted it by
word of mouth and, according to Thomas of Celano, dismissed him
and his companions with the words: "Go with God, my brethren,
and as God will deign to inspire you, preach penance to all. But if
Almighty God increases you in number and grace, report it to me
joyfully, and I shall grant you more than this, and with greater
security I shall entrust you with greater tasks."[171] There are some
indications that Innocent, about the time of the Lateran Council,
approbated the companionship in due form.[172] In the last year of his reign
the pope may also have granted to St Clare the assent to the *altissimae
paupertatis propositum*, the privilege of poverty.[173]

There is no conclusive evidence that Innocence had commissioned
Diego of Osma and the subprior Dominic, when in the begining of
1206 they stayed in Rome, to preach against the heretics in apostolic
spirit and in an apostolic manner of living.[174] But he is sure to have
welcomed with joy the fact that they and, prompted by them, his
legates, resolved to wander preaching through the heretical districts in
poverty and simplicity. At the end of 1206 he explicitly orders that,
for preaching against heretics, religious be drawn upon who, emulating the poor Christ's poverty, did not shrink from contacting, in
despicable attire and in the glow of the spirit, those held in contempt.[175]

In view of Innocent's attitude to the new forms of monastic life
and to the new ways of pastoral care, and in view of the weight which
the Council attaches to preaching and to engaging preachers as the
bishop' assistants, it comes as a surprise that the Lateran Council
prohibited the foundation of new orders[176] just at the time when
Dominic was in Rome in order to obtain the pope's assent to the

foundation planned by him of the Order of Preachers. This prohibition was certainly not initiated by the pope.[177] If he yielded to a
demand of the Council, it was only because he knew that the new
religious communities which grew up under his protection were not
endangered by the prohibition. One should not read more into the
prohibition than its wording clearly says. It is not the foundation of
new companionships which is forbidden, but the binding to new
*ordines*, to new rules of monastic life. Neither did Innocent by any
means prohibit St Dominic from founding his companionship, but he
caused him, first, to select one of the approved rules in common with
the brethren, and then to return to receive approbation.[178] This restriction did not stand in the way of the devotion to a special task nor
obviously of complementing the rule in view of the special objective
set to the foundation.[179] Jordan of Saxony, therefore, also seems to
regard Innocent's demand as being no obstacle to the foundation of
Dominic's order. He reports that the brethren, after the pope's
command had been made known to them, had selected St Augustine's
rule, had complemented it by some more severe practices and also
decided to hold no landed property (*possessiones*), in order to prevent
the office of preaching from being handicapped by concern for
worldly goods.[180] Innocent surely approved of, and welcomed, the
speciality of the order projected by Dominic, that it saw its main task
in preaching. At that time the Order of St Francis seems to have
already been formally approbated by the pope, so that it too was not
affected by the prohibition enacted by the Council.[181]

By taking away from the idea of apostolic poverty the blemish of
heretical suspicion[182] and by furthering and protecting movements
which incarnated new forms of monastic life and of Imitation of
Christ and also actualized new forms of ministry and preaching,
Innocent III deserved well of church reform and of the restoration of
the purity of Christian life in a measure it is impossible to evaluate
rightly. The *Legenda secunda* of Thomas of Celano[183] relates that the
pope in a dream saw the basilica of the Lateran near collapsing; but a
humble, mean-looking man had supported it with his shoulders and
prevented the collapse. "Truly", the pope had said, when shortly
afterwards St Francis appeared before him, "this is the man who by
work and teaching will support the Church." Therefore, Thomas
continues, the pope had readily acceded to Francis's request and had
always shown to the servant of Christ his special affection. This legend, if not in the literal, yet still in a deeper, spiritual sense, rings true.

**Notes to Chapter 6**

[1]Migne PL. 217, 398. Cf. also *ibid.* 311, 381.

[2]Cf. Reg. I 358 and Chapter 10 below.

[3]For the Council's reform work see the collection of reform decrees in Fliche, 144ff.; Gibbs and Lang, 99f. On the Council in general see Gibbs and Lang, 96ff.

[4]See above all Canones 21 (Leclercq 1350) c. 12 X 5, 38; 10 (Leclercq 1340) c. 15 X 1, 31; 11 (Leclerq 1341) c. 4 X 5, 5; 33 (Leclercq 1351) c. 23 X 3, 39; 26 (Leclercq 1355) c. 44 X 1, 6; 22 (Leclercq 1351f.) c. 13 X 5, 38.

[5]Cf. Mandonnet, 13ff.

[6]Can. 22 (Leclercq 1351f.). c. 13 X 5, 38.

[7]Cf. also Gibbs and Lang, 97.

[8]Prior to this the canonical norm had been that of communion three times a year, but it had long since been disregarded, see Browe, 27ff. By his decree of 1215 with its clear and well-considered regulations Innocent ensures that the sacrament is received at least once a year.

[9]Chron. Angle. 96.

[10]Cf. the requirement made of the confessor in can. 21: *Sacerdos autem sit discretus et cautus, ut more periti medici superinfundat vinum et oleum vulneribus sauciati; diligenter inquirens et peccatoris circumstantias et peccati, per quas prudenter intellegat, quale illi consilium debet exhibere, et cuiusmodi remedium adhibere, diversis experimentis utendo ad sanandum aegrotum* (Leclercq 1350).

[11]Can. 10 (Leclercq 1340).

[12]The sources frequently refer to Innocent III's sermons. The Chronicon Sublacense (34f.) mentions a sermon in Subiaco (the sermon itself in Migne PL. 217, 589ff.). In Monte Cassino Innocent is forced to forgo mass and preaching because of the summer heat and the throng of the crowd (Ann. Casin. 319). He preaches in public in Rome during a general supplication on the occasion of the Saracen war in Spain (Reg. XV 181, Migne PL. 216, 699). A Dutchman who spent almost two months at the Curia reports the piety with which Innocent read mass and preached in the 'stations' churches (Emonis chron. 471). Innocent himself instituted a 'stations' service at the Hospital of the Holy Spirit at which future popes were to preach annually on the works of charity (Gesta c. 144). John Capocci, the leader of the Roman opposition, is reported to have interrupted Innocent in the middle of a sermon with the invective "Your words are God's words, but your works are the devil's works" (Caesarius, Strange 1, 103). According to Humbert de Romanis, in a sermon on the feast of St Mary Magdalene, Innocent III once translated a homily of Gregory the Great word for word from the Latin into the Italian and, when he could not remember the wording of the text, had the cleric who held the book help him on. On the cleric's question why he who had enough of his own to say, was doing this, Innocent answered that he did so in order to reprove and shame those who despised the words of others (quoted in Mandonnet, 16, n. 23). A similar story, but in the manner peculiar to the narrator brought to a wittier point, is told by Salimbene: occasionally when preaching to the people Innocent held a book in his hand. When a chaplain asked him why, he replied: "I do it for your sake, who cannot speak freely and yet think it a shame to read something out" (MG. SS. 32, 31). Seventy-eight sermons are extant, partly in a collection arranged by himself. In the preface to this collection Innocent writes: "I have preached and dictated a number of sermons to the clergy and the people, partly in learned words and partly in the

vernacular (*vulgari lingua*) lest I should, for the care of the worldly things weighing heavily on me because of the wickedness of the time, altogether neglect the spiritual things which, due to my apostolic office, are my principal concern" (Migne PL. 217, 311). In view of the allusions to specific situations (cf. for instance Migne PL. 217, 337, 393, 395, 596, 675) there is no doubt that a number of these sermons were in actual fact preached. For Innocent's high regard for the office of preaching see also above pp. 212ff. We learn from England that in 1200 Innocent had sent the abbot of Saint-Germer-de-Fly there to preach against the practice of Sunday markets, which in consequence were actually abolished for some time (Great Roll of the Pipe of the Ninth Year of the Reign of King John, quoted in EHR. 63, 1948, 131). Innocent also authorized the great preacher Fulk of Neuilly to engage Cistercians and Benedictines as well as regular canons to assist in preaching (Reg. I 398).

[13]Cf. the opening paragraphs of Chapter 6 above, and Chapter 10 below.

[14]Can. 10 (Leclercq 1340) c. 15 X 1, 31.

[15]Can. 27 (Leclercq 1356) c. 14 X 1, 14.

[16]Can. 26 (Leclercq 1355) c. 44 X 1, 6.

[17]Can. 18 of the Third Lateran Council of 1179 (Leclercq 1101).

[18]Can. 11 (Leclerq 1341) c. 4 X 5, 5.

[19]Can. 29 (Leclercq 1357) c. 28 X 3, 5.

[20]Can. 32 (Leclercq 1359f.) c. 30 X 3, 5. This canon refers to the fact that in some areas the parish priest only recived one sixteenth of the tithe and that it was in consequence scarcely possible to find an even moderately educated cleric there. Several of the canons drawn up at the Council are aimed at securing the churches their due tithes against the claims and privileges of third parties, lay, secular or regular priests (can. 53, 54, 55, 55, 56–Leclercq 1374, 1375, 1376, 1377–c. 32, 33, 34 X 3, 30, c. 7 X 1, 35).

[21]Can. 29.

[22]Can. 50 (Leclercq 1372) c. 8 X 4, 14. Cf. Tenbrock, 29f. and Vincke, 146f., 158.

[23]Some time earlier Innocent, with regard for the difficulties suffered by the newly baptized, had already mitigated the stringency of the Church's marriage rules for the Christianized Livonians, and at the same time had recommended the bishops to show leniency towards them in penitential practice (Rainer of Pomposa t. XL, Baluze, Epistolarum Innocentii III libri undecim 1, 1682, 604).

[24]Cf. Vincke, 108f., 163.

[25]Can. 51 (Leclercq 1373f.) c. 3 X 4, 3.

[26]Can. 52 (Leclercq 1374) c. 47 X 2, 20.

[27]Can. 51.

[28]Can. 62 (Leclercq 1381) c. 15 X 3, 45.

[29]Can. 62 (*ibid.*) c. 14 X 5, 38.

[30]Can. 23 (Leclercq 1352) c. 41 X 1, 6.

[31]Can. 24 (Leclercq 1353) c. 42 X 1, 6.

[32]Migne PL. 217, 675f.

[33]Can. 6 (Leclercq 1334f.) c. 25 X 5, 1.

[34]Can. 12 (Leclercq 1342ff.) c. 7 X 3, 35.

[35]Can. 30 (Leclercq 1358) c. 29 X 3, 5.

[36]Can. 6 (Leclercq 1334) c. 25 X 5, 1.

[37]Reg. I 79, 80; Can. 32 (Leclercq 1359f.) c. 30 X 3, 5; William of Puylaur, 119f.

[38]Can. 7 (Leclercq 1335f.) c. 13 X 1, 31. The cathedral chapters retain, where such is the custom, the correctional power over their members. But if, despite the bishop's

warnings, they should fail to exercise the duty corresponding to the law within the time limit set by the bishop, then the bishop's correctional power becomes effective against them too. See also can. 48 (Leclercq 1376f.) c. 25 X 2, 28.

[39]Can. 55–58 (Leclercq 1376–1378) c. 34 X 3, 30; c. 7 X 1, 35; c. 24 X 5, 33; c. 25 X 5, 33. Can. 60 (Leclercq 1380) c. 12 X 5, 31. Cf. Chapter 3 above.

[40]Reg. XVI 30; P. 4707, 4708.

[41]The Credo formulated at the Council, can. 1 (Leclercq 1324f.), even as regards the wording, was conceived at least with the pope's keen personal co-operation. Compare, for example: ...*verus homo factus, ex anima rationali et humana carne compositus una in duabus naturis persona...* (can. 1) with: ...*cum secundum eorum sententiam ex anima et carne Christi nulla constet substantia vel persona...* (*Compost. archiep.* Migne PL. 217, 1176), and: ...*accipiamus ipsi de suo quod accepit ipse de nostro...* (can. 1), with: ...*Per id ergo quod suscipit ipse de nostro, accipimus ipse de suo...* (*De sacro alt. myst.* Migne PL. 217, 886). In both cases the statement refers to the Eucharist as the *Mysterium unitatis.* Cf. also in can. 2, in connection with the condemnation of a treatise by Joachim of Fiore, the phrase *quae* [scil. Romana ecclesia] *cunctorum fidelium disponente Domino mater est et magistra...*with...*quae* [apostolica sedes] *disponente Domino ceterarum ecclesiarum mater est et magistra...*(*De sacro alt. myst.* Migne PL. 217, 774). Cf. also Chapter 1 above.

[42]See amongst others: *Qualiter...debeat praelatus procedere ad inquirendum...sicut olim aperte distinximus, et nunc sacri approbatione concilii confirmamus* (can. 8, Leclercq 1337, c. 24 X 5, 1)–*Constituta super hoc edita sacri approbante concilio revocantes...*(can. 50, Leclercq 1372, c. 8 X 4, 14).

[43]See for instance the decrees concerning provincial councils and general synods.

[44]If, for example, the collator fails to collate within three months a benefice which has become vacant *de iure* because its incumbent has accepted a second benefice, he is held liable with his own income for the revenues which the actual holder of the benefice has unlawfully drawn from it (can. 29, Leclercq 1357, c. 28 X 3, 5.).

[45]For the community of the diocese of York Innocent as early as 1207 orders annual general chapters to be held. If a monastery were in need of reform, the chapter was to appoint two or three correctors for the church concerned. The chapter further has the duty and the authority to deliberate on the ways of reforming monastic orders and to correct, without regard to appeals, all that needs correction in the monasteries (Reg. X 32). The pope was approached with requests of this kind by Denmark and northern France (cf. Hilpisch, 236f.). It is significant that Innocent on one such occasion calls upon the Benedictine abbots of the province of Rouen to provide him with an accurate account of the results of the reform measures he had approved, so that, if he saw that monastic life had profited from them, he could all the more safely and cautiously order that they be observed permanently (Reg. XIII 124). The preventive and remedial measures taken by the Council against appeals whose sole purpose was to hinder the competent superior in the execution of his duty of correction, or against the unjust challenge of the competent ecclesiastical judge (can. 48, Leclercq 1370f., c. 25 X 2, 28; can. 35, Leclercq 1362, c. 59 X 2, 28), Innocent had in substance already resorted to in the fourth year of his reign in a special case on the complaint made by the archdeacon of Metz (Alanus 2, 16, 8 P. 1447, von Heckel, Dekretalensammlung, 259).

[46]In keeping with the pope's consistent declarations on procedures in matrimonial matters and on questions of separation of marriage, and in conformity, word for word, with a decretal of Innocent III on the assessment of testimony by witnesses *de auditu*

(Reg. XII 61, Comp. IV c. 1 1. IV t. 3), can. 52, which declares such witnesses against the validity of a marriage impugned for a too close relationship admissible only to a limited extent and only under precautions, closes with the words: *Tolerabilius est enim aliquos contra statuta hominum copulatos dimittere, quam coniunctos legitime contra statuta Domini separare* (Leclerq 1374, c. 47 X 2, 20). Can. 42 reflects both in formulation and content an often repeated reasoning of the pope: *sicut volumus, ut iura clericorum non usurpent laici, ita velle debemus ne clerici iura sibi vendicent laicorum... ut quae sunt Caesaris reddantur Caesari et quae sunt Dei Deo recta distributione reddantur* (Leclercq 1366). The demand of the Lateran Council that in cases of illness it is the curer of souls who should be summoned first (can. 22, Leclercq 1351, c. 13 X 5, 38), corresponds to a minutely substantiated advice given by Innocent III in his commentary on the psalms of penance (Migne PL. 217, 990f.). On the origins of can. 19 cf. Chapter 10 below.

[47]Can. 38 (Leclercq 1363f.) c. 11 X 2, 19.
[48]Can. 48 (Leclerq 1370f.) c. 25 X 2, 28.
[49]Can. 37 (Leclercq 1363) c. 28 X 1, 3. Cf. Chapter 3 above.
[50]Chapter 10 below and pp. 189–90 above.
[51]Cf. his treatise on the seven psalms of penance (see Chapter 10 below).
[52]Cf. p. 190 above.
[53]Cf. pp. 189ff. above and Chapter 10 below. Given the vast extent of obligations which fall to the supreme head of the Church, we can scarcely expect that Innocent III, besides preaching, personally practised pastoral care. However, individual cases which by chance are extant show that Innocent proffered personal pastoral advice to visitors to the Curia when the opportunity arose. Gerald of Wales on his own accord renounced into the pope's hands the benefices which he might have obtained by unlawful means and confided himself, as he tells us, to the pope's fatherly advice concerning his future life and the salvation of his soul. Before he left the Curia Gerald received these benefices back from Innocent together with salutary instructions as to their future use and the conduct of his future life (Girald. Cambr. 1, 138). In the case of a priest, where the question whether he was free or bound to live in an order was at issue, Innocent did not content himself with the judicial decision declaring him to be free, but advised him as his pastor none the less to choose the monastery. Whether he remained in the world or left it, in any case he was to serve God and walk in the paths of the commandments, lest it should turn out that he had deceived himself (Reg. XV 132). Innocent probably feared that the priest's case was the one often referred to in the pope's writings, in which someone, though loosed before the Church, might still be bound in the eyes of God (see Chapter 2 above and Appendix 2 below). A story told by Caesarius of Heisterbach, a contemporary of the pope, may well reproduce the gist of the experience of many a visitor to the Curia of Innocent III's pastoral sense and priestly lenience towards penitent sinners: Innocent dismisses a woman who had committed a grave sin with no more than a mild penance. To a cardinal who pharisaically takes offence, Innocent answers: "If I have done wrong in respect of this woman and if her penance is not sufficient in the eyes of God then may the devil possess me and torment me in front of you all, if not, may the same happen to you." The cardinal is possessed by the devil, and when healed by the prayers of all, he declares that he would never again in future insult God's mercy (Caesarius, Strange 1, 77f.). It is worth mentioning in this context that Innocent declared it to be a pious and meritorious work to marry a prostitute in order to rescue her from her wicked way of life (Reg. I 112, cf. Fliche, 90, 133f.).

[54]Migne PL. 217, 528ff. In an effective small treatise, the *Dialogus inter Deum et peccatorem* (**Migne PL.** 217, 691ff.), Innocent in a similar way elaborates his thoughts in the form of a dialogue between God and the sinner.

[55]Can. 67ff. (Leclercq 1385ff,).

[56]Reg. VII 186.

[57]Can. 68 (Leclercq 1386).

[58]As does Reg. X 190.

[59]Can. 67 (Leclercq 1385f.).

[60]In addition to the letters quoted see also Reg. VIII 121.

[61]Reg. VIII 186.

[62]Cf. Chapter 8 below, the opening paragraphs.

[63]For England see Robertson, Frequency of Preaching in Thirteenth-Century England (Speculum 24, 1949, 377ff. Refs. to France, *ibid.* 377 n. 11). Davy (29f.) notes a revival of preaching at the beginning of the thirteenth century which he ascribes to the reforms by the Lateran Council and the foundation of the Mendicant Orders.

[64]More detailed studies of the effects of the reform decrees in general exist only for England: Gibbs and Lang, esp. Part III: The Reform Work on the Lines laid down by the Lateran Council of 1215, esp. 94ff; in addition Robertson *op. cit.* and Williamson, Some aspects of the legation of Cardinal Otto in England 1234–1241 (EHR. 64, 1949) 160, 165, and Cheney, Legislation of the Medieval English Church (EHR. 50, 1935) 198ff. On the execution of the decree establishing the general chapters see Berlière, Honorius III et les monastères bénédictines 1216–1277 (Rev. belge 2, 1923, 249ff.), Gibbs and Lang, 148ff., Williamson, 167, Hilpisch, 238ff. The assessment of the effects of this decree varies. Of the contemporaries of the Council, Gerald of Wales rates its significance high (Girald. Chambr. 4, 95).

[65]The statements by Gibbs and Lang (174ff.) on the development in the English church correspond to the picture which the decrees of the Council offer for the development of the western Church as a whole in the latter half of the thirteenth century. There is noticeable a stubborn insistence on the rights granted, especially on the material rights of the clergy.

[66]The widespread disregard of the canon decreeing an annual assembly of provincial synods is shown for England by Gibbs and Lang, 143ff. and Cheney, Legislation, 198ff., and for Germany Hauck, Kirchengeschichte 5 (1911) 135ff.

[67]Gibbs and Lang, 174ff.

[68]Cf. Browe, 13f., 44, 114ff.

[69]Can. 68 (Leclercq 1386f.), 5 X 6, 15. Cf. G. Kisch, The Jews in Medieval Germany (1949), 151, 206f., 293ff., 300; see also Browe, Die Judenmission im Mittelalter und die Päpste (Misc. Hist. Pont. VI 1942), 66.

[70]Reg. I 76 of 3.4.1198. The obligation of alimentation referred not only to those promoted to the higher orders which since Innocent's reign finally include subdeacons (c. 9 X 1, 14), but also to the lower grades (Reg. III 25). Reg. I 76 in Gregory IX's decretals is referred only to the clerics of the higher orders (c. 16 X 3, 5). Though this letter of Innocent III is concerned specifically with the case of a subdeacon, the obligation of alimentation is laid down as a general principle for all clerics ordained without appointment to a definite church. Cf. von Heckel, Ordination, 285f. Von Heckel shows that Innocent satisfied the ordained priests' claims to alimentation by judicial decree and not by provision and he, well aware of the innovation, incorporated the first of his letters containing such a decree into the Register, contrary to the normal practice of the chancery.

[71]Migne PL. 211 No. 194, 476f.

[72]P. 5036, c. 13 X 1, 14.

[73]On one occasion the bishop of Poitiers extracted such an oath from almost 200 priests (Reg. XV 186; cf. also von Heckel, Ordination, 289).

[74]C. 13 X 1, 14. The bishop's complaints are unjustified also in that Innocent, when providing for priests who were not known to him, always made the actual granting of the provision dependent on an examination of the qualification of the candidate to be provided (c. 13 X 1, 14; Reg. X 152).

[75]Von Heckel (Ordination, 289) assumes that in his later years Innocent had tacitly forborne from his more extensive demand that the provision be granted also to the lower grades ordained without appointment to a definite church. He points to Innocent's letter to the archbishop of Braga already referred to (c. 13 X 1, 14; P. 5036). In this letter, he claims, Innocent had at least not directly objected to the archbishop's view, voiced in his complaint, that the obligation to alimentation be restricted to the sacri ordines. The relevant passage reads: *accepimus te nostris auribus intimante, quod quidam clerici, qui ad sacras ordines sunt promoti, te... super beneficia obtinenda infestant.* In my opinions these words do not express such a restriction. The archbishop only states the facts of his case, namely that certain clerics of higher orders are pressing him for alimentation.

[76]In October 1212 he reprimands the bishop of Poitiers for the oath which he had had sworn to him in order to circumvent the apostolic decree by which he, the pope, had bound the consecrators and their successors to take care of the alimentation of the priests ordained without appointment to a definite church. By this he, the bishop, had sinned against the law and the Apostolic See, had opened up a means of violating the canons, and had attempted to block the way for the alimentation of poor clerics which he in his mercy had opened to them by his constitution (Reg. XV 186). It is not to be assumed that all the 200 to be ordained had received higher orders.

[77]C. 13 X 1, 14; c. 16 X 3, 5.

[78]On the nature of the pope's provision rescripts see Barraclough, 90ff. Barraclough sees the complaints against papal provisions in their true light and also stresses the positive side of provisions.

[79]Gesta c. 147.

[80]Such cases in Reg. I 210, 368, 337, 460; II 26, 289; III 4, 26; V 32, 123; VII 70, 90, 98: VIII 52, 78; IX 73, 260; X 9, 80, 186; XV 17, 38; P. 1041, 1082, 1084, 1442.

[81]Reg. VII 165; cf. also Chapter 7 below, n. 137.

[82]On the difficult financial situation of the Curia during the eleventh and twelfth centuries, see Jordan, 34.

[83]The main source is a letter from Honorius III (Recueil 19, 763, P. 7349, 7350 of 28.1.1225). Gerald of Wales also reports the plan. According to his account Innocent attempted to secure a tenth of the revenues from all the cathedral churches in the world for the needs of the Apostolic See, but the greater and 'more authentic' part of the Council members refused to burden themselves with such a contribution (Girald. Cambr. 4, 304f.). On the plan to reserve prebends see Gottlob, Servitientaxe, 57f., and Pfaff, Kaiser Heinrichs VI. höchstes Angebot an die Kurie (1196), 1927, 27f., 44ff., 78ff.

[84]Cf. also Gottlob, Servitientaxe, 60ff. Honorius III, who as Innocent III's chamberlain will have been closely involved in the preparation of the proposal, took up the attempt (P. 7349, 7350), but with no more success than his illustrious predecessor (Gottlob, *op. cit.* 58f.).

Innocent did not make it easier to effectuate the reform by summoning representatives of the chapters to the Council. According to the pope the chapters were to take part because matters would have to be discussed at the Council which were their particular concern (Reg. XVI 30) and among these certainly was the attempted reform. It seems that Innocent from the onset was willing to put the plan into effect only with the goodwill of all those concerned.

[85]Prior to this, in the case of defamation, that is of imputation by public decry, the deposition of the defamed office holder was possible, but only as an administrative measure by the competent superior, if the defamed person had not been able to effect the canonical compurgation inflicted on him, by his own oath and by the help of compurgators. An investigation into the merits of the imputations themselves was excluded in his procedure. The object of the investigation was the fact of the defamation itself alone.

[86]Reg. I 277.

[87]Reg. II 156, P. 806.

[88]Reg. II 63 (c. 10 X 5, 34).

[89]Reg. II 260.

[90]Reg. II 236.

[91]Can. 8 (Leclercq 1337ff.), c. 24 X 5, 1. Any discussion on the historical derivation of Innocent III's inquisition (cf. R. von Hippel, Deutsches Strafrecht 1, 1925, 188) must, in my opinion, take into consideration the use of the inquisitorial procedure in matters of heresy prior to Innocent's reign.

[92]Besides the process by inquisition Innocent also knows the process by denunciation. In this form of procedure the legal proceedings are initiated by trustworthy information. The informant, in contrast to the accuser, does not bear the full burden of responsibility for the opening of proceedings, nor the full onus of proof, since the accusations are examined and the witnesses heard ex officio. None the less the frivolous and malicious informant is punished, too (Reg. XI 58). The process by denunciation merges into the process by inquisition.

[93]Public decry and frequent imputations must have made the offence notorious to the judge so that he could not drop the matter without causing a public scandal (can. 8 Conc. Lateran.–Leclercq 1338–c. 24 X 5, 1).

[94]The abbot of Gembloux had informed Innocent that monks of his monastery without his, the abbot's, knowledge and against his will, had paid money to the bishop of Liège for his confirmation. Upon this information Innocent does not order an investigation to be opened against the simoniacs, but declares that those who had given or received the money would have to be punished according to canon law if their crime were notorious to the Church, which did not pass judgement on what was concealed (Reg. II 172). Bishops from the vicinity of Rome had unlawfully and partly simoniacally ordained foreign priests (Reg. XV 218). Proceedings seem not to have been taken against them, since they had neither been accused nor publicly defamed.

[95]Can. 8 Conc. Lateran. (*op. cit.*).

[96]Can. 8 Conc. Lateran. (*op. cit.*) Cf. also Reg. XV 191.

[97]Reg. VI 174.

[98]The Gesta record that, in his careful concern to reform and correct the abuses in the Church, Innocent had delegated shrewd visitators to various provinces, had the condition of the churches and the line of conduct of the prelate examined by them, and had those found guilty deposed (c. 130). Apart from southern France and northern Italy there is no trace of the delegation of special visitators. The Gesta probably include the

activities of monastic visitators and of the visitations undertaken by the cardinal legates, whose principal or subsidiary rôle was always also of a reforming nature. We know of a more detailed reform, and consequently, visitation activity, by cardinal legates in France: Peter Capuano (Reg. V 12), Guala (Reg. XIII 1, Hon. Ep. I 98 = Horoy 2, 128) and Robert Courçon (see for instance Hon. Ep. II 39 = Horoy 2, 516, III 30 = Horoy 3, 38). In England the activities of Cardinal deacon John of S Maria in Via Lata had been principally concerned with internal church matters (cf. Tillmann, Legaten, 92f., and C.R. Cheney, The Papal legate and the English monasteries in 1206, EHR. 46 1931). We know, too, that the legate Nicholas of Tusculum made journeys of visitation in 1213 and 1214 and deposed the unworthy abbots of Westminster, Evesham and Bardney (cf. Tillmann, *op. cit.* 105). In Ireland and probably in Scotland, too, the cardinal legate John of Salerno in the years 1201 to 1203 indulged in extensive activity as reformer and visitator. He was certainly not charged with a political mission. He was in London on 21 August 1201 on his journey through England and thereafter is traceable in York (cf. Tillmann, *op. cit.* 90). He will, therefore, have gone to Scotland in the first place. By September 1202 he must have been active for some time already in Ireland, for Innocent at that time answers his question concerning the appointment to the archbishopric of Armagh and praises him for his efforts to reform the Irish church (Reg. V 83). In February 1203 Innocent replies to a letter in which the legate reports on the *enormitates* he had found in the Irish church. The answer (Reg. V 158; Delisle, Lettres, 402f.; P. 1832) shows that the legate, according to the pope's assumption, will have to stay even longer in Ireland. On special monastic visitations for particular regions see pp. 203ff. above.

[99]Innocent also personally undertook visitations of monasteries, for example S Scholastica's at Subiaco (cf. Chapter 10 below) and Monte Cassino (Reg. XI 281; cf. Berlière, 40ff.).

[100]Examples of inquisitions in episcopal churches are to be found in Reg. VIII 116 (Toulouse), VII 209 (Viviers), VIII 200 (Novara), VIII 76 (Agde), XV 191 (Valence). These are not the inquisitions which were usual even in earlier times in cases of defamation. These latter were only concerned with the defamation as such, not with the facts underlying it, and could only lead to a procedure of compurgation against the defamed priest.

[101]Prior to Innocent's pontificate inquisitorial procedures of this kind had only been admissible in cases of suspected heresy.

[102]Cf. Chapter 7 below.

[103]Reg. III 24, VII 75.

[104]Reg. XVI 5.

[105]Cf. Chapter 7 below.

[106]Bishop Lothair of Vercelli, the Cistercian abbot Gerard of Tilieto, later bishop-elect of Novara, and then as the elect of Albano a member of the college of cardinals, the priest Albert of Mantua, the saintly bishop Peter of Ivrea, sometime abbot of the Cistercian monastery of La Ferté (Reg. VIII 200, IX 168, X 64, XI 187, 192; BF. 12402 Migne P. 217, 210; BF. 12395 P. 1242, 1243; Reg. XIII 134, XV 192, 197, 223, XVI 19, 160), Sicard of Cremona and Albert of Vercelli (Reg. XV 139, 142, 195, 197, XVI 13, 19, 160; BF. 12397, 12402 Migne PL. 217, 210).

[107]Reg. V 159.

[108]Alberic of Troisfontaines (MG. SS. 23) Reg. I 291; P. 4154 Migne PL. 217, 203f.

[109]On Odo of Paris see Rob. Autissiod. 272.

[110]P. 1374.

[111]Reg. XI 177.

[112]See n. 106 above and Chapter 10 below.

[113]Cf. Sappok, 68f., 97; Maschke, 48ff.

[114]For Andrew see Reg. XVI 10; P. 4724; Reg. XVI 181. For Albert: P. 2542; Delisle, Lettres, 411; Ambrose of S Teresa, 19ff. Innocent was generous enough to approve measures which were adequate only to the specific conditions of the countries concerned. So he refused, indeed, to confirm formally certain of Archbishop Andrew of Lund's regulations lest he should appear to create a commonly applicable law, but directs with words of high praise for the archbishop's wisdom and zeal that these regulations should continue to stand in the church province of Lund by virtue of papal authority. Andrew, in concord with the abbots of the Benedictine Order and in the interest of the reform of orders, had for instance directed the centralization of the monasteries under the control of the rector of Lund. Innocent declares that this measure for the present is to stand for four years, since such innovations easily give rise to the need for modification. If, in the initial four years, the measures should prove a success there would be no objection to his confirming them (Reg. VIII 198). Being far from the scene of events he was not in a position to assess the suitability of the measures definitively, but, highly confiding in the archbishop, he authorized them, because, as he says, from the shrewdness of the legislator the rightness of his regulations was to be deduced. For another instance where Innocent gave the archbishop a free hand, see Horoy 1, 171. Cf. also Reg. XVI 181.

[115]Reg. XIII 92.

[116]Reg. XVI 12.

[117]Reg. XV 186.

[118]Reg. X 194. Cf. also Reg. V 95 and P. 992, 1334. Cf. on Rainald de Forez and his dispute with the city and the feudal aristocracy of the diocese, H. Kleinclausz, Histoire de Lyon 1 (1939), 153ff., 160, 162.

[119]Such imputations were made against the bishops of Viesti, Motula, Benevento, Melfi, Sorrento (Reg. XVI 139).

[120]Reg. II 236.

[121]Reg. XVI 139.

[122]Thomas of Capua, Dict. Epist. (Hahn, Coll. 1) 343f.

[123]Reg. XV 115, 235.

[124]On the proceedings see Reg. V 13; VII 87; IX 51, 55, 259; XII 149, 150.

[125]Reg. VIII 151. Cf. also Reg. XI 62, XII 91, XVI 74.

[126]Reg. VIII 200. Cf. also Reg. XI 192.

[127]Cf. the rigorous regulations he decreed in the monastery of Subiaco (Reg. V 82, complete text in Alanus 3, 19, 15, see von Heckel, Dekretalensammlung, 277), and the enthusiastic praise by the chronicler on the pope's justice and mercy during his visitation of the monastery (Chron. Sublacense, 34f.).

[128]*Illam autem maturitatem et temperantiam in exsequendo visitationis officium observetis, ut ii ad quos vos declinare contigeret non minus in vestro recessu gaudeant quam accessu* (Reg. XI 177).

[129]*Remotisque laicis, viros religiosos adhibuit ad quotidianum ministerium mensis, ut ei a personis regularibus honestius serviretur, consuetis tamen officiis viris nobilibus reservatis, qui festivis diebus secundum morem deserviebant in eis* (Gesta c. 148 Migne PL. 214 CCXXVf.).

[130]*Nobilium filios, quos valettos appellant, ab aula sua prorsus amovit* (Gesta c. 150 Migne PL. 214, CCXXVIII). Cf. Fliche, 111.

[131]Gesta c. 150.

[132]Gottlob, Servitientaxe, 23ff. deals extensively with these committees. Cf. also Jordan, 80ff.

[133]See Chapter 5 above.

[134]Text in Gottlob *op. cit.* 754. Cf. *ibid.* 27.

[135]Cf. Gottlob, *op. cit.* 28f.

[136]Typical of Innocent's reaction to such blackmail is a letter he wrote on 12 August 1202. He authorized the archbishop of Canterbury to institute investigations throughout England concerning the sums which his nuncio, Master Philip, who had collected the fortieth for the Holy Land in 1200, had received or extorted on his own account or on behalf of the pope, to the latter's humiliation. The archbishop was to report the results of his investigation to the pope without delay (Cheney, Master Philip, 343f.).

[137]Gesta c. 41.

[138]*Ibid.*

[139]*Ibid.*

[140]See Chapter 3 above; cf. Gottlob, *op. cit.* 42ff. For presents to the pope and the cardinals see also Eichmann, Die Krönungsservitien der Kaiser (ZRG. Kan. Abt. 28, 1939), 2ff.

[141]Cf. Barraclough, 50ff.; Berlière, 42.

[142]Reg. XI 28. Cf. Chapter 7 below and *ibid.* n. 4.

[143]Gervase of Canterbury 2, App. to Pref. LXXXIII.

[144]Two of many examples may be cited. Replying to an enquiry as to whether those appointed to a definite parish church who had been presented by their rector for ordination without the approval of the patron, were to be given precedence over others who were presented by the patron, Innocent decides that the patrons' rights were in no way prejudiced by such intitulation and that the patrons could present alternative candidates for the vacant churches (Reg. XI 258). When Innocent permits a bishop to dispose of churches the presentation of which was disputed between third parties on the condition that the question of the right of patronage could not be solved within four months, he does not forget to add a reservation concerning the right of the person who proved to be in possession of the patronage (Reg. I 521). Cf. Reg. X 150.

[145]For the following text see Ladner, L'ordo praedicatorum avant l'ordre des Prêcheurs (in Mandonnet 2, 1937) and Vicaire, La Sainte Pédication de Narbonnaise (*ibid.* 1, 1938). Cf. also Fliche, 140ff.

[146]See p. 205 above; Chapter 7 below and *ibid.* n. 8.

[147]See pp. 192–3 above; Cf. also Berlière p. 24, 34, 38. Innocent had the statutes of the new order of the Humiliati examined by Cistercians, the abbots of Locedio and Cerratto, as well as by Brother Rainer (Tiraboschi 2, 135).

[148]Reg. I 358 (Migne PL. 214, 336; cf. also Reg. I 398).

[149]P. 1026.

[150]In 1213 the pope intended to engage Cistercians to preach in Tuscany or had already so engaged them, Canivez, Statuta Capitulorum Generalium Ordinis Cisterciensis (1116–1786) 1 (1933), 414, No. 52 (cf. Mandonnet 1, 123 n. 38).

[151]Reg. VII 76.

[152]Cf. Mandonnet 1, 27ff., 39; 2, 40ff., 123.

[153]Grundmann, 57ff.

[154]On the decisive change effected by Innocent III in the policy of the papacy towards the religious lay movements in the Church cf. Grundmann, 10ff., 70f., Mandonnet 2, 43f.

[155]On the Order in general see Grundmann, 65ff.

[156]Privilege of 16 June 1201 (Tiraboschi 2, 139ff., cf. Grundmann, 76f.).

[157]Privilege of 12 June 1201 (Tiraboschi 2, 135ff., cf. Grundmann *loc. cit.*).

[158]Privilege of 7 June 1201 (Tiraboschi 2, 128ff., cf. Grundmann, 78ff.).

[159]See Reg. II 228. Also Grundmann, 72ff., Mandonnet 1; 37.

[160]Böhmer, Analekten, 65.

[161]James of Vitry (Moschus), 334ff.

[162]Cf. Schnürer, 339.

[163]Warmth is the feature of the edifying letters to the Humiliati of 8 December 1214 in which Innocent admonishes them to be sober, pious and righteous in their lives in this world *nobis ad gaudiam, vobis ad meritum et alios ad exemplum* (Tiraboschi 2, 157).

[164]On the Catholic Poor cf. Grundmann, 100ff., Mandonnet 2, 49f.

[165]Within the limits of his competence Innocent even freed those of its brothers who lived in the outside world from war service and the obligation to take oaths in temporal matters as well (Reg. XI 196–198), even though refusal to perform military service or to take oaths were both considered to be characteristics of heresy.

[166]Reg. XII 67, 68.

[167]Reg. XII 69.

[168]Reg. XIII 63. Cf. also Reg. XIII 77, 78, XV 90ff., 96. Grundmann (166) believes, and Mandonnet agrees with him, that after 1212 the Curia had discontinued labouring for the strengthening of the community since Innocent's letters after that date no longer mention the Catholic Poor. I find this an unconvincing argument, the more so since the registers of the last years of the pope's reign (1214–1216) are lost.

[169]Reg. XIII 94 (Migne PL. 216, 191), XV 176 (*ibid.* 668).

[170]On the encounter and Francis' request cf. Grundmann, 127ff.

[171]Thomas of Celano (Alençon), 35. A more recent examination of the origins of the Franciscan Order, Quaglia, L'originalità della regola francescana, 1943, was not accessible to me.

[172]Cf. nn. 173 and 181 below.

[173]See Grundmann, 148ff.; M. Fassbinder, Über die Quellen zum Leben der hl. Klara (Franziskan. Studien 23, 1936), 312ff.; Grau, Das *Privilegium Paupertatis* Innocenz' III. (Franziskan. Studien 31, 1949), 337ff. Since this privilege was issued in writing a written confirmation also of St Francis' Rule or, at the least, of his manner of living may be presumed.

[174]The question is last discussed by Grundmann p. 103ff. and Vicaire (in Mandonnet 1), 141ff. Both assume that the Spaniards adopted this new means of countering heresy in accord with the pope (as does Fliche, 132f.). This otherwise very credible assumption is, in my view, questioned by the letter of 17 November 1206 referred to above, in which Innocent grants this permission only by way of the legate Ralph of Fontfroide to those monks who had volunteered to preach against heresy but did not dare to do it on their own responsibility (Reg. IX 175). This will not refer to Diego or Dominic, yet it would be strange if Innocent in the presumed discussion he had with both on the new plan during their stay at the Curia, should only have granted them permission to preach and not have envisaged and permitted that they engage companions.

[175]Reg. IX 175.

[176]Can. 13 (Leclercq 1344) c. 9 X 3, 36.

[177]So also Grundmann, 141ff., Mandonnet 1, 49f., and Vicaire (Mandonnet 1) 156ff., 148ff.

[178]Jordan of Saxony (Opera, ed. Berthier, 1891), 14.

[179]Cf. Mandonnet 1, 178ff.

[180]Opera, 14.

[181]Cf. Grundmann, 142ff. Salimbene the Minorite renders the Lateran Council's prohibition in a form in which it appears to be directed against the formation of new Mendicant Orders (*Inter que statuit papa, quod decetero nulla religio mendicans consurgeret*, MG. SS. 32, 22). He complains that by the carelessness on the part of the prelates this constitution was not observed and that as a consequence there were not enough alms available for those who really wore themselves out in preaching and teaching and who were bound by God to live by the gospel. Salimbene thus interprets the Council's prohibition against the orders as being a form of protection for the 'old' Mendicant Orders or even for his own order only against any future competition.

[182]According to Grundmann (132f.) Cardinal John of St Paul, who introduced St Francis at the Curia and defended his ideal of life against objections (on John himself see Chapter 7 below and Chapter 1 n. 93), had accepted for the first time the ideal of the *perfectio evangelica* in the form in which it inspired the whole religious movement of the age as the legitimate way of life within the Church, not only for tactical reasons, but for the sake of its true evangelical demands. Against this it should be remembered that Innocent himself in a sermon contrasts the Mosaic law which promises worldly riches: *Dabo vobis terram fluentem lacte et melle* with the law of the gospel which preaches temporal poverty: *Si vis perfectus esse, vade et vende omnia quae habes et veni et sequere me* (Migne PL. 217, 537f.), and that in another sermon he teaches that it is inherent to perfection to follow Christ *ut nudus sequatur nudum, pauper pauperem* (*ibid.* 573).

[183]Thomas of Celano (Alençon), 182. Cf. also Legenda Trium Sociorum (AASS. 2 October) 737.

# CHAPTER 7

# The defender of the faith

Although Innocent, as a pastor, professed to his duty to lead back, like a good shepherd, those who had strayed from the Lord's flock,[1] he called people to arms against the Albigensians, for the Crusade against the heretics in southern France, in which in Christ's name and under the sign of His Cross, the blood of tens of thousands was shed and inhuman cruelties were committed. That the war took a course which he had neither intended nor wanted, partly exonerates Innocent III as a man, but does not relieve him from his responsibility at the bar of history.

When Innocent invoked the strength of the sword against the heretics, he himself did not see any contradiction with the task set to him by his pastoral office. In the spirit of his age he felt that precisely as a pastor he was obliged to proceed against the heretics with temporal as well as spiritual weapons. For him heresy was the worst menace to the Christian people, since it mortally endangered their souls. In his own eyes he would be an unfaithful overseer in the vineyard, if he shunned force where the duty of guarding the Lord's possession against devastation by the foxes was involved, and a hireling, not a true shepherd, if he did not use his sword to protect the sheep from the rapacious wolves.[2]

Innocent, though, only decided to crusade against heresy when he saw no other way of saving Catholicism in southern France from destruction.[3] For a long time he had been trying to bring Philip of France to proceed against the local magnates, Philip's vassals, who had failed to purge their country from heresy.[4] He hoped that, by way of an intervention of the feudal overlord, heresy could be crushed in the main heretical regions without much bloodshed, perhaps without waging war.[5] When in the end he formally proclaimed the Crusade, he still tried to give it, in a certain measure, the character of a punitive expedition at the hands of the royal overlord by requesting Philip to appoint, by virtue of royal authority and, thus, not by order of the Church, the commander of the army who should head the Lord's warriors under God's protection and under the king's standard.[6]

Innocent laid such weight on the king taking over the leadership of the war because he feared that otherwise the special interests of the participants, as had happened on the previous Crusade to Jerusalem, might gain the upper hand and dissension might arise, so that the campaign would cause harm to the Church instead of advantage and further heresy instead of extinguishing it.[7] Since he was unable to direct the enterprise himself from afar, Innocent saw the unity of the command and, what is more, of a command from a higher level, only guaranteed if King Philip took the supreme command into his own hands.

When Philip refused to accede to the pope's wishes, because, in view of his enmity against John of England and the uncertain conditions prevailing in the Empire, he was unwilling to tie himself down in the south, Innocent transferred the command to his legates, with Abbot Arnold of Citeaux at their head.[8] In Arnold Innocent believed he had found the man who better than any other was qualified to take the pope's place in the difficult and dangerous conditions which prevailed in the fighting areas. The abbot, who for years had been active in the heretical districts as a legate and who previously had been abbot of Grandselves, one of the great Cistercian monasteries of Languedoc, became, indeed, the very heart and soul of the Crusade. By his superiority of mind and by his iron strength of will he amalgamated the forces which had a natural tendency to diverge, and orientated them towards the aim he had passionately seized on. And yet, events did not take the straight and consistent course which the pope and the abbot had in mind, because the pope and his legate themselves became antagonists. A strange, almost dramatic conflict developed between these two strong personalities, in which Innocent was not to win.

Arnold wished to pursue the war until the threat of heresy had been radically suppressed by way of removing all the magnates who had proved unreliable in the matter of faith, in particular Count Raymond of Toulouse,[9] the most powerful of the supporters of heresy in southern France. Innocent, on the other hand, wished to end the reluctantly started war as quickly as possible, and therefore was prepared to take the incriminated lords into favour again if they submitted themselves to the demands of the Church. There were grave dangers in such forbearance. Innocent was aware of them as was his legate. It was not easy to attach credit to the sincerity of the submission of the supporters of heresy[10] and to their true faith which they asseverated just when the crusading army was approaching or had scored its first unexpected successes. But any attempt at overthrowing these lords could only result in driving them to side again with the heretics and in giving new strength to heresy. Taken into favour again, they might, being warned, refrain from opposing the execution of the constitutions against heresy, if a purged and renewed episcopate showed vigilant zeal.

It is true that Innocent, before the beginning of the war, had himself considered the radical solution. He would have been happy if King Philip had seized the heretical districts into his hands.[11] But now, after the king had refused to co-operate, such a solution would have left no option but to replace the local powers, which were deeply rooted in the country, by foreign noblemen from northern France drawn from the ranks of the crusaders, that is by persons who, of their own strength, would neither be able to conquer the lands nor to keep hold of them. The war, therefore, would have dragged on indefinitely and would have had to keep on its character as a crusade.

The disparity of views between Innocent and Arnold was not exclusively a matter of a differing assessment of political expediency, but also corresponds to the difference of their characters. Arnold's iron rigour, which in matters of faith went to the point of cruelty, fitted in with a way of proceeding which was only satisfied when the adversary was crushed. To Innocent's more gentle disposition, however, a policy of forbearance appeared to be more adequate.

The disparity became apparent already before the war started. Arnold would have liked best to throw the army straight away against the excommunicate count of Toulouse, although Raymond, alarmed by the preparations for the Crusade, asked to be absolved from the ban. But Innocent recommended that the count be treated with consideration for the time being,[12] and in June 1209 he ordered a legate, his notary Milo, sent out from the Curia for that particular purpose, to release him from the ban.[13] Thereupon Arnold, after the crusading army had conquered the vicomtés of Béziers and Carcassonne,[14] hastened, as it seems, to achieve a fait accompli at least in this matter before the pope could take a possibly divergent decision and thwart his legate's intentions again. By way of election through the army Arnold, in August 1209,[15] gave the country a new lord in the person of the northern French count Simon de Montfort,[16] whose energy and religious zeal guaranteed that the territories entrusted to him would be purged from heresy.

We do not know whether Innocent for his part would have decided differently, in any case he approved what had happened without his knowledge and confirmed to Simon de Montfort his new possessions. But contrary to Simon and Arnold, he hoped to bring the war to an early end. Great successes had been scored. The local lords no longer dared protect heretics openly or even avow their cause. They all gave themselves out to be good Catholics. In one of the districts most strongly infested with heresy a vast number of heretics had been extirpated or banished, the land itself had passed from the hands of a supporter of heretics into those of one of their assiduous persecutors. In neighbouring Provence the local barons and municipal authorities had pledged themselves on oath to fight effectively against heresy and, by way of surrendering castles, had given security for the fulfilment of their pledge. Moreover, because of the success attained by the crusading army, the Catholic party seems to have regained the upper hand in many places which had been spared the war. Consequently, when confirming to Simon his possessions, Innocent gives him to understand that he can rely on papal support only for the maintenance of the acquisitions, but not for new conquests.[17] Referring to the distress of the Holy Land he also refuses to issue, as he had apparently been requested, a new call to take up the cross against the heretics. The defenders of the Holy Land were already complaining, Innocent significantly states, that, because of the indulgence granted for the war against the heretics, support for the Holy Land was dangerously hampered.[18] Innocent gives clearly to understand that he wants to turn his own and Christendom's force towards the true crusade, the expedition to Jerusalem. Simon's wish to become liege vassal to the Roman Church for the conquered territories,[19] he passes over in silence. It seems as if he was unwilling to burden himself or his successor with a solemn guarantee in favour of the foreign conqueror.

The abbot legate did not accede to the pope's policy of forbearance. He and his co-legate Hugh Raymond of Riez even succeeded in winning the support of the curial legate Milo for a policy of proceeding ruthlessly.[20] The legates' attacks are concentrated on the person of Raymond of Toulouse, whose reconciliation with the Church they try to undo. Scarcely three months after the count's absolution and despite his active participation in the Crusade, Raymond is anathematized again and his lands are placed under interdict. The sentence is to become effective if Raymond fails to fulfil his obligations within a brief period of time.[21] The legates' proceeding was shockingly precipitate, an act, therefore, of malevolence and injustice and, since Raymond was about to travel to the Curia, a demonstrable anticipation of the papal decision into the bargain.[22] Raymond's excommunication under the pretext of breach of oath served for the preparation of an offensive war and of a war of conquest against him and his lands.[23]

Innocent decided against his legates. He regards the count as not being excommunicate and the legal consequences of breach of oath and of excommunication as not having become effective and, whilst Raymond is staying at the Curia, gives him a chance to clear himself for ever, by way of a canonical compurgation, from the charges of heresy and of complicity in the murder of the papal legate Peter of Castelnau.[24] The proceedings of compurgation had naturally to take place at the scene of the alleged offences, but the pope had so fixed its form that, without papal co-operation, it could only result in the count's exculpation, that is, therefore, could not be used to lay a snare for him.[25] A warning to the legates not to impede maliciously or frivolously the execution of his mandate shows how much he was in earnest about the enforcement of his own policy of reconciliation against the divergent opinion of his representatives.[26]

Arnold and his collaborators deliberately counteracted the pope's pronounced intentions.[27] In July 1210,[28] at the Council of Saint-Gilles, they refuse to admit the count to the canonical compurgation on the grounds that he had not fulfilled, and was not fulfilling, the obligations which had been imposed on him at his absolution and which he had confirmed by oath.[29] At the beginning of 1211 Raymond was excommunicated again by the legates and was eventually manoeuvred into the fight against the crusading army, in which he lost almost the whole of his country.

Innocent let himself be persuaded that Raymond had culpably offended against his sworn obligations,[30] and confirmed his legates' sentence.[31] He also regarded the fiefs, which Raymond held from the

Roman Church, as well as his other church fiefs, as forfeited and
devolved upon their former possessors,[32] and consented to the temporary occupation of the county of Toulouse by the crusading army.[33]
Since at the same time, in April 1211, Innocent was requiring or
accepting the resignation of the dissolute archbishop of Auch and of
other unworthy and unsuitable members of the southern French
episcopate,[34] the realization of the legates' aim, the complete renewal
of the conditions of temporal and spiritual rule in the heretical
districts, seems to be near at hand.

But Innocent had by no means abandoned his policy of reconciliation. He refuses to declare Raymond of Toulouse's sovereignty
forfeited or to transfer it to Simon de Montfort until Raymond had
been sentenced pursuant to the procedure which he had prescribed.[35]
In June 1212 he angrily requires again that his mandate be executed
without delay,[36] and towards the end of the year he welcomes with
new hopes the prospect of being able to enforce his policy of
forbearance with less dangers to the faith than before. King Peter II
of Aragon, a ruler sincerely devoted to the Roman Church and proven
as an enemy of heresy, had, with Raymond's, his brother-in-law's,
consent, declared himself prepared to take Raymond's lands into his
own hands, to protect them for Raymond's son, the younger Raymond, and to take care of the latter's upbringing in the Catholic faith.
He had also interceded on behalf of Raymond's vassals, the count of
Foix[37] and the lords of Comminges and Béarn, and had accused
Simon and the legates of having unlawfully robbed the barons of their
possessions.[38] Innocent reserves to himself the decision on the
proffered guarantee on which he first intends to take the expert
opinion of the spiritual and temporal notables concerned, among them
the municipal authorities.[39] But he already lets the legate Arnold, now
archbishop of Narbonne, know that he, the pope, regards the Crusade
as ended. Arnold, he writes, together with King Peter of Aragon,
should labour for peace and no longer trouble the Christian people on
behalf of the indulgence against heresy. The danger threatening from
the Saracens, he continues, was now more serious than the affair of
heresy, which had taken so favourable a turn. The Christian people
must now turn to the Saracen war.[40] The pope uses a different tone in
his letter towards the man he had formerly treated with so much
consideration. Without a comment of his own, thus not repudiating
them, he puts forward to Arnold and to Count Simon the serious
charges which Peter of Aragon had raised against them, among them

the reproach that they had also held out their "greedy hands" for lands which had never been suspected of heresy.[41] At the same time he orders those barons to be restored, for whom Peter had interceded with him.[42]

At the time when Innocent set out to put an end to the policy of conquest pursued by Simon de Montfort and the legates, the defenders of this policy prepared for a counter-blow. When at Lavaur in January 1213 they convened a council, they knew of the king of Aragon's proposals, they probably also knew that the Curia had favourably accepted them. They now tried at the last moment to anticipate the decision on Peter's offer. Basing themselves on the expert opinion of the assembled bishops, headed by the legate and Archbishop Arnold, the delegates again refuse Raymond's admission, requested by the pope, to the canonical compurgation.[43] Moreover, the legates and delegates, together with the assembled bishops, openly and solemnly turn against the papal policy of forbearance and reconciliation. "To save their souls", they unanimously present to the pope the crimes which the count of Toulouse had committed personally or had caused to be committed by his son and the lords of Foix, Comminges and Béarn, particularly, as they significantly point out, after his return from the Curia, meaning: after the pope's attitude had roused his courage to commit further outrages. They beseech Innocent for God's sake to bring the affair, which was a matter of their own and their churches' liberation and peace, even of their very lives, to a fortunate end by laying the axe to the pernicious tree and hewing it down.[44] The bishops from the Rhône valley describe how much their region had suffered from the heretics and the excommunicate bands of mercenaries. In lavish terms they thank Innocent that he had restored their faith and peace, but then warn him that Toulouse, almost the only city in the county still unconquered, was again infesting the neighbouring regions, and that what the pope had so much toiled to build up and to reform at great expense, was again doomed to chaos. They also implore the pope to constitute himself judge and abandon the city, which for them is no less wicked than Sodom and Gomorrah, to being razed to the ground. If this coil, too, was broken, they would be liberated. They assure him by the Truth, which is God Himself, that the tyrant of Toulouse, once he was allowed to raise his head again, would devastate all and everything, and then the Church would be worse off than under the domination of barbarian peoples.[45] The archbishop of Bordeaux, together with two of his suffragans, expresses the warning that the Church and the clergy would inevitably be threatened with doom if a task, begun so obviously with justice and power, was left half finished.[46] Bishop Bernard of Béziers laments that his own and the other prelates' throats would be threatened by the sword and the church property with destruction, if the count and his sons rose again. If Toulouse, the nest of heresy, remained in their hands, then a flame would again flare up from it and harm the neighbouring cities worse than before.[47]

The envoys sent by the Council of Lavaur, headed by Thedisius, the papal special commissioner for the compurgation proceedings against Raymond, were at first not lent a ready ear by Innocent,[48] but in the end he could not avoid being impressed by the information conveyed to him. It was not only his representatives, but also the entire local episcopate and the bishops of the neighbouring provinces, who fervently demanded the overthrow of the house of Toulouse, the restoration of which, they predicted, would result in the greatest possible evils for the Christian faith and for the Church, evils which they laid at his, the pope's, charge, if he continued to take the count under his protection. One thing at least seemed to be a fact, that Raymond was not willing or at least not able himself to purge his territory from heresy. If Innocent was none the less willing to hold Raymond and his son, he had to rely wholly on the guarantee the king of Aragon had offered for the purging of the county from heresy. But Peter seems to have somewhat shaken confidence in his reliability by asserting that the territories of his vassals of Foix, Comminges and Béarn had never been infested with heresy, an assertion which the envoys sent by the Council of Lavaur would have had no difficulty in disproving.[49]

Innocent does not decide in favour of either party. He does revoke the orders of restoration issued in favour of the above-mentioned lords as being obtained surreptitiously,[50] and he no longer insists on Raymond being admitted to the canonical compurgation, but, on the other hand, he neither abandons the count and the other lords, nor the city of Toulouse.[51] A cardinal legate is to replace Arnold and the other legates who have themselves become parties to the confrontation;[52] he is to end the war, to decide the various legal claims or at least to examine them, and to absolve the lords of Conserans and Béarn as well as the city of Toulouse.[53] At that time Innocent, after his great call, in April 1213, for a crusade to the Holy Land, was more than ever intent on establishing peace in Christendom. In September 1213 he tries to bring those Germans who had taken the cross against the heretics to pledge themselves for the expedition to Jerusalem instead, because this enterprise was more deserving.[54]

The papal legate, Peter of Benevento, cardinal deacon of S Maria in Aquiro,[55] who in the spring of 1214 had set out for his area of legatine jurisdiction, succeeded in re-establishing peace in southern France. He absolved the citizens of Toulouse, the counts of Foix and Comminges,[56] and probably Gaston of Béarn as well.[57] Through his mediation Raymond of Toulouse was reconciled with the Church, at the price, though, of an unconditional capitulation.[58] At the council of legates, opened at Montpellier on 8 January 1215, the assembly resolved to appoint Simon de Montfort governor of the county of Toulouse and of the territories conquered by the crusading army.[59] The legate duly left the final decision to the pope, but the resolution of the council gives rise to the conjecture that the cardinal, just as the former legates or delegates as soon as they came to know conditions at first hand, had become an opponent of the pope's policy of forbearance, at least in the matter of the count of Toulouse. Robert Courçon, the cardinal legate for France who, during Peter of Benevento's absence in Aragon, had for a short time been active in the heretical districts, had gone to the length of granting to Simon and his successors all the territories conquered within the range of his legatine jurisdiction, and of formally confirming them to him and to his successors.[60] Courçon had not at first favoured Simon's and the crusaders' cause, but after his arrival in the heretical districts had soon changed his mind.[61]

Innocent now left the question which had become insoluble for him for the forthcoming general council to decide, but he still entrusted Simon with the administration of those possessions of the count of Toulouse which the crusaders had conquered.[62]

( The fight against heresy in general was one of the chief tasks facing the Fourth Lateran Council. The existing legislation against heresy was integrated and made more efficient.[63] ) The solemn proclamation of a creed brought into strong relief the tenets which the Cathari denied: the doctrines of Trinity and of Incarnation, the creation of all things, including those corporeal, by God, the resurrection of the flesh, the original goodness of all creatures, even of evil spirits, the pleasingness to God also of married life, the validity of the christening of infants, the doctrines of the sacraments of baptism, penance and the Eucharist, including the dogma of trans-substantiation,[64] as well as the doctrine of the Church as the only way of salvation.[65]

At this Council the balance which had been wavering so long tilted against Raymond. He was found guilty in the matter of heresy and of breach of oath and on these grounds, and because under his rule the country could not be kept in the true faith, was excluded from rulership for ever. His lands conquered by the crusaders, with the exception of his wife's dowry, were transferred to Simon de Montfort. The important Provençal possessions, which had not been conquered, Innocent promised to the count's son on the chance that he should prove a true catholic.[66] The pope did not consent to the condemnation of the other lords.[67]

As to the final phase of this strange struggle, the papal letters leave us in an embarrassing position, since the registers of the last years of Innocent's reign are lost. But from chronicle reports we learn that Innocent was averse to Raymond's condemnation to the last.[68] In the circles of the count's friends the tale went about that Innocent had allowed the condemnation to be extorted from him. He is said to have declared that Raymond was unjustly removed from his rulership, and that he, the pope, would never tolerate the cross to be preached for the purpose of sustaining Simon, the new lord of the country, in its possession.[69] This rôle of Pilate is unbecoming in Innocent, and these cannot have been his words. But even an enemy of Raymond admits that the count's condemnation was by no means a foregone conclusion.[70] Another reliable contemporary writer, a court chaplain of Philip of France, reports that Innocent had apparently been inclined to restore the dispossessed count of Toulouse, but that nearly all the participants of the Council had opposed to such a course.[71]

The Fourth Lateran Council was in no way a demonstration of papal absolutism[72] and the assembled bishops were not assigned the rôle of mere supernumeraries.[73] It seems that Innocent did not dare to assume, in defiance of the Council's opinion in the matter of faith, the responsibility for a policy to which the first and foremost affected local episcopate and the papal envoys themselves, however many of them had been appointed during the war against heresy, had demurred. The resistance shown by his representatives, above all by those directly sent from the Curia, could, indeed, only be grounded in their conviction that the full restoration of Catholicism in southern France was not to be thought of, if the local authorities, particularly the counts of Toulouse, remained in power. Only because he was aware of this will Innocent have over and over again put up with his intentions being thwarted by the legates. But for all that, the sentence might well have turned out differently if King Peter of Aragon's death on 12 September 1213 in battle against Simon de Montfort had not swept away the guarantee for the purgation of the county and for the Catholic upbringing of the younger Raymond.

It remains, however, strange that Innocent did not decisively drop Raymond already before the convening of the Council, if he did not intend simply to push through the policy to which he was personally inclined against the opposition of the local episcopate and of his own representatives on the spot. We must not put it past a statesman of his kind and rank that he failed to take a decision because of the risks involved in either course. The only explanation is that Innocent felt himself hampered in his decision by reasons of law and fairness.[74] It is true that, in the matter of heresy, the count was most heavily incriminated. Innocent himself had charged him with complicity in the death of Peter of Castelnau. If the respective mandate was really published, Innocent at that time had released Raymond's subjects and allies from their oaths and offered his lands to the Catholics.[75] But after that he had accepted Raymond's surrender and thereby had created a new legal situation. What had happened before, could now no longer be preferred against Raymond in an offhand way. It seems that Innocent, above all, could not get over the legates' having prevented the count's compurgation from the suspicion of heresy and of complicity in the murder of Peter of Castelnau. Even if the reasons why they refused to institute the proceedings of compurgation were more or less valid, there was no doubt that they were adverse to this compurgation and that they pursued the count's overthrow, no matter what he did or offered. Innocent's sense of justice and his priestly feeling revolted against condemning a man who was ready to give any satisfaction and guarantee,[76] revolted even more against robbing the innocent young son.

The policy corresponding to Innocent's personal views would not only have been more just and more priestly, but probably also more useful. Simon de Montfort and his son could not gain a footing in the conquered territory. The house of Montfort remained the object of bitter hatred in the south. The counts of Toulouse, father and son, reconquered their rulership, and again war raved in the unfortunate country for more than a decade. The course of events would have been the same if Innocent had consented to the more radical solution,

demanded at the Council, of totally disinheriting Raymond's son and
of removing other incriminated magnates. A consistent implemen-
tation of the pope's policy of reconciliation, on the other hand, would
also have helped the wounds which the Crusade against heresy had
inflicted upon the soul of the southern French lands to heal sooner.[77]

Even though the course and outcome of the war in its particulars
fell short of the pope's wish and will, it still staved off from the
Church a direct and serious menace. Catholicism in southern France
was saved, the political power of heresy was broken. But at what
price?

The Albigensian war[78] is said to have destroyed for ever the
flowering of the south, to have spread the silence of death over the
smiling landscape of the troubadours. There is much exaggeration in
this assertion. Even before the Albigensian wars the south was
anything but a paradise of serenity and peace.[79] Outrage, viciousness
and all the evils which are inseparably linked with an anarchy of the
nobility were rampant.[80] The bands of Spanish mercenaries and the
other gangs[81] taken into service by the barons were a veritable pest
for the country. Already the Lateran Council of 1179 had bracketed
them with the heretics and called people to fight against them.
Raymond of Toulouse had been banned in 1207, that is before the
beginning of the Crusade, because, among other grounds, he kept
such mercenary bands.[82] A chronicler well acquainted with the conditions then prevailing tries to exonerate the count, stating that he
could not help but take such bands into his service and allow them to
take all possible liberties, since he himself was constantly harrassed
by his own vassals.[83] A decade or more before Innocent III's accession to the papal throne Stephen of Tournai had warned Bishop
John of Poitiers against accepting an appointment to the archbishopric of Narbonne. In those regions, he writes, dishonesty,
trickery, hunger and sorrow were prevalent. On a recent journey to
Toulouse he had often seen there the ghastly picture of death,
churches which were half decayed or razed to the ground, unin-
habited human dwellings which served wild beasts for shelter. He had
shuddered and gone pale at the news of his friend's move to Narbonne.[84] Anarchy was the basic evil from which the country suffered,
and Innocent was on the right lines, as regards the temporal welfare
of the inhabitants too, when, before the Crusade and with a view to
avoid it, he proposed to Philip Augustus that he should annex the
territories to his crown lands. In Provence Innocent III's legates truly

deserved well of the country and his inhabitants. They promulgated a land peace, caused the magnates to be bound to it and to swear to watch over the security of the highways, to grant the travellers free passage by water and land, to abolish unjust tolls and to disband the gangs of mercenaries.[85] The lords had to stand them security by delivering fortified castles and to surrender their thieves' lairs for destruction.[86]

Even though the Crusade against heresy did not destroy the peace of a country blessed with happiness, it still caused a world of terror, suffering and destruction. The fate of the city of Béziers alone offers ample proof. On the evidence of the crusading legate himself,[87] nearly twenty thousand persons, men, women and children, were massacred by the crusading army during the storming of the town. It is a blemish on Innocent's memory that, at least in public,[88] he passed over the atrocious deed in silence and even praised the doings which comprised it. In his view, God gave the cities of Béziers and Carcassonne miraculously into the hands of the holy army, and he feels he must thank God for what He had mercifully and miraculously done, through those filled with true zeal for the faith, against His abominable enemies.[89] The terms "mercifully" and "miraculously" refer to the surprising speed, stressed by the legates, of the first successes, and not to the massacre itself. But against the background of the slaughter the pope's words leave an extremely repulsive impression. Innocent will have regarded the ghastly destruction of Béziers as a divine judgement and have thought it inadmissible to argue with the crusaders about it.[90] Perhaps a word of Innocent's lifts the veil a little which disguises what he personally felt when he received the terrible news: "We would have wished that the destroyers of orthodox faith ... not only had kept what belonged to them, but also, returning to the purity of the Catholic faith, had possessed in love and peace what belongs to us."[91] Innocent later saved Toulouse from the fate of unhappy Béziers.[92] Contemporaries were fully aware that the uncompromising severity of the spokesmen of the Crusade against heresy was contrary to Innocent's mental attitude. "Of your inhuman feelings, of the fanaticism in which, against my will, you indulge in your sermons, of all this I know nothing.... My lords, the Church accepts the repentant sinners",[93] these are the words which, at the Lateran Council, he is said to have directed against the implacable fighters for the faith.

The way Innocent proceeds against heretics and supporters of heresy in other cases leaves no room for doubt that the proclamation of the Crusade against heresy was not meant as a call to mass slaughter, and that he disapproved of the lawless massacre of Béziers.

A great number, even most, of the victims of Béziers Innocent would never have convicted of heresy by way of legal process. He used every precaution in proceeding against those suspect of heresy, since, according to his own statement, he deemed it his task not to disperse what was gathered, but to gather what had been dispersed, and since he did not wish to condemn the innocent together with the guilty ones.[94] In the first place, he made a sharp distinction between the heretic by inclination and the Catholic who, without wishing or willing, espoused heretical views. At the Lateran Council, though, he condemns a treatise by the late Abbot Joachim of Fiore, but at the same time puts beyond doubt the author's Catholic spirit.[95] In the same way Innocent seems to have regarded the Parisian *magister* David of Dinant as being Catholic, although David was an exponent of a materialistic pantheism.[96] Small minds took offence at the pope's intercourse with the *magister* and attributed it to a predilection for sophistry.[97] Innocent, in the second place, sharply limits the concept of heretic. Heretics for him are, first and above all, the teachers of heresy, the perfect, also called comforters, and, besides, all those who publicly profess to a false doctrine or defend it, but not the mere adherents, the followers, the simple believers,[98] that is the category to which the bulk of the victims of Béziers certainly belonged.[99]

Where the precautions which Innocent personally exercised in proceedings against heresy were used, there was little danger of an innocent person or of a mere adherent of the heretics being condemned as a heretic. Notwithstanding Raymond of Toulouse's contention that a heretic he knew could prove that the belief of the Cathari was better than the Catholic faith,[100] Innocent regards him as only suspect of heresy, but not as a notorious heretic. An accused who in a disputation had earnestly defended heretical errors, in view of Innocent's definition would still be able to escape condemnation if his defence and the examination of his reputation in public furnished facts which exonerated him. Even against persons infected by heresy who persuaded sick people to forgo confessing to their priests, since a confession heard by bad priests could not put them in the way of salvation, who also abhorred marriage and in many other respects objected to the Catholic faith, Innocent does not immediately institute proceedings for heresy.[101] An example of the precaution he used, where there was strongest suspicion of heresy, is his attitude towards members of secret conventicles in the city and diocese of Metz.[102] They read the Bible in French translation, expounded it to each other, preached to each other, avoided and despised all who did not join them, and contemptuously looked down upon the uneducated priests. Innocent in an affectionate letter advises them that the wish to become acquainted with the Scriptures was not blameworthy, but recommendable, but that he could not approve of the secrecy which they made of it, nor of their seclusion, of their arrogation to themselves of the office of preaching, and of their mockery of their pastors. He gathers more detailed information from the bishop about the person of the translator and his intention, about the belief of those involved as well as about their attitude to the Church and the Apostolic See, and besides warns the bishop to use every precaution in judging and condemning. One should take care to beware, he writes, of gathering the tares before the harvest and of pulling out thereby the wheat, too. As little as the wickedness of heresy could be tolerated, so little must one curtail the display of pious simplicity, lest either the patience of superiors should embolden the heretics, or their impatience embarrass the simple-minded and just thereby make them heretics. Not even the fact that the more influential members of the sect refuse to obey the pope's orders, that they continue to preach and declare that obedience was due only to God, and that they keep to the translation against their bishop's orders, is sufficient for Innocent to condemn them. Cistercian abbots are commissioned to summon, in co-operation with the bishop, the charged persons into their presence and to see redressed what is blameworthy, but in the case of failure they are to institute a thorough inquiry and to report to him. Only a man of exceptional generosity was capable of facing, amidst an embittered fight against heresy, suspicious symptoms with such an impartiality and composure.[103] That he did not snuff out the glimmering wick, but nursed its glowing, is one of the most likeable traits of the great pope's character.

In view of Innocent's cautiousness and conscientiousness in the face of charges of heresy it would be inexplicable if he had refused to those accused of heresy the right to a counsel for the defence.[104] There obviously is some misunderstanding here. It is true that Innocent prohibits advocates from giving legal assistance to heretics.[105] But this prohibition naturally refers to the assistance given to notorious and condemned heretics in their civil lawsuits and legal transactions, not to the heretical proceedings themselves. No accused person, and consequently no one suspected of heresy either, was considered guilty before he had been sentenced. Under Innocent the procedural position of a person suspected of heresy was not inferior to that of any other person accused in the canonical process.[106]

It must be regarded as quite a blessing that Innocent, referring to the divine ordinance forbidding the temptation of the Lord, strictly rejected the proof by ordeal even in heretical proceedings.[107]

When Innocent insists that the secular power punish the heretics, he either speaks of the penalty prescribed by law[108] or else names the customary punishments of confiscation of goods and of expatriation.[109] The Inquisition, later, handed the heretic it had sentenced over to the temporal judge with the request not to punish him with death.[110] We can hardly, however, put Innocent III's renunciation of the demand for the death penalty on a level with the mere formalism of that request emanating from hypocrisy or self-deception.[111] In single cases Innocent's directives regarding the treatment of heretics even exclude the possibility of the death penalty having been executed. He orders that a recidivous heretic, a priest who had already spent seven years in confinement for publicly preaching heresy and who, after having been pardoned by his bishop, had again canvassed for the false doctrine, is to continue to be detained by his bishop.[112] In another case he decides that a highly placed cleric charged with heresy, in the event of his condemnation, is to be ousted from office and benefices and to do penance in a monastery of strict observance.[113]

When Innocent III summoned the Crusade against heresy and tolerated the execution by the secular power of the heretic handed over to it, he departed from the long-standing and noble principle that the Church does not thirst for blood;[114] and yet, this principle was still so much alive in him that he neither himself imposed the death sentence, nor demanded directly or indirectly, openly or covertly, that it be executed.[115]

Through Innocent III the existing legislation against heresy was not aggravated, but rather mitigated,[116] in any case made more effective. He held the spiritual and temporal authorities even more strictly responsible for the eradication of heresy than had been the case before,[117] and issued detailed regulations against adherents and friends of heretics. Since he was more concerned to prevent heresy from making further headway than to punish heretics, his regulations deal more thoroughly with the adherents of heresy than with the heretics themselves. Anyone who harbours heretics, defends them, believes in their teaching, or favours them, was liable, after he had been twice warned in vain, or, since the Lateran Council, after he had persevered for one year in the state of excommunication, to infamy, which meant total legal incapacity in civil law matters, the exclusion from any communion with others and the loss of one's entire property.[118] In the Patrimony Innocent punished recidivous adherents of heresy, aggravating the general legislation, with expatriation as well.[119] The friends of heretics, therefore, were no longer threatened, as under Lucius III, with the same punishment as the heretics themselves, but they became more easily entangled in the fine meshed net of Innocent's statute, the effectiveness of which, even as regards the civil consequences of infamy, no longer depended only on the goodwill of the authority in office for the time being. In any case the precariousness of legal transactions made by those declared infamous, being legally invalid, remained. Innocent surrounded, as it were, the heretics proper with a cordon sanitaire, which was to minimize as much as possible the danger of contagion.

But Innocent did not think that force was the only and ultimately decisive means to be used in the fight against heresy. He reopened the gates of the Church to *those* heretics who in truth had never intended to separate themselves from the Church and who had only been squeezed out of it by lack of understanding and narrow-mindedness on the part of the episcopate and of his own predecessors.[120] He also realized that an inner conquest of heresy was dependent on a revival of preaching and pastoral care, on a purification and restoration of the Church.[121] Both were an affair of the heart for him and the objective of his unremitting efforts. By initiating an intensive preaching activity in the heretical districts he tried to convert the apostates and to prevent heresy from making further headway. With particular vigour he pursued church reform in the heretical districts of southern France and in the cities of Lombardy,[122] which were seriously endangered by heresy.

In southern France and Provence, where the outrageous evil conditions in the churches cried aloud to Heaven, numerous bishops were deposed or forced to resign, mostly by way of inquisitions carried through by the legates or by other papal commissioners. Already before the Crusade against heresy the bishops of Toulouse,[123] Béziers[124] and Uzès, all three suffragans of Narbonne, had been swept from office. Against a fourth bishop of the church province, the bishop of Agde, an inquisitorial proceeding at least was taken.[125] At that time also the bishops of Viviers[126] and Vence[127] were removed. It was not easy to depose unworthy prelates who were often powerful themselves or supported by powerful relatives and friends. Two of the most seriously incriminated prelates, Archbishop Berengar of Narbonne and the dissolute archbishop Bernard of Auch, were only swept from their seats after the balance of power, due to the successes of the Crusade against heresy, had radically changed. In June 1210 Innocent charged his legates with the inquisitorial process against the two archbishops[128] and in April 1211 he demanded the resignation of Bernard of Auch[129] and the bishops of Valence[130] and Rodez[131] and accepted the resignation of the bishop of Carcassonne.[132]

When the new elections to the episcopal sees were held Innocent did not leave the cathedral chapters to themselves, since they would certainly only have replaced one unworthy or unsuitable bishop by another. Instead he arranged for the elections to be held under the supervision and with the co-operation of his legates and delegates and, circumstances permitting, even delegated to them the formal appointment of the new bishop.[133] A series of excellent men was thus raised by way of the direct or indirect intervention of the pope and his representatives. No matter how much the severity which Arnold of Citeaux, Berengar's successor to the see of Narbonne, had shown in the war against heresy may repel us, the blamelessness of his life and his will and strength to reform his bishopric and church province cannot be questioned. The same may be said of the new bishop of Carcassonne, the Cistercian abbot Guido of the monastery of Vaux de Cernay,[134] and of Fulk of Toulouse,[135] the former troubadour who had forsaken the world and become a Cistercian monk. Garsias of Horto, the new archbishop of Auch, who from 1210 till 1213 had been bishop of Comminges, is praised by a contemporary chronicler as a man of wondrous sanctity.[136] It may also be due in some measure to the participation of the legates and of other papal representatives that the sees of Conserans, Riez and Uzès, in the persons of Bishops Navarro, Hugh Raymond and Rainald, were filled with prelates whom Innocent could entrust with his representation as legates.[137]

The legates, delegates and preachers whom Innocent, up to the beginning of the Crusade against heresy in southern France, had charged with fighting against heresy by means of preaching and enacting statutes against heresy, almost without exception belonged to the Order of the Cistercians which he held in such high esteem. It was of still greater consequence, for the time to come as well, when at the end of 1206 he ordered that for preaching against heresy religious should be drawn upon who, as he states, felt moved by the glow of the spirit to preach in the streets, but who did not dare to perform the office of preaching on their own authority, men who, emulating the poor Christ's poverty, did not shrink from contacting, in despicable attire and in the glow of the spirit, those held in contempt.[138] It is Innocent's great merit that he freed the idea of apostolic poverty from the blemish of heretical suspicion and that he bent it to the needs of the fight against heresy and of the renewal of church life.[139] It is perhaps significant that Innocent III's only cardinal legate in southern France before the time of the Crusade against heresy was the characterful and deeply religious John of St Prisca, the 'cardinal of St Paul'.[140] As the first friend and protector of St Francis at the Curia, this cardinal showed how much his mind was open to the idea of the Imitation of Christ in humility and simplicity.

By means of legislation, by the call to arms, and also by resolute personal engagement[141] as well as by his reformatory activity and the support he gave to the Catholic movement of holy poverty,[142] Innocent III fought successfully against heresies in the Occident. On the other hand, he himself at times furthered their growth in the Italian cities through his over-frequent conflicts with the communes and the means he thereby put to use. During his conflict with Orvieto, a town in the Patrimony, the heretics gained the upper hand there. Innocent himself had paved the way for their propaganda by laying Orvieto under interdict, thus forcing the clergy to leave the town.[143] During the struggles over the immunity of the clergy Lombard cities had, sometimes for years, to do without religious service and the receipt of the Eucharist, which turned out to the advantage of heresy. In these struggles the cities also often made common cause with the heretics. In the first year of Innocent's reign the citizens of Treviso, a city which he had placed under interdict, refused to proceed against the heretics on the grounds that they themselves were enemies of the Apostolic See.[144]

After the conflicts over the immunity of the clergy had abated in the latter half of Innocent's reign, heresy, also in northern Italy, was doubtless strongly curbed by the reforming activity of papal legates and commissaries and by measures immediately directed against heresy, in particular by visitations which sometimes spread over years.[145] But the bitter conflict between the pope and Milan and the other Welf-minded cities after his rupture with Emperor Otto IV, gave a fresh impetus to heresy in Lombardy. Innocent already thought of organizing a crusade against Milan, because there, he writes, the heretics were allowed to preach in public and were so favoured that they flocked there from all sides. In Milan everything deviant from Catholic truth was accepted as religion.[146]

In his later years Innocent was more cautious in the use of the two-edged sword of interdict in his conflicts with the cities.[147] But he could never make up his mind to renounce the dangerous weapon which in the long run never failed. He regarded the immunity of the clergy as so momentous an issue and the task of establishing and securing papal power in Italy as being so pressing for the Church, that he accepted the conflicts which resulted from this, with all their inherent dangers, even the danger of heresy making headway. As so often in Innocent's life, religious and pastoral needs came unfortunately into conflict with the legal claims of the Church and with the exigencies of politics.

## Notes to Chapter 7

[1] Reg. XIII 63, XV 94. Cf. also ibid. 78.

[2] Reg. I 95, II 1.

[3] See Belperron, 121ff., 135. He also provides a survey of the popes' efforts during the twelfth century and of Innocent III's endeavours prior to the Albigensian Crusade to bring heresy under control in southern France. On the Cathari and the Waldensians see R. Morghen, Osservazioni critiche su alcune questioni fondamentali riguardanti le origini e i caratteri delle eresie medievali (Arch. Dep. Rom. di stor. patr. 67, 1944), 97ff., with a critical survey of the sources and literature. Cf. also Grundmann, 14ff. Shannon, The Popes and Heresy in the thirteenth century, published in the U.S.A. in 1949, was not accessible to me.

[4] In 1201 Innocent had already considered requiring Philip to take up arms against Raymond of Toulouse, the most powerful of the supporters of heresy in southern France. (P. 1549, 1550). Appeals dated 1204 and 1205 are extant in which Innocent urgently requests the king to oblige the magnates of southern France to expel the heretics and to incorporate into the crown land the territories of those who refused to comply (Reg. VII 79, 212). The crusading indulgence was already at that time promised to those who were prepared to fight for the defence of the faith (Reg. VII 76). By the close of 1207 Innocent confesses that his attempt to master the heresy had been fruitless and that he had no alternative but to summon the king and the magnates of France to take up arms against the heretics and their supporters (Reg. X 149. The king's reply is in Vaissete 8, 557f.). After the murder of the legate Peter of Castelnau early in 1208 Innocent, after a futile new appeal to the king, formally proclaimed the Crusade

against the heretics (Reg. XI 28; William of Nangis Chron. Recueil 20, 753. The king's answer in Vaissete 8, 558f.).

[5]Years earlier he had appealed to King Imre of Hungary against the heretics in Bosnia and their protector, the banus, Imre's vassal, and by threatening royal intervention had caused the banus to submit to the demands of the Church. For these events see Reg. III 3; V 110; VI 140, 141, 212. Cf. Acta Inn. Introd. 65ff.

[6]Reg. XI 229. Cf. also Peter des Vaux 1, 72ff.

[7]Cf. Reg. XI 229 and Belperron, 146ff.

[8]On Arnold see Belperron, 128f. Besides Arnold, Bishop Navarro of Conserans, who probably since May 1207 at the latest had replaced the deceased Cistercian monk Ralph of Fontfroide (Reg. X 68), was at first active. In 1208 Bishop Hugh Raymond of Riez was adjoined to both, probably as the successor to the murdered Peter of Castelnau (Reg. XI 158). In 1209 the papal notary Milo as legate co-operates with Arnold and Hugh Raymond, but he died in the same year (See Reg. XII 158). At the end of 1210 at the latest Rainald, bishop of Uzès, must have been appointed legate (Reg. XIV 32–49). In June 1210 Hugh of Riez is named besides Arnold (Reg. XIII 87, 88). The renewed excommunication of Raymond of Toulouse early in 1211 was pronounced by Arnold and the bishop of Uzès (Reg. XIV 36). In May 1213 Rainald is reported as having died (Reg. XVI 5).

[9]On the count's personality see Belperron, 141ff.

[10]On the armed expedition mounted by Cardinal legate Henry of Clairvaux in 1181 under Alexander III the viscount Roger II Trencavel of Béziers, the father of the now deposed viscount Raymond Roger, had declared his submission. But once the legate had left, the heretics openly resumed their former activities (Belperron, 126).

[11]Reg. VII 79, XI 28.

[12]Innocent advances reasons of expediency only which were plausible also to the legate. He advises him to treat the king with consideration to begin with, regardless whether he had honest intentions or not, if such an approach could persuade Raymond to give less support to those separated from the Church. If Raymond were dishonest he could then, isolated as he would be, later be crushed easily (Reg. XI 232). Perfidy would be the word for this directive (Belperron 153 speaks of a ruse of war) if Innocent had had in mind the count's ruin as it was pursued by his enemies. Probably, however, these reasons were *ad hominem* and Innocent's directive contained rather more goodwill for the count than the choice of words would suggest.

[13]Despite the extremely kind and considerate form in which Milo's mission was communicated to the abbot legate (to be concluded from the account given by Peter des Vaux 1, 71 though it may be exaggerated; cf. also n. 26), it met with a bad reception by Arnold and his circle who regarded it as frustrating their aims. This emerges from an account provided by Peter, an admirer of the abbot legate, who alleges that Raymond was beside himself with joy when he heard of the mission (Peter des Vaux, 1, 69). William of Tudela, the author of the first part of the Chanson de la Croisade contre les Albigeois, also interprets Milo's mission as a victory for the count (Chanson, Chabot, vv. 235ff.). In any case the mission of a legate direct from the Curia was in response to a request of Raymond himself (Peter des Vaux 1, 67f.).

[14]On the course and on details of the Crusade see Belperron, 158ff.

[15]See Peter of Vaux 1, 102, n. 1, and Belperron, 175f.

[16]Cf. Belperron, 175ff. On Simon's character of cf. *ibid.* 181ff. Simon writes to the pope informing him that, in agreement with the army, the conquered territory had been

conveyed to him through the legate, the abbot of Citeaux, by God's and the pope's side (Reg. XII 109). From Peter des Vaux we know that the army appointed two bishops, four knights and the abbot legate to act as electors (1, 101). He styles the abbot *huius negotii pater et magister.* Simon later reports that he had assumed the dominion *ad instantiam tam baronum exercitus Domini quam et legati et praelatorum qui presentes erant* (quoted in Guébin-Lyon 1, 102, n. 1).

[17]The legates gave the pope to understand that after the withdrawal of the greater part of the crusaders so many knights and experienced men were still left to Simon that he would be able to defend the territory he had gained and to occupy all the rest with the exception of Toulouse if only he were supported by the Church *in expensis* (Reg. XII 108). Innocent, in his reply, invites Simon to consider that it was no less worthy to preserve what had been gained than to gain it, and assures him that he would never have to miss his advice and assistance if he were prepared to hold what had been gained and preserve it in the holy religion (Reg. XII 123).

[18]He contents himself with a series of individual appeals, probably solicited from him, for Simon's support to the emperor, the kings of Aragon and Castile and other temporal and spiritual lords (Reg. XII 123–125, 129, 136, 137). Perhaps, he writes to Simon, he would have done more if some time earlier he had not issued a general appeal for help for the Holy Land in its desperate need, the results of which he would impair if a second appeal in the heresy affair were to follow so swiftly (Reg. XII 123).

[19]The offer of vassalage was made in a veiled form which reflects how unsure the applicant felt. The legates inform the pope that Simon, in recognition of the *dominium* of the Roman Church, was prepared to pay a fixed annual tribute (Reg. XII 108). Simon himself does not mention the offer, but hints at it by noting that with the agreement of the army the territories had been conveyed to him through the legate by God's and the pope's side (Reg. XII 109). In his answer Innocent pointedly corrects Simon's interpretation of his investiture as lord of the territory, indicating that the princes of the army had conveyed it to him on the advice of the legates. There is no mention of the offer of a tribute *in signum dominii.* Yet Innocent accepts for the household the annuity of three dinars fixed by Simon, but forestalls any later misinterpretations of *in signum dominii* by defining that it was meant to show that Simon intended to hold the territories in the devotion of the Apostolic See and in the Holy religion (Reg. XII 123).

[20]Cf. Peter des Vaux 1, 72, 75f.

[21]Reg. XII 107. Cf. also Peter des Vaux 1, 143f.

[22]The legate Milo feels himself entitled to admonish the pope that if Raymond should come to Rome he must find in Peter's successor all the steadfastness of the rock (Reg. XII 107).

[23]Should the count break his oath, the seven castles given to Milo as a pledge and the county of Mauguio as well as the count's rights in a number of Provençal cities were to relapse to the Roman Church (Reg. XII 106, 107 Forma iuramenti, Migne PL. 216, 129ff.). These cities, as guarantees, were also liable to participate, when occasion arose, in the fight against the count. Milo frankly declares to the pope that, under the conditions given, it would be easy enough to drive the count from his territory (Reg. XII 106). Innocent at that time replied that it would not be fitting for the Church to enrich itself at the expense of others, and therefore reserved the count's right to the castles in view of the possibility that he might after all fulfil the obligations laid upon him (Reg. XII 152).

[24]If the count should purge himself he is to be returned the castles which he had

pledged as security at his absolution and he is to be publicly declared a good Catholic and to be guiltless of the legate's death (Reg. XII 152, 153). At the end of July on receiving news of his absolution Innocent had written the count a kind letter and assured him that he had no intention of unfairly burdening him (Reg. XII 90).

[25]If no denunciator should come forward against the count he is to undergo canonical compurgation in a form to be laid down by the papal delegates with the approval of an assembly, summoned for that express purpose, of the relevant bishops, prelates and laity. If such compurgation should fail or if the count should regard its form as being an encumbrance, then the pope's decision is to be sought. If an unjust denunciator should come forward, the proceedings are to be carried through barring the passing of the final sentence which the pope reserves to himself (Reg. XII 152, 153).

[26]According to Haller (Papsttum, 449) Innocent had allowed the legates a free hand by interpolating a deliberately ambiguous parenthesis into his instructions for the procedure against the count: *si ante completum concilium contra praefatum comitem, quem interim ea quae iniuncta sibi sunt praecipimus adimplere... apparuerit accusator....* This is an extremely artificial interpretation in clear contradiction to the pope's apparently sympathetic intention (see also Reg. XII 154, 155), which is in fact emphasized by the exhortation stated above and by Innocent's later attitude. When Innocent, in an eulogizing letter, informs the abbot legate of the authorization vested in Thedisius of Genoa (for whom see Guébin-Lyon 1, 69 n. 2) to conduct the compurgation proceedings in the abbot's stead, and when he declares it his will that Thedisius should regard himself as the abbot's instrument (Reg. XII 156), then the intention becomes obvious: to inform the highly esteemed man of the decision taken against him, the same as in the earlier case of Milo's mission, in as considerate a form as possible. Peter des Vaux's account (1, 143) of Raymond's bad reception at the Curia in 1210 is contradicted both by quite concrete statements of the Chanson (Chabot, 104ff.), according to which Raymond had a friendly reception by the pope and the cardinals, and by the pope's own words: *licet nobilem virum R. comitem Tolosanum ad sedem apostolicam accedentem... curavimus honorare* (Reg. XII 156). As baseless as Haller's accusation of ambiguity in the case of the count is his charge that in 1212 Innocent had begun to exploit the conquered territory for the financial gain of the Church (Papsttum, 452). In reality the mission of the papal treasury official, which Haller has in mind, was concerned with the collection of the different tributes due to the Apostolic See from southern France (P. 4588–4596; cf. Fabre, Etude sur le *Liber censuum* de l'église romaine, 1892, 162) and with the subsidy of one thousand silver marks which Simon had promised (Reg. XV 171), but not by any means with a share of the spoils or with any new impositions laid upon the conquered territories.

[27]Peter des Vaux himself concedes that Thedisius, the pope's special agent in the matter, wished to thwart the procedure and in fact has thwarted it (1, 166f.).

[28]Cf. Belperron, 214, Guébin-Lyon 1, 167, n. 2.

[29]Reg. XVI 39.

[30]Reg. XIV 36. He had already at the end of 1210 remonstrated with the count that it was due to Raymond's negligence, not to say to his outright approval, that the heretics were still staying in his territories. Innocent's tone is mild, yet he warns him that if he does not expel them, his territories would be destined to be possessed by those who would expel them (Reg. XIII 188). In the same mild form he warns at the same time the counts of Toulouse, Foix and Comminges as well as Gaston of Béarn against molesting Simon de Montfort and the crusaders (Vaissete 8, 601f.).

[31]Reg. XIV 36.

[32]Reg. XIV 35, 37, 38. This was the first step in a process envisaged as early as 1207. At that time Innocent had warned the count that if he did not rapidly make amends he would first have the territories withdrawn from him which he held from the Church of Rome. If this failed to bring him to reason he would then declare him an enemy of Christ and a persecutor of the Church and have his territories offered to others (Reg. X 69). The count had recognized on oath at his absolution that, should he fail to fulfil the obligation laid upon him, he would forfeit, besides seven *castra* pledged as security, his rights to the county of Mauguio (*Processus negotii*, Migne PL. 216, 89ff; Peter des Vaux 1, 76).

[33]He directs the legates to have the county preserved in the interests of those who are entitled to it (Reg. XIV 163).

[34]See pp. 245ff. above.

[35]Innocent informs the king of France that Raymond had lost almost the whole of his territory as a result of his failure to allay suspicions of his heresy and because in these regions he was generally held to be a heretic. He, the pope, did not know, though, whether it was by the count's fault that a compurgation had not been effected (Reg. XIV 163). The following year Innocent firmly rejects his legates' proposal that the territory, which had not yet been legally withdrawn from the count and his heirs, should be given to a third party (Reg. XV 102).

[36]Reg. XV 102. He demands full and complete truth from the legates in their reports and forbids them from continuing to carry out his mandate in the desultory manner which they were hitherto reported to observe.

[37]For the count of Foix see Belperron, 192f.

[38]Reg. XV 212, 213.

[39]*Ibid.* 212, 215.

[40]*Ibid.* 215.

[41]*Ibid.* 212, 213.

[42]*Ibid.* 219.

[43]Reg. XVI 39, 46.

[44]Reg. XVI 41.

[45]Reg. XVI 40.

[46]Reg. XVI 42.

[47]Reg. XVI 44.

[48]Peter des Vaux 2, 97f.

[49]This statement was in no case true as regards the county of Foix (cf. Peter des Vaux 1, 199ff.; Vaissete 8, Preuves, 1034ff., 1150f.); as for the other counties, given the situation in southern France, it is altogether extremely unlikely.

[50]Reg. XVI 48.

[51]Consuls and council were banned and the city was laid under interdict because they had refused to hand over the heretics and their supporters to the crusaders. The citizens had declared their readiness to have those named by the legates brought up for trial in the bishop's palace before the legate and the bishop, and, should the abbot refuse that proposal, had claimed the pope's protection both for themselves and for those under threat (Vaissete 8, Preuves, 612ff.). Innocent ordered the absolution early in 1211 without insisting that the accused and suspected persons be handed over to the crusading army, and after many difficulties, caused by the legates, the absolution then took place. It was not long, however, before the city was again laid under ban and

interdict (Vaissete, *loc. cit.*). Innocent also resisted the stormy appeals by the bishops assembled under the guidance of the legate at the Council of Lavaur (Reg. XVI 40, 44) that the city be consigned to being razed to the ground. Although he was convinced that the city was protecting a number of known heretics and a greater number of supporters, abettors and defenders of heresy within its walls and that fugitive heretics from outside had found refuge there (Reg. XVI 40, 44), he orders Bishop Fulk of Toulouse, who had left the city with his clergy, but yet seems even then to have enjoyed a measure of trust with his opponents, to absolve, in conjunction with two shrewd and honourable men, those citizens who, after furnishing sufficient security, sincerely requested such absolution, but to punish the persistent heretics with the confiscation of their goods and banishment from the city, to which they were never again to be admitted unless they proved by their deeds that they were true Catholics (Reg. XVI 48). Thereafter the city, being reconciled with the Church, was to enjoy the protection of the Apostolic See and no longer be molested by Simon and the other Catholics (Reg. XVI 48). In actual fact the city was not absolved by the bishop, but by the legate Peter of Benevento on the authority of the pope (Reg. XVI 172, Vaissete 8, 647ff., Peter des Vaux 2, 201, William of Pylaur 139).

[52]Arnold will have lost his position as legate at the same time, at the latest with the appointment of the cardinal legate (P. 4880 of 15 January 1214, addressed to Arnold as legate, belongs in fact to 1213, see P. 4648). In P. 4985 (Recueil 19, 596) of 2 January 1215 he is referred to only as archbishop of Narbonne (as in P. 5010 and 5276, both of which, however, are extant in the form of *regesta* only). Peter des Vaux makes no mention of Arnold during the whole of 1214. On 8 January 1215 Peter mentions Arnold as a participant at the Council of Montpellier designating him as *archiepiscopus Narbonensis* (2, 237). Arnold finally fell out with Simon de Montfort on account of the duchy of Narbonne which they both claimed (Arnold to Honorius III in Recueil 19, 620, Peter des Vaux 2, 253ff., P. 4985). At the Lateran Council he no longer seems to have been among the implacable adversaries of Raymond, and may even have stood up for him (Anonymous continuation of the Chanson, Meyer, vv. 3472ff.).

[53]Reg. XVI 167, 171, 172.

[54]Reg. XVI 108.

[55]For Peter see Heyer, 395ff, also containing significant details of his legation in southern France and Aragon 1214/5 (397ff. Cf. also Belperron, 286ff., 289ff.).

[56]Cf. Heyer, 398. The counts of Foix and Comminges were granted absolution on less stringent terms of submission than those imposed on Raymond of Toulouse (Vaissete 8, 643ff.).

[57]The legate in any case had explicitly been charged with the absolution of Gaston as well as of Roger of Comminges (Reg. XVI 172) and of the city of Toulouse (*ibid.*). Before his departure the legate, on papal mandates (P. 4967–4969), handed the castle, delivered to him by the count of Foix, as a security, over to Simon (Vaissete 8, 682).

[58]Vaissete, 6, 442f. Cf. Peter des Vaux 1, 197f.

[59]Peter des Vaux 2, 238ff. Cf. Vaissete 6, 452.

[60]Vaissete 8, 653ff. Cf. Belperron, 290f.

[61]Vaissete 8, 682.

[62]P. 4967–4969. If Innocent requests Simon, *hanc pro Christo legationem recipere* (P. 4967), this indicates that the pope's decision was a disappointment for Simon who had reckoned with the definitive conveyance of the territories.

[63]See pp. 244ff. above.

[64]See E. Mangenot, article 'Eucharistie' in Dict. de théologie catholique 5[2] (1939), col. 1290ff., for a more detailed account of the concept of *transsubstantiatio* which is in frequent use from the second half of the twelfth century onwards. See also Ott, 106 n. 53; Forest-van Steenberghen-de Gandillac, 160, 171.

[65]*Una vero est fidelium universalis Ecclesia, extra quam nullus omnino salvatur*, can. 1 (Leclercq 1324f) c. 1 X 1, 1.

[66]P. 5009; Recueil 19, 598f.; Peter des Vaux 2, 263.

[67]On their complaints the counts of Foix and Comminges, who had been deprived of part of their lands by Count Simon, are given a favourable provisional reply which shows that Innocent is not considering the ruin of the two lords (Recueil 19, 600; P. 5015; Migne PL. 216, 992). See also the Anonymous continuation of the Chanson (Meyer) vv. 3655f. Cf. Luchaire, Innocent III 2, 258.

[68]See Belperron, 340ff., for details of the negotiations and events at the Council concerning the case of Raymond and the other magnates from southern France.

[69]Anonymous continuation of the Chanson (Meyer) vv. 3381ff., 3548ff., 3571ff., 3639ff.

[70]Peter des Vaux 2, 261.

[71]William Brito (Delaborde 1) 306.

[72]Heiler (266) characterizes the Council in these terms. This view is contradicted however by the fact that Innocent leaves intricate questions to the Council to decide besides the case of the count of Toulouse, the conflict between King John of England, the episcopate and the barons (P. 4990, Wendover 2, 145) as well as the questions of the competence of the temporal and spiritual courts in England (Hampe, Registerbände, 556f.) See also Chapters 2 and 6 above.

[73]In addition to n. 72 above see above Chapter 6. Innocent is reported to have designated the patriarch of Aquileia, who opposed him at the Council in the question of celibacy, as Paphnutius (Boncompagni, Rhetorica novissima, Bibl. iur. Med. aevi 1892, 281), doubtless in reference to the saintly Egyptian confessor who at the Council of Nicaea had appealed for a more lenient practice in the question of priest marriage (cf. Wetzer-Welte, Kirchenlexikon 9, 1895, 1378f.). Innocent knew of the event from Gratian's *Decretum* (Dist. XXXI c. 12). In connection with the passage of the *Decretum*, this could only have been meant as an acknowledgement.

[74]Belperron, 307f., puts it somewhat differently: "Le juriste proclame le droit, mais l'homme hésite". He notes that the pope tried to be humane in the matter.

[75]Reg. XI 26, 28. On Innocent's attitude to the count from the mission of Peter of Castelnau to the Crusade, see Belperron, 135ff., 141ff.

[76]"Si jamais il a fait chose qui soit déplaisante à Dieu, il s'est rendu à moi, soupirant et gémissant, pour accomplir vos décisions et mes ordres" (Anon. continuation of the Chanson, Meyer, vv. 3469-3471).

[77]A present-day priest in southern France attributes the great distrust and the very strong instinctive resistance to the Church, which his parishioners and the people in southern France as a whole feel to this very day, partly to the cruel crusade waged by the medieval Church against the country ("Die Welt", No. 197, 24 August 1950).

[78]For an evaluation see Belperron, 10f.

[79]Cf. Belperron, 22ff., 35ff.

[80]Cf. Peter des Vaux 2, 62.

[81]Cf. Grundmann, Rotten und Brabanzonen, DA 5 (1942), 419ff.

[82]Reg. X 69.

[83]William of Puylaur, 125.

[84]Ep. 75 (Migne PL. 211, 373f.). Cf. also Ep. 73 (*ibid.* 371f.).

[85]See Grundmann, Rotten und Brabanzonen, 431ff., 437 n. 1, 439 for an account of the efforts of the popes and their legates against the employment of mercenary bands and 'brabanzons'. However, Simon de Montfort also took such troups into service (*ibid.* 438f.).

[86]Reg. X 69, XII 106, 107; *Processus negotii* (Migne PL. 216, 90ff.) and *forma iuramenti* (Migne PL. 216, 128ff.); Reg. XII, 154, XIV 39, XVI 40; Vaissete 6, 266. One of Celestine III's legates had already endeavoured to bring about a land peace in Provence (Vaissete 6, 172).

[87]Reg. XII 108. See Belperron, 164ff. for the slaughter. He assumes that Arnold exaggerated the numbers in order to emphasize the significance of the victory (166f.).

[88]Of the pope's answers to the reports of the conquest of Béziers and Carcassonne are extant only the official letters for the use of Simon de Montfort, not the answers to the legates themselves. The atrocities committed by the Latins at the conquest of Constantinople Innocent also at first reprobated in personally styled letters only (Reg. VIII 126, 133, and later also to the Greek emperor Theodore Lascaris, Reg. XI 47), but not in his official letters.

[89]Reg. XII 122, 123.

[90]Despite his condemnation of the atrocities of Constantinople (Reg. VIII 126, 133) Innocent writes to Emperor Theodore Lascaris that it was often God's way to make use of evil to punish the evil ones. He did not, he writes, excuse the Latins, but had frequently reproved them for their excesses. But even if the Latins were by no means free from guilt, still it was, in his belief, through them that the Greeks in a just procedure had been punished by God (Reg. XI 47).

[91]Reg. XII 126.

[92]Cf. above pp. 236–7. To be noted is also the letter of protection for Montpellier of 1 March 1209 in which Innocent forbids the legates to allow the city to be molested by the crusading army on the basis of any malicious imputations whatever (Migne PL. 216 187). This letter of protection, by chance extant, is certainly not the only one issued.

[93]...(d)els vostres durs ni dels vostres prezics engoiches e cozens que faits outra mon grat dor eu non so sabens... Senhors ja recep Glieiza pecadors penedens... (Anon. continuation of the Chanson, Meyer, vv. 3461ff. On the historical value of the description of the Lateran Council by this anonymous contemporary, see Meyer 2, LXVIff.).

[94]Reg. II 235, 228; XVI 17.

[95]Can. 2 (Leclercq 1327ff.); Alberic of Troisfontaines (MG SS 23), 879. Cf. Huck, 131f.

[96]Cf. Chapter 1 above. For David of Dinant see M. de Wulf, Gesch. d. mittelalterl. Philosophie (German transl. by Eisler, 1913), 181; Théry, Autour du décret de 1210: David de Dinant (Bibl. thomiste 4, 1925); Grabmann, 30ff. Théry believes that he can identify David with one of the pope's chaplains (9f.). It is striking that David was not condemned at the Lateran Council even though his doctrine had been branded heretical by a Paris synod as early as 1210.

[97]Anonymous of Laon (MG. SS. 26) 454.

[98]Unauthorized preaching was no longer condemned forthwith as being heresy as had been the case in 1184 under Lucius III at the Council of Verona (see Mansi 477–c. 9 X 5, 7). Such preaching is forbidden, though, and penalized in the heresy statute of the

Lateran Council, but is not qualified as being heresy. The statute deals with such transgression as something separate from the measures provided against heretics and their supporters. It falls into the heresy statute merely because unauthorized preachers laid themselves open to the suspicion of heresy.

[99]In Toulouse, which was considered to be a nest of heretics, were living according to Innocent *quidam haeretici, plures vero credentes, fautores et receptatores ac etiam defensores* (Reg. XVI 48).

[100]Reg. X 69.

[101]Reg. IX 208.

[102]Reg. II 142, 235. The people were identified as Waldensians and the sect was exterminated (Alberic of Troisfontaines 878).

[103]Cf. above Chapter 1.

[104]Thus mistakenly Schnürer, 435.

[105]Reg. VIII 85.

[106]Cf. Reg. II 63. The regulation that the accused who fails to purge himself of the suspicion of heresy is to be punished as a heretic if he remains in the state of excommunication for more than one year (can. 3 Conc. Lat., Leclercq 1350), does not lay upon the accused the burden of proof that the facts on which the imputation is based are wrong, but requires him to substantiate in the usual form of canonical compurgation by means of his own oath and the support of compurgators that, despite the facts adduced and proven against him, he is not a heretic. When discussing the heretical inquisition under Innocent III, that is the search for heretics by the competent bishop and the taking and carrying through of heresy proceedings ex officio, any thought of the procedures which later on were to give the name of Inquisition such a gruesome ring must be dismissed (see Chapter 6 above). The two procedures have nothing in common, apart from the initiation of the prosecution on the initiative of the ecclesiastical superior, not on the accusation of some third party. At the Lateran Council Innocent emphasized again the procedure introduced by Lucius III in 1184 at the Council of Verona (c. 9 X 5, 7).

[107]Reg. XIV 138 (see also can. 18 of the Lateran Council, Leclercq 1348, c. 9 X 3, 50). Cf. Grundmann, Religiöse Bewegungen, 137f.

[108]Reg. X 130, "due punishment": can. 3 Conc. Lat. (Leclercq 1330) c. 13 X 5, 7.

[109]Reg. I 94, 81; VII 76; can. 3 Conc. Lat. A statement made by the pope can, superficially considered, be misconstrued as constituting a demand that heretics should face the death penalty. Innocent writes "If the goods of those punished to death for lese-majesty are confiscated, ... how much more readily should those who, deviating from faith, offend God, be severed from our Head, Christ, by ecclesiastical punishment and be deprived of their worldly goods" (Reg. II 1). But when comparing the punishments for the two crimes Innocent uses the term decapitation with reference to heresy explicitly in the metaphorical sense, meaning an exclusion from the Church, whilst the confiscation of goods is meant in the literal sense of the word. Even when Innocent demands the *exterminatio* of heretics we are not allowed to think simply of their extermination. Only an expulsion can be meant in his order to the Toulousians to "exterminate" the heretics from their city and not to readmit them until they have proved themselves true Catholics (Reg. XVI 48). The *exterminatio* used in the heresy canon of the Lateran Council has the same meaning; according to it the superiors are required *quod de terris suae iurisdictioni subiectis, universos haereticos, ab ecclesia denotatos, bona fide pro viribus exterminare studebunt*. Cf. Ch. Moeller, Les bûchers et les auto-dafé de l'inquisition depuis le moyen-âge (RHE. 14, 1913) 724f.

[110]Schnürer, 437.

[111]Cf. Reg. XI 257, in which Innocent decrees that if the Church hands over a cleric, who is condemned of serious crimes and then degraded, to the temporal authority, then it is to stand up effectively (*efficaciter*) against the infliction of the death penalty.

[112]Reg. XI 62.

[113]Reg. XI 63. In a third case Innocent justifies a sentence of confinement with the fear that the cleric deposed for heresy might become desperate enough to pass finally over to the heretics and infect others (Reg. II 99). At the Lateran Council Innocent, reverting to the legislation enacted by Lucius III (whether of his own accord, is uncertain), ordered that heretical priests and others convicted of heresy should be handed over to the temporal power for punishment (can. 3, Leclercq 1330).

[114]Innocent III's attitude is perhaps elucidated by the answer he gave to the enquiry of a bishop whether it was allowable to evoke the assistance of the royal power against those who persistently refused to pay their tithes, even though such individuals could hardly be forced to pay their dues without shedding blood. Innocent decides that the bishop was entitled to institute normal legal proceedings against such offenders. If the king were then to use against such rebels the power entrusted to him, their obstinacy was to blame for it (Reg. XVI 26). He is likely to have adopted the same attitude regarding the question of heresy.

[115]Innocent orders the removal of a bishop from office because he had attended a trial by ordeal and the consequent execution of the individual found guilty, and had thereby given in his authority (Reg. XI 187). Can. 18 of the Lateran Council of 1215 forbids priests from taking any part in pronouncing a sentence of death or in an execution (Leclercq 1348, c. X 3, 50). Even Arnold of Citeaux, the hammer of the heretics, still felt himself bound by this principle. His admirer relates that Arnold was saddened when the fate of the garrison of the heretical Minerve was put into his hands. He had wished them to die, but as a monk and a priest he had not dared to sentence them to death (Peter des Vaux 1, 158). The fact is notable that the podestà Peter Parenzi, who had been personally charged by Innocent III with the suppression of heresy in Viterbo, punished the heretics with all kinds of penalties, but not with the death penalty, which had already been used in Viterbo in the past (AASS. 21 maii tom. V 87f.). Could the explanation for this moderation rest in the fact of Parenzi's papal mission?

[116]Lucius had forthwith inflicted the penalty for heresy on those suspect of heresy who had not submitted to canonical compurgation (Mansi 477; c. 9 X 5, 7); according to Innocent they were only to be condemned as heretics if they had remained in the state of excommunication for more than one year (can. 3 Conc. Lat. Leclercq 1330, c. 13 X 5, 7). Lucius III only granted pardon to heretics, if they showed repentance immediately after discovery; he required that recidivists should forthwith be handed over to the temporal power for punishment without the benefit of a further hearing. Innocent's legislation makes no mention of such restriction of pardoning and in practice, at least in the early years of his reign, he allowed recidivists to forestall their deliverance to the temporal power by confessing their error and by providing satisfaction and guarantees (Reg. V 36, VI 66; cf. also Reg. XVI 48 and IX 18).

[117]Lucius III's decree on the diocesan bishop's duty to search for heretics was in substance adopted by Innocent. Lucius had threatened the bishop who would not regularly publish the excommunication against heretics with suspension from office for a period of three years. Innocent demands that everyone be punished with deposition who fails actually to purge his diocese from heresy (can. 3 Conc. Lat., Leclercq 1332). Lucius had threatened only counts, barons, rectors, and consuls of cities with the loss

of their honours if they failed to support the Church against heresy to the best of their ability. Innocent extends the loss of office and land to all magnates, including sovereign magnates, and moreover, the procedure which is to lead to their deprivation is precisely laid down (*ibid.* 1331).

[118]Reg. II 1; can. 3 Conc. Lat. (Leclercq 1331).

[119]Gesta c. 124, Reg. X 130. If according to the statute of Viterbo, the heresy statute for the Patrimony, a quarter of the goods of a supporter of heresy is liable to confiscation, whereas the general legislation declares his total possessions confiscated, the explanation seems to be that in the Patrimony every supporter of heresy is liable to the loss of the quarter, even those who submit at the first warning and therefore escape punishment under the terms of the general legislation. There can be no doubt that persistent offenders in the Patrimony were also punished with the loss of their total possessions. In Reg. III 3 Innocent stresses that he is having the possessions of those who support heretics in the Patrimony confiscated.

[120]Cf. Chapter 2 above.

[121]Cf. Chapter 6 above.

[122]Cf. Chapter 6 above.

[123]Reg. VIII 115, 116; Gesta c. 130; William of Puylaur, 126.

[124]Gesta c. 130. Cf. Reg. VI 242.

[125]Reg. VIII 76.

[126]Reg. VII 209, Gesta c. 130.

[127]Reg. VII 84 (cf. also *ibid.* II 34), Gesta c. 130.

[128]Reg. XIII 88.

[129]Reg. XIV 32.

[130]*Ibid.*

[131]Reg. XIV 33.

[132]Reg. XIV 34. Bishop Bernard Raymond of Rochefort may have resigned more or less voluntarily, possibly because his mother was a heresy suspect and because his brother was a notorious enemy of the Church (Peter des Vaux 1, 135, 188).

[133]Reg. VII 75, 209; VIII 76; X 68; XIV 34; XVI 5.

[134]For Guido see Guébin-Lyon 3 (1939) XIff.

[135]Baluze, Misc. 6, 457; William of Puylaur, 125. A supporter of the count of Toulouse, the friend of heretics, draws a black picture of Fulk (Anon. continuation of the Chanson, Meyer, vv. 3309ff.). Cf. on Fulk also Vaissete 6, 243ff.

[136]Peter des Vaux 2, 152. Peter styles both Garsias and Bishop Navarro of Conserans elsewhere (2, 55) *viri venerabiles et Deo pleni.*

[137]The removal of unworthy or of heresy-suspect canons in the course of inquisitions and visitations (cf. Reg. VIII 116) as well as the appointment of canons by papal legates and commissaries when the filling of benefices had devolved to the pope (Reg. VII 165), resulted in the renewal of the cathedral chapters and thus contributed to the improvement of conditions for future episcopal elections.

[138]Reg. IX 185.

[139]See Chapter 6 above.

[140]See above Chapter 1, n. 93. He was referred to as Cardinal of St Paul after the Benedictine monastery in Rome whose abbot he had been before his promotion to cardinal. For John see Wenck, Päpste, 456ff., and Paschini, Il cardinale Giovanni di San Paolo (Studi di storia e diritto in onore di Carlo Calisse 3, 1940) 107ff.

[141]The events in Viterbo are significant. Innocent had succeeded in overthrowing the

domination of the Patarenes by setting about calling up the neighbours against the city. But the commune still could not make up its mind to expel the heretics. Innocent, therefore, set out in person for Viterbo to deal the deathblow to heresy there. As he drew near the heretics fled. Innocent had their supporters identified by name, forced them to provide guarantees and satisfaction and ordered all houses to be destroyed in which heretics had been harboured (Gesta c. 123).

[142]See Chapter 6 above.

[143]Vita Petri Parentii (AASS. 21 maii tom. V) 87.

[144]Reg. II 27.

[145]Cf. Chapter 6 above. Innocent was never content with merely counteracting heresy but was also constantly at pains to eliminate the causes of its germination and growth as far as they were rooted in deleterious conditions prevailing within the Church itself (cf. Reg. X 54). It is in this spirit that the papal legate entrusted with the suppression of heresy in Bosnia, on completion of his mission, proposes to the pope that the hitherto sole bishopric of that vast country be divided and three or four new ones be created (Reg. VI 140).

[146]Reg. XV 189. The letter may be one for conditional delivery only (cf. Tillmann, Über päpstliche Schreiben, 192ff.) On heresy in Milan in the year of Innocent III's death see the letter written by James of Vitry quoted in Böhmer, Analekten, 65.

[147]See above, Chapter 4, n. 103. It is possible that Innocent for the same reason absolved Milan and its adherents after Otto IV's defeat without the cities abandoning Otto.

[148]See Chapter 4 above.

# CHAPTER 8

# Towards the unity of the Church

The union of all men and peoples in the one Church of Christ, the ultimate object of the faith, the hope and the working of the Church from the days of its foundation, seemed to come true in substance during Innocent III's pontificate in consequence of the subordination of the Greek Church to the obedience of the Latin Church. When, in 1204, Innocent thought that, with the creation of the Latin Empire of Constantinople, the union of the Greek Church with the Roman Church had been established, he regarded what had happened, along with the coincidental successes of the Church in Livonia, Bulgaria and Armenia, as an overwhelming fulfilment of everything for which his predecessors had hoped and striven in vain, a fulfilment which involved a new promise: "Be confident in your trust that, after you have caught the fishes, that is led the Christians back to the true faith, you will catch men, namely convert Jews and heathens .... When all Christians have returned to the obedience of the Apostolic See, then the host of non-believers will turn to the faith, and thus all of Israel will be saved".[1]

As early as the first years of his reign great prospects presented themselves to Innocent for the union of the Slav churches of the Balkans with Rome. In 1198 a legation from King Vulk of Dioclea and Dalmatia, the coastal areas of what was then Serbia,[2] requested that conditions of the church of his country be adjusted and a separate church province be constituted for his territory.[3] Innocent made use of the opportunity also to get into contact with Vulk's brother, the great zupan Stephen of Serbia, with a view to uniting the Serbian church with Rome.[4] At the turn of 1199/1200 he also sent an envoy on the arduous and dangerous journey to Johannitza, the tsar of the

Bulgars who, according to reports received at the Curia, was inclined to break off the ties of the church of his country to the patriarchate of Constantinople and affiliate it to the Roman Church.[5] In 1208 he charged the Latin archdeacon Nicholas of Durazzo with a mission to Demetrius, prince of the Albanians, who wished to join the Roman Church together with his people and who had requested that a legate be sent to his country.[6] Innocent extended his efforts to win over the Slav peoples beyond the Balkans also to the Ruthenians.[7]

His endeavours failed to come to a sure and lasting success, as the Lateran Council of 1215 manifested. No Bulgarian, no Serbian, no Ruthenian bishop was willing or able to follow the papal invitation.

The Lateran Council reveals the collapse of almost all of Innocent III's efforts to restore the churchly unity of the Orient and the Occident. From all the episcopates of the countries which, under his reign, had dissociated themselves from the Schism, or which the pope had endeavoured to unite with the Roman Church, he could only welcome at the Council the patriarch of the Maronites of Lebanon, Jeremias.[8] The absence of the catholicos or of a representative of the head of the church of Cicilian Armenia even points to a setback as compared with the times of his predecessor.[9]

Political circumstances had been the cause for the contacts taken up by the peoples of the East with Rome, as in the case of the Serbians, Bulgarians and Armenians, or had forced them to subordination, as in the case of the Ruthenians. Changes in the political sphere were also accountable for the recurred estrangement, if not complete breach of relations.

Innocent cannot be exonerated from some responsibility for this disappointing development. He is not, though, to blame for the cooling of relations between Armenia and Bulgaria and the Roman Church. King Leo of Armenia demanded, as price for his subordination to the Apostolic See, that the pope, in the Antioch succession dispute, side with Armenia without caring about right or wrong. For the Bulgarians who had turned away from Constantinople ecclesiastically, because they were in opposition to Eastern Rome politically, the union with the Latin Church lost all relevance when a Latin emperor in Constantinople, wholly contrary to the pope's wishes, made the claims of Eastern Rome against Bulgaria his own. But Innocent had a share in the failure of his efforts regarding the Serbians and Ruthenians. In deference to King Imre of Hungary he renounced the already prepared mission of a cardinal legate who was to convey the royal crown to the great zupan and to effect the union of his church to Rome.[10] After King Imre had conquered Serbia and Stephen had been replaced by Stephen's brother Vulk, Innocent then, in the interest of Hungary, had charged not a cardinal legate, but the Hungarian archbishop of Kalocsa, with the same commission.[11] Perhaps for political reasons the archbishop delayed executing the commission and, thereby, effecting the union of the Serbian church with Rome, until in the event the brothers Vulk and Stephen came to an understanding, in concerted action regained Serbia's independence from Hungary, and lost their interest in a union of the Churches. Also in the case of Ruthenia Innocent served the church union badly by allowing it to become linked with extraneous political aspirations, namely the subjection of Ruthenia to Hungary. He made his first attempt to come into contact with the Ruthenians in 1207, when King Andrew of Hungary had assumed the guardianship of the sons of the late prince Roman of Volhynia and Halich,[12] and his second attempt, when in 1214 Andrew had forced his son Coloman upon the Ruthenians of Halich as their king.[13] After Coloman had been expelled, Innocent tried in vain to come into direct contact with the Ruthenian church.[14]

That Innocent's several endeavours at establishing the union of the Churches failed to achieve a decisive and definitive success is not only due to his mixing up the question of union with political aims. The ultimate cause of his failure is that he was unable to interpose the decisive keystone into a union of the schismatic churches of the East with Rome, so that only a pretended, not a real union was established between the Greek and the Roman Churches.

When, in August 1198, Innocent raised the question of church union in a letter to the Eastern Roman emperor, it became apparent how fatefully he had misunderstood the question of reunion of the separate churches as being in substance a question of obedience. In this letter he speaks of the union of the churches as amounting simply to the return of the Greek Church to the obedience of the Apostolic See.[15] When in the following year Alexius proposed to him to convene a council which should deal with the question of church union, Innocent at once deprived the church assembly, which he, too, had been planning, of the character of a council of union. He insisted on the patriarch's participation being regarded as an act of obedience to the Roman Church.[16] Innocent failed to realize how deeply the separation of the two Churches was rooted in the ethnical parti-

cularities and in the separate historical development of Orient and
Occident, and regarded the separation as being, in substance, the
result of overbearance and of culpable disobedience on the part of the
patriarchs of Constantinople and of the emperors who supported
them. The disobedience of the Greeks towards the Apostolic See,
their rejection of the doctrine of *filioque*, were for him unforgiveable
deviations,[17] and he was convinced that the Greek Church in consequence of the Schism had sunk from its former theological heights
and was now in need of being instructed by the Latins.[18]

This misunderstanding of the origins of the Schism and of the
particularities of the Greek Church explains Innocent's belief that,
with the translation of the imperial rule to the Latins and with the
foundation of the Latin patriarchate of Constantinople, the union of
the Churches had been effected; it also explains why he kept to this
fiction. If Innocent, in a moment in which the constellation of power
had given a great part of the Greek Church into his hands, had set
about working for a real union of the Churches in the spirit of
unprejudiced love, the separate Churches would have been likely to
draw, inwardly at least, nearer again to each other. Innocent missed
the great historical chance, and perhaps could not but miss it, because
the prejudices which opposed the right course of action were then
still insuperable.[19]

It is true that Innocent was not the founder of the most unfortunate creation of the Latins in Constantinople, the Latin patriarchate. He not only recognized the Greek bishops as generally being
lawfully consecrated, but also regarded them as the lawful holders of
their sees,[20] and for his part would certainly have left the patriarchate,
in subordination naturally to the Roman Church, to the Greeks.[21] But
he assumed the responsibility when, from political reasons,[22] he
legitimized the illegal reorganization of the Greek Church effected
by the conquerors and, thereby, consented to the subjection, in the
literal sense of the word, of the Greek Church not only to the
Apostolic See, but also to the Latin Church. Political reasons would,
however, have hardly turned the scale, if Innocent had been fully
aware of the absurdity of a Latin patriarchate for the Greek Church.

Barring the question of obedience, Innocent cannot be reproached
with inflexibility in the treatment of the Greeks. His moderation,
shrewdness and generosity towards the Greek Church and the Greek
clergy in the Latin Empire have often been recognized.[23] After the
establishment of the rule of the Latins in Constantinople Innocent

had first thought of altering the Greek rite of mass regarding the use of leavened bread, to which the Latins took offence,[24] and, perhaps, of assimilating the Greek rite to the Latin rite even in other items.[25] But already in the following year he directs the Latin patriarch that, if the Greeks were unwilling to desist from their rites of mass and sacraments, he should tolerate them, until the Apostolic See, after mature deliberation, should decide differently.[26] Such tolerance amounted almost to generosity for the successor of Celestine III, who for his part had congratulated the Cypriots that, desisting from the abominable schism of leavening (*a beluato fermentorum scismate*), they had returned to the true faith of the Church.[27] But Innocent even went beyond this stage of reluctant toleration. His treatise on the sacrament of the Eucharist mirrors the change to greater broadmindedness. In one passage of the work, the first version of which dates back to his cardinalcy, the author states that the Greeks, persisting obstinately in their error, celebrated the Eucharist with leavened bread;[28] in another passage, belonging, therefore, to the later version not completed before 1208,[29] he declares that many celebrated, this very day, mass with leavened bread with whom, as being true Catholics, the Roman Church held communion.[30] In the question of the rite of consecration, too, Innocent arrived at greater liberality. When the Bulgarian Church joined the Roman Church in 1204, he had ordered the Bulgarian bishops to be subsequently anointed with chrism, because this anointing, unknown in the Greek Church, was prescribed not, in the first place, by the Roman rite, but by divine law.[31] On the other hand, he ordered the new Greek bishops of the Latin Empire to be consecrated by their Latin superiors according to the Roman rite, but desisted from forcing those already consecrated to have themselves subsequently anointed.[32] His esteem of Greek monasticism was manifested in the way he not only allowed the Greek monasteries and nunneries to keep to their traditional way of life, but expressly bound them to it,[33] in that he took Greek monasteries under his protection[34] and bestowed great praise upon the monks of Mount Athos.[35] Lastly, at the Lateran Council, he shows an attitude towards the Greeks which, in the questions of rite and customs, seems to set aside all narrowness and illiberality. He only forbids two of their customs, the ablution of the altars at which Latins had said mass, and the repetition of baptisms administered by Latin priests. The relevant canon begins with the assurance that the pope was willing to favour (*fovere*) and to respect all the Greeks who, during his pontificate, had returned to obedience to the Apostolic See, and to sustain (*sustinere*) their rites and customs, as far as with God he could.[36] The Lateran Council does not leave matters at the toleration of the Greek rite or of other non-Latin rites, but strictly orders that in areas where believers of different tongues and different rites live side by side, their own priests are to be appointed for the believers of each rite, who in the wonted language and according to their custom say mass to them, administer the sacraments and instruct them through word and example.[37] At the Lateran Council the legal validity of the marriage of the clergy in the Eastern Church is presupposed by Innocent as a fact.[38] If he were to be supposed to have ever intended a Latinization of the churches of the East,[39] at the Lateran Council he abandoned its execution for good. It is perhaps worth noting that, at the Council, Innocent did not legalize his own provision, under which, in the case of new elections within the Greek Empire, Latins are to be given preference in bishoprics, in which Greeks and Latins live side by side.[40] He obviously did not want the Greeks to appear, in the face of the entire Church, to have an inferior legal status. It is also possible that he no longer regarded his provision as being the last word on the question of the bishops in the church of the Latin Empire. He may have come to feel how fatefully the traditional practice of the Latins, who also in the kingdom of Sicily, in the Holy Land, in Antioch and elsewhere had claimed for themselves the most important bishoprics and the most famous monasteries,[41] hindered the separate Churches from getting nearer to each other.

But not even at the Lateran Council was Innocent able to make up his mind to show that unlimited generosity, which alone could have led, even though perhaps not yet to a real union, still to an inner rapprochement of the Churches of the Orient and Occident. He did not admit that the union of the Churches in actual fact still had to be realized, and that it had to be discussed and concluded with the Greek episcopate of the Greek Empire, including the unconquered regions, with the Greek patriarch at their head.[42] In the treatment of the question of obedience Innocent remained as hard and as rigid as he had been prior to the Latin conquest of Constantinople,[43] though he ascribed the blame for the perseverance of the Greeks in the state of separation partly to the atrocities committed by the conquerors, and though he did not hesitate to state that, after what had happened, the Greeks had every right to despise the Latins more than dogs.[44]

When measured by the standards of his age, Innocent's policy towards the Eastern churches must be sized up as broad-minded, but when viewed with regard to its substance, it makes evident a personal failure on the pope's side. It reveals the tragic limitation inherent in this great man, that in his conception of the union of the Churches he kept to a narrow legalistic view, and that above all he did not understand the need to keep this question so crucial for Church and Christendom from becoming involved in the vicissitudes of political expediency. He misunderstood and misjudged things, but also was, indeed, too little gifted with that love, which suffers everything, which is patient and forbearing, and which does not follow political considerations where religious decisions are involved.

## Notes to Chapter 8

[1]Reg. VII 203. Innocent himself displayed no initiative in respect of the conversion of the heathen world, yet effectively supported the missionary work in Prussia and Livonia. Cf. also Chapter 6 above and *ibid.* n. 23 and Fliche, Chrétienté, 86ff.; Haller, Papsttum 3, 433f., 550.

[2]Cf. Acta Inn. Introd. 37ff.

[3]Reg. I 526 (Acta Inn. P.I no. 7).

[4]*Ibid.*: *Scriptum est super hoc in eundem modum....*

[5]Reg. II 266 and Reg. V 115 (Acta Inn. App. 8, 562f.).

[6]Reg. XI 7. Acta Inn. P.I no. 106, cf. *ibid.* 338f. The Albanian church was re-incorporated into the Greek Church in 1213 after Michael Comnenus Ducas' conquest of Albania (cf. *ibid.* 120, 339, 370).

[7]Reg. X 138 (Acta Inn. I no. 105).

[8]Acta Inn. I no. 216.

[9]For Armenia's relations with the Roman Church see Acta Inn. Introd. 37ff. Oliver, a crusade-preacher and participant in the Fifth Crusade, reports however that the Armenians had confessed to submission to the Roman rite and like the Latins celebrated mass with unleavened bread (Hist. Damiat. 265f.).

[10]Reg. V 18 (Acta Inn. I 33).

[11]Reg. VII 127 (Acta Inn. I 63).

[12]Acta Inn. P. I 336 note. The cardinal legate, Gregory of S Vitale, was authorized for Hungary too (Reg. X 138 = Acta Inn. P. 1 no. 105). Since he died in the following year it is unlikely that he ever set foot in Ruthenia (Acta Inn. P. I 336 n.).

[13]This information stems from a letter written by the king to the pope informing Innocent that the magnates and people of Galicia who were his subjects had asked him to give them his son Coloman as king and that it was their intention to remain obedient to the Roman Church in future, with the reservation of their own rite. Lest this intention should be unnecessarily delayed he requests that the coronation and the acceptance of the oath of obedience, i.e. the pledge to recognize and uphold the union,

be not delegated to a legate *a latere* but to the archbishop of Gran (Fejér 3, 163ff. a. 1214). A letter from Honorius III to Andrew shows that the coronation was in fact performed by the archbishop on the pope's authority (Fejér 3, 355).

[14]Innocent sent special envoys to invite the Ruthenian bishops to attend the Lateran Council. Andrew, who hoped to reconquer the country, prevented the envoys from continuing the journey and promised them that he himself would send the bishops to the Council as soon as he was in a position to do so (Acta Inn. Introd. 103).

[15]Reg. I 353, 354 (Acta Inn. P. I nos. 4, 5, 178ff.).

[16]He declares that the submission of the Greek Church and of its head must precede the council, which he, the pope, for several reasons was prepared to convene. If the patriarch should fail to attend or to send representatives he would take measures against the emperor, the patriarch and the Greek Church (Reg. II 209, 211, Acta Inn. nos. 9, 10, pp. 193f., 198).

[17]Reg. VIII 55, Acta Inn. P. I no. 79, p. 301.

[18]*Quae* [the Greek Church] *debuerat propter tempus esse magistra, rursus indigere videtur, ut doceatur, quae sint elementa exordii sermonum Dei...* (Reg. VIII 55, Acta Inn. P.I. no. 79, p. 301). *Quae primo sanis affluebat doctrinis, et pene magistra vocari poterat propter tempus, errorum postmodum circumfusa caligine, coepit plurimum indigere, rursus divini eloquii rudimenta mendicans...* (Reg. XVI 105, Acta Inn. P. I no. 211, p. 450).

[19]The Greeks were no less prejudiced. Cf. Luchaire's analysis of a Greek memorandum from Innocent III's time (Innocent III 4, 238ff.).

[20]Reg. IX 140, X 51, XIII 6, XV 134 (Acta Inn. P. I nos. 91, 100, 139, 198).

[21]On the news of the capture of Constantinople Innocent orders a Latin prefect to be appointed for all the Roman priests in Constantinople (Reg. VII 164, Acta Inn. P. I no. 66). It seems that it was his intention to give the Romans an exempt spiritual head the same as the Pisans in Constantinople had in the so-called Prior of the Pisans. There would have been no point to this measure if Innocent had then intended to establish a Latin patriarchate.

[22]Cf. Chapter 9 below.

[23]Norden, 18, 196; Luchaire, Innocent III 4, 244; Haller, Papsttum, 381.

[24]*Translato ergo imperio, necessarium est ut ritus sacerdotii transferatur, quatenus Ephraim, reversus ad Judam, in acymis sinceritatis et veritatis, expurgato fermento veteri, epuletur...* (Reg. VIII 55, Acta Inn. P. I no. 79).

[25]In response to a request by Emperor Baldwin of Constantinople he requisitions missals, breviaries and other liturgical books from the French bishops *ut... Orientalis ecclesia in divinis laudibus ab Occidentali non dissonet, et, sicut est unus Deus et fides una, ita uno ore ipsum laudat et glorificet oriens et occasus...* (Reg. VIII 70, Acta Inn. I no. 81). The editor of the Acta assumes that Innocent had in fact intended at first to establish the *unitas cultus divini et ritus* (Introd. 130). However, I believe that we should not think of a suppression of the Greek rite as such since it was tolerated by the Roman Church in southern Italy, Sicily and Hungary; the pope himself performed ordinations of priests of the Greek rite (Reg. XI 23). At the beginning of his reign Innocent repudiated the non-Greek bishop forced by the temporal power on the Greek chapter of S Anastasia, the cathedral chapter of S Severina in southern Italy, confirmed the chapter's right to hold free elections, and used the occasion to emphasize that the Church *sub obedientia sedis apostolicae perseverans, Graecorum hactenus et ritum servavit et linguam* (Reg. I 16, Acta Inn. P. I no. 1, p. 169). Innocent confirms the

privileges granted to the Basilian monastery of Grottaferrata of observing the Greek rite and his relations with it are in no way different from those with Latin monasteries (Acta Inn. P. I no. 3, p. 170ff., no. 20, p. 210ff.). When a schism occurred in several places in southern Italy because the Greeks were only prepared to attend a service conducted by Greek priests and the Latins only one taken by Latin priests, though the separation was not easily feasible, Innocent sends delegates to try to compose the issue. They were instructed to proceed *sine personarum acceptione, cum non sit distinctio Judaei et Graeci, sed in omni gente, qui facit iustitiam acceptus sit Deo* (Reg. III 27, Reg. VI 139 = Acta Inn. P. I no. 40, p. 240f.). It is true that the latter case, taken by itself, is not conclusive evidence for Innocent's recognition of the Greek rite, but other facts indicate that he recognized the substantial autonomy of the united Greek churches in the Occident. In Hungary, Innocent, on a request by the king, orders enquiries to be made on the advisability of combining the Greek churches in Hungary into a single exempt bishopric (Reg. VII 47, Acta Inn. P. I no. 60). He raises no objections to the sons of married Greek priests being elected bishops nor to their being consecrated by their Latin superiors in southern Italy, since the oriental Church did not allow the vow of celibacy (Reg. VI 139, Acta Inn. P. I no. 40, p. 240). He decides that a Greek priest who had been ordained by a Greek bishop with the, though culpable, consent of his Latin diocesan bishop, may exercise his *ordo*, even if, in contravention of the Latin regulation, he had not received all the orders at the same time or not in the Ember period, but reserves to himself to decide finally on this hitherto tolerated custom (Acta Inn. P. I no. 18, p. 208, P. 1056).

[26]Reg. IX 140, Acta Inn. P. I no. 91, p. 399.

[27]JL. 17329.

[28]Migne PL. 217, 855. The conclusion of the chapter is no less pointed:... *Graeci vero postquam tunicam Domini inconsutilem diviserunt, ut perpetuae divisionis scandalum interponerent, sacrificii ritum temere mutavere...* (*ibid.* 858). Cf. also Reg. VIII 69.

[29]Cf. Chapter 1 n. 90.

[30]Migne PL. 217, 878.

[31]Reg. VII 2, 3, Acta Inn. P. I no. 51, p. 258ff.; Reg. VII 231.

[32]Reg. XI 155, 179, Acta Inn. P. I nos. 120, 122.

[33]Reg. XI 155, Acta Inn. P. I no. 120, p. 352.

[34]Reg. XIII 36, 40, Acta Inn. P. I nos. 145, 147.

[35]Reg. XVI 168, Acta Inn. P. I no. 214.

[36]Can. 4 (Leclercq 1333, Acta Inn. P. II no. 1).

[37]*Quoniam in plerisque partibus intra eandem civitatem atque diocesim permixti sunt populi diversarum linguarum, habentes sub una fide varios ritus et mores: districte praecipimus, ut pontifices huiusmodi civitatum sive diocesum provideant viros idoneos, qui secundum diversitates rituum et linguarum Divina officia celebrent, et ecclesiastica sacramenta ministrent, instruendo eos verbo pariter et exemplo* (can. 9, Leclercq 1339, Acta Inn. P. II no. 3, p. 483f.). In cases of urgency the bishop is even to appoint a priest of the nationality concerned as his vicar for the particular matters of the rite particular to that nationality (*si propter praedictas causas urgens necessitas postulaverit, pontifex loci catholicum praesulem nationibus illis conformem... constituat sibi vicarium in praedictis, qui ei per omnia sit obediens et subiectus...*, ibid.).

[38]*Qui* [priests of the higher orders] *autem secundum regionis suae morem non abdicarunt copulam coniugalem, si lapsi fuerint, gravius puniantur, cum legitimo*

*matrimonio possint uti* (can. 14, Leclercq 1345, Acta Inn. P. II no. 4, p. 485).

[39]As Heiler, 266f., maintains. But the reproach is not sufficiently substantiated. In Bulgaria a modification of the rite can hardly have been intended. On assuming the Roman rite either Latin would have had to become the church language or else the Roman liturgy would have had to be translated into the church language hitherto used. In any case the whole range of liturgical texts would have had to be replaced by Latin ones, but, given the total ignorance of Latin in the Bulgaria of that time, such a course was out of the question. After the conclusion of the union, in fact, the tsar of the Bulgars had to send two young men to Rome so that they might learn Latin and be able to translate the pope's letters for him since there were no linguists (*grammaticos*) in the country (Reg. VII 230). The circumstantial way in which Innocent justifies one single ritual modification, namely the anointing of bishops and priests with chrism at their ordination (Reg. VII 3, Acta Inn. P. I no. 52 p. 258ff.; the exposition stretches over more than four columns in Migne), and his emphasis that the Bulgarians by effecting the ordination in this form would not be following the Roman rite in the first place, but the divine command (Reg. VII 2, Acta Inn. P. I no. 51 p. 258), all this does not suggest that a demand had been made for far-reaching modifications in the rite practiced by the Bulgarian Church. Innocent surely allowed the Ruthenians to retain their rite, for according to the king of Hungary it was the condition they had made for their submission to the Roman Church (Acta Inn. App. I 23, p. 598, Introd. 103). If later on the king or the Hungarian clergy after all tried to appoint Latin priests or bishops (Acta Inn. Introd. 104), we cannot lay the blame for this unwise procedure on Innocent. It is true, however, that the council of legates of Antivari in 1199 decreed priestly celibacy for the kingdom of Dioclea and Dalmatia. There is no mention in the council canons of the rite, apart from the fixing of the time for ordinations on the Ember days as usual in the Latin Church, and similar regulations (Reg. II 178, Migne PL. 214, 727f.). The legates almost certainly insisted on priestly celebacy because they considered the kingdom to belong to Latin Christendom. According to the editor of the Acta Innocenti the Latin rite was dominant in Dioclea, and all its bishoprics were under the jurisdiction of the Roman See, in contrast to Serbia proper, whose bishoprics were subordinate to the patriarch of Constantinople and which followed the Byzantine-Slav rite (Acta Inn. P. I no. 34, p. 234 n). When Innocent requires the Maronites to conform *ecclesiae Romanae consuetudinibus se in omnibus studiosius* (Acta Inn. P. I no. 216, p. 459f.) it seems indeed to indicate the Latinization of this oriental church. But when placed in its proper context Innocent's demand reads differently. He decrees, *ut pontifices vestibus et insigniis pontificalibus sibi congruentibus iuxta morem Latinorum utantur, ecclesiae Romanae consuetudinibus se in omnibus studiosius conformantes.* It cannot be assumed that Innocent explicitly denotes a minor demand and glosses over far-reaching demands in a general wording, nor is it likely that he would have required the patriarch, who had just attended the Council (the Acta Inn. date the letter, instead of January 1216, wrongly January 1215), which had recognized the autonomy of the non-Latin rites, to give up their own rite or to effect considerable modification in it. The assumption that Innocent had in view the adaptation in matters of minor importance only, is confirmed by a statement of James of Vitry: ... *cum omnes alii orientales Praelati, exceptis dumtaxat Latinis, annulis et mitris pontificalibus non utantur, nec baculos, pastorales gestent in manibus, nec usum habeant campanarum, sed percussis baculo vel malleo tabulis populum ad ecclesiam soliti sunt congregare; hi praedicti Maronite in signum obedientie consuetudines et ritus observant Latinorum* ... (Mos-

chus, 153). The legate Peter Capuano, when accepting the Maronites' submission to the Roman Church, had imposed on them the profession of the *filioque*, the duality of wills in Christ, and several modifications concerning the taking of sacraments and sacramentals which, judging by the nature of those explicitly named, were of minor importance (Acta Inn. P. I no. 216, p. 459f.). Neither does the statement of Oliver, the crusade-preacher and participant in the Fifth Crusade, that the Maronites celebrated the liturgy given them by Innocent III to the extent that their language, the Chaldaic, allowed it (Hist Damiat., 265), give any more detailed clues for the assessment of the extent to which the Maronite church was 'Latinized'. According to Joachim of Fiore in his *Tractatus tres super Evangelia*, the Armenians had already before Innocent III's pontificate sought the pope's permission to celebrate mass with unleavened bread and according to the rite of the Roman Church (Huck, 163).

⁴⁰Reg. IX 140, Acta Inn. P.I no. 91.

⁴⁰See Acta Inn. Introd. 21, 31f., 28. Cf. also G. Stadtmüller, Michael Choniates, Metropolit von Athen (Orientalia Christiana XXXIII, 1934), 196.

⁴²The Greek bishops and other clerics assembled in Constantinople had made a request to Innocent in that sense (Acta Inn. App. I 22 p. 593ff.). Cf. Norden, 226f. It is doubtful whether he ever received the memorandum (see Acta Inn. Introd. 136).

⁴³This is not contradicted by the fact that Innocent practically had his legates negotiate with the independent Greeks on the subject of union and that the legates, certainly not against their mandator's will, had held disputations with the Greek theologians even within the confines of the Latin Empire (see Norden, 182ff., 215ff.; Heisenberg, Neue Quellen zur Geschichte des lat. Kaiserreichs und der Kirchenunion I, SB. München, 1922, 7ff.; Acta Inn. Introd. 133ff.). On the mission of one of these legates, Cardinal Pelagius of Albano, see D. Mansilla in Anthologia Annua (Inst. Esp. de Est. Eccl., Rome 1953), 11ff., a publication which was not accessible to me.

⁴⁴Reg. VIII 126, Acta Inn. P.I no. 84, p. 308.

# CHAPTER 9

# "For the inheritance of Christ crucified"

After the establishment of the Latin Empire of Constantinople Innocent had for a moment cherished the exultant hope that, the two
sisters, the Greek and Roman Churches, being united, the other two
sisters, the Churches of Alexandria and Jerusalem, would also be
liberated from Egyptian captivity.[1] Their liberation was Innocent's
aim from the first day of his reign to the last. Already in the
notification of his elevation he had promised the patriarch of Jerusalem powerful support for the Holy Land.[2] It was when setting out on
a journey to reconcile by personal action the antagonistic Italian cities
in the interest of the Holy Land,[3] that death befell him. In the
intervening sixteen years Innocent organized one crusade, made
elaborate preparations for a second, and accepted innumerable troubles and sacrifices for the sake of the Holy Land and its defenders.

What was the incentive for the pope's crusading ardour? Innocent
is said to have regarded the crusades as a means with which to realize
his hierarchical plans or as a possibility for the display and exercise
of papal leadership in Christianity.[4]

Those who see political calculations at the bottom of all of Innocent's activities could deduce his crusading ardour with greater
reason from the recognition that the Christian world was threatened
by the Moslem world, and that the Christian states in the Orient were
an outpost of occidental Christianity. Innocent regarded the followers
of Mohammed as *one* of the enemy forces, which faced the confessors of the Cross. In his address of 1198 calling for a crusade he
puts these words into their mouths: "Where is your God to rescue
you from our hands? We have desecrated your holy places and hold
them in our hands after we have taken them by storm. We have

broken the lances of the Gauls, brushed aside the assaults of the English, cut to pieces the forces of the Germans, and tamed the *Spaniards* for a second time. Where is your God? May he rise up, help you and protect himself and you![5] It is only logical that Innocent regards the fights of the Spanish kings against the Moors as being a holy war, too, and, therefore, exhorts kings and peoples to succour them in the face of the dreadful threat, with which in 1211 they were confronted by Mohammed Ben Jacub's offensive. It is right now, Innocent gives them to understand, that all must stand by each other, since the enemy of the Cross seeks to oppress not Spain alone, but Christians everywhere.[6] At that time he grants the fighters in Spain the same indulgence as those taking part in the campaign to Jerusalem,[7] thus recognizing the war as a crusade. He orders intercessory prayers to be held for Spain, similar to those for the Holy Land. He himself takes part in the great intercessory procession in Rome on 23 May 1212, speaks to the people on the greatness of the danger and summons them to intercession for the fighters. After the battle of Las Navas on 16 July 1212, in which the power of the Moors in Spain was broken, Innocent celebrates a thanksgiving feast in Rome, thus manifesting his awareness of the importance of the battle, which is one of the decisive battles in world history. But whatever importance the pope attaches to the war against the Saracens in Spain, he still does not put it on the same level as the fight for the Holy Land. When in 1213 he calls again for the campaign to Jerusalem, he repeals the indulgence granted for the fighters in the Moorish war, excepting the Spaniards themselves.[8] It is that, for Innocent, the campaign to Jerusalem was more than a fight against the common enemy of Christianity at a special sector of the front line – seen from this angle, the Spanish war would have been of incomparably greater importance; it was, rather, a fight for the places which Christ had sanctified by his earthly life, a fight for the Holy Grave and for the wood of His Cross, a fight for the inheritance of Christ crucified. The Spaniards for their part Innocent excepted from his call for the crusade, because he dared not denude the second front of Christianity whilst the battle on the first broke out; but in the common efforts of Christianity the campaign to Jerusalem then as ever took priority, except at the moment of extreme threat on the Spanish front. Innocent also deems it more deserving to take part in the fight for the liberation of the holy places than in the Crusade against heresy, their liberation is also more important to him than the union of the

Churches. As much as he wished, he once declares, that the Greek Church return to obedience, he was more set on support for the Holy Land.[9] On another occasion he declares that, though he welcomed the profession by Constantinople of obedience to the Roman Church, he would have liked better to see Jerusalem return into the power of the Christian peoples.[10]

It was in fact, though this is often hard to grasp for the modern way of thinking, the very liberation of the holy places of Christianity for which Innocent was concerned. Just as he regards it as the duty of every Christian to support the Lord and to follow Him loyally, to die for Him as He died for us, and just as the kings and peoples must rise to fight the Lord's battle and to avenge the shame inflicted on Christ crucified, so he felt that he, as the first servant of the King of Kings, as the Vicar of Christ, was most strongly responsible for the salvation of the Lord's inheritance. On a solemn occasion, at the Lateran Council, he assures the fathers that he is prepared to travel to the ends of the earth,[11] in order to rouse kings, princes and peoples with a strong voice, so that they may rise to fight the Lord's battle and to avenge the shame inflicted on Christ crucified, who, by our sins, had been driven from the throne of the Land which he had won with his blood and in which he had worked all the mysteries of His redemption. He spoke extremely severely when he felt that the shepherds of the Church were neglecting their duties towards the cause of the Holy Land. He writes to the bishops of the French episcopate, who had not paid the crusading tax of a fortieth, although some of them had even promised of their own free will to pay the thirtieth, that they were blamed by laypeople for preferring to use the revenues from their ecclesiastical offices (*de patrimonio Christi*) for the support of jugglers rather than of Christ Himself, and for spending more on their hounds and hawks than they were willing to spend for coming to Christ's aid.[12] He reproaches the English bishops for being worse than the Saracens, since they were prepared to overthrow the *one* king who could be expected to come to the help of the Holy Land.[13]

The Holy Land was the objective of Innocent's painstaking efforts, even without counting the preparations for two crusades. He deserves thanks, still more than for his liberal generosity,[14] for his own and his legates' truly thorny exertions to establish peace and to redress the disastrous conditions in the Christian Orient. Here, far worse than in the Occident, everybody was at variance with everybody, the patriarch of Jerusalem with the patriarch of Antioch, the Templars with the Hospitallers, the king of Armenia with the count of Tripoli, the king of Jerusalem with his over-powerful vassals. It was impossible to resolve certain questions, such as that of the Antioch succession dispute between King Leo of Armenia and Count Bohemond of Tripoli, by way of peaceable agreement. But for all that, the pope's permanent interventions for the sake of peace were not altogether in vain. Even though Innocent virtually only brought to pass shorter or longer lasting truces between the fighting parties, without his exertions, particularly without the pressure which in the interests of peace he brought to bear on the Orders of Knighthood at odds with one another, a state of unremitting warfare between the wielders of power would probably have persisted. On two occasions, one the Antioch succession dispute, the other the death of Queen Mary, wife of John of Brienne, king of Jerusalem by his wife's right,[15] the Christian Orient, but for Innocent's intervention, would probably have openly split into two opposing military groups.[16]

Still more than by quarrels between the wielders of power, Innocent was often disheartened by the acts of outrage which happened in the Holy Land and by the bad example which clerical circles set through dispute and discord and in their entire conduct of life. He once indignantly reproaches Patriarch Aimerico Monaco of Jerusalem for the hatred and malevolence through which laymen and clerics, his subordinates and he himself, had brought God's anger upon their country and, indeed, upon the entire Christian people, whilst they had better implore His mercy by prayers, vigils, fasting and works of charity. In his embitterment he even went to the length of declaring that it was perhaps downright worse if false believers were resident in the land rather than Saracens.[17] His admonitions and warnings will have been of little avail. But Innocent conferred a true blessing on the unfortunate land in that he assisted in the appointment of saintly men to the patriarchal sees of Jerusalem and Antioch, Albert of Vercelli[18] and Peter of Ivrea, who till then had been his co-operators in the ecclesiastical affairs of Lombardy. Unlike their predecessors, Albert of Jerusalem and Peter of Antioch did not aggravate the feuds prevailing in the Holy Land, but saw their task as establishing peace, and by their conduct gave to clergy and people a noble example of Christian life.

Pious prayer, pure intention, works of penance and charity were for Innocent the prerequisites for the liberation of the holy places.[19] In order to ensure that the malice of the people across the sea no longer frustrated his own, his legates' and the Christian Orient's endeavours, he demanded from the overseas clergy to so comport itself and to so instruct the people entrusted to it in the works of piety that the Lord, reconciled, would return His inheritance to God's heirs.[20] He was also at pains to keep alive in those who had taken the cross the awareness that they were preparing themselves for a holy war, by imposing on them the duty of leading a strict life, by urging them to reduce the sumptuosness of their standard of living and by most strictly forbidding tournaments.[21]

It needs no stressing that a man like Innocent left nothing undone to prepare the ground for the fight for the reconquest of the holy places. Realizing that in an age so filled with religious enthusiasm, with eagerness to fight and with the spirit of enterprise, his main problem was not to gather men who were ready to fight, but to raise the necessary funds, he paid special attention to this aspect of crusading preparation.[22] He extended the crusading indulgence to everyone who equipped fighters at their expense, granted also a share in the indulgence to all those who contributed to the costs of the crusade to the best of their ability,[23] and in his call to the crusade, published in 1213, ordered offertory-boxes to be put up in every church,[24] those offertory-boxes which Walther von der Vogelweide later made the object of his wicked misinterpretation.[25] Innocent resolved also to introduce a momentous innovation in that, on 31 December 1199, he imposed a crusading tax[26] of a fortieth upon the clergy and the non-privileged monastic orders. Innocent himself and the cardinals even contributed a tenth of their yearly incomes.[27]

In 1199 he had not yet considered introducing ecclesiastical punitive measures against those who were disobedient, but had contented himself with the purely moral obligation laid upon the secular and regular clergy. But he was soon to learn that the appeal to conscience was insufficient.[28] The failure of the Fourth Crusade was partly due to the unsatisfactory result of fund-raising. Since the crusaders could not pay the Venetians the costs of their transport overseas, they lost, and the pope lost with them, the freedom of decision.[29]

The first crusade which Innocent set on foot truly became the most painful disappointment of his life. The Venetians misused the crusading army, which had gathered in Venice in 1202, first to help them conquer Zara and the Dalmatian coast, and then to take part in the enterprise against Constantinople which, even though not initiated by the crusaders, was still carried through with the approval of a number of barons from the crusading army. The crusaders led back to Constantinople Prince Alexius, son of the dethroned Emperor Isaac Angelus and nephew of the usurper Alexius III, and, after the prince, as Emperor Alexius IV, had met with a violent death, established a Latin Empire under Count Baldwin of Flanders. They never set foot on Palestinian soil.

The question remains whether Innocent, for all his ardour, has a share in bringing about the failure of this Crusade; whether in the hope of gaining both Jerusalem *and* Constantinople for the Occident, of liberating the holy places and of establishing the union of the Greek and Roman Churches, he failed to exert all his power to prevent the diversion of the crusading army to Constantinople. It is true that Innocent did not bring his deadliest weapons into action against this attempt at diversion: the imposition and publication of anathema, even by name with regard to the army leaders, the interdict, the exclusion from the crusading indulgence, the formal challenge to the army to defy orders and to offer resistance.[30] But the reason was not that he had secretly approved of the happenings. Innocent opposed both enterprises, the expedition against Zara as well as that against Constantinople, as far as he could, without jeopardizing the Crusade itself. His ultimate aim was not to further or to prevent the restoration of a Greek pretender, or any other such enterprise, but only to promote the Crusade and make it a success. He did not intend to enforce at the expense of the Crusade the prohibitions, issued in the interests of the Crusade, of attacks against Christian countries,[31] that is to run the risk of a complete or partial disbandment of the army. But he had to capitulate to the impossibility of forcing his will upon the Venetians, the authors of the first diversion and the supporters and beneficiaries of the second one. He could well have prevented the crusading army from moving against Zara and Constantinople, but he would have never been able to bring the Venetians against their will to transport the crusaders to Syria. He would have had no way of adopting spiritual coercive measures if the Venetians had refused to carry over in their ships the army which still owed them the charges of transport due to them under the terms of the transportation agreement. The pope knew that, in the case neither of Zara nor of Constantinople, could he force the doge and his followers to forgo the possibility of exploiting to the full an uniquely advantageous situation. Doge Henry Dandolo, whom Innocent on a later occasion once admonished to serve God in future, after he had so far served the world,[32] was far less within reach of the moral power of the Church than most of his contemporaries, and the position of Venice was far too powerful for the pope to resort to temporal sanctions against the republic as he had against the Lombard cities and even against crowned heads. The crusading legate, Peter of Capua, therefore certainly entered into the pope's ideas when, prior to his departure from Venice, he confidentially expressed the wish that the army should stay together at all costs, even if its course was at first bound for Zara;[33] and it is equally certain that the abbot of Locedio, one of the pope's two confidants with the army, could count on the pope's consent when he yielded to the resolution of the army to set sail for Constantinople.[34] Innocent himself advised a legation of crusaders which called on him after the fall of Zara to overlook and let pass many things, until they had reached the overseas areas, in case the Venetians were looking for an occasion to disband the fleet.[35] But for a totally unforeseeable event, the conquest of Constantinople by the Latins, Innocent would probably have in fact succeeded in ensuring that the mass of the crusading army held together and in a body crossed over to Syria, whereas if he had reacted more severely, certainly a minor part only would have reached its destination.[36]

The pope's compliance was by no means motivated by considerations of an eventual advantage accruing from the Greek enterprise. It is true that the Greek pretender had promised the union of the two Churches and most effective support of the Crusade, to pay a subsidy of 200,000 silver marks, to provision the crusading army fully for one year, to take part personally in the expedition or to supply 10,000 men for one year at his own expense, to maintain 500 knights in the Holy Land for life,[37] and thereby had offered all and even far more than the pope had tried to get from Alexius III, the pretender's uncle. We also know that the offer was supported by some members of the Curia,[38] among them the crusading legate Peter of Capua.[39] But Innocent, as it seems, saw no occasion to place any greater hopes on the younger Alexius than on the elder, and he was far from expecting that a change on the throne would also lead to a change of system. It is true that the negotiations concerning the union of the Churches, which Innocent so far had had with the emperor,[40] had shown little prospect of success. But Innocent, surely, still expected more from an agreement made with a hard-pressed ruler on the basis of a political alliance, than from promises made by a young pretender who granted whatever might seem desirable, probably without fully realizing the import of his concessions and certainly without rightly assessing his possibilities of fulfilling them. Innocent regarded the Greek adventure as a loss of time and of energy for the Holy Land, which was made up for, at best, by an uncertain advantage.[41] He himself, in 1199, had threatened the emperor with an armed intervention if he were to oppose the union of the Churches,[42] but he had never considered taking action in favour of a Greek pretender. He, therefore, greets with reserve and scepticism the news of Alexius' restoration, his declaration of personal obedience and his promise to reduce the Greek Church to the obedience of the Roman Church.[43] Then as before he demands that the crusading vow be at long last fulfilled, though he must be aware that after the departure of the Latins nothing would happen in the matter of the union of the Churches that had not been achieved during their presence. He insists on the crusaders devoting all their energies to regaining the Holy Land, since that was most deserving in the face of God and most glorious in the face of men. However much he, the pope, wished for the Greek Church to return to obedience, still more was he desirous of help for the Holy Land.[44] Innocent is unlikely to have wished for an adventure which, even after its fortunate, but by no means surely foreseeable success, he still faces with such cool scepticism.

But Innocent then greeted with exaltation the establishment of the Latin Empire in April 1204, to which he had contributed no more than he had to the restoration of the pretender.[45] As poorly as he thought of Alexius' promises, so exuberantly he hoped for the transference of the Empire and its means of power into the hands of a Latin ruler. Totally misjudging the Greek way of thinking, he believed that in view of the Caesaro-papal system of the Greek Church the question of the union of the Churches was in substance resolved. The holy war, on the other hand, seemed to have won an invaluable base and invaluable resources. In view of the gain which was to be expected, it did not matter too much that the crossing over to Syria had to be postponed again.[46] And thus Innocent allowed himself to be enticed into continuing his course of complaisance and to slacken the reins, which he had long ago let slip out of his hands. After Zara the crusaders knew that Innocent was inclined to overlook many things in order to prevent the Crusade from being jeopardized; the Venetians knew, thereafter, which liberties they could take, since the fate of the Crusade depended on them. Now the fate of the Latin Empire, too, lay in their hands. Unscrupulously they exploited the situation to despoil the Church of Constantinople and to establish the Latin patriarchate of Constantinople, which in effect was to become a Venetian one. Saving the forms of law, Innocent approved of the totally uncanonical new order[47] and, by legalizing the subordination of the Greek Church to the Latin Church, made it impossible for the Schism to be inwardly overcome. With such complaisance he not only acceded to the urgent requests of the emperor who was dependent on the Venetians. He rather kept on reckoning with the crossing of the crusading army to the Holy Land. But the realization of the Crusade was out of the question if the Venetians refused to support the new Empire, or if they declined to co-operate in the cause of the cross or even placed difficulties in its way. Again Innocent was mistaken in his calculations. When, in the spring of 1205, Johannitza, the tsar of the Bulgars, thoughtlessly challenged, in league with the Kumans, Turks and Greeks successfully fought against the Latins, the crusading legate Peter of Capua released the crusaders from their vow, provided that they remained in Constantinople for one year to defend it. Innocent censured his legate's action,[48] but it is hardly questionable but that the cardinal did what, as matters stood, was imperative. The departure of the crusaders would promptly have resulted in the collapse of the newly-established Empire. On the other hand, the crusaders could have hardly been expected to remain in Constantinople if their crusading vow remained in force. When some little time later the fearful piece of news of Emperor Baldwin's defeat and capture reached the Curia, Innocent himself realized that, in the interests of the union of the Churches and of the Holy Land, nothing was left for him but to give up any hopes for the Crusade for the time being and to sustain the shaking edifice of the Latin Empire.

When Innocent had the entire unfortunate course of events before him, he may have asked himself whether it would not have eventually been wiser and more successful to walk straight on in the royal ways, rather than to keep on making well-calculated allowances for what, for the moment, appeared to be useful and necessary.

Less than a decade after the failure of the Fourth Crusade Innocent began with increased energy to make preparations for a new crusade. In his great call to the cross in the spring of 1213 he implored princes and lords, bishops and prelates, chapters, towns and villages, to equip an appropriate number of fighters, in so far as those called up did not take the field in person.[49] Everybody, regardless of physical fitness which Innocent in 1199 had ordered to be carefully examined, is to be admitted to taking the cross. It goes without saying that the pope did not wish to burden the crusading army with disabled persons now or in the future. Therefore, the vow of those permanently disabled was later to be commuted to the obligation of offering a corresponding sum of money. Such commutations had also occurred in earlier times. By systematically applying them, Innocent now taps a new source of fund-raising for the crusade,[50] a proceeding which, from the point of view of morals, was hardly free from scruples, since it could easily lead to buying oneself out of one's vow if those granting the dispensation, unlike Innocent himself,[51] no longer kept strictly to the reasons which legitimatized the commutation.\At the Lateran Council, only after the consent of the entire Church as represented by the participants in the Council, did Innocent impose on the clergy a new crusading tax, this time of a twentieth for three years instead of the former fortieth for one year, the payment of which was now to be enforced under penalty of excommunication.[52]\ He taxes himself and the cardinals again with a tenth, moreover makes all the money he could spare, 30,000 pounds, available for the holy cause, and equips at his own expense the ship which is to transport the crusaders from Rome and its outskirts.[53] Relying on the authority of the General Council, Innocent even ventures to impose, in view of the forthcoming crusade, a four-year peace upon the Christian world.[54] It would not be so easy for a prince, even if he held the view, as did Philip of France, that the quarrels between kings were none of the pope's business, to disregard the peace which the entire Church imposed on him in the common interest of Christianity.

Innocent sought to rule out everything which had contributed to the failure of the previous Crusade. The transport of the army should not again become a business transaction, nor should the crusading army be dependent again on the goodwill of a single power over which he had little influence. He, therefore, prevailed upon the maritime towns to make their contribution to the crusade by way of providing transport vessels[55] and, also in other respects, encouraged the building and procuring of ships.[56] This time he is careful to fix himself the place and the date of departure. All crusaders travelling by sea were to gather, on 1 June 1217, in the Sicilian kingdom, namely in Brindisi, Messina and the neighbouring harbours. He himself intended to be on the spot in order to help with the organization of the embarcation and to give his farewell blessing to the warriors of the Lord.[57]

The successes of preaching the cross and of his own endeavours justified, at about the beginning of 1216, Innocent's confident hope that, at the appointed date, a force would be gathered sufficient to attack the enemy on his own ground.[58] There were three kings among the crusaders. King Frederick had taken the cross on the day of his coronation in Aachen, on 25 July 1215;[59] King John of England already the previous March.[60] King Andrew of Hungary had been signed with the cross for years and was now ready to fulfil his vow. But the pope was still faced with the difficult task of establishing peace in those areas of the Christian world where wars had broken out in defiance of the threats of punishment, strictly executed by him, which the Lateran Council had issued.[61]

On the journey whose object was to reconcile Genoa with Pisa and the two hostile power groups in Lombardy with one another,[62] Innocent died in Perugia on 16 July 1216. At the Lateran Council, the previous year, he had declared that it was his ardent desire to see the work he had begun accomplished,[63] but at the same time had expressed his submission to God's will, if this were denied him.[64] We do not know whether death spared Innocent yet another extremely painful disappointment. Whether under him the crusade would have led to eventual success or not, it would certainly have taken another course than the crusade which took place under Honorius III.[65] Honorius was imbued with the same ardour for the cause of the cross, but he lacked the firm hand and the unparalleled prestige of his predecessor. For a second time Innocent's preparations for a crusade, this time probably the most elaborate preparations ever made for a crusade, were wasted. Just as in his efforts to secure peace between papacy and emperorship, so in the crusade, Innocent III's death had come one hour too soon.

## Notes to Chapter 9

[1] Reg. VII 203.
[2] Reg. I 11.
[3] Cf. above, at the end of this chapter.
[4] Cf. Cramer, 181. Cramer's assumption that the crusading legates were to be the true leaders of the crusading army (186) cannot, in my opinion, be reconciled with the phrase *qui* [the legates] *exercitum Domini humiliter et devote praecedant* (Migne PL. 214, 310). Innocent merely did for the crusades what no temporal lord could do in his stead. He neither appointed the leader of the crusading army nor attempted to appoint him, nor did he interfere with the conduct of the crusade, with the exception of the

obvious and obligatory attempt to prevent the crusading army from being misused for selfish purposes. In order to secure a successful issue of the crusade he even swallowed grave insults done to his prestige by the overbearing arrogance of the Venetians.

[5]Reg. I 336.

[6]Reg. XIV 144, 145.

[7]We hear of this on the occasion of the repeal of the indulgence in 1213 (Reg. XVI 28, Migne PL. 216, 820).

[8]Reg. XVI 28.

[9]Reg. VI 230.

[10]Reg. IX 139.

[11]*Transire ad reges et populos et nationes, adhuc autem et ultra* (*Sermo VI in Conc. Lateran. hab.* Migne PL. 217, 676).

[12]Gesta c. 84, Migne PL. 214, CXXXIII.

[13]Rymer 1[1], 138.

[14]See for instance Reg. XII 27, 28.

[15]See Böhm, Johann von Brienne, König von Jerusalem, Heidelberg thesis, 1938.

[16]Cf. Reg. XV 209–11.

[17]Reg. X 214.

[18]Cf. Ambrose of S Teresa, 19ff.

[19]Reg. I 11, XVI 28, 36, Migne PL. 216, 820f.; Exped. pro recup. terrae sanctae, Leclercq 1391.

[20]Reg. V 26. Cf. also *ibid.* XVI 36.

[21]Gesta c. 84 (Migne PL. 214, CXXXVIf.).

[22]Cf. Martini, 309–335 for an exhaustive account of Innocent III's fund-raising for the crusades.

[23]*Huius quoque remissionis volumus esse participes iuxta quantitatem subsidii ac praecipue secundum devotionis affectum, qui ad subventionem illius terrae de bonis suis congrue ministrabunt* (Reg. I 336, Migne PL. 214, 311; and almost identical Reg. II 270, 271 Migne PL. 214, 831. Cf. also Reg. XVI 28). Burdach interprets the regulation as a debasement of the indulgence to the level of a trade commodity subject to specific taxes, as a sale of God's gifts at fixed rates (Walthers Kampf, 469), but there is no merit in that argument. There is no question of a somehow numerically fixed or fixable share in the indulgence, the less so as the share is to depend in the same measure on the strength of the piety and on the size of the gift; it thus offers a partaking which escapes worldly calculation.

[24]Reg. II 270, 271; cf. also Reg. XVI 28.

[25]Sagt an, hêr Stoc, hât iuch der bâbest her gesendet,
daz ir in rîchet und uns Tiutschen ermet unde pfendet?
Swenne im diu volle mâze kumt ze Laterân,
sô tuot er einen argen list, als er ê hat getân:
er seit uns danne wie daz rîche stê verwarren,
uns erfüllent aber alle pfarren.
ich waen des silbers wênic kumet ze helfe in gotes lant.
Grôzen hort zerteilet selten pfaffen hant.
hêr Stoc, ir sit uf Schaden her gesant,
daz ir ûz tiutschen liuten suochet toerinne und narren.
See Walther von der Vogelweide, Gedichte, Insel-Bücherei No. 105, 32.

[26]See Chapter 2 above.

[27]Reg. II 270–272, III 47. He required an appropriate contribution from the privileged orders which was, however, to be at least a fiftieth (Reg. II 268. Cf. also Reg. II 47). The Cistercians defended their exemption from taxes with obstinacy and in the end Innocent gave in (Chron. Angl. 130. Cf. also Caesarius, Strange 2, p. 7). In the summer of 1201 Innocent thanks the abbot and chapter of Citeaux for the 2,000 marks which they had voluntarily offered for the support of the Holy Land (P. 1935).

[28]Martini (318ff.) speaks of total failure. Cf. the pope's letter to the French bishops complaining bitterly at their failure to pay the fortieth (Gesta c. 84, Migne PL. 214, 132f.). The pope's letters of 1206/7 reveal that the fortieth from the English Church had failed to reach its destination. English prelates had retained money which had been paid towards the fortieth or for the redemption of the crusading vow and had regarded themselves, as to their *temporalia*, as being exempt from the tax (both letters are published in Cheney, Master Philip, 348ff.).

[29]See Martini, 319.

[30]Innocent appears not to have transmitted the excommunication of the Venetians after the conquest of Zara for publication to his confidants in the army and thus enabled Marquis Boniface of Montferrat, the leader of the crusading army, to withhold the letter until he had reassured himself of the pope's intentions, being convinced, as the margrave excuses himself with good reason, that the publication of the excommunication would result in the immediate dissolution of fleet and army (Reg. IX 99, 100). In his reply Innocent insists on the delivery without stressing it (Reg. VI 101), but once again fails to choose the safe way of publication by someone in his confidence. Innocent would probably have been glad to grant the requests made by the crusaders to ignore the excommunication of the Venetians (Reg. VI 99) who did not even think of applying for absolution, if the crusading army itself had not made such a course impossible for him. It seems that Innocent intended to pass over the excommunication of the whole crusading army for the enterprise against Zara. The Register contains a letter (Reg. V 161) from the end of the fifth year of his reign in which Innocent, though withholding his blessing from the crusaders before Zara, yet regards them as excommunicated only if they should continue to destroy the city or approve of such destruction or refuse to return their spoils to the emissaries of the king of Hungary. In all probability this letter was not issued, but replaced by another (Reg. V 162), by which the absolution of the crusaders is entrusted to the cardinal legate regardless of the absolution already given by the bishops (this seems to be the letter to which Peter des Vaux refers 1, pp. 109f., when saying that he had seen the letter which contained the apostolic excommunication). Before a statement of the pope's opinion had arrived, the crusaders had had their ban lifted by the bishops in the army by swearing on oath that they would obey the pope's commands (Reg. V 62). Once the crusaders themselves had admitted that they were excommunicate, Innocent could no longer ignore the excommunication of those who were truly guilty.

[31]Reg. V 161, VI 101.

[32]Reg. VII 206.

[33]Anonymous Halberst. 12; cf. Gunther of Pairis, 72f.

[34]According to Villehardouin, 444, he implored those who resisted to accept the treaty with Alexius since that was the best way of helping the Holy Land.

[35]Reg. VI 99, 100, 102; Villehardouin, 444.

[36]If Innocent before the capture of Constantinople speaks of an *occasio* which the Venetians might seek to dissolve the fleet, he seems to have not yet definitely made up

his mind as to whether the Venetians seriously intended Alexius' restitution or whether they regarded it, i.e. its prevention by the pope, as the desired *occasio.* The very fact that the Venetians took part in the enterprise suggests that they set considerable store by it, and if the crusaders had still had the freedom to decide in this matter, Innocent would certainly have taken more energetic measures. The possibility is also not to be excluded that the leaders of the army, who had pledged themselves to the prince, were all too ready, before the mass of crusaders suspected what was going on, to yield to the pressure of the Venetians in this matter. It may even be that these selfsame leaders, by fixing too high the number of those to be ferried over in the transportation contract had, not altogether unvoluntarily, brought on themselves their later strained position. But a dissolution of the army would not only have to be feared from a possible sabotage of the crusade by the Venetians, but would also have been likely to happen as a direct consequence of a rigorous intervention by the pope. Once it was made known that the pope had prohibited the attack on Zara, a number of nobles immediately broke away from the army and sailed to Syria via Apulia (Villehardouin 442; Peter des Vaux 1, 110). After the capture of Zara and the conclusion of the treaty with the prince, again sizeable groups departed to make their own way by Apulia or Hungary (Anonymus Halberst. 13; Villehardouin 444; Devastatio 88). Some had sought permission from the Curia to return home some time before this, a permission which Innocent had reluctantly given on condition that they would later redeem their vows (Gunther of Pairis, 72). After the capture of Zara a thousand men are reported to have left the army with permission, more than another thousand without it (Devastatio, 88). On Corfu still another part of the crusaders, with the acclamation of the others, declared their intention to send for ships to Brindisi to Count Walter of Brienne, the leader of the papalists in the kingdom (Villehardouin, 446). Robert de Boves, a member of the delegation sent by the crusading army to the pope after the capture of Zara, once he had learned of the treaties concluded with the pretender, did not return to Zara despite the oath which the delegates had, significantly, been obliged to swear, but sailed to Syria by way of Apulia, presumably with the pope's approval (Villehardouin, 445; Clary 11). But even if Walter was able to transport fragments of the crusading army to Syria, he certainly would not have been in a position to ferry over, in a relatively short time, the army proper, nor surely to provision it. The army was at the mercy of the Venetians, and any rigorous papal intervention would only have resulted in its dissolution, and never in its prompt passage to the Holy Land.

[37] MG. Const. 2, 9; Villehardouin, 443; Reg. V 122.

[38] Reg. V 122.

[39] He made himself bearer of a formal inquiry from the crusading army concerning the restitution of Alexius (Reg. V 122) and Marquis Boniface of Montferrat later apologized to Innocent, maintaining that it was the cardinal who had advised him to proceed with the undertaking (Reg. VIII 133). Naturally this statement is not to be understood as meaning that the cardinal himself had inspired the undertaking. See Anonymus Halberst. 12, Gunther of Pairis, 73, for the cardinal's indulgent attitude out of concern for the realization of the crusade.

[40] Reg. I 352, 354, II 211, V 122. See Chapter 8 above.

[41] Alexius' restitution played a part in the peace offers which Philip of Swabia made to the pope in the spring and summer of 1203. Through the monk Otto of Salem, who arrived in Rome in the latter half of April at the latest, Philip promised the pope, should he reverse his decision in the throne dispute to his advantage, among other things church union, provided God handed over the Greek Empire to him or to his brother-in-

law, the prince. This promise is contained also in the detailed offer upon which Philip then came to an agreement with a papal negotiator in June or July (see above Chapter 5 n. 164). Before 21 April 1203 Innocent had already learned of the conclusion of the treaties between the crusading army and the pretender (Reg. VI 48, Gunther of Pairis, 76ff.). When he discussed Philip's offer he could, therefore, scarcely still hope to prevent the Greek enterprise. In the event of it taking place against the pope's wishes and being successful, it could well be an advantage if Philip guaranteed to fulfil the promise of church union and if he made this guarantee effective by undertaking the crusade which he offered to Innocent at the same time. In this way the enterprise would have lost to some extent the character of being a dangerous and at bottom fruitless adventure. Long before these negotiations, as early as 16 November 1202, Innocent had informed the Greek emperor that he had rejected the application of the prince (Reg. V 122) who had made a personal visit to the Curia and for whom the leader of the crusading army, Marquis Boniface of Montferrat, had stood up during his visit to the Curia (Gesta c. 83). In June 1203, not knowing that the fleet was already under way for Constantinople, he writes to the crusaders that no one should pride himself that he could occupy or plunder Greece only because it was less obedient to the Apostolic See or by reason of what the emperor had done to his brother. It was not for the crusaders to judge this and they had taken the cross not to avenge such sin but in view of the disgrace done to Christ. He urges them now to hasten to the relief of the Holy Land without further delay, putting aside all trivial excuses and pretexts (Reg. VI 101). Significantly, Innocent refers to the emperor as his most beloved son in Christ and adds that he would be writing to him about the scarcity of supplies since he had already offered to provision the army (Reg. VI 102).

[42]Reg. I 335.

[43]Reg. VI 210, 211, 2.

[44]Reg. VI 230.

[45]Reg. VII 153, 154, 203.

[46]Cf. Delisle, Lettres, 409f.

[47]Reg. VII 203.

[48]Reg. VIII 126.

[49]Reg. XVI 28.

[50]See Martini, 321, 326f.

[51]Martini, 330.

[52]Martini, 322. By the papal agents who were to receive the money Burdach (Walthers Kampf, 521) understands Italian collectors of the pope. However they were no more curial officials than the agents of 1213 who were to promote the cause of the crusade in the individual church provinces and most likely they were the same men. Appointed as agents were, for instance, for the church province of Mainz the abbot of Salem, the former abbot of Neuberg, the dean of Speyer and the provost of Augsburg (Reg. XVI 28, 29); for the provinces of Halberstadt and Bremen the resigned bishop of Halberstadt and the former abbot of Sichem; for the province of Cologne Master Oliver, the Cologne scholastic, and Dean Hermann of Bonn (*ibid.* 29).

[53]Available for that purpose are 3,000 silver marks, being the residue of alms given by some believers, the bulk of which he had already assigned to the patriarch of Jerusalem and to the Orders of Knighthood (Exped. pro recup. = Leclercq 1392; Migne PL. 217, 269ff.; P. 5012).

[54]Exped. pro recup. terrae sanctae (Leclercq 1394).

[55]Reg. XVI 28.

[56] *Ad liberandum* (Migne PL. 217, 270 = P. 5012).

[57] Migne PL. 217, 269.

[58] Hampe, Registerbände, 559.

[59] According to Kantorowicz (71) Innocent was embarrassed by Frederick's zeal, who by a brilliant diplomatic trick had placed himself at the head of the crusading movement and thereby had unexpectedly deprived the papal *imperator* of the control of the crusade. Kantorowicz seems to draw this bold conclusion from the fact that there is *no record* of any statement by the pope on Frederick's taking the cross. However, it would be inadmissible for Kantorowicz to maintain that Innocent had never mentioned the king's decision even if the registers of the last years of Innocent's reign were still extant and showed no record of any such statement.

[60] Innocent was not disposed to allow John to wear the cross merely for his personal security. Until the opening of the Lateran Council he had required the king to inform him of the date of his departure for the Holy Land (Rymer 1[1], 129. Cf. Tillmann, Legaten, 107).

[61] John could not think of fulfilling his crusading vow before internal peace had been restored in England. Consequently the English barons and the pretender, the French dauphin Louis, whom they had invited to England, were excommunicated for obstructing the cause of the crusade (cf. Rymer 1[1], 138f.). The long-standing truce (1214–1220) between England and France, however, remained in force. Philip dissociated himself from his son's enterprise and did not support him publicly nor with full or even sufficient engagement of his powers. Luchaire is wrong to assume that Innocent had laid King Philip himself under ban and interdict (Innocent III 5, 273f., and L'avènement, 673). One of Innocent's last mandates (P. 5299) orders the publication of the sentences against Louis, not against Philip himself. The mandate was issued in May at the earliest, probably not before the second half of the month, since P. 5267, entered in the rubrics under a much earlier date, is identical with P. 5111 of 20 May. By the end of May Innocent, moreover, is still in normal contact with the king (P. 5268). And then, Luchaire's source, William Brito, never reports that Innocent had ordered the French bishops to publish his sentences against the king, but states that Innocent when the fatal disease befell him, had just begun to dictate intolerable decrees against King Philip and the kingdom (Delaborde 1, 308).

[62] Milan and Piacenza had been laid under excommunication and interdict by the papal legates who were to prepare Innocent's visit to Milan and other cities in Lombardy (P. 5280, 5281, 5329), since both cities had refused to make peace with Pavia (MG. Epp. saec. XIII 1, 1f., 3f.; Ann. Placent. Guelfi 431). The Pisans were also under ban at the time of Innocent's death (Horoy 1, 317). The chronicle of Nicholas Trivet names Pisa and Genoa as the destinations of Innocent's travel (quoted in Potthast Vol. 1, 461).

[63] Migne PL. 217, 673. Cf. also *ibid.* 267 and Reg. XVI 34.

[64] Migne PL. 217, 673.

[65] Luchaire (Innocent III 4, 296ff.) assumes that the preparations for the crusade had already proved abortive before Innocent III's death. This mistake derives from the fact that Luchaire takes the date of the start of the crusade to have been 1 July 1216 instead of 1217 (*loc. cit.* and 6, 56). Martini (322f.) attributes the failure of the Fifth Crusade primarily to the scanty attendance of the French barons and to the French episcopate's poor spirit of sacrifice, which for its part he connects with the indignation, felt by the higher ranks, at the preference shown to the lower ranks and with the unqualified admission to the crusading vow of suitable and unsuitable aspirants.

# CHAPTER 10

# The man

In August 1202 Innocent III made a stay at Subiaco, a colourful description of which we owe to a happy find of Karl Hampe.[1] It is a letter which a superior official, but not of the rank of cardinal, sent in those days from Subiaco to an absent colleague. The report is a witty, but genuinely felt jeremiad on the hardships to which the curials, in a tent-camp under the blazing sun of Subiaco, are exposed. Above the lake, enclosed by rugged and gloomy mountains, lies the place where the tents are pitched for the pope, the curial officials, and the baggage personnel. On the south side the chief cook had pitched his smoke-stained tents. From there resounds constantly the squabble of the kitchen helps over tallow and grease. On the east side the apothecary, in the early morning, holds his phials with urine up to the light and all day long molests his surroundings with the unpleasantly monotonous pounding of pestle and mortar. On the north side the crowd of buyers and sellers flocks together in the morning to hold market. The squabbling and shouting puts an end to sleeping. Tired, the curials turn out of their beds; tired they remain all day, and the pope, whose humble shelter is pitched on the west side,[2] often sees his fellow workers sleeping over their work. Despite the cool breeze blowing from the lake, the heat is hard to bear. From sunrise on the gnats, whose buzzing alone is a torture, do their tormenting work, and from three hours after dawn the shrill sound of the cicadas disturbs the sleep. At night the chirping of the crickets drives sensitive nerves to despair. No less oppressing is the moaning and wailing of the sick lying all around.[3] On the other hand, the view over the lake is

magnificent. The chaplains[4] frequently refresh themselves in its cool
water, so that it seems to be alive with fish. To the letter-writer
himself the lake, though, causes tantalizing torments; he dreads the
neck-breaking descent and the toilsome re-ascent, which made him
forget any pleasure the lake had given.

Innocent will have felt the hardships of the provisional camp in
the hot sun of Subiaco hardly less than the letter-writer. We know
that, once at Monte Cassino, he had to forgo saying mass and
preaching because of the stifling heat which the throng of people had
brought to the point of intolerability.[5] For his extremely shaky health[6]
the summer months were always critical.[7] He therefore spent them
outside Rome, unless special reasons made his presence in the city
imperative. In Subiaco Innocent could well have escaped many of the
hardships behind the protecting walls of the monastery. But he
apparently wanted to share them with his retinue, or perhaps to spare
the monastery an extra burden. In his unassuming simplicity, and
defying the hardships of place and season, he contented himself with
a humble tent or hut, did not demand any special regard from his own
entourage, but appears to have put up patiently with the noise, the
shouting and groaning. To him the curials could flee when the torment
of the heat became unbearable. According to the letter-writer's words
they even forced him to set all work aside like themselves and, sitting
intimately at his feet and engaged in lively talk, they forgot the
summer torture.[8]

In this description Innocent does not stand before us as a man
unapproachable in the feeling for the dignity of his office and in the
consciousness of the heavy weight of his responsibilities. Thus it is
that the letter-writer, with a smile of intimacy and still respectfully, in
the language of the curials speaks of Innocent as the third Solomon,
our most reverend father, the successor of the Prince of Apostles and
Vicar of Jesus Christ, the spring of living water who had been allotted
the treasure of all wisdom and eloquence.[9] Even trifles concerning the
pope are important to him: the third Solomon likes to stay on the isles
in the lake,[10] and thus, unlike the letter-writer, does not fear the
neck-breaking descent and the toilsome re-ascent. He dips "his holy
hands" into the water and uses it for a refreshing gargling. When the
letter-writer mentions that he has consulted the doctor on the sick
friend's behalf, he does not forget to add that the third Solomon, too,
regards the doctor with deserved respect.

Like the letter-writer, the visitors to the Curia attest to Innocent's

responsive and humanly simple nature and to his amiability. A monk
from the monastery of Andres near Boulogne, still rejoicing in
retrospect, gives an account of his audience with the pope. He called
on him just when Innocent had woken from his after-dinner nap and
was still free from business.[11] Innocent called the kneeling monk to
him, greeted him with a kiss and, after their business was done, told
him about a visit he had paid to Andres, where he had enjoyed
hospitality when, during his student days in Paris, he had made a
pilgrimage to the tomb of St Thomas of Canterbury. To the monk
Thomas Marleberge of Evesham Innocent twice made a present of
game at Christmas-time.[12] This will not have been the only time that
the pope showed small kindnesses to strangers who spent some time
at the Curia. It fits in with his amiable nature[13] that, on a journey – in
summer – to the southern regions of the Papal State, he allowed the
nobles of Ceccano to perform tournaments before him[14] and that, so it
is asserted,[15] he enjoyed the skill at jumping of the youth in Viterbo.

In the lively description by Gerald of Wales, the famous author, of
his visits to the Curia, Innocent faces us in the same amiable and
humanly simple nature. On an excursion to Fonte Vergine, Innocent
once talked with Gerald for some time both jestingly and seriously
and laughed heartily over the rough manner in which Gerald had
proved that a monk, who alleged that Gerald had robbed him of a
horse, was a slanderer.[16] Gerald even wants us to believe that Innocent joined him and the cardinals in making fun of the poor Latin
and the lack of theological education of Archbishop Hubert Walter of
Canterbury, Gerald's opponent in his lawsuit.[17] The Welsh monk is
undoubtedly telling fibs here, as he did in his spiteful talk about the
archbishop which he himself retracted as being, for the most part,
mere prattle.[18] Innocent could not allow himself to forget so far his
own dignity and the consideration due to a prominent member of the
episcopate. Easiness in social contacts for Innocent was certainly not
tantamount to go-as-you-please. He possessed an outspoken sense for
what is fitting and proper. When, after the death of Pope Celestine
III, a number of cardinals immediately left the Lateran Palace in
order to resort to the better protected Septizonium for the purpose of
preparing the new election, Innocent was one of those cardinals who
remained in the Lateran to attend to the pope's exequies.[19] Feelings of
personal affection had no effect on this behaviour of Lothair, since he
had not, at least not intimately, been connected with the deceased.
We are occasionally informed that Innocent, even when going for a

walk, had the cross carried before him,[20] thus not even when relaxing
did he try to sever himself from the bonds which tied him as holder of
his high office. Gerald may be correct in his assertion in so far as the
pope will not always have hidden a smile at Gerald's wittily produced
spiteful comments. He seems to have enjoyed the Welshman's company, but because of Gerald's immoderate vanity and unshakeable
self-confidence and because of the almost childlike manner in which
he displayed both features, he will not always have taken Gerald too
seriously. Gerald himself once notes how the pope, shaking his head
at his, Gerald's, speech, casts a smiling glance at Cardinal Ugolino
seated at his side.[21]

Gerald is not the only one who noted and recorded the happy trait
of wit and humour in the pope's character. A visitor to the Curia
observes how Innocent, in the midst of official business, with a jest in
Italian (*vulgariter loquens*) turns to the cardinals.[22] When a procurator
once complains that the opposing party had taken away his advocates
(*copia advocatorum*), Innocent smilingly replies: *Nunquam defuit
alicui copia advocatorum in Curia Romana*, nobody, indeed, has so
far been short of legal advisers at the Roman Curia.[23] *Felix ille casus*,
oh what a happy "fall" (*casus* meaning both "case" and "fall"), he is
said to have exclaimed at the news that Archbishop John of Trier,
who, vacillating between the pope and the king, and not daring either
to attend the Staufen's court-day or to stay away, had fallen from his
horse.[24] Even if this is only an anecdote, it still pins down, as does
another told by Salimbene, the knowledge contemporaries as well as
posterity had of the pope's humorous vein. The Franciscan relates the
jocose conversation the pope had with a juggler to whom Innocent
answered in the same bad Latin in which he had been addressed, and
gives the comment that the pope was a man who had allowed himself
pleasure in the midst of his worries.[25] Now and then Innocent's wit
and humour took on the more biting form of irony. He is prepared to
give the bishop of Fiesole the opportunity of testing in his presence
whether he could, as he had boasted, buy himself out of his guilt with
money.[26] "Behold, Adam has become one of us...", he ironically
states, when the bishop of Penne after his elevation forgot that as a
Cistercian he was particularly committed to lead a simple life, and at
the same time reminds the man, whom he himself had appointed, of
the relevant words of Genesis: "I repent having made the man".[27] I
would regard it as an amiable joke rather than irony, when in his
chambers one evening he greeted Gerald of Wales, who was pursuing

at the Curia the recognition of his election as bishop of St David's and at the same time of the metropolitan status for the bishopric, as elect of St David's and another time as archbishop.[28]

The Welsh writer to whom we owe so many fascinating details of Innocent's private life, also gives us important information about the pope's interests. When in the pope's presence verses were once recited in his praise, Gerald asserts that he received the most applause for his poem.[29] It is no undue generalization if we assume that reciting poetry and readings from literature were a feature of the social entertainments at the Curia. Innocent was himself in large measure acquainted with the classical literature of Rome[30] and had some notion of the splendour of Greek culture. Athens for him is the city from which the wealth of learning had flowed out almost to the whole world, the city of shining name and of perfect beauty, the first city to teach the art of philosophy and to bring forth poets, the mother of all arts, the city of learning (*litterarum*).[31] He had himself a smattering at least of Greek.[32]

It is significant that Gerald, who was exceptionally well-read and who, proud as he was of his education and knowledge, was quick to look down arrogantly on others, recognized the pope's wide reading and praised him as a lover of literature,[33] by which he not only meant theological literature. We can therefore give credit to the pope's biographer when he emphasizes Innocent's erudition in secular knowledge.[34] Gerald often had occasion to talk with Innocent. On one of his visits to the Curia he presented six of his writings to the pope. As the author is proud to relate, Innocent kept them lying at his bedside for almost a month, called the attention of cardinals visiting him to the delicacies of style and content, and eventually lent them out to them one by one. But he had had no mind to part with the *Gemma ecclesiastica*.[35] It is certain that Gerald, in his vanity as an author, exaggerated, but his truly fascinating writings, for example along with the *Gemma*, the topography of Ireland[36] and the conquest of Ireland, must have appealed to Innocent's lively mind. It shows the pope's broad-minded impartiality that he enjoyed a book such as the *Gemma ecclesiastica* or at least smilingly stomached it. A lesser mind would have found in it so many passages which are exceptionable. Thus, the author offers objections to the compulsory celibacy of the clergy[37] and, while attacking the Church's worldly power, repeats the legend that the devil, on the day of the Donation of Constantine, had triumphantly exclaimed: "Now I have instilled the poison into the

Church",[38] and hints at an immoderate financial burdening of the
prelates in view of the many expenses they had at the Curia with the
cardinals, its nepotists and legates.[39]

His vivid sympathy for scholarship is already testified by his close
connections with the Universities of Bologna and Paris.[40] His historical knowledge and his critical talent appear to us as admirable for his
age. This knowledge he will partly have gained while scrutinizing the
papal archives. The comparison of sources, for which the Curia gave
him a unique possibility, offered him the opportunity of training and
utilizing his critical faculties and his flair, rare at that time, for
historical developments.[41]

Besides literature and poetry, Innocent appreciated the fine arts.
He had a portico built in front of his titular church of SS Sergius and
Bacchus, which he had had restored during his cardinalcy.[42] He also
made large-scale alterations among others to the Lateran and to the
Vatican Palace. He rebuilt the Hospital of the Holy Spirit and, under
the name of his brother Richard of Segni, erected the tremendous
tower which came to be called the Torre dei Conti.[43] Hospital and
tower were extolled by later generations as true wonders.[44] When, in
the time of Petrarch, an earthquake laid the tower in ruins, the poet
deplored the fall of a building that was unique in the whole world.[45]
Innocent had the mosaics in the ceiling of St Peter's renovated and
his portrait inlaid, a feature which reminds us of the popes of the
Renaissance. To numerous churches within and outside Rome he
made gifts of valuables of the goldsmith's art, of miniature-painting
and of embroidered mass-requisites, or contributed to their restoration and architectural embellishment. Experts judge that in the
drawing-up of his bulls Roman *maiestas* is in a most beautiful manner
combined with aesthetic sensitivity.[46] The "E" in the *Ego* of the
pope's signature and the Rota cross, which each pope drew himself,
stand out for their beautiful clarity.[47] The signatures of the cardinal
deacon of SS Sergius and Bacchus already show fine perception of
form and sureness and firmness of lineation.[48]

The picture of the rich and many-sided personality of Innocent III
is completed when we are informed that he was skilled in singing and
psalmody,[49] and that his ear was sensitive to dissonant voices and
harsh modulation.[50]

His external appearance corresponds well to the impression we
gain of the man Innocent: a small, delicate figure with attractive,
finely-drawn features and a clear, sonorous voice.[51]

The great variety of testimonials which allow us an insight into Innocent's private life and into the range of his interests show that he was no fanatic for work who, consumed by a passionate desire to be active and regardless of his frail body and of human wishes and needs, kept on labouring until his strength was exhausted. Rather he was imbued with the virtue of moderation which prevents work from becoming an obsession, a scourge of life. He allowed himself his siesta and, in the evening, probably some social entertainment. He frequently made excursions into the surroundings of Rome and liked to regale himself with the beauties of nature.[52] Gerald of Wales provides a charming account of one such excursion.[53] The bell of the Lateran Palace announces that Innocent has just left. The pope is taking one of his favourite outings to Fonte Vergine, "that very beautiful spring, situated to the south not far from the Lateran, which emits a flow of fresh water and sends a delightful rivulet down into the plain". Gerald hurries after the pope and finds him sitting, together with some of his entourage, a little apart from the rest of the retinue, by the bubbling spring, just as if in a room encompassed on all sides by water and waves. When the pope catches sight of the archdeacon, he has him called, invites him to join the group, and talks with him until their return to the town. At Ferentino, where Innocent liked to sojourn, it probably was, as at the Fonte Vergine near Rome, "the rich and beautiful spring" he himself had had dug, which attracted him.[54] Despite his manifold pursuits, Innocent found time to be active as an author[55] and to carry on a correspondence on theological questions.[56] His tremendous achievement may only have been possible because he was gifted with a mental strength which prevented him from becoming enslaved to work, and because his orderly and harmonious nature enabled him to seek and find relaxation and recreation in his writing, in entertainment and in the enjoyment of nature, even in jesting and playing.

It is striking that none of the men who report on the pope and his entourage from their own experience at the Curia, ever mention the name of his brother Richard or of any other member of the pope's family. Not a single personally couched word of the pope's to one of these relatives has come down to us in his letters, nor do the *Gesta* of the pope give any indication that a closer personal relationship existed between the pope and his lay relatives. We do know that Innocent availed himself of the services of these bellicose noblemen of Rome and the Campania in his political activities.[57] But clerics from his entourage, such devoted men as the cardinals Octavian[58] and Ugolino,[59] the later Gregory IX, will inwardly have appealed more to the finely educated intellectual man. How far Innocent was still interested in furthering his family, we cannot decide. He may have welcomed the glorious future which was opened to it by the matrimonial alliance agreed with the Staufen house. But when circumstances changed, he readily abandoned the project.[60] The family interest was in any case subordinate to the interests of church policy.

Innocent III's personal relationships to his fellow men were doubtless not only determined by the amiability of the man of the world and by personal affection or even aversion. He was by disposition kind and humane. Though easily flaring up and inclined to be impatient,[61] he was still quick to forgive.[62] The chronicler of Subiaco attests to Innocent's true kindliness when, after the pope had thoroughly visited and reformed the badly run-down monastery,[63] he praises him, with regard to this very visit under such depressing conditions, as righteous, as the mildest, holiest and kindest of men.[64] Warm-heartedly Innocent felt the woes and disappointments of those who came within his ken.[65] The monk of Evesham, who had been staying at the Curia for some time, knew that it was Innocent's way to comfort generously those afflicted.[66] One of the many to experience Innocent's kindness was probably Conrad of Querfurt, the deposed bishop of Würzburg and Hildesheim. When after his humiliation he offered the pope presents, Innocent hesitated to accept them. He did not wish Conrad to think that he could pave the way for his restoration by presents. But, on the other hand, he was reluctant to reject them, since he was loath to disoblige the humiliated bishop. He tactfully found a neat way out in that he accepted the bishop's presents, but sent him a present of greater value in return.[67]

The large-scale charitable activity which Innocent displayed was a matter of the heart for him, not only a duty of his office. On the news of a famine having broken out in Rome he at once hurried back to the city. How much he gave on that occasion, his biographer writes, was known to Him who is omniscient.[68] It was at this time that Innocent preached a particularly insistent sermon on the duty of charity. Anyone, he said, who in this emergency not contenting himself with keeping what was necessary, held onto surpluses, should know that he was guilty of murder as often as poor people died because of his avarice. For, the pope continues, if someone possessing riches of this world saw his brother suffer need, but still refused to proffer him the breasts of pity, how could the love of God live in him? Nobody should plead that it was enough to give according to one's means. He who possessed much, rather, had to give superabundantly, and he who possessed little, had to give even from this little sufficient to deprive himself of some of what he needs and of all that is superfluous.[69] The hospital by the church of S Maria in Sassia, the old foundation of the Anglo-Saxon kings, which Innocent rebuilt at his own expense, extended, and richly endowed, became the institution in which focussed and from which emanated the activities of Christian charity for the sick, for orphans and foundlings and for the poor. Legend has it that a fisherman with his net had saved two infants from the water and that, moved by this, the pope had instituted the hospital. The house accommodated at least three hundred inmates.[70] Innocent must be regarded as the co-founder of the Order of the Hospital of the Holy Spirit,[71] which he described as "his" order.[72] In any case, it was only through him that the order gained universal importance.[73] More than eight thousand public beggars were fed every day in the hospital. Innocent's biographer reports with praise that he had the hungry fed, the naked clothed, poor maids wedded, abandoned children tracked down and, through his almoners, found out the poor and infirm who were too ashamed to show their poverty openly; he helped them in secrecy.[74] The oblations due to him in St Peter's he employed for the poor, as well as a tenth of his total income and, according to ancient custom, those oblations which were made to him personally (*ad pedes ipsius*).[75] He frequently visited needy monasteries and released them from their debts or granted them generous relief.[76] It is significant that at his visitations of monasteries he laid particular stress on the monks fulfilling their duties of hospitality, of aid for the sick and of care for the poor,[77] and that he demanded from them, as when he visited the abbey of Monte Cassino, that they set aside unjust and excessive impositions, with which the dependents of the monastery were burdened.[78] Innocent's charitable work must be valued all the more highly because his political commitments must have cost enormous sums and he had at all times a wide open hand for the Holy Land.[79] His humanity is placed into full relief when he renounces returns due to him, if they are too heavy a burden for the debtor. During his stays at Ferentino in 1206 and 1208 he refuses to accept the provisions (*fodrum*) due to him from the churches in the bishopric, since, in view of his frequent visits to the city, they would have been unbearably burdened if they had to provide for his maintenance each time.[80] That Innocent also felt the distress of prisoners of war and of those wrongly oppressed and did all in his power to liberate them or to mitigate their miserable lot, we would assume, even if we had no evidence for it.[81] In fact, he approved and supported the Trinitarian Order of John of Matha in its efforts to ransom Christian prisoners and to have Christian prisoners exchanged for Moslem ones.[82] We are in no position either to affirm or to deny, whether his human feeling was totally irresponsive when, biassed by the convictions of his age, he ordered or tolerated harsh measures against the Jews and other "enemies" of the Church.[83]

*Vir multae discretionis et gratiae* Innocent is styled by a monk from the Alsatian monastery of Pairis.[84] He, indeed, possessed the *discretio*, the faculty of discernment, the judiciousness which knows how to differentiate between and to deal with people. It is not easy to translate the term *gratia*. It oscillates between the meaning of charm and amiability and the deeper sense of grace and benignity. It may be that the monk had only in mind the pope's amiability and the impression of his external appearance. But perhaps *gratia*, in the wide range of its implication, is also apt to fathom the character of the man Innocent in its most happy features.

Are we allowed to go beyond stating the range of Innocent's interests and his attitude towards men, and try to penetrate into the deeper psychic strata of his nature? May we venture to make statements on his relationship to God, on his inner attitude towards the demands of Christian moral law? Overabundantly the sources seem to flow in the wealth of his sermons, his writings and letters. But the letters, even in so far as Innocent himself drafted them, are to their very wording mostly of an official nature and, therefore, bear the stamp of officialdom. His writings and also some of his sermons sometimes repeat thoughts of others. Even if a critical edition of the pope's works[85] allowed us to distinguish reliably his own contribution from that of others, it would still prove difficult to gain access to the nature of his personality. The values to which the religious writer professes, the ideal of virtue which the scholar of moral theology and preacher sets up, correspond to an objective order of values and are not necessarily predicative of the natural echo which they found in his human existence, nor of the extent of his endeavours to realize them in his own life. The fact, for instance, that the pope – by full conviction – presents God and things divine as being for man the only good worth aspiring after, does not yet allow us to infer that he lived up to this conviction, nor even that he felt a strong personal relationship to the supernatural.

There are some personal statements of the pope on religious matters which do allow us some insight into his inner religious attitude and the nature of his religiosity. When the pope is informed that the inmates of a house living together in a religious community, despite a life of piety and penance, were bodily possessed and tormented by demons, that they spoke unholy and blasphemous words and from time to time forbore to do works of piety and to attend service, he gives no credence to the reports. It must be admitted, he answers, that the devil lays snares for the righteous, since he had tempted Christ himself. But he knew of no case nor had he ever read, that a person who had done true penance and was devoted to works of piety, had ever been bodily tormented by the devil. "Be it far from the Catholic faith", he exclaims, "that God's temple ever be the devil's abode and the sanctuary of the Holy Ghost a demon's lair. For there is no community between light and darkness and no agreement between Christ and Belial. We admit that, on occasion, saints such as Job have been outwardly threatened by demons, but We deny that they were inwardly tormented like men possessed." Christ himself, he continues, had testified in the Gospel: "If someone loves me, he will beware my word, and my Father will love him and we will come unto him and make our abode with him." "How then", he argues, "could the Evil One dare dwell in *him* whom Father and Son had chosen? We, therefore, hold what is reported to be a fabrication, unless those people are tormented because they pride themselves with such torments, or unless, being mentally deranged in consequence of leading too strict a life, they mistake mental illness for demoniacal torments."[87] To this very personal answer corresponds the profession to a *living* faith in God's mercy and in Christ's work of redemption and in His will to redemption, to which he once gave expression on the feast of the Conversion of St Paul: "Nobody should despair about the amount and gravity of his sins, because God not only accepts the penitent, but also draws the sinners to him as well . . . . Cain sinned gravely when he killed Abel, but he sinned even more gravely when he said: My sin is too grave for me to deserve remission. Far be it that a sin committed by men is greater than God's mercy. Nobody, therefore, may despair of God's mercy, because His mercies are above all works . . . . Is it, indeed, in vain that Christ rose from the dead and ascended to Heaven? Far

from it! That is the Catholic faith: His blood always calls to the
Father on our behalf . . . . We have an advocate with the Father, Jesus
Christ, the Righteous, who always prays for us by showing the
stigmata of His suffering."[88]

The pope's religious and dogmatic outlook manifests an occasionally surprising breadth and freedom. He does not stop at the letter,
the legal formula. As christening in water, without the supernatural
love of God, is for him mere fiction (*figmentum*), christening in tears
mere lamentation (*lamentum*), and christening in one's own blood
nothing but torment (*tormentum*), so faith and love, in his view, can
replace any sacrament. For one who is dying, but owing to an interdict
cannot receive the Eucharist, the Lord's Word is valid: *Crede et
manducasti*, believe and you have eaten.[89] Innocent stresses that
remission of sins is even effected before confession and absolution by
virtue of repentance and infusion of God's love.[90] A Jew who, in
danger of his life, had baptized himself and then died, even though
the baptism was invalid, would have at once hastened to the land of
the Father, not *propter fidei sacramentum*, but *propter fidem
sacramenti*, because of his faith in the sacrament.[91] When, in the
consistory, Innocent once deliberated with the brethren on the question whether a priest, who later discovered that he had not been
christened, was validly ordained, he opposed the view that before
baptism nobody could receive any other sacrament. He holds the
view that everybody, not only by virtue of the sacrament of faith, but
also by virtue of faith in the sacrament, doubtless becomes a limb of
Christ, and that everybody who possesses Christ by virtue of faith,
possesses, even if unchristened, the foundation without which
nothing could be erected: Jesus Christ.[92] However, he orders the
ordination of the priest to be repeated, but only in order to be on the
safe side and to pay respect to a decree of the Council.

Innocent's own piety is orientated towards the substance of Christian faith, it is Christo- and theocentric. His sermons even on Lady
Days and the commemoration days of other saints are entirely focussed on God and Christ and often put the person of the saint himself in
the background. In his sermons and writings, as well as in the
execution of his official functions, he also opposed excesses in the
worship of saints, images and relics, and naive and superstitious
religious fancies.[93]

The pope said mass with a piety which edified the pilgrims to
Rome.[94] He himself undertook to reform the ordinary as well as the

breviary for the use of the Roman Curia.[95] On the treatise which he devoted to the sacrifice of the mass,[96] he worked as cardinal and as pope.[97] It is the most voluminous, the most profound and the most personal of his writings.[98] Already in the book on the fourfold species of marriage which, on the whole, leaves the reader cold, personal engagement is noticeable in the words with which the author speaks about the sacrament of the Eucharist, the great banquet feast of the bridegroom for his bride in the New Testament.[99] When the then cardinal emphatically states that the altar table should be covered with precious clothes, the corporal woven from finest linen, and the mass-requisites made of gold and silver and decorated with precious stones,[100] we hear the future pope who had enquiries made in all the churches in Rome about the number of silver chalices and who endowed the 133 deficiencies "in awe of the sacred mystery of Christ's Body and Blood".[101] The very same pope who reduced his household to strict simplicity[102] and who ordered the silver and golden household effects to be replaced by those of wood and glass, provided his chapel with requisites made of gold and precious stones and with sumptuous chasubles.[103] He most strongly expressed his conviction of the great significance of the Eucharist in the Christian's life in that he imposed, at the Lateran Council, the duty on every Christian, once arrived at the years of discretion, of receiving the Eucharist at least once a year under penalty of exclusion from the Church.[104]

Innocent's entire literary work is ascetic-religious in nature. It is still surprising that among the works of this highly gifted lawyer there is not a single one devoted to canonistics, and that he did not even himself compile his decretals, but entrusted their compilation to his notary.[105] Innocent himself adduces as reason for his literary activity during his time as pope[106] his pastoral intention and his need to hold communion with himself, to directly concern himself with things divine, because of the worry that his religious life be endangered by his enmeshment in worldly affairs. "I am encumbered by so many legal cases brought before me and hampered by the fetters of so many pursuits.... No time is left to me for contemplation, not even enough time to breathe. I am so much at the mercy of others and that I am almost deprived of my own self", thus he writes to Abbot Arnold of Citeaux when sending him a collection of his sermons which, he states, he had preached and dictated so that, besides his care of the temporal affairs lying so heavily upon him because of the wickedness of the time, he should not altogether neglect his care for the spiritual matters which, by virtue of the duty of his apostolic office, were his prime concern.[107] We may believe the pope that, amid the overwhelming quantity of his pursuits, he struggled to preserve for himself a small part of his inner life, to regain his own self, to regale himself on the spring of religious life and, thereby, to fulfil the demand which, in his treatise on the sacrament of the Eucharist, he makes on the prelate: the combination of active and contemplative life.[108] His work, the commentary on the seven penitential psalms, Innocent completed three months prior to his death, on Easter Sunday, 10 April 1216.[109] In its preface he writes that, in order to avoid being dragged completely down by the many duties and the profound worries to which by the burden of the office (*ex cura regiminis*) and by the wickedness of the time he saw himself exposed beyond his powers, he liked to steal himself an hour or two to recall his mind to his inner self, so as to avoid becoming a stranger to himself and being so much at the mercy of others that he never rediscovered his own self. He who touched pitch would be defiled, he continues. He had taken for his subject the penitential psalm because the activities and troubles of this world often led to grave guilt, which must be expiated by grave penance.[110] Was Innocent thinking with these words also of his own grave guilt which he incurred through his enmeshment in temporal affairs? He who touches pitch will be defiled; the picture with which he characterizes the act of becoming guilty, he used to apply, according to the author of his *Gesta*, to his efforts in the Papal State,[111] to his political activities in general we may add without undue generalization. Could Innocent, in retrospect, have justified before his own conscience his policy of recuperations, his attitude in the throne contest between Philip of Swabia and Otto of Brunswick? Did he not impute it to his own guilt that he had made war and prolonged wars,[112] that he had taken too violent measures against defiant vassals in the Patrimony?[113] Had he not in an un-Christian way hated Markward of Anweiler and rejoiced at the excommunicate's death in a manner unbecoming a priest?[114] Was he aware that, when political necessities seemed to be at issue, he had misused ecclesiastical punitive measures without regard for the danger to the souls, that, for instance when lifting and imposing the interdict on Pisa purely for reasons of political expediency, he almost played fast and lose with all that is holy?[115] Did he realize that he had guiltily let pass things in silence, about which he ought not to have kept quiet,[116] that in the crooked ways of diplomacy he had denied truth?[117] John Capocci, the leader of the Roman-civic opposition, is said to have interrupted one of the pope's sermons with the invective: "Your words are God's words, but your works are the devil's works".[118] Here, the hatred of the political adversary, in a coarsening and distorting manner, points to a discrepancy in Innocent's life, to the discrepancy between Innocent the priest and pastor and Innocent the statesman and territorial sovereign. Did Innocent feel the deep import of the tragic involvement in this discrepancy which, indeed, was a general symptom of the medieval papacy? It is true that even for him, the bright and clear thinker, the state of facts may have more easily become obfuscated than for the modern observer, since he lived in an age and in an environment which was less precise in distinguishing between the honour of, and the service to, God and the honour and advantage of the Church in its earthly manifestation. But he, too, could not but recognize an obvious violation of Christian moral law as such, which thereby constituted a guilty act. Innocent III has been labelled an unscrupulous politician. It is certain that he did not *unscrupulously* do wrong. Nor was he unscrupulous in the sense that *any* means was acceptable to him to attain a political aim. At least he did not sacrifice the sanctity of the bonds of marriage, not even to the most pressing political needs.[119]

Innocent bowed in reverence to men who, endangered similarly to himself, had still in piety remained pure in this world of entanglements, to men such as Gregory VIII, the man of saintly memory,[120] and Bishop Peter of Ivrea,[121] the former abbot of the Cistercian monastery of la Ferté and later patriarch of Antioch. These men, of whom he had convinced himself that they obeyed the voice of conscience without regard to the consequences, he treated with high esteem. It is reported that, during the German throne contest, the pope's visitor Bishop Conrad of Halberstadt, who was a loyal follower of Philip of Swabia, departed in his good grace, probably because he had come to know him as an upright and truly religious man.[122]

A last question, to what extent Innocent was susceptible to the relish for fame and honour, to the relish, above all, for power,[123] is hardly to be answered with certainty. It is unlikely that such sentiments played a significant rôle in the pope's life. The sense of moderation peculiar to him and his conservative mind do not allow us to regard him as a man possessed by the demon of power, as among his contemporaries was Emperor Henry VI and as before him had been Gregory VII. Innocent was devoid of anything that is daemonic. His strength was not rooted in instincts. His strong will responded to the guidance of a keen intellect and of a clear and wide-ranging comprehension. Love of the Church and abandonment to the idea of papacy were in any case the paramount motives for his actions.

Innocent III was only fifty-five years old when, at Perugia on 16 July 1216, he fell victim to fever which had already once during his reign brought him to the verge of the grave. "He who so recently had been sitting in great glory on the throne, now lies unnoticed (*despectus*) in his grave; he who so recently had in brilliant array been shining in the high hall, now decays (*sordet*) naked in his coffin."[124] What the young cardinal had written in his work on human misery, came conspicuously true in his own case. In the night following his death burglars plundered his corpse. The next morning his body was found naked and already in a state of decomposition. Shocked, James of Vitry reports: "But I entered the church and saw with my own eyes how transitory and vain the deceiving splendours of this world are."[125] The funeral was held in the church of St Laurence at Perugia.[126] At some later date his bones were heedlessly thrown together with those of Urban IV and Martin IV in a box which was stored in a cupboard in the sacristy of the new cathedral. When this box was opened in 1605 on the occasion of its transfer to the cathedral chapel of St Stephen, the only remains found of the great pope were a few broken and jumbled bones.[127] Leo XIII ordered the bones of his great predecessor to be brought home to Rome, to the Lateran Palace, the main place of Innocent's activities. A priest brought them, packed up in a suitcase, back to Rome by rail.[128] It was as if the dead testified once again that the splendour of the world is transient.

### Notes to Chapter 10

[1]Sommeraufenthalt, 511ff.

[2]*A quarto latere, quot calentem solem plenius intuetur...* (Hampe, Sommeraufenthalt, 531).

[3]According to Hampe (*op. cit.* 521) probably those who were given no nursing in the run-down monastery which Innocent was then trying to reform (cf. Berlière, 39f,),

[4] See Elze, 171ff., for the papal chaplains under Innocent III.

[5] Ann. Casin. 319.

[6] In the sermon he gave at his ordination he himself confesses that his strength was not that of stones nor his flesh of iron (Migne PL. 217, 656). In the first six months of his pontificate we hear of an illness which, at the least, handicapped him in his affairs (Reg. I 456). Towards the end of November of the following year he mentions a weakness which had hampered him in his work (Reg. II 207). In October 1203 he was ill for some length of time and indeed so seriously that he was reported to be dead (Gesta c. 37; Reg. VI 191; RNI 91, 96). Towards the end of 1209 we hear again of the pope having fallen ill (RNI 177). With the exception of his illness in 1203 all reports of such illnesses are extant by sheer chance. We therefore must consider it possible that in fact he was ill even more often. One of his addresses to the Lateran Council is imbued with presentiments of death (Migne PL. 217, 673ff.) and indeed he succumbed to an attack of fever in the following year when he was still in his prime.

[7] See Chron. Andr. 737f.; Girald. Cambrens. 3, 195; Gesta c. 135; Ann. Casin. *loc. cit.*

[8] *Sed datum est nobis remedium graciosum: quocienscumque in talibus fatigamur, ad fontem currimus aque vive ad vicarium Jesu Christi, cui thesauri sunt tocius sapiencie et eloquencie commodati, qui licet a Martha* [the *m* which follows in the wholly corrupt manuscript is corrected by Hampe to *non*, but a negative at this point does not make for good sense] *fuerit hospicio susceptus, cum Maria tamen a nobis cogitur hospitari, cum qua circa pedes eius familiariter residentes in verbis gracie delectamur et sic diucius commorantes haurimur aquam in gaudio de fontibus salvatoris et . . . utriusque hominis indigencie satisfacimus copiose . . .* (Hampe, 535). We learn from a letter of Thomas of Capua that when on one occasion Innocent was obliged to stay in Rome during the fever days of high summer, he gave leave of absence to a number of curial officials – to the timid ones it seems – until the weather changed for the better (see Summa dictaminis, Heller, 259).

[9] A miniature in the second volume of Innocent III's Registers may shed some light on the pope's attitude to his fellow workers at the Curia. The cardinal chancellor and two secretaries are offering Innocent the seventh book of the register. The secretaries are lying at the pope's feet and he is blessing them with the words written on the banderol: *Sic pueri, nostra vobis benedictio prosit. In fructu vitae presentis ut auxilietur* (Luchaire, L'avènement, 705). From the pope's correspondence with his legates we know that he was always ready to express his thanks and recognition to his colleagues and to console them in their difficulties. He measured their work not only by the success it had and did not blame them for failures which were not their fault. When Cardinal Soffred of St Praxedis complained of the trials and disappointments he had suffered in the Holy Land (Gesta c. 118), Innocent writes to him a warm consoling letter. He assures the cardinal of his sympathy, adding that everyone would be rewarded by the measure of their efforts. He must not, he writes, be grieved if he should not achieve all he had wished, provided only that he did not omit anything that ought to be done. He shared, he writes, the cardinal's suffering, his pains were his own pains and he would do all he could to ease his burden. He would not forget him, even if owing to the great distance he could not send letter or messenger as often as he wished (Reg. VI 130). Urging the same cardinal to accept the call to the patriarchate of Jerusalem, Innocent takes pains to forestall the impression that he forewent Soffred's company and collaboration with indifference. He emphasizes how much he would miss him and how close he felt to him in personal respects (Reg. VI 129). He encourages and

comforts the cardinals Ugolino of Ostia and Leo of S Croce, his legates during the difficult negotiations to bring to an end the throne dispute, when matters seem not to be going as desired or not speedily enough (RNI 147–149). On one occasion he writes to them that even though they were, in the first instance, working for God, he knew that they were also working for him. They could, therefore, confidently expect to be rewarded by him, the pope (RNI 148). Once he sends a warmly-worded letter of recognition to Cardinal legate Peter Capuano, Soffred's colleague as crusading legate (Reg. VI 209). He praises Cardinal John of St Paul, cardinal priest of S Prisca, in a letter to third parties, for the cardinal's successful accomplishment of a task he had been given (Reg. I 557). Innocent's amiability and benevolence towards his colleagues naturally do not preclude him, in case of a serious violation of duty, from giving them a stern reprimand as happened to the above-mentioned cardinals Soffred and Peter Capuano, when on the news of the capture of Constantinople by the Latins they had forsaken the Holy Land without permission and had hurried to Constantinople (Reg. VIII 126).

[10]The writer of this letter relates that "when we descend to the charming island spots under the thick crowns of the trees to stroll about there, then we carry the crucifix not on horseback but as pedestrians ... in an unseemly manner on our shoulders" (Hampe, 513). This seems to refer to a descent of the pope and his entourage, in the van of which, as usual, the cross was carried.

[11]Chron. Andr. 737. Thomas Marleberge, the monk of Evesham, confirms what the report of the chronicler of Andres leads us to believe, that it was not difficult to gain access to the pope. Such difficulties as there were are more likely to have been due to the doorkeepers than to the pope's will (Chron. Evesham 169). Cf. also Caesarius (Schönbach 2), 34.

[12]Chron. Evesham 184.

[13]In addition to the comments already quoted cf. the characteristics given the pope by Gunther of Pairis (75): *vir multae discretionis et gratias... praesul amabilis et venerabilis, ac generosus,* and the statements by Thomas Marleberge of Evesham (Chron. Evehsam, 199): *dominus papa ut erat curialissimus, more suo liberalissime oppressos consolans,* and by Gerald of Wales who held the pope's attitude to him to have been always kind and benevolent (Girald. Cambr. 3, 165; cf. also *ibid.* 241).

[14]Ann. Cecc. 296f.

[15]See Hurter 2, 744 note 244.

[16]Girald. Cambr. 3, 252ff.

[17]*Ibid.* 254f.

[18]*Ibid.* 1, 426.

[19]*Ipse cum quibusdam aliis apud basilicam Constantinanam voluit decessoris exsequiis interesse* (Gesta c. 5).

[20]See n. 10 above.

[21]Girald. Cambr. 3, 267.

[22]Chron. Evesham 160.

[23]*Ibid.* 153.

[24]Gesta Trevirorum Cont. IV (MG. SS. 24) 391.

[25]MG. SS. 32, 31f. Cato's words *Interpone tuis interdum gaudia curis,* which Salimbene adapts, Innocent himself had addressed to his listeners in sermons at Gaudete and Laetare (Migne PL. 217, 338, 393).

[26]Reg. VII 20.

[27]Reg. III 10.

[28]Girald. Cambr. 3, 176, 181.

[29]*Ibid.* 94.

[30]As can be seen from the copious quotations in his works, especially the *De misera.* Such quotations may occasionally even be found in his official documents; he seems to have had a predilection for Horace.

[31]From the arenga of a privilege for the Latin bishop of Athens (Reg. XI 256).

[32]He frequently uses Greek words in his writings, often in Greek script (Migne PL. 217, 411, 489, 633f., 635, 675, 781f.). The following reference to Greek is particularly significant: Innocent interprets the passage from the psalms *Unxit te Deus, Deus tuus* with *Deus Pater unxit te, Deus Fili,* justifying his interpretation: *Quod in Graeco satis elucet, in quo vocativus a nominativo distinguitur* (Migne PL. 217, 959). See also *ibid.* 359, 988.

[33]Girald. Cambr. 1, 119.

[34]Gesta c. 1. Innocent also seems to have had some knowledge in natural science. In his works he refers on a number of occasions to the views of those, *qui de rerum naturis edisserunt* (Migne PL. 217, 582, 680) or of the *physici* (Migne PL. 214, 1121) although such views could have come to him second hand.

[35]Girald. Cambr. 1, 110 and 3, 336.

[36]According to Holmes, Gerald the naturalist (Speculum 11, 1936) 110ff., the description of the fauna of Ireland reveals such a high degree of accurate observation that the work approaches the best parts of Albert the Great's *De animalibus.*

[37]Girald. Cambr. 2, 187f.

[38]*Ibid.* 188f., 360.

[39]*Ibid.* 332.

[40]For Paris see above Chapter 1; for Bologna, Maccarrone, Innoc., 80f.

[41]When asked why no collects were directed specifically to the Holy Ghost in the same way as to the Father and the Son, Innocent holds the view that the early Church had at first addressed the Father only in the collects, later also the Son when the divinity of Christ had been denied by heretics. When subsequent heretics had challenged even the divinity of the Holy Ghost, the Church had drawn up in hymns and litanies special prayers to the Holy Ghost, but left the traditional form of the collects as it was (Reg. VI 193 col. 218ff.). A possible explanation of the absence of a *Commemoratio* of the confessors in the canon of the mass Innocent sees in the assumption that the canon developed at a time when the Church had not yet begun to venerate the confessors (*De sacro alt. myst.* Migne PL. 217, 849). To answer this question Innocent made use of the *Liber pontificalis* (as testimony for the transformation of the pantheon under Boniface IV into a church of the Virgin Mary and All Martyrs; Lib. pont. 1, 317), of St Jerome (as witness for the form of the catalogue of apostles in the earlier manuscripts), of the register of Gregory the Great (as testimony for the composition of the *secreta super eucharistiam*) and probably of the so-called sacramentary of Gelasius as well. He arrives at his conclusion from the statements in the sources, from his study of the catalogue of saints contained in the canon and the names of the saints to whom the early bishops' churches were consecrated. In his works Innocent has regard to differing readings and translations of his texts (in commentaries on the Epiphany he notes that it was called Epiphaniarum in earlier codices, Migne PL. 217, 485, Sermo VIII in solemn. apparit. Cf. also Migne PL. 217, 849, 983, 987f., 1006, 1009, 1028, 1058, 1091). He makes it a point to use authentic sources. Thus he tried to establish the

history of the mass from authentic sources. In respect of one ceremony he once says that he had heard the reason, the historical, that is, not the allegorical, from a number of people. But since he had not been able to find any mention of it in an authentic text, he thought it better to pass it over in silence than to state it light-heartedly as a fact (Migne PL. 217, 911).

His critical attitude to documents, which seems to anticipate modern lines of approach, is as surprising to us as it was amazing to his contemporaries (Gesta c. 42. For further details see Krabbo, Die Urkunde Gregors IX. für das Bistum Naumburg vom 8. November 1228, MIÖG 25, 275ff.). He discovers the falsification of a single word in one of Nicholas II's bulls for the monastery of S Felicita in Florence by an erasure and by the different shades of ink and restores the original text in his confirmation of the privilege of 22 June 1209 (see the *Regestum* in Davidsohn, Forsch. 1, 187).

[42]Gesta c. 4, 145.

[43]On Innocent's own building activity and his efforts to decorate and enrich churches and other buildings in and around Rome see Gesta c. 4, 14, 145, 146, 127; Ptolemy of Lucca (SS. rer. Germ., ed. Schmeidler, 1930), 90; Gilberti Chron. Pont. et. Imp. Rom. (MG. SS. 24) 134. Literature: Reumont, Geschichte d. Stadt Rom 3 (1868), 453f.; Gregorovius, 648ff.; Hurter 2, 781ff.; Luchaire, Innocent III 1, 211f.; Burdach, Walthers Kampf, 499ff.; Cabrol-Leclercq 12 (1935) 269ff.

[44]Ptolemy of Lucca *loc. cit.* Cf. Gregorovius 5, 649f.

[45]See Gregorovius, *loc. cit.*

[46]Katterbach u. Peitz, Die Unterschriften der Päpste und Kardinäle in den "Bullae Maiores" vom 11. bis 14. Jahrh. (Misc. Fr. Ehrle, Studi e Testi 40, 1924), 243.

[47]*Ibid.* 243f. Cf. the plates appended to the essay, esp. nos. 62B, 65A, 66.

[48]See plates nos. 61, 62B in Katterbach-Peitz. Cf. *ibid.* 243.

[49]Gesta c. 1.

[50]*De sacro alt. myst.* (Migne PL. 217) 775.

[51]*Statura mediocris et decorus aspectu* (Gesta c. 1); *forma conspicuus* (Gunther of Pairis 75); *pusillus statura, sed pulcher... vox eius sonora, et, si suppresse proferebatur, audiebatur ab omnibus et intelligebatur* (Codex of Perugia, cf. Bonazzi 1, 268). On portraits of the pope see Luchaire, L'Avènement, 70ff. According to H. Thode (Franz von Assisi und die Anfänge der Kunst der Renaissance in Italien, 1934, 91) the fresco portrait in the chapel of Gregory IX in the Sacro Speco of Subiaco is one of the paintings completed in 1228. A portrait in the abbey of St Peter in Ferentillo, which was restored by Innocent, also seems to depict the pope (Marchetti-Longhi, 287f.). A study by G. Ladner on papal portraits of antiquity and the modern age was not accessible to me.

[52]Besides the exposition in the following text see the report by the curial official in Hampe, Sommeraufenthalt, (p. 290 above).

[53]Op. 3, 252ff.

[54]Gesta c. 137.

[55]See Chapter 6 n. 64, and pp. 300–2 above.

[56]Reg. V 121, VI 193, XX 7; Rainer of Pomposa 1, *Si personas* (Migne PL. 216, 1175 to the resigned Archbishop John of Lyons, Bishop Uguccio of Ferrara and the archbishop of Compostela).

[57]For Richard and his son see Chapter 5 above; for his relatives and in-laws in general, see Seeger, 42ff.; for his cousin, the marshal James, Chapter 5 above and for his cousin Trasimund of Segni see Chapter 5 n. 274.

[58]The cardinal, Lothair's erstwhile fatherly friend (see above Chapter 1 n. 20 for the supposed descent of the cardinal from the house of Segni), writes to him as "his Octavian", asking him, his most beloved father and most noble lord, to think of him in love (Reg. III 15). To a rebuke to Octavian which Innocent feels he is obliged to give and which he expresses, though distinctly, as considerately as possible, he subjoins the remark that he had spoken to him about the matter *familiariter et fiducialiter*, confidentially and trustingly, as the friend to the friend whom he embraces in purest love (Reg. III 16. See also Girald. Cambr. 3, 270).

[59]Familiarity combined with a deep respect and devotion on the part of the subordinates is evident in a letter Ugolino wrote to inform the pope of his return from a legation which had been completed sooner than expected. He was hastening to return to Innocent whom he had left regretfully albeit obediently (RNI 152. Hints to the close and trusting relationship between Innocent III and Ugolino in Girald. Cambr. 3, 181f., 267). Richard of San Germano reports (70) that Gregory IX formally celebrated the anniversary of Innocent's death when visiting Perugia in 1228.

[60]See Chapter 5 above.

[61]*Naturae aliquantulum indignantis, sed facile ignoscentis* (Gesta c. 1). His gruff demeanour towards Archbishop Peter of Sens (Reg. VI 151) for disobedience to papal mandates, his cutting reproof of the French episcopate (cf. Chapter 9 above and *ibid.* n. 28) for its indifference to the cause of the cross, and of the English episcopate for its attitude in the conflict of the king with his barons (Rymer 1[1], 138), may owe their sharpness partly to Innocent's personal indignation.

[62]Gesta c. 1. When he learns how deeply Archbishop Peter, his former teacher (cf. Chapter 1 above), grieves over the treatment he had received by the pope, he sends him a consoling letter in which he explains in a kind manner the reason for his severity and asks him not to doubt his love (Reg. VI 236).

[63]Hampe, Sommeraufenthalt, 521.

[64]Chron. Sublacense 34f. Innocent's human and brotherly attitude in the case of the severely inculpated bishop of Pecs (see above Chapter 3) is particularly appealing.

[65]Cf. Chapter 3 above.

[66]Chron. Evesham 199.

[67]Gesta c. 44.

[68]Gesta c. 143. These events took place in the early months of 1202 (cf. Reg. V 6).

[69]Migne PL. 217, 441ff.

[70]On the occasion of the service of the stations of the cross, which Innocent had inaugurated there and in which the pope in office is to preach on the works of charity, a distribution of bread, wine and meat to one thousand poor people from outside and to three hundred inmates of the hospital is arranged (Gesta 144, Reg. X 179).

[71]The rule which he gave the Hospital of the Holy Spirit, founded by him, and whose direction was entrusted to Guido of Montpellier (Reg. VII 95), has in any case not been adopted solely by Montpellier. We need not investigate here how accurately the text of the rule in Migne PL. 217, 1137 conforms to the rule given by Innocent.

[72]He speaks of the *religio hospitalis nostri Sancti Spiritus* (Reg. XI 169). See Fliche, 138f., for the relationship between the Order and the pope. See also Reiche, Das deutsche Spital und sein Recht im Mittelalter 1 (Kirchenr. Abh., ed. Stutz 111, 1932), 166ff.

[73]Donations such as those from King John of England (Mercati, 285ff.), perhaps also from the bishop of Chartres (Reg. X 223) and the count of Blankenburg (Reg. XI 69) may have been bestowed upon the Order owing to its powerful protector.

[74]Gesta c. 143.

[75]*Ibid.*

[76]Thus he offered a thousand pounds to clear the debts of a monastery near Viterbo and held out the prospect of further assistance (Reg. X 205, Gesta c. 149). He made a gift of a thousand pounds in gold to the nuns of Acre for the acquisition of landed property and of one thousand silver marks once to the Hospital of the Holy Spirit (Gesta c. 149).

[77]Reg. V 82, XI App. Migne PL. 215, 1593.

[78]Reg. XI *loc. cit.* He makes it easier for the monastery to meet his demand by granting it an annuity of two pounds of silver during his lifetime. Also to the monastery of Subiaco he assigns revenues in order to lighten its duty of *hospitalitas* again imposed upon it (Reg. V 82, P. 1721a.).

[79]See above Chapter 9.

[80]Ann. Cecc. 296f.

[81]Innocent regarded the miserable captivity of thousands of Christians in Saracen dungeons as one of the necessary reasons for taking up a crusade (Reg. XVI 28). At the end of a war between Florence and Siena he urges the victors to repatriate the prisoners (Reg. X 62). When he establishes peace in April 1201 between the cities of the March of Ancona he ordered, after hearing the parties and examining the documents, that all prisoners be handed over to his procurators in the first instance. All ransoms which should have been paid after the arrival of the pope's order to release the prisoners are likewise to be handed over to the procurators (BF. 5749). After Rome's victory over Viterbo, with whom he himself was at odds at the time, he takes pains to ease the lot of the miserably treated prisoners (Gesta c. 134, 135). During the war with Terracina he orders the Frangipani, his allies, to hand over the prisoners to him. When he has to return them to the Frangipani because the citizens did not give them satisfaction according to the pope's decision (cf. the granting of the revenues due to the Roman Church in Terracina to the Frangipani by Celestine II, 1143, Falco, 704), he makes the prior condition that no harm be done to them (Contatore, D.A., De Historia Terracinensi libri quinque, 1706, 176). During the last campaigns in the border regions of the Patrimony and the Sicilian kingdom (see Chapter 5 above) the commanders of the papal army, in deference to the pope, forgo the usual methods of torturing and mutilating the prisoners and pay money instead for the surrender of the castle whose garrison refused to capitulate in defiance of the promise given by the enemy commander on his capture (Gesta c. 39). Innocent intervenes with the dukes of Poland and Pomerelia on behalf of the newly-converted Prussians who were being so heavily harassed with slavish tributes by the princes that those converted to the freedom of the Christian faith were worse off than at the time of their subjection to heathendom. He instructs the archbishop of Gnesen to protect the new converts from unjust oppression, if necessary by imposing ecclesiastical punishments (Reg. XV 148. See also Reg. XVI 121). Innocent's embitterment, even hatred, towards Markward of Anweiler may, therefore, be due also to the terrible atrocities which had been perpetrated in Sicily by Henry VI, and, as Innocent believes, with Markward's complicity (cf. Reg. III 23).

[82]Reg. I 481. See also Reg. II 9, XIV 146–148; Leclercq 1735; Horoy 2, 251 (Hon. Ep. I 206). Cf. Fliche, 139f. and Maccarrone, Innoc., 78f.

[83]On this question, as regards heretics and schismatics, Chapter 7 above.

[84]Gunther of Pairis 75.

[85]A critical edition of the work *De misera condicione hominis* by M. Maccarrone is forthcoming in the *Thesaurus mundi.*

[86]Fliche, Chrétienté, 16ff., seems to disregard this fact. Nor does his assessment of the pope's letters pay sufficient attention to the realities of the situation in which they were written.

[87]Reg. VIII 157.

[88]Sermo IX in festo convers. (Migne PL. 217), 491ff.

[89]Reg. XI 102 bis.

[90]Comment. in VII psalm. poenit. (Migne PL. 217), 1016. See amongst others Pr. coll. t. 31 de sent. exc. (Migne PL. 216), 1248.

[91]Reg. IX 159.

[92]Reg. IX 54.

[93]To a piety which although showing true zeal is not according to wisdom, he opposes, in sharp distinction to the adoration due to God alone, the true manner of veneration of saints and images (Migne PL 217, 436ff.). By a clear exposition of the essence of saintliness and canonization (Reg. I 530) he corrects devious conceptions (cf. Chapter 2 above). At the Lateran Council he forbids the display of newly-discovered relics without papal approval. The bishops are not to permit visitors to their churches to be deceived by vain fictions and false documents nor to allow the alms collectors to narrate anything that differs from their letters of authority (can. 62 Leclercq 1381, c. 2 X 3, 45 and c. 14 X 5, 38). In response to a request by the patriarch of Constantinople, Innocent does confirm the patriarch's decision against the Venetians who, by a sacrilegious act of force, had seized one of the paintings hung in the church of Hagia Sophia and allegedly painted by the Evangelist Luke, but he adds that in no case did he approve, as being superstitious, of the opinion of some Greeks who seemed to value the picture beyond its due, being convinced that the spirit of the Holy Virgin rested in it (Reg. IX 243).

[94]Emonis chron. 471.

[95]Salimbene (MG. SS. 32) 31. On the ordinary revised on the basis of Innocent III's liturgical reform see Andrieu, Le missel de la chapelle papale à la fin du XIIIe siècle (Misc. Fr. Ehrle, Studi e testi 38, 1924), 374ff.; Jungmann, Missarum sollemnia 1 (1949) 128f. Cf. also Andrieu, Le pontifical p. 319, and Baumstark, Missale Romanum (1929), 144f., Cabrol, Missel romain (Cabrol-Leclercq 11, 1934) 1481, Maccarrone, Innoc., 110f., and Elze, 172. On Innocent III's reforms of the breviary see Batiffol, Histoire du bréviaire romain ([3]1911), 238ff. A chance comment in *De sacro alt. myst.* (see above, Chapter 3, n. 67) might be an index to a point of view which was a criterion for Innocent's reform, that of simplification (cf. lately Moeller, Un cas d'abbréviation de l'office romain au XIIIe siècle: les litanies du samedi saint, Misc. Hist. in hon. L. van der Essen 1947, 340ff.).

[96]Migne PL. 217, 773ff.

[97]Cf. Chapter 1 above.

[98]Thalhofer-Eisenhofer, Handbuch der Katholischen Liturgik ([2]1912), 127f. (also containing a summary of the work). Cf. Jungmann 1, 142, and Maccarrone, Innoc., 110ff. In this work, too, Innocent subscribes to the allegorical way of thinking which is so unfamiliar to the modern mind. As usual he holds the meaning of the ceremonies of the mass to be the depiction of the life of Christ. However, material and historical annotations are given their right as well as deeply pious contemplation on the Holy mysteries.

[99]Migne PL. 217, 945ff.

[100]*Ibid.* 947.

[101]At the Lateran Council he lamented before the whole Church that sometimes not

only the churches were in a neglected state but that even the holy vessels, the altar cloths and the corporals were so dirty as to be repulsive. It was altogether contrary to common sense to tolerate filth, which was disgusting enough in the profane world, in the sanctuary (can. 19, Leclercq 1349, c. 2 X 3, 44).

[102]See Chapter 6 above.

[103]Gesta c. 144. Gregorovius describes a chasuble in the church of Anagni which he ascribes – unfortunately without giving reasons – to Innocent III, as being richly interwoven with gold and adorned with pictures of such striking beauty that they reminded him of paintings by Giotto or Fiesole (Wanderjahre in Italien 2, 1883, 109).

[104]Can. 21.

[105]Petrus Collivaccinus of Benevento (See Heyer, 395ff.), formerly master in Bologna and later cardinal deacon of S Maria in Aquiro. As such he acted as legate in southern France in 1215 (see Chapter 7 above).

[106]The extant works dating from his time as cardinal he wrote, according to his own statement, the one to fill in some leisure time, the other on the initiative of and to a theme given him by a third party (Migne PL. 217, 701, 921f.).

[107]Migne PL. 217, 311f. In the *Conclusio* of the *De sacro alt. myst.* he writes in similar vein: *Cum ex officio tot causarum sim impeditus incursibus, tot negotiorum nexibus irretitus, ut infra breve temporis spatium, nec ad meditandum otium nec ad dictandum quiverim nacisci quietem. Et quidem minor in singulis, divisus ad singula vix potui meditata dictare, nedum meditando concipere (ibid.* 914). Cf. also *ibid.* 381.

[108]Migne PL. 217, 798.

[109]See Maccarrone, Innoc., 108f.

[110]Migne PL. 217, 967ff.

[111]Gesta c. 17.

[112]Cf. Chapter 5 above.

[113]He had the crops of the nobles of Narni and Gabriano and such noblemen-highwayrobbers as the nobles of Raspampano devastated, the fruit trees felled, the mills broken and all chattels carried away (Gesta c. 15, 134).

[114]Reg. V 89.

[115]Davidsohn (Gesch. von Florenz 1, 623f.) is not wrong when he characterizes the events in such terms. Being the supreme defender of justice, Innocent could hardly justify the punishment of bishops and their churches respectively, by curtailing their legal position for offences committed by their diocesans (cf. Böhmer, Acta, 631f.; BF. 6112; Reg. I 123; Tillmann, Über päpstliche Schreiben, 193).

[116]Cf. Chapter 7 above.

[117]The register of the throne dispute is tendentiously compiled. It was its particular aim to veil the pope's real reasons for his decision in Otto's favour. Otto's first renunciation of the recuperations of 1200 is, therefore, no more included (cf. Grundmann in his review of Kempf, Regestum, ZRG. Kan. Abt. 37, 1951, 428f.), than the written and sealed pledge on the renunciation made by his envoys (RNI 20 refers to this) and all the documents on the negotiations with Philip of Swabia about the recuperations.

RNI 65 contains a palpable falsehood in that Innocent holds out to Otto the hope that the king of France might alter his policy, referring to a letter, which he, the pope, had recently received from the king. The letter (RNI 63 it seems) contains nothing which would support such interpretation, on the contrary it was to destroy any hope whatever of the king changing his policy (for further discussion see Kempf, Regestum, 187 n. 6).

It is another distortion of the truth when Innocent states that the ancestors of Philip of Swabia had nearly always been persecutors of the church of Cologne (RNI 80, Kempf, Regestum, 217) and that Henry the Lion had been deprived of his inheritance by the emperor on account of the Lombard case (RNI 92, Kempf, Regestum, 244). At least light-hearted is the charge that Philip of Swabia *ambitionis vitio* had arrogated the dominion to himself in his nephew's stead. It is indeed most unlikely that Innocent, by a perusal of the imperial privileges granted to the Roman Church, had in fact satisfied himself of the right of the Curia to Tuscany (Reg. I 15, cf. Chapter 5 above). While it would be wrong to dismiss the pope's statements on Philip's aims in Sicily as deliberate falsifications, yet they scarcely reflect the whole truth (Cf. Chapter 5 above, n. 34. Cf. also Kempf, Regestum, 79). The same must be said for his assertion, which sounds improbable though, that Markward intended to make himself king. A seemingly false statement by the pope on a betrothal of Frederick of Sicily to Constance of Aragon, Frederick's later wife, must be set aside since the text of the register does not give the fiancée's name. It refers not to Constance but to Sancha of Aragon. When the letter with the allegedly false statement (RNI 111) was issued (27 October) Constance's first husband, Imre of Hungary, was still living (he died on 30 November). Cf. Kempf, Regestum, 277 n. 3. Often quoted as a conspicuous piece of evidence of a direct lie is the pope's statement in Reg. V 128 that Philip of France had married Agnes of Meran before he had been served the papal prohibition. In Reg. I 171 and II 197 Innocent had stated the contrary, namely that Philip had got married despite many prohibitions by the Church, one of which had been read in the king's presence by a notary and by the deceased Cardinal legate Melior (cf. Tenbrock, 82f.). I am far from whitewashing Innocent from the imputation, yet the facts of the case are by no means as clear as they appear to be on first sight. As Innocent relates the facts in the letter of legitimation of November 1201, Philip, in the time between the issue of Reg. II 197 and V 128, had asserted *vehementer* that the prohibition had not, probably meaning 'not before the marriage', been delivered to him. The king might perhaps have maintained that he had contracted his second marriage before receiving Cardinal Melior. Such an assertion would have been difficult to disprove because the formal act of marriage, then, was not so easily ascertainable as nowadays, since it need not be performed solemnly in the sight of the Church. Philip also might have denied the fact of a formal notification. Even if the pope personally need not believe these reasons he could not officially disregard them forthwith. I should like to point to two events which might show certain parallels to the case in question. In 1213 Innocent allows the bishop of Treviso, who maintained that he had not received a mandate of suspension from the papal legate, to continue to administer the bishopric until the mandate was delivered to him, always provided that he did not prevent the letter from being served on him (Reg. XV 195). In this case a mandate whose existence is known both to the pope and the addressee, is ignored because it has actually or allegedly not been delivered in due form. The second case shows how strictly Innocent distinguished between what he personally knew and what he had learnt in his official capacity. On the confidential intimation by Thomas Morosini, patriarch of Constantinople, of an oath he had sworn to the Venetians concerning appointments to ecclesiastical offices, Innocent stresses in his reply that he had already some time before come to know something of the affair *ex certa relatione* (Reg. IX 130), i.e. that he could use his knowledge against the patriarch. Later, when the patriarch is accused at the Curia of having sworn this same oath Innocent declares that thereby, *si ita est* or *si dictis veritas suffragatur*, Thomas had committed a grave sin (Reg. XI 76). The patriarch's procurator had disavowed the oath at the Curia. Innocent makes use of the patriarch's confession neither against the patriarch's delegates nor against Thomas himself, but on the basis of the reports forwarded to him in the matter directs that the oath he publicly repudiated if the patriarch freely confessed that he had sworn such an oath. We must also be careful not to assume want of the pope's veracity whenever two letters seem to be contradictory. In such cases the question arises as to whether the contradictions do not derive from the fact that one of the letters was for conditional delivery only (thus, for example, of the letters Reg. VI 164 and 167, the letter numbered 164 is only for conditional delivery; see Reg. VI 165, 166).

[118]Caesarius (Strange 1) 103.

[119]Cf. Chapter 3 above and Appendix 2 below.

[120]Cf. Chapter 1 above, n. 60.

[121]On Innocent's order Peter had accepted the bishopric of Ivrea, but a few days later had fled to live in solitude again because, amongst other reasons, the church possessed revenues which he had realized were unlawful. In an amiable letter Innocent requested Peter to return to his bishopric and, wholly contrary to his normal practice in such cases, which he regarded as a grave contravention against church discipline if not against divine law, he explains to him without using a single sharp word that he had not been entitled to leave his bishopric without the pope's permission (Reg. IX 172). He had designated him, Innocent writes, for the small poor church, not that he should care for it alone, but in the interest of the whole of Lombardy which he would be able to instruct by the example of his life and his teaching since he was powerful both in words and deeds (Reg. XVI 15). When on a later occasion Peter, now patriarch, is charged with having robbed the nephews of his predecessor, Innocent appoints him to be judge in his own case, since he could not leave the investigation into his doings to anybody more trustful than him and since he could not uphold the plaintiffs' rights in any better way. Innocent is convinced that Peter would never knowingly encumber anyone against justice, since he sought not for his own, but for that which is Christ's (Reg. XV 181). A similar sympathetic feeling as that shown to Peter of Ivrea we find in Innocent's attitude towards the saintly patriarch Albert of Jerusalem, the former bishop of Vercelli. When the patriarch of Antioch, Peter's predecessor, had died in the dungeons of the count of Tripoli. Innocent almost beseechingly appeals to Albert, as his most beloved and sorely missed (*desideratissimum*) brother in Christ, who must feel the tragedy as deeply as he himself, but who could perhaps counter it with greater merit (Reg. XI 110). Innocent once declined to reply to a question of law which the patriarch had put to him, because Albert was himself well versed in legal matters and his own answer might differ from the patriarch's view (Reg. IX 254. Cf. also Reg. XII 8, and Ambrose of S Teresa, 39f.).

[122]Gesta episc. Halberst., 119f. Cf. Chapter 5 above, n. 101. When Conrad later resigns from his bishopric against the pope's will and withdraws to a monastery, he is suspended and summoned to appear at the Curia (Gesta episc. Halberst., 122f.), yet seems to have been permitted the *cessio*. Even later he enjoyed the pope's high esteem and had to undertake many a papal commission (see Chapter above 9, n. 52).

[123]We could point here to such trifles as the fact that on one occasion verses in praise of the pope were recited in his presence (see p. 293 above), that he had his portrait inlaid in the apse mosaic of St Peter (see p. 294 above), that he self-assertively dilated on the success of his recuperations (see Chapter 5 above). In contrast to these,

however, stand indications of the pope's modesty. The dedications in both the works he wrote as cardinal please by their unpretentious style, avoiding excessive intimations of humility as well as exaggerating panegyrics to the addressee (Migne PL. 217, 701, 921f.). As pope, Innocent never assumes the attitude of being endowed with superior, let alone infallible, knowledge. "I would rather be taught in this question than teach and rather comment on a judgement than pass one. However, since I could not discover anything about this matter from my predecessors, I would say, without detriment to the faith and without prejudice to a more correct view . . ."; with these words he begins the exposition of his own view in one particular question (Reg. I 349. Cf. also Reg. VII 169 and XV 40). The fact that a man of such predominant importance before his pontificate was scarcely known outside the narrow circles of the Curia speaks for modest reserve (cf. Chapter 1 above, n. 68). The fact that he possessed self-control, and that he seems not to have tried to gain, by way of party influences, a standing which Celestine III was not prepared to grant him of his own accord, does not suggest that Innocent had a driving ambition to hold the reins of power.

[124]Migne PL. 217, 737.

[125]Cf. James's letter in Böhmer, Analekten, 65f.

[126]Bonazzi 1, 269.

[127]Bonazzi *loc. cit.*

[128]Reported by Cramer, 191 n. 2.

# CHAPTER 11

# The verdict of history

History has denied Innocent III its highest distinction, the title of 'the Great'.[1] Decisions of this kind are irrevocable. Would we be well advised to lodge an appeal, if this were possible? Must not the fact that Innocent III led the spiritual and temporal power of the medieval papacy to its apogee and that, unlike his successors, he still observed moderation in his aspirations, suffice to secure him the claim to paramount greatness?

It was a supreme achievement that, through the new Papal State and the Sicilian vassal state, he protected the papacy against the vicissitudes of political events. It does not lessen the greatness of Innocent's achievement that this protection, relative like all protections, was to a great extent weakly abandoned by his successor. What speaks in favour of his historical greatness are the results of his fight for the liberty of the Church, his reforming work, and the protection and encouragement he gave, in an epoch-making manner, to the movement of Catholic poverty. If the Catholic Church had to thank Innocent for nothing else than this protection and the issue of the one command, which even today obliges the Catholic to receive at least once a year the sacrament of the Eucharist, the importance of his pontificate for the development of Christian life in the Church would be assured. Innocent's reign became decisive for the further development of canon law.[2] It marks a turning point in the history of Germany, England, Italy and France.[3] A tremendous, though eventually fruitless, accomplishment was the preparation of two crusades. And the man who had to bear on his shoulders the vast amount of work, worry and responsibility involved in the great events and decisions of his pontificate, was a man of poor health, who had been seriously ill more than once during the eighteen years of his reign. The establishment and maintenance of papal rule in Rome and in the Papal State, the constructive work in the Patrimony, the papal regency in Sicily, all this involved no end of toilsome and exhausting wrestling with a thousand difficulties and thousands of often malicious acts of opposition. The ordinary tasks of administration and jurisdiction, given the attention and care Innocent bestowed on their performance, would for themselves have almost been enough of a strain. It can be assumed that not even in less important affairs did any real *decision* leave the chancery without his definite knowledge. All or by far the greater part of his letters, as far as they are not couched in a purely formal manner, he drafted himself, even to the wording.

Innocent's faculty for sharp critical thinking and for strong and determined action, as well as his sense of moderation, attest to the rank of his abilities as a statesman and as a man. He sets himself clear objectives, keeps them fixedly in view, but is still highly flexible in the choice of the ways and the preparation of the means to achieve them. Conservative by disposition, he is still open to everything that is new and conducive to success, and he himself pioneers new ways. With a sober sense for what is real, possible and attainable, he combines the knowledge of what ought to be, of what is necessary and the ultimate aim of the idea.

Posterity, which denies Innocent III the title of 'the Great', may take into account that he, for all the far-sightedness with which he worked for the future, was still not always able to rise above his age and the circumstances tied to it. The failures, occurring not without his guilt, of his policy in the Fourth Crusade and on the question of the union of the Churches, or his ambiguous attitude in the Crusade against heresy, could be adduced as arguments against admitting his outstanding historical and personal greatness.

But considerations of this kind are, in themselves, hardly sufficient to explain that Innocent III does not live on in history as the Great. The person of a pope cannot solely be judged by the standards of excellent statesmanship, but must also, and above all, be measured according to the demands of the office and the dignity of a Vicar of Christ. Innocent met these requirements in part. With holy ardour he strove for the reform of the clergy and of the Church; the purification of the sanctuary was his ardent desire and the object of constant efforts in his pontificate. He deeply felt the duties resting upon him as defender of the faith and of moral law. His priestly life was blameless and his piety genuine and deep. But it was not always the highest interpretation of his office which guided his actions, and the values of law and morality, which he had often high-mindedly advocated, he sometimes sacrificed to his political aspirations.

So it is due, perhaps, to a fine sense of value that history, for all Innocent III's eminent importance in world history, refused to him who was unable to resolve the inner conflict between the Vicar of Christ and the statesman and politician, the honorific epithet of the Great, which it awarded to Leo I and Gregory I, popes who also rank with the saints of the Catholic Church.

## Notes to Chapter 11

[1]According to Haller (Papsttum, 471) Innocent, if any pope at all, would have deserved the epithet 'the Great'. E. Kantorowicz also thinks it justified when the pope is occasionally styled *Innocentius magnus* (Ergänzungsband 20). It is noteworthy that the dean Albert of Passau speaks of the 'great Innocent' when making mention in 1256 of his activity as advocate at the Curia under Innocent III and Honorius III (BF. 11745).

[2]His reign marks an epoch in the history, too, of papal documentary practice and of the papal chancery. He drew up fixed rules for dealing with documents and papal diplomatics in the succeeding centuries rests on the foundations he had laid. That the registers of the popes since Innocent III are to a great part extant is attributable to his organizational acitivity (Schmitz-Kallenberg, Urkundenlehre, Meisters Grundriss d. Geschichtswiss. 1, 1912, 99).

[3]As a consequence of his intervention in southern France.

# APPENDIX 1

# Innocent III's alleged claim for the fullness of temporal power

Two statements made by Innocent III have been misinterpreted as expressing the pope's view that the dual power centered in Rome was embodied in the papacy. The most striking statement is: "Both powers deserved to have the seat of their primacy in Italy, which by divine providence has been given the principate over all the other provinces, and, therefore, it is befitting that We, though having to extend Our care to all provinces, bestow Our paternal care to Italy in particular . . . , where owing to the primacy of the Apostolic See also the principate of priesthood and of kingship excels".[1] The thought of the primacy of St Peter being the cause of Rome's spiritual and temporal power was not alien to the Middle Ages and does not presuppose a union of spiritual and temporal power in the papacy. The elements of this conception we find in a sermon of Pope Leo the Great preached at the Feast of SS Peter and Paul.[2] After an eulogy of the two princes of the apostles, who had raised Rome to greater magnificence than it possessed in heathen times, Leo expresses his conviction that divine providence had created the Roman Empire in order to make it easier for Christendom to gain ground. One town had been given sovereignty over many peoples so that they would be more quickly accessible for the preaching of the gospel. He then continues that, after the apostles had divided the lands of the world amongst themselves, Peter had been sent to the seat of the Roman Empire so that the light of truth might more effectively pour from the head through the whole body of the world.[3] From this conception it was only a small step for the Middle Ages to develop the idea that

Rome had been given the sovereignty over the world because it was chosen as the town of the prince of the apostles, that consequently the primacy of Peter was the *causa finalis* of Rome's world domination. Otto of Freising took this step before Innocent III. According to him, it was not accident that Rome received sovereignty over the world. The world, he argues, had been given a new peace in order that the work of the messengers of the gospel might be made easier: "But as to why God has given this favour to that people or to that town before others, we cannot decide, unless I may venture to say that it was in recognition of the deserts of the prince of the apostles, whom He foresaw would have his seat there . . . , on whom He had promised to build His Church, so that the place, which on account of the prince of the apostle's magisterial chair was to have the principate over the entire Church, should first rise to unlimited domination over the peoples from whom the believers were to be recruited. Fortunately, therefore, the same town, which was later to become the head of the Church, had before been the head of the world."[4] No other meaning should be read into Innocent III's statement of Peter's primacy being the cause also of the temporal principate of Rome.

The second of Innocent's misinterpreted statements occurs in a sermon he preached on the Feast of SS Peter and Paul. Closely following to some extent Leo the Great's above-mentioned sermon, Innocent argues that Rome had had and still had the primacy and the principate over the whole world. God had willed to so raise it that, just as in heathen times it alone had held the domination over all the peoples, so in Christian times it should alone hold the *magisterium* over all the believers. It had been deserving and appropriate that the prince of the Church, by the will of providence, should have established his seat in the town which was in possession of world domination. It had been manifest, he continues, how much God had loved this town which he had destined to be the priestly and royal, the imperial and apostolic town, in that it held and exercised not only domination over bodies, but also *magisterium* over souls. Owing to the Lord's dignity it was now far greater and gifted with more honour than it had once been owing to its temporal power. Owing to the former it possessed the keys to the kingdom of heaven, owing to the latter it held the reins of the whole world. In order to prevent so high an honour going to another town, Christ Himself had, by way of His Epiphany, held back Peter when he was about to flee from persecution.[5] Nowhere in this sermon does Innocent claim that the papacy embodies the dual power of Rome.[6] Even if the high honour, whose loss Christ had averted, refers to the dual power, Innocent still does not mean to say that Peter's leaving Rome would have deprived it, together with the spiritual power, of its temporal power as well. That Innocent, speaking of imperial Rome, still regarded it in fact as the seat of the worldly empire, follows from another of his sermons on the Feast of SS Peter and Paul, in which he declares that Rome as the seat of the *magisterium* was now more magnificent than it had once been during the imperial Principate, since to its *magisterium*, as was well known, even the *Roman princeps himself* was subject.[7]

The apostle James, Innocent writes to the patriarch of Constantinople, had yielded up to Peter not only the entire Church, but also the whole world.[8] This statement, isolated from its context, can scarcely be understood other than in the sense of a claim to papal world domination. Innocent intends to refute the patriarch's assertion that, if any Church should enjoy the primacy, then it must be the Church of Jerusalem and not the Church of Rome. Innocent therefore, following Bernard of Clairvaux,[9] states that St James had contented himself with the Church of Jerusalem and, in view of St Peter's unique privilege, had left it to him to rule *non solum universam ecclesiam, sed totum saeculum.* He continues that St Peter's letting himself down into the sea, whereas the others had to use the boat to come to Christ, also manifested the privilege of his unique pontificate, *per quod universum orbem susceperat gubernandum, caeteris apostolis vehiculo navis contentis, cum nulli eorum universus fuerit orbis commissus, sed singulis singulae provinciae vel ecclesiae potius deputatae....* Also by walking on the see Peter had shown, since many waters meant many peoples, that he had been invested with the power over many peoples. The claim to world domination, which seems to be expressed in these words, is in total contradiction to the clear and unambiguous opinion which Innocent, at different times and on different occasions, had given of the nature and the limits of his temporal jurisdiction. Since the pope was an unusually clear and logical thinker and since there is no evident reason why he should have unusually increased his temporal claim in this letter, we should not content ourselves with stating a contradiction while there is a possibility of reconciling his statement with what we can ascertain to be his fundamental view in these matters. The purpose of this very comprehensive letter is to prove the spiritual primacy of the Roman Church. The *occasional* interspersion of a seemingly so extremely far-reaching claim, therefore, appears very strange. The *universum orbem*, mentioned in the second passage of the letter, must in any case be understood in a spiritual sense, since it stands for the totality of all the churches. The *totum saeculum*, which seems to be differentiated from the universal Church, we may think means the world external to the Church, namely that part of the world which is still to be converted.[10] But the passage under discussion has probably nothing to do with contrasting the world with the universal Church, but is merely a linguistic redundancy. Elsewhere Innocent once wrote that God had not only placed the Roman Church at the head of all believers, but had also raised it above all other Churches, and, further, that the bishop of Rome had received the *magisterium* and the primacy over all the Churches and all the superiors of churches, and even over all believers.[11] To contrast, in substance, the totality of believers with the totality of Churches does not make sense, for the *magisterium* over all the churches must include the *magisterium* over the superiors of these churches and over all believers. The redundance of the expressions used by Innocent in his letter to the patriarch explains itself as an accumulation of the various expressions which Bernard of Clairvaux employs in the relevant passage to characterize Peter's primacy: *Jacobus...una contentus est Hierosolyma, Petro universitatem cedens...signum singularis pontificii Petri, per quod non navem unam, ut caeteri quique suam, sed saeculum ipsum susceperit gubernandum...unicum se Christi vicarium designavit, qui non uni populo, sed cunctis preesse deberet...Ita cum quisque caeterorum habeat suam tibi* [Bernard addresses Pope Eugenius III] *una commissa est grandissima navis, facta ex omnibus ipsa universalis ecclesia, toto urbe diffusa....* Also a linguistic redundance is doubtless the formulation that Peter had been entrusted not *specialiter aliqua specialis ecclesia*, but the *totus mundus* and the *ecclesia universalis*. God, therefore, had accepted Peter *in plenitudinem potestatis*, while the others were called *in partem sollicitudinis*.[12] Here the context is also purely spiritual.

In Innocent's consistorial address to the Staufen legation of 1199/1200 the precedence of the *sacerdotium* over the *regnum* is justified in these terms among others: "The princes are given power in the world, but the priests are given power also in the heavens, the princes only over the bodies, the priests also over the souls", and in another passage: "For the several magnates have several provinces and the several kings several kingdoms, but Peter is far superior to all of them both in *plenitudo* and in *latitudo*, since he is the vicar of Him to whom the earth belongs and its plenitude, the whole world and all who live in it".[13] In the second passage Innocent in no way intends to describe the several kingdoms as being parts of the universal monarchy of Peter. He compares nothing but the *latitudo* of the priestly and the royal power, and comes to the conclusion that the former is by far the more extensive. The latter never stretches over more than several provinces, the former, even though in a different sphere, over the whole world. It is this same idea which, in 1024, had been expressed to John XIX: "Even if the power of the Roman Empire, which was once the sole ruler in the whole world, is now divided between countless sceptres in all the corners of the world, the power to bind and to loose in heaven and on earth remains with the *magisterium Petri*."[14] The paraphrase of God's name in the second passage cannot serve as proof for the pope's claim to world domination.[15] It is sufficiently explained by the fact that Peter's spiritual power extends over the whole earth and thus, in this one sense, represents the divine domination over the world. On the other hand, the power of the priests over bodies is not necessarily of the same kind as that which the princes exercise over bodies. The most plausible explanation, indeed, of the power of the priests in heaven and on earth is to regard it as that power which refers to the Lord's words: "Whatsoever you will bind on earth will be bound in heaven..."; the power of which Innocent says that those whom the spiritual power binds or looses on earth, God regards as also bound or loosed in heaven;[16] the ecclesiastical criminal jurisdiction, which Innocent describes as the sword which binds what it strikes, not only on earth but also in heaven.[17] It is more difficult to explain the power of the priests over bodies. Innocent may have been thinking of the exclusion of those excommunicated also from life in the community, of the refusal of the excommunicate's body to be buried in consecrated earth. But we can also point to the formula of the anathema: "We deliver his flesh to Satan, so that the soul be saved at the Day of Judgement". If in the passage under discussion Innocent had in mind the domination over the world, it would be striking if just here he were referring to priests in general.

In a letter of 1212 written to the people of Milan, Innocent speaks of a principate of the Apostolic See over the whole world.[18] The passage itself gives no indication of the import of this statement. But a glance at the development of the term 'principate', and at the

manner in which Innocent generally uses it, shows that only a
spiritual interpretation is admissible. Likewise having a purely spiritual meaning is the principate which Innocent, in a sermon on the
apostles, in a sermon on the Feast of Gregory the Great and in his
treatise *De quadripartito specie nuptiarum*, attributes to the apostles,
following the verse from the Psalms *Pro patribus tuis sunt nati filii,
constitues eos principes super omnem terram.*[19] Innocent designates
the bishops, too, as *principes super terram,*[20] as *principes super
omnem terram;*[21] he uses here a formulation frequently occurring in
the liturgy of the feast of the princes of the apostles,[22] which goes
back to the early days of Christendom and which lacks any political
colouring. In Augustine we read: *Pro patribus tuis nati sunt tibi
filii.... Patres missi sunt Apostoli, pro Apostolis filii nati sunt tibi,
constituti sunt episcopi.... Haec est catholica ecclesia: filii eius
constituti sunt principes super omnem terram, filii eius constituti sunt
pro patribus....*[23] Later, Gregory the Great, in his commentary on
Hannah's song of praise, gives to the verse *Ut sedeat cum principibus, et solium gloriae teneat* the following comment: *Qui vero principes hoc in loco nisi sancti apostoli designantur? De quibus nimirum
principibus Deo per Palmistam dicitur: Constitues eos principes....*[24]
Nicholas I speaks of himself in a purely spiritual context that We are
*pro patribus nati filii* set up in the house of the Lord as *principes
super omnem terram.*[25] On another occasion he writes: *Pro quibus
patribus nos... nati sumus filii et constituti... principes super omnem
terram, i.e. super universam ecclesiam....*[26] Bernard of Clairvaux also refers the phrase of the Psalms *Constituti sunt* to the
apostles and their heir, the pope.[27] The *Decretum Gratiani* understands by the *principatus in populos,* of which St Jerome speaks in his
commentary on the Epistle to Titus, the episcopal office,[28] and
occasionally points to a statement by Gregory of Nazianzus: *Dedit
enim et nobis potestatem, dedit principatum multo perfectiorem prin-
cipatibus vestris* (that is, of the emperors).[29] These examples already
show that this use of the term 'principate' is not restricted to the
Latin world. Indeed, St Chrysostom in his Greek work on the priestly
office calls the priesthood an 'arché'.[30]

In the sermon preached on the day of his consecration Innocent
asks himself who he was himself or what was the house of his Father,
that he was permitted to sit above kings and to possess the throne of
glory, for to him was said in the Prophet: "I have placed you above
peoples and kingdoms, that you may uproot and destroy...."[31] In

this passage Innocent expresses his precedence over the kings, but he does not say that this precedence was based on anything other than his purely spiritual position. Innocent frequently used Jeremiah's words, doubtless in a spiritual sense. He once compares the preachers of the gospel to victorious kings who ordered salt to be sown on the sites of destroyed towns, so that not even a stalk might sprout. The destroyed towns, he preaches, were the peoples converted to the faith, in whom the kingdom of the devil had been destroyed. God, he continues, spoke of this destruction through the Prophet: "I have placed you over peoples and kingdoms...."[32] To the king of France, who had refused to let himself be forced into making peace with John of England, Innocent writes: "Does not the Lord speak to us in the Prophet 'See, I have placed you above peoples and kingdoms...', so that we do not now uproot the seeds of evil and gather the gifts of virtues?".[33] In a letter to the French episcopate on the same matter he quotes these words again, in order to show that he was justified in using ecclesiastical coercive measures against the king, "for", he adds, "it is certain that all mortal sin must be uprooted, destroyed and dissipated".[34] Once Innocent argues that he, whom God had placed above peoples and kingdoms in order that he, according to the Prophet, may uproot..., must be very careful to uproot vices and to plant virtues, to destroy what is evil and to build up what is good.[35] Innocent declared null and void the oath which the Venetians had forced on the patriarch of Constantinople Thomas Morosini, because God had placed the bishop of the Apostolic See, who possessed the *plenitudo ecclesiasticae potestatis*, above peoples and kingdoms, so that he, following the word of the Prophet, should uproot and destroy what he found to be barren or noxious on the Lord's acre entrusted to him.[36] In the preamble of a monastic constitution we read: "Placed above peoples and kingdoms by God's ordinance to uproot and to destroy, to build likewise and to plant, we are bound to give apostolic confirmation to that which has been prudently... decreed, so that the occasion be removed for any slackening in monastic discipline and encouragement be given to the strengthening of virtues".[37] Innocent also used these words to describe the bishops' right and duty. He rebukes the archbishop of Sens because he had let Peter's sword grow rusty, so that he was no longer able to uproot, to destroy and to dissipate what the Lord has ordered to be uprooted, destroyed and dissipated, saying: "See, I have this day placed you above peoples and kingdoms...".[38] On the other hand, he praises the archbishop of

Torres, who was intending to replace the unspiritually living members
of his cathedral chapter by regular canons, for having not only
superficially retained the Lord's word to the Prophet: "See, I have
this day placed you above peoples and kingdoms".[39] We see that the
words can be applied to every reforming activity, even in the smallest
circle, and that the first part of the verse has thus sometimes completely lost its significance. Not at first sight in the spiritual sense,
Innocent uses the phrase in his letter to the German princes announcing his intervention in the throne dispute. Since the princes, he writes,
had not so far put an end to the evils of discord and civil war, he, who
according to the word of the Prophet had been placed above peoples
and kingdoms to uproot and to destroy and to build up and to plant,
warned them to live in the fear of God and to take greater care for the
Empire.[40] He writes to King Leo of Armenia that he had received the
diadem in honour and praise of the Apostolic See, of which Leo had
known that it was placed above peoples and kingdoms.[41] In both cases
one seems at first sight justified in regarding Jeremiah's words as
being used in the sense of the pope having a temporal authority over
the kings of the world. But the wording still does not preclude their
referring to the pope's spiritual position.[42] And the spiritual interpretation, as long as it is at all possible, must be given precedence, if
only for the reason that Innocent once emphasizes that the *spiritual*
jurisdiction of the Apostolic See, in *contrast with the temporal one*,
extended over peoples and kingdoms.[43] In the sense in which Innocent generally uses Jeremiah's words, is doubtless also to be
understood his statement to Philip of France that God had raised him,
the pope, to the throne of glory, in order that he sit in judgement not
only with the princes, but also over them.[44] This statement is contained in a hortatory letter occasioned by the king's marital deviation,
and it ends with the threat that in this case the pope would be sitting
in judgement without respecting persons. In a letter to the French
clergy Innocent uses a similar phrase to justify the intended imposition of the interdict because of the marriage affair.[45] Innocent's
declaration that he was entrusted with Peter's sword *ut vindictam in
nationibus et increpationes in populos faciamus*,[46] is to be compared
with the reproach he made to the archbishop of Sens, that in his
mouth the Lord's word was tied down and that he did not know how
to utter the right word *ad faciendam vindictam in nationibus et
increpationes in populis.*[47]

   In his much quoted letter to the rectors of the Tuscan League,[48] which was incorporated into the first collection of his decretals as evidence of the precedence of spiritual over temporal power,[49] Innocent seems to espouse an original dependence of temporal on spiritual power, saying: "As the Creator of the universe, God, has put two great lights in the firmament, the greater one to preside over the day, the lesser one over the night, so he has instituted in the firmament of the universal Church ... two high dignitaries, the greater one ... to reign over the souls, and the lesser one ... to rule over the bodies; namely the episcopal authority and the royal power. As the moon receives its light from the sun and is the lesser of both as regards size as well as nature, site and effect, so the royal power draws all the splendour of its dignity from the pontifical authority. The more the royal power remains within the range of its vision, the greater will be the light with which it is adorned, and the more it distances itself from the sight of the pontifical authority, the more it will lose in splendour." It must be noted that Innocent does not say that, as the moon receives its light from the sun, so the kingship derives its power from the sacerdotal authority. The second clause of the comparison rather reads: so the royal power draws the *splendour* of its dignity from the pontifical authority. What is borrowed, need only be the splendour of royal dignity,[50] not the sovereign power itself. Innocent may have been thinking of the consecration of Christian kings and, above all, of the coronation of the emperor by the pope. This would explain the phrase "the more it remains within the range of its vision, the greater will be the splendour with which it is adorned". The highest splendour of temporal dignity is bestowed, at the imperial coronation, by the pontifical authority on the emperor, who is closest to its seat, who derives his title from that seat and who, in the idea, is most intimately connected with it. In the sense of a dependence of the splendour only of royal power on the pontifical power Frederick II made Innocent's comparison his own: *In exordio nascentis mundi ... Dei providentia ... in firmamento celi duo statuit luminaria, maius et minus: maius, ut praeesset diei ... Que duo, sic ad propria officia in regione zodiaca offeruntur, ut et si se multotiens ex obliquo respiciant, unum tamen alterum non offendit; immo, quod est susperius inferiori suam communicat claritatem.*[51] Caesarius of Heisterbach knows how to combine Innocent's comparison with a recognition, in principle, of the independence of temporal power, without laying stress on a distinction itself between *splendor dignitatis* and *dignitas* or *potestas regalis*. According to him, the sun means the pope, because he *sicut sol dicitur quasi solus lucens comparatione* far outshone any office in this world in glory, power and dignity. The image of the moon he declares to be appropriate to the emperor because, when the pope crowned and blessed him, he was lighted as the moon is by the sun. And yet, both regimentations were from God and received their light from God.[52] Caesarius's interpretation assumes a greater dependence of the emperorship from the pope than is necessarily implied in Innocent's words. In Caesarius's version, the emperor receives his power, even though deriving from God, only through the pope's mediation performed at the coronation, whereas according to the interpretation which we suggest, the already existing imperial power, by way of coronation, only receives dignity and sacred virtue.

## Notes to Appendix 1

[1]Reg. I 401. Cf. Maccarrone, Chiesa, 152.

[2]Cf. Maccarrone, *loc. cit.*

[3]Sermo 82 c. 2, 3 (Migne PL. 54, 423f.).

[4]Chronica (SS. rer. Germ. ed. Hofmeister, 1912) 134. The idea of orientating Rome's world domination to the pope's spiritual position is also found with the decidedly pro-imperial author of the Vita Caroli Magni at the time of Frederick I. He relates of Charlemagne that nothing had seemed to him more fitting than that the ancient power of the city of Rome be re-established and that the city of the prince of the apostles again bear the diadem over all the realms of the world (Rauschen, Die Legende Karls des Grossen im 11. und 12. Jahrhundert, 1890, 24). On one occasion Frederick II roundly confessed to this idea: ... *cum ad hoc, disponente Domino Imperii sceptrum sumpserimus, et Romanum Imperium nostrum ex antiquo fuerit ad praedicationem evangelii praeparatum, ut catholicam fidem et matrem ecclesiam a cunctis hostium incursibus ... eruamus ...* (Albert von Beham, ed. Höfler, 1847, 59).

[5]Sermo XXII *De sanctis* (Migne PL. 217, 556f.).

[6]Cf. Maccarrone, Chiesa, 12ff.

[7]*Ibid.* 556.

[8]Acta Inn. P.I. n. 9 p. 188; P. 862. Cf. the detailed evaluation of the letter in Maccarrone, Chiesa, 16ff.

[9]*De consideratione* lib. 2. c. 8 (Migne PL. 182, 752). Cf. Maccarrone, Chiesa, 19ff.

[10]In a sermon on the Feast of SS Peter and Paul Innocent once compared the world, the *saeculum*, with the sea into which the nets of preaching are thrown from Peter's boat in order to convert the peoples of the world to the true faith (Sermo XXII *De sanctis*, Migne PL. 217, 555ff.). Eichmann evaluates the phrase discussed above as being only a characterization of the pope's dominant position, not a claim to world domination (Acht und Bann, 49).

[11]Reg. II 220, Acta Inn. P.I. n. 12, 201.

[12]Reg. VII 1.

[13]RNI 18; Pr. coll. t. 2 In Genesi (Migne PL. 216, 1180). Cf. Maccarrone, Chiesa, 100ff.

[14]Hugh of Flavigny, Chron. (MG. SS. 8) 392.

[15]Cf. Tillmann, Zur Frage, 145ff.

[16]RNI 32.

[17]Reg. VI 181.

[18]Reg. XV 189.

[19]Migne PL. 217, 599, 515, 966f. On Innocent's use of this psalm word see Maccarrone, Chiesa, 27f.

[20]Reg. VI 171.

[21]Migne PL. 217, 966f. Cf. also *ibid.* 82.

[22]See Maccarrone, Chiesa, 27.

[23]*Enarratio in Psalm.* 44 (Migne PL. 36), 513.

[24]*In prim. reg. Expos.* lib. 1 c. 3 (Migne PL. 79, 73).

[25]MG. Epp. sel. 6, 296.

[26]*Ibid.* 475.

[27]*De consid.* lib. 3, 1, 3 (Migne PL. 182, 758, 764). The numerous passages in the patristic and medieval literature in which the apostles, the bishops, the saints with and without further qualifications, are described as *principes*, need not be enumerated here.

[28]Qu. 1 causa 8 c. 6. Cf. Hugelmann, Die deutsche Königswahl im Corpus Juris Canonici (1909), 32.

[29]C. 6 Dist. X.

[30]Migne PG. 48, 643.

[31]Sermo II *De diver.* (Migne PL. 217, 657). On Innocent's use of the passage see Maccarrone, Chiesa, 28ff.

[32]Sermo IV *ibid.* 668.

[33]Reg. VI 163.

[34]Reg. VII 42.

[35]Reg. I 376.

[36]Reg. IX 130. Cf. also Reg. XVI 5.

[37]Reg. X 14.

[38]Reg. VI 151.

[39]Reg. VII 112.

[40]RNI 2.

[41]Reg. II 220, Acta Inn. P.I n. 12, p. 202.

[42]A similar difficulty presents itself in the arenga of the feudal privilege for King John of England (Reg. XVI 131). It reads that the king of kings etc. had so secured the *regnum* and *sacerdotium* in the Church that the *regnum* was priestly and the *sacerdotium* royal, placing one before all others, namely the one whom He had appointed as His vicar on earth, so that, as every knee bowed to Him in Heaven, on the earth, and below the earth, so everyone should obey His vicar so that there is one flock and one fold. The kings for the sake of God so venerated his vicar that unless they took care to serve him devotedly they did not think they were reigning properly. Here Innocent seems to regard himself quite simply as the superior of the kings, and yet his subsequent comments show that in these words he only has in view his spiritual power over the kings. For Innocent continues that it was in this spirit that John had decided to

submit himself and his kingdoms also *temporaliter* to him to whom he knew them to be subject *spiritualiter*, so that in the single person of Christ's vicar, *regnum* and *sacerdotium*, like body and soul, were united for the great profit and advantage of both. It was divine dispensation that the provinces which from old had had the Roman Church as their proper teacher in *spiritualibus*, now had her as their peculiar sovereign also *in temporalibus*. Since Innocent recognizes that before the feoffment John was subject to him only *spiritualiter*, he cannot have been willing to maintain in the same breath that the kings of the world by God's ordinance were subject to him also *temporaliter*. In even greater perfection, Innocent's train of thought will have run, the concept of the priestly kingdom and of the royal priesthood has been realized by John's step, in that he, who is set by God as spiritual lord over the kings, has now become also *temporaliter* the king's superior. It is noteworthy that for Innocent the statement that the king of France does not recognize anyone besides the pope to be his superior amongst men, is equivalent to his other statement that *in temporalibus* the king did not recognize anyone to be his superior. Cf. Tillmann, Zur Frage, 178f.

[43]Reg. II 4.
[44]Reg. I 174.
[45]Reg. II 197.
[46]Reg. XV 189.
[47]Reg. VI 151.
[48]On this letter see Maccarrone, Chiesa, 98ff.
[49]Reg. I 401; Pr. coll. t. 2, *Sicut universitatis* (Migne PL. 216, 1186).
[50]The comparison is seen in the same light by Carlyle, 146 and Maccarrone, Chiesa, 99f.
[51]Huillard-Bréholles 5¹, 348.
[52]Sermon on the Second Sunday in Advent (Caesarius, Schönbach 1, 44f.).

# APPENDIX 2

# The marriage case of Philip Augustus of France and other marriage cases under Innocent III

The description which Davidsohn,[1] Tenbrock[2] and Haller[3] give of the papal proceedings in the marriage conflict between Philip Augustus of France and his second wife, Ingeborg of Denmark, I am unable to subscribe in all details. The reproach more or less strongly emphasized by these scholars of Innocent having utilized the marriage matter as a means of bringing the king to heel politically, does not, to my view, withstand close scrutiny.[4]

Papal diplomacy in the years between 1200 and 1204[5] kept on striving to perform the hopeless task to winning the king over to its German policy, that is of separating him from Philip of Swabia and reconciling him to a Welf kingship,[6] or at least of establishing a peace between Philip and John of England, which left John the possibility of supporting his Welf nephew.[7] In the conflict with Philip of Swabia the highest political interests of the pope were involved, namely the securing of the newly-founded Papal State and the recovered vassal kingdom of Sicily, the securing, indeed, of the very independence of the papacy.

If Innocent had made use of Philip's marriage conflict as a weapon in the political struggle, it would have to have happened during these decisive years. The fact that the papal legate Octavian of Ostia was staying at the French court in 1200 and 1201 on a political mission and played a significant and not always unobjectionable rôle also in the marriage matter, seems indeed to point to the legal matter having been improperly mixed up with political affairs. The cardinal lifted the

interdict by the pope's order, after Ingeborg had been formally
re-instated, and he then accepted the king's action for annulment of
his marriage on the ground of the impediment of too close a degree of
affinity. Octavian seems to have been more compliant towards the
king in carrying out his mission than was fit.[8] As Ingeborg complains
to the pope, the condition made by him for the lifting of the interdict,[9]
namely her reinstatement in her rights as wife and queen, had only
been fulfilled pro forma. In any case, Octavian accepted Philip's
action for annulment, contrary to the pope's directive,[10] at once and
not six months after Ingeborg's re-instatement.[11] Octavian seems to
have hoped to gain political concessions by being compliant in the
marriage matter. Philip would scarcely have bought his happiness at
the expense of the vital interests of the crown. But he may have been
prepared to make concessions as long as there was no danger
threatening from Otto of Brunswick. The king concludes a letter to
the pope, in which he heatedly complains of having been forced to
re-accept Ingeborg and of the legate's alleged severity, by requesting
that Innocent instruct Octavian to proceed more kindly towards him
in this matter which redounded or seemed to redound (*cedat et cedere
videtur*) to the honour of the Roman Church. He continues: "Your
holiness should also know that we have requested, entreated and
implored his lordship the cardinal as our friend, as legate and as
priest, to accept from us the oath that we have never intended to ally
ourselves with anyone (namely with Philip of Swabia)[12] against the
Roman Church, although we have often been solicited to do it . . .".[13]
Here, Philip in a veiled manner threatens the possibility of his giving
more active support to the German king, or surely links, in some
other respect, the matter of his marriage to his position in the throne
dispute.

Whatever intentions the king and the legate may have had, the
pope's attitude is unequivocal. He was not willing to tolerate foul play
and acted in this case not as a politician, but as a keeper of law and
morality. He, though, in correspondence with Ingeborg, rejects the
complaints against the legate as being scarcely credible.[14] But it
follows from a postscript to a letter sent to the legate on 31 October,
added after the arrival of Ingeborg's envoy at the Curia, that Innocent
fears, even believes, that her complaints might not be unfounded. He
declares to Octavian that he would not tolerate deceit and foul play
(*figmentum et colludium*) in the matter, and instructs the cardinal to
be guided in his decision rather by God than by man, by the pope

rather than by the king, by the entire Church rather than by only one person, by considerations for his own salvation rather than by the royal will. Innocent, further, warns Octavian against holding constant communion with people who did not dare to say a word in favour of the queen for fear that it might be bandied about, and he requests him, as his dearest friend, not to let himself be prejudiced against the queen either in sentiment or in deed, but rather to be well-disposed to her, since her cause deserved it.[15] He leaves the legate in as little doubt as the king that he requires his instructions to be genuinely executed, not only pro forma.[16] At the turn of 1200/1201 the legate is instructed not to begin the proceedings until the queen has been restored to full freedom and to the honour due to her.[17] Some little time later he reiterates the instruction[18] and thus, in the very days when he was preparing Otto of Brunswick's public recognition, gives the king not even the slightest indication of being compliant in the marriage matter.

The conduct of the proceedings was not entrusted to Cardinal Octavian alone. Together with him, the characterful and deeply pious cardinal John of St Prisca, known as the 'cardinal of St Paul', the later friend and protector of St Francis,[19] was to act as judge and to pass the judgement. His name guaranteed the pope that justice would be administered and no diplomatic game be played.[20] The marriage case was heard before the two legates at the Council of Soissons in the middle of March 1201. When Philip realized that the decision was going against him, he prevented the passing of a judgement by declaring that he renounced a decision.[21]

Later that same year Philip was urging that a new proceeding be instituted. He speaks in the peremptory manner of a man who knows that the addressee has reason to show himself compliant to him. Alleging the thin argument that Ingeborg had forborne to produce witnesses at the last hearing, he demands that the judgement be passed on the basis alone of the statements of the witnesses he had produced.[22] It is to this time that a letter must belong, incompletely extant only in Bernard of Compostela's collection of decretals, in which Innocent as pastor admonishes Philip to consider that, if a divorce decree should be obtained on the basis of false evidence and if thereupon Philip should conclude a new marriage, it would pass for a marriage in the eyes of men but before God would be held to be an adulterous alliance, and that he committed a grave sin into the bargain by allowing an innocent woman to lose her case. He asks Philip what he would do if after the divorce, for instance in fear of death and in view of the Day of Judgement, he should repent, since he would not then be able to return to his legitimate wife, nor to dismiss his illegitimate partner.[23] At the beginning of the following year Philip insists again that his process be facilitated, probably by being committed to a French ecclesiastical court. This time he enters, along with the objection of too close affinity, the plea of consanguinity and of enchantment (*maleficium*), which had prevented him from consummating the marriage. Innocent replied to him in July 1202, saying that he could not give up two demands: that the queen be given a sufficient chance to defend herself and that the hearing take place before disinterested judges.[24] At the same time the pope charges the archbishop of Rheims, Philip's uncle, with dissuading the king from demanding from the pope anything that he could not fulfil without twisting the law and without bringing dishonour and disgrace upon their souls.[25] The degree to which Innocent is anxious to accommodate the king, as far as it was reconcilable with his conscience, is shown by his offer to send authorized persons to Denmark at his own expense to hear the queen's witnesses there, lest the case should be delayed against the king's wishes; it is shown still more by his legitimizing Philip's children from his alliance with Agnes of Meran.[26] Far from being a means of pressure, the marriage conflict, in these years, is for Innocent only a cumbersome hindrance to his policy. Since he left Philip in no doubt that in his case he would not sacrifice law and justice, Philip was rather strengthened in his resistance to papal policy by a deep personal embitterment. In the truly insulting letter with which Philip replies to the papal recognition of his Welf arch-enemy, he also mentions that the pope had destroyed his personal happiness: *Gravamina, que vos nobis irrogastis, equanimiter sustinuimus, ista vero, que ad detrimentum honoris nostri et regni nostri exheredationem manifeste imminere videmus, nullatenus pateremur.*[27]

Philip seems to have renounced the institution of a new divorce suit under the conditions fixed by the pope[28] and to have tried instead to bring Ingeborg, by abusive treatment, by threats and pressure, to testify to what she was expected to declare. He seems to have now regarded the plea of enchantment, which had allegedly made it impossible for him to consummate the marriage, to be the most conducive to success, and to have demanded that Ingeborg testify accordingly.[29] The queen complained to the pope of the ill-treatment, requesting him not to allow new proceedings to be instituted until she was in a position to conduct her case without restraint, and not to accept any statement extorted from her, which was prejudicial to the legal validity of her marriage.[30] Thereupon Innocent in June 1203 most firmly interceded with Philip to treat Ingeborg in a humane manner worthy of a queen. Gravely concerned for Ingeborg's life, he warns the king that he would be held responsible for his wife's death and would never be able to marry again, if anything should happen to the queen in the misery of her captivity.[31] He requires that free access to the queen be granted to a papal emissary, the abbot of Casamari, and his companion, the queen also having complained that the pope's letters were not delivered to her. Tenbrock assumes that the abbot, who sought to establish peace between France and England,[32] was to bring, by way of interceding on behalf of the queen, pressure to bear on Philip in the interest of Innocent's imperial policy. This assumption has no foundation, since the pope's intercession for the queen was occasioned by Ingeborg's desperate calls for help, which the pope could not ignore. Another letter too, much sharper in tone, of December of the same year, is in answer to complaints about the treatment of the queen delivered, as it seems, by a Danish legation,[33] which in France had apparently been denied free access to their mandator's sister.[34] But neither does this letter call for the political interpretation which Tenbrock gives to it.[35] This time Innocent declares to the king that he could no longer close his eyes to Ingeborg's misery, nor accept patiently such an insult to the Apostolic See, nay to the entire Church, but that he would be forced to fulfil the duty of his office without respecting persons.[36] Innocent did not need to live up to his threats. At least the worst abuses in the treatment of the queen were redressed.[37]

If in the years 1200 to 1204, in which for Innocent everything depended on winning Philip over to his German policy, he made no questionable concessions in the marriage matter nor used the marital conflict as a means of political pressure, we must be wary of searching after political motives behind the pope's proceeding in the marriage case in 1205, in which year no interests of high rank are ascertainable which could have influenced it.

On 5 July 1205 Innocent informs the queen that he would not be able to refuse to accept the king's action for annulment of his marriage on the ground of enchantment, along with the count of affinity. He had done all in a man's power, but had not persuaded her

husband to show her marital affection, as he was unable to instil love
into the king's heart. Indeed, neither she nor the king, he writes, could
keep on living in this miserable plight.[38] It is obvious that Innocent
has a mind to decree the divorce. There are no imperative political
motives ascertainable. Why should we not believe that he was willing
to put an end to an untenable situation, if this was possible by way of
a legal proceeding, in the interest not only of the king, but also of the
unfortunate woman?

That Innocent, in his efforts to maintain law, was concerned for
more than the purely formal law, would indeed appear to be more
than doubtful if a notice from the king's register was credible which,
according to Davidsohn, a royal legate made after his interview with
the pope, or which was made in Philip's chancery on the basis of
the legate's report after his return.[39] According to this *forma in
qua consulit dominus papa de divortio celebrando*,[40] Innocent advises
the king to plead both grounds for the divorce, affinity and enchantment. If the queen did not intend to call witnesses on the first count,
he would agree to it, but he could not prevent her from calling them.
Should this happen, the king need not feel fear, since he would have
these witnesses examined by his own procurator. In the matter of
enchantment the king would be given credence if he swore by his soul
that he had been unable to consummate the marriage, and that mainly
for this reason the queen was odious to him, provided that the queen
did not swear to the consummation—a course of action from which
she could probably easily be dissuaded. But if the king feared that the
decision would go against him, it could be postponed, so that the king
would be in the same position again as before. He could not, though,
be spared the necessary attempt at consummating the marriage, since
such enchantments could be broken by prayers. Davidsohn, following
Delisle, ascribes this notice to the year 1207 and to the mission of the
abbot of St Geneviève's.[41] In my view it belongs to July 1205. In its
unusually optimistic view of a separation being possible, the letter
Reg. VIII 113 of 5 July 1205 harmonizes well with the *forma in qua
consulit*. Also in this letter, the two counts for annulment, *affinitas*
and *maleficium*, are considered as equivalent, whereas previously the
stress lay on the count of *affinitas*,[42] and later, in 1207 the only point
at issue is the non-consummation of the marriage because of
enchantment,[43] and also in the years after 1207 the question of
consummation remains decisive.[44] The strongest argument for assign-
ing the *forma in qua consulit* to 1205 is the fact that on 9 December

1208 Innocent writes to Philip, that more than three years previously the queen had declared by word of mouth and in writing under her seal that the marriage had been consummated, and that she had requested him to give no credence to her, if under duress she should make a declaration to the contrary. If the queen, he writes, now made such a reverse declaration, her simple word could not be credited, but she would have to swear to her statement.[45] It follows that an explicit admission by Ingeborg of her marriage having been consummated must have been made in 1205, before December. If such an admission existed, it could scarcely any longer be maintained, the pope's view being that the queen would easily be dissuaded from rejoining to the king's sworn statement of having been unable to consummate the marriage by making a sworn statement to the contrary. Ingeborg's admission explains why the new process did not come about, despite the pope's inclination, clearly expressed in the *forma in qua consulit* and in the letter of July 1205, to clinch the marriage conflict.

Did Innocent indeed accommodate King Philip in 1205, exceeding the bounds of what is permissible, to the extent which the *forma in qua consulit* seems to suggest? In the *forma* the pope's view is rendered by a third party, and for this reason alone it must be accepted with caution. As early as 1202 Innocent in his letter explains the offer to Philip, which he is forwarding him through the royal envoy, *ne sinistra interpretatione depravetur.*[46] On 2 April 1207 Innocent informs Philip that he was writing to the abbot of Sarnai, in order that the prelate might deliver and expound the pope's letter to him, lest it should, as once had happened, be unfaithfully explained to him by a third party.[47] In April 1209 Innocent writes to Philip again, explaining that he knew for certain that the papal letters were often interpreted to him less faithfully, since a wicked expositor explained to him sometimes more, sometimes less, or sometimes even something that is quite different, or that he explained it in a quite different form, thereby culpably deceiving the king, dazzling his insight, and insulting the pope whose intention he discredited.[48] It is very possible that the pope's criticisms of April 1207 and 1209 refer precisely to the interpretation given to his proposal made in July 1205. To those items wrongly attributed to the pope may well belong, among others, the assertion that Innocent believed that the queen could be readily dissuaded from swearing to the consummation of her marriage. The assumption of an unfaithful rendering of the pope's intentions gains in probability, since there is no political reason to be seen which might have caused Innocent to offer an accommodation in the marriage matter in 1205 which in the years before, under stronger pressure of political necessities, he had refused.

Neither does Innocent's attitude to the demand for a new divorce proceeding, which Philip submitted to the pope in 1207, show any compliance to the king. He could not refuse the king permission for a new proceeding to be instituted, since no judgement had so far been passed. In 1205 the institution of the proceeding may have failed owing to Philip's reluctance to fulfil Innocent's precondition: a renewed attempt to consummate the marriage with Ingeborg. Now, in 1207, Philip gives to understand through the abbot of St Geneviève's that he was ready to conform to the demand, provided that in the case of failure the attempt would not redound to his prejudice.[49] Innocent charged Guala, cardinal deacon of St Maria in Porticu, who had been appointed legate on 29 May 1208 primarily in the interests of the Crusade, also with the enquiry into the king's action for enchantment and with taking a canonical decision, provided that both parties agreed. The legate is instructed to ensure Ingeborg's full freedom during the proceedings.[50] Philip regarded the legate's authorization as insufficient.[51] He now demands point-blank that the pope give the legate full powers to dissolve the marriage without any right to appeal, whether on the grounds of affinity or of enchantment, whether on account of the queen's taking the veil or on any other ground on which, in the times of the king's and the pope's predecessors, a divorce used to be based.[52] The proposal is in fact that Ingeborg should take the veil and that he, in view of his oath that the marriage had not been consummated, should be allowed to get married again. Innocent urgently admonishes the king to control himself, to renounce the case, and to show marital love to the queen.[53] A second letter points out to the king how objectionable it would be if the ground for divorce, which he produced and which in itself was not free from doubt, was applied in his case, since there could be no question of the queen having made either a voluntary or a rightly-motivated decision and since, not even in view of the queen's state-ments before the legates and of her repeated declarations to him, could it be accepted that the marriage had not been consummated. None the less he authorizes Guala to institute the proceedings on the basis of the king's causes of action. The legate is to proceed accord-ing to the instruction given to the earlier legates in respect of the ground of affinity, according to the instructions given to him person-

ally as regards the ground of enchantment, and under careful observation of the expositions the pope is forwarding him as regards the
ground that the queen had taken the veil. He is empowered to pass
the final decree only if both parties agree. In any case, a precondition
for the acceptance of the action is that the queen's full freedom is
safeguarded.[54] Philip interpreted the pope's answer as a refusal and
informed the legate in deep displeasure that, if he had no other
business to perform, he need not, for the sake of the divorce suit, stay
on in France, since the pope was anyway unwilling to release him
from his marriage bond.[55] This is no expulsion, but it meant that the
legate in his other pursuits, the cause of the Holy Land and probably
also the reconciliation of the king with Otto IV, could no longer
count on much readiness on the king's part. On 23 April 1209
Innocent entreated the king again to remove the only stain on his
honour, the matter of his marriage, and this in a letter in which he
implores the king in view of the straightened situation of the Holy
Land to provide effective support for Count John of Brienne, called
to be king of Jerusalem.[56] The close political alliance with Philip
against Emperor Otto IV, which Innocent in his desperate situation
sees himself forced to conclude in the following year, is no reason for
him to alter his refusal to be compliant to the king as contrary to
divine and canon law. On 5 May 1210 he expresses his hope to
Ingeborg that she would still gain her husband's love.[57] In that year
Philip tried to influence Innocent in favour of a divorce through the
intercession of the landgrave of Thuringia, his and the pope's ally.[58]
The king's last attempt at enforcing a divorce failed in 1212. The
pope's confidential agent, Magister Robert Courçon, the later cardinal,
had been charged with a new enquiry, which had shown that the
marriage must be considered consummated. Since the other grounds
for nullification of the marriage had, as it seems, already dropped out,
Innocent, on 9 June 1212, had to declare definitely to the king that,
much as he wished to be compliant, he could not separate him and his
queen on grounds of conscience and in view of the danger that
otherwise he would lose office and sacred rank as a heretic. The king,
therefore, should no longer pester him in this matter, lest he should
have the appearance of exploiting the present persecution of the
Church to extort the divorce from the pope.[59] The following spring,
when preparing to embark on his English expedition, Philip became
reconciled with Ingeborg.[60] When Davidsohn denies Innocent any
credit for this reconciliation and ascribes it to political calculations on

the king's part,[61] he overlooks that, whatever its immediate cause may have been, its precondition lay in Philip's definite loss of any prospect of being released from the fetter of marriage.

If there is nothing to support the charge that Innocent used the king's marriage conflict as a means of political pressure, there is as little reason to accuse him of not having taken a strong enough line against the king. Two phases must be sharply distinguished in the marriage matter during Innocent III's reign. In the first, the issue is not the validity or invalidity of the marriage, but the validity or invalidity of the divorce decree. This phase ends with Ingeborg's formal re-instatement in the beginning of September 1200,[62] enforced by the imposition of the interdict on France. In the second phase the validity of the marriage itself is at issue, since the quashing of the divorce decree was not tantamount to the final recognition of the legal validity of the marriage. The marriage matter had returned to its starting-point, to the king's decision to become divorced, with the only difference that now, instead of pursuing the divorce at a French episcopal court, he had to pursue it at the Curia. The situation had completely changed, a fact which is all too readily overlooked in assessing Innocent's attitude. Up till now the pope held the initiative in the marriage conflict. It rested with him to cause his predecessor's decree to be recognized and to dissolve an alliance which, as long as the first marriage was not lawfully terminated must be held to be adulterous and in the general opinion was adulterous. Now, the initiative had passed to Philip. Now it was the king, not the pope, who was interested in a new proceeding. All Innocent could wish was that Philip would accept the existing legal situation, that is renounce the institution of a new proceeding, for which he saw, doubtless from the beginning, little prospect of success and which was bound to weigh so heavily upon the relationship between Philip and the Curia. In the main issue Innocent had no demands to make on the king, but on the contrary had to ward off demands made by the king. If he allowed a new process, he would not be acting against the king, but making concessions in his favour, or at least be taking steps in direct response to the king's insistence. The pope only kept his initiative in matters which, though of highest import from the aspect of humanity, were less relevant in political terms: in the matter of the treatment of the queen and of her real, not only formal, re-instatement in her rights as wife and queen. It would not be doing justice to Innocent to ignore the considerable difference which exists between using ecclesiastical

punitive measures to enforce the dissolution of an illegitimate marriage and using the same measures to assure better treatment for the
wife and the fulfilment of the conjugal duties. But for the divorce suit,
the Curia would have scarcely had occasion to intervene in these
matters, and nobody would have expected the pope, in such a case, to
go beyond administering religious admonitions and warnings.

As Ingeborg in France against King Philip, so in Bohemia Adela,
the repudiated wife of King Ottokar, sought right with the pope
against her husband, who had contracted a second marriage with
Constance, the sister of the king of Hungary. According to Tenbrock[63] the course as well as the duration of the proceedings were
influenced by political considerations on the pope's part.

In October 1199 Innocent mentions in a letter to the French
bishops that, according to reports he had received, Ottokar, following
the example of Philip Augustus, had repudiated his legitimate wife
and had contracted an adulterous second marriage.[64] A few days
previously he had appointed a commission which was to examine the
queen's appeal against the divorce decree passed by the episcopal
court.[65] Up to 1209 a series of papal delegates and subdelegates was
engaged in the matter. In 1210 the case was heard at the Curia itself,[66]
until Adela's death in the same year brought it to an end. Decisive for
the question whether Innocent used this process as a means of
political pressure against Ottokar in the throne dispute are the events
up to 1206. The most prominent members of the various commissions
appointed in this period,[67] Archbishop Ludolf of Magdeburg, Archbishop Everard of Salzburg and Bishop Gardolf of Halberstadt, were
outspoken supporters of Philip of Swabia. It goes without saying that
the pope did not instruct these men to proceed in Ottokar's case
according to his readiness to oppose the pope in the matter of the
throne dispute. In the very months in which Innocent did his utmost
to win Ottokar for Otto's cause, at about the beginning of June 1201,
the archbishops of Magdeburg and Salzburg, together with the provost of Seeburg, are directed to examine the witnesses without
further delay and to assign the parties a date for the hearing to be
held at the Curia.[68]

Johannes Vincke's treatise on the marriage suit of Peter II of
Aragon and his wife Mary of Montpellier in the years between 1206
and 1213 and the publication of the records of the lawsuit[69] bring out
in full relief the difficulties inherent in a lawsuit of this kind and, at
the same time, testify to the objective manner in which cases were

conducted at the Curia. The procedure in general was stodgy, precisely because of the efforts to maintain punctiliously the rights of the parties,[70] but it thereby gave them ample opportunity to put obstacles maliciously in each other's way.[71] The fact that Ottokar only divorced himself from his wife because he wanted to be free of her and to marry another woman, must not influence our judgement on the course of the proceedings. It is natural that the pope too was aware of these personal reasons, and indeed he once enounced them.[72] But that was irrelevant before an ecclesiastical court; what mattered was only whether the alleged blood relationship really existed, and that could be as difficult to establish as it was easy to understand Ottokar's inner reasons for the divorce.

The soundness of the contention that Innocent, where the validity or invalidity of a marriage was concerned, was not guided by opportunist motives, is confirmed by his attitude to the Spanish marriage cases, in which he insisted on the dissolution of marriages and enforced his decision, even though he thereby jeopardized the peace between the Christian kingdoms in Spain so close to his heart and so necessary in the interests of defence and the fight against the Saracens.

The rulers of Castile, Aragon, Leon, Portugal and Navarre were all closely related to one another, and nowhere was it more desirable politically than here that through marriage alliances between the royal houses frontier-hostilities should lose their basis and antagonisms be ended, since the frontiers between the various kingdoms and those with the Moorish territories were uncertain and since all these rulers shared a common aim: to dislodge the Saracens from the peninsula. Peace and the maintenance of fighting strength, both were certainly a matter of the heart for Innocent, but the canonical ordinance was too sacred for him to have tolerated for either reason marriages which were held incestuous.

The marriage settlement between Alfonso IX of Leon and Berenguela, the daughter of his cousin Alfonso VIII of Castile, completed and secured an effort toward peace. Under the title of the princess's dowry, the Castilian held a number of castles belonging to the son-in-law, which she, that is her father, was to retain, if her husband were to dismiss her.[73] The divorce of the marriage, which Innocent enforced,[74] resulted, as was to be feared and as Innocent indeed feared,[75] in a war between Castile and Leon about this dowry.[76] The political consequences of the divorce worked out disastrously up to the year 1213, to the detriment also of the Saracen wars. It was not before autumn of 1213 that a true peace came about.

The marriage, too, of a sister of Sancho VII of Navarre with Peter II of Aragon, stipulated in the peace treaty between Sancho and Peter, was prohibited by Innocent on 11 February 1199 on the ground of blood relationship in the third degree. Sancho, who as the vanquished party had perforce concluded the treaty, had himself made complaints to the pope.[77] As in Alfonso IX's case, Innocent ran the risk of jeopardizing peace whenever the maintenance of the canonical marriage laws was involved.[78]

## Notes to Appendix 2

[1]Philipp II.

[2]Tenbrock, 74ff.

[3]Papsttum, 343ff.

[4]However Tenbrock stresses that Innocent had not lent himself to a radical miscarriage of justice. In the conflict between the statesman and the representative of the Church the latter had been victorious in the crucial issues. But the intensity with which Innocent had championed the strict law of the Church, in Tenbrock's view, had been determined by the political necessities (89).

[5]In 1200 Innocent begins to advocate Otto's cause openly with the French and English kings (RNI 25, 28; cf. Chapter 5 above). In the summer of 1204 Innocent has to accept that his attempts to force Philip Augustus to make peace with King John have failed (cf. Tillmann, Legaten, 91f).

[6]RNI 25, 47, 48, 50, 63, 64, 81, 82.

[7]Cf. Tillmann, Legaten, 90ff.

[8]Cf. also Gesta c. 54.

[9]Gesta c. 53.

[10]Gesta c. 54; Reg. III 16.

[11]Reg. III 16.

[12]Cf. Recueil 19, 460.

[13]Reg. III 18.

[14]Reg. III 11.

[15]Reg. III 16.

[16]Reg. III 18. Davidsohn accuses the pope of failing to renew the interdict when he realized that its raising had been obtained by deceit (150ff.). Yet it would have been impossible for the pope to give the lie to the legates and to the French bishops and to renew the interdict on the basis of the statement by only one of the parties, even though personally he might have been convinced that the complaint was well founded, the less so as the main issue had been settled: the recognition by the king that his marriage with Ingeborg had for the time being to be regarded as standing by right and the connection with Agnes of Meran as being void.

[17]P. 1218–1220.

[18]P. 1288–1289. Davidsohn maintains, without giving reasons, that the pope's demand had not been complied with, and he accuses Innocent of weaknesses for failing, therefore, to postpone the beginning of the divorce proceedings. However, Innocent *did* insist on the precondition; if it was disregarded, of which we know nothing, it would be the legate who was to blame.

[19]See Chapter 7 above.

[20]Cf. also Davidsohn, 122f.

[21]Gesta c. 55; Reg. V 50; Rigord (Delaborde 1) 149. For more details see Davidsohn, 161ff.

[22]Delisle, Cat. 667.

[23]Singer, 99f.

[24]Reg. V 49, 50.

[25]Reg. V 49.

[26]After Agnes' death Innocent on 2 November 1201, to the offence of many, pronounced the legitimation on the king's petition. (The legitimation decree is extant in the collection of decretals compiled by Bernard of Compostela, Singer, 89ff.; its communication to the French bishops P. 1499, Migne PL. 214, 1191ff.; Rigord, Delaborde 1, 151).

[27]RNI 63.

[28]The king's envoys refused to accept the conditions (Reg. V 50).

[29]The plea of enchantment is first mentioned to the archbishop of Rheims (Reg. V 49) in the document cited above. It is not, however, mentioned in a letter written to the king at the same time and may thus be assumed not to have played a major rôle at that stage. The statement which according to Reg. VI 85 was to be forced out of Ingeborg makes no reference either to *affinitas* or *consanguinitas*, to neither of which Ingeborg could possibly have borne evidence herself.

[30]Reg. VI 85.

[31]Reg. VI 86.

[32]Cf. Tillmann, Legaten, 90ff.

[33]Along with the hortatory letter to King Philip (Reg. VI 86 P. 2036) a letter is issued to King Waldemar (P. 2034), Ingeborg's brother, as well as to Archbishop Andrew of Lund (P. 2038), the king's friend. The latter contains the answer to a question raised by the archbishop.

[34]See Reg. VI 182.

[35]Tenbrock, 84.

[36]Reg. VI 86.

[37]Davidsohn accuses Innocent of not even having attempted to live up to his threat by deed, but then brings forward himself the references showing that at that time the queen's position had changed for the better (205ff.). How could the pope have straight away taken a strong line against the king, perhaps by inflicting ban or interdict, if Philip had already ceased maltreating the queen?

[38]Reg. VIII 113.

[39]Davidsohn, 214ff.

[40]Davidsohn *loc. cit.* and Migne PL. 217, 68f.

[41]Davidsohn p. 214ff. As do Tenbrock, 86, and Haller, Papsttum, 394, 545.

[42]See pp. 333ff. above.

[43]Reg. X 176.

[44]Cf. p. 340 above.

[45]Reg. XI 181.

[46]Reg. V 50.

[47]Reg. X 42.

[48]Reg. XII 27.

[49]Reg. X 176.

[50]Reg. XI 68.

[51]Davidsohn, who accepts the *Forma in qua consulit* as a true rehearsal of the pope's proposals and dates it November 1207, finds it difficult to explain why Innocent, between 18 November 1207 and 28 May 1208, departed from his accommodating approach to Philip. He believes (223ff.) the reason to be the poor enthusiasm with which King Philip had received the pope's demand to take up the fight against the Albigensians, but this is a rather unsatisfactory argument. At about the time of Guala's mission, Innocent was still trying to win the king over to the Albigensian cause, and for his special mission in the cause of the cross the legate was entirely dependent on the king's goodwill. Concessions once made Innocent could hardly have been able to revoke. If he had ever approved of another way of proceeding in the matter of the *affinitas*, as according to the *forma* was the case, Innocent would hardly have been in a position to refer the king, if later he should bring an action for *affinitas*, to the instruction given to his legates Octavian and John of S Prisca (Reg. XI 182). If Innocent had ever departed from the path of law in the marriage affair he would never have been able to bring the king to renounce his divorce. Moreover the fact that the legate is not instructed to dissolve the marriage by reason of affinity, needs no explanation if the *Forma in qua consulit* belongs to the year 1205. Davidsohn assumes that in the interim Philip had investigations instituted with a view of making the allegation of affinity appear credible.

[52]Reg. XI 180.

[53]Reg. XI 181.

[54]Reg. XI 182.

[55]Delisle, Cat. 1111.

[56]Reg. XII 27.

[57]Reg. XIII 180.

[58]In November 1210 he promises to marry one of the landgrave's daughters, provided she is not too ugly, if the landgrave could persuade the pope to divorce him from Ingeborg (Delisle, Cat. 1248; Baluze, Misc. 7, 245).

[59]Reg. XV 106.

[60]William Brito (Delaborde 1), 246.; Rob. Autissiod. (Cont. II), 279.

[61]Philipp II, 259. The alleged political considerations (Davidsohn, 252ff.) are rather dubious.

[62]An instruction to the legate in July/August 1198 even directs him to lay an interdict on the kingdom if the king should fail within a month to dismiss Agnes and to restitute Ingeborg (Reg. I 447). According to a letter of October 1199 the legate was given the authority, should he see fit, to content himself with the more lenient coercive measure of inflicting a personal interdict on the king, on Agnes and on the retinue of both (Reg. II 197). The former letter seems to have been for conditional use only (cf. Tillmann, Über päpstliche Schreiben, 199) and in any case was not produced at first. Davidsohn fails to see through the true state of facts and conjectures that political motives were at the bottom of the apparent change in the pope's instruction and of the legate allegedly missing the term set by the pope (Philipp II, 8ff.).

[63]Tenbrock, 68.

[64]Reg. II 197.

[65]Reg. II 188.

[66]See the following note and Codex diplomaticus et epistolarius regni Bohemiae, ed. Friedrich, 2 (1912), 45f.; Reg. XI 184, XII 50.

[67]The first commission is given to Archbishop Ludolf of Magdeburg and two abbots (Reg. II 188, Cod. dipl. Boh. 2, 8), a second to Bishop Gardolf of Halberstadt and two co-delegates (Reg. IX 60, XII 50). In early June 1201 are appointed the archbishops of Salzburg and Magdeburg together with the provost of Seeburg (Cod. dipl. Boh. 2, 14; Bernard of Compostela in Singer, 60ff.; cf. Reg. IX 60) and in April 1206 again Everard of Salzburg and two co-delegates (P. 1376, Cod. dipl. Boh. 2, 48ff. cf. also Reg. IX 60).

[68]P. 1376, Cod. dipl. Boh. 2, 48ff. Cf. Reg. IX 60.

[69]Vincke, 108–189.

[70]Cf. Barraclough, 80f., 98.

[71]Cf. Chapter 3 above.

[72]Reg. II 197; *Ecce enim dux Bohemiae ... expavit.*

[73]Reg. I 99 P. 81; Reg. VI 80.

[74]Cf. Reg. VII 67, 94.

[75]Reg. I 92.

[76]Cf. Reg. I 99, II 75, VI 80, VII 93, IX 2; Rod. Tolos. (Recueil 19) 264.

[77]Reg. I 556.

[78]In the last period of Innocent's pontificate the marriage, already stipulated by contract, between the young King Henry I of Castile and the sister of Alfonso II of Portugal is dissolved by papal mandate on the grounds of relationship in the third and fourth degrees (Rod. Tolos. 280). Yet after that Innocent seems to have ordered an investigation into the degree of relationship (P. 5313), probably to make out whether a dispensation could be granted.

# APPENDIX 3

# Conrad of Würzburg's alleged 'treachery'

The question of the so-called 'treachery', allegedly committed by Bishop Conrad of Würzburg, cannot be wholly cleared up. Apart from Leopold von Borch,[1] who goes so far as to discount any hostility of Philip of Swabia against Conrad in the last days of the prelate's life, Conrad is generally accused of shameful treachery and of, eventually, open defection from Philip, thereby paying the pope the price for his translation to the see of Würzburg. Only Otto of Sankt Blasien,[2] writing some time later, finds it possible to report an actual conspiracy and open rebellion. The Chronicle of Lauterberg records that Philip had suspected his chancellor in 1200 of having approved of Otto's cause for the sake of the pope's favour[3] and relates, on the occasion of the bishop's murder in 1202, that Conrad had begun to turn to Otto's faction.[4] The Chronicle of Reinhardsbrunn records that the many discussions between Conrad and the landgrave of Thuringia after the court session at Würzburg had aroused Philip's suspicion of Conrad, adding that Philip had instigated the bishop's murder.[5] The reports in not strictly contemporary sources must be used with every caution. The allegation in the Chronicle of Lauterberg of Philip having entertained suspicions against the chancellor as early as 1200 is based, as it seems, on an unfortunate combination of facts. From a report which is also the source of Arnold of Lübeck's account[6] and of the Magdeburg Schöppenchronik,[7] the chronicler had come to know that Henry of Glinde,[8] the dean of Magdeburg, had aspired to the chancellorship for himself and, therefore, had been blinded by the chancellor's brother on 15 August. The suggestion that the dean's application was connected with a suspicion against Conrad seems to be a later addition. Neither Arnold nor the Magdeburg Schöppenchronik make any mention of this. It can also be proved to be false. On

27 March 1199 Innocent expresses his condolence with the dean of
the cathedral church of Magdeburg for the unexpected loss of his
eyesight and confirms him in his deanship.[9] In the latter half of 1200
Innocent gave permission for Conrad's brother to be absolved from
the excommunication for the crime he had committed against the
dean.[10] The blinding, therefore, happened at a time when Conrad,
openly defying the pope, was maintaining his ground both in Hildesheim and Würzburg. As to the Chronicler of Reinhardsbrunn we
must, from the first, be very guarded, since he occasionally construes
downright fantastic connections of events. The reports which, apart
from Otto of Sankt Blasien's much later written chronicle, attest only
to Philip's suspicion against his chancellor and to the beginning of
Conrad's turning to Otto, even if we were to put full confidence in
them, would not be sufficient to reproach Conrad with perfidious
treachery as if it were an established fact. According to Winkelmann, Conrad had sold himself, probably already in the spring of 1200
on the occasion of his stay in Rome, to the pope's policy for the price
of his ecclesiastical rehabilitation. From autumn 1201 onwards he had
then, Winkelmann argues, secretly made preparations for his open
defection, which had in particular comprised his coming to an understanding with the landgrave. His open rebellion had then occurred,
prematurely, in early November.[11] Winkelmann holds that there is no
other explanation for the pope's indulgence towards Conrad after the
bishop's submission than his treachery to Philip. Theodor Münster,
too, assumes that Conrad, for the price of his reinstatement at
Würzburg, had had to commit himself to abandon the Staufen policy
and to support the pope's policy, at least by remaining neutral.[12] But
the pope holding the see of Würzburg open for Conrad *after* his
submission, is no more suspicious than the fact that he had done the
same *before*, and when, in 1201, he still allowed Conrad's postulation
and effected his translation, this was, as shown above,[13] by no means
an unparalleled, not even an exceptional, proceeding towards a
supporter of Philip. It is interesting in this context that, in about
December 1200, Innocent still approved of the election, at Lorsch, of
Bishop Lupold of Worms, who had certainly not committed himself to
the pope in the imperial cause, and that he required the monks to be
obedient to him.[14] As late as March 1202 he had been prepared to
leave Lupold the see of Worms, which he had by right forfeited, if
only he abandoned the see of Mainz, and he held the see of Worms
open even for the excommunicated and deposed bishop, since in-

structions for a new election in Worms were never issued.[15] In his attitude towards the Staufen-minded bishops Innocent, as far as possible, took into account the site of the bishoprics. Bishops within the Staufen sphere of influence were less importuned than bishops in regions bordering it. In' the case of Würzburg, Innocent may have been content to see the powerful bishopric, in which he could not possibly have brought a supporter of the Welf to be recognized, in the hands of a man who had come to experience his power and mercy. He could not but prefer as bishop of Würzburg a Staufen partisan, who was devoted also to him, to an exiled supporter of the Welf who would only have had the name of a bishop of Würzburg. It is, therefore, not at all so astounding, as it seems to Winkelmann and others, that Philip continued to place confidence in his chancellor, despite the favour the pope showed him. The Chronicle of Reinhardsbrunn, in this instance, assesses the state of affairs probably not altogether incorrectly, when it ascribes the pope's approval for the chancellor's renewed elevation to Philip's intervention with the pope.[16] In the same year Philip seems also to have interceded with the pope on behalf of Henry of Jacea, the Staufen bishop-elect of Liège.[17] If secret treachery had been the price for the pope's favour, it would certainly have been less openly conferred on the chancellor. The fact also that Conrad took no part in the Protest of Bamberg-Hall, though he was then staying at Bamberg, militates against a perfidious treachery on his part. A perfidious traitor would have joined in the Protest so as to give Philip no occasion for suspicion. Winkelmann's interpretation of RNI 52 as proof of the chancellor's treachery is, in my view, altogether inadmissible.[18] This letter reads as follows: *de Suevo ... mentio non habetur, nisi quod aliquando ascitis aliquibus episcopis, quos potest difficulter habere, Warmaciensi videlicet, et Spirensi et cancellario suo, langravio etiam, et quibusdam comitibus, qui cum eo non ambulant recto corde. Nam dux Boemie ... et domnus Argentinensis ac plures de superioribus nobiscum sunt.* In the first place, the chancellor is certainly not counted among those already won over. The words describing those who do not stand single-heartedly by the duke can refer either to the *quidam comites* alone or to the *comites* and the landgrave or even to *comites*, landgrave, chancellor and the two bishops. In any case, according to the construction of the sentence, the chancellor belongs to one class together with the bishops of Worms and Speyer, Philip's loyal supporters. If the letter-writer wanted to cast doubt also on their loyalty, he would not say more than that Philip had no reliable friend at all left. From the fact that the chancellor is mentioned in the same breath with two declared supporters of Philip I would rather deduce that, at about the time of the Bamberg court session, the papal agent knew nothing of any treachery on Conrad's part. An apparently convincing argument in favour of treachery is the fact that in the last days of Conrad's life matters came to hostilities, even to Philip's launching an expedition against the bishop.[19] But, on the other hand, there are indications that the dissension between Philip and his chancellor did not at all result from high-political reasons. On 23 December 1202 Innocent reproaches Archbishop Siegfried of Mainz for failing to bring Conrad help against the maliciousness of his enemies. He had come to know, he writes, that the duke of Swabia, bearing a grudge against the bishop, was persecuting him and had himself proposed to rage against his church. Philip, he continues, had surrendered the goods of the clerics and the church people to plunder and pillage and had not even spared the womanhood of the nuns nor the vocation of the monks. The archbishop is prohibited, under penalty of loss of office and benefice, from daring to offer *help or counsel* to the duke and his supporters against the bishop, and is required to forbid his diocesans by the pope's order from molesting, under whatever pretext, the bishop and his church for the benefit of the duke, who was raging against justice and ecclesiastical liberty.[20] This letter does not, in my view, refer to Philip's expedition *ad episcopum Herbipolensem*, to which the abbot of St Gall had committed himself by oath at a court session at Ulm in 1202 and in which he also took part. Since Philip is traceable in Speyer as late as 8 November, the court session can scarcely have taken place before the middle of the month and the incursion into the Würzburg territory can only have occurred towards the end of November at the earliest. On the other hand, the events Innocent is describing must have stretched over some period of time, since otherwise Innocent could hardly have reproached the archbishop for not having helped Conrad. It, therefore, was not a sudden rebellion of the bishop in November 1202 which occasioned the expedition, but it was rather preceded by hostilities on Philip's part. It is strange that Innocent regards the Welf archbishop as nothing short of an ally of the Staufen king against the bishop.[21] This strange alliance is perhaps the key to events. The Chronicle of Lauterberg reports that Bishop Conrad and the brothers Henry and Botho of Ravensburg, nephews of Philip's marshal Henry of Kalden, had become deadly enemies because of the murder by the brothers of one of Conrad's confidants. Being threatened by the bishop, the report says, they had murdered their victim at their uncle's instigation, after even the king's intercession had proved of no avail.[22] That the two Ravensburg brothers in the first place had a hand in the murder is confirmed by papal letters[23] and by the evidence of Burchard of Ursberg.[24] But Siegfried of Mainz was, at least in 1213, linked by personal ties with one of the brothers, with Henry of Ravensburg, who after the murderous deed by papal order had been deprived of his prebend at Würzburg against compensation in other respects. In his capacity as legate Siegfried, in 1212, had tried to procure for this Henry the see of Würzburg. In his letter to the archbishop Innocent writes that he confided in Siegfried's cleverness so far as to assume that, however great his affection for Henry might be, he would not have made this attempt if he had known of the then already issued papal order.[25] We are scarcely wrong in associating the joint front of the Staufen king and the Welf archbishop against Conrad of Würzburg with their mutual partisanship for the Ravensburg brothers. The fact of an antagonism existing between Conrad and Siegfried also shakes the credibility of the suspicion, based on the Chronicle of Reinhardsbrunn, of Conrad having formed a secret conspiracy with Landgrave Hermann of Thuringia. The landgrave, shortly afterwards, appears as a close ally of Siegfried. The support he gave to the Welf archbishop was the occasion for the break with Philip. But how did it come about that the king sided with the Ravensburg brothers, thus turning against the man previously so close to him? The brothers had a strong advocate at the royal court in the person of Philip's marshal. Perhaps the cause of the Ravensburg brothers was the cause of the imperial *ministeriales* in general,[26] whom Philip did not wish to displease. But also Philip himself came into conflict with Conrad over the claims made by the Empire on the bishopric. After Philip's death, Conrad's successor complained before an assembly of princes that Henry VI and Philip had imposed on his church the duty of paying an annual sum of one thousand marks, and this injustice had also been the cause of Conrad's murder.[27] If we add that Innocent accuses Philip in connection with his hostilities against the bishop of raging against justice and ecclesiastical liberty, that he regards Conrad's death as the consequence of the prelate's intercession for the liberty of his church,[28] and that, according to Arnold of Lübeck, Conrad, who is described as a fanatical defender of justice, came into dispute with Philip's *ministeriales*, who had impudently seized upon church property, then it is not unjustified to assume that, when Conrad tried to redress conditions in his bishopric, seriously damaged by its vacancy, a conflict developed between him and the imperial *ministeriales* as well as King Philip himself over the rights and claims of both sides. The beginnings of the conflict point also to the Würzburg period. At the court session at Bamberg Philip is still making presents to Conrad.[29] On 20 September he is for the last time traceable as being together with Philip at Nürnberg. If the letter, in which Philip orders the vassals, militia and citizens of Würzburg to receive their new bishop with honour and to serve him loyally, is – as in all probability it should be – placed at this time,[30] then Conrad was dismissed graciously by the king to his diocese shortly after the court session at Bamberg. This does not, of course, exclude the possibility that Conrad's failure to take part in the Protest of Bamberg-Hall prepared the ground for a certain estrangement between him and the king, since Philip may have been more offended with his chancellor for his hesitation, whilst formerly he had so defiantly opposed the pope, than with the other bishops. It is also possible that Conrad's enemies later used this hesitation to throw suspicion on him. That Conrad, once he had got into serious conflict with Philip, glanced his eye to the Welf side, we would have to presume, even if the Chronicle of Lauterberg did not state it. But whether Conrad could actually have changed sides is very much open to doubt in view of the site of Würzburg and of the certainly not pro-Welf feelings amongst the people of the diocese.

### Notes to Appendix 3

[1]Geschichte des kaiserlichen Kanzlers Konrad, Legat in Italien und Sizilien, Bischof von Hildesheim und von Würzburg (1882).

[2]Chronica, 68.

[3]Chron. Mont. Ser. 168.

[4]*Loc. cit.* 170.

[5]Chron. Reinhardsbr. 565f.

[6]Arnold of Lübeck 231.

[7]P. 127.

[8]On Henry ,see Kittel-Beaumann-Erdmann, Das Briefsiegel Heinrichs von Glinde (1180–1194) DA. 3 (1939), 420ff.

[9]Reg. II 21, v. Mülverstedt, Regesta Archiepiscopatus Magdeburgensis 2 (1881) No. 116.

[10]P. 1136, v. Mülverstedt No. 134.

[11]Philipp, 231ff., 265ff.

[12]Konrad von Querfurt (Leipzig thesis 1890), 51.

[13]Pp. 189ff.

[14]P. 1204, 1205.

[15]Cf. above Chapter 2, n. 105.

[16]*Loc. cit.* 563. When Innocent, probably in September 1200, asks Conrad to count on the pope's mercy in connection with requests which had come to the pope's hand on Conrad's behalf (P. 1135), Staufen partisans or their agents were staying at the Curia (P. 1131, 1132, 1133, 1136).

[17]See above Chapter 5, n. 70.

[18]On the nature of this letter by the papal notary Philip see above Chapter 5, n. 80.

[19]Reg. V 134, P. 1793; Casus S Galli (MG. SS. 2) 162.

[20]Reg. V 134.

[21]Siegfried had also failed to heed the summons by Cardinal legate Guido of Palestrina to come to Cologne. The legate reports to Rome that a number of those summoned had locked their cities and houses in the messengers' faces so that they should not receive them, and particularly names the bishops of Mainz, Speyer and Worms (RNI 51, Kempf, Regestum, 138). By the time of Otto's proclamation on 3 July 1201 Siegfried's attitude, therefore, was at least undecided, but before 30 September, the day of his consecration, he seems to have again avowed himself loyal to Otto. At the beginning of 1202 he apparently was staying in Rome (RNI 65, Kempf, Regestum 186f.).

[22]Chron. Mont. Ser. 170.

[23]Reg. VI 113, XVI 50.

[24]Chron. 95.

[25]Reg. XVI 50.

[26]Cf. Reg. V 155 in which Innocent lays the murder to the charge of the imperial ministeriales.

[27]Arnold of Lübeck 245.

[28]Reg. VI 114.

[29]BF. 57.

[30]BF. 57, 58. Cf. also v. Borch, 351.

# APPENDIX 4

# The timing of Emperor Otto IV's revocation of the papal recuperations

The generally accepted view that Otto, already before his march to Rome, had regarded the recuperations as void and that Innocent had tacitly put up with this and in September, though probably under reserve of all rights, had even approved of the restitution,[1] is, in my view, without any convincing foundation, particularly as regards the pope's attitude. The appointment of the imperial legate also for the March of Ancona, the duchy of Spoleto and *all* of Tuscany is no cogent proof, unless we were to conclude that Otto's claims even at that time widely exceeded those of Henry VI, who had indeed restituted the greater part of Roman Tuscany to the Roman Church. It seems impossible that Otto already at that time had not even intended to leave the Church the frontiers of 1197. Moreover, if this appointment was indeed meant as a measure directed against the policy of recuperations, it was superseded by the Privilege of Speyer of 22 March. Up to the day of his coronation there is only *one* event from which Otto's claim to parts at least of the recuperations could be deduced, namely Otto's dispatch, reported by Maurisius, of Azzo of Este to the March of Ancona already from his camp at Imola.[2] Even if this information is correct, it is still not a matter of course that Azzo was charged to bind the March by oath to the Empire. His official mission may have been to collect the *fodrum*, even though in point of fact it may have been directed towards the revocation of the recuperations. Only the pope was, though, entitled to collect the *fodrum*, but Otto, like Frederick II on his later march to Rome for coronation, may have deliberately or unintentionally disregarded this. It is, moreover, possible that Azzo also held the pope's authorization.

The pope's tacit approval of the revocation of the March and the duchy has been deduced, for one thing, from his having crowned Otto emperor and his having continued to hold allegedly friendly communion with him despite the re-incorporation of these territories into the Empire; secondly, from a papal letter to Otto of 1210 which, though fictitious, is believed by Winkelmann to be genuine, in which Innocent complains that Otto, not satisfied with the frontiers with which his predecessors had contented themselves, had made bold to invade the Tuscan Patrimony; and lastly, from the fact that Innocent gave as motive for his later proceeding against Otto the emperor's assault on the kingdom of Sicily. The presupposition that Otto, before his coronation, had challenged the recuperations from the point of view of legitimacy or in a form clearly recognizable for Innocent, has been shown to be very doubtful. The friendly communion with the emperor up to his coronation which, by the way, can only be accepted if more attention is paid to the extreme politeness of the form of negotiations than to their substance, can thus easily be explained. The privilege of Matelica of 12 October is the first of Otto's acts known to us from which it clearly follows that he disavowed his promises. It is true that, from the time after that, three of the pope's letters to Otto are extant which give no indication of discord. But the letters of 13 and 31 October as well as that of 11 November prove in fact no more than that diplomatic relations between Otto and the Curia had not yet been broken off. On 13 October, when Innocent called upon Otto to see the abbot of St Sisto's righted against Cremona,[3] he may not necessarily have known of Otto's measures, which are first testified by the imperial privilege for Matelica of 15 October. The letter of 31 October was written in the interests of Waldemar of Denmark and at his request.[4] The letter of 11 November, in favour of Simon de Montfort against the heretics,[5] was not addressed to Otto alone but in the same words also to the kings of Castile and Aragon,[6] and to all three of them at Montfort's request. Innocent's letter of 13 November sent at the same time to Otto in the matter of the bishop of Bamberg clearly shows how strained relations had already become at that time. In sharp words Innocent deprecates and then quashes the proceedings against the bishop of Bamberg charged with complicity in the murder of Philip. Otto is required to put no obstacles in the way of a new proceeding to be conducted before papal delegates, and to restore for his part what he retained from the possessions of the bishop and his church.[7] The above-mentioned passage in the pope's alleged letters to

Otto of 1210, which seems to contain only a complaint about the
infringement of the Tuscan Patrimony, with its genuineness loses its
main probatory force.[8] We can, however, point to another letter
which, though fictitious, seems to reflect the true state of affairs, a
letter allegedly written by Wolfger of Aquileia, which purports to be
an answer to the pope's demand to Otto's legates to proceed less
harshly and to bring the emperor to restore the duchy, the March and
the Matildine estates.[9] That Innocent, in justifying his proceeding
against Otto, brought into prominence, particularly vis-à-vis the
German princes, the emperor's assaults on Sicily, is natural. In this
connection we may also point to a statement made by the pope in a
letter of 1201 to the German princes. After an exposition of the sins
committed by the Staufen house against the Apostolic See, Innocent
continues: *Reales autem iniurias subticemus, quas ei circa possessiones ecclesiasticas intulerunt, ne cui posset perverse intelligenti
videri, quod pro iure ac honore imperii defendendo iniurias huiusmodi
perpetrarint.*[10] But Innocent complained also about the spoliation of
the Patrimony, and that even before the assault on Roman Tuscany,
for example on 18 January 1210.[11] Oblivious of his promises, Innocent
writes, Otto had *suddenly* begun to persecute his mother, the Church.
Innocent refers to Otto's written and sworn securities, to the
privileges that is, the substance of which he thus regards as still
relevant. He demands that the emperor desist from the persecutions
he had begun of the Roman Church and of the king of Sicily, and that
he make reparation for the *wrongs* he had *committed (de offensis)*.[12]
When Honorius III, in 1226, writes to Frederick II that the Church
had borne with patience all the insults done to it until Otto had
attacked him, Frederick,[13] he speaks the truth in so far as the ban of
excommunication was only published after Otto had crossed the
border to the Sicilian kingdom. But it would be wrong to deduce that
the excommunication would not have been effected, if Otto had
contented himself with the revocation of the recuperations. Direct
testimonials of Innocent having insisted on the maintenance of the
whole of the recuperations are provided by the patriarch's fictitious
letter and by the report given in the Reimchronik of the last negotiations between pope and Otto before his coronation as emperor,
amounting to the demand that the pope should return to the emperor,
what the emperors had possessed before the pope.[14] Reiner of Liège's
testimony also belongs here, according to which the emperor, after
his coronation, had disregarded his oath, *quod bona illa non repeteret,*

*quae idem apostolicus tempore dissensionis regum occupaverat et possederat.*[15]

## Notes to Appendix 4

[1]Cf. Ficker, Forsch. 2, 398; Winkelmann, Otto IV, 192, n. 1.
[2]Leibniz, Scriptores rerum Brunsvicensium 2 (1710) 30.
[3]BF. 6075.
[4]Reg. XII 104 P. 3810.
[5]Reg. XII 124.
[6]Reg. XII 123, 125.
[7]Reg. XII 118.
[8]Hahn, Coll. 1, 150.
[9]Böhmer, Acta, 825, BF. 12365.
[10]RNI 33.
[11]BF. 6081; Winkelmann, Acta imperii inedita 2 (1885), 676ff.
[12]Böhmer, Acta, 630.
[13]Huillard-Bréholles 2¹, 593.
[14]Reimchronik vv. 6646–6649.
[15]Reiner of Liège 662.

# Index

Aachen 283
Abaiamonti 128, 129
Acqui, bishop 102 n.99
Acre 168 n.102, 310 n.76
Adela of Blois, queen of France 14 n.51
Adela, wife of King Ottokar of Bohemia 343, 344
Adolf of Altena, archbishop of Cologne 89, 98–9 n.54, 112, 120, 121, 122, 124, 138, 163 n.45, 164 n.62, 166 n.73, 168 n.104, 182 n.264
Aegidius, Magister 117, 118
Agnes of Meran 24, 313 n.117, 336, 345 n.16, 347 n.62
Aimerico Monaco, patriarch of Jerusalem 276
Aimo, archbishop of Tarentaise 162 n.35, 170 n.116
Albanian church 267 n.6
Alberic of Troisfontaines 223 n.108
Albert, archbishop of Magdeburg 132, 138, 145, 148, 171 n.116, 175 n.171, 182 n.264
Albert, bishop of Vercelli and patriarch of Jerusalem 183 n.272, 205, 223 n.106, 276, 314 n.121
Albert de Morra, see Gregory VIII
Albert of Mantua 223 n.106
Albert of Liège 16 n.62
Albert the Great, De animalibus 307 n.36
Albertus, Magister 75 n.79
Albigensian Crusade 47 n.99, 205–6, 229–42, 244, 245, 246, 247, 248 n.3, 340, 347 n.51
Aldobrandini 176 n.181

Aldobrandino, count palatine and marquis of Este 135, 185–7 n.279
Alessandria 102 nn.95, 99; bishop, 53
Alexander III, pope 4, 6, 14 n.51, 38, 45 n.37, 46 n.93, 111, 212, 249 n.10
Alexandria, church 273
Alexius III, Byzantine emperor 43 n.21, 263–4, 278, 279
Alexius IV, Byzantine emperor 174 n.164, 278, 279, 280, 285 n.34, 285–6 nn.36, 39, 41
Alferius, archbishop of Sorrento 207
Alfonso VIII, king of Castile 250 n.18, 344
Alfonso IX, king of Leon 344, 345
Alfonso II, king of Portugal 66, 94, 101 n.89, 348 n.78
Alfonso III, king of Portugal 101 n.89
Alps 125, 130, 136
Amadeus, archbishop of Besançon 170 n.116, 201–2, 206
Amelia 185 n.279; county 184 n.276
Amphusus de Rota, count of Tropea 179 n.234
Anacletus II, anti-pope 9 n.7, 115
Anagni 312 n.103
Ancona, March 104, 109, 114, 125, 126, 130, 133, 142–3, 150, 176 n.184, 205, 310 n.81, 357–9
Andres monastery near Boulogne 11 n.26, 13 n.51, 54–5, 291, 306 n.11
Andrew, archbishop of Lund 91, 205, 224 n.114, 346 n.33
Andrew, II, king of Hungary 65, 70, 99 n.57, 263, 268 nn.13, 14, 283
Angers, bishopric 97 n.9

Angevin Empire 76 n.99, 80ff.
Annales Casinenses 179–80 n.245
Anselm, archbishop of Naples 180 n.245
Antioch 262, 266; patriarch 275, 314 n.121 *and see* Peter, abbot of La Ferté
Antivari, council 270 n.39
Apulia 106, 126, .137, 161 n.33, 286 n.36
Aquapendente 184 n.276
Aquileia, patriarch, *see* Wolfger
Aquino, county 151; lords 181 n.258
Aragon 70, 90, 237, 253 n.55; king 250 n.18, 344
Arelate 175 n.178
Aristotle 3, 12 n.35
Armagh 223 n.98
Armenia 261, 262, 267 n.9, 271 n.39
Arnold, abbot of Citeaux and archbishop of Narbonne 230–2, 234, 235, 236, 246, 249 nn.8, 13, 250 n.16, 253 n.52, 257 n.115, 301
Arnold of Lübeck 349, 353–4
Ascoli, bishop 178 n.227
Assisi 156 n.7
Athens 293; bishop elect 48 n.119
Athos, Mount 265
*auditor* 6, 7
Augsburg, provost 287 n.52
Augustine of Hippo 326; his rule 215
Avignon, papacy 153
Avranches, bishopric 97 n.9
Azzo, marquis of Este 143, 186 n.279, 357

Baldwin, archbishop of Canterbury 13 n.51, 36
Baldwin of Flanders, Latin emperor of Constantinople 268 n.25, 278, 281
Bamberg 137, 351, 352, 354; bishop 358
Bamberg-Hall Protest 118, 174 n.162, 351, 354
Bardney, abbot 223 n.98
Bari 160 n.26
Basel, diocese 181 n.255
Beatrice of Staufen 138
Benedictine Order 224 n.114
Benevento 16 n.61, 62; 1156 treaty 85

Berard of Bari, archbishop of Palermo 76 n.99
Berengar II, archbishop of Narbonne 204, 206, 246
Berenguela of Castile 344
Bergamo 102 n.103
Bernard, archbishop of Auch 204, 206, 234, 246
Bernard, bishop of Béziers 236
Bernard, duke of Carinthia 182 n.267
Bernard of Clairvaux 23, 40 n.5, 42 n.16, 323, 324
Bernard of Compostela 62, 75 n.79, 335, 346 n.26
Bernard Primus of Milan 214
Bernard Raymond of Rochefort, bishop of Carcassonne 258 n.132
Berthold, provost of Bamberg and archbishop of Kalocsa 65, 76 n.103, 99 n.57
Béziers 241–2; vicomté 231–2
Blankenburg, count 309 n.73
Blasius, archbishop of Torres 327–8
Bobbio, monastery 60
Boboni family 6, 16 n.61, 128
Bohemia 99 n.57, 120–1
Bohemond, count of Tripoli 276, 314 n.121
Bologna 312 n.105; University 3–4, 13 n.51, 14 n.52, 294
Boniface, marquis of Montferrat 174 n.164, 285 n.30, 286–7 nn.39, 41
Boniface IV, pope 307 n.41
Boniface VIII, pope 27
Bosnia 249 n.5, 259 n.145
Botho of Ravensberg 352–3
Bouvines, battle 149, 186 n.289
Braga, 59; archbishop 221 n.75
Bremen, archbishopric 76 n.107, 134, 170 n.112, 287 n.52
Brenner Pass 160 n.26
Brindisi 282, 286 n.36
Brittany 60
Brixen 160 n.26
Bruno of Sayn, archbishop of Cologne 99 n.54, 138, 171 n.116, 175 n.171, 177 n.201
Brunswick 131

Bulgarello, count 184n.278
Bulgaria 41n.12, 261–2, 265, 270n.39
Burchard of Ursberg 175n.176, 180n.247, 181n.256, 353
Burgundy 134, 201, 210

Caesarius of Heisterbach 219n.53, 329–30
Cagliari 183–4n.274
Calais 14n.51
Calano, count 179n.234
Camaldoli, prior 174n.164, 205
Camerino 186n.279
Calixtus III, anti-pope 2, 11n.21
Campania, the 2, 10n.16, 14n.51, 114, 156n.7, 164n.62, 176n.184,295
Canterbury 13–14n.51; archbishopric 79, 81–5, 162n.35; monastery 17nn.65, 70, 53–4
Capua 180n.245
Carcassonné 241; vicomté 231–2; bishop 246 *and see* Bernard Raymond, Guido
Carrefou, monastery 54–5
Castel Fumone 185n.279
Cathari 237–8, 242, 248n.3
Catholic Poor 213–14, 226nn.164, 168
Cato 306n.25
Ceccano 291
Celestine II, pope 310n.81
Celestine III, pope 1, 6, 7, 8, 10n.11, 11n.20, 16n.62, 17n.68, 19n.95, 35, 56, 85, 104, 107, 108, 155n.5, 156n.7, 158nn.12, 13, 16, 160n.25, 173n.142, 255n.86, 265, 291, 315n.123
Cerratto, abbot 225n.147
Certaldo 158n.13
Charlemagne 154n.3, 155n.6, 330n.4
Chartres, bishop 309n.73
Cistercian Order 17n.65, 28, 46n.71, 192–3, 211–12, 243, 246–7, 249n.8, 285n.27, 292
Città di Castello 114, 185n.279
Clare, St 214
Clement III, pope 2, 5, 6, 7, 9n.1, 10–11n.20, 15–16n.61, 16n.62, 17n.66, 18n.80, 52, 54

Cnut, king of Denmark 66
coinage 45n.40
Cologne 118; archbishopric 99n.55, 138, 169n.107, 313n.117
Coloman, son of King Andrew of Hungary 263,267n.13
Comminges, lord 234, 235, 236, *and see* Roger
communes 29, 93, 94–6, 104, 127, 148, 157n.9, 175n.167, 205, 247–8; *see too* Lombard League, Tuscan League
Compostela 59
Conrad, bishop of Constance 149
Conrad, bishop of Halberstadt 138, 167–8n.102, 171n.116, 175n.171, 182n.264, 303, 314n.122
Conrad, bishop of Speyer 170n.116, 351
Conrad, bishop of Strasbourg 164n.62
Conrad III, king of the Romans 115–16
Conrad of Irslingen 156n.7, 158n.13, 159n.18
Conrad of Querfurt, bishop of Hildesheim and Würzburg 3, 99n.55, 162n.38, 171n.117, 296, 349–55
Conrad of Wittelsbach, archbishop of Mainz, cardinal bishop of the Sabina 9n.11, 111, 112–13, 116, 165n.70
Conradin, grandson of Frederick II 152
Conserans 236
Constance 149; Peace of 134, 157n.9
Constance, empress of Henry VI, and queen of Sicily 65, 85–6, 105, 106–7, 109–10, 158–9n.18
Constance of Aragon 136, 172n.122, 313n.117
Constance, second wife of King Ottokar of Bohemia 343, 344
Constantine, Donation of 293
Constantinople, church of Hagia Sophia 91–2, 100n.74, 311n.93; Council 37; Latin conquest 268n.21, 278–80, 306n.9; Latin Empire 66, 91–3, 100–1nn.76, 84, 255n.88, 264–6, 273, 280–1; patriarch 323; patriarchate 78n.143, 262, 264–7, 268n.21, 281, 311n.93; Pisans in 268n.21
Conti, family 10n.16

Corneto  135
Corsica  149
Cracow  100 n.61
Cremona  180 n.245, 358
Crimerius, bishop of Piacenza  72 n.10
Crusade  140,  151;  *see*  Albigensian;
   Fifth  36,       271 n.39,       288 n.65;
   Fourth  277–81, 285 n.30, 285–6 n.36
Cyprus  99 n.57, 265

David of Dinant  3, 242, 255 n.96
Demetrius, prince of the Albanians  262
Denmark  43 n.25, 66, 131, 137, 168 n.102,
   179 n.239, 218 n.45, 336
Diego, bishop of Osma  59, 214
Diethelm,    bishop    of    Constance
   167 n.102, 168 n.104
Dietrich, archbishop of Cologne  149,
   182 n.264, 183 n.268
Dietrich, bishop of Merseburg  167 n.102,
   169 n.109
Diniz II, king of Portugal  101 n.89
Dioclea and Dalmatia  270 n.39; king, *see*
   Vulk
Dipold  of  Schweinspeunt,  count  of
   Acerra  and  Spoleto  143,  159 n.18,
   164 n.62, 184 n.277, 185–6 n.279
Dol, bishopric  60
Dominic, St  214–15
Dominican Order  214–15
Dover  14 n.51
Durandus of Huesca  213

Egbert  of  Meran,  bishop  of  Bam-
   berg  145,  149,  169 n.109,  171 n.116,
   175 n.171, 182 n.264, 183 nn.268, 269
Eger, Golden Bull or Privilege of  1213,
   88, 149, 184 n.275
Elbe, river  168 n.102
Elias Malmort, archbishop of
   Besançon  206
Engelhard,   bishop   of   Naumburg
   (Zeitz)  99 n.55, 183 n.268
England  11 n.26, 12 n.31, 13–14 n.51, 25–
   6, 43 n.21, 65, 66, 67–8, 73 n.26, 77 n.122,
   79–85, 89, 98 n.33, 102 nn.103, 104, 111,
   117, 120, 121, 130, 131, 139, 145, 146,

220 n.64,  223 n.98,  225 n.136,  254 n.72,
   285 n.28, 288 n.61
Eugenius III, pope  59
Everard,   abbot   of   Salem   160 n.31,
   168 n.104, 169 n.109, 174 n.164, 287 n.52
Everard, bishop of Brixen and archbishop
   of  Salzburg  132,  160 n.26,  169 n.110,
   171 n.116, 182 n.267, 343, 348 n.67
Evesham, abbot, 223 n.98; monastery  52,
   54, 57, 61–2, 63; *see too* Thomas Marleberge

Fabriano  164 nn.57,     58,     178 n.227,
   186 n.279
Fano  156 n.7
Ferentillo, St Peter's monastery  308 n.51
Fermo, diocese  40 n.11
Ferrara  134, 143, 178 n.211
Fiesole, bishop  53, 292
Florence  163 n.45, 310 n.81; bishop  205;
   monastery of S Felicita  308 n.41
Foix, count  234, 235, 236, 237, 251 n.30,
   253 nn.56, 57, 254 n.67; county  252 n.49
Foligno  159 n.18, 184 n.277, 184 n.279
Fondi  151; count  179 n.234
Fonte Vergine  291, 295
Fossanova, monastery  136
France  12 n.31, 25–6, 29, 47 n.99, 70, 80,
   83,  89,  90,  96,  111,  117,  118,  120, 121,
   131, 139, 140, 145, 153, 193, 201, 203,
   205, 210, 222–3 n.98, 229, 230ff., 245–7,
   254 n.77
Francis   of   Assisi  214,   226 n.173,
   227 n.182, 247, 335
Franciscan Order  214–15
Franciscus Pipini  181 n.259
Frangipani  2, 9 n.7, 310 n.81
Frankfurt  139, 182 n.260
Frederick I Barbarossa, emperor  6, 108,
   109, 111, 115 n.3, 165 n.70, 330 n.4
Frederick II, emperor  29, 36, 45 n.47, 61,
   69–70, 76 n.99, 83, 86–7, 88, 105–7, 115,
   117, 126, 131, 137, 139, 143–4, 146, 147–
   8–9–50,  51,  52–3–4,  158 nn.15,  17,
   159 n.18, 160 n.23, 161 n.34, 171–2 n.122,
   172 n.130,       176–7 n.194,       178 n.211,

179n.234, 181–2n.260, 283, 288n.59, 313n.117, 329, 330n.4, 357, 359
Frederick, bishop of Halberstadt 783n.269
Frederick of Malveti 159n.18
Frederick, provost of St Thomas's near Strasbourg 160n.27
Fulk, bishop of Toulouse 246, 253n.51, 258n.135
Fulk of Neuilly 217n.12

Gabriano 312n.113
Galicia 267n.13
Gallura 183–4n.274
Gardolf, bishop of Halberstadt 343, 348n.67
Garigliano, river 151
Garsias of Horto, bishop of Comminges and archbishop of Auch 246, 258n.136
Gaston of Béarn 234, 235, 236, 237, 251n.30, 253n.57
Gavignano 2
Gelasius, theory of two swords 23, 42–3nn.16,17
Gembloux, abbot 222n.94
Genoa 111, 115, 148, 283, 288n.62
Geoffrey, archbishop of York 55–6, 163n.45
Gerald, abbot of Casamari 337
Gerald of Wales 54, 63, 73n.21, 98nn.28,34, 129, 219n.53, 221n.83, 291–4, 295, 306n.13, 307n.36
Gerard, abbot of Tilieto, bishop elect of Novara and elect of Albano 180n.245, 223n.106
Gervase of Canterbury 13n.51, 17n.65
Gervase of Heraclea, Latin patriarch of Constantinople 92
Gimualdo of Fumone 185n.279
Giotto 312n.103
Glastonbury, monastery 71nn.5, 10
Gnesen, archbishop 310n.81
Grado, patriarch 180n.245
Grammont, Order 13–14n.51, 46n.71, 205
Gran, archbishopric 56–7, 99n.57
Gratian, cardinal deacon of SS Cosmas and Damianus 10n.11

Gratian's *Decretum* 254n.73, 326
Greece 101n.84
Greek Church, union with Latin Church 19n.92, 37, 174n.164, 261–2, 263–7, 268nn.16–25, 271n.43, 273, 275, 279–80, 286–7n.41
Gregory, cardinal priest of S Maria in Porticu 9n.11
Gregory, cardinal priest of S Vitale 267n.12
Gregory of Nazianzus 40n.5
Gregory Pierleone Raynerii 129
Gregory I the Great, pope 307n.41, 319, 326
Gregory VII, pope 27–9, 45n.47, 93, 148, 210–11, 303–4
Gregory VIII, pope 5, 12n.31, 13n.51, 15–16n.61, 16n.62, 303
Gregory IX, pope 29, 43n.23, 45n.47, 73n.26, 177n.210, 178n.211, 189, 197, 200, 292, 296, 306n.9, 308n.51, 309n.59
Gregory X, pope 178n.211
Grottaferrata, monastery 268–9n.25
Guala, cardinal deacon of S Maria in Porticu 340–1, 347n.51
Guala, cardinal priest of SS Silvester and Martin 67, 185n.279, 223n.98
Gubbio 184n.276
Gué Saint Remy 13n.51
Guido, abbot of Vaux de Cernay and bishop of Carcassonne 246
Guido, cardinal bishop of Palestrina 117, 123, 166n.81, 355n.21
Guido of Montpellier 309n.71
Guillelmus de Monterotondo 78n.141
Gunther of Pairis 298

Hadrian IV, pope 85
Hagenau 149
Halberstadt 287n.52
Hariulf, abbot of Oudenburg 49n.121 74n.59
Hartbert, bishop of Hildesheim 169n.109, 182n.264, 183n.269
Hartwig, archbishop of Bremen 168n.102, 170n.112
Hartwig, bishop of Augsburg 169n.109

Hartwig, bishop of Eichstädt 183 nn.268–269
Helen of Gallura 183–4 n.274
Henry, count palatine of the Rhine 124, 149, 170 n.112
Henry Dandolo, doge of Venice 278–9
Henry I, duke of Brabant 120, 124, 148, 164 n.62, 170 n.112, 171 n.122, 177 n.195
Henry II, emperor 155 n.6
Henry V, emperor 142, 176 n.181
Henry VI, emperor 1, 6, 85, 86, 100 n.74, 103–5, 107, 108, 109, 112, 115, 133, 134, 137, 144, 152, 160 n.26, 303, 310 n.81, 353, 357
Henry Kietlicz, archbishop of Gnesen 91, 205
Henry I, king of Castile 348 n.78, 358
Henry II, king of England 80
Henry, son of King Henry II of England 162 n.35
Henry III, king of England 67
Henry of Clairvaux 249 n.10
Henry of Flanders, Latin Emperor of Constantinople 101 nn.83,84
Henry of Glinde, dean of Magdeburg 349–50
Henry of Jacea, elect of Liège 123, 165 n.70, 351
Henry of Kalden 138, 352–3
Henry of Ravensburg, bishop elect of Würzburg 182 n.264, 352–3
Henry of Veringen, bishop of Strasbourg 149, 169 n.110
Henry, son of Frederick II 151, 152
Henry the Lion, duke of Saxony 156 n.8, 313 n.117
Hermann, dean of Bonn 287 n.52
Hermann, landgrave of Thuringia 124, 145, 164 n.62, 165 n.73, 341, 347 n.58, 349, 353
Hildesheim, bishopric 99 n.55, 162 n.38, 296
Holland 124
Holy Land 9 n.11, 48 n.119, 66, 77 n.129, 111, 112, 118, 225 n.36, 230, 232, 236, 250 n.18, 273–81, 285 n.27, 286 n.36, 297–8, 305 n.9, 341
Honorius II, pope 9 n.7

Honorius III, pope 71 n.5, 94, 152, 186 n.281, 201, 221, 268 n.13, 283, 359
Horace 307 n.30
Hospitallers, Order of Knights of St John 275–6
Hubert Walter, archbishop of Canterbury 16–17, 225 n.136, 291
Hugh, bishop of Auxerre 64
Hugh, bishop of Rodez 246
Hugh Nonant, bishop of Chester 13–14 n.51
Hugh of Pierrepont, bishop of Liège 123, 165 n.70
Hugh of St Victor 44 n.38
Hugh of Wells, bishop of Lincoln 82, 97 n.18
Hugh Raymond, bishop of Riez 232–3, 246, 249 n.8
Humbert, bishop of Valence 223 n.100, 246
Humbert de Romanis 216 n.12
Humiliati, Order 212, 225 n.147, 226 n.163
Hungary 56–7, 65, 66–7, 70, 99 n.57, 111, 121, 262–3, 267 n.12, 269 n.25, 286 n.36

Ildebrandini, counts 184 n.278
Imola 357
Imre, king of Hungary 56, 65, 67, 99 n.57, 249 n.5, 262–3, 313 n.117
Ingeborg of Denmark, wife of Philip Augustus 333–4, 336–43, 345 n.16, 347 nn.58,62
Innocent II, pope 9 n.7, 16 n.62, 74 n.59, 115–16
Innocent IV, pope 27, 29, 45 n.47, 71 n.5, 153
inquisition, 202–3, 222 nn.91, 92, 223 n.101, 244, 256 n.106
Investiture Contest 27, 87, 103–4
Ireland 83, 99 n.57, 223 n.98, 293
Isaac Angelus, Byzantine Emperor 278
Isola Farnese 142
Italy 29, 93, 103–4, 107, 108, 112, 113, 114, 116, 121, 125, 130, 131, 133, 134, 140, 142, 148, 150, 152–3, 205, 222 n.98, 247–8, 268–9 n.25

James, count of Andria, marshal 125, 126, 185 n.279, 308 n.57
James I, king of Aragon 70, 78 n.141
James of Vitry, bishop of Acre 51, 70 n.1, 212, 259 n.146, 270 n.39, 304
James the Apostle 323
Jeremias, patriarch of the Maronites of Lebanon 262
Jerome, St 307 n.41, 326
Jerusalem 230, 232, 237, 274–5; church 273, 323; patriarchate 275, 287 n.53, 305 n.9
Jews 197, 198, 298, 300
Joachim of Fiore 4, 242
Johannes Galensis 62
Johannes Oddonis 129
Johannes Teutonicus 62, 75 n.79
Johannitza, tsar of the Bulgars 261–2, 281
John, archbishop of Kalocsa and of Gran 99 n.57, 263
John, archbishop of Lyons 19 n.92, 308 n.56
John, archbishop of Trier 112, 120, 121, 122, 132, 164 n.62, 166 n.73, 167 n.102, 171 n.116, 292
John, bishop of Antivari 78 n.143
John, bishop of Cambrai 170 n.112
John, bishop of Orvieto 184 n.278
John, bishop of Poitiers 206, 221 nn.73, 76, 240
John Capocci 129, 216 n.12, 303
John, cardinal deacon of S Maria in Via Lata 223 n.98
John Chrysostom 326
John, count of Brienne and king of Jerusalem 341
John de Gray, bishop of Norwich 81, 82
John Kamateros, patriarch of Constantinople 48 n.120
John, king of England 25, 43 n.21, 48 n.119, 65, 66, 67, 73 n.26, 77 nn.129, 130, 79–85, 97 nn.12, 21, 98 n.28, 121, 131, 139, 140, 146, 151, 211, 230, 254 n.72, 283, 288 n.61, 309 n.73, 327, 331 n.42, 333, 345 n.5
John of Anagni 10–11 n.20, 15 n.61
John of Damascus 40 n.5

John of Matha, Trinitarian Order 298
John of Naples 16 n.61
John of St Paul, cardinal priest of S Prisca 9 n.11, 19 n.95, 227 n.182, 247, 258 n.140, 306 n.9, 335, 347 n.51
John of Salerno, 10 n.11, 223 n.98
John XIX, pope 325
Jordan of Novafossa 10 n.11
Jordan of Saxony 215
Justinian, emperor 24

Kalocsa, archbishopric 56–7, 76 n.103
Kumans 281

Ladislas, king of Hungary 65, 70
Lambeth, chapel 36
Languedoc 230
Laon 63
Las Navas de Tolosa, battle 274
Lateran, basilica 64; palace 1–2, 51, 128–9, 174 n.159, 291, 294, 295, 304
Lateran Council, Third, 1179 58, 191, 199, 200, 212, 240
Lateran Council, Fourth, 1215 4, 12 n.45, 23, 34, 38, 57, 58–9, 63, 64–5, 69, 71–2 n.10, 79, 92, 94, 96, 101 n.84, 150, 189–202, 214, 217 n.20, 218–19 nn.41, 45, 46, 220 nn.63, 64, 227 n.181, 237–40, 241, 242, 245, 253 n.52, 254 nn.72, 73, 255 nn.93, 96, 98, 256 nn.106, 109, 257 n.113, 262, 265–6, 268 n.14, 275, 282, 283, 288 n.60, 301, 305 n.6, 311 nn.93, 101
Laurentius Hispanus 62
Lauterberg, chronicle 349, 352
Lavaur, council 235, 236, 253 n.51
Lecce 125, 126
Leo, cardinal priest of S Croce in Jerusalem 177 n.210, 306 n.9
Leo, king of Armenia 262, 276, 328
Leo of Anticoli 185 n.279
Leo I the Great, pope 319, 321, 322
Leon 344
Lerida, bishopric 59
Lesko, duke of Silesia 100 n.61
*Liber censuum* 78 n.143
*Liber pontificalis* 8, 155 n.6
Liège, bishopric 123, 165 n.70, 222 n.95
Limoges 13–14 n.51

Livonia   217 n.23, 261, 267 n.1
Locedio, abbot   225 n.147, 279
Lodi   183 n.272
Lombard League   140, 157 n.9, 166 n.77
Lombardy   72 n.10, 90, 94–6, 121, 127,
    138, 148, 149, 154 n.2, 156 n.8, 175 n.167,
    178 n.211, 205, 212, 245, 247–8, 276, 283,
    314 n.121
London   223 n.98
Lorraine, dukes   207–8
Lorsch   350
Lothair, bishop of Vercelli   223 n.106
Lothair of Supplinburg   115–16
Louis,   dauphin   of   France   67,   83,
    288 n.61
Louis VII, king of France   14 n.51, 146
Louis the Pious, emperor   155 n.6
Lucius   III,   pope   17 n.65,   212,   245,
    255 n.98, 256 n.106, 257 nn.113,116,117
Ludolf, archbishop of Magdeburg   31,
    162 n.38, 167 n.102, 168 n.104, 169 n.109,
    343, 348 n.67
Ludwig I of Wittelsbach, count palatine
    of the Rhine   184 n.275
Ludwig, duke of Bavaria   182 n.267
Lund, archbishopric   76 n.107
Lupold, bishop of Worms   87, 88, 123,
    125, 130, 131, 149, 150, 168 n.106,
    174 n.164, 178 n.229, 186 n.281, 350–1
Lutold, bishop of Basel   149, 181 n.255
Lyons, council   187 n.292

Magdeburg, *see* Schöppenchronik
Magna Carta   68–9, 77 n.129
Mainz, archbishopric   88, 99 n.55, 111,
    123, 138, 150, 168 n.106; province
    287 n.52
Maledetti family   14 n.51
Manegold, bishop of Passau   183 nn.268,
    269
Marbach, provost   181 n.255
Marittima   1, 127
Markward of Anweiler, count of Mol-
    ise   104, 110, 112, 114–15, 121, 125,
    126, 159 n.18, 161 n.33, 164 nn.58,62,
    172 n.130, 173 n.136, 302, 310 n.81,
    313 n.117
Maronites of Lebanon   262, 270–1 n.39

Martin IV, pope   187 n.292, 304
Martin de Summa   71 n.5
Mary of Brabant, betrothed to Otto
    IV   149, 165 n.73, 171 n.122
Mary of Montferrat, wife of John of
    Brienne   276
Mary of Montpellier, wife of Peter II of
    Aragon   343–4
Mary, wife of Philip of Swabia   175 n.165
Matelica   178 n.227, 358
Matthew   of   Lorraine,   bishop   of
    Toul   207
Matthew Paris   71 n.10
Mauger, bishop of Worcester   57
Mauguio, county   250 n.23, 252 n.32
Maulbronn, monastery   170 n.116
Maurisius   357
Mauritius, bishop of Poitiers   221 n.73
Melchisedech   23
Melior, cardinal priest of SS John and
    Paul   313 n.117
Messina   282
Metz   243
Michael Comnenus Ducas   267 n.6
Milan   71 n.5, 102 nn.99,103, 148, 151,
    175 n.167, 212, 248, 259 nn.146,147,
    288 n.62, 325; archbishopric   102 n.100,
    180 n.245
Milo,   notary   231–3,   249 nn.8,13,
    250 nn.22,23, 251 n.26
Minerbe   257 n.115
Modena   102 n.99
Mohammed Ben Jacub   274
Montalto   135
Monte Cassino   69, 110, 151, 216 n.12,
    223 n.99; abbot   179 n.234, 181 n.258,
    290
Montecelli family   14 n.51
Montefiascone   108, 127, 135, 143, 147,
    156 n.7, 160 nn.25,30, 184 n.276
Montmartre, abbess   57
Montpellier   78 n.141, 255 n.92, 309 n.71;
    council   237, 253 n.52
Morimund, abbot   180 n.245
Moslems   273–4, 298
Motula, bishop   224 n.119

Naples   152

Narbonne, archbishopric 240, 245–6
Narni 127, 185n.279, 312n.113
Naumburg, bishopric 99n.55
Navarre 344
Navarro, bishop of Conserans 246, 249n.8, 258n.136
Neuss, Privilege, Promise or Pledge 117–18, 138, 139, 150, 178nn.211, 216
Neustift 160n.26
Nicholas, archdeacon of Durazzo 262
Nicholas, bishop of Viviers 223n.100, 246
Nicholas, cardinal bishop of Tusculum 77n.122, 223n.98
Nicholas de Ajello, archbishop of Salerno 86, 87, 108
Nicholas I, pope 16n.62, 46n.90, 60, 326
Nicholas II, pope 308n.41
Nicholas Trivet 288n.62
Nonancourt 13n.51
Nordhausen 166n.73
Normandy 80, 97n.7
Norway 91
Novara, bishopric 223n.100
Nürnberg 183n.268, 354

Octavian, cardinal bishop of Ostia 2, 4, 5–6, 9–10n.11, 10–11n.20, 12n.31, 13–14n.51, 15–16n.61, 166n.73, 174n.149, 333–5, 347n.51
Octavian, cardinal deacon of SS Sergius and Bacchus 14n.51, 296, 309n.58
Odo of Poli 174n.149
Odo of Sully, bishop of Paris 3, 205, 223n.109
Oliver, Magister 287n.52
Orvieto 127, 184nn.276,278, 185n.279, 247
Ostia, cardinal bishop, *see* Octavian
Otto IV of Brunswick, emperor 22, 26, 27, 29, 44n.31, 49n.121, 55, 61, 66, 83, 87–9, 106, 110, 111, 115, 117–25, 130, 131, 132, 134, 137–52, 156–7n.8, 160n.23, 162n.35, 166n.79, 183nn.269,272, 207, 248, 259n.147, 302, 312–13n.117, 334, 335, 341, 343, 345n.5, 350, 357–9

Otto, bishop of Würzburg 149, 182n.264, 183n.269
Otto, duke of Meran 145
Otto, monk of Salem 286–7n.41
Otto of Freising 322
Otto of Sankt Blasien 175n.178, 349, 350
Ottobeuren, monastery 148
Ottokar I, king of Bohemia 120–1, 124, 145, 343, 344

Palermo 126, 161n.34, 172n.130; archbishopric 76n.99, 86, 87, 125
pallium, the 41n.12, 78n.143, 169n.110, 171n.116, 175n.171
Pandulf 72n.10, 77n.129, 129
Papal State(s) 23, 77n.132, 104, 105, 126–7, 131, 134, 135, 136, 150, 152, 176n.184, 291, 302, 333
Parano 184n.278
Paris 12n.29, 13–14n.51; council at, in 1210 12n.35, 255n.96
Paris, St Geneviève's abbey 10n.20, 11n.26; abbot 338, 340
Paris, University 3–4, 12n.30, 13–14n.51, 15–16n.61, 291, 294
Parma 157n.9
Paschal II, pope 142
Paschal III, anti-pope 2
Passignano, monastery 163n.45
Patarenes 173n.139, 212, 259n.141
Patrimony, the 40n.11, 69, 108, 113, 114, 126–7, 130, 131, 135, 136, 137, 145, 147, 151, 176n.184, 245, 247, 258n.119, 302, 310n.81
Paul Scolari, *see* Clement III
Paul of Segni 73n.26
Paulus Hungarus 179–80n.245
Pavia 288
Pecs, bishop 56, 99n.57, 309n.64
Pelagius, cardinal bishop of Albano 9n.11, 101n.84, 271n.43
Penne, bishop 292
Peregrine, papal chaplain 179n.243
Périgueux, bishop 206
Perugia 51, 150, 152, 156n.7, 184n.276, 185n.279, 283, 304, 309n.59
Pesaro 156n.7

Peter, abbot of La Ferté, bishop of Ivrea and patriarch of Antioch 78 n.135, 205, 223 n.106, 276, 303, 314 n.121

Peter, abbot of Neuburg 174 n.164, 287 n.52

Peter Annibaldi 129

Peter, archbishop of Compostela 308 n.56

Peter, bishop of Arras 205

Peter, bishop of Vence 246

Peter, cardinal bishop of Porto 9–10 n.11

Peter Collivaccini of Benevento, cardinal deacon of S Maria in Aquiro 62, 70, 237, 253 n.51, 312 n.105

Peter des Roches, bishop of Winchester 48 n.119, 82

Peter des Vaux 249 n.13, 250 n.16, 251 nn.26, 27, 253 n.52, 285 n.30

Peter Ismael, bishop of Sutri 2, 10 n.19, 121

Peter II, king of Aragon 45 n.40, 65, 90, 234, 235, 236, 239, 343–4, 345, 358

Peter Lombard 3, 4, 12 nn.37, 42, 13 n.46

Peter of Blois 12 n.31, 19 n.92, 40 n.5

Peter of Capua or Capuano 9 n.11, 223 n.98, 271 n.39, 279, 281, 306 n.9

Peter of Castelnau 16 n.62, 233, 239, 248 n.4, 249 n.8, 254 n.75

Peter of Corbeil, bishop of Cambrai and archbishop of Sens 3, 37, 309 n.61

Peter Parenzi, podestà of Viterbo 173 n.139, 257 n.115

Petrarch 294

Petrus Annibaldi 185 n.279

Phara, bishopric 99 n.57

Philip II Augustus, king of France 10 n.20, 11 n.25, 14 n.51, 23, 24–5, 41 n.11, 42 n.16, 66, 80, 110, 121, 139, 141, 144–5–6, 147, 161 n.34, 190, 210, 229–31, 240, 248 n.4, 252 n.35, 282, 288 n.61, 312–13 n.117, 327, 328, 332 n.42; marriage case 29–30, 46 n.67, 55, 170 n.115, 333–348

Philip, Magister, notary 166 n.81, 178 n.216, 225 n.136

Philip of Namur, regent of Flanders 170 n.112

Philip of Swabia 3, 6, 26, 48 n.119, 49 n.121, 61, 87–9, 98 n.52, 99 n.55, 105–

6, 108–15–17, 119, 120–1–2–3–4–5, 130, 131, 132, 133, 134, 135, 136, 137, 138, 140, 141, 142, 147, 148, 150, 151–2, 156 n.7, 158–9 n.18, 159 n.18, 160 n.25, 161 n.34, 162 n.35, 174 n.164, 175 n.165, 286–7 n.41, 302, 303, 312–13 n.117, 333, 334, 343, 349, 350–4

Piacenza 95, 102 nn.99, 100, 157 n.9, 288 n.62; bishopric 100 n.74

Pisa 54, 111, 158 n.13, 180 n.245, 183–4, 268 n.21, 274, 283, 288 n.62, 302

plenitudo potestatis 22, 34, 36, 39, 41 n.12, 47 n.118, 321ff.

Poland 90–1, 100 n.61; dukes 310 n.81

Poli 128, 129, 174 nn.149, 155

Policastro 87

Pomerelia 310 n.81

Porto, cardinal bishop, see Peter

Portugal 59, 66, 93, 94, 101 n.89, 199, 344

Praeneste, cardinal bishop 9 n.11

Preachers, see Dominican Order

Provence 69, 232ff., 240–1, 245–6, 255 n.86

Proveno 184 n.278

Prüm, abbot 57

Prussia 267 n.1, 310 n.81

Radicofani 127, 143, 178 n.230, 184 nn.276, 278

Radulf, bishop of Sutri 108, 109, 110, 160 nn.25, 26, 162 n.35

Ragusa, archbishopric 78 n.143

Rainald, bishop of Uzès 246, 249 n.8

Rainald de Forez, archbishop of Lyons 206, 224 n.118

Rainer, Innocent III's confessor 225 n.147

Rainer of Pomposa 62

Ralph, monk of Fontfroide 226 n.174, 249 n.8

Ralph of Coggeshall 17 n.65

Raspampano 173 n.139, 312 n.113

ratione peccati 25–6, 43 n.28, 167 n.88

Ravenna duchy 176 n.184; exarchate 104, 109

Ravennika, treaty 101 n.84

Raymond, bishop of Agde 223 n.100, 246

Raymond VI, count of Toulouse

170n.115, 230–1, 233–40, 248n.4, 249nn.8,12,13,251nn.26,30,252nn.32,35, 253nn.52,56, 254n.72
Raymond, son of Raymond VI of Toulouse 238–40
Raymond de Rabastencs, bishop of Toulouse 245
Raymond Roger, vicomte of Béziers 249n.10
*regalia* 88, 89, 123
Regensburg, bishop 179n.240
Reimchronik 359
Reiner of Liège 177n.202, 359
Reinhardsbrunn, chronicle 349, 350, 351, 353
Rhône, valley 235
Richard of San Germano 159n.18, 309n.59
Richard of Segni, count of Sora 10n.16, 73n.26, 128, 129, 134, 136, 150, 174nn.149,155, 175n.176, 181n.258, 294, 295
Richard I the Lionheart, king of England 54, 97n.9, 110, 115, 117, 140, 162n.35, 163n.46, 190
Richerius, bishop of Melfi 207, 224n.119
Rieti 156n.7, 184n.277
Robert Courçon 3, 223n.98, 237, 341
Robert de Boves 286n.36
Roger, archbishop of Benevento 207, 224n.119
Roger, count of Comminges 237, 251n.30, 253nn.56,57, 254n.67
Roger Hoveden 9–10n.11, 163n.46
Roger II Trencavel, vicomte of Béziers 249n.10
Romagna, the 134, 161n.33, 178n.211
Roman, prince of Volhynia and Halich 263
Rome 2, 72n.10, 73n.23, 113, 121, 124, 127, 130, 137, 140, 141, 142, 148, 150, 151, 160n.27, 162n.38, 175nn.167,171, 185n.279, 214, 216n.12, 222n.94, 274, 282, 286n.41, 290, 294–5, 296–7, 300–1, 305n.8, 310n.81, 350; buildings mentioned 294, 297; commune 1–2, 9n.1, 127–9, 140, 166n.77, 209, 303; *see* Lateran; Septizonium 2, 9n.6, 291

Rome, Hospital of the Holy Spirit 294, 309nn.71,72, 310n.76
Rome, S Anastasio's, abbot 109
Rome, St Andrew's monastery 2, 9n.7, 10n.19
Rome, St Peter's 314n.123
Rosellae, county 135
Rouen, archbishopric 48n.119; province 218n.45
Ruthenia 262, 263, 267n.12, 268n.14, 270n.39

Sabina, the 1, 127
St Albans, monastery 71n.10
St Davids, bishopric 54, 63, 73n.21, 293
St Gall, abbot 352
St Homobonus 33
St Paul 46n.71
St Peter 28, 40n.11, 41n.12, 66, 118, 321ff.
St Sisto's, abbot 358
Saint-Germer-de-Fly 217n.12
Saint-Gilles, council 233
Salem, abbot, *see* Everard
Salimbene 216n.12, 227n.181, 292, 306n.25
Sancha of Aragon 172n.122, 313n.117
Sancho, count, uncle of King James I of Aragon 70, 78n.141
Sancho VII, king of Navarre 345
Sancho I, king of Portugal 94, 101n.89
Sancho II, king of Portugal 101n.89
Sandwich 14n.51
San Germano 136
Sanseverino 164n.58
Santa Severina, Calabria, chapter 86, 268n.25
Saracens 77n.129, 94, 136, 216n.12, 234, 274, 275, 276, 344
Sardinia 149, 183–4n.274
Sarno 87
Sassovivo, abbot 205; monastery 184n.277
Schöppenchronik of Magdeburg 181n.256, 349
Scotland 223n.98
Scotti 2, 6, 10n.17, 128
Seeburg, provost 343, 348n.67

Segni 10 n.16, 14 n.51
Sens, archbishop 47 n.99, 48 n.119
Serbia 261–2, 263
Sergius Scrofa, bailiff of Amalfi 172 n.133
Sicard, bishop of Cremona 180 n.245, 183 n.272, 223 n.106
Sichem, abbot 287 n.52
Sicily, kingdom of 6, 45 n.47, 65, 84–7, 104–9, 112, 113, 114–15, 116, 125–6, 130, 131, 133, 134, 136, 137, 139, 143–4, 145–7, 151–4, 206, 282, 310 n.81, 333, 358–9
Siegfried of Eppenstein, archbishop of Mainz 48 n.119, 88–9, 123, 138, 145, 148, 149, 169 nn.109, 110, 170 n.114, 171 n.116, 182 n.264, 352, 353, 355 n.21
Siena 140, 310 n.81
Silvester, bishop of Sées 48 n.119, 80
Silvester Hispanus 62
Silvester II, pope 16 n.62
Simon de Montfort 70, 232, 234, 235, 237–9, 249–50 nn.16–19, 250–1 n.24, 251 nn.25, 30, 253 nn.51, 52, 57, 62, 254 n.67, 255 nn.85, 88, 358
Slavs 261–3
Soffred, cardinal priest of S Praxedis 305–6 n.9
Soissons, council 335
Sora, county 10 n.16, 136, 150–1, 175 n.176
Sorrento, bishop 224 n.119
Spain 7, 59, 65, 102 n.103, 216 n.12, 274, 344
Spalato 99 n.57
Speyer 352; dean 287 n.52
Speyer, Protest, Promise or Privilege of, 1209 49 n.121, 88, 98 n.52, 112, 139–40, 161 n.34, 163 n.39, 164 n.49, 167 n.83, 177 n.202, 178 n.211, 357
Spoleto 185 n.279; duchy 104, 114, 127, 130, 133, 143, 150, 176 n.184, 205, 357–9
Stade, county 170 n.112
Staufen (Hohenstaufen) 105, 109–16, 118, 122, 124, 130, 131–2, 134, 135–8, 149, 152, 162 n.38, 296, 350–1
Stephen, abbot of St Geneviève's and bishop of Tournai 10 n.20, 11 n.26, 15 n.61, 46 n.71, 198, 199, 240

Stephen Langton, archbishop of Canterbury 3, 12 n.29, 13 n.46, 73 n.26, 77 n.129, 81–4, 211
Stephen, papal chamberlain 185 n.279
Stephen, zupan of Serbia 261, 263
Strasbourg 151, 160 n.27
Stroncone 185 n.279
Subiaco 216 n.12, 289–90; monastery 224 n.127, 296, 310 n.78; Sacro Speco, 308 n.51; S Scholastica's, 223 n.99
Sutri 160 n.25
Sverre, king of Norway 91
Swabia 138, 148, 160 n.31, 175 n.178
Sweden 67, 91
Syria, *see* Holy Land

Tancred of Bologna 62, 74 n.60
Tancred of Lecce, king of Sicily 85, 109, 125, 172 n.130
Taranto 125, 126
Tarragona, archbishop 70, 78 n.141
taxation 36, 47 nn.97, 99, 94, 101 n.86, 225 n.136, 275, 277, 282, 285 nn.27, 28
Templars, Order of Knights 76 n.108, 78 n.141, 275–6
Terni 185 n.279
Terra di Lavoro 115, 126, 136, 177 n.194
Terracina 310 n.81
Thebes, bishop elect 48 n.119
Thedisius, canon of Genoa 236, 251 n.26, 251 n.27
Theodore Lascaris, Byzantine emperor 255 nn.88, 90
Thomas Becket, archbishop of Canterbury 80, 82; shrine 4, 13 n.51, 291
Thomas Marleberge, monk of Evesham 52, 53, 56, 61–2, 63, 72 n.10, 73 n.23, 291, 306 nn.11, 13
Thomas Morosini, Latin patriarch of Constantinople 92, 313–14 n.117, 327
Thomas of Capua 186 nn.279, 281, 305 n.8
Thomas of Celano 214–15
Todi 185 n.279; county 174 n.184, 184 n.276
Tolentino 173 n.136
Torre dei Conti 294
Torres 183–4 n.274

Tortona, bishop 157 n.9
Toulouse, bishopric 223 n.100; county, 234–41, 250–3 nn., 256 n.99
Tours, archbishopric 60
Trasimund of Segni 2, 183–4 n.274, 308 n.57
Trent 148
Treviso 95, 157 n.9, 247; bishop 313 n.117
Trier, archbishopric 88, 122, 154–5 n.3
Tripoli 99 n.57; count, see Bohemond
Turks 281
Tuscan League 107, 140, 155 n.5, 156 n.7, 157–8 nn.9,12,13, 166 n.77, 328
Tuscany 104, 108, 114, 127, 130, 133, 134, 135, 143, 150, 137, 176 n.184, 205, 225 n.150, 357–8; Matildine estates 104, 134, 138, 140, 155–6 nn.4,7, 177 n.202, 359
Tusculum 174 n.159; cardinal bishop 9 n.11

Ueberlingen 149
Ugolino, cardinal bishop of Ostia, see Gregory IX, pope
Uguccio of Pisa, bishop of Ferrara 5, 15 nn.53,59, 23, 24, 41–2 n.16, 43–4 nn.21,31,32, 45 n.60, 46 n.87, 308 n.56
Ulm 352
Urban II, pope 46 n.71
Urban III 16 n.62, 17 n.65, 155 n.3
Urban IV, pope 304

Velletri 127–8
Venice 91–2, 100–1 nn.73,74,76,84, 277–80, 285 n.30, 285–6 n.36, 310 n.93, 313 n.117; peace of 1177 127
Verona 157 n.9; council 255 n.98, 256 n.106; March 178 n.211
Vetralla 143
Vézelay, monastery 17 n.65
Victor IV, anti-pope 14 n.51
Viesti, bishop 224 n.119
Vincentius Hispanus 62
Visconti de Valentano 184 n.278
Viterbo 127, 135, 136, 138, 141, 150,

176 n.184, 257 n.115, 258 n.119, 258–9 n.141, 291, 310 nn.76,81
Vladislav Odonicz, duke of Kalish and Greater Poland 100 n.61
Vulk, king of Dioclea and Dalmatia 42 n.16, 261, 263

Waldemar, bishop of Schleswig 43 n.25, 66, 76 n.107, 131, 179 n.239
Waldemar II, king of Denmark 66, 121, 131, 144, 346 n.33, 358
Waldenses 213, 248 n.3, 256 n.102
Waldes of Lyons 212
Walter, count of Brienne 125–6, 172 nn.128,130, 286 n.36
Walter Guarnerii 173 n.136
Walter Pagliari, bishop of Catania 144, 161 n.34, 179 n.234
Walther von der Vogelweide 108, 159–60 n.23, 277, 284 n.25
Welfs 111ff., 117ff., 130, 134, 137–41, 145, 146, 166 n.79, 168 n.102
Westminster, abbot 223 n.98
Wgyed, monastery, Smogyvar 99 n.57
William, archbishop of Bordeaux 236
William, archbishop of Bourges 33, 205
William, archbishop of Ravenna 179 n.240, 180 n.245
William, bishop of Uzès 245
William Brito 181 n.259, 288 n.61
William Capparone 126, 136, 159 n.18, 172 n.122
William, count of Montpellier 25, 40 n.11, 167 n.88
William I, king of Sicily 85
William II, king of Sicily 85
William of Andres 13–14 n.51, 63, 97 n.13
William of Cagliari 183–4 n.274
William of Champagne, archbishop of Rheims 336, 346 n.29
William of Pusterla, podestà of Alessandria 102 n.95
William of Roquesel, bishop of Béziers 245
William of Staufen, bishop elect of Constance 48 n.119, 169 n.110
William of Tudela 249 n.13

Winchester, bishopric 80–1
Wolfger, bishop of Passau and patriarch
  of Aquileia 123, 132, 140, 160–1 n.31,
  162 n.38,        169 n.110,         170–1 n.116,
  175 n.171,    177 nn.202,211,    180 n.245,
  183 n.268, 254 n.73, 359
Worcester, bishopric 54–5, 57, 61, 63
Worms, Concordat 90

Würzburg 354;          bishopric 99 n.55,
  162 n.38, 349–52

York 223 n.98; archbishopric 162 n.35;
  diocese 218 n.45

Zacharias, pope 43 n.31
Zara 277–80, 285 n.30, 286 n.36